FILM
AN INTRODUCTION

Preface to the Third Edition

THE BOOK BEFORE YOU REPRESENTS close to thirty years of research, experimentation in teaching, and writing. I developed and wrote *Film: An Introduction* in the twofold hope that its readers will better understand and appreciate individual films and gain a fuller understanding of the film medium's variety, achievements, and possibilities. It is gratifying that the book has been used as a major text in an immense variety of courses, including Introduction to Film, Writing about Film, Women in Film, Religion and Film, Latinos in Film, Film and Literature, Introduction to Video Art, and many others. *Film: An Introduction* has been used at community colleges, liberal arts colleges, state universities, and private universities throughout the United States, and in Canada, Australia, Ireland, and England. Such wide-ranging adoptions have helped motivate me to undertake the considerable task of doing a third edition. So, too, have the positive responses from film instructors. Their suggestions and the responses of my own students have helped shape this major revision.

FEATURES

THE MOST COMPREHENSIVE INTRODUCTION TO FILM *Film: An Introduction* includes a wider array of films, more help for students, and a broader selection of images than any other introductory film book. In addition to introducing students to the technical, aesthetic, theoretical, historical, and cultural aspects of film, every chapter offers an incomparably broad discussion of film, from the silent classics of D. W. Griffith and Sergei Eisenstein to the Hong Kong cinema of John Woo, the documentaries of Errol Morris, and classic and contemporary experimental films.

EXTENSIVE STUDY AIDS ENHANCE THE TEXT'S ACCESSIBILITY A wealth of study aids reinforce key concepts and make review easier: class-tested figures and tables; features that showcase a variety of supplementary information, such as excerpts from the U.S. Production Code; chapter summaries; an appendix containing helpful tips on writing about films; and a comprehensive four-column chronology detailing major historical and artistic events.

DETAILED, COMPREHENSIVE CAPTIONS ENHANCE LEARNING In-depth captions explain the important aspects of each image, providing coverage beyond the main text. So extensive are the book's photos and captions that they could function alone as a brief introduction to or review of the book's scope and content and, indeed, the major aspects of the film medium.

FILM'S STRUCTURE ALLOWS INSTRUCTORS TO TAILOR THE TEXT TO THEIR CLASSROOM NEEDS The structure of *Film* leads its readers from the most familiar and accessible material (the expressiveness of film techniques) to increasingly unfamiliar and somewhat more demanding subjects. Part One considers many of the techniques used in making a film and, more importantly, the consequences for viewers of the filmmakers' choices. Because fictional films have so dominated film viewing and film studies, Part Two explores the sources and major components of the fictional film. Part Three considers the immense variety of films (types of fictional films and alternatives to live-action fictional films). Part Four examines ways to understand a film: how viewers can better understand a film when they consider its contexts, how their changing expectations influence their responses to the film, and how viewers learn or formulate meanings. Many instructors will find that the arrangement of chapters reflects the order of the topics they cover in the course. Others may want to teach the chapters or parts of chapters in a different order. Because of the chapter headings and subheadings and the brief marginal definitions of important terms, they may easily do so.

THOROUGH ATTENTION TO FILM LANGUAGE PROVIDES ADDITIONAL SUPPORT Brief marginal glosses put film definitions at students' fingertips, and an illustrated glossary defines each term more fully and provides examples. To help students identify and understand major concepts, key terms in each chapter are set in boldface and further defined in the glossary, which now includes forty new terms. In addition, a new list of major terms at the end of each chapter helps students review the concepts essential to understanding the chapter.

NEW TO THE THIRD EDITION

NEW COVERAGE OF THE VARIETY OF FILMS With new sections on Bollywood, the action films of Hong Kong, the musical, and Dogme 95, *Film* continues to provide the most varied coverage of any introductory film text.

Even More Attention to Diversity in Film New sections cover the changing representations of African Americans, Latinos, and Latin Americans in historical and contemporary films. In addition, the third edition includes more coverage of films by female filmmakers; Third World films, including Iranian and Senegalese; and works by Mexican and Canadian filmmakers.

Increased Coverage of Filmmaking Choices and their Consequences *Film*, third edition, provides new or expanded discussion of costuming, color, the use of shadows, scripts, animation, fiction as a source for films, multiple sources for fictional films, and the influence of multiple cultures.

New Frame Enlargements The third edition includes frame enlargements from frequently taught older movies such as *The Godfather*, *The Graduate*, *Blood Simple*, and *West Side Story*. The new edition also features images from recent movies, such as *About Schmidt*, *Bamboozled*, *Hedwig and the Angry Inch*, and *Road to Perdition*.

New "Close-Up" Sections Apply Major Concepts to a Single Film Featured at the end of each chapter, new "Close-Up" sections demonstrate how a subject introduced in that chapter can be applied to a particular film. For example, the "Close-Up" for Chapter 4, "Sound," is a description and discussion of the soundtrack in an excerpt from *The Conversation*. In addition, a comprehensive appendix, "Close-Up on *The Player*: A Sample Film Analysis," applies many concepts from the book to a single film.

New, More Specific Film Citations Because many instructors like to show video or DVD excerpts for many of the examples discussed in *Film*, the approximate time into the film is often supplied. For example, instead of "early in *Citizen Kane*," readers are now informed "16¼ minutes into *Citizen Kane*."

New Sections on Important Film Concepts The third edition includes other important new sections: goals of documentary films; satire; gender issues in films and film studies; and the consequences of viewing different versions of the same film.

INSTRUCTOR'S MANUAL AND WEB SITE

The Instructor's Manual Has Been Updated and Revised The Instructor's Manual includes a new section of viewing, listening, reading, and writing exercises. These exercises, many of which can be used in the classroom, help students become more aware of particular aspects of a film. The Instructor's Manual also includes teaching strategies for each chapter, revised test questions and an answer key to accompany each chapter, sample syllabi, and assignments for essays, journals, group presentations, a sample quiz, and two types of final examinations. There are also sections on how to help students write more effectively about film and on the course review, as well as useful sources for film teachers: film and video distributors, books, and articles.

THE WEB SITE HAS BEEN MADE MORE USEFUL The Web site for the third edition focuses on supplementary resources for both instructors and students, including:

(a) materials from previous editions, such as Chapter 5 (on the expressiveness of film techniques in *The Third Man*) from the second edition

(b) sample student essays, and

(c) the Instructor's Manual (for instructors only), which can be downloaded and modified to more closely fit each instructor's needs.

The Web site also includes information about how to contact the author.
    The site is located at <bedfordstmartins.com/phillips-film>.

Acknowledgments

The following libraries and archives have aided me in my research: McIntyre Library, University of Wisconsin–Eau Claire; L. E. Phillips Memorial Public Library, Eau Claire, Wisconsin; Pacific Film Archive, Berkeley; Library and Film Center, Museum of Modern Art; and Motion Pictures, Broadcasting, and Recorded Sound Division, U.S. Library of Congress. The following film distributors have also cooperated: Anthology Film Archives, California Newsreel, Canyon Cinema, Chicago Filmmakers, Creative Thinking International, Film-makers' Cooperative, Flower Films, International Film Bureau, Kino International, Michael Wiese Productions, National Film Board of Canada, New Line Productions, New Video Group, New Yorker Films, Pyramid Film and Video, and Women Make Movies.

REVIEWERS Over the many years as I wrote and rewrote this book, I consulted scores of professional filmmakers and film scholars about the accuracy and clarity of various sections of the book. The following people, generous professionals all, gave of their precious allotment of time and provided feedback appropriate for my introductory audience: Les Blank, Flower Films, El Cerrito, California; Rose Bond, Gaea Graphics, Portland, Oregon; Stan Brakhage, University of Colorado, Boulder; Jim Gardner, Sound One, New York; Cecelia Hall, executive sound director, Paramount Pictures; Michael B. Hoggan, past president, American Cinema Editors and now adjunct professor of filmmaking at University of Southern California and California State University, Northridge; Ken Jacobs, independent filmmaker, New York; George Kuchar, independent filmmaker, San Francisco, California; Tak Miyagishima, Panavision International, L.P.; Errol Morris, Fourth Floor Productions, Cambridge, Massachusetts; J. J. Murphy, University of Wisconsin, Madison; Robert Orlando, Coppola Pictures, New York; Lee Parker, Daedalus Corporation, Turlock, California; Jeff Wall, University of British Columbia; and technical representatives of the IMAX Corporation, Toronto. These professional filmmakers supplied information or photographs (or both), or corrections, suggestions, and encouragement about different sections of the manuscript.

Many people have read the entire manuscript for the first or second edition or parts of it and made helpful suggestions and corrections: Barbara L. Baker, Central Missouri State University; Bob Baron, Mesa Community College; Frank Beaver, University of Michigan; Peter Bondanella, Indiana University; Christine Catanzarite, Illinois State University; Jeffrey Chown, Northern Illinois State University; Marshall Deutelbaum, Purdue University; Carol Dole, Ursinus College; Bernard Duyfhuizen, University of Wisconsin–Eau Claire; Charles Eidsvik, University of Georgia; Jack Ellis, Northwestern University; Douglas Gomery, University of Maryland; Charles Harpole, University of Central Florida; Ken Harrow, Michigan State University; William H. Hayes, professor emeritus of philosophy, California State University, Stanislaus; Ron Heiss, Spokane Community College; Nel Hellenberg, Spokane Falls Community College; Tim Hirsch, University of Wisconsin–Eau Claire; Deborah Holdstein, Governors State University; Barbara Klinger, Indiana University; Ira Konigsberg, University of Michigan; Don Kunz, University of Rhode Island; Karen Mann, Western Illinois University; Mike McBrine, Amherst College; Scott MacDonald, Utica College; Dale Melgaard, University of Nevada, Las Vegas; Avis Meyer, St. Louis University; Wayne Miller, Franklin University; James Naremore, Indiana University; David Natharius, Arizona State University; Marty Norden, University of Massachusetts, Amherst; Samuel Oppenheim, California State University, Stanislaus; Kimberly M. Radek, Illinois Valley Community College; August Rubrecht, University of Wisconsin–Eau Claire; Eva L. Santos-Phillips, University of Wisconsin–Eau Claire; Paul Scherer, Indiana University, South Bend; Carol Schrepfer, Waubonsee Community College; John Schultheiss, California State University, Northridge; John W. Spalding, Wayne State University; Terry Steiner, Spokane Falls Community College; Sonja Swenson, Taft College; Kristin Thompson, University of Wisconsin–Madison; Frank Tomasulo, Southern Methodist University; and Tricia Welsch, Bowdoin College.

QUESTIONNAIRE RESPONDENTS The following instructors of an introduction to film course responded to Bedford/St. Martin's questionnaires, sharing strategies for teaching the course and their requirements in a textbook: Richard Abel, Drake University; Ernesto Acevedo-Muñoz, University of Colorado–Boulder; Marilyn K. Ackerman, Foothill College; Dr. Robert Adubato, Essex County College; William A. Allman, Baldwin-Wallace College; Ann Alter, Humboldt State University; Bob Alto, University of San Francisco; Victoria Amador, Western New Mexico University; Lauri Anderson, Suomi College; Robert Arnett, Mississippi State University; Bob Arnold, University of Toledo; Paul Arthur, Montclair State University; Dr. Maureen Asten, Worcester State College; Ray Barcia, Goucher College; Dr. Bob Baron, Mesa Community College; Karen Becker, Richland Community College; Edward I. Benintende, County College of Morris; John Bernstein, Macalester College; Robin Blaetz, Emory University; Alex Blazer, Ohio State University; James Bozan, University of Missouri–Rolla; Bruce C. Browne, University of Wisconsin–Sheboygan; Carolyn R. Bruder, University of Southwestern Louisiana; Lawrence Budner, Rhode Island College; Ken Burke, Mills College; George Butte, Colorado College; Jim Carmody, University of California, San Diego; Ray Carney, Boston University; Harold Case, Allan Hancock College; Lisa Cartwright, University of Rochester; Dr. Christine J. Catanzarite, Illinois State University; Rick Chapman, Des Moines Area Community College; Rick Clemons, Western Illinois University; Jay Cofield, University of Montevallo; Lois Cole, Mt. San Antonio College; David Crosby, Alcorn State University; Rita Csapó Sweete, University of Missouri–St. Louis; Ramona Curry, University of Illinois; Joan Dagle, Rhode Island College; Dr. Kathryn D'Alessandro, Jersey City State College; Mary Jayne Davis, Salt Lake Community College; Margarita De la Vega-Hurtado, University of Michigan–Ann Arbor; Larry R. Dennis, Clarion University; Carol M. Dole, Ursinus College; Fredric Dolezal, University of Georgia; Gus Edwards, Arizona State University; John Ernst, Heartland College; Thomas L. Erskine, Salisbury State University; Jim Everett, Mississippi College; Patty Felkner, Cosumnes River College; Peter Feng, University of Delaware; Jody Flynn, Owensboro Community College; Linda Fuller, Worcester State College; Mike Frank, Bentley College; Arthur M. Fried, Plymouth State College; Don Fredericksen, Cornell University; Keya Ganguly, Carnegie Mellon University; Dr. Joseph E. Gelsi, Central Methodist College; Jerry Girton, Riverland Community College; Joseph A. Gomez, North Carolina State University; John M. Gourlie, Quinnipiac College; William J. Hagerty, Xavier University; Mickey Hall, Volunteer State Community College; James Hallemann, Oakland Community College; Ken Harrow, Michigan State University; Rolland L. Heiss, Spokane Community College; Thomas Hemmetier, Beaver College; Bruce Hinricks, Century College; Tim Hirsch, University of Wisconsin–Eau Claire; Allan Hirsch, Central Connecticut State University; Rosemary Horowitz, Appalachian State University; Sandra Hybels, Lock Haven University; Frank E. Jackson, Lander University; Susan Jhirad, North Shore Community College; Kimberlie A. Johnson, Seminole Community College; Edward T. Jones, York College of Pennsylvania; Leandro Katz, William Paterson College; Thomas K. Kegel, Oakland Community College; Harry Keyishian, Fairleigh Dickinson University; Les Keyser, College of Staten Island; Helmut Kremling, Ohio Wesleyan University; Barry Laga, Mesa State College; Al LaValley, Dartmouth College; Don S. Lawson, Lander University; Carol S. Layne, Jefferson Community College; Paul Lazarus, University of Miami; Peter Lev, Towson State University; Danny Linton, University of Memphis; Susan E. Linville, University of Colorado–Denver; Dr. Cathleen Londino, Keans College of New Jersey; Frances Lozano, Gavilan College; Jean D. Lynch, Villanova University; Karen B. Mann, Western Illinois University; Walter McCallum, Santa Rosa Junior College; James McGonigle, Madison Area Technical College; Jay McRoy, University of Wisconsin–Parkside; Marilyn Middendorf, Embry Riddle Aeronautical University; Joseph Milicia, University of Wisconsin–Sheboygan; Mark S. Miller, Pikes Peak Community College; Mary Alice Molgard, College of Saint Rose; James Morrison, North Carolina State University; Charles Musser, Yale University; Marty Norden, University of Massachusetts–Amherst; Barry H. Novick, College of New Jersey; Kevin O'Brien, University of Nevada, Las Vegas; Brian O'Leary, Pennsylvania State University–Erie; Jan Ostrow, College of the Redwoods; Richard Peacock, Palomar College; Richard Pearce, Wheaton College; Ruth Perlmutter, University of the Arts; David Popowski, Mankato State University; Joyce Porter, Moraine Valley Community College; Maria Pramaggiore, North Carolina State University; Cynthia Prochaska, Mt. San Antonio College; Leonard Quart, College of Staten Island; Clay Randolph, Oklahoma City Community College; Maurice Rapf, Dartmouth College; Jere Real, Lynchburg College; Gary Reynolds, Minneapolis Community & Technical College; David Robinson, Winona State University; James Rupport, University of Alaska–Fairbanks; Jaime Sanchez, Volunteer State Community College; Kristine Samuelson, Stanford University; Richard Schwartz, Florida International University; Richard Sears, Berea College; Eli Segal, Governors State University; Dr. Rick Shale, Youngstown State University; Craig Shurtleff, Illinois Central College; Charles L. P. Silev, Iowa State University; Joseph Evans Slate, University of Texas–Austin; Thomas J. Slater, Indiana University of Pennsylvania; Claude Smith, Florida Community College at Jacksonville; Elana Starr, Villanova University; Terry J. Steiner, Spokane Falls Community College; Kevin M. Stemmler, Clarion University; Ellen Strain, Georgia Institute of Technology; Judith A. Switzer, Bucks County Community College; Julie Tharp, University of Wisconsin–Marshfield; John Tibbetts, University of Kansas; Marie Travis, George Washington University; Robert Vales, Gannon University; Jonathan Walters, Norwich University; Shujen Wang, Westfield State College; Dr. Rosanne Wasserman, U.S. Merchant Marine Academy; J. R. Welsch, Western Illinois University; Tricia Welsch, Bowdoin College; Bernard Welt, the Corcoran School of Art; Robert D. West, Kent State University; Mary Beth Wilk,

Des Moines Area Community College; Deborah Wilson, Arkansas Tech University; Gerald C. Wood, Carson-Newman College.

Dennis DeNitto (City College of New York) provided advice and encouragement and generously made available more than a dozen frame enlargements. The photographs of models in Chapter 2 were taken by Jon Michael Terry of Jon Michael Terry Photography, Turlock, California. Prints for many of the older black-and-white frame enlargements were done by the Snap Shot, Eau Claire, Wisconsin. At the Museum of Modern Art/Film Stills Archive, Terry Geesken and Mary Corliss helped me secure many photographs used in the book.

Particularly helpful as I worked on the third edition were the video artist Bill Viola and the filmmakers Rodney Graham, Bill Morrison, and Shirin Neshat. For help in securing photos thanks are due to the Academy Foundation of the Academy of Motion Picture Arts and Sciences; Barbara Gladstone Gallery (New York); 303 Gallery (New York); California Newsreel (San Francisco); Marc Wanamaker, Bison Archives (Hollywood, California); and the British Film Institute Stills, Posters and Designs (London).

Various other people have also made significant contributions to the third edition. Three people contributed new sections: Corey Creekmur, University of Iowa (early and late drafts on Bollywood and Hong Kong cinema); Michael Newman, a graduate student at the University of Wisconsin–Madison (early draft on the musical); and my colleague Stacy Thompson at the University of Wisconsin–Eau Claire (an advanced draft on Dogme 95). Professors Ernesto Acevedo-Muñoz, University of Colorado–Boulder; Alan D. Chalmers, University of South Carolina–Spartanburg; Nel Hellenberg, Spokane Falls Community College; and my colleagues at the University of Wisconsin–Eau Claire—August Rubrecht, Robert Nowlan, and Bernard Duyfhuizen—all provided valuable feedback on new or rewritten sections. Jack Ellis, Northwestern University, provided corrections and suggested revisions of the updated chronology. Three of my former students—Bret Lampman, William Meyer, and Zach Finch—contributed essays that serve as both sample analyses at the end of a chapter ("Close-Ups") and as model essays for students to learn from. Amélie Strohschänk, Zach Finch, and Eva Santos-Phillips were a huge help with the proofreading.

Finally, I want to thank the dedicated, hardworking, and skillful people at the New York office of Bedford/St. Martin's who helped with the production of the third edition. Producing a new edition of this book is an usually long, complicated, and costly endeavor. There were not only the words to be written and rewritten, edited, and later copyedited, but also photographs to be secured and reproduced in an appropriate size and shape and with the right amount of contrast. A few publicity stills needed to be cropped to help more clearly make the desired points. Some frame enlargements had scratches that needed to be digitally removed or minimized. There were also figures, tables, marginal glosses, footnotes, and features to juggle. The peo-

ple whose responsibility it was to see that all these tasks and more were accomplished skillfully and on time are listed in the top grouping of page iv.
All deserve praise and thanks, but four people deserve special thanks. As de-
velopmental editor, Joshua Levy pointed out ways to improve the manuscript and worked with me to develop the cover. The copy editor, Rosemary
Winfield, was helpful in spotting wordiness and ineffective repetition, and
the book is easier to read because of her labor. Bernie Onken was a cooperative project editor who ensured that the production work was done well and
on time. Finally, in working with me on the many photos, Pat Ollague once
again proved to be professional and attentive to detail.

ABOUT THE AUTHOR

William H. Phillips received his B.A. from Purdue University, his M.A. from
Rutgers University, and his Ph.D. (in dramatic literature and film studies)
from Indiana University. His postdoctoral studies in film include three sab-
baticals to write and to do research at major film archives, libraries, and film
distributors in the United States and Europe; participation in an eight-week
National Endowment for the Humanities Summer Seminar for College
Teachers on the history of film at Northwestern University; and attendance
at the first (two-week) American Film Institute Center for Advanced Film
Studies Symposium for College Film Teachers. He has also taught short
scriptwriting many times and served as producer of readings of original
short film scripts for live performance then rebroadcast on cable TV.

Phillips has taught introductory film courses at the University of
Illinois–Urbana; Indiana University–South Bend; California State University–
Stanislaus; and the University of Wisconsin–Eau Claire. His publications include the books *Analyzing Films* (1985), *Writing Short Scripts* (2nd ed., 1999),
and *Writing Short Stories: The Most Practical Guide* (2002).

Brief Contents

Contents

FILM
AN INTRODUCTION

Introduction

THE IMPULSE TO GO TO THE MOVIES IS AT ONCE simpler and more complicated than anyone could predict. Going to the movies is an act that takes many forms. We go to the movies in adolescent packs, on timid first dates, with minivan-loads of children or busloads of friends from the senior center and also alone, on foot, in the middle of the day. We talk back to the characters on the screen, or shush the people behind us who are doing it; we walk out in disgust, or come back the next night, or buy each successive DVD release of something we didn't much care for in the first place. We weep, we rage, we snore, we aspirate our popcorn in bursts of helpless laughter. (Scott)

The lines at the movie theater stretch down the block. At the neighborhood video store, all the copies of the latest hit movie are rented out. As a group of people in a remote Cuban village see their first film, their faces radiate joy and wonder, and a short documentary Cuban film, "For the First Time," records the event. Immigrant children watch a movie and are captivated by it and united in pleasure (Figure I.1). A young American filmmaker born in Vietnam returns there to make a documentary and interviews former Vietnamese leaders, who ask her "a lot of questions about American film stars." In a scene from the 1988 Senegalese film *Saaraba* (meaning "Utopia"), alienated youths in Dakar are seen in the foreground smoking drugs; in the background hangs a poster for *Apocalypse Now*. Audiences watching the 1995 Academy Award–winning documentary *Anne Frank Remembered* glimpse photos of movie stars on Anne Frank's bedroom wall (Figure I.2). And here was the scene at an Afghan movie theater late in 2001:

> The usher carried a rubber whip and the policeman on duty toted a submachine gun. Patrons had to check their knives, brass knuckles and other weapons at the door. And audience members had enough combat experience to criticize the film's climactic shootout scene as unrealistic.
> On Friday, hundreds of teenage boys enjoyed an afternoon at the movies in Kabul, something they could not do for the past six years. The object of their curiosity—*Elan*, an Indian action movie—was outdated, blurry and damaged. None of them could understand the dialogue. And the smell of the overcrowded theater they fought to enter was revolting. But no one seemed to care. (Rohde)

FIGURE I.1 **The joy of movies**
Immigrant children from different countries and ethnic groups are mesmerized by "The Immigrant," a 1917 silent film starring Charlie Chaplin. *Courtesy of Rebecca Cooney and New York Times Pictures*

FIGURE I.2 **Photographs of movie stars**
Anne Frank—a girl who with her family hid in a secret apartment in an Amsterdam house during the Nazi occupation—is the subject of the documentary film *Anne Frank Remembered* (1995). At several points in the film audiences see her bedroom wall, on which are hung photographs of movie stars (at the top of the image shown here)—yet another indication of the widespread influence of movies on modern lives. *Sony Pictures Classics*

At various times in history, Mickey Mouse, Charlie Chaplin, Rudolph Valentino, Marilyn Monroe, John Wayne, Arnold Schwarzenegger, and other stars have been more widely known throughout the world than presidents, popes, and athletes. These examples attest to the power and pervasiveness of film, especially American commercial cinema. (For a variety of accounts by filmmakers, film critics, and film scholars about how they "first fell in love with film," see the *Film Quarterly* article titled "Filmic Memories.")

No one questions the entertainment value of movies: the proof is in the huge number of people who watch them. Many people, though, disagree about whether films have any additional value. To some viewers, movies' preeminent ability and commercial proclivity to show sex and violence have made them seem unworthy of study. Movies have been dismissed as "ribbons of dreams" and Hollywood as a "dream factory." Nonetheless, films can be more than commercial entertainment, and studying them and the film medium has many benefits.

STUDYING FILMS AND THE FILM MEDIUM

Some people fear that studying films will spoil their enjoyment of them. But with guidance and a chance to reach their own conclusions, nearly all viewers find that studying films increases their enjoyment of them and often their appreciation of the effort and creativity involved in making them. Many people find, too, that they enjoy a wider variety of films for more reasons than they did before studying films.

Film study helps viewers understand how different filmmakers have used the medium. It also reveals the medium's possibilities and limitations. For example, considered together, the films *Citizen Kane* and *Pulp Fiction* suggest how complex and varied the structure of a nonchronological film story may be. The experimental "Un chien andalou" shows how a film may be used not to show a story or present facts but to suggest something of the bizarre, irrational, yet sometimes striking images of dreams.

Film study also helps viewers understand and appreciate the wide variety of films, including long films and short films; fictional films, documentary films, experimental films, and combinations of those films; and various groupings of fictional films, such as Italian neorealistic films, Bollywood films, musicals, and combinations of fictional film types, such as a film that combines elements of horror and science fiction. Film study also helps viewers understand the indebtedness of later films to earlier ones. Studying films will help you understand familiar films in new ways. For example, examining the story of *Gladiator* can reveal how that popular film, like so many popular American movies, celebrates individualism and the potential of one person to make a major difference in the course of major events.

Viewers trained in film studies tend to notice more significant details while viewing a film. They are more likely to appreciate the expressiveness of the lighting, composition, camera angles, camera distances from the subjects, and other filmmaking techniques.

Studying films can make you more aware of how contexts influence the making of films. As illustrated in this book, when and where a film is made and which sources it draws on influence what the film will be like. A film made under a third world dictatorship, for example, will differ fundamentally from any film made in modern Japan. A musical will be influenced by earlier musical films: it will accept some conventions or traditions of musicals and reject others.

People who have studied films and the responses they bring forth tend to understand the films' meanings in greater depth and to be more aware of how and why others might interpret the same film differently. They are also more likely to be aware of how the viewer's situation—where and when the viewer lives, for example—influences his or her responses to a film.

Finally, films can help us understand different places, people, and cultures—whether a foreign country or a region of the viewer's own country. However, films, even documentary films, should never be accepted as objective accounts. The films' subjects must be considered in light of the film medium's inherent properties and the filmmakers' motives, methods, and skills. In the case of experimental films, the worlds glimpsed often exist only in the filmmakers' imaginations.

ABOUT THIS BOOK

Film: An Introduction, Third Edition, attempts to help readers understand the film medium more completely: the medium's general characteristics, possibilities, achievements, and limitations. Consequently, the book includes discussions of a wide array of films, including some that have received less than glowing reviews—or have not been reviewed at all. The intention here, however, is not to evaluate films or to include only critically acclaimed films but to understand films and the film medium itself. These issues are illustrated by the following exchange I had with a colleague who does not teach film courses:

COLLEAGUE: Did you really see *Natural Born Killers*? I guess that's one of the downsides of specializing in film—kind of like correcting tests if you're a teacher.

AUTHOR: I see a huge variety of films and enjoy nearly all of them in some way or other. I do not so much try to judge them by some aesthetic standards (after all, my background and assumptions may not be the same as yours) but to see them in some sort of context (for example, a creative variation of a genre). Or I may enjoy a film for its structure or editing or something else. All films, on one level, are an exercise in and celebration of human creativity.

COLLEAGUE: True, but still . . . *Natural Born Killers*??? (Which I haven't seen but have read a lot about.)

AUTHOR: *Natural Born Killers* is worthwhile for me to know. In fact, I will be discussing it briefly in the second [and third] edition[s] of my film book as a critique of a type of TV news reporting. Parts of the film also exemplify black humor. Then, too, [director Oliver] Stone's movies are always well filmed and edited. *NBK* is certainly not to everyone's taste. For many viewers, it is probably Stone's least accessible film. But seen in different contexts, the film is at least interesting on a number of levels.

To help readers understand unfamiliar terminology, many terms in this book are explained within the paragraph or in the margin. The marginal definitions allow readers to read any chapter out of order without interruptions for trips to the glossary. Because of this feature, many terms, such as *genre*, are defined in multiple chapters.

This book includes many other features for the beginning film student:

- Features that provide interesting supplementary information;
- New Close-Up sections at the end of each chapter that apply concepts from that chapter to one or two films;
- A summary of the major points of each chapter;
- Annotated suggestions for further reading;
- An appendix on reading, researching, and writing about films;
- An extensive chronology that relates certain historical events to other events and helps readers find dates and check spellings;
- An illustrated glossary that includes over fifty drawings and photos; and
- More than six hundred illustrations (photographs, tables, and drawings), most with extensive informative captions.

Occasionally, readers of film books do not understand the concepts being explained because they have not seen the films used as illustrations. To try to minimize that problem, I have often supplied more than one example and included photographs, drawings, tables, and detailed descriptions.

Throughout the book, the titles of short films (those less than sixty minutes) are enclosed with quotation marks, and the titles of long films (sixty or more minutes) are set in italic type.

CREDIT WHERE CREDIT IS DUE

As we discuss a film and our responses to it, to whom should we give credit? If the film required only modest resources to make it—as is the case with many experimental films—often one person deserves most or even all of the credit. But what one person could create a full-length movie? To write, costume, direct, light, perform, film, edit, and score a movie is beyond the powers of one mortal. Nonetheless, many film reviewers and critics credit and blame a single person, usually the director.

In the case of a novel or painting, assigning responsibility to one person is reasonable enough. With films made by many people, however, it is often difficult to know which contributor affected which aspect of the finished product, and in most cases the director is unlikely to be responsible for the creativity of every aspect. For instance, did the writers, director, or actors rewrite crucial lines of dialogue? Did the writers, director, editors, actors, or producer insist that certain scenes be dropped? Examining the film or even reliable film publications usually yields no answers to these and many other questions about creative contributions. To compound the problem, screen credits often inaccurately report who did what on a film. Many questions about specific contributions to the finished film remain unanswerable.

For compactness and ease of identification, this book often identifies films by director, but readers should remember that the director alone is not responsible for all the film's creativity. Consider the original *Psycho*, which was directed by Alfred Hitchcock and was first shown in 1960. A reading of the source novel and the script that describes the finished film reveals that author Robert Bloch and scriptwriter Joseph Stefano deserve partial credit for the shape and texture of the finished film. Many of the performers—especially Anthony Perkins, Vera Miles, and Martin Balsam—do more than adequate work. Bernard Herrmann's music contributes to every scene in which it is employed: when any section is viewed without it, its absence is pronounced. The title work by Saul Bass at the beginning and the end of the film is unusually imaginative and appropriate. Hitchcock does deserve much credit for supervising and coordinating all these and other efforts, and various filmmaking strategies that Hitchcock favored reveal his influence on *Psycho*. Nonetheless, thinking of *Psycho* as "Hitchcock's *Psycho*" glosses over the contributions of many others. (For details on the creation of this film, see Stephen Rebello's *Alfred Hitchcock and the Making of* Psycho.)

When someone gives the director full credit or blame for a film that many people helped make, I sometimes am reminded of an account, apocryphal though it may be, of the American director Frank Capra and his frequent collaborator, scriptwriter Robert Riskin. According to Richard Walter's version of the story, Capra expounded on "the Capra touch" in a lengthy interview but did not once mention Riskin. After the interview was published, Riskin sent Capra a manuscript with this note: "Frank, let's see you put the Capra touch on this." Inside were blank pages (4).

WORKS CITED

"Filmic Memories." *Film Quarterly* 52.1 (Fall 1998): 54–71.

Rebello, Stephen. *Alfred Hitchcock and the Making of* Psycho. New York: Dembner, 1990.

Rohde, David. "Film Critics with a Keen Eye for Violence." *New York Times* 26 Nov. 2001 (late ed., final): B:5. <http://query.nytimes.com/gst/abstract.html?res=F40615FD3A5E0C758EDDA80994D9404482>.

Scott, A. O. "The Lasting Picture Show." *New York Times* 3 Nov. 2002 (late ed., final): 6:41. <http://query.nytimes.com/gst/abstract.html?res=F60917FE3F5B0C708CDDA80994DA404482>.

Walter, Richard. *Screenwriting: The Art, Craft and Business of Film and Television Writing.* New York: NAL, 1988.

Part One
THE EXPRESSIVENESS OF FILM TECHNIQUES

W HAT ARE THE CONSEQUENCES FOR VIEWERS OF THE INNUMERABLE decisions filmmakers make while creating films? Some answers will be explored in this, the first and largest, part of the book.

Part One, The Expressiveness of Film Techniques, discusses what the settings, subjects, and composition may contribute to a film; how the film stock, lighting, and camera can be used to create certain effects; how the resulting footage might be edited and with what consequences; and what the soundtrack can contribute to viewers' experience of a film. It focuses on the impact of the many choices filmmakers make.

To create a desired effect, a technique such as lighting or camera lenses or camera angles may be changed as the film progresses—for example, to give a sense of walls and ceiling closing in on the characters.

◀ In *Secrets & Lies* (1996), a woman (on the right) realizes that the woman on the left is her daughter, the result of a brief liaison. The entire scene consists of only two shots, the second one more than seven and a half minutes long. In this publicity still, which closely approximates a frame from the second shot, the two subjects are centered and are the same height in the image: they are the main objects of interest and are of equal importance. The camera distance and lens make the subjects large enough that viewers can see the many shifting, complex feelings suggested by the actors' expressive faces. The background, a restaurant, is slightly out of focus and empty. The subjects and setting are clearly and evenly illuminated. The scene conveys many contrasts: the two women are of different races, social classes, and temperaments. The woman on the left is dressed professionally, holds briefcase and papers, and does not smoke. The woman on the right is casually dressed, disheveled, and smokes. The woman on the left has an enunciation and accent of an educated person; the woman on the right does not. The woman on the left largely reins in her emotions; the woman on the right gets extremely emotional. Although the two subjects are quite unlike, they share and help communicate a complicated, difficult emotional situation. Change the arrangement of the subjects within the frame, background, camera distance, camera lens, clothing, lighting, editing, or actors, and the scene and the audience's response to it would be altered. *October Films*

9

Usually such changes are gradual and imperceptible, especially in mainstream movies.

A particular technique, such as a camera angle, may have one effect in one part of a film and a different effect elsewhere in the same film or in a different film. Often a low camera angle reinforces the sense that the subject is large, dominant, imposing, or powerful, but not always. Sometimes, for example, the filmmakers simply want viewers to notice the relationship of the subject in the foreground to a tall object in the background. Similarly, a high camera angle does not always make the subject seem small, vulnerable, or weak, although in many contexts it does. It depends on the contexts and on other techniques used at the same time.

Finally, several techniques used together create a particular effect. For example, in some desert shots in *Lawrence of Arabia* (Figure 1.8a), viewers may be struck by how much the characters are engulfed by an inhospitable environment. But it's not just the camera distance and smallness of the subjects in the image that create that effect: the high angle diminishes the size of the subjects, the (hot) color is unvarying and inhospitable, and the focus is shallow, as if even close by there is nothing worth seeing. To illustrate the expressiveness of various cinematic techniques, the following chapters focus on them one at a time, but in films they never function in isolation.

ISE EN SCÈNE—PRONOUNCED "MEEZ AHN SEN," with a nasalized second syllable—originally meant a director's staging of a play. Often in film studies the term refers to everything put before the camera in preparation for filming. As used in this book, **mise en scène** consists of the major aspects of filmmaking that are also components of staging a play: the settings; the subject(s) being filmed, usually actors or people as themselves; and the composition, the arrangement of the settings, lighting, and subjects. In French *mise en scène* means "staging." The phrase is used in the opening credits for some French films where English-language films would use "direction," as in "Mise en scène de Luis Buñuel," meaning "Direction by Luis Buñuel." Although the **designer** and **cinematographer** are often deeply involved in matters of mise en scène, in large productions of movies, the director usually makes the final decisions about mise en scène.

So expressive can mise en scène be that sometimes entire major **scenes** use only visuals to convey moods, characterizations, and meanings. The opening scene of the western *Rio Bravo* (1959), for example, introduces the main character (the sheriff), an alcoholic who later proves to be his deputy, and a murdering antagonist—all in a wordless scene of two minutes and thirty-two seconds. Mise en scène can be so expressive that sometimes only a few carefully selected images can convey a good deal of a film's story, moods, and meanings. In *Shall We Dance?* (1996), an office worker in modern-day Japan surreptitiously takes up dance lessons that lead to unexpected complications at work and even more so at home. Much of the film's story is conveyed by only the four images shown in Figure 1.1.

SETTINGS

The **setting** is the place where filmed action occurs—either on a **set**, which is a constructed place used for filming (Figure 1.2), or on **location**, a real place that is not built expressly for the filmmakers (Figure 1.3). A film's setting—such as the wide-open spaces of a western or the cramped confines of a prison—can have tremendous impact on the viewer's experience and, as is

Terms in **boldface** are defined in the Illustrated Glossary beginning on page 621.

designer or **production designer:** The person responsible for the appearance of much of what is photographed in a movie, including architecture, locations, sets, costumes, makeup, and hairstyles.

cinematographer: The person responsible for the motion-picture photography during the making of a film.

scene: A section of a narrative that gives the impression of continuous action taking place in continuous time and space.

FIGURE 1.1 Mise en scène conveying much of a story
The settings, subjects, and compositions of carefully selected images reveal much of the story of *Shall We Dance?* (1996). (a) In the background, a man is leaning against a train door, dozing in a crowded commuter train after a day's work. (b) Surreptitiously, he begins ballroom dance lessons and gets so caught up in them that he practices with a back brace, at night, and in the rain. (c) Because he is gone from home so much learning to dance, his wife spends more and more time alone and grows unhappy. (d) Eventually, the man dances gracefully and skillfully. These four images show the main character tired and lifeless and then dedicated and exhilarated as his wife grows despondent. But the main character succeeds (and, not illustrated, his wife's fears are put to rest). These few frame enlargements cannot convey the many (often amusing) complications in the man's life after he begins dance lessons, but the basics of the story are clear from just the mise en scène of these four images. Frame enlargements. *Shôji Masui & Yuji Ogata; Miramax*

shown below, is often used to imply a time and place or to reveal or enhance style, character, mood, and meaning.

Types of Settings

Filmmakers have many options in selecting and creating settings. In recent years, settings for certain movies, especially science fiction and action films, have been created in a computer and then eventually transferred to film. Usually, though, most of a film's scenes are **shot** on a set or on location. Many films combine **shots** made on a set with those made on location.

shot (verb): Filmed (as in "They shot the movie in seven weeks").

shot (noun): An uninterrupted strip of exposed motion-picture film or videotape.

A setting may be the main subject of the scene, as in the famous set from *Intolerance* (1916, Figure 1.4). At the opposite extreme, a setting may draw no attention to itself: for example, it may be blank (**limbo**) or out of focus (Figure 1.5).

Besides limbo sets, two other main types of settings are used by film-makers: realistic settings, as in that huge set for *Intolerance*, and nonrealistic settings, as in a scene from the musical *The Band Wagon* (1953, Figure 1.6).

Realistic settings are used in most movies to try to convince viewers that what they are seeing could exist—and thus to help viewers get caught up in the world and action of the film. In *Shall We Dance?* (see Figure 1.1c), for example,

FIGURE 1.2 Early film set
Interior of Georges Méliès's glassed-in film studio, one of the world's first sets, which was built in France in 1897. Many windows were necessary be-cause early films were made without artificial light. The studio was used for preparations for filming—for instance, for painting scenery—and for filming Méliès's early, very short films. Méliès himself is seen on the left. *The Museum of Modern Art/Film Stills Archive*

FIGURE 1.3 Filming on location
For "Feeding (the) Baby" (1895), the Lumière Brothers of France took a camera outside and recorded brief actions as separate films, such as a train arriving at a station, workers leaving a factory, children digging for clams, and a family having a meal. The film illustrated here is one of the earliest home movies. Frame enlargement. *The Museum of Modern Art/Film Stills Archive*

FIGURE 1.4 The setting as subject
This set of Babylon for *Intolerance* (1916), directed by D. W. Griffith, is the largest, most elaborate set ever built for a U.S. movie. The towers were 165 feet high. The set serves as the main subject of this shot, filmed from the gondola of a balloon. Because *Intolerance* was a box office disaster, there was not enough money to tear down the set after filming, and for years its remains stood on the corner of Sunset and Hollywood Boulevards. *The Museum of Modern Art/Film Stills Archive*

FIGURE 1.5 Limbo set
An indistinct background, sometimes called a *limbo* or *limbo set*, sets off Gene Kelly and Cyd Charisse in one of the dance numbers from *Singin' in the Rain* (1952). With such a background, viewers have no choice but to give full attention to the two dancers. *Arthur Freed; Metro-Goldwyn-Mayer*

the room where the wife waits for her dancing husband to return looks very much as one would expect such a room to look in modern-day Japan.

Sometimes settings are deliberately non-realistic: they may be exaggerated or lack the right details to convince audiences that they closely represent the world they know. Non-realistic settings may include unexpected colors. They may look misshapen or contain abstract shapes. Such settings may be enjoyed for their creativity or whimsy, as in *The Band Wagon*. They may be used to reveal the main character's state of mind, as in the classic German film *The Cabinet of Dr. Caligari* (1919, Figure 1.7). Non-realistic settings also appear in many animated films, as in *Tim Burton's The Nightmare before Christmas* (1993, see Figure 8.36 on p. 391), and in symbolic or allegorical stories, such as "Neighbours" (1952, see Figure 8.37b on

FIGURE 1.6 Nonrealistic set establishing a scene's location and mood
An imaginative, playful, childlike setting for "Triplets," a whimsical and satirical song and dance number in *The Band Wagon* (1953). As in many musical numbers, the set is nonrealistic; the designers made no attempt to re-create a background that viewers would accept as true to life. None is needed. *Arthur Freed; Loew's Incorporated*

FIGURE 1.7 Nonrealistic sets reflecting a character's mental state
In the classic German film *The Cabinet of Dr. Caligari* (1919), viewers see a story told by an insane narrator, and the sets of his story are done in an expressionistic style complete with many irregular, unexpected shapes. In the scene represented here, as in many scenes in this film, part of the image was also blocked out, or masked. Frame enlargement. *Decla-Bioscop; The Museum of Modern Art/Circulating Film Library*

p. 392). In "Neighbours," a detailed, realistic setting would serve no purpose: the film focuses not on setting or the characters' relationship to setting but on the symbolic significance of two neighbors' actions. Often filmmakers on a tight budget use nonrealistic sets because it may be cheaper and faster to construct them than detailed realistic ones.

Functions of Settings

Above all, settings indicate place and time. When the action shifts to Cuba in *The Godfather Part II* (1974), we can see that the location has a warm, humid climate (a long shoreline, palm trees, men dressed in short-sleeve shirts and lightweight hats, most people dressed in white or light-colored clothes). From the variety of skin tones of the many people on the sidewalks and from the uniforms of the police or military authorities, we can infer that the story has shifted to a country with a tropical climate, probably somewhere in the Caribbean. From the car Michael is riding in, a 1950s Chevrolet we see earlier in the movie, another 1950s car parked by the curb, and the ankle-length skirts on the women, many viewers can infer that the time is the late 1950s or so. We scarcely need the soundtrack to reveal that the action shifts to Cuba.

In action movies set in nature or outer space, the filmmakers may dwell on the settings by using frequent shots of settings without people or with people seen only from a distance. They may use shots of the setting that do not advance the story or that last longer than necessary for **narrative** purposes. Such shots often stress the beauty, wonder, and vastness of nature (see Plate 21 in Chapter 2). When a shot presents the main subject with abundant space around it, the framing is called **loose framing** (Figure 1.8a). At the opposite extreme, **tight framing** leaves little space around the subject, and such settings often convey a sense of confinement and stress (Figure 1.8b). Occasionally, tight framing is used until someone abruptly intrudes into the image. For example, a hand may quickly emerge from offscreen and grab a character, as often happens in eerie, frightening scenes (memorably in *Night of the Living Dead*). Sometimes this technique is used to frighten a character and viewers, but then both quickly realize that the intruder is not a threat. In *Fatal Attraction* (1987), the Michael Douglas character is seen near an edge of the frame, listening to a menacing tape from his former lover;

narrative: A representation of a series of unified events situated in one or more settings.

a)   b)

FIGURE 1.8 Loose framing and tight framing
Framing refers to how the main subject is positioned within the frame. (a) In loose framing, the main subject of the shot has ample space and does not seem hemmed in by the edges of the frame and the background. Such is very much the case in this image from *Lawrence of Arabia* (1962, 1989). (b) In tight framing, there is little visible space around the main subject. As a consequence, the subject usually seems to be trapped or at least confined somewhat, as in this still for *The Bicycle Thief* (1948) that shows the main character hemmed in by the wall in the background and the hostile crowd on the right. (a) *Horizon; Columbia;* (b) *Vittorio De Sica; PDS-ENIC; British Film Institute Stills, Posters and Designs*

then his wife's hands quickly enter the frame to give his shoulders a massage. He and the viewers jump and then are relieved, and perhaps viewers are a little amused.

Settings are often used to help reveal what a character is like or to create or intensify moods. In the Iranian *Taste of Cherry* (1997), most of the film is given over to a middle-aged man, Badii, driving around Teheran and vicinity looking for someone to cover up his body if he commits suicide, which he intends to do. "Instead of talking about his suicidal feelings, Badii passes over and over through a hellish stretch of industrial debris, abandoned machinery, and brown, dry, or dying vegetation. The land itself looks ready to give up. It's an emblematic use of landscape . . . simultaneously a real landscape and a projection of Badii's mental state" (Erickson 53). Near the end of the Japanese film *Gate of Hell* (1953), the agitated setting mirrors the feelings of the samurai who intends to kill the husband of the woman with whom the samurai has become obsessed. The first, brief shot of the samurai's approach to the couple's house is of plants buffeted by wind. The next shot is of plants in the foreground blowing in a strong wind and the appearance of the samurai far in the background, waist-high in vegetation. As he approaches the house (and camera), the wind agitates the plants that surround him. Toward the end of the shot, he disappears off to the right of the **frame**; only the plants and the sky remain briefly in the background. In the next, very brief shot, a few plants blow in the wind. The message conveyed by the setting is that the samurai is like the wind: his agitated presence powerfully affects what is around him.

Where characters live or work, which objects surround them, and how they arrange those objects can also tell us much about the characters. The **expressionistic** castle of Dr. Frankenstein in *Frankenstein* (1931) seems entirely appropriate for its occupant (Figure 1.9).

FIGURE 1.9 Setting reflecting character
In *Frankenstein* (1931), Dr. Frankenstein's castle is made up of massive, roughly hewn stone blocks suggesting a fortress. The building's few, small windows and relative absence of natural light reinforce the sense of Dr. Frankenstein's illegal and immoral deeds away from the light of the world. The steep, wet, and uneven stairs, which lead up to the laboratory, are dangerous and uninviting. The outer door is massive and contains a small, heavily barred window similar to the one seen here in the background. Frankenstein's workplace is a lot like a prison. The building is largely given over to its upstairs laboratory, with its opening to the sky and the lightning that vitalizes the corpse Dr. Frankenstein steals from a grave in the film's opening scene. Frankenstein's building contains nothing to beautify or soften the interiors: no plants, no artworks, no fabrics, just barren surfaces of stone blocks and the equipment Dr. Frankenstein needs in his obsessive work. With its shadows, odd angles in its corners and wooden beams, and irregularly shaped windows, the setting is strongly reminiscent of expressionism. The castle of *Frankenstein* is appropriate for a scientist who has twisted out of line in daring to play god and create life. *Carl Laemmle; Universal*

expressionism: A style of art, literature, drama, and film used to represent not external reality in a believable way but emotions in striking, stylized ways.

a)   b)

FIGURE 1.10 Setting helping to establish mood and meaning
During the initial shots of *Blood Simple* (1984, reissued slightly revised in 2000), a narrator says
that no matter who you are, "something can all go wrong," that what he knows about is Texas, and
that "down here you are on your own." Seen here are frames from two of the film's opening seven
shots. All seven are extreme long shots of dry, flat Texas landscape. In all seven shots, the only
movement is of oil pumps, and the lighting is subdued or darkish. The film's first shot (a) is of a
blown-out tire on a highway that fills most of the frame. A few shots later, viewers see the screen
of a drive-in movie theater (b). The film's opening seven shots are void of vibrant life and are
melancholic and uninviting. Frame enlargements. *Ethan Coen; USA Films*

Sometimes a film's initial setting establishes mood and perhaps even
characterization and meaning, as in *Blood Simple* (1984, 2000, Figure 1.10).
Settings can also be used throughout a film to mirror changes in situation
and moods, as in *American Beauty* (1999, Figure 1.11).

SUBJECTS

Like settings, subjects are crucial in understanding the expressiveness of
mise en scène. In a fictional film, the subject is usually the film's characters.
In a **documentary film**, real people are often a shot's main concern.

documentary film: A film or
video representation of actual
(not imaginary) subjects.

Action, Reaction, and Appearance

We learn about characters and people by observing their actions, such as
dancing, marrying and divorcing, writing a novel. Viewers may also learn volumes from facial reactions. As writer and director Jim Jarmusch said about
the reactions of Forest Whitaker, the star of Jarmusch's *Ghost Dog: The Way of
the Samurai* (1999), "Reacting . . . I think is the essence of acting. And just tiny
things can fleet across his face and say a lot more than probably pages of dialogue." In movies, actions and reactions are the usual means of revealing

a)   b)

FIGURE 1.11 Work and home settings revealing changing character
At the beginning of *American Beauty* (1999), the Kevin Spacey character, Lester Burnham, is a
middle-aged man bored with his job and unengaged with his home life. He is cynical, lethargic,
and unassuming. Appropriately, the film's settings reinforce the story and meanings. (a) An office
at work has desaturated colors, black objects, hard surfaces, contemporary furniture, and artificial
light. There is lots of blank space on the wall opposite the man's desk and evidently only one inconspicuous plant in the room. The only painting is abstract and in the same style as the office:
simple, full of straight lines, and without vibrant colors. The desk is clear of clutter and family
pictures. This man, who was hired to sniff out inefficiencies and suggest who should be laid off,
has been in the position for only a month or so, and there is no sense that he has moved into his
office. The setting suggests cold functionality, monotony, and sterility. There is more of the setting in the occupant than the occupant in the setting. (b) Behind the chair and unseen here is a
remote-controlled toy vehicle that seems to attack the feet of Lester's wife, suggesting Lester's
rebellious return to childhood and its messy fun. Like his workplace, Lester's home is full of
shades of gray or desaturated colors and expensive modern furniture. Here clutter has begun to
appear in the previously immaculate room: Lester's bare feet on the coffee table, an open beer
bottle, and a banana peel. Later in this scene, the wife is so concerned that Lester will spill beer
on the $4,000 couch (seen on the right) that he gives up his attempt to seduce her and never again
tries to approach her intimately. Frame enlargements. *Jinks/Cohen Production; DreamWorks*

characterization. Perhaps this is because films are superbly suited to single
out actions and reactions, focus attention on them, and show them vividly and
memorably. No one in the western *High Noon* (1952), for example, tells viewers that the town marshal lives by his principles and that his integrity and
willpower are mightier than his fear. Those characteristics are shown by his
resolute movements, proud carriage, and creased and worried face.

Often a character's possessions suggest something about the owner. Cars
are a favorite means of characterization: station wagons for family members,
sports cars for independent singles, VWs for the unassuming, and Volvos for
the cautious and middle-aged. As in the choice of actors, the choice of vehicle may surprise and amuse audiences because characters may drive vehicles
that audiences would not expect. An example is the Oldsmobile minivan that
the John Travolta character, a Miami loan shark, drives and promotes in *Get
Shorty* (1995).

We also learn about characters by their appearance, including physical characteristics, posture, gestures, clothing, makeup, and hairstyle. Charlie Chaplin's world-famous tramp outfit serves as an example (Figure 1.12). When a film has multiple main characters, appearance can be used to individualize them, as in *Mystery Men* (1999, Figure 1.13). Clothing can be used to show or reinforce an aspect of a character, as in *The Graduate* (1967), in which one of the main characters occasionally wears a certain type of cloth-

FIGURE 1.13 Appearance setting off characters from each other and from everyone else
In *Mystery Men* (1999), the story of superhero wannabes, six men and one woman with special but limited skills join forces to fight crime—with varying degrees of effectiveness. This image is from late in the film, when the wannabes have quit squabbling and are united in trying to thwart a catastrophic threat to their city, engineered by the gleefully evil Casanova Frankenstein. The fork-hurling character on the right (Jeff) insists on the moniker Blue Raja, and he dresses as one, though, as his colleagues point out, he wears hardly any blue at all. The character in the middle, called Shoveler, often wears his son's baseball catcher's chest protector, a coal miner's light, and a large shovel on his back. Significant details are revealed in the characters' choices of adornments. For example, Bowler (on the left) always carries a clear plastic bowling ball containing the skull of her dominating father and wears a jacket embossed with a skull and crossed bowling pins. The varied costumes help viewers quickly identify characters, even in long and extreme long shots in action scenes. As befits their hardworking wearers (none of the characters seems to be wealthy), the costumes look like purchased party costumes or—in the case of the reluctant Mr. Furious—simple clothing with eccentric accessories, such as the metal Chevrolet insignia serving as his belt buckle (second from right). The costumes proclaim the characters' resourcefulness and individuality. Frame enlargement. *Lawrence Gordon Productions; Universal*

FIGURE 1.12 Costume revealing character
Charlie Chaplin in his now classic tramp outfit that he wore in many films, including here in *City Lights* (1931). At first glance, the character seems to be dressed as a gentleman: tie, hat, cane, jacket, vest, and carefully trimmed mustache. Closer inspection reveals, however, that the jacket is too tight, its sleeves too short, the trousers too loose. The cane is the flimsiest, cheapest one imaginable. His gloves are full of holes; his shoes are worn out and have holes. In some Chaplin films, including *City Lights*, the jacket elbows are patched or holey. He is not a wealthy gentleman, though he tries to look like one. His is a constant but amusing battle to retain his sense of class and dignity. *Charles Chaplin; United Artists*

FIGURE 1.14 Costume revealing an aspect of a character
About twenty-eight minutes into *The Graduate* (1967), Mrs.
Robinson, wearing a leopard-skin coat, shows up at a hotel bar to
meet young Ben Braddock before they go to a hotel room to initiate their affair. Later in the film, the leopard-skin motif is
picked up again both as Mrs. Robinson prepares to pack for the
wedding a black jacket with leopard-skin lapels and cuffs and as
she wears that jacket and a small leopard-skin hat at the wedding.
The leopard is a ferocious wild cat. Similarly, Mrs. Robinson reacts with a controlled ferociousness in pursuing her goals: seducing Ben and later trying to thwart his relationship with her
daughter. Frame enlargement. *Lawrence Turman; Embassy Pictures*

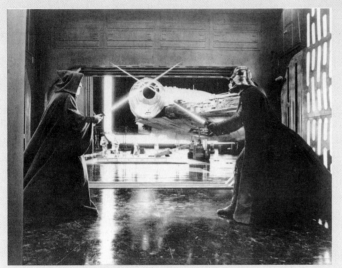

**FIGURE 1.15 Contending appearances, contending
characters**
In *Star Wars* (1977), the softness of Obi-Wan Kenobi's
robe and hood (left) contrasts with the heavier fabric
and metallic helmet of Darth Vader. Obi-Wan Kenobi
looks like a monk. Darth Vader looks militaristic, his
helmet a blending of a helmet worn by German soldiers
during World War II and one worn by warriors in the
earlier Soviet film *Alexander Nevsky* (1938). Take away
the light sabers and setting and one can almost imagine
a monk confronting an armored knight. It looks as if
Obi-Wan is poorly protected, but then the force is with
him. *Gary Kurtz & George Lucas; Lucasfilm Ltd.*

ing (Figure 1.14). Appearance may serve many other functions. It may be
used to heighten the contrast between adversaries, as in the appearances of
Obi-Wan Kenobi and Darth Vader (Figure 1.15), and even to hide a character's identity, as in Darth Vader's costume (see Figure 5.19a on p. 235). Often a
character's changing appearance reveals the character at different ages or under changed situations (Figure 1.16). As even the most casual viewer has noticed, costumes are often used to help show a place and time, and sometimes
also to show the character's status and power (see Plate 1 in Chapter 2). Appearance, including clothing, can be so expressive that a single image sometimes conveys the essence of a story. In *Star Wars* (1977), much of the story
is conveyed by contending forces who dress differently and face each other
from opposing sides of the frame against a backdrop of high-tech danger
(see Figure 1.15).

a)

b)

c)

d)

FIGURE 1.16 Clothing used to reinforce many messages
In *The Royal Tenenbaums* (2001), clothing is used to show how one of the major characters, Chas, the son played by Ben Stiller, was a formal, disciplined boy capitalist who wore a suit and tie as he conducted business (a). Years later, as a young man, Chas wears a red jogging suit on nearly all occasions. Even when he goes to the hospital, he and his sons wear their red jogging suits (b).

Chas's father, Royal, on the other hand, wears a greater variety of clothing and is presented as a more complex and variable character than Chas. He has been barred from practicing law, spent some time in prison, and lost his wealth, when he finally attempts to rejoin his family. At first, like Charlie Chaplin in so many of his films (see Figure 1.12), Royal tries to appear wealthy—in his case, by wearing a suit, tie, and shirt with French cuffs and by carrying an umbrella—though his usual means of transportation, a beat-up taxi, suggests that he is impoverished (c). In spite of his fast talking, scheming, and charm, Royal is eventually reduced to working as an elevator operator in the hotel where viewers first saw him ensconced as a seemingly wealthy guest (d). Frame enlargements. *Wes Anderson; Buena Vista*

Appearance reveals character. It can also create character. As film scholar James Naremore explains:

> Costumes serve as indicators of gender and social status, but they also shape bodies and behavior. "[We] may make them take the mould of arm or breast," Virginia Woolf wrote in *Orlando*, "but they mould our hearts, our brains, our tongues to their liking." . . . Who shall say how much the lumbering walk of Frankenstein's monster was created by [Boris] Karloff and how much by a pair of weighted boots? We even have Chaplin's word that the Tramp grew out of the costume, not vice versa: "I had no idea of the character. But the moment I was dressed, the clothes and make-up made me feel the person he was." (88–89)

Characters and Acting

Characters are imaginary personages in a fictional story. They are often based in part on real people—as the main character in *Ed Wood* (1994) is based on the real movie director Ed Wood—or on a combination of traits from several people. But some characters—such as the characters in most action movies—are entirely imaginary. In a fictional film, humans usually function as characters, but characters can be anything with some human features, such as a talking animal or visitors from outer space. Characters' actions and language—and sometimes their thoughts, dreams, and fantasies—are the main ways we viewers come to understand them and to involve ourselves in the story. Depending on the needs of the story, characters may be round or flat. Round characters are complex, lifelike, multidimensional, sometimes surprising, and changeable. They tend to be the most important characters in a story. Flat characters are simple (stereotypical or minor), one-dimensional, and unchanging. They tend to play minor roles in a story, appearing in few scenes and rarely affecting the most significant actions. Narrative films tend to have only a few round characters because there is time to develop only a few characters in depth, and most viewers find it confusing to keep track of more than a few major characters.

TYPES OF ACTORS

> Far from the movies not being an actor's medium, there's probably been no other artistic medium in this [twentieth] century whose appeal rests so strongly on the human presence, and in which the human image has occupied a place of such primacy and centrality. (Pechter 69)

In the earliest years of cinema, film acting was considered so disreputable that in the United States and elsewhere, stage actors who appeared in movies would not let their names be publicized. How different is the situation today! Now American movie actors generally have more prestige, power, and wealth than anyone else involved in making a movie. The most popular actors can command many millions of dollars per movie. And by agreeing to do a particular film, a famous actor often ensures that it will be funded and made. Critics and film theorists have divided actors into various sometimes overlapping types, including stars, Method actors, character actors, and nonprofessional actors.

Some film industries—such as those of India, Brazil, France, and the United States—have film stars, famous performers who usually play a major if not the major role. Some American stars—such as Arnold Schwarzenegger and Sylvester Stallone—play a narrow range of characters but often generate widespread interest, command enormous salaries, and often guarantee a large box office, both in the United States and abroad. "Stardom seems more a state of being than a learned skill. . . . For a performer like Stallone . . . the ability to convey subtle shades of emotion, to enter personalities foreign to him, is essentially irrelevant. His skill is that of existing intensely on screen, of communicating his uniqueness and inviting audiences to enjoy it and identify with it" (Kehr). With stardom come prestige and power. A star's power may extend to the choice of the director and even to the script. Sometimes stars and their previous roles are so well known that scripts are written with them in mind or are rewritten to suit them better once they are signed up for a movie. Sometimes the stars' contracts give them the right to insist on script changes. Writer John Gregory Dunne details how Michelle Pfeiffer and Robert Redford—who both had script approval before and during the filming of *Up Close and Personal* (1996)—suggested or insisted on many changes in the script (132–75).

Dustin Hoffman (Figure 1.17), Robert De Niro, Tom Hanks, Marlon Brando, Al Pacino, Jeff Bridges, Jack Nicholson, Peter Sellers, Alec Guinness, Daniel Day-Lewis, and others have been regarded as stars yet have played a wide range of roles, sometimes within the same film. In *Kind Hearts and Coronets* (1949), Alec Guinness plays eight brief roles, including a woman; and in *The Nutty Professor* (1996) and *Nutty Professor II: The Klumps* (2000), Eddie Murphy plays multiple roles, including all the members of the Klump family (Figure 1.18). Female stars—such as Vanessa Redgrave, Anjelica Huston, Jessica Lange, Meryl Streep, Maggie Smith, Faye Dunaway, Ellen Burstyn, and Glenn Close—have been no less versatile and accomplished though they rarely get to play multiple roles in the same film (Figure

a)    b)

FIGURE 1.17 Versatile acting
In *Tootsie* (1982), Dustin Hoffman plays a male actor who sometimes plays a female actor. Here Hoffman is seen as (a) Michael Dorsey, an actor, and (b) Dorothy Michaels, who is in fact Michael Dorsey made up to look like a woman. With this film, Hoffman proved he was versatile enough to play two different yet related roles convincingly within the same film. Frame enlargements. *Sydney Pollack; Mirage; Columbia*

a)
b)
c)

FIGURE 1.18 **One actor, one film, multiple roles**
In *The Nutty Professor* (1996), Eddie Murphy plays (a) exercise guru Lance Perkins and all five members of the Klump family: Papa Klump, Ernie Klump, Mama Klump, (b) Grandma Klump, and (c) Professor Sherman Klump. On the right in (c) is Rick Baker, a special-effects makeup artist who won the first Academy Award for makeup for *An American Werewolf in London* (1981) and also worked on *The Exorcist* (1973), *King Kong* (1976), *Star Wars* (1977), *Starman* (1984), *Gremlins 2: The New Batch* (1990), *Men in Black* (1997), *Mighty Joe Young* (1998), *Nutty Professor II: The Klumps* (2000), *How the Grinch Stole Christmas* (2000), *Planet of the Apes* (2001), *Men in Black II* (2002), *The Ring* (2002), *The Hulk* (2003), and *The Cat in the Hat* (2003). *Brian Grazer & Russell Simmons; Universal City Studios*

1.19). Versatile foreign stars include the French actor Gérard Depardieu and Gong Li of China (Figure 1.20).

Some actors (for stage and screen), such as Marlon Brando, Al Pacino, and Joanne Woodward, are **Method actors**. These performers were trained at the Actors Studio in New York, which was founded by Elia Kazan and two others in 1947 and later brought to prominence by Lee Strasberg. Before filming begins, the Method actor tries to figure out the character's biography and psychology and immerses herself or himself in the role (for example, by not sleeping enough if the actor needs to create an exhausted or distraught character). During filming, Method actors try to become the character and

a)   b)

FIGURE 1.19 The versatile Vanessa Redgrave
Vanessa Redgrave (born in England in 1937) and her younger sister, Lynn, are the actor daughters
of Michael Redgrave, who himself had a distinguished career on the stage and screen. Of Vanessa,
David Thomson has written, "There is a case for her as the best actress alive, ready for further
challenge" (719). Critic Stephen Holden has written, "Vanessa Redgrave fuses the passion of a
true believer with a gift for empathy that allows her to get so thoroughly wired up to her characters' nervous systems that their minutest emotional responses detonate across her face like tiny
time bombs. At the same time, this riveting actress conveys the unsettling radar-like intuition of
someone who can see beyond the moment to a larger truth, and this gives her an aura of imperial
power. Not only does she seem more sensitive than the rest of us, but she also appears stronger
and more resolved." (a) In the biographical *Isadora* (1968), Redgrave plays the title role of Isadora
Duncan, the famous unconventional 1920s dancer. (b) In *Orpheus Descending* (1990), which is
based on a Tennessee Williams play and was made for TV, Redgrave plays a frustrated woman
running her husband's mercantile store in a Southern town as he is dying of cancer and often verbally abusing her. Other films from Redgrave's long and varied career include *Blow-Up* (1966),
Camelot (1967), Ken Russell's *The Devils* (1971), *Julia* (1977), *Wetherby* (1985), *The Ballad of Sad
Cafe* (1991), *Howards End* (1992), the documentary *Looking for Richard* (1998), *Cradle Will Rock*
(1999), *A Rumor of Angels* (2000), and many others. (a) *Hakim, Universal; Universal;* (b) *Nederlander
Film; Turner Pictures*

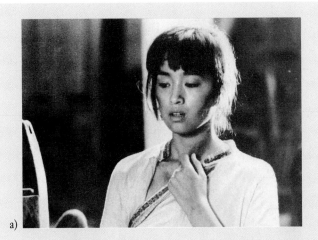 

a)   b)

FIGURE 1.20 Chinese star Gong Li in two diverse roles
Gong Li (a) as an abused wife who takes a lover, has a son by him, and years later suffers misery from the boy in *Ju Dou* (1990) and (b) as an innocent university-educated young woman trapped into becoming the fourth concubine of a wealthy man in *Raise the Red Lantern* (1991). Gong Li has also played such diverse roles as a golden-hearted prostitute in *Farewell My Concubine* (1993) and, as Berenice Reynaud wrote, "an unglamorous, heavily pregnant, touchingly obstinate heroine" in *The Story of Qui Ju* (1992). She has also appeared in a comedy. (a) *Miramax;* (b) *Fu-Sheng Chiu; Orion*

feel and act as the character would, in part by using people they know as models and by remembering situations from their own lives that evoke much the same emotion. Some Method actors, such as Robert De Niro, may also change their bodies drastically to look and feel the part (Figure 1.21).

Character actors specialize in more or less the same type of secondary roles. Dennis Hopper, for example, has often played antisocial or deranged characters (Figure 1.22). Actors such as Sydney Greenstreet, Peter Lorre, Harrison Ford, Gene Hackman, Morgan Freeman, and Kathy Bates began as character actors then became stars; but most character actors do not.

And then there are nonprofessional actors, people with no training or experience before the camera or theatrical audiences. Famed Soviet director Sergei Eisenstein preferred nonprofessional actors for ideological reasons: the Communist masses, not individuals, were the main subjects of his films. Eisenstein also believed that nonprofessional actors could best represent the types of working-class men and women and their oppressors, such as capitalists, Russian Orthodox priests, and tsarist military forces. With nonprofessional actors, directors do not have to worry about audiences being distracted by the actors' previous roles or their activities in their private

a)   b)

FIGURE 1.21 Method acting
In *Raging Bull* (1980), Robert De Niro as Jake La Motta (a) in his early years when he was a boxer
and (b) in later years after his fighting days were over. To play the role of the aging prize fighter
turned nightclub owner, Method actor De Niro put on more than fifty pounds. *Robert Chartoff &*
Irwin Winkler; United Artists

lives. For reasons of novelty and greater authenticity, some filmmakers use at
least some nonprofessional actors. Sometimes they have no choice. Films
such as *Salt of the Earth* (1954, see Figure 7.30 on p. 320) and many films
made in countries with widespread poverty may use few or no trained film
actors because none are available locally and the production lacks the money
to bring them in. Sometimes nonprofessional actors are so awkward and
self-conscious, as in the low-budget *Night of the Living Dead* (1968), that they
are distracting, even unintentionally laughable, unless the film becomes a
cult classic whose acting limitations have become part of the film's appeal.
But some directors, such as Vittorio De Sica of Italy, are especially adroit at
casting nonprofessional actors and eliciting effective performances.

A **cameo** is a small part usually limited to one scene and often unbilled.
Though cameos are usually played by famous actors, they may also be played
by famous people playing themselves or by insiders in the film community—

a)   b)

FIGURE 1.22 A character actor
(a) Dennis Hopper as a drug-dealing and drug-consuming hippie cyclist in *Easy Rider* (1969).
(b) Hopper thirty years later in a cameo as a rehab patient who had been shot in the mouth by
a former wife in *Jesus' Son* (1999). In addition to the roles illustrated here, Hopper plays a free-
lance photographer into drugs and his own mental world in *Apocalypse Now* (1979). In *Blue
Velvet* (1986), Hopper plays a sadistic, deranged, gas-inhaling, kidnapping lowlife whose mood
ranges all the way from angry to furious. He plays the town drunk in *Hoosiers* (1986), a drug-
crazed recluse in *River's Edge* (1987), a Vietnam marine veteran turned double-crossing hit
man in *Red Rock West* (1994), a vengeful terrorist in *Speed* (1994), and in *Waterworld* (1995) a
witty aquatic gang leader ironically called Deacon who has a shaved head, piratelike eye-patch,
and codpiece. In all these and other roles, he is so compelling that many viewers automatically
expect his characters to be unstable, unreliable, menacing, and perhaps into drugs or alcohol.
(a) *Peter Fonda; Raybert Productions; Columbia;* (b) *Jesus' Son Productions; Lions Gate*

a type of cinematic insider's joke. Often cameos are little unexpected treats
for viewers, who enjoy spotting the cameo, as when attorney Johnnie
Cochran and Reverend Al Sharpton appear briefly as protesters outside a
building in *Bamboozled* (2000). Perhaps the best-known cameos in cinema
were done by film director Alfred Hitchcock, who put himself in *The Lodger*
(1926) and every film he directed after it. Because he appears early in his

FIGURE 1.23 Hitchcock cameo
In Hitchcock's first American film, *Rebecca* (1940), as in other films he directed since 1926, the director makes a brief, silent, and in this case not very subtle appearance early in the film that has no impact on the story. *Selznick International; United Artists*

producer: A person in charge of the business and administrative aspects of making a film.

films for only seconds and says nothing, Hitchcock contributes little as an actor to the movies he made. But his cameos are playful and enjoyable tests of viewers' powers of observation and a challenge to Hitchcock's inventiveness because he did not want to make the same type of appearance twice (Figure 1.23).

CASTING

Once an actor becomes strongly associated with certain behavior outside the movies, for many viewers the actor in a film becomes more than the character. Sometimes those extra qualities supplement a role. Thus John Wayne, who was well known for his conservative political beliefs, was cast in many conservative and patriotic roles. Conversely, Jane Fonda, who was well known for her liberal political views, has often played liberal characters. To make a character even more unappealing than the script does, filmmakers sometimes choose an actor who is well known for playing offensive roles. In *Contempt* (*Le Mépris*, 1963), the part of the arrogant and pushy American film **producer** is played by Jack Palance, who was known for his portrayal of unsavory characters in such earlier films as the western *Shane* (1953).

Stars sometimes decide to be cast against type: to play a role unlike their usual previous roles. One of the most famous examples of casting against type is Henry Fonda's role in a 1968 Italian ("spaghetti") western:

> In Sergio Leone's *Once upon a Time in the West*, a homesteader and his two children are spreading a picnic in their front yard. This frontier idyll is shattered by the materialization of five menacing figures, who kill the family in cold blood. The sense of violation is exacerbated by the familiar, reassuring smile on the face of the leader of these merciless specters. It's the smile of young Abe Lincoln, Tom Joad [Figure 1.24a], Wyatt Earp, and Mister Roberts, a smile which for four decades in American movies has reflected the honesty, moral integrity, and egalitarian values synonymous with its owner—Henry Fonda.
>
> By casting him as an almost abstract personification of evil . . . [Figure 1.24b], Leone dramatically reversed the prevailing image of Fonda, at once complicating and commenting on our responses to that image. (Morris 220)

Another example of casting against type can be seen by comparing and contrasting two films with Tom Hanks (Figure 1.24c–d). Yet another example of being cast against type is Jennifer Aniston, popular star of the long-running

FIGURE 1.24 Casting against type

Throughout most of his career, Henry Fonda, the father of movie actors Peter Fonda and Jane Fonda and a grandfather to movie actor Bridget Fonda, played a succession of largely admirable characters. In 1939, he played Abraham Lincoln in *Young Mr. Lincoln*. (a) Fonda played the sympathetic Tom Joad in the film adaptation of the John Steinbeck Depression-era novel, *The Grapes of Wrath* (1940). He also played a low-keyed, trustworthy, and honorable Marshal Wyatt Earp in the western *My Darling Clementine* (1946). In *12 Angry Men* (1957), he played an intelligent, fair-minded juror whose actions ensure that justice is served. (b) But in the western *Once upon a Time in the West* (1968), in a striking example of casting against type, Fonda plays a killer without a conscience.

Tom Hanks has played mostly characters that are decent, likeable, sometimes romantic, sometimes funny. Generally, he has played characters viewers admire. (c) In *Saving Private Ryan* (1998), he plays an army officer who is under enormous pressure yet is dedicated to following commands, protecting the men under his command, and finally paying the ultimate price of duty to country. (d) In *Road to Perdition* (2002), however, Hanks is cast against type and plays a stoical, trustworthy, lethal enforcer for an early 1930s Midwestern Irish mob boss. In *Perdition*, Hanks's performance was a bit of a stretch for him, and most viewers and critics find it credible. The role, however, did not call for Hanks to display a wide range of emotion or to play a character less admirable than the movie's other adult male characters. And occasional critics were unconvinced. John Powers, for example, said that Hanks "makes the hit man seem like a lumbering and doleful plumber rather than a killer burning with the need for revenge." (a) *20th Century–Fox; The Museum of Modern Art/Film Stills Archive;* (b) *Paramount; Rafran; San Marco; The Museum of Modern Art/Film Stills Archive;* (c) Frame enlargement. *Steven Spielberg; DreamWorks; Paramount;* (d) Frame enlargement. *Sam Mendes; DreamWorks*

FIGURE 1.25 Two stars cast against type
Before *Mad Dog and Glory* (1992), Bill Murray (left) had played various amusing laid-back characters, and Robert De Niro had often played urban criminals. In *Mad Dog and Glory*, they switch roles. Murray plays a Chicago hood who goes to a psychoanalyst and wants to be a stand-up comedian, but he also enslaves others and sanctions murders. De Niro plays a sensitive, mild-mannered police photographer ironically called "Mad Dog" by his co-workers. Frame enlargement. *Barbara De Fina & Martin Scorsese; Universal City Studios*

TV show *Friends*, who grew tired of doing mainly romantic comedy and agreed to star in *The Good Girl* (2002), in which she plays a Texas variety store clerk bored with work and marriage and dangerously attracted to a much younger, unstable male co-worker.

Casting against type is chancy. Some viewers want an actor to play the same type of role repeatedly and may reject the actor in the new role. But as is illustrated by the casting of Henry Fonda in *Once upon a Time in the West*, casting against type can be effective. It can make viewers entertain new ideas: in this case, perhaps to be jolted into the realization that someone who looks virtuous and has a good reputation may in fact be evil. Casting against type may also intrigue viewers into seeing if the actors can succeed in the challenge they have undertaken (Figure 1.25).

In some animated films and some documentaries, the voices of famous actors are used. In those cases, actors may also be cast against type. Usually, though, actors' voices are used as one might expect. In *Toy Story* (1995) and *Toy Story 2* (1999), Don Rickles, who is known for his insulting grouchiness, supplies the voice of the caustic, cynical Mr. Potato Head, and Wallace Shawn, who has played uncertain and insecure characters, supplies the voice of the unassertive (Tyrannosaurus) Rex. In *The Lion King* (1994), little Simba says to his malevolent uncle Scar, "You're so weird." In reply Scar, played by Jeremy Irons, says, "You have no idea." Scar's response echoes one of the most famous lines from one of Irons's earlier films, *Reversal of Fortune* (1990). In *The Lion King*, Irons's voice conjures forth the ironic, evil, duplicitous, weary characters he has played, whereas the deep, masculine, confident, commanding voice of James Earl Jones as the lion king evokes the mostly admirable characters from earlier in his career (Figure 1.26). In Ken Burns's nine-part documentary film *Baseball* (1994), offscreen Gregory Peck—who has played a variety of well-known movie heroes—reads letters or statements by admirable men, such as the 1919 Chicago White Sox manager, who was unaware that eight of his players were involved in throwing the World Series. Elsewhere in the baseball documentary, Peck reads a passage from the Bible. In contrast, less recognizable actors were chosen to read the statements of "Shoeless" Joe Jackson, who was involved in the 1919 scandal, and the parts of other men the film represents partially negatively, such as Ty Cobb.

a) b)

FIGURE 1.26 Earlier roles, earlier characteristics
(a) Jeremy Irons as complex twin gynecologists who come to a messy end in David Cronenberg's *Dead Ringers* (1988). Irons also played Dr. Claus von Bülow, a man charged with trying to murder his socialite wife in *Reversal of Fortune* (1990). More recently, he enacted the snarling Uber-Morlock in the 2002 *Time Machine*. (b) James Earl Jones as an African American U.S. senator who becomes president of the United States in *The Man* (1972). In plays, on TV, and in films, Jones has brought a seriousness to the many admirable characters he has played, including a professional prize fighter in *The Great White Hope* (1970), actor Paul Robeson, writer Alex Haley, a writer in *Field of Dreams* (1989), and a South African backwoods minister in *Cry, the Beloved Country* (1995). (a) *David Cronenberg & Marc Boyman; 20th Century-Fox;* (b) *Lee Rich; Lorimar Television; Paramount*

PROCESS AND PERFORMANCE

A good part for an actor begins with an effective script and shrewd casting. Without a well-written part, usually an actor can achieve little. Often a successful screen performance also owes much to the casting. Many film directors, including Martin Scorsese, say that if a movie is cast well, the acting will largely take care of itself. As Robert Altman has said, "Once I get a film cast, 85% of my creative work is finished, and the actors really kind of take over. . . . I have to be there because they would all be fighting with each other if I weren't" (quoted in Cheng).

Unlike stage actors, movie actors in big productions do their scenes one shot at a time, often doing multiple **takes** (versions) of each shot. Often actors have to do scenes out of order and with long waits between shots. Because filming is so time-consuming and costly, usually all the scenes at one setting are filmed together; then the crew moves to another setting and films all the scenes that take place there. Over many days, actors enact snippets here and snippets there. Unlike stage actors, film actors must be able to focus and deliver an appropriate performance after much waiting for the right weather, the right lighting, the right something or other.

Sometimes actors improvise during filming: they say spontaneously what they think their characters would say under the circumstances. Although many directors allow no improvisation, in some films directed by

FIGURE 1.27 Understated comic acting
In *Mr. and Mrs. Bridge* (1990) with Joanne Woodward and Paul Newman, Newman's and Woodward's body language and facial expressions subtly and amusingly convey their doubts about the merits of the painting they are looking at. *Ismail Merchant; Miramax*

Robert Altman, Mike Leigh, Rainer Werner Fassbinder, and Martin Scorsese, improvisation plays a major role.[1] Those directors believe that what is improvised by an actor immersed in the character and the scene is likely to be truer to the character and situation than what has been imagined by the writer beforehand.

The actor's best allies are usually a skillful scriptwriter and a director who sets the contexts and establishes the moods for each shot. As is discussed in Chapter 3, the film actor can also be helped by an editor who selects the best take of each shot, shortens an ineffective shot, or **cuts** to a **reaction shot** during a lapse in the performance. Music can also cover weak moments in a performance. In films with many action scenes and frequent brief shots, the writer, director, and editor may strongly shape a performance.

Usually an effective performance persuades viewers that the character is believable and helps keep viewers involved in the story. However, there is no one type of effective performance: what works depends on the film's **style** and to some extent on the viewers' culture. Droll, understated comedy—such as that found in *Mr. and Mrs. Bridge*—calls for restrained acting (1990, Figure 1.27). Many films, including many comic films, work best if the acting is exaggerated. Film acting should be judged not by one absolute standard but in light of the kind of film it is in.

cut (verb): To sever and splice film while editing.

reaction shot: A shot, usually of a face, that shows someone or occasionally an animal reacting to an event.

style: The way subjects are represented in a text, such as a film. Styles for films or parts of films include farce, black comedy, fantasy, realism, abstract, magic realism, and parody.

---

[1] Some critics would add John Cassavetes to this list of directors, but as Todd Berliner demonstrates, "John Cassavetes' dialogue comes so close to real speech that it often sounds peculiar, like ad-libbing. Many people think Cassavetes films are, in fact, ad-libbed, but they are not. . . . For all his later films, Cassavetes wrote complete scripts, and, although he and the actors changed the script in rehearsals, they rarely improvised on camera" (7).

Judging a performance of what is usually meant to be an invisible art is difficult after only one viewing. A second viewing, a comparison of a script and the performance, or a viewing of other films with the same actor can help viewers see the actor's successes and failures.

COMPOSITION: THE USES OF SPACE

Composition is the third and final major aspect of mise en scène. Composition refers to how lighting and subjects are arranged in relation to each other and to the sides of the frame. Before filming each shot, filmmakers may consider the following questions: What shape should the image be? When should empty space be used? Should the arrangement of subjects on the sides of the frame or in the foreground and background be used to convey or reinforce a meaning or mood? Should the width and depth of the image be used expressively within the same shot? Should the objects of main interest within the frame balance each other or not? In this section, we examine some of the consequences of answers to those and related questions.

Shape of Projected Image

The **aspect ratio** indicates the shape of an image, specifically the relationship of the image's width to its height. Thus an aspect ratio of 4:3 means that the image is wider than it is tall by a factor of 4 to 3. Throughout film history the screen has nearly always been rectangular, but at different times the projected image has been relatively wider than at other times. From about 1910 to the early 1950s, most films were shown in the **standard aspect ratio**: approximately 4:3 or 1.33:1 (Figure 1.28a). Since the 1950s, wider

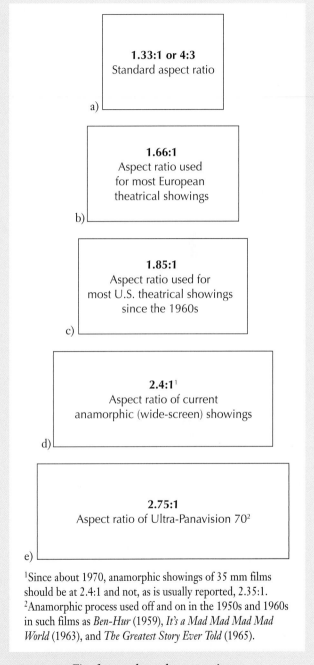

a) **1.33:1 or 4:3**
Standard aspect ratio

b) **1.66:1**
Aspect ratio used for most European theatrical showings

c) **1.85:1**
Aspect ratio used for most U.S. theatrical showings since the 1960s

d) **2.4:1**[1]
Aspect ratio of current anamorphic (wide-screen) showings

e) **2.75:1**
Aspect ratio of Ultra-Panavision 70[2]

[1]Since about 1970, anamorphic showings of 35 mm films should be at 2.4:1 and not, as is usually reported, 2.35:1.
[2]Anamorphic process used off and on in the 1950s and 1960s in such films as *Ben-Hur* (1959), *It's a Mad Mad Mad Mad World* (1963), and *The Greatest Story Ever Told* (1965).

FIGURE 1.28 **Five frequently used aspect ratios**
Movies have been shown in different rectangular shapes. Here are five of the most often used ones. They are drawn to scale.

wide-screen: A film format
with an aspect ratio noticeably
greater than 1.33:1 (a shape wider
than that of an analog TV screen).

formats have dominated in theatrical showings (Figure 1.28b–e). Figure 1.29 illustrates how **wide-screen** films can be made and later projected by using an **anamorphic lens**, which makes possible the widest images by compressing the image onto the film during filming and expanding the image back to its original width during projection.

As wide-screen formats became commonplace in the 1950s to counter the growing popularity of TV, some skeptics claimed that the wider images would be suitable only for wide subjects, such as snakes and funeral processions! But

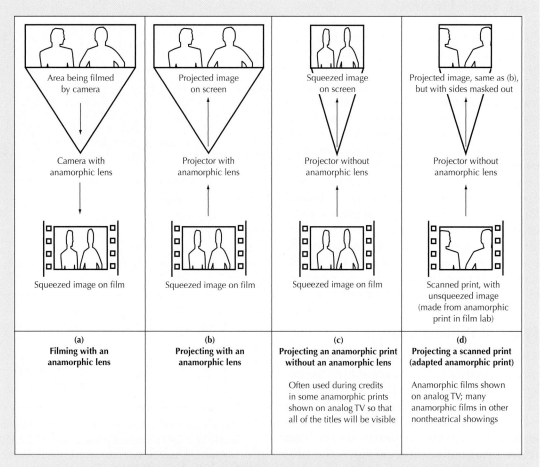

| (a)
**Filming with an
anamorphic lens** | (b)
**Projecting with an
anamorphic lens** | (c)
**Projecting an anamorphic print
without an anamorphic lens**

Often used during credits
in some anamorphic prints
shown on analog TV so that
all of the titles will be visible | (d)
**Projecting a scanned print
(adapted anamorphic print)**

Anamorphic films shown
on analog TV; many
anamorphic films in other
nontheatrical showings |

FIGURE 1.29 The anamorphic lens
An anamorphic lens can be used to compress a wide filmed image onto the film in the camera. Another anamorphic lens can be attached to a movie projector to unsqueeze the image during projection. These images are not to scale.

FIGURE 1.30 Composition and meaning
Composition can suggest major meanings in a story. With the characters at different distances from the camera and spread across the image, this composition from approximately 105¼ minutes into (*The*) *Red Desert* (1964) reinforces the sense of the characters' alienation from each other, which is one of the film's main meanings. *Film Duemila; Cinematografica; The Museum of Modern Art/Film Stills Archive*

filmmakers learned how to use the wide space effectively, as in the Italian film (*The*) *Red Desert* (1964). At various points in that film, loose framing is used, and the characters are appropriately scattered across the wide frame at various distances from one another and from the camera (Figure 1.30).

Although few filmmakers change the aspect ratio or shape of the image during filming, they can, though it was more often done in the silent era than since. A frame enlargement from *The Cabinet of Dr. Caligari* (see Figure 1.7) illustrates another way to change the shape of an image: parts of the image have been obscured by a process called **masking** to create an **iris shot**, here a diamond-shaped image. Other filmmakers change the shape of the image by simply illuminating only part of what is being filmed. As the frame enlargement from *Caligari* shows, obscuring part of the image directs viewers' attention to the visible subject.

Because films have been made in a variety of rectangular shapes and the TV screen is a fixed shape, videotape versions of movies and films broadcast on analog TV sometimes show the sides of the original image lopped off. In extreme cases—films intended for theatrical presentation in a 2.75:1 aspect ratio, such as *Ben-Hur* (1959, see Figure 9.20c on p. 442) and *It's a Mad Mad Mad Mad World* (1963, see Figure 1.28e)—less than half of the original image remains when the film is viewed in the standard aspect ratio.

A **scanned print** is a version made in the standard aspect ratio from an original anamorphic film. In making a scanned print, a technician—not the

iris shot: Shot in which part of the frame is masked or obscured, often leaving the remaining image in a circular or an oval shape.

FIGURE 1.31 Showing wide-screen films shot with spherical lenses Many theatrical films since the 1960s have been shot with a spherical lens with theaters *and* analog television in mind and can be shown in 1.85:1 in theaters (inner rectangle) or 1.33:1 elsewhere (outer rectangle). As illustrated by this frame from *Schindler's List* (1993), the visual information cropped from the top and bottom of the full image is of no importance. The wide-screen image is thus slightly more compact and ensures that the time viewers spend looking at the image will be used looking at the image's most expressive parts. Frame enlargement. *Steven Spielberg, Gerald R. Molen, and Branko Lustig; Universal*

FIGURE 1.32 The letterbox format The letterbox format is used to retain the original aspect ratio (or a close approximation of it) of a film shot with anamorphic lenses when the film is shown on TV or a video monitor, here *2001: A Space Odyssey* (1968). Letterbox images are more or less in the shape of a business envelope. Usually, the blacked-out bottom and top parts of the image are the same size, though occasionally only the bottom part of the screen is blacked out, which leaves more space for subtitles. Frame enlargement. *Stanley Kubrick; Metro-Goldwyn-Mayer*

film's editor or director—decides which part of the complete anamorphic image to show at each moment of the film or video (see Figure 1.29d). Often in scanned prints, the camera seems to glide sideways during a shot. To trained viewers, however, these horizontal movements are distracting, since they rarely occur when and how camera movements do during filming.

For years, filmmakers have known that their nonanamorphic (spherical) films might be shown in theaters and on analog television sets and have filmed in the standard aspect ratio mindful that later some of the top and bottom of the image would be cropped for wide-screen theatrical showings (Figure 1.31).

Some videotapes include a message that the image has been "formatted to fit your screen" or some similar message. But for a film originally shot with an anamorphic lens (for example, a film in **CinemaScope** or any other process with *scope* as part of its name), the full image will be visible only in a videotape, laser disc, or DVD in the **letterbox format** (Figure 1.32). Some videotapes of foreign-language films in the letterbox format include subtitles in the darkened area under the images so that viewers can see the original images in their entirety and read distinct subtitles.

CinemaScope: A wide-screen process introduced in 1953 made possible by filming and projecting with anamorphic lenses.

When considering the shape of an image on the screen, consider whether you are seeing the whole picture. If not, what you say about composition will probably not be true to the film as it was intended to be seen.

Empty Space

Empty space is often used to convey a sense of loss as in the Japanese film *Ugetsu* (*Monogatari*) (1953, Figure 1.33). Another film that uses empty space to suggest the feeling of loss is *Fargo* (1996), in which a husband arrives home and finds that his wife has been kidnapped, as he had arranged. The reality of what the husband has set in motion, however, is quickly and visually conveyed largely by empty space (things being badly out of order also contributes to the effect) (Figure 1.34).

Like everything else in a film, empty space has no inherent meaning: its impact depends on context. Empty space is not always used in a negative context. It often reinforces a sense of power and freedom, as in countless scenes of flying airplanes, or a sense of energy and free-spiritedness, as in enormous vistas in many a western and scenes of the open road (Figure 1.35).

If we see largely empty space in a shot followed by something intruding abruptly, the results can be startling. A famous example occurs in *The Shining* (1980), where viewers see a locked bathroom door, then an ax cutting through it, followed by the face of the Jack

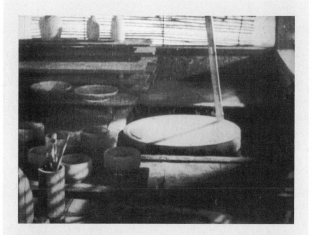

FIGURE 1.33 Empty space to convey a sense of loss
This frame from a shot late in *Ugetsu* (1953) parallels an earlier shot of the same composition with the potter's wife powering the wheel used to help make pottery. Coming late in the film, after the wife's murder in a civil war, this empty image suggests that the home is now drained of movement and life. Because of its composition and context in the film, the image here is poignant. A different camera angle or camera distance, a different framing, and the shot would not have been as effective. Frame enlargement. *Masaichi Nagata; Daiei Motion Pictures*

FIGURE 1.34 Empty space suggesting disruption of order
Four shots from three consecutive scenes beginning more than twenty-three minutes into *Fargo* (1996) in which the husband returns home and discovers that his wife has been kidnapped. (a) In the first scene, as in an earlier happier scene, the husband enters through the front door. (b) and (c) In the second scene, from inside an upstairs bathroom in which one of the kidnappers had found the wife, we see no one, no life, no movement, just a mess, including an empty shower curtain rod seen from the husband's point of view. (d) In the third scene, downstairs again, viewers see the crumpled shower curtain and the TV that the wife had been watching when the two kidnappers broke into the house. Now the TV shows no picture—not because it would likely lack a signal at that time of day or because one of the kidnappers somehow disrupted the signal input but because the empty screen contributes to the lifeless feeling of the scene: it's a dramatically appropriate detail. Frame enlargements. *Ethan Coen; PolyGram Film Productions*

Nicholson character—his face all exposed teeth, flared nostrils, staring eyes, scruffy beard, and straggly hair—eager to get to his wife to murder her. Suddenly, he has burst into his wife's space—and the viewer's. A more recent and even more dynamic example occurs in *The Bourne Identity* (2002, Figure 1.36).

FIGURE 1.35 Empty space to convey freedom
In *Wish You Were Here* (1987), the empty space and loose framing of this shot help convey a sense of freedom of movement and freedom from social convention. In a British town of the early 1950s—the place and time of the film's story—women were discouraged from displaying their bodies, but the young woman here does so defiantly. *Sarah Radclyffe; Zenith; Film Four; Atlantic Entertainment Group*

a)  b)

FIGURE 1.36 Violating space
A little more than forty-four minutes into *The Bourne Identity* (2002), (a) Matt Damon's Jason Bourne is standing before a large opaque glass window. He seems to sense something is not right. (b) Just then a would-be assassin swinging on a rope comes bursting through the window—toward Bourne and toward the viewers. This abrupt, in-your-face entry is about as rapid and startling a violation of someone's space as cinematically possible without 3-D images. Frame enlargements. *Hypnotic; Kennedy/Marshall; Universal*

Taking Sides

The width of the film image may also be used expressively. Films often show two people on opposite sides of the frame to suggest their alienation from each other. Late in *Raging Bull* (1980), the Jake La Motta character spots his brother Joey, from whom he has been estranged for years. Joey glances at Jake and walks away without a word. As Jake follows Joey, the camera moves

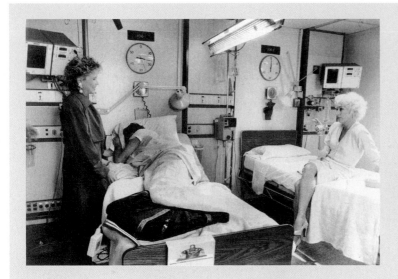

FIGURE 1.37 **Framing to display contending forces**
An often used composition, illustrated by a shot from *The Grifters* (1990): two opposing forces on opposite sides of the frame, with the object of contention between them. *Robert A. Harris & Martin Scorsese; Cineplex Odeon Films Production; Miramax*

parallel to them, and all the while we see Joey near the left edge of the frame and Jake near the right edge. The composition—the two remaining on opposite sides of the frame, Joey keeping his back to his brother—conveys the physical and emotional distance Joey wants to maintain. As in many films and staged plays, *The Grifters* (1990) often shows two opposing forces on opposite sides of the frame, with the subject of their conflict between them (Figure 1.37).

Occasionally filmmakers use split-screen **techniques** to show two or more images simultaneously on the same screen. *Napoléon* (1927) occasionally divides one standard aspect ratio screen image into three tall rectangles and early in the film divides the screen space into nine equal small rectangles, each one showing a different action. A split-screen effect may also be achieved by using separate films projected onto separate screens placed side by side, as in the ending of *Napoléon*. Often in *Napoléon*, multiple images allow the simultaneous viewing of events that are presumably happening at the same time (Figure 1.38).

A split screen may also contribute to a situation's suspense. In *Run Lola Run* (1998), the split screen shows time running out as Lola tries to reach her lover, Manni, before he foolishly tries to rob a grocery store in broad daylight (Figure 1.39). In one shot in *The Grifters*, the split screen is used to emphasize the characters' similarities (Figure 1.40).

The split-screen technique may be used for many different purposes within a film. The documentary *Woodstock* (1970) uses many variations of split screen—for example, to show action and simultaneous reactions; to show actions and someone commenting on them; to show different actions occurring simultaneously; and to show simultaneous views (different dis-

film(making) technique: Any aspect of filmmaking, such as the use of sets, lighting, sound effects, music, and editing.

a)

b)

FIGURE 1.38 Split screen serving different functions
Until near the end of Abel Gance's *Napoléon* (1927), only the middle screen of three side-by-side screens is used. During the concluding approximately eighteen minutes, three projectors and all three screens are used. (a) Viewers sometimes see one vast subject spilling over onto all three screens. Here Napoleon looks at his encamped troops. (b) More typically, late in *Napoléon*, three different images are projected at the same time, thus giving the audience the opportunity to absorb more information than is typical in a movie shown on a single screen. Frame enlargements. *Images Film Archive; The Museum of Modern Art/Film Stills Archive*

FIGURE 1.39 Split screen intensifying suspense
In *Run Lola Run* (1998), Lola is trying desperately to reach her boyfriend, Manni, before he attempts to rob a grocery story when the clock's minute hand reaches 12. The split screen intensifies the tension of the situation as the two major characters briefly share the frame with a clock whose hand is quickly approaching a fateful moment. This example illustrates how split screen can be used as an alternative to editing—here, for example, instead of separate shots of Lola, Manni, and the clock. Frame enlargement. *Stefan Arndt; Sony Pictures Classic*

FIGURE 1.40 Split screen suggesting similarities and competition
Early in *The Grifters* (1990), the main characters, who are all grifters or con artists, appear on the same screen split vertically into three areas: mother, son, and son's lover. The three characters stop almost simultaneously, turn, and look around carefully before turning back and continuing with their work: the mother to enter a racetrack and cheat her mob boss out of some winnings, the son to enter a bar where he cons two men, and the son's lover to enter a jewelry store where she tries to con the jeweler. Filming the three characters in the same position (and having all three wear sunglasses) suggests that they have much in common. Here the young man is positioned between the two women, who will soon be in fierce competition for him. Frame enlargement. *Robert A. Harris & Martin Scorsese; Cineplex Odeon Films Production; Miramax*

tances and angles) of the same subject, usually musical performers. In *Woodstock*, the extensive use of two or three simultaneous images also suggests that although the film runs nearly four hours, the events were too widespread and significant to be conveyed by one mere image at a time, even large wide-screen images.

An effect similar to split screen can be achieved without using multiple separate images or editing by showing a reflection of someone looking through a window on one side of the frame and, on the other side and through the window, what that person is looking at (Figure 1.41).

Shots involving a window, a looker, and a subject looked at are also used in *The Godfather Part II* (1974), *The Silence of the Lambs* (1991), and *Chinatown* (1974); in those films, however, the reflection is not of the looker but of what he or she sees (Figures 1.42–1.44). Another option for filmmakers is to show the looker and what is looked at in basically the same position within the frame (Figure 1.45).

A shot including a reflective surface allows filmmakers to show simultaneously a person and what he or she looks at and to maintain continuity of action,

FIGURE 1.41 Window and reflected looker
A window and carefully chosen camera angle and lighting are used in this shot from *Schindler's List* (1993) to show simultaneously Schindler looking at his factory workers and the workers he sees. If the filmmakers had instead used two shots to convey much the same information—a shot of Schindler looking and a shot of what he sees—they would have had to determine how much time to give to each shot, and the effect would have been much different. Frame enlargement. *Steven Spielberg, Gerald R. Molen, and Branko Lustig; Universal*

FIGURE 1.42 Window and reflected subject looked at
In this publicity still for *The Godfather Part II* (1974), viewers see the subject through the window and, elsewhere on the window, a reflection of what he sees. The filmmakers could have shown the boy followed by a point-of-view shot of what he sees, or vice versa. Instead they chose to present all the visual information in this one shot, which maintains continuity of action, space, and time. *Francis Ford Coppola; The Coppola Company; Paramount*

FIGURE 1.43 Window and reflected subject behind the looker
This publicity still for *The Silence of the Lambs* (1991) shows the character on the right looking and the character she is looking at being reflected off a glass or plastic barrier separating them. *Edward Saxon & Kenneth Utt; Orion*

FIGURE 1.45 Looker and reflective surface revealing object looked at
In *Chinatown* (1974), a detective takes photographs of a man and a young woman, and viewers see the detective at work and the object of his camera all within the same frame. As with the earlier examples of looker and a reflection of the object looked at within the same frame, this shot in *Chinatown* conveys much information quickly and economically and without editing: a shot of the detective then a shot of the man and young woman, or vice versa. Frame enlargement. *Robert Evans; Long Road Productions; Paramount*

FIGURE 1.44 Reflection of looker superimposed on subject looked at
This photo from *My Darling Clementine* (1946) shows the looker's face superimposed on what he sees. Doc Holliday, who is seriously ill and getting worse, drinks a shot of whiskey, looks at his medical certificate, says his own name scornfully ("Doctor John Holliday"), throws the whiskey glass, and breaks the glass protecting the certificate. Frame enlargement. *Samuel G. Engel; 20th Century–Fox*

time, and space rather than divide the information into a shot of the person looking and a shot of what is looked at. In other words, they choose to communicate the information by the composition of a single shot, not by the editing of two or more shots.

Foreground and Background

How filmmakers position people and objects in the background and how they situate them in the foreground are options that influence what the images communicate. The background of an action may go unnoticed because it is obscurely lit or out of focus or because subjects in the foreground draw much of the viewers' attention. However, in some contexts, such as when a dangerous character is lurking nearby, a dark or out-of-focus background may command viewers' attention. Often the background is in focus, and details there affect how viewers respond to something in the foreground, or details in the foreground may influence how viewers react to something in the background.

A filmmaker may use **rack focus**: changing the focus *during* a shot (usually rapidly) from foreground to background or vice versa. Rack focus directs viewers' attention to the relationship of foreground and background or to the action of a different subject. Often this shift in focus is done during a dramatic moment or while the primary subject of the shot is moving, or both, so that viewers do not notice the change in focus (Figure 1.46). In *Fatal Attraction*, the Michael Douglas character is being stalked by a former

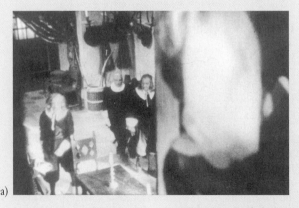

a)   b)

FIGURE 1.46 Rack focus
In this shot from early in Cocteau's *Beauty and the Beast* (1946), rack focus is used to shift the focus from the background subjects to a foreground subject *during* the shot. As in many examples of rack focus, simultaneous movement (here Beauty turning her head) helps disguise the change in focus during the shot. Frame enlargements. *Jean Cocteau; Anthology Film Archives*

lover. As he reaches into his car for a rabbit cage and the cage momentarily crosses the screen, rack focus is used quickly and unobtrusively, and the previously out-of-focus background is replaced with a focused image of the stalker's black car. Like the use of reflective surfaces discussed in the previous section, rack focus is an alternative to editing and maintains continuity of action, space, and time.

Foreground and background elements can be positioned to show how important something in the background is to the subject in the foreground, as in *The General* (1926, Figure 1.47). Another example of background subjects revealing the values of a subject in the foreground is seen in *Do the Right Thing* (1989, Figure 1.48).

Sometimes viewers can see something significant in the background that a character in the foreground is unaware of. Such is the case in a scene in *Local Hero* (1983). The citizens of a small Scottish village have been meeting in a church but do not want the main character in the

FIGURE 1.47 Background conveying something about subject in foreground
This photograph is Johnnie's gift to his sweetheart early in Buster Keaton's *The General* (1926). Overemphasizing the background at the expense of the human subject in the foreground effectively—and amusingly—demonstrates the extreme importance of the train to Johnnie. Frame enlargement. *Joseph M. Schenck; United Artists*

FIGURE 1.48 Expressiveness of background elements
In *Do the Right Thing* (1989), part of a setting often seen in the background reveals the values of the Italian American owner of the pizzeria seen here in the foreground. Although his clientele is mostly African American, he hangs photos of only Italian Americans, thus conveying a message of exclusiveness, not inclusiveness. *Spike Lee & Monty Ross; Forty Acres and a Mule Filmworks; Universal*

FIGURE 1.49 Foreground affecting mood and meaning
About twelve minutes into *The Graduate* (1967), Mrs. Robinson has lured recent college graduate Ben Braddock into her home where she gives him a drink, puts on music, tells him her husband should not be home for several hours, and sits exposing most of her legs. Next occurs this shot, during which Ben says "Mrs. Robinson, you're trying to seduce me," and she begins to laugh. Her leg is the largest, most prominent subject in the frame, and Ben is seen under it, smaller than part of her and lacking dominance. The shot's composition helps convey both Mrs. Robinson's attempt to test if Ben is sexually attracted to her and Ben's lack of control in the situation. Frame enlargement. *Lawrence Turman; Embassy Pictures*

foreground to know about it. As the main character talks to his assistant in the foreground, viewers can see the villagers scampering out of the church in the distant background.

Conversely, the foreground may be used to comment on the background (Figure 1.49). Sometimes filmmakers film *through* a foreground object, but viewers are so interested in the main subject in the background that they may not consider how the foreground object relates to the subject in the background. For example, when filmmakers impose something with bars (a door, a window, a headboard) in the foreground, often the suggestion is of entrapment or imprisonment for the subject in the background. An example occurs in *Wish You Were Here* (1987). Lynda—an insecure teenage woman involved with Eric, a much older man—goes to live with Eric after her father learns of the affair. Eric calls her to his bed where he has stretched out. As she approaches the bed and sits on the edge of it, the camera moves so that it looks through the bars of the headboard at the two figures. The image suggests that being there with Eric is or will be a prison for Lynda. Another example of filming through something in the foreground occurs early in *Easy Rider* (1969). After the two bikers have bought drugs, they stay outside overnight near what looks like an abandoned house. The next morning as they ride off on their motorcycles, somewhat ominously, they are seen from within the decaying abandoned house, whereas the two departing bikers could easily have been filmed without any intervening object. Or a shot may show the relationship of foreground, background, and intermediate subjects (Figure 1.50).

Occasionally, both width and depth are used expressively within the same shot. In *The Bicycle Thief* (1948; also known as *Bicycle Thieves*), when a boy is angry at his father, he is seen in the background and on the opposite side of the frame from the father (Figure 1.51).

FIGURE 1.50 Foreground, background, and in between
Nine minutes into *Unforgiven* (1992), as the Clint Eastwood character, William Munny, is trying to sort his sick pigs from the healthy ones, unexpectedly a stranger shows up. Before we viewers see him, we hear him addressing Munny ("You don't look like no rootin', tootin', son of a bitchin' cold-blooded assassin"); then we see a very long shot of the man on his horse, though we cannot see his face very well. Neither Munny nor the audience knows the stranger's mission. The composition of the following shot, seen here, and in a later shot helps sustain the possibility that he is dangerous: in the foreground, the stranger, largely unseen off the left side of the frame with his rifle within easy reach and in a line with Munny's daughter; in the background Munny's daughter; and in between the stranger and the girl and off to the right, the unarmed Munny. Frame enlargement. *Clint Eastwood; Warner Bros.*

FIGURE 1.51 Image's width and depth used expressively
After the father slaps his son in the Italian neorealist classic *The Bicycle Thief* (1948), the sulking boy keeps his physical and emotional distance. Their estrangement is suggested by the framing: they are on opposite sides of the frame and the boy is deep in the background. Frame enlargement. *Vittorio De Sica; PDS-ENIC*

Symmetrical and Asymmetrical Compositions

In symmetrical compositions with only one major subject, the subject is seen in the approximate center of the frame (Figure 1.52). In symmetrical compositions with two subjects, typically both are on the opposite sides of the frame (Figure 1.53), or both may be near the center (Figure 1.54). Even an image with many subjects can be symmetrical (Figure 1.55).

In asymmetrical compositions, major subjects are not offset or balanced by other subjects elsewhere in the frame. An expressive asymmetrical composition occurs at the end of the **French new wave** film *Shoot the Piano Player* (1960). By the penultimate scene, Charlie, the main character, has lost the woman he loves. In the last shot of the film, Charlie is on the extreme left side of the wide-screen frame; on the right side is a plain wall. Charlie appears alone and out of balance—and he is. (This effect is lost if the film is not seen in its original wide-screen aspect ratio.) A film may use asymmetrical

French new wave (cinema): A movement made up of a diverse group of French fictional films made in the late 1950s and early 1960s in reaction to the carefully scripted products of the French film industry and often as explorations of more current subjects, sometimes rendered with untraditional techniques.

FIGURE 1.52 Symmetrical composition with one subject
In a symmetrical composition from *The World of Apu* (1958), the single subject appears in the middle of the frame with nothing in focus around his head to draw the viewer's attention. Frame enlargement. *Satyajit Ray; Edward Harrison*

FIGURE 1.53 Symmetrical composition with two subjects on opposing sides of the frame
This symmetrical composition from *The Apostle* (1997) shows two subjects in conflict, one on each side of the frame. This composition seems so natural that it has long been widely used in painting, plays, and films. Frame enlargement. *Butcher's Run Films; October Films*

FIGURE 1.54 Symmetrical composition with two subjects near center of frame
A symmetrical composition from *Henry and June* (1990) shows two subjects near the center of the frame. Visually and emotionally, they are close and in harmony. Frame enlargement. *Peter Kaufman; Universal*

FIGURE 1.55 Symmetrical composition with multiple subjects
In this image from *Cabaret* (1972), characters on the right balance characters on the left, and characters in the foreground are offset by characters in the background. The image, though filled with subjects, could scarcely be more symmetrical. *Cy Feuer; Allied Artists–ABC Pictures*

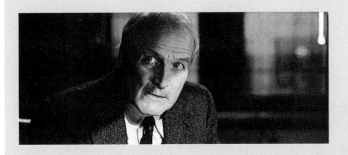

FIGURE 1.56 **Asymmetrical composition**
As illustrated here, in many (perhaps most) shots of a criminal character in *Road to Perdition* (2002), he is off to the left side of the frame, and there is nothing of corresponding interest on the opposite side of the frame. Those in the criminal world of *Road to Perdition* are out of balance with the world they live in. Frame enlargement. *The Zanuck Company; 20th Century-Fox/Dreamworks*

compositions more than only occasionally. Michelangelo Antonioni's *L'Avventura* (1960) uses them repeatedly, including in the film's last shot, an image of the two main characters off to the left of the wide-screen frame. In *L'Avventura*, typically the setting or part of it on one side of the frame offsets character(s) on the opposite side; this composition suggests the importance of the film's settings—which have little movement, vegetation, or life—and reinforces the sense that some human element is missing in the characters' lives. A more recent example of a film that uses many asymmetrical compositions is *Road to Perdition* (2002, Figure 1.56).

For an examination of some of the choices filmmakers make about mise en scène, see the feature about a shot in *Citizen Kane*, on pp. 54–55.

MISE EN SCÈNE AND THE WORLD OUTSIDE THE FRAME

Sometimes filmmakers use settings, subjects, and composition to comment on the world outside the frame—for example, to express a political viewpoint or promote a product. Mise en scène can also be used amusingly to imitate human behavior outside the film, including another film, or to pay tribute to another film.

Filmmakers may use an image to express political ideas that relate to the story yet promote the filmmakers' political views (Figure 1.57).

Mise en scène can also be used to promote businesses or corporations, products, or services. Moviemakers often make agreements with companies to display their products or services in exchange for money, promotion of the movie, or, much more often, goods and services (such as airline tickets or hotel accommodations). Sometimes the products and services shown are cited in the film's closing credits, as in "The Producers Wish to Thank Stanley Furniture, . . . Coca-Cola, . . . Black Death Vodka, Folgers Coffee, . . .

product placement: The practice of including commercial products or services, such as Coca-Cola or a particular airline, in films so that viewers can notice them.

American Tobacco." (Businesses, products, and services acknowledged under "Special Thanks To" in the closing credits for *The Player* [1992] can be found on pp. 618–19.) So widespread has **product placement** become that some large companies pay specialists to arrange for placements in movies.

Movies may plug a related corporation. *Contact* (1997), released by Warner Bros., features Cable News Network (CNN) repeatedly. That's no accident. At the time *Contact* was being made, both Warner Bros. and CNN were owned by Time Warner (Figure 1.58). Sony used its Columbia Pictures branch to make *Panic Room* (2002), which conveniently and prominently features Sony video monitors. Increasingly in multicorporate businesses, one branch promotes another.

Product placement can be excessive and intrusive—sometimes for comic effect, sometimes not. A good example of egregious and amusing product placement is from a scene in *Wayne's World* (1992) that shows five name-brand products in a row, including Garth suddenly dressed in Reebok shoes, a Reebok jogging suit, and a hat with "Reebok" emblazoned under the brim and above it. So dressed, Wayne flaunts the Pizza Hut logo while declaring he would never do a product placement. More often, intrusive product placements are not amusing. During a three-minute stretch well into *EDtv* (1999), we hear that a major character prefers Pepsi over Coke, see a Pepsi machine, and see several characters with Pepsi cans.

Product placements may be subtle and go unnoticed by many viewers. The documentary film *The Big One* (1998) focuses on a book tour and many side trips that satirist and filmmaker Michael Moore takes in hopes of ques-

FIGURE 1.58 Using mise en scène to promote a (related) corporation
During *Contact*, which shows humans establishing contact with extraterrestrial life, viewers often see TV coverage of spectacular unfolding (fictional movie) events, and that coverage is supposedly by CNN. Curious that CNN is so prominent, one might think. The reason: at the time *Contact* was released by Warner Bros. (1997), Time Warner controlled both Warner Bros. and CNN. The makers of *Contact* could either have made up a fictitious network or paid an existing network (say, NBC), or used CNN (for free or for lesser permissions fees). For the parent corporation Time Warner, the choice would be obvious. Frame enlargement. *Steve Starkey and Robert Zemeckis; Warner Bros.*

tioning CEOs about corporate downsizing and sending jobs abroad even though the companies have been making huge profits. Moore gives considerable screen time to his visits to bookstores to give talks and to the long lines of people waiting for him to sign their copy of his book. There's also a shot of his book as number 1 on the *New York Times* list of best sellers. The message: his book is important (and so is Michael Moore). One could argue that promoting his book and the messages it contains indirectly supports the other main subject of the film: the pain suffered by workers who are victims of downsizing. But it could be argued that the emphasis on his book's popularity is also a self-promoting product placement. Regardless of Moore's motives, in *The Big One* Michael Moore's book functions as a pervasive product placement.

Some filmmakers sometimes conceal product identity to avoid possible lawsuits. If a movie shows someone committing a crime, filmmakers are usually careful not to associate the crime with a commercial product. That is why viewers will not see a character listen to a particular heavy metal number or drink a famous whiskey and then go out and murder someone.

Mise en scène can also be used to **parody** someone or something. A parody is an amusing imitation of human behavior or of a **text** (such as a book or film), part of a text, or texts. For example, the mise en scène of a shot inside Han Solo's spaceship in *Star Wars* is amusingly re-created in many later parodies, such as the 1987 movie *Spaceballs* (see Figure 5.15a and c on p. 230). Mise en scène can also be used to pay an **homage**, a tribute to an earlier text (such as a film) or part of one. For instance, some shots of the main character in the French new wave film *Breathless* (1959) re-create mannerisms that Humphrey Bogart used in his films (see Figure 7.32a–b on p. 314).

text: Something that people produce or modify to communicate meaning. Examples are films, photographs, paintings, newspaper articles, operas, and T-shirts with a message.

CLOSE-UP: MISE EN SCÈNE IN *CITIZEN KANE*

FIGURE 1.59 Expressive composition in *Citizen Kane* (1941)
Seen here is part of a publicity still that closely approximates the composition of a few frames of the scene that begins nearly sixty-six minutes into the film where a rival politician is trying to blackmail Kane (center) into quitting the governor's race or face public disclosure of Kane's affair with a single woman (left). Kane's wife, Emily, is seen on the right of the frame. *Orson Welles; RKO General Pictures*

For each scene, filmmakers decide how much to rely on mise en scène—settings, subjects, and composition.

In one scene in *Citizen Kane*, which begins 65¾ minutes into the film, Charles Foster Kane, a wealthy newspaper publisher, and his wife, Emily, have gone to the residence of Kane's mistress, Susan, where they are met by Susan and a crooked politician (Gettys). During the scene Gettys tries to pressure Kane into withdrawing from the governor's race against him or face public exposure of Kane's affair with Susan. Early in the scene, one shot lasting 117 seconds contains the following compositions and major movements:

1. At the beginning of the shot, Kane is near the left of the frame facing Emily, who is on the right of the frame.

2. Susan joins Kane on the left (the camera pivots slightly to the left to accommodate her), and the three characters are positioned much

as they are in Figure 1.59, although in the film Kane is closer to Susan than to Emily.

3. Kane turns away from the two women and starts to walk toward the background. As he walks, the camera pivots slightly to the right to follow him, excluding Susan from the frame, and Emily pivots and looks toward the background, where Kane joins Gettys. Emily is in the left foreground; the two men are in the background.

4. Gettys walks forward while staying on the right of the frame. Kane remains in the background, in the center of the frame between Emily on the left and Gettys on the right. For the rest of the shot, Gettys and Emily remain in the foreground and on opposite sides of the frame.

5. Susan rushes into the frame from the left and joins Kane in the background, center.

6. Susan steps forward a few steps; Kane remains in the background.

7. Susan takes another step forward; Kane remains in the background.
8. Toward the end of the shot, Emily, Susan, and Gettys, all in the foreground, turn their heads and look toward Kane, who remains in the background (they await his response to Gettys's blackmail attempt).

Much is going on in this lengthy shot, both in groupings of characters (shifting alignments and confrontations) and in dramatic impact (who commands attention, who has power, who does not).

For example, the shot begins with Kane between his wife and mistress, though closer to the mistress than his wife, and with the blackmailer out of the frame—in fact, waiting in a dark part of the room. The shot ends with Kane in the center of the frame facing his wife, mistress, and blackmailer in the foreground. By his own choice, he is physically and emotionally alone. In spite of his wife's practical advice and his mistress's emotional appeals, he is determined that only he will make the decision he is about to announce.

SUMMARY

In this and other publications, the term *mise en scène*, which is originally a theatrical term, signifies the major aspects filmmaking shares with staging a play. It refers to the selection of setting, subjects, and composition of each shot. Normally in complex film productions, the director makes final decisions about mise en scène.

Settings

- A setting is the place where filmed action occurs. It is either a set, which has been built for use in the film, or a location, which is any place other than a film studio that is used for filming.
- A setting can be the main subject of a shot or scene. Depending on the needs of the scene, settings may be limbo (indistinct), realistic, or nonrealistic.
- Settings often reveal the time and place of a scene, create or intensify moods, and help reveal what people (in a documentary film) or characters (in a fictional film) are like. Throughout a film, changes in the settings can also mirror changes in situations and moods.

Subjects

- In films, fictional characters or real people are the usual subjects, and their actions and appearances help reveal their nature.

- Performers may be stars, Method actors, character actors, or nonprofessional actors. There is some overlap among these categories: a star, for example, may also be a Method actor. Depending on the desired results, actors may be cast by type or against type.

- Usually film actors must perform their scenes out of order, in brief segments, and often after long waits.

- Effective performances may depend on the script, casting, direction, editing, and music. There is no one type of effective performance: what is judged effective depends in part on the viewers' culture and the film's style, its manner of presenting its subject.

Composition: The Uses of Space

- Filmmakers, especially cinematographers and directors, decide the shape of the overall image. They also decide how to use the space within an image: when and how to use empty space and what will be conveyed by the arrangement of significant objects on the sides of the frame, in the foreground, or in the background. Filmmakers also decide if compositions are to be symmetrical or asymmetrical.

- Composition influences what viewers see positioned in relationship to the subject and how the subject is situated within the frame; what information is revealed to viewers that the characters do not know; and what viewers learn about the characters' personalities or situations.

- Many films are seen in an aspect ratio (or shape) other than the one the filmmakers intended, and the compositions and the meanings and moods they help convey are thus altered, sometimes severely.

Mise en Scène and the World outside the Frame

- Mise en scène can be used to promote a political viewpoint or commercial product (the latter practice is called *product placement*).

- Mise en scène can be used to parody human behavior or a text (such as a film). It can also be used to pay homage to an earlier text or part of one.

Major Terms about Mise en Scène

Below, numbers in italics refer to the pages where the terms are explained. All terms are defined in more detail in the Illustrated Glossary beginning on p. 621.

anamorphic lens *36*	character actor *27*	designer or production
aspect ratio *35*	CinemaScope *39*	designer *11*
cameo *28*	composition *35*	expressionism *17*

QUESTIONS ABOUT MISE EN SCÈNE

The following questions are intended to help viewers understand mise en scène and their responses to it. Not all the questions are appropriate for every film. In thinking out, discussing, and writing responses to those questions most appropriate for the film being examined, be careful to stick with the issues the questions raise, to answer all parts of the questions, to explain the reasons for your answers, and to give specific examples from the film.

Settings

1. Can you tell where sets are used and where the filmmakers filmed on location? If so, what does each type of setting contribute to the film?

2. Where and to what effect is each of the following type of setting used: limbo, realistic, or nonrealistic?

3. Where are settings used to reveal time and place?

4. Where and to what effect are settings used to create or intensify moods?

5. Where and to what effect are settings used to help reveal what people (in a documentary film) or characters (in a fictional film) are like?

6. Are settings used to mirror changes in situations and moods? If so, explain.

Subjects

7. What are the film's major subjects?

8. If the major subjects are people or characters, which actions are especially expressive?

9. If the film is fictional, who is the protagonist or main character? Why do you say so? Describe the character's appearance and personality.

10. Explain which performers are stars, Method actors, character actors, or nonprofessional actors.

11. Are any of the actors cast against type? If so, explain how so.

12. Are any of the actors cast to type? If so, cite some previous roles, and explain how they are consistent with the present role.

Composition

13. What is the film's intended aspect ratio? Are you seeing the film in its intended aspect ratio? If not, how does the changed aspect ratio alter the film's compositions?

14. In significant excerpts from the film, how do background and foreground elements relate to each other?

15. In significant parts of the film, how do subjects on the sides of the image relate to each other?

16. Are significant subjects bunched up within the frame or spread apart? Are they in the center of the frame or off to a side?

17. In the fictional film, is composition used to reveal to viewers information that the characters could not know?

18. Are significant subjects arranged in such a way as to balance out the composition or to create an imbalance?

Mise en Scène and the World outside the Frame

19. Where is mise en scène used to promote a political viewpoint?

20. Where is mise en scène used to promote a business or corporation, a commercial product, or a service?

21. Where is mise en scène used to parody human behavior or a text (such as a film)?

22. Where is mise en scène used to pay homage to an earlier text or part of one?

WORKS CITED

Berliner, Todd. "Hollywood Movie Dialogue and the 'Real Realism' of John Cassavetes." *Film Quarterly* 52.3 (Spring 1999): 2–16.

Cheng, Scarlet. "It's All in the Acting." *Los Angeles Times* 8 April 1999. Accessed at <http://www.calendarlive.com/home/calendarlive//calendar/t000031433.html> (no longer accessible at this site).

Dunne, John Gregory. *Monster: Living off the Big Screen*. New York: Random House, 1997.

Erickson, Steve. "*Taste of Cherry*." *Film Quarterly* 52.3 (Spring 1999): 52–54.

Holden, Stephen. "A Rumor of Angels: A Friendship Based on Tough Love and Phony Tears." Review. *New York Times* (late ed.) 1 Feb. 2002: E20.

Jarmusch, Jim. *Fresh Air*, National Public Radio, 11 April 2000.

Kehr, Dave. "Big Stars in Little Movies." *The New York Times on the Web* 12 Sept. 1999. <http://www.nytimes.com/library/arts/091299ns-small-films.html>.

Morris, George. "Henry Fonda." *The National Society of Film Critics on the Movie Star*. Ed. Elisabeth Weis. New York: Penguin, 1981.

Naremore, James. *Acting in the Cinema*. Berkeley: U of California P, 1988.

Pechter, William S. "Cagney vs. Allen vs. Brooks: On the Indispensability of the Performer." *The National Society of Film Critics on the Movie Star*. Ed. Elisabeth Weis. New York: Penguin, 1981.

Powers, John. Review of *Road to Perdition*. *Fresh Air*, National Public Radio, 12 July 2002.

Reynaud, Berenice. "Gong Li and the Glamour of the Chinese Star." *Sight and Sound* Aug. 1993: 12–15.

Thomson, David. *The New Biographical Dictionary of Film*. New York: Knopf, 2002.

FOR FURTHER READING

Affron, Charles, and Mirella Jona Affron. *Sets in Motion: Art Direction and Film Narrative*. New Brunswick, NJ: Rutgers UP, 1995. On the status of art direction in cinema and how set design can function in narrative films, with interpretations of many specific sets and films.

Bruzzi, Stella. *Undressing Cinema: Clothing and Identity in the Movies*. London: Routledge, 1997. Citing detailed examples from a variety of mostly popular films, Bruzzi demonstrates how clothes are key elements in the construction of cinematic gender, identity, sexuality, and desire. The chapters are divided into three parts: "Dressing Up," "Gender," and "Beyond Gender."

By Design: Interviews with Film Production Designers. Ed. Vincent LoBrutto. Westport, CT: Praeger, 1992. Interviews with twenty film production designers; the book includes a glossary and a bibliography with many annotated entries.

Carringer, Robert L. *The Making of Citizen Kane*. Rev. and updated. Berkeley: U of California P, 1996. An in-depth examination that includes a chapter on the art director. Many black-and-white illustrations.

Dyer, Richard. *Stars*. 2nd ed. London: British Film Institute, 1998. Discusses stars in terms of social phenomenon, images, and signs and includes Dyer's detailed interpretations on such stars as Marlon Brando, Bette Davis, Jane Fonda, Marilyn Monroe, and John Wayne.

Garnett, Tay. *Directing: Learn from the Masters*. Lanham, MD: Scarecrow, 1996. Directors such as Scorsese, Spielberg, Malle, Fellini, and Truffaut discuss their decisions in making films.

Heisner, Beverly. *Production Design in the Contemporary American Film: A Critical Study of Twenty-three Movies and Their Designers*. Jefferson, NC: McFarland, 1997. American films from the 1980s and 1990s are discussed under five headings: "Realistic Films Set in the Present Day," "Stylized Films Set in the Present Day," "Period Films," "Period Films That Move through Several Decades," and "Science Fiction and Fantasy Films."

Lumet, Sidney. *Making Movies*. New York: Knopf, 1995. On filmmaking by a famous American director. Chapter 6 is on art direction and clothes.

Michaels, Lloyd. *The Phantom of the Cinema: Character in Modern Film*. Albany: State U of New York P, 1998. Focuses on the representation of character in film and includes discussion of a variety of films with elusive and ambiguous main characters.

Miller, Mark Crispin. "Advertising: End of Story." *Seeing through Movies*. Ed. Mark Crispin Miller. New York: Pantheon, 1990. 186–246. A detailed discussion of product placement, sometimes called *product plugging*.

Screen Acting. Ed. Alan Lovell and Peter Kramer. London: Routledge, 1999. Argues for the centrality of the actor's performance to a film's impact, offers directions for studying film performances, and discusses the acting styles of various movie actors.

Sennett, Robert S. *Setting the Scene: The Great Hollywood Art Directors*. New York: Abrams, 1994. Includes chapters on art direction in the silent film, the Hollywood musical, classic horror films, science fiction, and the western. Each chapter focuses on a few (usually famous) movies. Many photographs and sketches.

Tashiro, C. S. *Pretty Pictures: Production Design and the History Film*. Austin: U of Texas P, 1998. Shows how production design, which is broadly defined to include all processes used to create a film's visuals, can support or contradict a film's story or exist in its own parallel realm of meaning.

CHAPTER 2

Cinematography

WHAT MOVIES DO IS MAKE PERCEPTION EASIER. The darkened theater cuts out the claims of peripheral vision. The large images on the screen open up the perceived world for analysis . . . and allow [viewers] to see details simply not available in ordinary experience. Because film makers can further assist perception by careful lighting, lens choice, and camera placement, and can guide expectations and discriminations in a thousand more subtle ways, they can radically enhance the efficiency of seeing. . . . And, in a sense, the film maker can make the viewer more intelligent perceptually, at least while the film is running. Movies use perception in ways that make being "perceptive" remarkably easy. That is one reason why they are so involving. (Eidsvik 21, 23)

Terms in **boldface** are defined in the Illustrated Glossary beginning on page 621.

In the previous chapter we saw how **setting**, subjects, and **composition**—all essential components of staged plays—can function in a film. In this closely related chapter, we explore some of the cinematic aspects of filming, such as some of the many ways the film stock, lighting, camera lenses, camera distances and angles, and camera movement affect the finished images. We take up these topics in a temporal order: the film stock that is put into the camera; some of the ways the camera itself may be manipulated during filming; and after filming is completed, the ways that the cinematography may be corrected or supplemented digitally. Whether through the latest digital equipment or through photochemical equipment, cinematography always strongly influences how viewers respond to the finished film: it helps convey the subject matter in expressive ways and powerfully shapes the viewers' emotional responses and the meanings viewers detect in films.

setting: The place where filmed action occurs, either a set, which has been built for use in a film, or a location, which is any place other than one built for use in a movie.

composition: The arrangement of settings, lighting, and subjects (usually people and objects) within the frame.

FILM STOCK

Film stock is unexposed and unprocessed motion-picture film. It is made up of two basic components (Figure 2.1). The clear, flexible base resembles the **leader** on microfilm—the clear or opaque piece of film that is threaded into

grain: One of the many tiny light-sensitive particles embedded in gelatin that is attached to a clear, flexible film base (celluloid).

scene: A section of a narrative that gives the impression of continuous action taking place in continuous time and space.

documentary film: A film or video representation of actual (not imaginary) subjects.

footage: A length of exposed motion-picture film.

a microfilm reader. On top of the base is a thin gelatin coating called the **emulsion**, which contains millions of tiny light-sensitive **grains**. After the emulsion is exposed to light, it can be chemically developed to hold an image. The emulsion is also what has been scratched when you see continuous unwanted vertical lines in a projected movie.

The film or video stock influences the film's finished look, including its sharpness of detail, range of light and shadow, and quality of color. Cinematographers try to select film stocks that give the finished film an appropriate look. In preparing to film *Eve's Bayou* (1997), a family drama set in Louisiana in 1962, cinematographer Amy Vincent did extensive location scouting, shot hundreds of stills at various locations, and studied photographs of the period and place to be re-created in the movie. Later she chose different film stocks to achieve different effects. One stock was used for day interiors, one for day exteriors, one for night exteriors, and yet another for a character's "vision" **scenes** ("Newcomers"). Many **documentary films** combine older documentary **footage** with more recent footage shot on a different film stock. *Hearts of Darkness: A Filmmaker's Apocalypse* (1991), for example, combines footage shot during the making of *Apocalypse Now* (1979) with footage of interviews shot on a different film stock decades later.

The different film stocks help viewers differentiate between the reactions of cast and crew then and their later recollections of the same events.

With the commercial viability of digital videotape in recent years, some cinematographers film parts of the movie on a particular film stock and shoot other parts using digital video, which is later transferred to film. Examples include Errol Morris's documentary *Fast, Cheap & Out of Control* (1997), the German fictional film *Run Lola Run* (1998), and Spike Lee's *Bamboozled* (2000). As we see in more detail in the next chapter, for various reasons, including costs and ease of use, more and more filmmakers film entirely on digital tape, edit the material with computers, and transfer the results to film for theatrical showings.

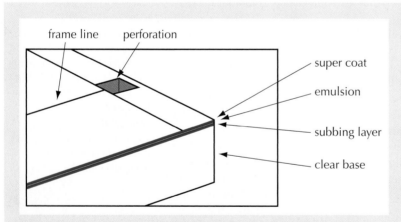

FIGURE 2.1 Film's components (not to scale)
A piece of film consists of a clear base, which constitutes most of the film's overall thickness, and the emulsion, which consists of a thin layer of gelatin in which are suspended the tiny light-sensitive crystals that make up the image after exposure to light. The emulsion is attached to the base by a clear adhesive called the *subbing layer*. A super coat on top of the emulsion protects it against scratching. Most film also has an antihalation backing (not shown) to prevent light reflection back through the base that would cause a blurred effect (halation) around the bright part of an image, as with bright oncoming headlights. (Adapted from Malkiewicz 50)

Gauge

Film stocks are available in various **gauges** or widths (Figure 2.2). The most common width used for filming and projecting movies in commercial theaters is 35 millimeter (mm), though movies may be filmed in 16 mm, enlarged, and copied onto 35 mm film. Increasingly, films such as *Time Code* (2000) are shot mostly or entirely on digital video and transferred to 35 mm film for theatrical showings. Occasionally, movies are shot on 65 mm stock and copied to 70 mm film for showings, though few movie theaters have the equipment to show 70 mm films. Generally, the wider the film gauge, the sharper the projected images (the laboratory work is also a determinant of sharpness). A 35 mm print of a movie, for example, is less grainy than a 16 mm print of the same film (if both are seen on the same screen and projected from the same distance). Although both prints have the same density of particles or grain in the film emulsion, the area of the 35 mm frame is much greater than that of the 16 mm frame (see Figure 2.2b and a), and to fill up the screen the 16 mm film needs to be magnified much more than the 35 mm print. With the increased magnification comes increased graininess, just

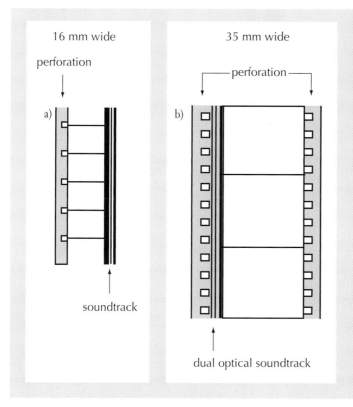

16 mm wide

perforation

a)

soundtrack

35 mm wide

perforation

b)

dual optical soundtrack

FIGURE 2.2 Four film formats (actual size)
(a) 16 mm wide. Occasionally used by small commercial theaters, TV stations, industry, military, and schools and universities. Usually, the aspect ratio of the projected image is 1.33:1. Other formats in 16 mm include anamorphic (squeezed) prints with an aspect ratio of 2.4:1 when projected with an anamorphic lens. (b) 35 mm wide. Used in most commercial theaters, sometimes for major TV showings, and showings at some large universities. When projected, the screen image may have an aspect ratio of 1.33:1; 1.66:1 for many European theatrical showings; 1.85:1 for most U.S. spherical (nonanamorphic) theatrical showings; or 2.4:1 for anamorphic showings.

(continued on p. 64)

FIGURE 2.2 (continued)
(c) 70 mm wide, nonanamorphic (unsqueezed) image. Used only in selected large theaters. Aspect ratio: 2.2:1. In the United States and western Europe, films shown in 70 mm usually are shot on 35 mm and enlarged or are filmed in 65 mm and printed on 70 mm stock.

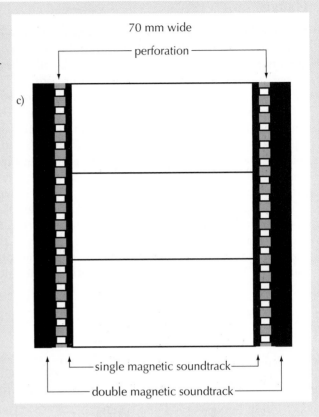

70 mm wide

perforation

c)

single magnetic soundtrack

double magnetic soundtrack

(continued on p. 65)

as when you hold a piece of processed film up to a light and look at it through a magnifying glass, you will see more of the grain than if you look at it with the naked eye.

Speed

The quality of an image also depends on the speed of the film stock, its sensitivity to light. **Slow film stock**, which often requires considerably more light than **fast film stock**, can produce fine grain and a detailed, nuanced image. Often slow film stocks are used for musicals filmed on **sets** and for other films in which detailed images are important and the lighting can be carefully controlled during filming (Figure 2.3).

Fast film stock requires less light than a slow film stock. Often it is used in documentaries, especially when lighting options are limited, and in fictional films hoping to capture a documentary look (Figure 2.4). Fast film stock is also used in fictional film scenes with little available lighting. In older

set: A constructed setting where action is filmed; it can be indoors or outdoors.

FIGURE 2.2 (concluded)
(d) 15 perforation/70 mm format. Used by IMAX. Filmed and projected by running the film horizontally through the camera and projector. The space for each frame is about ten times larger than the area of the 35 mm frame. The projector aspect ratio is 1.43:1.

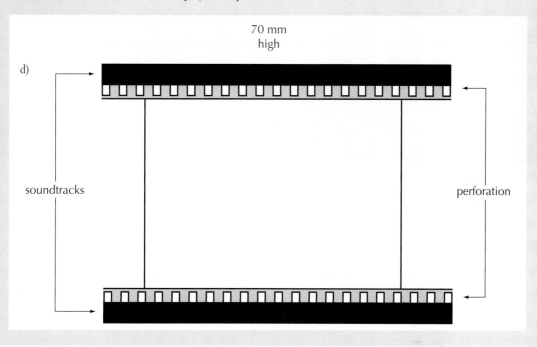

FIGURE 2.3 Fine-grain image
This fine-grain image of Jennifer Lopez appears in *Maid in Manhattan* (2002), which is yet another loose remake of the Cinderella story. The choices made in film stock, lighting, and lab work ensured that this fine-grain image immediately reveals the details of the actor's jewelry, the warmth of her smile, and the radiance of her eyes. Fine-grain images tend to be associated with controlled shooting conditions and professional quality and can help nurture the impression that the shot was made on a set, not on location. Frame enlargement. *Revolution Studios & Shoelace Productions; Columbia*

FIGURE 2.4 Rough-grain or grainy image
Grainy images may be achieved with older fast film stock or by other means and tend to be associated with amateur filmmaking, newsreels, old footage, and old documentary films. Sometimes, as in parts of *Citizen Kane* and *Forrest Gump*, grainy images are deliberately created to support the illusion of old footage. In *Pi* (1998), film stock that produces very high contrast and depending on the light either washed-out, overly dark, or grainy images gives a documentary feeling to this film about the lifestyle and work of an eccentric, brilliant loner mathematician. Note especially here the grainy texture of the subject's right cheek, chin, and neck and of the door. *Eric Watson; Artisan Entertainment*

films, fast film stock produces graininess. However, today's fast film stocks—and **fast lenses**, which transmit light efficiently—can produce remarkably detailed results even when shot with low levels of lighting, though current black-and-white stocks produce grainier results than current color stocks.

Film processing can also affect graininess. Some filmmakers ask the laboratory to make the processed film grainier to create or enhance certain effects. This may be done, for example, to depict harsh living conditions.

Color

> It's funny how the colours of the real world only seem really real when you viddy [see] them on a [movie] screen. —Narrator of *A Clockwork Orange* (1971 film)

As early as 1896, some films had color. Some black-and-white films were hand-colored (each frame was painted with different colors using small brushes, sometimes in assembly-line fashion). Other early films, including many major **feature films** of the 1910s and 1920s, were **tinted**: whole scenes or groups of related scenes were dyed a color, and the same color was used for similar scenes or **sequences** throughout the film. Thus battle scenes might be tinted red, and night scenes blue. Different tints could also indicate **flashbacks** or fantasies, as in the classic French film *Napoléon* (1927). By 1932, Technicolor combined three **negatives**, each sensitive to red, green, or blue, and in 1935, the first three-color Technicolor feature film was produced. Initially, color was used in ways that might surprise modern viewers: "In the 1930s and 1940s, . . . [Hollywood] decreed that colour should be reserved for certain genres that in themselves were not particularly realistic—stylized and spectacle genres (musicals, fantasy, epics)" (Hayward 70). But by the early 1950s, to counter the growing popularity of black-and-white tele-

feature film: A fictional film that is at least sixty minutes long.

sequence: A series of related consecutive scenes, perceived as a major unit of a narrative film.

flashback: A shot or a few shots, a brief scene, or (rarely) a sequence that interrupts a narrative to show earlier events.

negative: Unexposed film stock used to record negative images.

vision, more and more movies were made in color, and color was well on its way to becoming the usual way of showing **celluloid** lives.

celluloid (adj.): movie

Unfortunately, when you study film color, you cannot be certain you are seeing the shades and intensities that the filmmakers intended. Prints of color films, including those for theatrical release, may vary in quality because most are mass-produced. Eastman color films, especially those made for many years after 1949, usually turn reddish with age. Many color photographs available for study are not from the finished film and do not convey the film's colors very faithfully.

There are also special considerations to be aware of when discussing the significance of color. Color may be used in so many ways that it is important not to overgeneralize. As with discussions of all cinematic **techniques**, discussion of color is most useful when it is considered in context, including where the color is used in the film and how the color is used in conjunction with other filmmaking techniques. It is also important to remember that color associations vary from culture to culture. For example, in pre-Communist China, yellow was often associated with the emperor, and saffron (orange-yellow) with Buddhist robes.

film(making) technique: Any aspect of filmmaking, such as the use of sets, lighting, sound effects, music, and editing.

Saturated color, which is intense and vivid, has been used in countless contexts, such as to render the heat and tension of a setting, to show powerful emotions, and to represent violent actions. Saturated color may be used throughout an image as in the Japanese movie *Princess Mononoke* (1997). In the movie, people intent on industrializing the wilderness threaten nature, and at one point warriors of the iron foundry's boss fire guns that seem to shoot fire. Next, viewers see one of their targets, a boar running in a blazing forest (Plate 2). (The color plates follow p. 70.) Saturated color may emanate from light offscreen. In *Blood Simple* (1984, 2000), a detective hired by a bar owner to kill his wife and her lover has broken into the lover's house, has taken the woman's gun from her purse, and is walking in the direction of the bedroom where the lovers are. The scene is bathed in a blue light originating inexplicably from outside the house. The unnatural lighting (along with the low angle and shadows on the side of the detective's face) adds to the strange mood of the scene (Plate 3). Saturated color may also be employed in only part of the image to draw attention to that part of it, as in Plate 4.

Desaturated color is muted, dull, and pale. Filmmakers may use it to suggest a lack of energy or the draining of life, as throughout Werner Herzog's *Nosferatu, the Vampyre* (1979) and in the late scenes of *Terms of Endearment* (1983), where the Debra Winger character is losing her bout with cancer. The desaturated color in the Robert Altman western *McCabe and Mrs. Miller* (1971) has two purposes: Altman wanted the film to have the look of old, faded color photographs, and the desaturated color is appropriate to the story, which is set in a damp, cold environment and ends in death for one of the two main characters. Desaturated color may establish and reinforce certain moods throughout a film, as in the world created for Tim Burton's *Sleepy Hollow* (1999)—a world where there are lots of clouds and fog, the sun never shines, nothing is in bloom, the trees are bare, it's cold, gloomy, and colorless, and the land is assaulted by a headless horseman intent on beheading those who still live (Plate 5). Other films use desaturated color only part of the time, as in *Gangs of New York* (2002, Plate 6).

A film may display only a limited color spectrum, as throughout *Road to Perdition* (2002, Plate 7). As that film's director said, the film's cinematographer deals in "muted shades of gray" (Zone 42). Conversely and more typically, color films have a wide range of color (Plate 8).

Different colors can be used to help viewers keep oriented as to location and **plotline**. *Traffic* (2000) shows a long, complicated story with many major characters and different settings in both Mexico and the United States. The story alternates between characters in one location and other characters in another location. Early in the movie, occasional title cards help viewers stay oriented. Throughout the film, the three basic color schemes have the same effect. Sequences in Northern Mexico and Mexico City, mostly about the Benicio Del Toro character and those with whom he interacts, are rendered in various shades of burnt yellow, which at times, as in the desert, intensifies the sense of heat and dryness (Plate 9). Sequences in California and Texas, of the Catherine Zeta-Jones character and many others, are seen in approximately normal coloring (Plates 10–11). Finally, the sequences of the Michael Douglas character at work in Ohio and Washington, D.C., of that character with his wife and daughter, and of the daughter's misadventures into drugs are all bathed in blue, except for interior night scenes (Plate 12).

Different color schemes can be used to contrast very different types of characters. In *One Hour Photo* (2002), the main character is a repressed, solitary photo processor at a Wal-Mart–like store. Outside work, he consistently wears desaturated, neutral colors; his apartment is the same except for his collection of stolen color photographs of the Yorkin family covering one wall; and his car is white (Plate 13). How very different are the colors of the Yorkin family, with whom he has long been obsessed; the three Yorkins live in a world of vibrant and varied colors (Plate 14). Similarly, in *About Schmidt* (2002) the Jack Nicholson character wears muted colors, whereas his daughter's future mother-in-law, played by Kathy Bates, sometimes wears loud colors.

Even more prominent in *About Schmidt* are the gray and light tans that Schmidt wears after he retires and the ubiquitous gray exterior lighting (Plates 15–16). "*About Schmidt* is visually awash in cold, almost steel-gray tones. 'That's kind of the feeling Omaha had at that time of year,' says [the film's cinematographer James] Glennon. '. . . I think it's much better and more appropriate to let the film have that rather cold look, instead of trying to warm things up with a kind of false optimism'" (Silberg 80).

Saturated and desaturated colors can be used to demarcate different locations and thus different types of action, as in the musical *Chicago* (2002, Plates 17–18). "The key to devising the film's look lay in creating a visual demarcation between the Onyx [Theater, where the musical numbers are staged] and the so-called 'book scenes,' or narrative segments. Marshall [the

plotline: A narrative or series of related events usually involving only a few characters or people and capable of functioning on its own as a story.

director], Beebe [the cinematographer] and Myhre [the production designer] decided that the former would be staged in saturated colors, whereas the latter would be rendered in muted blues and grays" (Pavlus 48).

In *Vertigo* (1958, 1996), contrasting colors are worn by contrasting yet related characters. Certain colors are associated with Madeline, and another group of colors with Judy (Plates 19–20). When Judy finally appears looking like Madeline, appropriately Judy emerges out of a hazy green light (a Judy color) wearing a gray suit (a Madeline color). In only the last scene does Judy/Madeline wear black, which forebodes an unhappy fate.

Colors are sometimes classified as "warm" or "cool." In most Western societies, warm colors (reds, oranges, and yellows) tend to be thought of as hot, dangerous, lively, and assertive and tend to stand forward in paintings and photographs. People trying to be sexy or feeling sexy may drive red sports cars, and women in Western cultures who want to emphasize their sex appeal (or sexual availability) have long been known to use red to draw attention to themselves. In Western cultures, the association of red with sexuality is at least as old as the "scarlet women" of the Bible. Warm colors may be used in countless other contexts—for example, to draw attention to nature's beauty. The western *Posse* (1993), like so many other westerns and so many other films, includes brief shots that momentarily and wordlessly draw attention to the environment's beauty (Plate 21).

Colors on the other side of the spectrum (greens, blues, and violets) are often characterized as "cool." In Europe and the United States, these colors tend to be associated with safety, reason, control, relaxation, and sometimes sadness or melancholy. Green traffic lights and blue or green hospital interiors are supposed to calm and reassure. In *Reversal of Fortune* (1990), blue light is used in all the scenes with Sunny von Bülow in a coma. The room, her bedding, and her skin are all bluish. In those scenes, the blue suggests cold and lack of vitality, the opposite of a lively, passionate red. In the scenes in which windows are open and it's zero degrees outside, and in a night scene in the von Bülows' bedroom after they have argued and turned out the light, blue adds to the sense of coldness. Blue is used in many other ways in our lives. In the United States, for example, dark blue has been worn with business suits, perhaps to downplay the clothing and body and to suggest restrained emotions. Cool colors can also emphasize the desolation and malevolence of a damaged environment, as in the brief views of the lifeless earth seen in *The Matrix* (1999)—the result of twenty-first-century warfare between humankind and a race of advanced machines spawned by artificial intelligence (Plate 22).

Films may use mostly cool colors in the early scenes and increasingly use warm colors as the film progresses. Conversely, films may initially use mainly warm colors and as the film progresses use cool colors. *The Iron Giant* (1999), which is initially set in autumnal rural Maine, at first uses warm colors (Plate 23). After the first snowfall and the action shifts to the American military attacking the extraterrestrial creature, the setting is awash in whites, grays, and black (Plate 24).

In Western cultures, white—which is not, strictly speaking, a color—has long been associated with innocence and purity, as in white wedding dresses. White may also imply lack of emotion or subdued emotions, as in men's white dress shirts. Those deeply ingrained associations are put to use in George Lucas's first feature film, *THX 1138* (1971), which is set in a repressive futuristic society where except for the robot police that are dressed in black and wear rigid silvery metallic masks, people are dressed entirely in white and all the interiors are off-white (Plate 25).

Black, which is strictly speaking also not a color, is often associated with death or evil, as in black hats on countless cowboy gunslingers; the black charioteer costume and black horses of the Roman tribune in *Ben-Hur* (1959); the black bra Janet Leigh has changed into when she decides to steal $40,000 in *Psycho* (1960); black capes on all those movie Draculas; and Darth Vader's helmet, face piece, and clothing. Darkness is also often used as in *The Blair Witch Project* (1999), where many scenes are set at night and the darkness and unidentifiable sounds may work on the viewer's imagination (Plate 26). Black is used in many situations, so it is important not to overgeneralize. For example, in Europe, the United States, Latin America, and Japan—though not in China—black is the preferred color for mourning. In some formal contexts, black clothing can seem stately and elegant, at least to those raised in Western societies.

From the early days of cinema, filmmakers have occasionally combined color shots and black-and-white shots in the same film. The most famous example is *The Wizard of Oz* (1939), which renders Dorothy's ordinary life in Kansas in black and white and her adventures in Oz in color. *Schindler's List* (1993) reverses the situation: the opening and closing are in color and are set in the present, whereas, with the exception of a red coat on a little girl, the body of the film is in black and white and is set in the past. Alternating between color and black and white throughout a film may draw attention to the practice. Such alterations are used in the documentary *Madonna: Truth or Dare* (1991), where most of the concert footage is in color and the off-stage action in black and white; in *JFK* (1991), where most of the flashbacks are in black and white; and in *The Hurricane* (1999), where black-and-white shots are used for past boxing matches (see Figure 5.4 on p. 207) and for other background events, such as demonstrations in the boxer's behalf. Filmmakers can reverse the usual usage. In the Chinese film *The Road Home* (1999), the gloomy present of death and grief is seen in black and white, whereas the glorious earlier times of youthful courtship and love are rendered in vivid colors.

As in many aspects of filmmaking, filmmakers often use colors intuitively, simply because they seem right. As cinematographer Allen Daviau has said of cinematographers in general, "We do some things that we don't even realize we're doing until we see the film put together. And we did them out of instinct." And as in other aspects of moviemaking, colors in films are often more true-to-movies than true-to-life. Many viewers know, for example, that real blood in movies wouldn't look real enough (or exciting enough?), so various substitutes are used during filming.

PLATE 1 The expressiveness of costumes
In *Shakespeare in Love* (1998), the costume seen here is worn by Queen Elizabeth of England and quickly and clearly conveys her wealth, power, status, and uniqueness. Frame enlargement. *Bedford Falls Productions, Universal Pictures, & Miramax; Miramax*

PLATE 2 Saturated color throughout a frame
In this image from *Princess Mononoke* (1997), saturated warm colors connoting the intensity of the fire and the ferocity of the situation permeate the image. Frame enlargement. *Studio Ghibli; Miramax*

PLATE 3 Saturated color from light offscreen
Saturated color may be used in the light illuminating a scene, as in this scene from *Blood Simple* (1984, 2000). Frame enlargement. *Ethan Coen; USA Films*

PLATE 4 Saturated color in part of frame
In this photograph for *La vie est belle* (Zaire [now Congo], 1987), the bright colors of the woman's dress (plus her girth and gesture) draw attention to her, even though she is at the extreme right side of the frame. *Courtesy of California Newsreel, San Francisco*

Plates 1–4

PLATE 5 Desaturated colors throughout a film
In *Sleepy Hollow* (1999), the colors are drained of intensity. Nearly all of the colors are desaturated: dull, drab, faint, grayish. Even the actors' faces are pallid. Frame enlargement. *Mandalay Pictures; Paramount*

PLATE 6 Desaturated colors, selective use
In *Gangs of New York* (2002), desaturated color is used in the scenes of poverty and the working class, as in this frame of an Irish immigrant newly arrived in New York. Frame enlargement. *Alberto Grimaldi & Harvey Weinstein; Miramax*

PLATE 7 Limited spectrum of colors throughout a film
Cinematographer Conrad Hall worked mightily to ensure that *Road to Perdition* (2001) is a color film that looks very close to black and white, as here in this period shot of Chicago. Frame enlargement. *Sam Mendes; DreamWorks*

PLATE 8 Wide spectrum of colors throughout a film
In this frame from *Smoke Signals* (1998), the many shadings of color in the woman's dress, her skin tones, her hair, and the indistinct background exhibit a broad range of colors. Frame enlargement. *Larry Estes & Scott M. Rosenfelt; Miramax*

Plates 5–8

PLATES 9–12 Color to demarcate different locations and plotlines

In films with complicated plots, color can be used to help the viewer stay oriented—in the case of *Traffic* (2000), to help the viewer always know which general location and which plotline is on the screen. Frame enlargements. *Laura Bickford, Marshall Herskovitz, Edward Zwick; USA Films*

PLATES 13–14 Different colors, different types of characters

As is illustrated in *One Hour Photo* (2002), filmmakers may use a certain color scheme for one character or group of characters (the loner seen here behind his car's cracked windshield) and a very different color scheme for a very different character or group of characters (the family he's obsessed with). Frame enlargements. *Pamela Koffler; Fox Searchlight*

PLATES 15–16 Character and environment in same basic desaturated colors

In *About Schmidt* (2002), Schmidt dresses in desaturated grays, charcoal, blues, and tans. In keeping with the character's personality, experiences, and moods, the exteriors are often rendered in desaturated shades of gray, as if his world is overcast. Frame enlargements. *New Line Cinema.*

Plates 13–16

PLATES 17–18 Saturated and desaturated colors to demarcate major locations
In *Chicago* (2002), musical numbers set inside a theater or within Roxie's mind are usually seen in saturated colored lights, usually blue but sometimes red or a red shaded with some orange, whereas most scenes in the jail and all the exteriors are rendered in grays. Frame enlargements. *Miramax*

PLATES 19–20 Colors to differentiate two major yet related characters
As seen in Plate 19, in *Vertigo* (1958, 1996), Madeline dresses in gray (suit), white, and a black and white combination. Her hair is blond, even white. In contrast, Judy is first seen dressed in green and has dark red hair (Plate 20) and later wears various colors, including green, red, violet, and taupe. Frame enlargements. *Paramount; Universal*

PLATE 21 Warm colors, nature's beauty
In this shot from the western *Posse* (1993), the warm colors help convey nature's beauty and the setting's heat and dryness. This shot is followed by a shot of the sun setting and a cactus in the right foreground, all still bathed in the same warm colors. Frame enlargement. *PolyGram Filmed Entertainment; Gramercy Pictures*

PLATE 22 Cold colors, nature's malevolence
In *The Matrix* (1999), what remains of earth are the types of ruins seen here, drained almost entirely of color, mostly shades of gray though with a faint tint of blue. Frame enlargement. *Joel Silver; Warner Bros.*

PLATES 23–24 Warm colors then cold colors in a film
Plate 23: In the first part of *The Iron Giant* (1999), warm, fall colors (shades of yellow, red, and orange) are used for the day scenes. (As usual, blues are used for night scenes.)
Plate 24: In the last part of the film, the military actions are associated with snow, cold, cloudy skies, and white, grays, and black. Frame enlargements. *Allison Abbate; Warner Bros.*

Plates 21-24

PLATE 25 Extensive use of white
THX 1138 (1971) is set in a futuristic society that attempts to suppress emotion. People and their residences are not individualized by colors, and all the feelings colors suggest and evoke are absent. *Lawrence Sturhahn; Warner Bros.*

PLATE 26 Extensive use of black
In *The Blair Witch Project* (1999), the leader of the student filmmakers is running in the dark, panting and screaming in confusion and fear. Blackness, and the possible dangers it might hide, engulfs both setting and characters, so that neither participants nor viewers can know where they are and what (or who) is nearby. Frame enlargement. *Haxan Entertainment; Artisan Entertainment*

PLATES 27–28 Black-and-white and color within the same frame
In *Pleasantville* (1998), the black-and-white world of the 1950s TV series that the two 1990s teens become trapped in gradually gains in color. Frame enlargements. *A Larger Than Life Production; New Line Cinema*

PLATES 29–31 Different sequences, different graphic styles and color schemes

"T.R.A.N.S.I.T." (1997) is a ten-minute nonchronological animated film composed of seven sequences, each made by a different animation team and each in its own style of graphic art. (See p. 395 for a description.) Plate 29: Early in the film but late in the fabula, the setting is on the deck of a luxury ocean liner. Plate 30: In a Venetian hotel room, Emily and the sleeping Oscar, who had slapped her. Plate 31: In a casino at Baden Baden, Germany, Oscar has won large stakes at roulette and soon will win Emily's affection. Frame enlargements. *Piet Kroon; Short 4: Seduction (DVD)*

PLATE 32 Appearance nurturing viewer expectations

"Vexation Island" (1997), which was shot on 35 mm film, has the color, resolution, and wide-screen format we expect to see when we go to a movie. Those qualities, along with the film's setting and subject, encourage viewers to initially expect a Hollywood-style movie, perhaps something like *Cast Away* (2000) set in an earlier era. (See discussion on p. 466.) Frame enlargement. *Rodney Graham, Vexation Island 1997, Courtesy Rodney Graham and 303 Gallery, New York*

LIGHTING

Light [is] the paintbrush of the cinematographer. (Turner 96)

Filmmakers often spend an enormous amount of time and money lighting their subjects. They do so because lighting can convey meaning and mood in subtle yet significant ways. The importance of lighting is evident in our lives: on sunny days, people are more likely to be cheerful; on cloudy days, people tend to feel subdued. Studies show that some people in northern climates are subject to severe depression in winter if they receive too little light. The importance of lighting in filming is suggested by the word *photography*, which literally means "writing with light."

Two Types of Light

Hard light tends to show people in unflattering ways—for example, by creating shadows in the eye sockets—so it may reveal characters or people as plain or even unattractive (Figure 2.5). Two excellent sources of hard light are a focused spotlight and bright (midday) sunlight, when the sun functions as an intense spotlight.

Soft light, which can be bright or dim or something in between, reflects off at least one object before it illuminates the subject. An excellent (and free) source of soft lighting is available during the so-called magic hour of each day. According to cinematographer Nestor Almendros, the best of the magic hour light is available for only twenty to twenty-five minutes after sunset (in the middle latitudes, with fewer minutes near the equator and more minutes near the earth's poles). Sunlight before dawn is an equally useful source of soft light. Soft lighting tends to have the opposite effects of hard lighting. It softens the border between light and shadow, so, for example, it fills facial wrinkles and makes people look younger; it makes young people look even more attractive (Figure 2.6). Typically, cinematographers use soft light to present subjects in an appealing way, as in romantic films, or to make actors look their most youthful or most attractive, as in many Hollywood studio films of the 1930s and 1940s.

Direction and Intensity of Light

The direction of light on a subject is another expressive option for filmmakers. Some ways to light a subject by using sources from different directions are illustrated in Figures 2.7 to 2.12. In all these examples, the model is the same and so is her makeup. The camera distance, lens, and angle are unchanged. But notice what different images a change in the direction of the lighting produces, what different moods and meanings. (You can usually detect the directions and intensities of most or all light sources by looking at the subject's eyes. **Catchlight**, a reflection of the light sources, is visible for all bright light that reaches the eyes.)

FIGURE 2.5 Hard lighting
The subject is illuminated by one direct, bright (spot) light. Hard light produces bright illumination; reveals many details, including imperfections in the subject; and creates shadows with sharp edges. *Model: Kimberlee Stewart; photographer: Jon Michael Terry*

FIGURE 2.6 Soft lighting
Soft light produces the appearance of smoother surfaces than hard light does by softening borders between light and shadow. If there are shadows, they will be faint. *Model: Kimberlee Stewart; photographer: Jon Michael Terry*

FIGURE 2.7 Backlighting
The model was illuminated by one light from behind. Often backlighting makes the subject seem threatening because viewers cannot interpret the subject's mood or perhaps discern the subject's identity. *Model: Kimberlee Stewart; photographer: Jon Michael Terry*

FIGURE 2.8 Top lighting
The model was illuminated by a single light from above. Top lighting used by itself is not flattering. Here the hair looks lighter than it is; a slight imperfection on the model's right cheek is visible; and she has shadows under her eyes. *Model: Kimberlee Stewart; photographer: Jon Michael Terry*

FIGURE 2.9 Bottom lighting
The model was illuminated by a single light from below. Like top lighting, bottom lighting is unflattering to the skin. Often bottom lighting also adds a touch of menace; it is often used to enhance a frightening mood, as in many horror films. *Model: Kimberlee Stewart; photographer: Jon Michael Terry*

FIGURE 2.10 Side lighting
Here the model is lit by one light from the side. Side lighting creates many shadows on the face, including prominent shadows under the eyes. It may be used to suggest someone with a divided personality or someone feeling contradictory emotions. *Model: Kimberlee Stewart; photographer: Jon Michael Terry*

FIGURE 2.11 Main, frontal lighting
The model was lit by a single light in front of her and a little to the right of the camera. This lighting presents the subject in an attractive way, though not quite as much so as main or key and fill lighting together. *Model: Kimberlee Stewart; photographer: Jon Michael Terry*

FIGURE 2.12 Key light and fill light
A combination of key light and fill light presents the subject's skin in the most appealing way. Here the slight imperfection on the model's cheek is less noticeable, and the right side of her face appears to be a little smoother than in the photo made with only main, frontal lighting (Figure 2.11). *Model: Kimberlee Stewart; photographer: Jon Michael Terry*

FIGURE 2.13 Three-point lighting
From the catchlight in Joel Grey's eyes in this publicity still for *Cabaret* (1972), we can see that the key light is to the right of the camera; a small fill light comes from slightly to the left and a little lower than the key light. Soft backlight is reflected off the back wall, but there is enough of it to highlight Grey's left shoulder a little and to set him off from the background. *Cy Feuer; Allied Artists–ABC Pictures*

For filming on a set, often at least three lights are used for each major subject: the **key light**, or main light; **fill light**, a soft light used to fill in unlit areas of the subject and reduce **contrast**; and a **backlight** (Figure 2.13). For filming, the key light is usually the first light set, or it may be handheld and moved around during a shot to keep the main subject illuminated appropri-

contrast: The difference between the lightest and darkest parts of an image.

FIGURE 2.14 Low-key lighting
A shot with low-key lighting is mainly dark, often with areas of deep dark tones. By using little or no frontal fill lighting, the filmmakers can immerse parts of the image in shadows, as is seen here in this frame from *Touch of Evil* (1958, 1998) of the film's complex main character played by Orson Welles. Low-key lighting often adds a dramatic or mysterious effect, as in many detective and crime films and in many horror films. Frame enlargement. *Albert Zugsmith; Universal*

ately. A key light and a fill light ensure adequate and fairly even illumination with few or no shadows on the subject. The backlight, often from above or below the subject, highlights at least some of its edges, such as the hair or shoulders, and helps set the subject off from the background to give a sense of depth. Lighting the main subjects and parts of a set is complicated and often requires more than three light sources.

One of the most fundamental decisions filmmakers make is how much light to shine on the objects within the frame. **Low-key lighting**, in which the subject is lit by very low levels of illumination and much of the image is bathed in darkness, may be the choice if the filmmakers want to create a dramatic or mysterious effect (Figure 2.14). At the opposite extreme, with **high-key lighting** the main subject is flooded with light, and nearly all parts of the frame are illuminated (Figure 2.15b).

It's not unusual to light different characters differently within the same scene, as director Leni Riefenstahl did: "I always made sure the men, actors or not, were lit differently from the women. They were lit from the side so their features stood out. . . . With a young woman, who must look beautiful, you need a very soft light from the front. No side-lighting at all, so no facial lines or flaws are visible."

Lighting can support the type of character an actor plays. As film scholar Richard Dyer points out, in *Butch Cassidy and the Sundance Kid* (1969) the lighting tends to glamorize the tongue-in-cheek, romantic character played by Robert Redford (Figure 2.15a). Conversely, in *All the President's Men* (1976) Redford plays a no-nonsense investigative reporter and is often lit by hard, bright lighting that does not conceal skin imperfections (Figure 2.15b).

a)

b)

FIGURE 2.15 A star lit two ways: soft lighting and hard high-key lighting
(a) Soft lighting softens lines around the eyes and enhances Robert Redford's looks in *Butch Cassidy and the Sundance Kid* (1969). (b) The bright, hard lighting often used on Redford in *All the President's Men* (1976) does not soften facial lines and enhance his looks. In this movie, he plays an investigative reporter, and lighting that glamorizes him would be inappropriate. Frame enlargement. (a) *John Foreman; 20th Century–Fox;* (b) *Wildwood Enterprises; Warner Bros.*

Shadows

Light and shadows can emphasize and deemphasize parts of an image and thereby create moods and meanings (Figure 2.16). Light and shadows are also used to draw attention to part of an image in a scene late in *Schindler's List*. Oskar Schindler has arrived at the Auschwitz concentration camp to try to save a large group of Jewish women from extermination. For much of one scene in which he bribes a Nazi officer, the top half of the officer's face is in shadows. It's as if he wears a mask, which is appropriate because he is like an impersonal outlaw hiding in the dark. The shape of shadows can also be used expressively, as in an early Hitchcock film *Blackmail* (1929, Figure 2.17).

In the 1960 *Psycho* and many other films, shadows are used to heighten mystery and suspense (Figure 2.18). When used in combination with other lighting, however, shadows can have a different effect (Figure 2.19).

a)

b)

FIGURE 2.16 Expressive use of shadows
(a) In *Citizen Kane* (1941), Charles Foster Kane signs his "Declaration of Principles" for a newspaper he has recently taken over as Jed Leland (left) and Mr. Bernstein (right) look on. Kane's face is in shadows, which undercuts this supposedly noble moment. Later in the film, we learn that Kane abandons these principles. The lighting on and the position of Bernstein remind us that Bernstein was a witness to this event, too. (This scene is part of Bernstein's version of events.) Frame enlargement. (b) A publicity still of approximately the same shot is less expressive because Welles's face is turned more toward the camera and is not obscured by shadows. This pose still fails to capture the irony of the moment: Kane's face in the dark as he makes a show of presenting his declaration of principles and signing them. The publicity still also does not capture Leland's admiration as successfully and sheds too much light on Bernstein, whereas, given the moment, most of the attention should be on Kane. *Orson Welles; RKO General Pictures*

FIGURE 2.17 **Shapes of shadows**
In *Blackmail* (1929), the main character has killed a man in self-defense. Late in the film, she has decided to surrender to the police. In this frame, the shadows of prison bars on and behind her suggest her possible fate. Frame enlargement. *BIP; The Museum of Modern Art/Circulating Film Library*

FIGURE 2.18 **Shadows to obscure the identity of a subject**
The lighting in this scene approximately forty-seven minutes into *Psycho* (1960) helps hide the identity of the attacker and make the attacker seem even more frightening. This effect is intensified by the low angle of the shot and a knife that seems as long as the attacker's forearm. Frame enlargement. *Alfred Hitchcock; Universal*

FIGURE 2.19 **Shadows, unusual lighting, unusual situation**
Near the end of the Senegalese film *Saaraba* (1988), the subject shown here believes that he has reached saaraba (a mythical place without life's misery and uncertainties). In the eleven-second shot represented here, the subject is driving a motorcycle at night, but the image was made indoors with the subject lit by three carefully positioned spotlights—one from each side and one from the back—and by one faint fill light. *Courtesy of California Newsreel, San Francisco*

Depending on context, shadows on the side of someone's face can convey different meanings. In many films, including *Touch of Evil* (1958), a shadow cast on someone's face by a character standing over her or him can convey a threatening situation (Figure 2.20). In many films, too, shadows on the side of a character's face suggest an evil, perhaps split personality, as in the image of one of Shakespeare's major villains, Richard III, from the documentary film *Looking for Richard* (1996, Figure 2.21).

Shadows and other areas of darkness can be central to an entire film or even series of films. Cinematographer Gordon Willis lit the *Godfather* films

FIGURE 2.20 Shadows to suggest a threat
Approximately seventy minutes into *Touch of Evil* (1958), several menacing men enter a woman's motel room and approach her as she is on the bed. Twice, as here, a man's shadow passes across her face as she clutches a sheet to her chest. In this scene, as in Western cultures in general, extinguishing a light or plunging some place or someone into darkness has long been associated with danger and perhaps even death. Frame enlargement. *Albert Zugsmith; Universal*

FIGURE 2.21 Shadows on the side of a face to suggest two aspects of a character
This image from about 17½ minutes into the documentary *Looking for Richard* (1996) shows the title character of Shakespeare's play *Richard III* illuminated from only one side. Given that Richard puts on one face for the public but shows a darker side when he is alone and plotting his ruthless ascension to power, the lighting seems entirely appropriate. That the lighting is also hard adds to the unglamorous results. Richard is not in any sense attractive. Frame enlargement. *Al Pacino and Michael Hadge; Fox Searchlight*

FIGURE 2.22 Shadows to obscure eyes
In this image from almost four minutes into *The Godfather* (1972), overhead lighting creates shadows around the eyes, largely obscuring them. Here and elsewhere in the film, the shadows make the eyes hard to "read" or interpret, unnatural, and a little frightening. Frame enlargement. *The Coppola Company; Paramount*

a)

b)

FIGURE 2.23 General uses of darkness and light in *The Godfather*
Beginning with the opening sequence, *The Godfather* (1972) often alternates between violent or dangerous actions in the dark and (generally) safer events that take place in the light. (a) Here, as in other films Gordon Willis has photographed, the lighting is minimal. In this scene, a corrupt police captain arrives on the scene in darkness. In many scenes in *The Godfather*, dangerous people, including the godfather himself, are often only partially visible, and the characters' eyes are obscured by darkness or seem to peer out of it (as here and as in Figure 2.22). For dangerous, powerful men—whose minds are difficult to read—the darkness seems appropriate. (b) Many other scenes in *The Godfather* are filmed outdoors or in bright light, often of happy family occasions, as in this photo of the family after the daughter's wedding. Frame enlargements. *The Coppola Company; Paramount*

as darkly as he dared—and darker than most other cinematographers would have dared. In the *Godfather* trilogy, many actors playing criminals are lit primarily from above, and frequently we can see their eyes only dimly, if at all (Figure 2.22). Given the dark and evil doings, the many dark scenes throughout the three *Godfather* films are appropriate. Then, too, darkness and shadows can be used in certain parts of a film, as in the criminal activities in *The Godfather*, and light used in contrasting parts of the film, as in most of the large family scenes (Figure 2.23).

Other Uses of Light

A film's contrasting settings may be lit differently. In *All the President's Men*, the newsrooms where the journalists work to shed light on the perpetrators of the Watergate break-in during Nixon's presidency are lit with bright, hard, white light that largely precludes shadows. In contrast, the parking garages where viewers glimpse the Watergate burglars and the unidentified informer are dark and shadowy. In *Desperately Seeking Susan* (1985), the suburban housewife's world is lit in soft light, whereas the punk world of the character played by Madonna is darker and more shadowed (Salt 288).

Filmmakers may change the lighting during a film to modulate mood and suggest meaning. Some films illuminate the main subject more and more as they proceed: for example, as the main character of *American Beauty* starts to loosen up and enjoy life, the illumination on and around him gradually increases. Some films begin in the dark and end in the dark (*Citizen Kane*). Other films begin in the light until the mood and scenes tend to turn dark, and the films end in darkness (*I Am a Fugitive from a Chain Gang*, 1932). And some films begin in the dark but end in the light (*Jaws*, 1975).

THE CAMERA

To film, cinematographers need film stock, light, and a camera. What lens or lenses are used on the camera and the location of the camera relative to the subject are crucial determinants of the final images and thus their impact on viewers.

Lenses and Focus

Images are filmed with three basic types of lenses: the **wide-angle lens**, the **normal lens**, and the **telephoto lens**. Each type of lens has different properties and creates different images (Figures 2.24–2.26). Often all three lenses are used at different times within the same film.

Striking uses of the wide-angle lens and the extreme wide-angle or **fisheye lens** occur in various parts of *Seconds* (1966, Figure 2.27). In other films, the wide-angle lens has also been used to suggest that something is not right. Near the end of *Murder on the Orient Express* (1974), the detective tells the assembled suspects about parts of earlier testimony; as he does so, snippets of interviews with the same suspects and a brief shot of a woman walking away are repeated from earlier in the film, but now we see that activity through a wide-angle lens. Again, a technique may be modified as the film's story progresses. For example, the lens used to film an important character may be changed as the story develops. In *Crossfire* (1947), an anti-Semitic character is seen early in the film through a normal 50 mm lens. As the story progressed, the director used shorter and shorter lenses. "Eventually in the last third of the picture . . . everything I shot with him was with a 25 [mm, a wide-angle lens]. . . . That slight subliminal distortion . . . made him a different kind of a character" (Dmytryk).

The normal lens is used most often in films because it most closely approximates what people see with their own eyes, and most films attempt to present the illusion of reality.

The telephoto lens has been used in many films to depict someone moving toward the camera laboriously slowly, as when the Dustin Hoffman character runs to prevent a wedding late in *The Graduate* (1967). Or it can

Three Types of Lenses

(camera distance from subjects is unchanged)

FIGURE 2.24 Wide-angle lens (here a 28 mm lens on a 35 mm camera)

- The wide-angle lens may be used to emphasize distances between subjects or between subjects and setting because it causes all planes to appear farther away from the camera and from each other than is the case with a normal lens.
- Deep focus: All planes are in sharp focus.
- Compared to a normal lens, as in Figure 2.25, more of the image's four sides are visible.
- With very wide-angle lenses or with the subject close to the camera, there is much distortion or curvature of objects, especially near the edges of the image, as in Figure 2.27b. This is sometimes called *wide-angle distortion*.
- Movements toward or away from the camera seem speeded up.
  Models: Kimberlee Stewart and Carlos Espinola; photographer: Jon Michael Terry

FIGURE 2.25 Normal lens (approximately 50 mm lens on a 35 mm camera)

At most distances, this lens causes minimal distortion of image and movement. As its name implies, the normal lens creates images close to what the normal human eye would see in the same circumstances. *Models: Kimberlee Stewart and Carlos Espinola; photographer: Jon Michael Terry*

FIGURE 2.26 Telephoto lens (in this example, 200 mm lens on a 35 mm camera)

- All planes appear closer to the camera and to each other than is the case with a normal lens (Figure 2.25).
- Shallow focus: only some of the planes very close to each other are in focus.
- Less of the image's sides is visible than is the case with a normal lens.
- Movements toward or away from the camera seem slowed down.
  Models: Kimberlee Stewart and Carlos Espinola; photographer: Jon Michael Terry

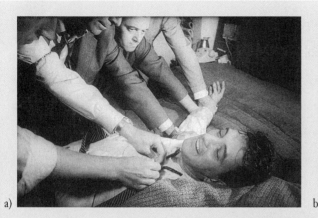

a)   b)

FIGURE 2.27 Wide-angle lenses
Seconds (1966) shows the story of a dissatisfied middle-aged man who pays a secretive company to fake his death, do major cosmetic surgery on him, and set him up with a new identity and lifestyle (he is given the name Mr. Wilson). To convey some sense of the unusual situations that Wilson then finds himself in, cinematographer James Wong Howe sometimes used wide-angle and extreme wide-angle lenses. At a party, for example, Wilson becomes roaring drunk and indiscreetly talks about his previous life. (a) A normal lens is used to show Wilson from the point of view of the sober party guests, who are also "reborns." (b) An extreme wide-angle lens—which causes major distortion of the image, especially near the edges—is used to show some of the other party guests from the point of view of the wildly intoxicated Wilson. Frame enlargements. *Edward Lewis; Paramount*

compress a long row of signs, to seemingly crowd them together, as if to suggest the dense forest of signs in modern life. The telephoto lens is used similarly in a number of the opening shots in *Short Cuts* (1993, Figure 2.28).

Choice of lens, the lens **aperture** or opening, and film stock largely determine the **depth of field**, or the distance from foreground to background in which all objects are in focus. In **deep focus**,[1] which is achieved by using a wide-angle lens or small lens aperture or both, much or all of the depth of the image is in sharp focus. In low illumination, fast lenses and fast film stock also help achieve deep focus. Film theorist André Bazin argued that deep-focus scenes consisting of **long takes** are more open to interpretation than heavily edited scenes. Certainly deep-focus shots of long duration can let viewers experience clear images for lengthy segments of uninterrupted time. Deep-focus scenes may be less manipulative than edited footage. Viewers

long take: A shot of long duration. Not to be confused with **long shot**.

---

[1]*Deep focus* is a term used by many film critics and scholars. For the same situation, filmmakers are more likely to use the phrase *great depth of field*. *Deep focus* can be confused with *depth of focus*, which refers to the distance between the camera lens and the film in the camera in which the image remains in acceptable focus.

may be freer to look at the details in the frame and select those that seem significant, though in deep-focus and other shots filmmakers can guide viewers' attention through lighting, focus, camera placement, and composition (see the feature on *Citizen Kane* on pp. 54-55). Unarguably, deep focus does give filmmakers more opportunities to use foreground-background interplay expressively (see Figure 1.47 on p. 47).

When filmmakers use **shallow focus**—for example, by using a telephoto lens or a large lens aperture in low light—usually either the foreground or the background will be in sharp focus, and viewers' attention is directed to the subject(s) in sharp focus (see Figure 2.26). Depending on the context, unfocused subjects may be ambiguous, disturbing, threatening (see Figure 1.43 on p. 45), or some other effect. Subjects may be out of focus because the director chose to focus on something else within the frame or because the lighting, film stock, and lenses available when the film was made precluded deeper focus.

FIGURE 2.28 Telephoto lens compressing subjects in different planes
Nearly thirteen minutes into Robert Altman's *Short Cuts* (1993), helicopters that have been seen spraying insecticide over Los Angeles are landing. Here—as earlier when they are seen spraying—they are filmed with a telephoto lens; consequently, they look slowed down in their forward movement and bunched up. Frame enlargement. *Cary Brokaw; Fine Line Features*

Films are shot with either a **spherical** (or flat) lens (which does not squeeze the sides of the image onto the film in the camera) or, less often, an **anamorphic lens** (which squeezes the horizontal aspect of a wide image onto a normally shaped film frame). On rare occasions, filmmakers use an anamorphic lens within a film otherwise shot with spherical lenses. Such shots make everything look tall and thin and easily suggest that something is not right or is out of balance. In *Summer of Sam* (1999), Spike Lee occasionally uses the anamorphic lens to increase the sense of the characters' and viewers' disorientation. In *Crooklyn* (1994), the anamorphic lens is used throughout the two sequences of a Brooklyn girl's stay with her relatives in what to her is an alien Virginia. The first sequence of anamorphic footage begins approximately sixty-eight minutes into the film and runs nearly twelve minutes; the second sequence begins approximately eighty-three minutes into the film and runs for nearly five minutes. The anamorphic lens is also used in a scene well into the 1997 version of *Lolita* to show Humbert Humbert and what he sees during an attack of hysteria after he learns that Lolita is seeing another man.

An image's resolution and mood may also be changed by using a **diffuser**—material such as a nylon stocking, frosted glass, spun glass, wire mesh, gelatin, or silk—placed in front of the camera lens or a light source to soften the image's resolution. Figure 2.29 illustrates how diffusers soften facial lines.

a)   b)

FIGURE 2.29 **Some functions of diffusers**
A diffuser is a material placed over a light source or camera lens to soften the image. (a) Depending on the context, a diffuser may glamorize, lend a more spiritual or ethereal look, obscure aging, or result in a combination of these consequences. (b) Heavy diffusion creates an even softer look. *Model: Eva L. Santos-Phillips; photographer: Jon Michael Terry*

Camera Distances

Camera distance helps determine what details will be noticeable in the frame, what details will be excluded, and how large the subject will appear.

Figures 2.30 to 2.35 illustrate six camera distances and the terms usually used to describe them. (In the last three photographs, a longer lens was used so the photographer would not intrude into the model's space.)

When a film begins or when it shifts to a new setting, filmmakers often use an extreme long shot that reveals the setting (an **establishing shot**). Once viewers are oriented, the camera normally moves in closer to the subject.

An extreme long shot or a long shot may create or enhance a humorous situation, perhaps because at that distance viewers cannot see the pain, discomfort, awkwardness, or embarrassment involved. The famous early film star and director Charlie Chaplin reputedly said close-up for tragedy, long shot for comedy, and his own movies repeatedly illustrate that practice, as do many later movies (Figure 2.36).

Often a camera distance is chosen for surprising reasons. Ang Lee, the director of *Sense and Sensibility* (1995), used no close-ups during the movie's

Camera Distances

FIGURE 2.30 Extreme long shot
The entire subject will be visible (if not obstructed by some intervening object) but very small in the frame, and much of the surroundings will be visible. This camera distance is often used to show the layout and expanse of a setting. *Model: Carlos Espinola; photographer: Jon Michael Terry*

FIGURE 2.31 Long shot
Usually the subject is seen in its entirety, and much of its surroundings is visible. This camera distance has many possible uses—for example, to stress how small a human subject is in relationship to its environment. *Model: Carlos Espinola; photographer: Jon Michael Terry*

FIGURE 2.32 Medium shot
This camera distance tends to give equal importance to a subject and its surroundings. When the subject is a person, the medium shot usually shows the body from the knees or waist up. *Model: Carlos Espinola; photographer: Jon Michael Terry*

FIGURE 2.33 Medium close-up
The subject fills most of the height of the frame. When the subject is a person, the medium close-up usually reveals the head and shoulders. *Model: Kimberlee Stewart; photographer: Jon Michael Terry*

FIGURE 2.34 Close-up
The subject fills the height of the frame, and the shot reveals little or none of the surroundings. When the subject is a person, the close-up normally reveals all or nearly all of the head. *Model: Kimberlee Stewart; photographer: Jon Michael Terry*

FIGURE 2.35 Extreme close-up
The subject or, frequently, part of the subject completely fills up the frame and thus looks very large to the viewer. If the subject is someone's face, only part of it is visible. This camera distance is used to show the texture of a subject or part of it. With this camera distance, typically none of the background is visible. *Model: Kimberlee Stewart; photographer: Jon Michael Terry*

FIGURE 2.36 Extreme long shot to create humor
In *Smoke Signals* (1998), twice viewers see a van at an Idaho country crossroad as we hear the radio traffic report. During the opening credits, this is the July 4, 1976, traffic report: "Big truck just went by. [pause] Now it's gone." Later in the film, the radio announcer informs listeners that the "KREZ traffic van [has been] broken down at the crossroads since 1972." The traffic reporter then gives the traffic report for the reservation: "Ain't no traffic, really." The amusing imitations of big-city traffic reports coupled with the extreme long shots revealing nothing for vast distances contribute to the humor of the shots. Frame enlargement. *Larry Estes & Scott M. Rosenfelt; Miramax*

opening ten to fifteen minutes because the thirty-five-year-old lead actor was older than the source novel indicated, and Lee wanted the audience to accept her in the part before he used close shots. At other times, an extreme long shot or a long shot distances viewers from a painful sight. In *Wish You Were Here* (1987), a teen, Lynda, feels unloved, so she seeks male attention in various ways, including displaying herself publicly and accepting as a sex partner her father's friend Eric, a man in his fifties who often belittles her. After her father discovers that Lynda has been having sex with Eric and evidently kicks her out of the house, she goes to Eric's. Soon in a medium shot we see Eric start to unbutton her blouse; then she starts crying. He responds, "Come on. . . . What's all the fuss?" She says, "Hold me, please; just hold me," but he doesn't. He keeps undressing her during most of the rest of the shot and the following medium close-up shot. In a second medium close-up shot, he talks to her briefly. Then in a long shot, we see him over her and still undressing her. Here the long shot prevents the viewer from spying too long or too closely at Lynda's emotional pain. The long shot also discourages viewers who find her sexually attractive from enjoying seeing her being further exposed. In a sense, it protects her from further (viewer) intrusion.

The long shot or extreme long shot requires viewers to be especially attentive to what is happening. Such a shot may also have emotional rewards. For instance, a long shot or extreme long shot may suggest that viewers cannot get close to or entirely understand someone (Figure 2.37).

For close-ups, the camera can be positioned near a performer's face, or, much more often, a telephoto lens will be used so the camera does not have to get close to the subject. Close-ups and medium close-ups may show the many nuances and complexities of human feeling. Directors especially fascinated with the nuances of emotions, such as the famed Swedish director

FIGURE 2.37 Extreme long shot to reveal character and environment
A frame enlargement showing Kyuzo, the master swordsman in *The Seven Samurai* (1954), as seen in an extreme long shot. Kyuzo practices, in part for the art of it, alone in the woods, and even from this distance we can detect his focus, power, and gracefulness. The extreme long shot is also effective for showing the relationship of the subject to the environment. The camera is far enough back that viewers can see all of the swordsman's body yet see much of the surroundings—the trees, the rain, the stream that runs before his feet and toward the viewers. The extreme long shot here might also suggest that we viewers (and the film's characters) cannot get close to Kyuzo; he is a loner. Frame enlargement. *Sijiro Motoki; Toho Productions*

Ingmar Bergman, may often use lengthy close-ups and **extreme close-ups** of faces. The usefulness of close shots to reveal emotions and character or personality cannot be overestimated. In his book *Kinesics and Context*, Ray Birdwhistell claims that the human face is capable of "some 250,000 different expressions" (8).

Perspective

By changing the camera lens and the camera distance, filmmakers can change **perspective**: the relative size and apparent depth of objects in the image. Figures 2.38 to 2.40 illustrate three ways that filmmakers can use perspective.

In these three photographs, the main subjects are approximately the same size in the frame and appear in about the same position within the frame. But everything else changes when camera distance and lens are modified together. By changing the lens and the distance together, cinematographers can emphasize or deemphasize certain areas of the image. They can change the relationships of people and objects in the frame to convey the information and the moods they intend. Often viewers cannot tell the distance of the camera from the subject or the type of lens used unless they know the subject and its setting well enough to detect distortion in their representation.

Filmmakers often change perspective from shot to shot, but occasionally they change perspective within a shot by **dollying** forward or backward as they simultaneously use a **zoom lens**—a lens that can be changed smoothly toward the wide-angle range or telephoto range while the camera is filming. Depending on the movement of the camera and the simultaneous changes in the focal length of the camera lens, the background will seem to recede or to move forward as the main subject remains the same size and in approximately the same position within the frame. In several shots in *Vertigo*, the camera dollies forward as the camera lens **zooms out** (changes from telephoto to wide angle). The net effect of these two simultaneous changes is that as the foreground of the image seems to change

dolly: To film while the camera is mounted on a moving dolly or wheeled platform.

zoom lens: A camera lens with variable focal lengths that can be adjusted by degrees during a shot so that the size of the subject and the area being filmed change.

Changing Perspective

In Figures 2.38–2.40, notice how the lens determines how many trees are visible, how large the trees appear, and the sharpness of the focus.

FIGURE 2.38 Wide-angle lens (28 mm) at 8 feet 10 inches
This photograph was made by positioning the camera closer to the human subjects than in the comparable photograph made with a normal lens (Figure 2.39). Here the camera angle seems to be a slight high angle, and the bench seat on the left seems elongated. This camera distance and lens could be used to stress the depth of the background, to show more of the sides, or to emphasize the distance of the subjects from the background. *Models: Kimberlee Stewart and Carlos Espinola; photographer: Jon Michael Terry*

FIGURE 2.39 Normal lens (50 mm) at 15 feet 6 inches
This photograph closely mirrors the distances and relationships the human eye sees. *Models: Kimberlee Stewart and Carlos Espinola; photographer: Jon Michael Terry*

FIGURE 2.40 Telephoto lens (200 mm) at 62 feet
This photograph was made by moving the camera back from its position for Figure 2.39 and using a telephoto lens. Here the background seems much closer and is more out of focus. The camera angle is not as high as in Figures 2.38 and 2.39, and the bench on the left now seems somewhat shorter. (To see how the camera angle seems to change, look again at the three photographs, and note the angles from which the camera seems to view the cement area under the picnic table.) *Models: Kimberlee Stewart and Carlos Espinola; photographer: Jon Michael Terry*

only slightly, the background recedes and comes into sharper focus and more of the sides of the background comes into view (Figure 2.41).

Another change in perspective during a shot occurs in *GoodFellas* (1990), but with the opposite camera movement and opposite simultaneous type of zooming. Approximately 134 minutes into the film, Jimmy is meeting Henry in a restaurant. Jimmy is about to try to betray Henry and send him to his death. They sit on opposite sides of the frame, with a large window between them. As they talk, the camera **tracks** backward as it **zooms in**, going from normal to telephoto. The two men stay the same size and in the same positions within the frame, but the background becomes larger and its planes be-

track: To film while the camera is being moved around.

FIGURE 2.41 **Changing perspective during a shot: background receding**

In several shots in *Vertigo* (1958, 1996), the main character, a detective, looks down, and from his point of view, viewers see the background receding with the background in the center of the frame receding much faster than objects off to the sides and in the foreground. The shot illustrated here begins nearly 76¼ minutes into the restored version of the film and lasts two seconds: (a) the first frame of the shot, the detective's view as he looks down the stairwell, (b) midway through the shot, and (c) the last frame of the shot. In *Vertigo*, shots like this—achieved by zooming out (from telephoto to wide angle) while moving the camera forward—help viewers experience something like vertigo. Frame enlargements. *Paramount; Universal*

a)

b)

c)

come more compressed: for example, the car parked across the street seems progressively closer to the large sign advertising sandwiches behind it. Perhaps the shot reinforces the sense that Jimmy's attempt to betray his friend is unnatural and unexpected.

These rapid but fluid changes in perspective within the shots from *Vertigo* and *GoodFellas* change the subjects and their relation to the setting in unsettling ways. They also briefly disorient viewers, in part because the changes are unnatural and unexpected. Although these changes in perspective last no more than a few seconds, they may momentarily draw viewers' attention to them.

Angles and Point-of-View Shots

Another important choice that cinematographers make is the angle from which to film the subject. Figures 2.42 to 2.45 illustrate four basic camera positions: **bird's-eye view**, **high angle**, **eye-level angle**, and **low angle**. The camera may be placed at any angle above or below those indicated in the figures.

FIGURE 2.42 Bird's-eye view
This bird's-eye shot very early in the German film *Run Lola Run* (1998), made with the help of computer animation, shows a soccer ball kicked high into the air and presumably heading toward the camera.

For a bird's-eye view, the camera is often mounted on a crane. A moving bird's-eye view is used memorably late in *Taxi Driver* (1976) when viewers look down on the aftermath of a violent scene; the camera movement makes the shot even more disturbing than the usual bird's-eye view. In all instances, the effect is disorienting, perhaps even dizzying, since viewers look straight down on the subject. Most filmmakers avoid the bird's-eye view, probably because it can attract attention to itself and be distracting. Frame enlargement. *Stefan Arndt; Sony Pictures Classic*

FIGURE 2.43 High angle
High angles make the subject appear smaller and in some contexts shut off from the surroundings (sometimes all that is visible of the background is a floor or the ground). In other contexts, the subject seen from a high angle appears isolated, dwarfed by the setting, or vulnerable, as in this image from the Chinese film *Not One Less* (1999). Frame enlargement. *Columbia Pictures Film Production Asia; Sony*

FIGURE 2.44 Eye-level shots

(a) An eye-level angle—such as this one of the actor Chow Yun Fat in *Anna and the King* (1999)—creates the effect of the audience being on the same level as the subject. Viewers look neither up nor down at the subject. Frame enlargement.

(b) The height of the camera may depend on the filmmaker and the culture in which the film is made. In films directed by Yasujiro Ozu of Japan, such as *Tokyo Story* (1953), eye-level shots are often taken with the camera approximately two feet above the ground when the subjects are sitting on the ground. In eye-level shots for films from Western societies, the camera is normally positioned five to six feet above the ground for standing subjects and three to four feet for sitting subjects. (a) *Fox 2000 Pictures*; (b) *Shochiku; The Museum of Modern Art/Film Stills Archive*

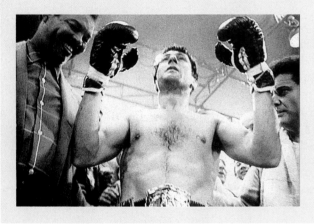

FIGURE 2.45 Low angle

In this frame from nearly eighty-two minutes into *Raging Bull* (1980), Jake La Motta is celebrating winning the world middleweight championship. At his moment of triumph, he is shown from a low angle that makes him seem prominent, dominating, and powerful. Low angles are often used in shots emphasizing a person's physique, sexual power, or powers of intimidation. As illustrated here, when the camera is positioned at a low angle, the surroundings are often minimized, perhaps with a lot of sky or ceiling visible in the background. Frame enlargement. *Robert Chartoff & Irwin Winkler; United Artists*

In a **Dutch angle** shot the subject appears to be on a slanted surface. It is often used to disorient viewers or make them ill at ease. As a point-of-view shot, the Dutch angle may suggest a character's confused state of mind. The Dutch angle is used in many scenes in *The Third Man* (1949), *Do the Right Thing*, and *Natural Born Killers* (1994). Documentarian Errol Morris often uses Dutch angles in his films, too. Dutch angles are also used in the early scenes of *Bagdad Café* (1988) to suggest unhappy personal relationships (Figure 2.46).

In **point-of-view shots** (often called *p.o.v. shots*), the camera films a subject from the approximate position of a character, a real person (in a documentary), or occasionally an animal. Such camera placements contribute to the viewer's sense of identification with the looking subject and of participation in the action. In *Vampyr* (1932), the main character hallucinates that he is in a coffin with a small glass window. He thinks he looks up and sees (and viewers feel as if they are seeing) what it looks like from inside a coffin (Figure 2.47). In parts of more modern films, such as the two murders in the 1960 *Psycho*, periodically throughout *Halloween*

FIGURE 2.46 Dutch angle
Dutch angles are used many times early in *Bagdad Café* (1988), particularly in shots of two quarreling couples. This image, approximately sixteen minutes into the film, shows a woman who has quarreled with her man, who then drives away. Here the Dutch angle reinforces the sense that the woman's life is now out of balance. Frame enlargement. *Zev Braun; New Yorker Films*

FIGURE 2.47 Point-of-view shot
In this point-of-view shot from within a coffin in *Vampyr* (1932), viewers see a vampire with a lighted candle looking down into the coffin. Later the coffin is carried outside, and viewers see the outside surroundings from within the coffin. Frame enlargement. *Julian West & Carl Theodor Dreyer; Filmproduktion Paris-Berlin*

FIGURE 2.48 Sustained point of view
Lady in the Lake (1946) was an experiment with sustained point of view: viewers see events from the main character's point of view, except for an occasional shot of a mirror showing the main character, detective Philip Marlowe. Here Marlowe is about to get slugged and knocked out. The image of the man in this shot is somewhat blurred because filming any extremely rapid movement at twenty-four frames per second results in some blurred individual frames. Frame enlargement. *George Haight; MGM*

(1978), and late in *The Silence of the Lambs* (1991), viewers are frequently put into the uncomfortable position of seeing horrendous events through the eyes of a killer. On a less threatening note, in *Toy Story* (1995) and *Toy Story 2* (1999), viewers are often allowed to see impending dangers, such as a large menacing dog, from the same point of view as one of the toy characters. In 1946, a rare attempt was made to present an entire film from the point of view of a single character in *Lady in the Lake* (Figure 2.48). Similarly, in the Belgian film *Thomas in Love* (2000), audiences see only what the main character sees on his computer screen, including the people he talks to.

Much more often in films, the camera is placed outside the action, in an objective camera shot, and the audience is more spectator than participant.[2]

Moving Camera

The camera may be moved during filming without moving it around in space because a camera operator can **tilt** a camera up and down and pan from side to side. Tilting is a camera movement achieved during filming when a camera operator pivots the camera down to up or up to down while the camera is attached to a stationary base or is handheld. It is often used to reveal a subject by degrees, frequently with a surprising or humorous conclusion. In **panning**, the camera is handheld or mounted on a tripod and pivoted sideways, as the two camera operators on the ground are doing in Figure 2.49. Panning is often used to show the vastness of a location, such as a sea, plain, mountain range, or outer space. As film scholar Ira Konigsberg points out, it may also "guide the audience's attention to a significant action or point of interest, . . . follow the movement across the landscape of a character or vehicle [as in Figure 2.49], and . . . convey a subjective view of what a character sees when turning his or her head to follow an action" (284). Rarely, as in Woody Allen's *Husbands and Wives* (1992), a 360-degree (circular) panning shot is used to show the surroundings on all sides of the camera, though that practice usually draws attention from the subject to the technique itself.

Panning too quickly causes blurred footage; such a result is called a **swish pan** (Figure 2.50). It is seldom used in commercial films. An exception is found in *Schindler's List*, where swish pans done with an unsteady handheld camera intensify the chaos when Nazis roughly sort naked prisoners. Swish pans may also be point-of-view shots. Late in *The Wild Bunch* (1969), Angel, a member of the wild bunch, is upset when he realizes he is now under the control of a Mexican general. From Angel's point of view, we see some laughing Mexicans, then after a swish pan other people laughing at him.

---

[2]For helpful explanations of lighting, color, camera angles, and camera lenses selected for the films he directed, see Sidney Lumet's discussion in Chapter 5, "The Camera: Your Best Friend," in his *Making Movies* (1995).

FIGURE 2.49 Panning

For this shot for *Little Fauss and Big Halsy* (1970), two camera operators (left) pivot their cameras sideways on top of a tripod to follow the speeding motorcycles. At the same time, a camera operator on the crane films onrushing action. *Brad Dexter & Albert S. Ruddy; Paramount*

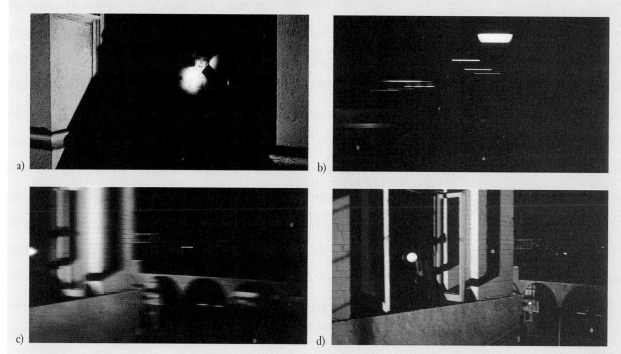

a)

b)

c)

d)

FIGURE 2.50 Swish pan

Approximately twenty-two minutes into *Touch of Evil* (1958), the Janet Leigh character enters her darkened hotel room and is immediately illuminated by a small light (a). A swish pan from right to left (b and c) ends with a clear view of the source of the light: a flashlight from a room across the way (d). Frame enlargements. *Albert Zugsmith; Universal*

FIGURE 2.51 Early cinematography
The early American cinematographer Billy Bitzer hand-cranking a large and bulky Biograph camera as he films some of the U.S. Army Field Artillery in approximately 1905. Later, Bitzer worked closely with D. W. Griffith for sixteen years and filmed such classics as *The Birth of a Nation*, *Intolerance*, and *Broken Blossoms*. *The Museum of Modern Art/Film Stills Archive*

After a very brief shot of Angel, we see another point-of-view swish pan in the opposite direction and more laughter at his expense. The point-of-view swish pans help convey his extreme frustration and disorientation.

It is also possible to move the camera through space while filming. In the early years of cinema, however, filmmakers simply plopped down a camera before the subject, aimed it, and started turning the hand crank. The first films were extremely short, often only a minute or so. Later, the camera was still so bulky it had to be mounted on a sturdy tripod and could be moved along with its subject only by placing the camera in some type of moving vehicle, such as the back of a flatbed (Figure 2.51). By the 1920s, however, various filmmakers had learned other ways to film while moving the camera. In a striking shot from *Napoléon*, the camera was mounted at the base of a huge swing device suspended from a very high ceiling, and the camera filmed a crowded room below as it swung back and forth over the room. Almost as notable are the concluding two shots of *The Crowd* (1928), which were taken from a camera above the film's central family and receding from it, showing the family more and more engulfed by a crowd at a theater. However, in the early years of synchronized sound on phonograph records or on the film itself (late 1920s), moving the camera during filming largely halted because the sound from the camera was being picked up by the sound recording equipment (see Figure 9.19 on p. 441). But gradually inventors developed camera shields (blimps and barneys) to muffle sound, and filmmakers learned how to record sound effectively while moving the camera. By the early 1930s, camera movement during shots had again become commonplace. For example, filmmakers could track or dolly. Such camera shots should not be confused with shots made with a stationary camera with a zoom lens. In zooming, the camera appears to move in or away from a flat surface, whereas in dollying or tracking, the camera is moved through space and viewers get some sense of contour and depth.

With a **crane**, a camera may be positioned at a particular location in the air or moved smoothly through the air (see Figure 2.49). A crane makes pos-

a) b)

FIGURE 2.52 Filming from a crane
In *High Noon* (1952), the town marshal—who knows he is soon to confront four armed men intent on killing him—is seen in a close-up revealing his worry and fear. The next shot begins as a medium shot; then nearly seventy-four minutes into the film (a) the camera begins moving backward and (b) continues moving backward and upward, stopping when it shows him in an extreme long shot even more distant from him than the image seen in (b). During this crane shot, viewers see the marshal wipe sweat from his brow, turn away from the camera, and walk away alone toward a deadly showdown. Rather than show the action of this thirty-second crane shot in two or more shots—for example, a medium shot followed by a high-angle, extreme long shot—the director chose to preserve continuity of space, time, and action. Frame enlargements. *Stanley Kramer Productions; United Artists*

sible otherwise impossible camera angles and distances. Crane shots may be unobtrusively slow, gracefully slow, or rapid and disorienting; depending on the contexts, the effect can be soothing, exhilarating, or threatening. They may create or heighten many different effects (Figure 2.52).

The **Steadicam**—a device consisting of a lightweight frame, torsion arm, movie or video camera, and small TV monitor—is another piece of equipment that allows the camera operator to move around smoothly while filming (Figure 2.53). Using a Steadicam has many advantages: "Visually, the Steadicam duplicates many benefits of handheld shooting without the lack of stability in the latter practice; indeed, to the crew, it can provide speed, flexibility, mobility, and responsiveness. And, of course, it can also energize the film with visual dynamism" (Geuens 12).

The Steadicam can be used in long, continuous shots, such as in a celebrated shot from *GoodFellas*. In this shot, which begins approximately thirty-one minutes into the film, Henry gives money to a car attendant across the street from the Copacabana nightclub; then Henry and Karen walk across the street, cut through a line of people waiting to get into the club, go in a side entrance and down some stairs, and walk through corridors and the kitchen to the nightclub itself. There a special table is set up for them, and Henry is greeted by men at nearby tables. Henry and Karen sit; they receive

Filmmakers Talk about Cinematography

The documentary film *Visions of Light* (1992) includes excerpts from interviews of many cinematographers and other filmmakers. All of the following quotations are from cinematographers, except for Robert Wise.

In the beginning all there was was a guy with a camera. There were no directors. . . . There was a guy and a camera, and he would shoot these subjects, and the subject may be twenty seconds long of a train coming at you, whatever it is. Then actors were brought in and because the cameramen were basically photographers and weren't that facile with performers, usually one of the performers directed the performers, so right in the very beginning you saw that there was the division of duties.
—Stephen H. Burum

A great DP [director of photography] adds to the material that already exists and really works to understand the subject matter and the language of the director they're working with.
—Lisa Rinzler

I think visually. I think of how if you turned off the soundtrack, anybody would stick around and figure out what was going on.
—Conrad Hall

Notice the beautiful jobs that were done on [actress] Marlene Dietrich where . . . if you light a set at 100 foot candles, she would be at 110, 15 foot candles. She would have just a little bit more light on her than anybody else so she would pop out amongst the crowd.
—William A. Fraker

By having the deep focus, he [cinematographer Gregg Toland] was able to give Orson [Welles] a lot more leeway on how he moved his actors and staged the scenes and freed him up. I think that was a tremendous contribution that Gregg gave to the film [*Citizen Kane*].
—Robert Wise

With [cinematographer John] Alton and the people in film noir they were not afraid of the dark, and in fact they were willing to sketch things just very very very slightly to see how you could use dark, not as negative space, but as the most important element in the scene.
—Allen Daviau

You see some of the scenes [from *Touch of Evil*, 1958], and you realize how much handholding [camera work] was done in the film, but it's extremely seamless. That film in particular was an inspiration to all of us because it was a textbook of what you could do. It was shot on a small budget in a short time, mostly on locations, and . . . you had almost simultaneously the breakout in France of the new wave. You had Orson Welles doing a new wave film in a Hollywood studio. And I think it has continued to be an inspiration to a lot of filmmakers.
—Allen Daviau

The films of the French new wave . . . captured a sense of life . . . by loosening up the camera and moving with it. . . . They would not think anything about picking up the camera and running with it. It had almost a documentary feel, and so that sort of quality about it would draw you into the film in the way that I think a more static camera would not.
—Caleb Deschanel

The director is going to be the author of the performances of the film, the story of the film. The cinematographer is the author of the use of light in the film and how that contributes to the story.
—Ernest Dickerson

Suddenly you're aware of the fact that things are not exactly as they seem. In other words, you create a representation of it, and lots of times that representation is more emotional than it is real.
—Caleb Deschanel

FIGURE 2.53 The Steadicam
This device for stabilizing moving handheld camera shots was first used in feature film production in the mid-1970s. Depicted here is a Steadicam Video SK with video monitor and Sony Hi-8 video camera below. A 35 mm movie camera is even larger and heavier than the video camera shown here. Operating a Steadicam expertly takes training and practice because it initially upsets the operator's sense of balance, especially when moving. It can also be tricky to maneuver in the wind, and achieving smooth starts and stops with one can be difficult. *"Steadicam" is a registered trademark of Cinema Products Corp., Los Angeles.*

a complimentary bottle of wine from men at another table and talk a little; then Henry and Karen watch the beginning of a comedian's routine. For a little more than three uninterrupted minutes, the use of a Steadicam allows viewers to see and to some extent experience the deference, attention, and favors that Henry enjoys as a mobster.

A Steadicam is also used effectively near the end of *The Shining* (1980). As the ax-wielding main character chases his son through a large, snow-covered outdoor maze, hoping to catch him and murder him, the Steadicam follows the pursued then the pursuer without making viewers nauseous. With the increased capacity of digital video, it is now possible to use a Steadicam to shoot an entire feature film in one shot, as was done in the making of *Russian Ark* (2002), a dreamlike guided journey through the famed Hermitage Museum in St. Petersburg during which the film's viewers glimpse artworks and meticulously costumed and choreographed reenactments of historical Russian events.

FIGURE 2.54 Camera movement to reveal subjects and setting
Four photographs approximating the opening tracking shot of *A Clockwork Orange* (1971). (a) The film begins with a close-up of the main character, Alex. Frame enlargement. (b) After a few moments the camera begins to dolly backward slowly, revealing Alex and the other drugged gang members, with Alex's feet propped atop one of two interlocking tables in the form of nude women. (c) As the camera continues tracking backward, viewers can see an attendant in the background to the far right and the first of the nude statues on pedestals. As the camera continues its backward movement, viewers see more and more of the setting, including more tables, more statues on pedestals, other immobile (and drugged) patrons on the sides of this futuristic bar, and the names of the liquid drugs available: Moloko (Milk) Plus and three others. (d) Toward the end of the shot, in the foreground viewers can see two more immobile attendants. Finally the camera stops moving, and during the last second or two of the shot the image looks much like this one, except a longer lens was used for this publicity still than in the movie so all planes look slightly more compressed than in the movie. *Stanley Kubrick; Warner Bros.*

Camera movement may be used in countless ways. It is often used so viewers can follow along with a moving subject, as in the Steadicam shot from *GoodFellas* described earlier. Sometimes camera movement is used to show the subject from a very different angle, as when the camera moves to

FIGURE 2.55 Tracking backward to reveal surprising information Sometimes a shot shows viewers its subject, then the camera moves backward and viewers see on the side of the frame someone watching the action they had recently seen, as is done in *Reservoir Dogs* (1992) seconds after the action depicted here. *Lawrence Bender; Miramax*

below Norman Bates's chin as the detective in the original *Psycho* questions him. Occasionally, camera movement is used to prevent the audience from learning information, as when a crane shot is used to position the camera overhead immediately before Norman carries his mother down the stairs in both the original version of *Psycho* and its 1998 remake.

Camera movement may allow viewers to see a subject more clearly. Moving the camera forward may create or intensify tension (what will we see next?) or slowly introduce viewers to the setting of the story, as in the beginnings of *West Side Story* (1961) and countless other films. Conversely, camera movement away from the subject can reveal more and more of a setting, as in the concluding two shots of *The Crowd* mentioned earlier and the opening shot of *A Clockwork Orange*. During this ninety-two-second shot, the camera reveals the main character in close-up, pulls back to show his collaborators in crime, then shows a major setting where the patrons are all drugged into immobility and where women are seen as sex objects to display and demean (Figure 2.54). Sometimes camera movement backward reveals someone watching what viewers have been watching (Figure 2.55). Moving the camera back may give a sense of release or conclusion, as in the shots used for the endings of *The Shawshank Redemption* (1994), *Hilary and Jackie* (1998), and *Dr. T and the Women* (2000).

Without a Steadicam, camera movement can disorient, confuse, or even sicken viewers, as in *Dr. Strangelove: Or, How I Learned to Stop Worrying and Love the Bomb* (1963). Immediately after a guided missile hits a bomber in *Dr. Strangelove*, the camera jars around vigorously and erratically and viewers feel momentarily at a loss. The erratic camera movement seen throughout *The Blair Witch Project*—which was intended to convince viewers that they were seeing amateur camera work—was so disorienting some viewers experienced "extreme nausea." Filming with a handheld camera while moving through a crowd usually results in footage that might make viewers feel something like the movement and excitement of crowd scenes.

Camera movement can also help control *when* during a shot viewers learn certain information. In *National Lampoon's Vacation* (1983), a shot begins with children asleep in the backseat of a moving car at night. The shot continues with the camera panning to the front seat, where the mother is also asleep; then the camera continues its movement, and we learn that the driver, the father, is also deep in sleep! Because of the context and camera movement, it's a hilarious moment.

(For a sample of cinematographers' views on the roles and expressiveness of cinematography, see p. 98.)

DIGITAL CINEMATOGRAPHY

Computers are increasingly being used to create or manipulate filmed images. Any image, just as any written language, can be scanned into a computer then changed in many ways. Computers can be used to composite (or combine) two or more images. They can also be used to **morph** images—to change the shape of the subjects—so that we can see a character's body change or even see a character morph into a different character (Figure 2.56).

Using a process called **digital intermediate**, filmmakers can transfer exposed film to digital, manipulate the colors and contrast with a computer program, then transfer the images back to film. The process was first used in *Pleasantville* (1998) to render parts of an image in color and other parts of the same image in black and white. In the movie, two teens from the 1990s are trapped in a black-and-white 1950s television series. As the two introduce the complexities of the 1990s world into the **stereotypical**, idealized, black-and-white vision of small-town life, gradually the **mise en scène** gains in color. Plate 27 illustrates how initially colors begin to appear on or near those who experience strong emotion—at first in the film, sexual desire. Plate 28 shows the soda shop owner painting from his imagination and from his memory of a Paul Cézanne still life he had recently seen in the library book. Using digital intermediate, filmmakers can use computers to alter color and contrast in part or all of a film. In such films as *O Brother, Where Art Thou?* (2000), *Frida* (2002), and *8 Mile* (2002), for example, they can bathe scenes in a dusty yellow tone, make colors vibrant and bold in scenes set in Mexico, or show downtown Detroit as blue green.

Computers can also be used to remove or cover up objects from images:

> They can eliminate scratches and remove objects which don't belong in period films. In one recent Western, bloodstains were removed from a character's shirt to make it acceptable for use in a trailer. In another PG-rated film, a brief bathing suit bottom was extended to cover some of an actress' exposed body . . . with the aid of "electronic paint." In *Wrestling with Ernest Hemingway* [1993], an

mise en scène: An image's setting, subjects (usually people or characters), and composition (the arrangement of setting and subjects within the frame).

FIGURE 2.56 Morphing

In morphing, filmed frames are scanned into a computer. Then the parts of the image that are to change are marked manually and transformed in stages by a sophisticated computer program. The images are then transferred to film stock and incorporated into the finished film. Morphing was used in many shots during postproduction of *Terminator 2: Judgment Day* (1991). An example is the shot represented here that shows the running, evil cyborg (a) transform into a man dressed as a police officer (b–d). Frame enlargements. *James Cameron; TriStar*

actor was clearly breathing after he was supposed to be dead. The image was fixed by scanning the film into digital format, literally erasing parts of frames where the actor's shirt was moving or breathing, and replacing it with cloned images from frames where the shirt was still. (Fisher 101)

After Brandon Lee was killed in an accident with three days of filming left in making *The Crow* (1994), for a few scenes a computer was used to move the image of his character to new settings. Now filmmakers with a large budget can use special effects during filming, as in *Wild Wild West* (1999), then clean up the images in the computer—for example, remove wires that supported actors as they were moved through the air.

Digital work allows filmmakers to correct mistakes that would be even more costly or impossible to correct (for example, perhaps the actor has moved on to another project and cannot return to reshoot an indispensable shot or scene). Like animation, computer work makes possible extensive manipulation of the film's images and makes visible what was previously impossible to show. For example, for one scene in *In the Line of Fire* (1993), footage of the first President Bush and his wife getting out of the presidential airplane was scanned into a computer, and their faces were replaced with the faces of the movie's characters. Digital cinematography, however, is not without its limitations. Some people think it still too often looks a little fake; then, too, it remains enormously costly and time-consuming. Even films known for their digital creativity—such as *Jurassic Park* (1993), *The Lost World: Jurassic Park* (1997), and *Jurassic Park III* (2001)—continue to combine digital visual effects with shots made by filming models (life-size or miniature), robots, **animatronics**, and the like. It seems certain that transferring video footage and film to a computer, manipulating the digitized visuals, and transferring the visuals back to film will grow in importance in large commercial films.

animatronic: A puppet likeness of a human, a creature, or an animal whose movements are directed by electronic, mechanical, or radio-controlled devices.

Digital cinematography will probably eventually replace traditional cinematography, but the history of film technology shows that technological advances alone do not bring about radical changes in filmmaking and film exhibition. At least for big-budget movies, profits for those involved in the production and distribution of moving images and sounds and the tastes of the viewing and paying public are also potent determinants. Now and in whatever future evolving technology and shifting economics bring us, cinematography will remain a powerful influence on films and in turn on viewer responses.

CLOSE-UP: CAMERA DISTANCES AND ANGLES IN A SCENE FROM *REVERSAL OF FORTUNE*

by Bret Lampman

In this flashback/vignette, which begins a little more than eighty minutes into the film (Table 2.1), the camera views a bedroom doorway (interior) in the first shot and shortly thereafter takes up the point-of-view shots of Claus and Sunny von Bülow: one representing Sunny's seated point of view from the settee (slightly low angle of Claus), the other Claus's standing point of view from near the window (slightly high angle of Sunny). The slightly high and low camera angles give the viewer a nearly point-of-view aspect at first, while about halfway through the scene we see Sunny and Claus closer to eye level. This technique seems appropriate for two reasons. First, the high and low angles at the beginning are conventional: since Claus is standing we get a high angle from his point of view, and likewise for Sunny. Also, as the confrontation heats up, seeing the characters more at eye level helps involve the viewer in the action.

This is an uncomfortable and emotional scene in which the two maintain a total physical separation. At no time in the scene do Sunny and Claus appear in the same frame. Two people casually chatting in a hotel lobby, keeping a respectful social distance, might have stood closer together than this man and his wife, who are in the privacy of their own bedroom. Even though Sunny eventually starts to fall apart emotionally, Claus does not approach to console or confront her. He does not even speak, despite her stinging barbs and her demand "Say something!" Their emotional distance is exquisitely portrayed as she remains on the settee, eventually beating her hands in her lap and sobbing, while he remains rooted in place. These two characters do not move; the camera moves instead, bringing viewers closer to each of them as the confrontation unfolds.

This is the closest we viewers come to either Claus or Sunny in the entire film spatially or emotionally. By this point, two-thirds of the way through the film, the background (their bedroom) is familiar to us, so the initial long shots do less to reveal mise en scène than to convey the characters' emotional distance. We find that Sunny is not so drugged up that she is beyond thinking or caring about her relationship with Claus; in fact, she is terribly upset that her marriage might be ending, that Claus might be leaving her or at least slipping from her control. Her plaintive emotional agony, honestly if angrily voiced, should have been enough to bring Claus to her side (there was plenty of room for two on the love seat), but he appears totally unprepared for her reaction; he does not move or even speak. His mostly passive face, even in medium close-up, is a stark contrast to Sunny's expressive face: she pleads, shouts, and sobs like a desperate child, for once holding nothing back.

As the emotional intensity builds, the camera brings us increasingly closer to Sunny and Claus (note particularly shots 8–14), while its eye-level angle involves us almost naturally in the confrontation. The predominant use of long shots earlier in this film leaves the viewer unprepared for the relative nearness of the camera here, making the viewer feel uncomfortably close. It is revealing that even a medium close-up should have the power to draw us into this exchange, presumably the last real communication Sunny and Claus ever had.

Of course, the flashback is Claus's, and we might believe that this is as near as Claus ever got to anyone, especially during an emotional display (except perhaps when making love). Were the memory related by Sunny, we may very well have found closer, higher, or lower camera distances

105

TABLE 2.1
Camera Distances and Angles in a Scene from *Reversal of Fortune*

SHOT	DIST.*	ANGLE	SHOT DESCRIPTION
1	LS	eye level	Alexander and Claus enter through open bedroom door.
2	LS	sl. high	Cosima on settee, looking toward Alexander and Claus (off frame). Bathroom door in background opens, and Sunny emerges, leans on door frame. Cosima looks over her shoulder, gets up, and walks to her mother.
3	MS	sl. low	As Sunny had requested, Alexander opens the window.
4	MS	POV**	Sunny leans unsteadily on Cosima as they walk toward the settee. Sunny stands on her own, smiles kindly, and kisses her daughter, who leaves her side (walks off frame). Sunny leans heavily on the settee.
5	LS	eye level	Claus kisses Cosima and walks her to the door. She and Alexander leave; Claus closes the door.
6	LS	sl. high	Sunny sinks onto the settee, leaning her head back.
7	LS	sl. low	Claus adjusts fluttering drapes over the open window. He takes a few steps toward Sunny, then stops suddenly, looking toward her.
8	LS	sl. high	Sunny is speaking to Claus. With effort, she sits up.
9	MS	sl. low	Claus is listening, standing still. He is silent.
10	MCU	eye level	Sunny continues speaking but remains seated. She looks arrogant but frightened, then angry.
11	MCU	sl. low	Claus reacts, looking injured, curious, or cautious (hard to read).
12	MCU	eye level	Sunny shouts angrily.
13	CU	sl. low	Claus remains still and silent, quietly controlled, stunned or uncertain (still hard to read).
14	MCU	eye level	Sunny begins to sob and beat her hands in her lap, seemingly at her wit's end.

*LS = long shot; MS = medium shot; MCU = medium close-up; CU = close-up.

**All following shots are point of view (POV).

and angles to reflect her feelings at the moment. But since this is Claus's narration, there is even here a feeling of distance that cannot quite bring us face to face with this sad couple.

They are separated by more than their physical distance. The emotional distance between them is equally noticeable. The camera brings us closer to Sunny, closer to Claus, than they are to each other. The scene is the film's most successful at helping us understand the relationship Claus and Sunny shared: even when they are together, they are somehow apart. Whether separated by a dinner table, a backgammon board, an affair, alcohol, night blinders and earplugs, or this emotional vacuum that not even Sunny's tearful collapse can bridge, the two are never close. We may believe that if only Claus had come as near to Sunny as this scene allows us viewers to, if only he had come down to her eye level as we do, rather than looking impassively down on her, she may have been reassured or encouraged. She may have lived.

But as we see in this scene, Claus keeps his social and emotional distance. In the end, so does Sunny.

SUMMARY

Cinematography involves the choice and manipulation of film stock or video, lighting, and cameras. Some of the main issues in cinematography are film grain, color, lenses, camera distance and angle from the subject, and camera movement. As with other aspects of filmmaking, the choices made in filming strongly affect how viewers respond to the film.

Film Stock

- Film stock, which is unexposed and unprocessed motion-picture film, influences the film's finished look, including its sharpness of detail, range of light and shadow, and quality of color. Often professional cinematographers use different film stocks or videotape in different parts of the same film to support certain effects.
- Generally, the wider the film gauge, the larger the film frames and the sharper the projected images.
- Slow film stock, which requires more light during filming than fast film stock, can produce a detailed, nuanced image. In older films, fast film stock usually produces more graininess than slow film stocks.
- Color associations vary from culture to culture, and a color's impact depends on context—where and how the color is used.
- In most Western societies, warm colors (reds, oranges, and yellows) tend to be thought of as hot, dangerous, lively, and assertive. Greens, blues, and violets are generally characterized as cool. In Europe and the Americas, these colors tend to be associated with safety, reason, control, relaxation, and sometimes sadness or melancholy.

- Color may be saturated (intense, vivid) or desaturated (muted, dull, pale), and saturated and desaturated colors can be used to heighten countless possible effects.

Lighting

- Hard lighting comes directly from a light source, whereas soft light comes from an indirect source. Hard lighting is bright and harsh and creates unflattering images. Soft lighting is flattering because it tends to fill in imperfections in the subject's surface and obliterate or lessen sharp lines and shadows.
- Low-key lighting involves little illumination on the subject and often reinforces a dramatic or mysterious effect. High-key lighting entails bright illumination of the subject and may create or enhance a cheerful mood.
- The direction of light reaching the subject can change an image's moods and meanings.
- Like light, shadows can be used expressively in countless ways—for example, to create a mysterious or threatening environment.

The Camera

- During filming, one of three types of lenses is used: wide-angle, normal, or telephoto. Often all three are used at different times within the same film. Each type of lens has different properties and creates different images.
- Choice of lens, aperture (or opening), and film stock largely determine the depth of field, or distance in front of the camera in which all objects are in focus.
- Diffusers may be placed in front of a light source or in front of a camera lens to soften lines in the subject, to glamorize, or to lend a more spiritual or ethereal look.
- Camera distance helps determine how large the subject will appear within the frame, what details will be noticeable, and what objects will be excluded from the frame.
- By changing the camera lens and the camera distance between shots or during a shot, filmmakers can change perspective: the relative size and apparent depth of objects in the photographic image.
- The angle from which the subject is filmed influences the expressiveness of the images. There are four basic camera angles—bird's-eye view, high angle, eye-level angle, and low angle—and countless angles in between.
- In point-of-view (p.o.v.) shots, the camera films a subject from the approximate position of someone, or occasionally something, in the film. Such camera placements contribute to the viewer's identification with one of the subjects and sense of participation in the action.

- A motion-picture camera may remain in one place during filming. While filming with a camera fixed in one place, the camera may be pivoted up or down (tilting) or rotated sideways (panning).

- Panning too quickly causes blurred footage. Such a result is called a swish pan.

- Ways to move the camera around during filming include dollying, tracking, using a crane, and employing a Steadicam. Like other aspects of cinematography, camera movement can be used in countless expressive ways.

Digital Cinematography

- Film and video images can be scanned into a computer, changed there, and transferred back to film. Computers can be used to modify colors and contrast, correct errors, and change the images in ways impossible or more troublesome and costly to do with film alone.

- Mainly for reasons of economy and convenience, more and more movies are being filmed in high-definition video and transferred to film for theatrical showings, though the results do not yet match the detail and nuances of the best film stocks.

Major Terms about Cinematography

Below, numbers in italics refer to the pages where the terms are explained. All terms are defined in more detail in the Illustrated Glossary beginning on p. 621.

anamorphic lens *83*
aperture *82*
backlight *72*
bird's-eye view *91*
catchlight *71*
close-up *86*
contrast *74*
deep focus *82*
depth of field *82*
desaturated color *67*
diffuser *83*
digital intermediate *102*
dollying *88*
Dutch angle *92*
emulsion *62*
establishing shot *84*
extreme close-up *86*
extreme long shot *85*
eye-level angle *92*

fast film stock *64*
fast lens *66*
fill light *74*
film stock *61*
fisheye lens *80*
footage *62*
gauge *63*
grain *62*
hard light *72*
high angle *91*
high-key lighting *75*
key light *74*
leader *61*
long shot *85*
low angle *92*
low-key lighting *75*
medium close-up *86*
medium shot *85*
morph *102*
negative *66*

normal lens *81*
pan *94*
perspective *88*
point-of-view shot *93*
saturated color *67*
shallow focus *83*
slow film stock *64*
soft light *72*
spherical lens *83*
Steadicam *97*
swish pan *94*
telephoto lens *81*
tilt *94*
tinting *66*
track (verb) *90*
wide-angle lens *81*
zoom in *90*
zoom lens *88*
zoom out *88*

QUESTIONS ABOUT CINEMATOGRAPHY

The following questions are intended to help viewers understand cinematography and analyze responses to it. Not all the questions are appropriate for every film. In thinking out, discussing, and writing responses to those questions most appropriate for the film being examined, be careful to stick with the issues the questions raise, to answer all parts of the questions, to explain the reasons for your answers, and to give specific examples from the film.

1. Are the images fine grain or rough grain? Are both looks used within the same film? What does the degree of graininess contribute to the film?

2. Does the film use "cool" or "warm" colors to achieve certain effects? Is color used in a symbolic way? Is color used to enhance mood? How lifelike is the color?

3. Does the film use "saturated" or "desaturated" colors to achieve certain effects? If so, explain.

4. Notice any particularly expressive uses of light and shadows.

   a. Where is lighting used to support or create a particular mood? What mood?

   b. Where is hard light used and with what consequences? Where is soft light used and with what consequences?

   c. Where are shadows used to conceal information? To enhance mood? To reveal what a character is like or is feeling?

   d. If a certain kind of lighting is used repeatedly, describe it, and explain its effects.

5. For an especially significant part of the film, what camera distances are used? To what effect? Are many close-ups used in the film? Generally, does the camera stay back from the subjects and show much of the setting?

6. For some of the most significant shots in the film, what lens seems to be used: wide-angle, normal, telephoto? With what consequences?

7. In the film, does the subject tend to be filmed in high, eye-level, or low angles? Where are camera angles especially significant or effective? Why do you say so?

8. Notice any especially expressive uses of camera placements.

   a. Where are point-of-view shots used? How often are they used? What effects do they have on your viewing experience?

   b. Where are camera placements used that make you feel like an outsider looking in on the action?

9. Characterize the camera movement.

   a. If the camera tends to remain stationary, what are the advantages and disadvantages of the stationary camera work?

   b. If moving camera shots are used, does the camera dolly or truck, or does it move up and down through the air? Are Steadicam shots used? If so, to what effect? What is the effect of the camera movement or lack of movement?

10. Does the camera pan or tilt? Where and with what consequences?

WORKS CITED

Almendros, Nestor (cinematographer). Interview. *Visions of Light* (documentary film). 1992.

Bazin, André. "The Evolution of the Language of Cinema." *What Is Cinema?* Ed. and trans. Hugh Gray. Vol. 1. Berkeley: U of California P, 1967.

Birdwhistell, Ray. *Kinesics and Context: Essays on Body Motion Communication*. Philadelphia: U of Pennsylvania P, 1970.

Daviau, Allen (cinematographer). Interview. *Visions of Light* (documentary film). 1992.

Dmytryk, Edward. Interview. *Hollywood: The Golden Years, Episode 5: Dark Victory*. BBC Television and RKO Pictures. 1987.

Dyer, Richard. *Stars*. 2nd ed. London: British Film Institute, 1998.

Eidsvik, Charles. *Cineliteracy: Film among the Arts*. New York: Random, 1978.

Fisher, Bob. "Looking Forward to the Future of Film." *American Cinematographer* Aug. 1994: 98–104.

Geuens, Jean-Pierre. "Visuality and Power: The Work of the Steadicam." *Film Quarterly* 47.2 (Winter 1993–94): 8–17.

Hayward, Susan. *Cinema Studies: The Key Concepts*. 2nd ed. London: Routledge, 2000.

Konigsberg, Ira. *The Complete Film Dictionary*. 2nd ed. New York: Penguin, 1997.

Lumet, Sidney. *Making Movies*. New York: Knopf, 1995.

Malkiewicz, Kris. *Cinematography: A Guide for Film Makers and Film Teachers*. 2nd ed. Englewood Cliffs, NJ: Prentice, 1989.

"Newcomers, director Kasi Lemmons and Amy Vincent, Set *Eve's Bayou* in the Spiritual and Geographic Heart of Louisiana." Accessed at *American Cinematographer* Nov. 1979 <http://www.cinematographer.com/magazine/nov97/bayou/pg1.htm> (no longer accessible at this site).

Pavlus, John. "Razzle Dazzle." *American Cinematographer* Feb. 2003: 42+.

Riefenstahl, Leni (filmmaker). Interview. *The Wonderful, Horrible Life of Leni Riefenstahl* (documentary film). 1993.

Salt, Barry. *Film Style and Technology: History and Analysis*. 2nd ed. London: Starword, 1992.

Silberg, Jon. "A Life Finally Examined." *American Cinematographer* Jan. 2003: 74+.

Turner, George. "A Tradition of Innovation." *American Cinematographer* Aug. 1994: 93–96.

Zone, Ray. "Emotional Triggers." *American Cinematographer* Aug. 2002: 32+.

FOR FURTHER READING

Alton, John. *Painting with Light*. 1949. Berkeley: U of California P, 1995. Alton, an accomplished cinematographer, explains the duties of the cinematographer and how lighting, camera techniques, and choice of location determine the visual mood of films. This edition includes new introductory material and a filmography.

Coe, Brian. *The History of Movie Photography*. New York: Zoetrope; London: Ash and Grant, 1981. A short history of evolving filmmaking equipment and processes. Many photographs, some in color.

LoBrutto, Vincent. *Principal Photography: Interviews with Feature Film Cinematographers*. Westport, CT: Praeger, 1999. In-depth interviews with thirteen cinematographers; each interview is preceded by a short biography and a selected filmography. The book concludes with a glossary, bibliography, and index.

Lowell, Ross. *Matters of Light and Depth: Creating Memorable Images for Video, Film and Stills through Lighting*. Philadelphia: Broad Street Books, 1992. The book's subtitle accurately describes its subject.

Rogers, Pauline. *Contemporary Cinematographers on Their Art*. Boston: Focal, 1998. Thirteen interviews cover such topics as preproduction, special effects, aerial photography, and second unit. Often the cinematographers tell how popular shots were lit and filmed.

CHAPTER 3

Editing

IN ONE OF THE FIRST SCENES OF *Road to Perdition*, taciturn mob enforcer Michael Sullivan . . . wends his car down the snowy driveway to his house.

Seamlessly, as if the audience were seeing Sullivan's wife and two boys as he would see them through the windshield, the camera captures their reactions to his arrival. In one cut, Sullivan's wife . . . smiles shyly. In another cut, his sons stop throwing snowballs at one another and anxiously dust themselves off.

Then, in the last cut, the camera is positioned so that the audience feels as if it is standing in the snow, watching Sullivan's black car pass by as his sons run along behind it.

In that brief, wordless scene, director Sam Mendes and the film editor Jill Bilcock deliver the first, telling impressions of each member of the Sullivan family. (Calvo)

As demonstrated by that early scene of *Road to Perdition* (2002), editing can be wondrously economical and expressive. In general, how do film editors work? After the many labeled strips of film have been developed, the film editor or editors—often in the later stages of the work, in cooperation with the director—select the best version, or best **take**, of each shot for the finished film. Often the editor shortens the shot; sometimes the editor divides a shot and inserts another shot or part of it (a **cutaway shot**) into the middle of the split shot. Often the editor consults a **master shot**, which records an entire scene, usually in a **long shot**. Sometimes parts of the master shot are used in the **final cut** of the scene; occasionally the master shot is used in its entirety. All of this work is usually done on an editing machine (Figure 3.1), though, as we see near the end of this chapter, increasingly digitized shots are edited with a computer and sophisticated software and the results transferred to videotape, DVD, or film.

It's often said that an impressive performance is made in the cutting (or editing) room. The editor can make an actor look effective by selecting only the best takes and by cutting to a reaction shot if an actor even momentarily lapses out of character. The editor can also make the writers look better, especially by dropping unnecessary dialogue and by ensuring an appropriate

Terms in **boldface** are defined in the Illustrated Glossary beginning on page 621.

cutaway shot: A shot that briefly interrupts the representation of a subject to show something else.

long shot: Shot in which the subject may be seen in its entirety and much of its surroundings are visible.

final cut: The last version of an edited film.

FIGURE 3.1 **An early flatbed editing table**
Acclaimed Soviet filmmaker Sergei Eisenstein (1898–1948) works at an editing table with takes of 35 mm film. In the background, light behind frosted glass illuminates the film strips that hang before it. *Courtesy Herbert Marshall Archives; Center for Soviet and East European Studies; Southern Illinois University*

pace to the dialogue and action. Editors can make everyone involved in the film look better by cutting the tedious and extraneous. In a movie, viewers never see, for example, all the reactions of someone in the film watching some important action. We should be grateful. As Hitchcock is reputed to have said, "Drama is life with the dull parts left out."

For a **feature film**, the editing process, which is often called "cutting the film," may require the efforts of two or more editors or an editor and assistants. Editing is so time-consuming that it's no wonder that for a feature film the job usually consumes months and can consume years. Although they faced extreme situations, the editors of *Crimson Tide* (1995) fashioned a 113-minute film out of 148 hours of **footage**. Documentary filmmakers often spend enormous amounts of time editing a film, too. Leni Riefenstahl had so much footage while making the **documentary film** *Olympia* (1936) that it took her ten weeks of ten-hour days just to view all the **dailies** (the prints made from a day's filming) and nearly two years to edit the film into its final version of more than three and a half hours (Riefenstahl). *Point of Order* (1963), a ninety-seven-minute documentary about the 1954 Army-McCarthy hearings, was fashioned during a three-year period from 188 hours of footage. Frederick Wiseman's *Belfast, Maine* (1999), which documents everyday life in a small coastal town, is 245 minutes long and is the result of 110 hours of filming and fourteen months of long days of editing. Even if the film is edited on computers, the process is demanding and extremely time-consuming.

In large productions, editors typically work within the boundaries set by the script and the footage **shot**. Nonetheless, by selecting shots and arranging, doubling, and shortening them, editors can expand or compress an ac-

feature film: A fictional film that is at least sixty minutes long.

footage: A length of exposed motion-picture film.

documentary film: A film or video representation of actual (not imaginary) subjects.

shot (verb): Filmed (as in "They shot the movie in seven weeks").

tion, promote continuity or lack of it, affect the film's pace and moods, and intensify viewer reactions. Sometimes editing can even salvage an otherwise mediocre film.

In this chapter, we first review major developments in early film editing and the building blocks of editing: shots, scenes, sequences, and transitions between shots. After that, we focus on how viewer responses can be affected by how the pieces of film or digitized images are selected and combined. We consider how editing can be used (1) to promote continuity or disruptions; (2) to superimpose and thus combine images; (3) to juxtapose images to make a point or to support a feeling or mood, intensify the viewer's reactions, or show parallel events; and (4) to affect the viewer's sense of pace, compress or expand time, and convey an enormous amount of information in a brief time. The chapter concludes with a discussion of how computers are increasingly used in editing.

EARLY FILM EDITING

> In the first quarter of the twentieth century, the film editor's room was a quiet place, equipped only with a rewind bench, a pair of scissors, a magnifying glass, and the knowledge that the distance from the tip of one's nose to the fingers of the outstretched hand represented about three seconds. (Murch 75)

reel: A metal or plastic spool to hold film.

In the first motion pictures, from the 1890s, filmmakers positioned the camera and filmed until the short **reel** of film ran out. That was it: one shot (Figure 3.2). Later, editing was limited to deciding the shots to include in the finished film and their order. Georges Méliès's early films, such as "Cinderella" (1900) and "A Trip to the Moon" (1902), were longer than previous films and consisted of a succession of scenes, each made up of one shot and showing continuous limited action in one place (see the feature on pp. 116–17). Film stories evolved further with the development of some scenes consisting of multiple shots.

In "The Life of an American Fireman" (1902) and "The Great Train Robbery" (1903), Edwin S. Porter tried more daring editing strategies, such as suggesting actions occurring at two places at the same time and combining footage he filmed with others' footage. However, Porter's innovation was surpassed by the **techniques** used by D. W. Griffith. In his

FIGURE 3.2 **Early film without editing**
The first films consisted of one shot. Technology did not yet permit editing. This frame shows two actors engaging in the first known screen kiss in the very brief, one-shot film "The Kiss" (1896). Frame enlargement. *Edison; The Museum of Modern Art/Film Stills Archive*

Editing of "A Trip to the Moon"

The most widely available version of Georges Méliès's 1902 silent film "A Trip to the Moon" runs about fourteen minutes and consists of fifteen scenes. Each scene in this French film is made up of only one shot. (The Roman numerals in the following outline indicate one way to divide the story into sequences.)

I. EARTH

1. Astronomers' Club: a gathering of men dressed as medieval wizards. Five female attendants bring in telescopes, which they give to men in the front row. Their leader arrives. The telescopes change into stools, and the men sit. The leader draws on a blackboard and leads the animated discussion. The leader and five others change clothes and leave.

2. Factory: workers constructing a rocket. The six men arrive, inspect the rocket, and leave.

3. Rooftop of the factory: the six explorers arrive and gesture toward the industrial scene with its smoking chimneys and a cannon barrel being cast.

4. Launch site on a rooftop: the six explorers arrive and get into the rocket; the hatch is closed; the female assistants push the rocket into the giant cannon and wave to the audience with their hats.

5. Launch site, another view of the cannon: uniformed man with female attendants, brief ceremony with the French flag. The rocket is launched (Figure a), and the onlookers wave good-byes.

II. FLIGHT

6. Space: long shot of moon. The rocket approaches the "man in the moon," who is hit in the eye by the rocket (Figure b).

III. MOON

7. Lunar surface: the rocket lands; the six explorers emerge from it; and the rocket disappears. The earth rises; the explorers bed down; their dreams: a comet, stars of a dipper, other astronomical sights. It snows, so the explorers get up and descend into the moon.

8. Interior of moon (Méliès's 1903 catalog calls it a giant mushroom grotto): the leader's umbrella is transformed into a mushroom then starts to grow rapidly. Moon creatures arrive, are hit by the earth leader, and vanish in puffs of smoke. Other moon creatures arrive and overpower the explorers.

9. Throne room of moon creature leader: the earthlings brought in. The earth leader tosses the moon leader to the floor where he explodes and disappears in a puff of smoke. The earthlings rush off.

10. Elsewhere on lunar landscape: the chase and further explosions, smoke puffs, and disappearing moon creatures.

11. Rocket perched over the edge of precipice: all but the leader have gotten inside. Nearby, the leader hits a moon creature (who disappears in a puff of smoke) and closes the rocket hatch. The leader of the explorers climbs down the rope suspended from the front of rocket; soon a moon creature is clinging to the rocket's base (Figure c). As the rocket falls, the moon creature holds on to the base of the rocket. Other moon creatures arrive at edge of precipice and gesture after the departing rocket.

a)

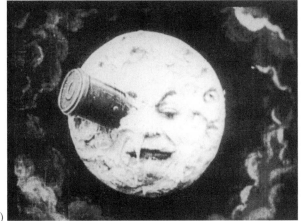

b)

c)

IV. RETURN TRIP

12. Space above ocean: the leader of the explorers, the rocket, and the moon creature are all falling.

V. HOME

13. Ocean: the rocket approaches the ocean and hits it.
14. Bottom of ocean: the rocket hits the bottom and floats upward.
15. Off a port: a ship tows the rocket toward land.

Early Editing

As in other early fictional films, throughout "A Trip to the Moon" (1902), the camera is stationary. The action plays itself out before it, and then a new shot and scene begin. (a) In one of the film's fifteen scenes, a huge cannon is fired, launching the rocket. Frame enlargement. (b) In the next scene, the rocket expedition from earth lands whimsically in the eye of the man in the moon. Frame enlargement. (c) As the leader of the moon explorers clings to a rope attached to the rocket, a moon creature clings to the base of the rocket right before it starts to fall. This is a drawing much like the corresponding frame in the finished film, though it shows the leader of the moon explorers, the man with a white beard, clinging to the rope, and the film does not. *Georges Méliès;* (a) and (b) *The Museum of Modern Art/Circulating Film Library;* (c) *British Film Institute Stills, Posters and Designs*

short films from 1908 to 1913 and his first features, Griffith proved to be one of cinema's most innovative and adept editors. Griffith's controversial *The Birth of a Nation* (1915) has more than thirteen hundred shots of widely varying length, and parts of the film—such as the Civil War battles and the assassination of President Lincoln—are edited in a manner today's audiences still find engaging.

Some later Russian filmmakers—especially Lev Kuleshov, Dziga Vertov, Vsevolod I. Pudovkin, and Sergei Eisenstein—were much impressed with Griffith's editing (it is said that Pudovkin had planned to become a chemist until he saw Griffith's ambitious 1916 film *Intolerance*). These filmmakers studied some of Griffith's films closely and discussed or wrote about the art, craft, and theory of film editing. These four were part of a group of Soviet filmmakers who experimented with editing, and though they developed somewhat different editing **styles**, they promoted what came to be called "Soviet montage" or simply **montage**. Such editing does not so much promote the invisible continuity of a story, strongly favored in **classical Hollywood cinema**; instead, it attempts to suggest **meanings** from the dynamic juxtaposition of many carefully selected

montage: A type of editing used in some 1920s Soviet films and advocated by some Soviet film theorists, such as the director Sergei Eisenstein.

classical Hollywood cinema: Films that show one or more characters facing a succession of problems while trying to reach their goals; these films tend to hide the manner of their making by using unobtrusive filmmaking techniques.

meaning: An observation or general statement about a subject.

FIGURE 3.3 Editing to suggest ideas
In the classic Soviet film (*Battleship*) *Potemkin* (1925), the editing of three consecutive shots makes a stone lion appear to come to life. The editing is used both to suggest a reaction to an event (the battleship begins to fire shells) and to suggest an idea (the *Potemkin* is so powerful that it brings stone to life). Frame enlargements. *Goskino; The Museum of Modern Art/Circulating Film Library*

details. As film theorist and scholar Dudley Andrew explains, Eisenstein

> was appalled at how inefficient and dull most cinema was, especially cinema which sought to give its audience the impression of reality. Reality, he felt, speaks very obscurely, if at all. It is up to the filmmaker to rip reality apart and rebuild it into a system capable of generating the greatest possible emotional effects. (69)

Soviet montage is illustrated in Eisenstein's *Strike* (1924), which uses a visual metaphor to express the situation of strikers in a capitalist society by cutting from shots of the striking workers and their families being attacked by police to shots of farm animals being slaughtered. Another example of Soviet montage occurs in Eisenstein's (*Battleship*) *Potemkin* (1925) after the tsar's troops and mounted Cossacks have attacked unarmed civilians in 1905 Odessa, Russia. In retaliation, the guns on the *Potemkin* have fired at the headquarters of the generals, and shells are starting to land. Then a sleeping stone lion seems to spring to life (Figure 3.3). The three consecutive shots suggest that the *Potemkin*'s guns are so powerful that they rouse even a stone lion or perhaps suggest that the Russian civilians (represented by the lion) are coming to life and will fight back; or perhaps these three shots suggest both meanings. The shots do not help develop the story; they do not even show any damage from the bombardment. Instead, they express an idea somewhat obtrusively (probably many viewers will be impressed and distracted by the editing of the three shots). Ever since the films of Griffith and those of the later Soviet masters Pudovkin and Eisenstein, the expressiveness and power of editing have been beyond dispute.

BUILDING BLOCKS

In constructing films that show stories, editors select shots to fabricate scenes and sequences. They connect shots in various ways and usually try to maximize continuity, which is an unobtrusive style of editing that helps viewers stay oriented as to time and location and follow the characters and action.

Shots, Scenes, Sequences

A **shot** is an uninterrupted strip of exposed motion-picture film or videotape made up of at least one **frame**, an individual image on the strip of film or videotape (Figure 3.4). A shot presents a subject, perhaps even a blank screen, during an uninterrupted segment of time. Typically, a feature film consists of hundreds of shots, sometimes more than a thousand. The original, uncensored version of (*Battleship*) *Potemkin* (1925) owned by the Museum of Modern Art in New York—which runs seventy-two minutes when projected at the silent speed of eighteen frames per second—has 1,346 shots. *Toy Story* (1995), which is 77½ minutes long, has 1,623 shots (Grignon). At the opposite extreme, some **experimental films** consist of a single, often very

experimental film: A film that rejects the conventions of mainstream movies and explores the possibilities of the film medium.

FIGURE 3.4 Frames, shot, and cut

The top twelve frames constitute a complete shot, and the bottom two the beginning of a new shot. The shots were spliced during editing of (*Battleship*) *Potemkin* (1925). When the film is projected at twenty-four frames per second, the top shot will last a half second. Frame enlargements. *Goskino; The Museum of Modern Art/Circulating Film Library*

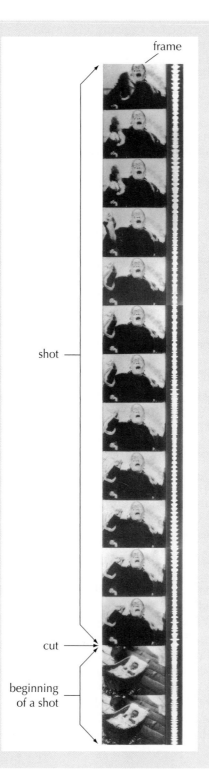

frame

shot

cut

beginning of a shot

lengthy, shot. Andy Warhol's *Empire* (1964), which is seemingly a single shot of a view of the Empire State Building and runs for hours, is an example of this sort of film.

A **scene** is a section of a **narrative** film that gives the impression of continuous action taking place during continuous time and in continuous space. A scene seems to have unity, but editors often delete tedious or unnecessary footage in such a way that viewers will not notice. For example, we may not see every step a character presumably takes in moving within a scene. A scene may consist of one shot and usually consists of two or more related shots, but on rare occasions a shot is used to convey multiple scenes, as in the more than eight-minute opening shot of *The Player* (1992). At various times during that shot, the camera moves closer to certain groups of characters so we can see them interact and then moves to different characters elsewhere nearby (Table 3.1). In the opening of *The Player*, as in the famous opening of *Touch of Evil* (1958), there is not the usual scene consisting of a shot or shots but a shot consisting of scenes.

Sequence lacks a universal meaning: filmmakers, critics, and scholars often assign it different meanings. And comparison of several published outlines of sequences for the same film reveals different "sequences." It is most useful to think of a sequence as a group of related consecutive scenes, although what unifies the scenes is not universally agreed on.

TABLE 3.1
The Opening Shot of *The Player*

SCENE NUMBER AND ACTION

1. A woman in Joel Levison's office takes a brief call from Larry Levy and hangs up. Another woman scolds her before sending her hurrying off for the day's trade papers.

2. Griffin drives into a parking space and gets out of his Range Rover. He is accosted by Adam Simon, who begins pitching a story for a possible movie. Griffin tells him to run the idea by Bonnie Sherow.

3. A man in a suit and another man who makes deliveries on a bicycle discuss tracking shots in movies.

4. Outside Griffin's office, we see through a window a man in a cap (Buck Henry) make a pitch for *The Graduate, Part Two*.

5. Adam Simon and Bonnie Sherow emerge from the same building; he is pitching his story to her. The delivery man on a bike has had an accident. Bonnie tries to help him.

6. A man in a Porsche briefly flirts with a young woman and asks where Joel Levison's office is. We learn that Levison is the studio head.

7. Another man is giving a studio tour to a group of Japanese.

8. Bonnie, still pursued by Adam Simon, tells him to write down his story for her.

9. Joel Levison arrives in a large Mercedes immediately after the young woman of scene 1 arrives back at the office and gives the papers to the other secretary.

10. Two men and a woman emerge from the building and talk about rumored upcoming changes at the studio, including the possibility that Griffin will be replaced.

11. In his office, Griffin hears two women make a story pitch.

12. The delivery man of scenes 3 and 5 mistakenly thinks that a man looking for Griffin Mill is the director Martin Scorsese.

13. The man in the suit from scene 3 and the man who made the pitch for *The Graduate, Part Two* discuss editing and tracking shots in movies.

14. While crossing the parking lot, Bonnie scolds her assistant for meeting with a writer.

15. The man from scene 12 makes a movie pitch to Griffin.

To better understand sequence, scene, and shot, consider the restored 1989 version of *Lawrence of Arabia*.

Sequence 1 (in England):

Scene 1: (consisting of two shots):

Shot 1: On the left side of the **wide-screen** frame, Lawrence fusses with a motorcycle as the opening credits roll in the center and on the right of the frame.

Shot 2: Lawrence starts the motorcycle, gets on it, and drives away until he is out of sight.

Scene 2 (consisting of twenty-three shots): As he rides quickly, even recklessly, up a hill, two bicyclists appear on his side of the road. He swerves and rides off the road.

Scene 3 (consisting of two shots): After Lawrence's funeral in St. Paul's Cathedral and before a bust of Lawrence, Colonel Brighton and a cleric exchange brief and somewhat opposing views of Lawrence.

Scene 4 (consisting of four shots): Outside St. Paul's Cathedral, four people are questioned about who Lawrence was; they are evasive, claim to have not known him well, or point out contradictory qualities.

The film's first sequence, then, is made up of four scenes, and those four scenes consist of thirty-one shots. The next sequence begins at an earlier time in Egypt.

Narrative films stitch scenes together; if a film follows the traditions of classical Hollywood cinema, the scenes are usually combined in an unnoticeable manner. Feature films vary enormously in the number of scenes, but a hundred or more is common.

Transitions

Shots may be joined in many ways. The most common method is to **splice**, or connect, the end of one shot to the beginning of the next. This transition is called a **cut** (or straight cut) because pieces of film are cut and spliced together (see Figure 3.4). In narrative films, normally only cuts are used within a scene.

A **match cut** (sometimes called a form cut) maintains continuity between two shots by matching objects with similar or identical shapes or similar movements or both similar shapes and similar movements. One of the best-known examples of a match cut is from *2001: A Space Odyssey* (1968), in which a bone slowly tumbling end over end in the air is replaced by an orbiting spacecraft with a similar shape (Figure 3.5). A match cut in which the second shot continues a movement begun in the previous shot is found in *M* (1931, Figure 3.6).

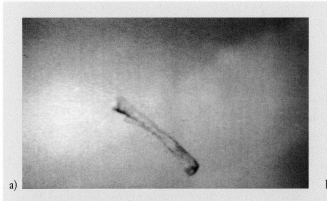 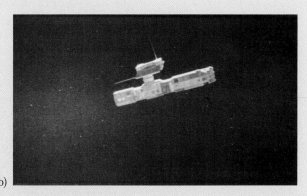

a)   b)

FIGURE 3.5 Match cut of similar forms
In *2001: A Space Odyssey* (1968), a shot of a bone is followed by a shot of an orbiting spacecraft.
The transition suggests that both the bone, which minutes before had been used as a weapon, and
the orbiting spacecraft are weapons. When projected, the film gives the appearance of the bone
becoming the orbiting spacecraft, and viewers do not notice that the angles of the two objects do
not match. Frame enlargements. *Metro-Goldwyn-Mayer*

a)   b)

FIGURE 3.6 Match cut of form and movement
In the German film *M* (1931), (a) the head of Berlin's underworld begins a sweeping motion with
his arm, and (b) the movement is picked up and completed by a match cut to the chief of police at
a different meeting. The suggestion is continuity and similarity between the groups: both have the
same goal—to catch a child murderer and restore order to their disrupted routines. Frame enlargements. *Nero Films; The Museum of Modern Art/Circulating Film Library*

A **jump cut** is a discontinuous transition between shots. For example,
one shot shows a woman running on a beach toward the water, and the next
shot shows her running away from the water. A jump cut is sometimes used

to surprise or disorient viewers (see Figure 3.16b–c). It may also occur if the film print or video has missing footage.

The **fade-out, fade-in** can provide a short but meaningful pause between scenes or sequences. Normally in a fade-out, fade-in, an image is gradually transformed into a darkened frame; then the next shot changes from a darkened frame into an illuminated one. However, many variations are possible. Early in *The Discreet Charm of the Bourgeoisie* (1972), a shot (and scene) ends with the camera **zooming in** as the image goes out of focus; the next shot (and scene) begins out of focus but quickly comes into focus. The transition functions much like the more traditional fade-out, fade-in. If a fade-out, fade-in is done slowly, it can serve as a leisurely transition; if done rapidly, it is less noticeable or not noticeable at all. Perhaps because of the current popularity of fast pacing in films, this transition is used far less often than it used to be.

In a **lap dissolve** or dissolve, one shot fades from view as the next shot fades into view then replaces it. Lap dissolves may be rapid and nearly imperceptible

zoom in: To use a zoom lens to cause the image of the subject to increase in size as the area being filmed seems to decrease.

a) b) c) d)

FIGURE 3.7 **Lap dissolve between scenes**
Lap dissolves are often used to convey what someone is thinking or remembering. In this example from a trailer, (a) the main character in *Amistad* (1997), a slave who led a rebellion on an 1839 slave ship, looks at a gift his wife back in Africa had given him. (b) and (c) By degrees, the image of the African wife emerges and gradually replaces the image of the man. (d) The transition is complete. In this case, in little more than a second the lap dissolve allows the filmmakers to change subjects, locations, and times. Frame enlargements. *Steven Spielberg; DreamWorks*

a)

b)

c)

FIGURE 3.8 Lap dissolve within a scene
Although lap dissolves are now rarely used within scenes, earlier films—as in this example from the experimental film classic "Un chien andalou" (1928)—occasionally used them. Frame enlargements.
Luis Buñuel; The Museum of Modern Art/Circulating Film Library

or slow and quite noticeable, creating a momentary superimposition of two images, sometimes suggesting similarities or even meaning (Figure 3.7). During the history of film, lap dissolves have been used in many ways. They have been used *within* a scene—for example, to introduce and conclude a cutaway that shows what a character is thinking. In Buster Keaton's *Our Hospitality* (1923), the Keaton character looks straight ahead, then a rapid lap dissolve introduces a brief shot showing what he is thinking about, and a second rapid lap dissolve returns to the shot of him looking straight ahead. Dissolves within a scene were occasionally used in early cinema to present a different view of the same subject (Figure 3.8). In the scene in *Citizen Kane* (1941) where the character in charge of the Walter Thatcher library walks across an enormous room, a lap dissolve not only serves to delete a snippet of uneventful time and action but also to suggest how large (and pretentious) the library was. Perhaps more often, lap dissolves within a scene have been used mainly to delete unnecessary time or action, as in the scene in *Vertigo* (1958, 1996) where the James Stewart character carries the Kim Novak character from the edge of the San Francisco Bay to his nearby car; in an early scene in *A Little Princess* (1995) when Sara and her father are alone in the "seminary for girls" where Sara will be staying; and in the

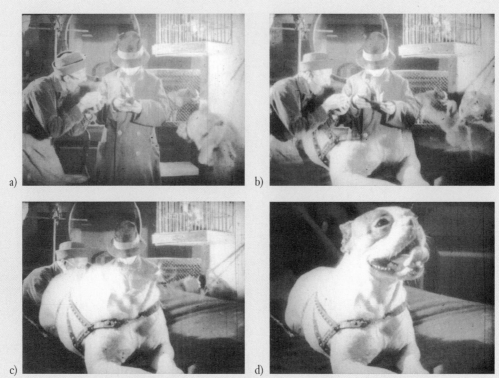

FIGURE 3.9 A wipe
In the Soviet film *Strike* (1924), a wipe is used between two scenes when the image of two men (a) is replaced with the image of a dog (b–d). Wipes may move across the frame from any direction: from below (as here), from above, from one of the sides, even on a diagonal. Frame enlargements. *The Museum of Modern Art/Circulating Film Library*

setting: The place where filmed action occurs.

serial: From the 1910s until the early 1950s, a low-budget action film divided into chapters or installments, one of which was shown each week in downtown and neighborhood movie theaters.

scene in *Election* (1999) when the Reese Witherspoon character rips down rival candidates' posters from a high school corridor's walls. For many years now, lap dissolves have mainly been used *between* scenes to suggest a change of **setting**, the passage of time, or both, as in nearly all of the many lap dissolves used in *Citizen Kane*.

A **wipe** seems to push one shot off the screen as it replaces it with the next shot (Figure 3.9). The wipe, which comes in many variations, has been popular in science fiction, **serials**, and action movies, but it has also been used in such diverse films as *It Happened One Night* (1934), *The Maltese Falcon* (1941), *The Seven Samurai* (1954), *Ed Wood* (1994), and *Battlefield Earth* (2000). Yet other examples are found in the opening and closing credits of some Pink Panther movies, where an animated pink panther seems to help push off one shot as it is replaced with the next shot.

TABLE 3.2
Six Frequently Used Transitions between Shots

CUT	The end of the first shot is attached to the beginning of the second shot. The most often used of all transitions, it creates an instantaneous change in one or more of the following: angle, distance, subject. See Figure 3.4.
MATCH or FORM CUT	The shape or movement of a subject at the end of the first shot matches or is very similar to a subject's shape or movement in the beginning of the second shot. See Figures 3.5 and 3.6.
JUMP CUT	A transition in which the viewer perceives the second shot as abruptly discontinuous with the first shot. See Figure 3.16b–c.
FADE-OUT, FADE-IN	The first shot fades to darkness (normally black); then the second shot fades in (by degrees goes from darkness to illuminated image).
LAP DISSOLVE or DISSOLVE	The first shot fades out as the second shot fades in, overlaps the first, then replaces it entirely. See Figures 3.7 and 3.8.
WIPE	The first shot seems to be pushed off the screen by the second shot. This is not a common transition but is not rare either. For a "wipe chart" illustrating 120 types of wipes, see Roy Huss and Norman Silverstein, *The Film Experience* (New York: Dell, 1968), 60. Examples they give include beginning with a small part of the second shot in one area of the frame and expanding the smaller area until it displaces the original, larger one. As Huss and Silverstein also explain, "a second image 'wipes' . . . a first from the screen . . . in several directional and formal ways: horizontally, vertically, diagonally, in the shape of a fan, like the movement of the hands of a clock, with a 'flip' (the frame revolves 360 degrees)" (59). See Figure 3.9.

The six transitions discussed thus far are summarized in Table 3.2.

Many other transitions are used less often than these six. In many films from the silent era and some sound films that try to evoke the silent era, an iris-in or iris-out may connect scenes. In the **iris-in**, a widening opening reveals more and more of the next shot until it is more visible (Figure 3.10). In an **iris-out**, the image is closed out by a constricting shape, usually a circle.

In some films, a dark object approaches the camera and concludes a shot or scene. In *Beauty and the Beast*, directed by Jean Cocteau (1946), a man and his horse are lost in a foggy forest. The man passes close by the camera; then his black horse approaches so close to the camera that its flank completely darkens the screen and ends the scene. After a rapid fade-in, viewers see a new setting. This transition is like a wipe to black, then fade-in.

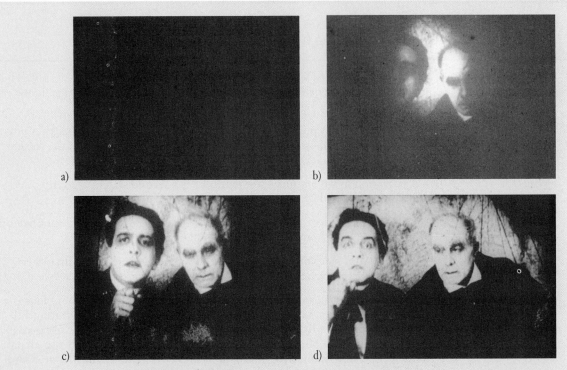

FIGURE 3.10 Iris-in
Four frame enlargements from early in *The Cabinet of Dr. Caligari* (1919) illustrate an iris-in: the image is gradually exposed by a widening opening, usually a circle. (a) The shot begins with four black frames, then (b–c) reveals more and more of the image by means of an irregularly shaped opening. (d) As is common in *Caligari*, part of the image remains in the dark (is masked). Frame enlargements. *Decla-Bioscop; The Museum of Modern Art/Circulating Film Library*

Easy Rider (1969) uses a series of quick cuts to bridge two scenes. Viewers see the last part of a scene's last shot, the beginning of the next scene, the last part of the previous shot, the first part of the next scene again, and the same repetition two more times—all this consuming little more than a second before the second scene is finally allowed to play itself out. If 1 stands for several frames at the end of a scene and 2 for several frames at the beginning of the next scene, the transition between the two scenes would be represented like this: 1 2 1 2 1 2 1 2.

Like other filmmaking practices, transitions between shots take on widely understood meanings or associations through repeated use. For instance, if enough filmmakers use lap dissolves to suggest that the action now shifts to a new setting, viewers come to associate lap dissolves with a shift to a new setting. (Similarly, people learn the meanings of most words by hearing or reading them in contexts, not by hearing, reading, or memorizing definitions.)

CONTINUITY EDITING

In narrative films and certainly in classical Hollywood cinema, **continuity editing** is normally used. Shots seem to follow one another unobtrusively, and viewers always know where the subjects of a shot are in relation to other subjects and in relation to the setting. Continuity editing allows the omission of minor details within scenes yet maintains the illusion of completeness. Continuity may be achieved in various ways. For example, **eyeline matches** may be used, in which a subject looks at something **offscreen**, and the next shot shows what was being looked at from approximately the point of view of the subject (Figure 3.11). Continuity is also maintained within scenes if all shots show the subjects from one side of an imaginary straight line drawn between them. This is sometimes referred to as the **180-degree system** (Figure 3.12).

A scene from *Life Is Beautiful* (1998) illustrates various ways continuity can be maintained within a scene (Figure 3.13). Eyeline matches are used in

a)  b)

FIGURE 3.11 Eyeline match
Approximately fifteen minutes into the Brazilian film *Central Station* (1998), (a) the main character looks off-frame, in this case directly at the camera. (b) Then from her point of view, the camera sees what she sees as the train doors are closing: a motherless boy she has reluctantly befriended. Such eyeline matches are one way filmmakers maintain continuity from shot to shot within a scene. Frame enlargements. *Martine de Clermont-Tonnerre; Arthur Cohn; Sony Pictures Classics*

a)   I, I'm a girl!   b)   I, I'm a girl!

FIGURE 3.12 180-degree system
These images from two consecutive shots of the Chinese film *King of Masks* (1996) illustrate the
180-degree system, sometimes called the 180-degree rule. Envision an imaginary line drawn
straight beneath the two subjects seen here. Notice how in both shots the camera is positioned
on the same side of that imaginary line. In all shots in this scene, viewers would see the right side
of the man and the left side of the little girl. No matter how many shots in a scene, filmmakers
using the 180-degree system would always keep the camera positioned on one side of that imaginary line, and the background would remain essentially the same, though different shots often
reveal different parts of that background. Frame enlargements. *Wu Tianming; Goldwyn*

this scene, as when the man on the bicycle looks offscreen to the left and
the next shot shows what he is looking at: the schoolchildren and the
woman. Throughout the scene the viewer sees the actor on his left side
or from behind but not on his right side (the 180-degree system). **Shot/
reverse shot** is another way to promote continuity. A shot from over the
first person's shoulder or to the side of it shows the face of a second person;
in the next shot the camera is behind or to the side of the second person,
and we now see the first person's face (Figure 3.13c–d). During both shots,
the background remains the same or is consistent with the previous shot.
Shot/reverse shot is often used for scenes with dialogue. Continuity editing
is also achieved by cutting on action: one shot ends during a subject's movement, and the next shot, usually from a different distance or angle, continues
or concludes the action (Figure 3.13d–e). In such instances, sometimes dead
time (some of the middle part of the movement) may be omitted, yet continuity is maintained because the same subject moves in a consistent and
seemingly uninterrupted way.

   Although continuity editing is the usual way narrative films are edited,
some filmmakers choose to ignore continuity from time to time, and other
filmmakers—such as the French actor and director Jacques Tati and the
Japanese director Yasujiro Ozu—often reject the conventions of continuity editing.

a)

b)

c)

d)

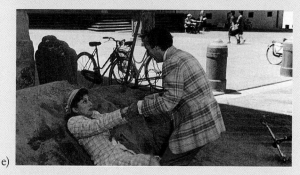
e)

FIGURE 3.13 Continuity editing within a scene
The scene from *Life Is Beautiful* (1998) represented here runs
twenty-nine seconds and consists of eight shots:

1. The man rounds a corner riding a bicycle in a hurry: an
   angry man is chasing him (a).
2. A line of schoolchildren and a woman to the left of them
   are walking toward the nearby piazza.
3. The man on the bike reacts with alarm because the children and the woman inadvertently block his path.
4. The man runs into the woman (b) and falls on top of
   her.
5. Her reaction when she sees who it is (c) (they had met
   briefly earlier when he broke her fall from a barn)
6. His reaction to her (d)
7. He helps her up (e), says good-bye, and runs off (he is
   still concerned that the man who had been chasing him
   might catch up with him).
8. Her reaction to his abrupt departure

In this scene, all shots of the man are from his left side or
from behind him, so viewers always know where he is in relationship to his surroundings. Applying the 180-degree system,
the camera operator filmed the subjects from one side of an
imaginary line drawn between the scene's main subjects: the
man and the woman. Sometimes, as in (b), the camera is positioned *on* or occasionally a little beyond that imaginary line. If
shots in a scene are filmed from the other side of that imaginary line—if, for example, we suddenly saw the man's right
side—the relationship of the subjects to each other and to the
setting shifts abruptly and perhaps confusingly. Here, as in
nearly all edited scenes, the continuity of space, time, and action or the illusion of them is maintained. Actually, in many
movie scenes, fragments of time and action are unobtrusively
deleted. Because of continuity editing, however, the action
seems to flow from shot to shot smoothly and clearly yet concisely. Frame enlargements. *Cecchi Gori Group; Miramax*

IMAGE ON IMAGE AND IMAGE AFTER IMAGE

Editors can combine two or more images into the same image—although it's usually hard for viewers to distinguish more than two images at the same time—or they can juxtapose images in expressive ways.

Superimpositions

superimposition: Two or more images photographed or printed on top of each other.

In creating a lap dissolve, editors **superimpose** images. The lap dissolve near the end of *Psycho* (1960) fleetingly juxtaposes three images (Figure 3.14). If a dissolve is slow enough—or even halts briefly midway, as is done on rare occasions—viewers are more likely to notice the superimposed images.

Near the beginning of *The Wild Bunch* (1969) occurs a complex example of combined images within a lap dissolve. Children in a western town are burning scorpions and ants. A slow lap dissolve combines images of the burning insects with images of many townspeople and railroad employees who had recently been shot in the crossfire between bounty hunters hired by the railroad and the wild bunch. During the dissolve from the children to the scene of carnage, viewers hear the giggles of the children burning the insects mingled with some crying and the moans of the injured people. The combination of images and sounds suggests that people can be like helpless scorpions and ants, painfully destroyed by powerful forces indifferent to their well-being. The blending of images also undercuts any notion of youthful innocence: the children who enjoy destroying insect life may grow up and destroy human life, as did the bounty hunters and the wild bunch.

FIGURE 3.14 **Superimposition of three images**
In a few frames near the conclusion of *Psycho* (1960), viewers may notice that three images are superimposed briefly: Norman from the shoulders up, a skull, and Marion's car being pulled from the swamp by a chain. In a 35 mm version of the film that is in good condition or a laser disc or DVD version viewed on a high-resolution monitor, viewers may notice the three superimposed images and consider their significance. (Viewers are unlikely to notice them on a videotape version.) The brief triple superimposition suggests that underneath Norman is his mother and that Norman is, in at least one sense, already dead. The superimposed images also suggest that Norman, his mother, and death are a swamp and that Norman embodies death and destruction. A psychoanalytic critic might see the swamp as the vast, untamed id near the human heart. Frame enlargement. *Alfred Hitchcock; Universal*

Juxtapositions

The **surrealist** film "Un chien andalou" (1928) begins with the following shots:

1. a title card: "Once Upon a Time"
2. a man's hands are sharpening a straight razor on a thick leather strap
3. a man is smoking and looking down
4. the man's hands are sharpening the straight razor; he seems to test the sharpness of the razor against one of his thumbnails
5. the man is smoking and looking down
6. the man opens the nearby door and walks through the opening
7. the man emerges on the other side of the door onto an exterior balcony and goes to the railing
8. the man looks up
9. a full moon in the dark sky
10. the man is still looking up
11. a woman looks straight ahead as a man stands next to her; the man holds open the eyelids of her left eye with his left hand and moves the razor blade toward the eye with his right hand (Figure 3.15)
12. a wisp of clouds seems to bisect the moon
13. a **close-up** of an eye being sliced by a straight razor
14. a title card: "Eight Years Later"

Since 1928, the film's opening has shocked and horrified audiences— pretty much what was intended by the filmmaker Luis Buñuel, who himself plays the man in the opening shots. But it is not merely the subject matter that provokes such strong audience response. It is also a matter of

surrealism: A movement in 1920s and 1930s European art, drama, literature, and film in which an attempt was made to portray or interpret the workings of the subconscious mind as manifested in dreams.

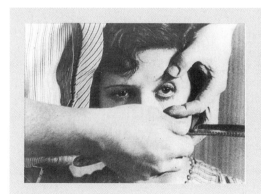

FIGURE 3.15 Editing to mislead
In this shot from the experimental film "Un chien andalou" (1928), a man seems about to cut the woman's eye, but he does not, and the next shot is of a wisp of cloud and the moon. Frame enlargement. *Luis Buñuel; British Film Institute Stills, Posters and Designs*

the selection and arrangement of the shots. Buñuel, after all, could have presented the main action in two shots, shots 11 and 13. Instead, the film delays the shock by beginning with somewhat curious action: why would a man be sharpening a razor when he does not seem to intend to shave, and why would he take that razor with him to the outside balcony? By near the end of shot 11, the action has become somewhat worrisome for viewers as the man moves the razor a little closer to the woman's eye. Shot 12, however, eases the tension for viewers, at least somewhat, only to be followed by the brief, explicit shot 13: a natural action (a wisp of cloud passing in front of the moon) followed by a brutal human action. This, perhaps the most shocking match cut in the history of cinema, seems to end with a brutal act, but if viewers have the stomach and curiosity to study the film's opening section, they will notice that the sliced eye and eyebrow do not match the woman's eye and eyebrow. (In fact, a dead cow's eye was used.) So powerful can juxtaposed images be that viewers do not notice prominent inconsistencies. Then, too, there is that matter of the initial title card seeming to promise a traditional narrative. Like "Un chien andalou" as a whole, this opening section proves to be neither traditional nor a narrative. The selection and juxtapositions of the film's opening thirteen shots illustrate how editing can help filmmakers guide and even mislead audiences and help intensify the audience's emotional responses.

Even in films that use continuity editing extensively (and as we saw illustrated above, "Un chien andalou" does not), filmmakers sometimes want to surprise, amuse, or confuse and may follow a shot with one viewers don't expect.

Occasionally the unexpected shot appears after a brief lap dissolve. In *Citizen Kane*, immediately after Kane marries Susan, his second wife, he has decided she'll have a career as an opera singer. As the newlyweds are about to be driven off, Susan tells the reporters surrounding the car that if necessary, Kane will build her an opera house. Kane shouts, "That won't be necessary." After a rapid lap dissolve, the next shot is a large newspaper headline reading "Kane Builds Opera House." The effect is surprising and amusing; the combination of shots also shows that Kane's judgment can be faulty.

Sometimes filmmakers use jump cuts to confuse or disorient viewers, as in several scenes in the classic **French new wave** film *Breathless* (1959, Figure 3.16). Editing can also be used to show contradictory qualities of a place or situation (see Figure 3.17).

Editors often join two shots to illustrate similarities. Near the end of *The Wild Bunch*, after the final shootout, we see a shot of perched vultures; two shots later a shot of gleeful bounty hunters swooping down on the dead to strip them of valuables, as birds (vultures?) fly across the frame in the foreground and a vulture is visible briefly in the background; then a shot of a vulture perched on a dead man. The juxtaposition of shots constitutes a none-too-subtle **filmic** metaphor suggesting that the bounty hunters are vultures.

French new wave (cinema): A movement made up of a diverse group of French fictional films made in the late 1950s and early 1960s in reaction to the carefully scripted products of the French film industry and as explorations of more current subjects sometimes rendered with untraditional techniques.

filmic: Characteristic of the film medium or appropriate to it.

FIGURE 3.16 Jump cuts that create discontinuity
In Jean-Luc Godard's *Breathless* (1959), a man driving a car pulls off a country road to elude two pursuing motorcycle police officers. A few seconds later, nearly five minutes into the film, an officer pulls off the road, and the man shoots him and runs away. The scene sometimes seems discontinuous, as if the camera were sometimes in the wrong position or shots or parts of them had been left out. The last seven shots of the excerpt illustrate three areas of confusion. Shots (a) and (b) are taken from one side of an imaginary line between the two subjects, with the man facing left; but shots (c), (d), and (e) are filmed from the other side of the line, and the man is now facing right. The scene is not edited using the 180-degree system. The police officer's location when he gets shot (f) is also puzzling: he is not on the path shown in shot (a). Finally, the relation of the last shot (g) to the preceding shots is unclear: viewers cannot know where the man is and how far he is from the shot police officer. Perhaps (g) is a new scene consisting of one shot. Although the seven shots are elliptical and confusing in some details, one could argue that the main action is clear and the discontinuous editing is appropriate for the subject: a sudden, unplanned murder. Frame enlargements. *SNC; New Yorker Films*

Less obvious yet still damning by association is some of the editing in the films of satirical documentary filmmaker Michael Moore. In *Roger & Me* (1989), we first see Miss Michigan riding in a car on which is affixed a sign for a Chevrolet dealer during a parade in Flint, Michigan, immediately after a shot of a man scooping up horse dung from the parade route. Later a man speaking of the poor labor conditions in Flint concludes that some people know what is going on and some don't; the next shot is of Miss Michigan. Later still, we see brief footage of the 1988 Miss USA pageant and learn that Miss Michigan won the national title; the next shot is a match cut of a man in Flint knocking on a door to evict people from their housing, presumably because they are out of work and behind in the rent. Because of the selection

a)

b)

FIGURE 3.17 Consecutive shots revealing contradictory aspects of a setting
These two shots early in *The Third Man* (1949) suggest the contradictory aspects of Vienna shortly after World War II: (a) a statue of Beethoven and (b) two black marketeers. The consecutive, discontinuous images quickly convey that the story will be set in a city of both culture and crime. Frame enlargements. *London Film Productions*

a)

b)

c)

FIGURE 3.18 Consecutive shots suggesting characters' situation
The Japanese film *Woman in the Dunes* (1964) begins with a city man collecting samples of insects in a remote setting near a sea. Some local men tell him that he has missed the last bus back into town and invite him to stay overnight with a woman in a shack in a sand pit. Soon the man realizes that the villagers and the woman intend for him to live with her and work with her. Later the man catches the woman off guard and ties up her hands and feet, but he fails to escape from the pit. Nearly forty-four minutes into the film occur the three shots represented here: (a) A bird's-eye view shows the two of them sleeping (she is still bound hand and foot). (b) The next shot shows a trapped insect trying to escape its glass prison. (c) The third shot is of sand falling down cliffs of sand, presumably nearby. Shot (a) shows that the couple is exhausted (they are motionless, and she sleeps even though her hands and feet are bound). Shot (b) suggests that though the man has tied up the woman, they are trapped, as is the insect the man had collected.

Shot (c), of falling sand, reminds viewers that sand continues to fall and endanger the shack (viewers earlier had learned that the woman has to shovel sand or it will overwhelm her shack). In a mere seventeen seconds, the three wordless shots convey that the man and woman are tired, trapped, and in danger. Frame enlargements. *Pathe Contemporary Films Release*

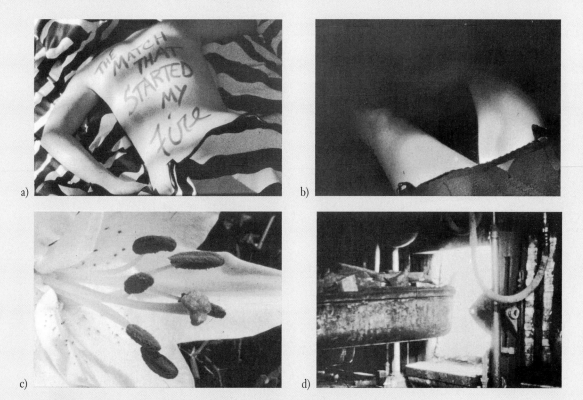

FIGURE 3.19 Consecutive shots creating meaning in a nonnarrative documentary
Three consecutive images from the nonnarrative documentary film "The Match That Started My Fire" (1991) illustrate how the selection and arrangement of shots can create meaning beyond what the shots convey individually. In the film various women describe their first awareness of their sexual feelings as viewers see a wide variety of images, some created for this film (b and c), some selected from existing footage (d). The three consecutive images shown here (b–d)—of a woman's bare legs illuminated in the dark, an open flower, and a mechanism pushing a load into a blazing furnace—suggest various facets of a woman's sexuality. Frame enlargements. *Cathy C. Cook; Women Make Movies, New York*

and arrangement of the shots (and because of how Miss Michigan responds to director Michael Moore's unexpected questions), she comes across as someone who cares not about labor and living conditions in Flint but only about winning the national title. In a bookstore in Michael Moore's *The Big One* (1998), viewers see three book covers: one with a photo of Senator Bob Dole, one with a photo of independent presidential candidate Ross Perot, and one with a photo of a dog.

Consecutive shots may serve yet other purposes. For example, they may subtly suggest the predicament that characters are in (Figure 3.18).

In nonnarrative films, the juxtaposition of shots may also be as expressive as in fictional films (Figures 3.19 and 3.20).

a)

b)

FIGURE 3.20 Consecutive shots creating a visual poem in a nonnarrative experimental film
In a shot from the experimental film "Un chien andalou" (1928), (a) a man begins to fall forward, presumably mortally wounded. In the next shot (b–c), now in the countryside, as he continues to fall, his hands brush the bare back of a seated woman; then the woman's image fades away. The two shots show that dying can figuratively be like momentarily brushing the bare back of a woman who quickly fades away and leaves the beauty of nature. The juxtaposition of shots suggests the fragility and beauty of life as human life ebbs away. Frame enlargements. *Luis Buñuel; The Museum of Modern Art/Circulating Film Library*

c)

Action and Reaction

How viewers react to a movie is often intensified by how subjects in the film react. In virtually all narrative films (fictional and documentary), many scenes show actions and other people's reactions, and those reactions tend to intensify the viewer's responses. Humorous scenes are usually funnier because someone is shown to be bewildered, stunned, or in some other way uncomfortable. Horrifying scenes can be more frightening because characters react to scary sights or sounds. Suspenseful athletic contests, as in the **narrative documentary** *Hoop Dreams* (1994), are even more involving because of how individuals in the crowd are shown reacting to events. Sometimes actions and reactions are shown within the same shot (Figure 3.21). Often, shots of action are followed by **reaction shots**, which are (usually brief)

narrative documentary: A film or video representation of an actual (not imaginary) narrative or story.

a)

b)

c)

FIGURE 3.21 Action and reaction within shots
A single shot may be devoted entirely to an action or entirely to a reaction. Sometimes, however, a shot combines action and reaction in different proportions: some shots are mostly of action; others mostly of reaction. For example, nearly two hours into *Pulp Fiction* (1994) occur two consecutive eventful shots. (a) The first is of a young man moving forward and firing a gun at the film's two main characters. The nervous young man misses all six attempts even though his targets are close by. Toward the end of the shot, after he realizes that he has fired his last bullet, for approximately two seconds he looks fearful and at a loss. (b–c) In the following shot, the two characters who were shot at look straight ahead at their assailant, down (as if to see if they are somehow shot but have not yet realized it), at each other, and straight ahead. Then they raise their guns and fire at the young man. The first of the two shots under consideration here is devoted mostly to the young man's actions and ends with a glimpse of his reaction to his predicament. The second shot continues and draws out the uncertainty and suspense with which the previous shot ends; it concludes abruptly with the two men's retaliation. Shot 1: action, then reaction; shot 2: more reactions, then action. Frame enlargements. *Lawrence Bender; Miramax*

shots showing someone's reactions to an event. Images of anguish can be more gripping if interspersed with reaction shots, as in *The Bicycle Thief* (1948, Figure 3.22). Filmmakers may even show a series of actions and then a character's reaction to them (Figure 3.23). Action shots followed by reaction shots can be used in a limitless variety of situations.

But action followed by reaction is not the editor's only choice. Sometimes editors show first a reaction and then what caused it (Figure 3.24). Part of a long scene in *Four Weddings and a Funeral* (1994) shows reactions to the solution to a problem and only later shows us the solution to the problem. Approximately seven minutes into the film, a wedding ceremony begins. Soon the best man realizes that in his rush that morning, he has forgotten to bring the rings. He pantomines to a friend in the congregation what the problem is, leaves the couple and the minister, and meets with his friend in the back of

a)

b)

FIGURE 3.22 Action, then reaction
Two consecutive shots show an action and reaction in the last scene of the Italian neorealist film *The Bicycle Thief* (1948). The boy has recently seen a crowd chasing, catching, and reviling his father, who in desperation tried to steal a bicycle so he would not lose his recently acquired job. (a) First viewers see the father's emotional pain, and then (b) the boy looks up, sees his father's anguish, and takes his hand. The reaction shot of the boy shows his anguish and empathy and intensifies viewers' response to his and his father's plight. Frame enlargements. *PDS-ENIC*

plotline: A narrative or series of related events usually involving only a few characters or people and capable of functioning on its own as a story.

FIGURE 3.23 Reaction to a series of actions
A shot can be in reaction to a succession of previous images. In *Vertigo* (1958, 1996), for example, the main character wakes up from a nightmare startled and fearful. Frame enlargement. *Paramount; Universal*

the church. The two rings the friend gives the best man surprise him, but we do not get to see them. Later in the scene, we see the minister's startled reaction to the rings and the reactions of the bride and groom. Only then do viewers see the rings the friend has borrowed from those in attendance: hers is large, heartshaped, and multicolored plastic; his looks like a pewter masked male's head with wings on both sides! Filmmakers may dwell on reaction shots rather than on the action and let viewers' imaginations supply the rest. An amusing example occurs in *There's Something about Mary* (1998, Figure 3.25).

Parallel Editing

In **parallel editing**, or cross-cutting, the film shifts back and forth between two or more actions, often suggesting that the actions are occurring simultaneously and are related but sometimes depicting events from different times. Parallel editing that suggests simultaneous events in different locations is used in an early sequence in the classic German film *M* (Figure 3.26). A much more complicated example of parallel editing occurs in *West Side Story* (1961, Figure 3.27).

Parallel editing is occasionally used throughout a movie to suggest two or more simultaneous **plotlines** and to generate suspense, as in *Dr. Strangelove: Or, How I Learned to Stop Worrying and Love the Bomb* (1963).

FIGURE 3.24 Reaction, then action
(a) In the last two shots for the trailer for *Antz* (1998), the main character, an ant named Z, looks at something off-frame. (b) The next shot shows viewers what Z is alarmed about: Princess Bala stuck in gum on the bottom of a shoe of someone walking. (In the film itself, the order of the two shots is reversed.) Frame enlargements. *PDI; DreamWorks Pictures*

FIGURE 3.25 Reaction to implied action
These four frames represent four consecutive shots from late in *There's Something about Mary* (1998). (a) Mary looks on. (b) The young man (Ted) helps Mary's brother get positioned in the batting cage. (c) A shot from the point of view of the boy in the batting cage shows a baseball whizzing forward. (d) Mary and Ted react with alarm and concern. By implication, the ball has hit the boy and knocked him down. Here the editing shifts the emphasis from the boy getting hit (which could be alarming to viewers) to the reaction of the two witnesses (which is amusing since viewers do not see the boy's pain). For a situation to be humorous, it usually has to be placed in a context where there is not too much pain to someone whom viewers care about. Frame enlargements. *Farrelly Bros.; 20th Century–Fox*

a)

b)

c)

d)

e)

FIGURE 3.26 Parallel editing to convey mood and meaning
In the German film *M* (1931), before the shots shown here, a young girl, Elsie, leaves school and plays with a ball. Viewers learn that a child murderer is on the loose and see Elsie being greeted by a stranger who buys her a balloon. Elsie's mother waits for her daughter and frets that she is late arriving back at their apartment. As the mother calls out Elsie's name, viewers see (a) an empty stairwell in the building where Elsie and her mother live and (b) an empty attic, presumably in their building. (c) In silence, viewers see Elsie's empty chair and table setting. (d) Somewhere outside the city, the ball Elsie played with earlier rolls into view and stops, and (e) the balloon the man had bought for her floats up and briefly gets caught in wires before being carried away by the wind. These five shots suggest that at approximately the same moment in time, Elsie is not in the stairwell, not in the attic, not at the table, and (somewhere outside the city) not in possession of her ball and the balloon. It is not only the parallel editing that contributes to the sequence's melancholic mood and ominous meaning: all five shots have no people, the last three shots of the sequence are without sound, and the last two shots end in disturbing stillness. Frame enlargements. *Nero Films; The Museum of Modern Art/Circulating Film Library*

Except for that film's expository prologue, its doomsday device finale, and its third sequence, which is located in undisclosed residential quarters, all the film's sequences occur at one of three locations: a U.S. Air Force base where General Jack D. Ripper decides to order a group of U.S. bombers to attack Soviet targets; an American bomber containing a crew trying to reach a target in the Soviet Union; and the Pentagon War Room, where the U.S. president and his advisers, the Soviet ambassador, and via phone the Soviet premier try to avert catastrophe. Although viewers get the sense of time moving forward as the film progresses, the parallel editing suggests that some of the events happen simultaneously.

a)

b)

c)

d)

FIGURE 3.27 Parallel editing with multiple subjects
Approximately ninety-three minutes into *West Side Story* (1961)
occurs a sequence using competing and overlapping music
("Tonight") and rapid parallel editing to convey the simultaneous actions by six subjects: a police officer and, much more
prominently, (a) the Jets, a gang on the way to a "rumble" or
showdown with the Sharks, (b) the Sharks, a Puerto Rican gang
on the way to a showdown with the Jets, (c) Anita, a Puerto
Rican looking forward to an amorous evening with her boyfriend, Bernardo, the leader of the Sharks, (d) Tony, the former
leader of the Jets, who is looking forward to meeting with his
lover, Maria, that evening, and (e) Maria, a Puerto Rican who
is looking forward to getting together with Tony. The parallel
editing between the six subjects quickly shows almost simultaneously how all the subjects are looking forward to the events
of the evening. Frame enlargements. *Robert Wise; United Artists*

e)

Often parallel editing shows someone being menaced while someone
else is on the way to help. Early in the twentieth century, D. W. Griffith per-
fected this technique and often used it in his films. It is still commonplace in
movies, as in *Toy Story 2* (1999), which incorporates parallel editing of two
plotlines during approximately half of the film (Figure 3.28). Parallel editing
may also be used to show one subject trying to achieve a goal as another subject tries to overcome various problems and prevent the first subject from
achieving the goal. A memorable example occurs near the end of Hitchcock's
Strangers on a Train (1951), where extensive and suspenseful parallel editing
shows one character on his way to plant incriminating evidence at a murder

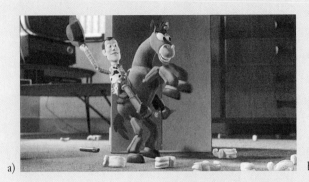

a)   b)

FIGURE 3.28 Parallel editing of two plotlines
Approximately half of *Toy Story 2* (1999) employs parallel editing of two plotlines: (a) Woody with
his horse from his earlier career and (b) Woody's friends on the way to rescue him (here four of
Woody's friends are in a toy car looking for Woody in the kidnapper's toy store). Frame enlargements. *Pixar; Walt Disney Pictures*

site as another character tries to overcome various problems and arrive there
before him.

Parallel editing can show a contrast. In *A Fish Called Wanda* (1988), it is
used amusingly to contrast a bored married couple getting ready for bed
with a young unmarried couple fully attending to each other as they undress
and have sex. In the documentary film "The Heck with Hollywood!" (1991),
which is about the difficulties of marketing one's own low-budget film, parallel editing is briefly used to contrast the views of an independent filmmaker with those of her distributor.

Parallel editing can also highlight a similarity. Throughout *M*, parallel
editing shows that the police, organized beggars, and organized crime in a
German city of the early 1930s are all trying to capture a child murderer.
Griffith also used parallel editing throughout the monumental silent film *Intolerance* to present four stories illustrating intolerance in four eras and places.

As we see so many times in this book, a technique is not restricted to a certain type of film. Parallel editing can also be used in films that tell no story, as
in the nonnarrative documentary *Titicut Follies* (1967), where it is used to compare and contrast the same subject at different times. Shots of an inmate being
force-fed by a psychologist in a mental hospital are alternated with shots of the
corpse of the same man being prepared for display before his burial.

PACE AND TIME

Pace is the viewer's sense of a film's subjects (such as succeeding events in a
narrative film or information in a documentary film) being presented rapidly

or slowly. Although it is a highly subjective experience and is influenced by many aspects of the film, a film's pace can help keep viewers involved or alienate them.

Fast and Slow Cutting

A shot may be as brief as one frame, but when it is, few viewers see its content. At the opposite extreme, as Hitchcock demonstrated in *Rope* (1948), a shot may run for as long as the reel of film in the camera, whereas a single shot in video may run more than two hours. Shots in feature films typically range from several seconds to about twenty seconds. **Fast cutting** refers to consecutive shots of brief duration (say, a few seconds or less) or editing dominated by brief shots. **Slow cutting** refers to consecutive shots of long duration or editing dominated by long-lasting shots. Because again so much depends on context, it's difficult to set a number here, but an average shot length (ASL) of fifteen or more seconds will seem slow to many viewers in Western cultures.

Fast cutting may impart energy to its subjects. It is also an effective way to convey a lot of information in a brief time, as in many **trailers** shown on TV, in movie theaters, and in videotape and DVD movies. Makers of music videos and other filmmakers often use fast cutting to intensify a sense of confusion or loss of control or to add urgency or energy. It's no accident, for example, that the opera montage in *Citizen Kane* uses fast cutting throughout. During that section of the story, Susan is under unbearable pressure, and the fast cutting reflects the fact that events seem to gallop out of her control.

trailer: A brief compilation film that advertises a movie or a video release.

For some descriptions of the opera montage in *Citizen Kane*, see the Web site for this book: <bedfordstmartins.com/phillips-film>.

Fast cutting is sometimes used to show images flashing through someone's mind during a crisis, as when late in *Spanking the Monkey* (1994) the main character has jumped from a high cliff and is plunging toward water. Fast cutting is frequently used for fights, climaxes to races, and montages summarizing past events. Editing may not only be fast but also have a regular rhythm (Figure 3.29).

Slow cutting can be used to establish a subdued mood before fast cutting injects energy. Slow cutting may also be used in scenes of calm or reflection. Filmmakers can also use slow cutting to slow the pace, just as the second movement of a symphony or concerto typically does.

Too much of any technique—fast cutting or slow—causes viewers to lose interest, so editing is used to vary a film's pace. Like poets writing in meter, filmmakers can establish a more or less regular rhythm, maintain it, or work expressive variations on it. In the last sequence of the classic Soviet

a)   b)

FIGURE 3.29 **Fast cutting and a regular rhythm**
Early in *October* (1928), which was codirected and edited by Sergei Eisenstein, two frames of a
soldier firing a machine gun are alternated with two frames of the gun being fired. This extremely rapid alternation between the soldier and gun, soldier and gun, soldier and gun, sets
up a regular rhythm, as if the man is relentless, as if he is a machine or part of one, or as if the
weapon consists of the man plus the gun. Through editing, the man and the gun become one.
To recapture some of the experience of seeing these two alternating images in the film, look at
the first frame only long enough to see its subject (much less than a second); then do the same
with the second frame; then allotting the same fraction of a second to each image, look back
and forth, back and forth, and so on. Frame enlargements. *The Museum of Modern Art/
Circulating Film Library*

film (*Battleship*) *Potemkin*, for example, the battleship *Potemkin* is steaming
along. The cutting is brisk but by no means hurried or frantic. After possible
rival ships are spotted and the men called to their battle stations, the cutting
becomes faster and faster until it is clear there will be no battle after all; then
the pace of the editing slows. Pace mirrors mood.[1]

Studies of editing show that since the mid-1970s, movies have had a
much shorter average shot length than in earlier decades. Film scholar Barry
Salt reports that from 1976 to 1987, the ASL of a large sample of movies was
about 8.4 seconds (296). Of course, some shots are twenty-five or even many
more seconds, but there are also many stretches of fast cutting. Why there is
so much fast cutting in recent movies, TV, and music videos in Western cultures is not easy to determine. Perhaps modern viewers absorb the meaning
of a shot more quickly. Perhaps we are visually jaded and need more of a kick.

---

[1]David Mayer's detailed cutting continuity script for (*Battleship*) *Potemkin* includes the number of frames for each shot in the film. The descriptions reveal that as the men on the
Potemkin prepare for possible battle, many shots are only a second or two long or even less
than a second (calculated at sixteen frames per second, which many experts believe is the
speed that best approximates the original showings). After it is clear that no confrontation
will occur after all, the average shot length tends to increase (208–52).

If a narrative is poor, editors may dazzle or distract viewers with exciting editing techniques, according to Michael Hoggan, a past president of American Cinema Editors. Or perhaps the fast cutting reflects the fast pace most people feel is an inescapable part of their lives. Maybe it's a combination of these or other causes. Music videos with their fast cutting and jump cuts bombard viewers with such an overload of information that it is often impossible to discern in them any coherence or meaning, and for many viewers this lack of coherence and meaning is characteristic of contemporary life.

Condensing Time and Stretching It: Montage and Other Editing Techniques

The Japanese director Yasujiro Ozu and Danish director Carl Theodor Dreyer, some experimental filmmakers, occasional documentary filmmakers, and a relatively few other filmmakers deliberately include shots that most directors and editors would consider unnecessary. For the vast majority of filmmakers, however, one of the main goals of editing is to eliminate dead time—any footage that does not contribute to the desired effects. The sense of dead time, however, depends on who is doing the viewing, and shots that were engaging in former eras often seem uneventful to viewers of a later generation. For example, the many shots in classic western films of cowboys riding and riding on and on are dead time to many of today's young viewers. One of the most effective means of cutting dead time and showing viewers much information quickly is a **montage**, or a "quick impressionistic sequence of . . . images, usually linked by dissolves, superimpositions or wipes, and used to convey passages of time, changes of place, or any other scenes of transition" (Reisz and Millar 112). One of the most famous montages in cinema is from *Citizen Kane*, the montage of breakfasts experienced by Kane and his first wife. In twenty-seven brief shots (plus brief blurry transitions that look like swish pans) lasting altogether only 133 seconds, the filmmakers show the couple's deteriorating marriage (Figure 3.30).[2]

Another use of a montage—this one without lap dissolves—occurs in *Raging Bull* (1980). One scene ends with the boxer Jake La Motta soaking his fist in a bucket of ice water. Then we see a **title card** announcing a La Motta fight, a few stills from the fight, and snippets from home movies. The same pattern is repeated, during which six fights are accounted for; Jake and Vicki date, marry, indulge in horseplay beside and in a swimming pool, and begin a family; and Jake's brother Joey marries and begins a family. In two minutes thirty-five seconds, the story jumps ahead more than three years, from January 14, 1944, to sometime after a March 14, 1947, fight. This montage

title card: A card or thin sheet of clear plastic on which is written or printed information included in a film.

---

[2]For a detailed description of the breakfasts montage in *Citizen Kane*, including ten frame enlargements and an analysis of the sequence, see Reisz and Millar (115-21).

a)   b)

FIGURE 3.30 **The breakfasts montage in** *Citizen Kane* **(1941)**
(a) At the beginning of the sequence almost fifty-two minutes into the film, Charles Kane and his
first wife are close to and attentive to each other; by stages they become alienated; (b) at the end
they are far apart, reading rival papers. In slightly more than two minutes, this montage shows
their growing alienation and failing marriage. Frame enlargements. *Orson Welles; RKO General
Pictures*

shows Jake's work and personal life and Joey's personal life all going well, but
the filmmakers chose to skim through those events.

Montages usually consist of many brief shots, often connected by lap dissolves, but a montage can be as simple as a few shots without lap dissolves. In
Hook (1991), we see three consecutive shots from behind a seated Wendy. Each
shot ends with Wendy turning around and revealing that she is older; this simple montage represents an expanse of forty or so years in a matter of seconds.

Montages are not the only method editors have of condensing time.
Sometimes editors provide much information by a succession of relatively
brief shots, as in the ending of *Breaking Away* (1979). The film presents the
story of four unemployed young living in a university town; they have
graduated from high school but have not yet found their places in life. The
most important of the four is Dave Stoller, whose father runs a used car lot
and disapproves of Dave's zealous imitation of professional Italian bicycle
racers and his attempts to emulate everything Italian. The four young men
are harassed by university students and decide to prove themselves by entering the annual university team bicycle race, which they win in a close race
against thirty-three fraternity teams.

After the race, the film has three more scenes, which presumably take
place at the beginning of the following fall semester:

Scene (two shots, twelve seconds)

    Shot 1. Used car lot: Mr. Stoller is leaving on a bike; his pregnant wife
             is talking about a car to an interested couple, though we do
             not hear her.

Shot 2. On a bike, Mr. Stoller leaves the Cutter Cars lot and rides into the street.

Scene (three shots, nineteen seconds)

Shot 3. On campus: a young woman with a French accent asks Dave where the "office of the bursar" is.

Shot 4. After hesitating, he replies, "You must mean the Bursar's Office."

Shot 5. She agrees and smiles.

Scene, the film's last (three shots, twenty-two seconds)

Shot 6. Dave and the French woman are biking; Dave tells her he was thinking about studying French and talks to her about the major French bicycle race.

Shot 7. Dave continues to talk to the French woman. Mr. Stoller is riding a bike from the opposite direction, passes Dave and the woman, and calls out to Dave. Dave replies hello in French.

Shot 8. Mr. Stoller's startled reaction and a **freeze frame** of it.

Without these last three scenes, the film would end after the bicycle race as a working-class success story, with four sons of limestone cutters as victors, working-class brothers united (one of the four young men and his police officer brother), and Dave and his parents reconciled. But the last three scenes, as in so many American movies, quickly shift emphasis from social class to individual psychology.

The last scene suggests that Dave may be about to take on a new role—that of would-be cosmopolitan student studying French rather than Italian. He's still an adolescent trying out roles. The Stollers also assume new roles, probably too many in too short a time to be believable if we think about the situation. Mr. Stoller has changed the name of the car lot from Campus Cars to Cutter Cars, suggesting that he will henceforth seek the town market and that the victory by the four young men has renewed his social class pride. The father has imitated the son and taken up bicycle riding. For the first time in the film, he allows his wife to help with the work at the car lot. Finally, the Stollers are going to start a new family. Mr. Stoller is more relaxed, more accepting of his son, more willing to accept his own limitations (his wife helping at the car lot). His calling out to Dave in the last scene reminds viewers of an earlier scene in which he snubbed Dave in public—when Dave was deep into his Italian period. The last two shots are of Dave (and the French woman) and Mr. Stoller, as it should be: throughout the film, Dave acts, and Mr. Stoller reacts. In these last eight shots, viewers are swept along on a rapid river of images until the final one, without noticing that all these changes in the lives of the Stollers are depicted in a very brief time. All this and more is conveyed by only eight shots, in fifty-three seconds of carefully edited film.

Editors nearly always try to condense time. But a few films—for the most part outside the classical Hollywood cinema—occasionally and briefly expand time, allowing more time to show an action than the action itself would take. Eisenstein used this technique in several of his films. In *October* (1928), he often stretches out an action slightly by including shots that repeat part of a movement, as in the toppling of a statue of a former tsar: one shot ends with the statue well on its way to the ground; the next shot begins with the statue not as far from the ground; the shot after that does the same thing. Three somewhat overlapping shots are used to show one brief action. Later, we see parts of the raising of a drawbridge more than once. Two other famous examples of expanded time are from Eisenstein's *(Battleship) Potemkin*. In one scene, an angry sailor breaks a plate, but the scene has been edited so that we see parts of the sailor's arm movement twice, from above first his left shoulder and then his right.[3] Later in the film, parts of the famous massacre of civilians on the Odessa steps are edited so that the running time is longer than the **story time**. Because of the surprising **structure** of the classic film "An Occurrence at Owl Creek Bridge" (1962), the film's running time (twenty-eight minutes) is longer than its story time (slightly more than ten minutes). Another example of expanding time slightly by repeating part of an action is found in *Bamboozled* (2000, Figure 3.31).

(Although it is not a matter of editing, time can also be expanded when the camera films at a faster rate than the film is projected, as when an explosion is filmed at three hundred frames per second but is projected at twenty-four: an explosion that would normally last approximately a quarter of a second will last about three seconds.)

For a sample description and an analysis that illustrates the expressiveness and impact of editing, see the Close-Up on pp. 153–54.

DIGITAL EDITING

As with other aspects of filmmaking, increasingly computers are being used in editing. Editing can be done by transferring videotaped or filmed images (and sometimes sounds) to a computer and using sophisticated software. With the power, speed, and flexibility of the computer, editors can do **nonlinear editing**—that is, access and edit shots in whatever order desired. Working on a computer with adequate hard drive space, editors can quickly

story time: The amount of time represented in a film's narrative or story.

structure: The arrangement of the parts of a whole text. In a narrative film, structure can be thought of as the arrangement of scenes or sequences.

---

[3]For frame enlargements for each of the sixty-one frames making up the eight key shots in this scene, see Mayer, 23–30. For Mayer's analysis of these shots, see 13–14, 15.

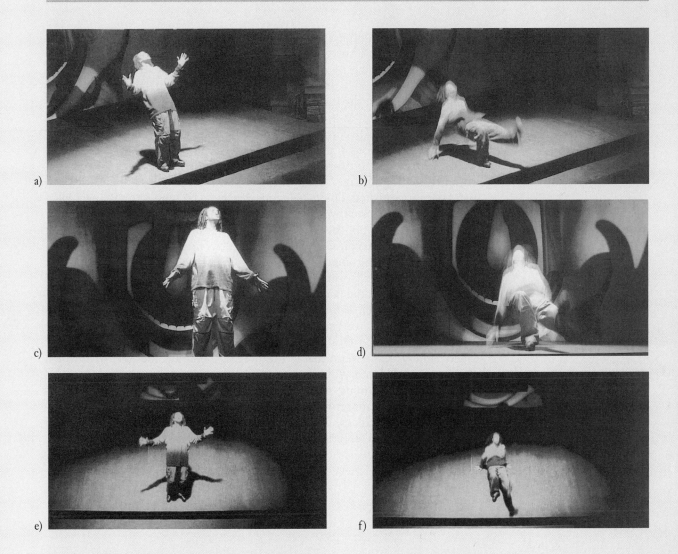

FIGURE 3.31 Expanding film time by repeating action
Approximately 112 minutes into Spike Lee's *Bamboozled* (2000), one of the two main performers in the TV minstrel show, who has become disillusioned with the show and is going to quit, comes onto the stage in his street clothes and tells the audience that he wants them to go to their windows and yell out, "I am sick and tired of being a Nigger and I am not gonna take it anymore." He then falls backward, an action seen in three consecutive, repetitive, brief shots. The beginning and ending of the first shot are seen in (a) and (b). The beginning and ending of the second shot are seen in (c) and (d). The last two images, (e) and (f), show the beginning of the third shot and the moment his hands hit the stage; this third shot continues beyond this moment and briefly shows him lying flat on his back. Using editing to expand the time prolongs slightly the already tense and suspenseful moment and gives it even greater emphasis. Frame enlargements. *Forty Acres and a Mule Filmworks; New Line Cinema*

access any of the digitized shots and select and combine them. Since the beginning of editing history, editors have been able to shorten any shot by deleting its beginning or ending or any fragment or fragments within the shot. With nonlinear editing, they can still do all that, but they can also lengthen or shorten the duration of a shot and thus change the speed of subjects within the shot, as is often done by editors working on trailers. Digital editors can also create certain effects, such as split screens and superimposed titles, and use various transitions between shots, such as lap dissolves and wipes. With some software and some films, editors can also select and synchronize sound to image. At any stage, editors can play back the results and see if they are satisfied. Digital versions may even be sent long distances electronically. If **film stock** was used during filming and the results will eventually be shown on film, the editor can transfer the shots to a computer, edit them, and use the computer to print out an *edit decision list* to use while cutting and splicing the final version of the film. If digital video was used for filming and the results were edited in a computer, the final edited results can be transferred from the computer to a videotape, DVD, or film for showings.

film stock: Unexposed and un-processed motion-picture film.

Some films, such as *Buena Vista Social Club* (1999) and *The Original Kings of Comedy* (2000), have been shot on digital video cameras, edited digitally, and transferred to 35 mm film for showings in theaters. Filming with digital video cameras has several major advantages, including the ease with which the content of digital videotape can be copied to a computer and edited there. As digital filming supersedes the older technology, digital editing is sure to grow even more widespread. Regardless of these and other technological editing advances, however, what will count for viewers are the skill with which the final creation is edited and the effect of the way the shots are chosen and arranged.

CLOSE-UP: THE EXPRESSIVENESS OF EDITING (AND OTHER TECHNIQUES): AN EXCERPT FROM *HIGH NOON*

In the 1952 western *High Noon*, Will Kane, the town marshal of Hadleyville, has learned that Frank Miller, a man Kane helped convict years ago, is on the noon train to Hadleyville. There he will be joined by three men; then the four men plan to kill Kane. For various reasons, the townspeople do not rally behind Marshal Kane. During the 11:55 a.m. to noon section, which begins almost 67½ minutes into the film, viewers see the following sixteen scenes (each scene is divided into its shots):

Scene 1: Kane's Office

1. Kane looks at the boy as the boy (who had volunteered to help Kane in the coming showdown) leaves. Kane turns and glances at the clock on the wall (it reads 11:55); then he starts to sit down.

2. Kane sits at desk, takes a pistol from the drawer, checks the hammer of its firing mechanism, tucks the gun between his belt and his abdomen, opens a box of bullets, and dumps them into his hand.

Scene 2: Train station

3. Near the train tracks, all three members of the Miller gang check to make certain their gun cylinders move freely and are full of bullets.

Scene 3: Kane's office

4. Kane takes out a sheet of paper and begins to write.

5. He writes at the top of the sheet: "Last Will and Testament."

6. He looks up from his writing.

7. As the music begins, the camera tilts up from a swinging clock pendulum to reveal it's 11:58.

8. Kane looks down from the clock and resumes writing his will.

Scene 4: Train station

9. The three members of the Miller gang are by the railroad tracks.

10. The empty railroad tracks*

Scene 5: Inside a church

11. Congregation at prayer

12. In a pew, Joe Henderson, a town leader, looks straight ahead.

13. Ezra, a man who urged the townspeople to stand by Kane during a debate that took place in the church, looks down.

Scene 6: Ramirez Saloon

14. At the bar, men smoke, wait, and look at each other.

15. A man with a dark eye patch gazes at his drink as he sits alone at a corner table.

16. The bartender, who is behind the bar, looks tense.

Scene 7: Kane's office

17. The swinging clock pendulum

18. Kane writing

Scene 8: Town street

19. View of a deserted town street

---

*According to Leonard J. Leff, shots 10 to 31 last 3.2 seconds each (159).

20. Another section of a deserted town street

Scene 9: Outside train station

21. View of empty train tracks (nearly the same shot as shot 10)
22. The three Miller men (presumably looking down the train tracks)

Scene 10: Above a town street

23. On a second-floor verandah, two old townsmen watch and wait.

Scene 11: Fuller house

24. Sam Fuller and his wife look at one another briefly, then look down (and the wife also turns away slightly).

Scene 12: Martin's place

25. Martin, the former sheriff, looks offscreen.

Scene 13: Mrs. Ramirez's residence

26. Mrs. Ramirez, Kane's former lover, waiting
27. Mrs. Kane waiting

Scene 14: Kane's office

28. The clock reads 11:59.
29. The swinging pendulum

Scene 15: Train station

30. The three Miller men looking straight ahead

Scene 16: Kane's office

31. Kane writing
32. The camera tilts up from the swinging pendulum and reveals that it is 12:00.

This excerpt uses parallel editing to show three major kinds of information:

- How Kane prepares for the coming showdown: he gets out his pistol and bullets and writes his will.
- What Miller's men do: they check their guns and wait for the arrival of the noon train.
- What the townspeople do: they do nothing to help Kane as they wait for the arrival of Frank Miller.

The editing here illustrates the enormous amount of simultaneous information edited film can convey. In little more than two minutes, we viewers see what characters are doing in nine settings. And the film shows what is occurring at different places at about the same time by rapidly cutting between Kane in his office, Miller's three men at the train station, and residents of Hadleyville in different parts of town. As the shots of the empty streets reveal, Kane's potential allies do nothing but wait indoors in safety.

Shots of brief duration are used within and between the scenes, but there is little movement within each shot. Indeed, many shots look like still photographs. It's as though the townspeople are frozen in inaction. People do little but wait, think, and feel (or try not to feel). And they do so alone. Many shots show only one individual. In shots of groups, there is little interaction, little community. Together the brief shots, regular rhythm of the editing, and inaction within the shots reinforce the sense that the people of Hadleyville are frozen in nervous, isolated paralysis as a momentous showdown moves steadily and inevitably toward them. All this—and more—the editing and other filmmaking techniques help us see and experience and understand.

SUMMARY

Editing involves decisions about which shots to include, the most effective take (version) of each shot, the duration of shots, the arrangement of shots, and the transitions between them. Regardless of the equipment used for filming and editing, editing can strongly affect viewer responses. It can be used, for example, (1) to promote continuity or disruptions; (2) to superimpose images; (3) to juxtapose shots to make a point, support a feeling or mood, intensify the viewer's reactions, or show parallel subjects or events; and (4) to affect the viewer's sense of pace, compress or expand time, and convey an enormous amount of information in a brief time.

Early Film Editing

- The first films of the 1890s consisted of one shot or a series of one-shot scenes.
- By the time of *The Birth of a Nation* (1915), editing was used to maintain continuity while telling complex stories.
- In the 1920s, the editing of some Soviet filmmakers conveyed a story and promoted ideas by the juxtaposition of shots.

Building Blocks

- The shot is the most basic unit of editing. It is a piece of continuous film or videotape depicting an uninterrupted action or an immobile subject during an uninterrupted passage of time.
- A scene is a section of a narrative film that gives the impression of continuous action taking place during continuous time and in continuous space. A scene usually consists of one or more shots.
- A sequence is a series of related consecutive scenes that are perceived as a major unit of a narrative film.
- Editors can use one or more of many possible transitions between shots, such as a cut, lap dissolve, or wipe. Depending on conventions and context, editing transitions can be used to convey or reinforce information or moods. For example, often a lap dissolve indicates that the next shot takes place at a later time or different location—or both.

Continuity Editing

- Continuity editing, which is used in most narrative films, maintains a sense of clear and continuous action and continuous setting within each scene.

- Continuity editing is achieved in filming and editing by using eyeline matches, the 180-degree system, and other strategies. The aim of continuity editing is to make sure viewers will instantly understand the relationship of subjects to other subjects, subjects to settings, and each shot to the following shot.

Image on Image and Image after Image

- A momentary superimposition of two or more images is possible in a lap dissolve, as in the ending of the 1960 *Psycho*.
- Consecutive shots can stress differences or similarities. They may also be used to surprise, amuse, confuse, or disorient viewers.
- Reaction shots often intensify viewers' responses. Usually a reaction shot follows an action shot, but it may precede one, or it may occur alone with the action not shown but only implied.
- Parallel editing can be used to achieve various ends, including to give a sense of simultaneous events, contrast two or more actions or viewpoints, or create suspense about whether one subject will achieve a goal before another subject does.

Pace and Time

- Usually fast cutting is used to impart energy and excitement; slow cutting may be used to slow the pace or help calm the mood.
- Depending on the context, a succession of shots of equal length may suggest inevitability, relentlessness, boredom, or some other condition.
- Shifting the pace of the editing can change viewers' emotional responses, as in the excerpt analyzed from near the end of (*Battleship*) *Potemkin*.
- Montage compresses an enormous amount of information, including story time, into a brief time, as in the montage of Susan's opera career in *Citizen Kane*.
- Editing usually condenses time (for example, by cutting dead time), but it can expand time—for instance, by showing fragments of an action more than once.

Digital Editing

- Increasingly, computers are being used for editing. Images are scanned into computers, edited there, and transferred back to videotape, DVD, or film for showings.

Major Terms about Editing

Below, numbers in italics refer to the pages where the terms are explained. All terms are defined in more detail in the Illustrated Glossary beginning on p. 621.

180-degree system *129*	iris-out *127*	reel *115*
continuity editing *129*	jump cut *123*	scene *120*
cut *122*	lap dissolve *124*	sequence *120*
cutaway shot *113*	master shot *113*	shot (noun) *119*
dailies *114*	match cut *122*	shot (verb) *114*
eyeline match *129*	montage *147*	shot/reverse shot *130*
fade-out, fade-in *124*	montage (Soviet) *118*	slow cutting *145*
fast cutting *145*	nonlinear editing *150*	splice *122*
final cut *113*	pace *144*	superimpose *132*
footage *114*	parallel editing *140*	take *113*
iris-in *127*	reaction shot *138*	wipe *126*

QUESTIONS ABOUT EDITING

The following questions are intended to help viewers understand the use of editing in a film and analyze their responses to it. Not all the questions are appropriate for every film. In thinking out, discussing, and writing responses to those questions most appropriate for the film being examined, be careful to stick with the issues the questions raise, to answer all parts of the questions, to explain the reasons for your answers, and to give specific examples from the film.

1. Generally, is the film's editing characterized by fast cutting or slow cutting? To what effect?

2. Is continuity editing used? If so, give examples and explain in at least one of the examples what strategies the filmmakers use to create continuity editing.

3. What transitions other than cuts does the film employ? What do those transitions contribute to the film's impact?

4. Where are shots joined for a particular effect, such as to stress similarities or differences or to create or enhance a mood? What do those special juxtapositions contribute to the film?

5. Does the film use parallel editing? If so, where and to what effect?

6. Where is editing used to delete time within a scene or section? Where is editing used to make viewers use their imaginations (for example, by use of a cutaway shot)? Is editing ever used to expand time? If so, explain how that is achieved and what the expanded time contributes to the film.

7. How would you characterize the film's overall pace? Did you notice changes in pace in particular parts of the film? If so, explain.

8. Does the film include any montages? If so, explain their components and functions within the film.

WORKS CITED

Andrew, J. Dudley. *The Major Film Theories: An Introduction*. New York: Oxford UP, 1976.

Calvo, Dana. "Eliminating the Short Cuts." *Los Angeles Times* (Home ed.). 23 July 2002: F1.

Grignon, Rex. Address. "The Making of *Toy Story*." Monterey, CA, Conf. Center. 10 Apr. 1996.

Hoggan, Michael, former president, American Cinema Editors. Telephone interview. July 1994.

Huss, Roy, and Norman Silverstein. *The Film Experience: Elements of Motion Picture Art*. New York: Dell, 1968.

Leff, Leonard. *Film Plots: Scene-by-Scene Narrative Outlines for Feature Film Study*. Vol. 1. Ann Arbor: Pierian, 1983.

Mayer, David. *Sergei M. Eisenstein's* Potemkin: *A Shot-by-Shot Presentation*. New York: Grossman, 1972.

Murch, Walter. *In the Blink of an Eye: A Perspective on Film Editing*. 2nd ed. Los Angeles: Silman-James, 2001.

Reisz, Karel, and Gavin Millar. *The Technique of Film Editing*. Enlarged ed. New York: Hastings, 1968.

Riefenstahl, Leni, filmmaker. Interview. *The Wonderful, Horrible Life of Leni Riefenstahl* (documentary film). 1993.

Salt, Barry. *Film Style and Technology: History and Analysis*. 2nd ed. London: Starword, 1992.

FOR FURTHER READING

Balmuth, Bernard. *Introduction to Film Editing*. Boston: Focal, 1989. An introduction for someone who wants to edit film.

Fairservice, Don. *Film Editing: History, Theory and Practice: Looking at the Invisible*. Manchester: Manchester UP, 2001. A comprehensive examination of the film editor's craft from the beginning of cinema to the present day.

Oldham, Gabriella. *First Cut: Conversations with Film Editors*. Berkeley: U of California P, 1992. Interviews with twenty-three award-winning editors, including editors of documentary films.

Rosenblum, Ralph, and Robert Karen. *When the Shooting Stops . . . the Cutting Begins: A Film Editor's Story*. New York: Viking, 1979. An account of editing and an acclaimed editor's experiences in editing.

Selected Takes: Film Editors on Editing. Ed. Vincent LoBrutto. Westport, CT: Praeger, 1991. Interviews with twenty-one film editors plus a glossary and bibliography.

Uring the 1986 Academy Awards ceremony, a clip from *Chariots of Fire* (1981) was shown of young men running on a beach accompanied by the sounds of feet splashing in water. Although the soundtrack may have been true to life, it was uneventful. Then the same **footage** was shown with the film's famous title music. The effect was so different that viewers felt as if they were seeing different footage. The runners gained the grace of dancers, and the action became special, more than life. It illustrated the importance of sound to the creation of vibrant cinema.

In movies, sounds usually seem lifelike. However, as with visuals, what seems true to life is an illusion. If you study sound in movies, you will notice that sounds we would normally hear are often omitted or replaced by music. Listen carefully and repeatedly to the sound that accompanies one character punching another, and you will notice that it is not entirely credible. In movies, we do not question such sounds (yet another movie **convention**). What are a few of the many ways that film sounds are created, how are film sounds used, and, most important, how do they affect viewers? This chapter gives some answers to those questions by examining some specific uses of a soundtrack's four major components, possible sound transitions, and general uses of sound in **narrative** films.

FILM SOUND: EARLY AND RECENT

Sound has always been a part of film viewing. Even during showings of the first short films in the 1890s, music was usually played to cover the sounds of the audiences and projectors and to reinforce mood and support **continuity**. Later in film history, the theater management also supplied sound effects. As is demonstrated repeatedly in *Monty Python and the Holy Grail* (1975), people could beat half coconut shells against a hard surface or against each other to make sounds like horses' hooves. Large pieces of sandpaper might be rubbed together to sound like a running river; a flexible strip could be stuck into

Terms in **boldface** are defined in the Illustrated Glossary beginning on page 621.

footage: A length of exposed motion-picture film.

convention: In films and other texts, a subject or technique that makers of texts and audiences have grown to accept as natural or typical.

narrative: A representation of a series of unified events situated in one or more settings. A narrative may be fictional or factual or a blend of the two.

continuity (editing): Film editing that maintains a sense of uninterrupted time and action and continuous setting within each scene of a narrative film.

159

FIGURE 4.1 **Allefex sound effects machine**
This sound effects machine was first marketed in Britain in
1909. Film historian David Robinson writes that the Allefex
"was capable of producing upwards of fifty sound effects from
storm noises, bird-song, and barking dogs to gun-fire, escaping
steam and the rattle of pots and pans" (159). Historian Brian
Coe includes a quotation that explains how some of the sounds
were made: "The shot of a gun is imitated by striking a drum
on the top of the machine, on which a chain mat has been
placed. . . . Running water, rain, hail and the sound of rolling
waves are obtained by turning a handle, which rotates a ribbed
wooden cylinder against a board set at an angle from the top of
which hang a number of chains. . . . The puffing of an engine is
made by revolving a cylinder with projections against a steel
brush. . . . Pendant tubes serve to produce the effects of church
bells, fire alarm, ship's bell, and similar noises; the sound of
trotting horses is caused by revolving a shaft carrying three tap-
pets which lift up inverted cups . . . ; the cry of the baby is emitted by the dexterous manipulation of plug-hole and bellows"
(91–92). *British Film Institute Stills, Posters and Designs*

spinning bicycle spokes to simulate the sound of an early airplane engine.
Some theaters even had a sound effects machine with a whistle, bell, horn,
chains, drum, and sheet metal. "Silent" films were rarely silent (Figure 4.1).

By the late 1920s, some sound films were shown using the **Vitaphone**
system, a large phonograph disc synchronized with the projector (Figure
4.2). Warner Bros. created a sensation with the Vitaphone system in *The
Jazz Singer* (1927), which was basically a silent film with synchronized musical numbers and a little ad-libbed dialogue. In 1928, Warner Bros. used the
system in *The Lights of New York*, the first all-dialogue motion picture. There
were drawbacks to the Vitaphone system: the records could be played only
twenty or so times before they became worn, and it was hard to keep the
record always synchronized with the images being projected.

In the same year as *The Lights of New York*, two rival and not entirely
compatible sound-on-film systems were used on **feature films**, and the days
of Vitaphone were numbered. With a sound-on-film system, the projector
displays the image on the screen as it simultaneously converts the optical information in the soundtrack into electrical information. That electrical in-

feature film: A fictional film
that is at least sixty minutes
long.

FIGURE 4.2 Vitaphone projection system
In the late 1920s, the Vitaphone system was used in the United States during filming and projecting.

During filming or often after filming, early film sound specialists recorded all the spoken words, sound effects, and music on a large phonographic disc, but they could not later remix. As Walter Murch has explained, "There was no possibility of cutting out the bad bits, because there *was* no way to cut what was being chiselled into the whirling acetate of the Vitaphone discs. It had to be right the first time, or you called 'Cut!' and began again" ("Sound Design" 240).

During projection of a Vitaphone movie, as seen here, the 35 mm projector was synchronized to the attached record player and disc. *The Museum of Modern Art/Film Stills Archive*

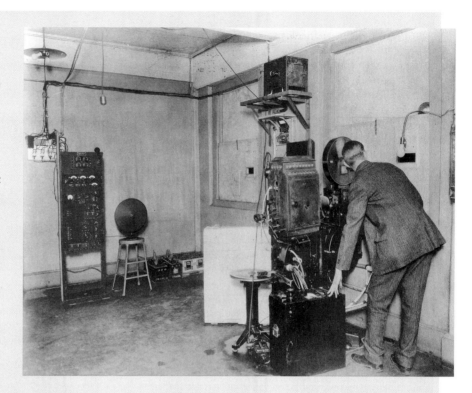

formation is amplified and sent to the theater speakers. (Figure 2.2 on pp. 63–64 illustrates where optical and the later magnetic soundtracks may be located on film.) Since 1928, if theaters have adequate sound equipment, audiences have been able to hear the spoken words, sound effects, music, and silence more or less the way the filmmakers intended. In the late 1920s and early 1930s, such directors as René Clair, Ernst Lubitsch, Rouben Mamoulian, Alfred Hitchcock, and Walt Disney experimented with film sound and discovered new uses for it, and in the 1940s and 1950s, Orson Welles, who did some innovative work in radio before turning to filmmaking, did highly original and influential work in film sound, beginning with his first film, *Citizen Kane* (1941).

In recent years, Robert Altman, George Lucas, Walter Murch, and other filmmakers have experimented with film sound and made major advances in its use. Today, sophisticated, dedicated film sound specialists can record and mix sound on audio tape on traditional analog equipment and can also create, store, manipulate, and mix sounds on computers. Many theaters have installed **THX sound**. Others have multispeaker sound systems that are vastly

THX sound: A multispeaker sound system developed by Lucasfilm and used in selected movie theaters to increase frequency range, audience coverage, and dialogue intelligibility while decreasing low bass distortion.

FIGURE 4.3 Digital and analog sound on 35 mm films
(larger than actual size)
There are three competing digital movie sound systems and one analog system.

(a) The Digital Theater Sound (**DTS**) system consists of a timing code that runs the length of the film print, a special optical reader, and a computer that controls one or more compact disc players and discs. The discs, which are the size of a standard CD but are incompatible with CD and DVD players, contain the film's digital soundtrack. Like the 1920s Vitaphone system (see Figure 4.2), DTS uses a separate disc for the soundtrack synchronized with the projector.

(b) The Sony Dynamic Digital Sound (**SDDS**) system includes an identical digital soundtrack on the two edges of the film. (If one strip of digital coding is damaged, the other acts as a backup.) On the projector, the digital sound is decoded with a reader. Unlike the other two digital sound systems, which create six channels of sound, SDDS creates eight.

(c) The Dolby Digital Sound (**DDS**) system consists of digital coding in the spaces between the sprocket holes on one side of the film print, a Dolby Digital reader in or on the projector, and a Dolby Digital Processor. DDS produces six channels of sound: five plus one for low rumbling sounds (often referred to as 5.1).

(d) Also still widely included on film prints is Dolby Stereo, an analog system consisting of two optical audio tracks that create four distinct channels of sound in theaters. Most current movie prints include more than one sound format—for example, one or two of the digital formats plus Dolby Stereo (with Dolby Stereo sometimes functioning as a backup). Because each of the available sound formats—three digital and one analog—uses a different area of the film print, movie prints such as the one seen here from *Saving Private Ryan* (1998) may include all three digital formats and Dolby Stereo. Frame enlargement. *Amblin Entertainment; DreamWorks SKG; Mark Gordon Productions; Mutual Film; Paramount*

(b) Sony Dynamic Digital Sound (SDDS)

(a) Digital Theater Sound (DTS)

(d) Dolby Stereo (dual analog tracks)

(c) Dolby Digital Sound (DDS)

superior to the sound systems that were available in the early years of sound cinema. And digital film sound systems—such as Digital Theater Sound (DTS) and Sony Dynamic Digital Sound (SDDS)—bring a new level of clarity, range, and fidelity that are now the standard in movie projection (Figure 4.3). Because of technology and human creativity, today film sound is more faithful, creative, dynamic, varied, and expressive than ever before.

COMPONENTS OF THE SOUNDTRACK AND THEIR USES

Filmmakers can include spoken words, sound effects, music, and silence in the soundtrack (Table 4.1). Each may be used in the usual manner, but each may also be used in surprising ways. "Dialogue is usually dominant and intellectual, music is usually supportive and emotional, sound effects are usu-

TABLE 4.1
Possible Soundtrack Components

SPOKEN WORDS	SOUND EFFECTS	MUSIC	SILENCE
Dialogues and monologues, including vocals that convey meaning. Example: "Hmmm" = "I don't know," "Let me think about that," or some other meaning depending on context.	**Sounds made by objects.** Example: a falling tree crashing onto an asphalt pavement	**Instrumental sounds** • Electronic. Examples: Moog synthesizer, Theremin, computer-generated music • Nonelectronic materials. Examples: wood, plastic, glass, a combination of materials • Electronic and nonelectronic combinations. Example: selective use of the Theremin and elsewhere orchestral music in *The Day the Earth Stood Still* (1951)	**No sound.** Example: an astronaut tumbling lifelessly through space in *2001: A Space Odyssey* (1968)
Narration = spoken comments about subjects on screen or off	**Sounds made by people (other than spoken words).** Example: a person walking on gravel	**Vocals.** Examples: singing, chanting, humming, rhythmic grunting, rhythmic forced laughing, whistling, yodeling, the throat singing heard in the documentary *Ghengis Blues* (1999)	
	Ambient sound = typical, usually unnoticed sounds of a place. Examples: the wind blowing through backyard bushes, indistinct conversations at a party	**Instrumental sounds and vocal combinations**	

symbol: Anything perceptible that has meaning beyond its usual meaning or function.

ally information. Their uses, however, are not inflexible. Sometimes dialogue is nonintellectual and aesthetic, sometimes music is **symbolic**, and on occasion sound effects may serve any of those functions. Any of these elements may be dominant or recessive according to the sharpness or softness of the sound and the relationship of the sound to the image" (Murch, "Sound Designer" 298). In this section, we consider some of the choices filmmakers make and the consequences of those choices.

Spoken Words

Most sound films since 1930 include dialogue, monologues, or narration. Movies such as *When Harry Met Sally* (1989) and *The Designated Mourner* (1997) have a dense mix of words, and dialogues and monologues cascade and swirl throughout them. These and other films may use overlapping dialogue. Viewers cannot make out all the words, but they hear most of them and sense the busy, chaotic atmosphere that overlapping dialogue can help create. In films using overlapping dialogue, characters speak without being entirely heard by those they speak at, and flash floods of words may be indicative of the characters' nervousness, isolation, or unconscious attempts to mask their painful situations. Many films directed by Howard Hawks—such as *Bringing Up Baby* (1938) and *His Girl Friday* (1940)—and several films directed by Orson Welles—perhaps most notably *Citizen Kane, The Magnificent Ambersons* (1942), and *Touch of Evil* (1958)—use extensive overlapping dialogue. Films directed by Robert Altman—such as *McCabe and Mrs. Miller* (1971), *California Split* (1974), *Nashville* (1975), *The Player* (1992), *Dr. T and the Women* (2000), and *Gosford Park* (2001)—also use extensive overlapping dialogue.

scene: A section of a narrative that gives the impression of continuous action taking place in continuous time and space.

Overlapping dialogue may also be used in a brief section of a film, as in *Saving Private Ryan* (1998). At the beginning of one **scene**, many typists are busy typing letters. Soon we begin to hear fragments of letters read by different male voices (presumably the commanding officers). The first voice begins, "Dear Mr. Brian Boyd: No doubt by now you have received full information about the untimely death of your son; however, there are some personal details . . . ," and is overwhelmed and replaced by another male voice reading another fragment of a letter. The voices are always cut off in midsentence. The images of many typists busily typing and the continuous typing sounds and overlapping and interrupted dialogue suggest how many letters had to be sent, how many men were lost in the battles of World War II, and how enormous the number of families devastated by the loss of their sons, brothers, and husbands. Overlapping dialogue is not restricted to fictional films. It is also used in the **documentary film** *Madonna: Truth or Dare* (1991). In the documentary "Personal Belongings" (1996), viewers hear many fragments of news reports about anti-Semitism and ethnic fighting in Central and Eastern Europe. During approximately thirty-two seconds,

documentary film: A film or video representation of actual (not imaginary) subjects.

seven or eight **sound dissolves** and extensive overlapping dialogue convey the rapidly escalating strife. At the beginning of *Contact* (1997), as we viewers see the receding earth, planets, and galaxies, we hear overlapping snippets of music and speech from U.S. TV and radio, generally representing earlier and earlier eras and suggesting that the earth has been proclaiming its life to the universe ever since the first radio transmission near the beginning of the twentieth century (see the feature on p. 166).

(see the feature on p. 166)

Often in a theater or in our home viewing environment, we hear film dialogue more distinctly than we could in a similar situation in real life (another movie convention). Usually dialogue in movies is louder and more distinct than it would be in actuality. At the beginning of a shot 6½ minutes into Woody Allen's *Manhattan* (1979), two male characters are seen perhaps fifty feet in the background ambling toward the camera as they talk. For more than thirty seconds, as they approach the camera, the volume of their dialogue remains essentially the same. In a comparable situation outside the movies, someone watching them at that distance could not initially hear them so clearly (and without at least occasional extraneous distracting noises), nor would the volume of their talk remain largely unchanged as they approach so closely.

Spoken words may also be deliberately distorted in movies to portray a character's confusion. In several scenes in *Nick of Time* (1995), what is being said to the main character is distorted. The effect is analogous to a visual **point-of-view shot**: viewers hear the same speech and other sounds as the distracted character presumably does.

Dialogue is invaluable for revealing a character's ideas, goals, and dreams, though often it does so more concisely, obliquely, and revealingly than conversation in life. Consider the following dialogue from *Betrayal* (1983). Robert and his wife, Emma, are on holiday. Robert has discovered a letter at the American Express office addressed to Emma and recognized the handwriting as that of his friend, Jerry. The next day Robert tells Emma there was a letter for her at American Express. After a while, she says that she got it and it was from Jerry. Shortly after that, their dialogue in the film runs as follows:

> ROBERT: What do you think of Jerry as a letter writer? [pause] You're trembling. Are you cold?
> EMMA: No.
> ROBERT: He used to write to me at one time. Long letters about Ford Madox Ford. I used to write to him, too, come to think of it. Long letters about, ooh, W. B. Yeats, I suppose. That was the time when we were both editors of poetry magazines. Him at Cambridge, me at Oxford. Did you know that? We were bright young men and close friends. Well, we still are close friends. All that was long before I met you. Long before he met you. I've been trying to remember when I introduced him to you. I simply can't remember. I take it I did introduce him to you. Yes. But when? Can you remember?
> EMMA: No.

sound dissolve: A transition in which a sound begins to fade out as the next sound fades in and overlaps the first sound before replacing it.

point-of-view shot: Camera placement at the approximate position of a character or person (or occasionally an animal) that gives a view similar to what that subject would see.

Opening Soundtrack for *Contact* (1997)

As images of the receding earth, solar system, and galaxies are seen, the following sounds can be heard:

Loud, indistinct, overlapping music
SONG: "Be There" by All for One
SONG: "Doot, doot, doot . . ."
Song by Hootie and the Blowfish
1997 SONG: "I Wanna be there when you're (gonna be there)" from "Wanna Be" by the Spice Girls
SONG: "God shuffled his feet" by Crash Test Dummies
SONG: "You wanna get with me, you gotta . . ."
Song: "Clearly, I've never been there, but it feels like . . ."
SONG: "Broken Wings" by Mr. Mister
1986, announcer at launch of *Challenger* space shuttle: "situation obviously a major malfunction"
Music for *Dallas* TV show

. . .

1979 (music), "Funkytown" by Lipps, Inc.

. . .

MUSIC: "Boogie Oogy"
MUSIC: "Sometimes you feel like a nut" commercial theme for Almond Joy
Song by The Trammps
Sounds of asteroids in space [these are the only sounds not originating from earth]
1973, President Nixon: ". . . your president's a crook. Well, I'm not a crook."
SONG: "Got to Give It Up" by Marvin Gaye
1969, Neil Armstrong on the moon: ". . . for man. One giant leap for man . . ."
SONG: commercial theme for Coca-Cola
1968, announcer: "Robert Kennedy was shot in that ballroom."
SONG: ". . . golden hair"
SONG: whistled theme for *The Andy Griffith Show* TV show
1963, Martin Luther King Jr.: ". . . God almighty, we are free at last."

Music theme from *The Twilight Zone* TV show
1963, announcer: "A sniper has fired at President Kennedy."
SONG: "Teeny Yellow Polka Dot Bikini"
SONG: "Mr. Postman"
1961, President Kennedy's inauguration: "Ask not what you . . ."
1958: Dean Martin singing "Volare"
1954 (?) Army-McCarthy hearings: "Communist Party or have you ever been a member of the Communist Party?"
1951, General Douglas MacArthur (addressing U.S. Congress): "Old soldiers never die . . ."
SONG: ". . . my lucky . . ."
Lone Ranger shouting "Hi ho Silver." Gunshots.
Dance music played by a big band
1942 (?) Edward R. Murrow broadcasting from England (?): "something before never experienced"
Dec. 7, 1941, President Franklin D. Roosevelt: "1941, a date that will live in infamy"
1940 (?): Hitler speech and crowd response
1939 song: "Somewhere over the Rainbow"
1939, announcer: "and we continue this evening's final edition of our *Maxwell House Good News of 1939*."
Walter Winchell radio broadcast: "Good evening, Mr. and Mrs. America and all our ships at sea. Let's go to press."
SONG: "We're in the Money"
ANNOUNCER: "lurks in the hearts of men" from *The Shadow* radio program
Man singing "happy times are here again"
1933: President Roosevelt's inauguration: "The only thing we have to fear is fear itself."
Early instrumental jazz music heard on radio
1920 (?), announcer of an early radio broadcast: "Let us know if this broadcast is reaching you. Please drop us a card."
1900 (?): Morse code (ends at two minutes seven seconds from beginning of film)
Silence

ROBERT: You can't?

EMMA: No.

ROBERT: How odd. [pause] He wasn't best man at our wedding, was he?

EMMA: You know he was.

ROBERT: Aah, yes. Well, that's probably when I introduced him to you. [pause] Was there any message for me in his letter? [pause] I mean in the line of business. To do with the world of publishing. Has he discovered any new and original talent? He's quite talented at uncovering talent, ole Jerry.

EMMA: [pause] No message.

ROBERT: No message? [pause] Not even his love?

EMMA: [pause] We're lovers.

ROBERT: Ah, yes. I thought it might be something like that, something along those lines. . . .

This passage reveals writer Harold Pinter's skill in creating characters that say one thing when they feel and think something else. In this passage, Robert also does not say directly what is important to him. Evidently he suspects his wife has been unfaithful, but he does not come right out and say so. Part of the time, he feigns forgetfulness: "He wasn't best man at our wedding, was he?" Part of the time, Robert muses about the past and brings up the points that Jerry is an old and dear friend, that he has known Jerry in fact longer than he has known Emma, that he introduced Jerry and Emma, and that Jerry was best man in their wedding.

By not coming right out and saying what he fears, Robert is able to hold Emma in painful suspense about whether he suspects her affair. Like many other Pinter characters, Robert knows when to pause for effect. Often he asks a difficult question and pauses; Emma doesn't reply, so Robert continues. Emma is soon put on the defensive. She gives short answers (less chance of a slip-up there). Reread all of Emma's responses. None is longer than four words! Toward the end of this exchange, she pauses before she replies, admitting, "We're lovers." Perhaps she thinks that Robert will at least stop his cat and mouse game.

After Robert hears Emma's admission, he again does not say what is bothering him, how painful for him Emma's words are: "Ah, yes. I thought it might be something like that, something along those lines." Elsewhere in the film, we see how painful his wife's affair is for Robert, but he never comes out and says so directly. Like most believable characters (and most people, for that matter), Robert often says one thing when he means another. And he never comes right out and says what is most important to him. We viewers must watch, listen, and figure that out for ourselves—and by doing so, we stay involved with the characters.

Sometimes word choices and accents provide clues about a character's background: country or region of origin, ethnic group, social class, occupation. Tone, volume, speed, and rhythm of speech also reveal what a character is like. So infinitely expressive is the human voice that the words "You had

irony: A statement, an event, or a situation involving an incongruity or a discrepancy between appearance and reality.

better go" can be threatening, pleading, sad, indifferent, questioning, **ironic**, amusing, matter-of-fact, or something else. Perhaps second only to an expressive face, a flexible voice can convey countless shades of emotion.

Many movies, however, use limited or no spoken words because given the settings or goals of the film, few or none are needed. In *Quest for Fire* (1981), which is set eighty thousand years ago, the hominids use an assortment of grunts, pants, screams, and so forth, but the film has no intelligible dialogue, only imaginary prehistoric languages that are not translated and are only vaguely understandable. The first and fourth parts of *2001: A Space Odyssey* (1968) are without intelligible dialogue, and only 43 of the film's 141 minutes contain dialogue. Other feature films employing little dialogue are *Blood Wedding* (1981)—which consists of backstage preparations, a brief warm-up session, and a flamenco version of most of Federico Garcia Lorca's famous play of the same title—and *Sidewalk Stories* (1989), which has no dialogue during its ninety-seven minutes except for a few lines near the end that are not integral to the story. Some short films use little dialogue; other short films that could use dialogue use none. The films' images, music, and perhaps sound effects convey story, meanings, and moods. "The String Bean" (1962) uses no spoken words, and they are used only occasionally and briefly in the classic French film "The Red Balloon" (1955).

Often films begin with music and no words: the opening scenes reveal the **setting**, major character(s), and mood without the help of the human voice. Many movie scenes with sound forgo the use of the human voice, and many movies use dialogue less than half the time. As scriptwriting books and scriptwriting teachers typically advocate, many filmmakers use dialogue only to reveal important information that cannot be conveyed visually.

setting: The place where filmed action occurs.

Sound Effects

sound effect: A sound in film other than spoken words or music.

Sound effects specialists tend to use sound effects highly selectively. In life we hear but usually ignore insignificant and potentially distracting sounds, such as an airplane overhead or a beeping digital watch. In cinema, such sounds are usually omitted from a soundtrack, and the sound effects that are included tend to be inconspicuous because they are usually played at low volume and often along with music or dialogue or both.

location: Any place other than a film studio that is used for filming.

Sound effects are often used to help create a sense of a **location**, and they can make a place seem more lifelike than it is (Figure 4.4). Sound effects can also make viewers feel more involved. In *Das Boot*, or *The Boat* (1981; expanded and reissued with eight-channel digital sound in 1997), when the German submarine is trying to evade detection deep below the surface, viewers hear sheet metal groaning and bolts popping from pressure they were not designed to withstand.

Effects are often used to intensify a mood. Sometimes a sound effect, such as a beating heart, intensifies the mood of the moment even though we

FIGURE 4.4 **Sound used to fill out a set** In *Citizen Kane* (1941), sound sometimes adds to the verisimilitude of a set. The budget for *Citizen Kane* was limited, and the set shown here was flimsy and incomplete (that's also a reason little or no lighting was often used in parts of the image). The set alone could not have nurtured the right sounds for the scene, but the reverberations in the soundtrack help mightily to convey the size, emptiness, and sterility of Kane's and Susan's lives in their huge Florida retreat. Frame enlargement. *Orson Welles; RKO General Pictures*

wouldn't hear such a sound outside the movies—yet another movie convention. Throughout most of *The Blair Witch Project* (1999), strange, unidentifiable sounds emanating from the dark woods contribute to the tension in the characters lost in the woods and in the viewers ensconced in the theater. In the theater or out, a sound from an unknown source—in the basement, in the attic, outside the window, under the bed—may frighten us. We are rattled by the unknown, so films often use sound from beyond the lighted **frame**, in the darkness. Even if we know the source of the sound, such as a tree limb brushing against a window, hearing a sound and not seeing its source leaves much to the imagination. We have paid to be emotionally involved, and filmmakers try to oblige us.

Another example of sound effects used to support a mood comes from *The Godfather* (1972). After Michael prevents an attack on his hospitalized father, a corrupt police captain and his men arrive at the hospital entrance. During the men's arrival and their confrontation with Michael, we viewers hear thunder three times: first as Michael pushes another man away and as police officers grab Michael, second as the police captain gets out of his car and approaches Michael, and third as we see the police captain's reaction after slugging Michael. We hear this thunder, though we may not much notice it, as we see the police in action. The thunder underscores the power of the police, especially the captain. In many other films, thunder often accompanies danger and violence and can be almost a cliché.

Sound effects are often used to enhance humorous or light moments. Early in Jacques Tati's *Mr. Hulot's Holiday* (1953), the sputtering and backfiring as Hulot drives his shaky, thirty-year-old car, which is not much bigger than a bathtub, are amusing in themselves, and the scenes in which they appear are funnier because of them. Sound effects from an unexpected source can create a humorous effect. In *Bowfinger* (1999), as the Eddie Murphy character is walking in a darkened parking garage, he hears the sounds of a woman's high heel shoes. Because he cannot see the source for the sound, he is puzzled and concerned. Soon viewers see the source: high heels on a dog's front paws.

Sound effects can be used just as effectively to intensify a sad or melancholy occasion. In the last shot of a documentary film about a much admired Italian actor, *Marcello Mastroianni . . . I Remember* (1999), Mastroianni, who died before the film was released, is off to one side of the frame, concluding his comments about the brevity of life while looking off-frame; then the sound of wind is heard before the final fade-out and continues into the end credits. The suggestion is of desolation, loneliness, and perhaps cold and death.

Sound effects can, in fact, be used to create or enhance any situation, including suspense and surprise. A famous example occurs about forty-four minutes into the 1942 *Cat People*. Alice is walking home at night in a deserted part of town and fears that she is being stalked by a woman whom the film has hinted transforms into an aggressive panther when she experiences strong emotions. Initially, we see and hear both Alice and the woman who might be following her; then we see and hear only Alice, who grows apprehensive, stops, and looks back. For a split second, the beginning of a large cat's low growl is heard and is immediately followed by the loud, startling sound of air brakes as a city bus abruptly pulls to a stop between Alice and the camera. But perhaps some viewers hear the beginning of a large cat's low growl because previous scenes have hinted that panthers have some special powers.

Another use of sound effects is to conceal an action. About sixty-eight minutes into *Chinatown* (1974), Jake, the detective, goes to the hall of records to investigate recent land sales. After he finds the page he wants, he lines up a ruler against the page and coughs loudly as he rips out part of the page. When Jake coughs, the clerk looks up but does not hear the ripping sound and resumes his work. A character also uses sound to conceal his action nearly two hours into *The Shawshank Redemption* (1994). As the main character attempts to break out of prison during a storm, he uses a large stone or piece of concrete to hit a sewer pipe, hoping to rupture it. To mask the noise he makes and thus his action, he hits the pipe only during the thunder.

Filmmakers may use one sound to mask another. In *On the Waterfront* (1954), the Marlon Brando character (Terry) unwittingly contributed to the murder of the brother of the woman Terry later becomes attracted to. Some sixty-three minutes into the film, in front of an industrialized riverfront, Terry finally tries to explain to her that he did not realize what the murderers had intended to do, but most of his anguished explanation is drowned out by a loud steam whistle. Viewers already know about his situation anyway and need not hear what he says here; instead, they can more readily concentrate on the two characters' extremely expressive faces.

Like light and shadow, sound effects often add to a film in significant yet inconspicuous ways. In many of the examples discussed above—such as the timely confluence of thunder and police in *The Godfather* and the amusing sound of the sputtering old car in *Mr. Hulot's Holiday*—the effects are not true to life. Only occasionally, however, are the effects so untrue to life as to draw attention to themselves, especially during a first or even second listening.

Sound effects specialists often use sound sources that viewers are unaware of. Frank Serafine has said that in the 1983 TV movie *The Day After*, he indicated the sound of a nuclear explosion by blending animal screams that had been processed so that viewers could not recognize the sources. Ironically, sounds that are faithful to their sources sometimes do not seem "real," so moviemakers substitute or add sounds, sometimes provided by a **Foley artist**, a person who creates and records sound effects as he or she watches the action in a film projected on a screen (Figure 4.5). The Foley artist may decide that the sounds of footsteps on snow that were recorded during filming don't sound right and may substitute the sound of walking on cornstarch. To simulate the sounds of walking in grass, a Foley artist may take tape from a cassette, crumple it, then walk on it in synchronization with the film's action. For the sounds of insects in *A Bug's Life* (1998), the sound engineer mixed such sounds as the cracking open of uncooked crabs and various World War II bombers in flight (Rydstrom).

A sound specialist may speed up or slow down the original recorded sound in digital format. At least as early as 1938, sounds were played backward to create new sounds. In that year Loren L. Ryder —the eventual winner of six Academy Awards in sound—recorded a pig's squeal and played it backward as the sound of an ice avalanche. Similarly, a suction sound may be made by running the sound of an explosion backward.

Sound effects may be recorded during filming, added later from a library of sound clips, or recorded on location for later use (Figure 4.6). Often sound effects are composite effects, made by combining simpler sounds (many of which might already have been modified themselves). For the sounds of the giant creature's "voice" in *Godzilla* (1998), six sound specialists worked on blending sounds from a rare two-CD set of

FIGURE 4.5 A Foley artist at work
Here a Foley artist clomps around in high heels on a hard surface in synchronization with the image being projected from the glassed-in room behind him as someone else records the sound for later inclusion in the film's soundtrack. Foley artists spend a lot of time in many different types of footwear walking on various surfaces. To facilitate the process, some Foley recording stages include various small troughs—each containing a different surface, such as concrete, grass, dirt, carpet, sand, or steel plate. *Brian Vancho, Foley artist; Sound One Corp., New York*

FIGURE 4.6 Recording sounds in nature
In the fictional film *Blow Out* (1981), the John Travolta character is a sound effects specialist who records and mixes sounds for movie soundtracks. Here he is shown with a microphone recording sounds of the night for storage on magnetic tape. *George Litto; Filmways Pictures*

Godzilla sound effects plus metal grinding and metal stressing sounds and modified animal cries (of bears, walruses, sea elephants, and a hawk) ("Making Godzilla Roar").

Sometimes synthetic sounds are created and blended. Other times, especially in action movies, animal sounds—such as a monkey screaming, a pig squealing, a lion roaring, or an elephant trumpeting—are distorted or used as is and blended with other sounds because many sound experts believe that animal sounds or variations of them can affect listeners more powerfully than human-made sounds. *Top Gun* (1986) includes many sounds of jet airplanes, but the recording of their sounds could not capture the excitement of the original noise, so animal sounds and human screams were blended in (Hall). In this and other uses of sound, the effect can be subliminal: viewers are unaware of why they respond as they do.

Music

Just how crucial music can be to a movie's dramatic texture was illustrated by an exercise [the lyricist] Mrs. [Marilyn] Bergman devised in which [the film composers] Mr. [Henry] Mancini, Mr. [Mark] Isham and Mr. [Dick] Hyman each provided music for the same 19-second film clip. The seemingly innocuous little scene shows a woman walking into a darkened house at the end of the day, turning on a light, mounting the stairs, entering a bathroom and starting to brush her teeth.

Mrs. Bergman gave each of the composers a different scenario to musicalize. Mr. Hyman was told that the woman comes home to a house that is blissfully empty and quiet now that her husband and his two children from a previous marriage have finally left. Mr. Mancini was told that she is coming home to the house that she shared with a husband who had walked out on her.

Mr. Isham's instructions explained that the woman is unaware of something the audience knows—that there is probably an intruder waiting for her.

While the scene was replayed, Mr. Hyman and Mr. Mancini each conducted a small orchestra on the stage. Mr. Isham played an electronic fragment written at home. In all cases, the clip came alive. Mr. Hyman's jaunty tongue-in-cheek music expressed quiet comic relief, Mr. Mancini's was wistfully romantic, Mr. Isham's tinglingly suspenseful.

—Stephen Holden

As is suggested above, music can serve countless functions and strongly affect a scene's moods and meanings. Music may, for example, mirror a film's central conflict while intensifying it, as in *The Omen* (1976). The movie shows what happens as Robert and Kathy come to realize that their son, Damien, is the son of the devil. Jerry Goldsmith created two types of music for the movie: "demonic music" and "Kathy and Robert's music." The demonic music is sometimes dissonant and electronic but more often is conveyed by many low male voices accompanied by relentless and pronounced rhythms. In contrast, Kathy and Robert's music is much more melodic and more varied to fit different moods. It is usually played on a piano or stringed instruments. Unlike the demonic music, Kathy and Robert's music is never loud and threatening, never persistently rhythmical, and never electronic. As Kathy and Robert's prospects grow more gloomy, though, their motif is played briefly and in minor keys: it's still beautiful but sadder and less prominent.

Throughout the film, the two kinds of music war with each other, mirroring the film's evil versus good conflict. Sometimes they battle within the same scene. By the end of the film, the demonic music triumphs over Kathy and Robert's music—within the scene and in the film as a whole—just as Damien and evil triumph over Kathy and Robert and those who have tried to help them.[1]

One use of music is to tag an important object that viewers will meet again much later in the film. In the animated movie *Antz* (1998), the first mention of the monolith (a Central Park water fountain) is accompanied by a specific musical motif. Later in the film, when viewers see the water fountain for the first time, the same music is heard.

Film music can help establish the place or time period of the story. In *Tom Jones* (1963), the lively harpsichord music helps establish the time of the narrative because the harpsichord was popular in the eighteenth century. In

---

[1]The Special Edition of the DVD for *The Omen* includes a bonus feature in which composer Jerry Goldsmith discusses four parts of the film score and corresponding excerpts from the finished film are shown. Another example of the use of two competing types of music to reinforce the film's central conflict is Quincy Jones's score for *The Pawnbroker* (1965), the making of which is described by the film's director, Sidney Lumet, in his *Making Movies* (175–77).

many movies, such as *American Graffiti* (1973), *Stand by Me* (1986), and *The Ice Storm* (1997), popular music establishes when the story takes place.

Often music suggests what a character feels. In *My Life as a Dog* (1985), as a girl plays a recorder with other students in front of a class, she sees another girl pass a note to the boy they both like and unintentionally starts playing badly. In the first scene of *The Purple Rose of Cairo* (1984), a young woman looks at a poster for a romantic adventure movie as viewers hear Fred Astaire singing. The woman's expression and the music show that she is lost in romantic thoughts, until her daydreaming and the music are abruptly cut off by the sound of a letter from the marquee crashing onto the sidewalk behind her. As in many films, music and an expressive face convey emotional nuances that words cannot.

As in *The Omen*, a musical motif may be played in different ways at different times to help convey something about a character. In *Citizen Kane*, Bernard Herrmann's music suggests how Kane feels at the six times his own song is heard. The first time it is played, Kane is near the height of his power and happiness. He has recently bought the staff of a rival newspaper, and a party has been arranged to celebrate the occasion. During the party, a band plays Kane's song loudly, briskly, and in a major key. After his affair with a young woman becomes known and he loses the election for governor, his song is played softly, slowly, and in a minor key. It is so subdued that many viewers do not notice it, though it adds to the melancholy of the scene. (The visuals of these two scenes also reinforce this contrast. At the party, the screen is alive with movement. The scene after the election defeat contains only two people: Leland and a man who is sweeping the sidewalk outside Kane's election headquarters, and their movements are lethargic, as if Leland and the worker were sapped of energy and hope.) Herrmann uses a similar strategy for his music for the breakfasts montage from *Citizen Kane* (approximately fifty-two minutes into the film). He begins with a romantic waltz that was heard about four minutes earlier in the film and follows it with increasingly unromantic variations for each of the montage's scenes.

Changing musical motifs can reinforce the changing moods of a situation. In a confrontation that begins approximately 132 minutes into *West Side Story* (1961), the mood changes from unfriendliness and taunting, to emotional and physical harassment, and then to the threat of a rape. When the Puerto Rican Anita enters Doc's store and is confronted by Jets gang members, one of the young men whistles part of "La Cucaracha," which means "the cockroach." Soon the same mambo played earlier at the dance is heard playing on the jukebox, and the Jets begin to taunt Anita and call her names. As the situation turns even uglier, "America," a song and dance number heard earlier in the film, begins. (In the earlier number, which begins a little more than forty-nine minutes into the film, Anita and five other Puerto Rican women sing about the merits of life in America and the limitations of life in Puerto Rico, and six Puerto Rican men sing about the limitations of life in America and the merits of life in Puerto Rico.) As the ethnically hateful treatment of Anita continues, off and on, one can hear the "America" music in the background, an ironic reminder of Anita's advocacy of American life (Figure 4.7). As two Jets pick up and carry a third Jet to place on top of Anita, who has been pushed to the floor, the same three chords are played repeatedly, as if to suggest the rape that presumably is about to occur. When Doc shouts "stop," the action and music cease simultaneously.

Another example of music played different ways at different times to reveal a character or situation occurs in *The War of the Roses* (1989). The song "Only You" is heard three times. The first time we hear it, Barbara Rose is watching and listening to the song on TV. The song is undistorted, but it is accompanied by her husband's snoring. Love has flown. Later in the scene, Barbara tells Oliver, her husband, she wants a divorce. The second playing

FIGURE 4.7 Musical motifs reinforcing the changing moods of a situation

In a scene late in *West Side Story* (1961), various musical motifs, some of them used earlier in the film, are used to support the changing moods of the scene. As the disrespectful treatment of the Puerto Rican Anita grows more threatening, a gang member holds her sash before her as if she were a bull and he a matador. As a running comment on much of this scene, off and on in the background can be heard the song "America." *Robert Wise; United Artists*

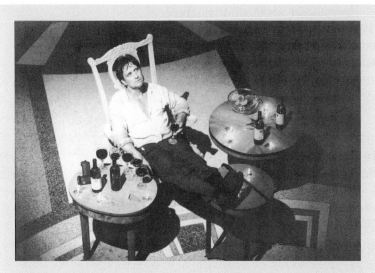

FIGURE 4.8 Music to express a changed situation
The Michael Douglas character uses a collection of partially full wineglasses to play part of "Only You" to his estranged wife in *The War of the Roses* (1989). "Only You" is heard three times in the film, each time more discordant than the last. *James L. Brooks and Arnon Milchan; 20th Century–Fox*

occurs after Barbara has led Oliver to believe that she has killed his beloved dog and used it to make the pâté Oliver has been savoring. In a fury, Oliver spits out the remaining pâté, overturns the table, and chases Barbara up the stairs. As he grabs at her and she kicks him down the stairs, "Only You" is played briefly, faintly, and in a minor key, accompanied by a sustained bass note (pedal point). The song is distorted and used ironically: it accompanies Oliver's attempts to hurt Barbara and her forceful rejection of him. The song is an appropriate choice because Oliver is obsessed with Barbara and wants only her, although she has declared she wants out of the marriage. The third time we hear the song, a drunken Oliver sings the first three notes as he tries to accompany himself with the music he makes by dipping a finger in wine and running it along the rims of partially full wineglasses (Figure 4.8). Again, how the music is played is appropriate. Oliver's mood is no longer loving, and he's no longer entirely in control of himself, so the song is crudely rendered: he sings somewhat drunkenly and off-key, and the wineglass notes are only crude approximations.

Sometimes a musical motif is associated with a character or group of characters, and the music is played the same way every time it accompanies the character or group. In *The Seven Samurai* (1954), the samurai who is an outsider has his own (jazzy) melody, and the other six samurai have their own group melody.

Music is often used to intensify an emotional effect. In *Jaws* (1975), a relentless, strongly rhythmical, and accelerating bass melody accompanies the shark attack on a boy. As the shark approaches its victim, the music is played more loudly and more quickly, suggesting the shark's power and acceleration. Once viewers have heard the shark theme and associated it with the shark, the mere melody sets their nerves on edge because music and viewers' imaginations are a powerful combination.

plot: The structure or arrangement of a narrative's events.

Filmmakers sometimes use music—knowingly or not—to distract viewers from a weak part of the script or to enhance a performance. *The Omen* illustrates both uses. Certain details about the film's **plot** may trouble viewers, but the music is so effective it helps involve viewers and keep them from dwelling on narrative weaknesses. Though the acting in *The Omen* is generally convincing, as in many films the music enhances the performances. Billie Whitelaw is exactly right as the frightening, evil governess, but she is often accompanied by a fiendishly able assistant: the demonic music. Gregory Peck is also well cast and is convincing, but in the scene where he learns of his wife's death, he is convincing only up to a point. As Peck buries his head in his hands in grief, the slow, melancholy strings and woodwinds increase in volume and build on the emotion he began.

In other films, the music is not as integral as in *The Omen*. Inappropriate or intrusive music can distract viewers—and insult them and the actors. As film composer Thomas Newman said, "I just don't want the actors to be angry with me. They've put all this work into the scene, come up with all these subtle moves and gestures to communicate what they're trying to get across, so the last thing they want is that the music just explodes all over the place. How insulting is that to the actors? It's like you're saying to the audience, 'You're not sure what they're doing? Okay, let me tell you what they're doing!'" (Edwards). Films may also use music to disguise shortcomings. If cooks cover their mistakes with mayonnaise and physicians bury theirs, perhaps filmmakers distract audiences from weaknesses with music.

Film music may reference earlier film music. Like visuals, music may be used **intertextually**—for example, to repeat earlier music or to make a joke. Sometimes, the music is the same as in an earlier film. Beginning approximately seventy-four minutes into the documentary *Wild Man Blues* (1997), viewers hear music before and after a Woody Allen press conference in Italy that was originally used in the press conference scene 122 minutes into Italian director Federico Fellini's *8½* (1963). Sixty-nine minutes into *Zoolander* (2001), the music of Richard Strauss helps develop a brief parody of part of *2001: A Space Odyssey*. Elsewhere, the music being referenced is not from the original film but approximates it closely enough that viewers can recognize the reference. Seventy-two minutes into *Zoolander*, the music evokes Nino Rota's music in the corresponding part of *The Godfather, Part II* (1974). Here, as in other movies, for copyright, budgetary, or artistic reasons, the original music was not used but is strongly suggested. Similarly, in the animated film *Jonah: A Veggie Tales Movie* (2002), after Jonah has been forced to walk the plank and is floating some distance from the ship, we hear music reminiscent of the famous prowling shark motif in *Jaws*. The music suggests that Jonah will soon be attacked from below. He is. By the whale.

More than ever, movies help sell recorded music. *Evita* (1996), *Buena Vista Social Club* (1999), and *O Brother, Where Art Thou?* (2000) are examples of movies that helped make their music into huge successes. In turn, the music sales and music videos—sometimes with clips from the films—created more interest in the movies. As never before, movies have a symbiotic relationship with tapes and CDs. The composer or performer may also be a

intertextuality: The relation of one text (such as a film) to another text or texts (such as a journalistic article, a play, or another film).

factor in selecting music for a movie. Names such as Elton John, Whitney Houston, and Jennifer Lopez generate interest not only in the movie but also in future music sales. In some movies, the music may be emphasized so that another division of the corporate conglomerate that made the film can sell tapes and CDs based on it.

At its most effective, music—which draws from the same creative well as poetry—helps elicit feelings and moods that are difficult or impossible to explain in prose. As Irwin Edman has written:

> But just because music cannot be specific it can render with voluminousness and depths the general atmosphere or aura of emotion. It can suggest love, though no love in particular; worship or despair, though it does not say who is worshiped or what is the cause of the despair. Into the same music, therefore, a hundred different listeners will pour their own specific histories and desires. . . . Words are too brittle and chiseled, life too rigid and conventional to exhaust all the infinity of human emotional response. The infinite sinuousness, nuance, and complexity of music enable it to speak in a thousand different accents to a thousand different listeners, and to say with noncommittal and moving intimacy what no language would acknowledge or express and what no situations in life could completely exhaust or make possible. (116–17)

Silence

Although they rarely do, filmmakers may use silence realistically. In *2001*, some scenes in outer space are aptly silent because space lacks air to carry sound waves. In the opening battle scenes of *Saving Private Ryan*, silence can plausibly indicate the loss of hearing due to injury and perhaps the nightmarish quality of intense, deadly warfare. Silence may also be used more symbolically.

From time to time, silence has been employed during dream scenes in sound films, as in Bergman's *Wild Strawberries* (1957) and Hallström's *My Life as a Dog*. The effect is unsettling and, if prolonged, is distancing.

Filmmakers have often used silence to suggest dying or death. In *2001*, as astronaut Frank Poole goes outside the spaceship, we hear Poole's breathing and the hiss of pressurized air. After the space pod has presumably cut Poole's air tube, all sounds stop as Poole struggles with his air tube and tumbles lifelessly through space. These deadly silent scenes outside the spacecraft are alternated with scenes containing **ambient sound** as the other astronaut, Dave Bowman, tries to help. Later when Bowman explodes the pod door of the spacecraft and is catapulted into the vacuum of the emergency air lock, at first we hear nothing. Then he pulls a switch that starts to close the spaceship's outer door and send air surging into the entry chamber, returning him and us listeners to the normal world of glorious sound. Silence can also be used to underscore the profound difference between life and death. One section of the documentary film *Titicut Follies*

ambient sound: The sound atmosphere of a place that people tend not to notice.

(1967) cuts back and forth between an asylum inmate being force fed and shots of his body being prepared for display before burial. The shots of his being force fed include the usual sounds; the shots of his corpse are silent. A similar use of silence occurs in *The Body Snatcher* (1945). A singing woman walks into the darkness in the background of the frame and is followed by a slow-moving horse-drawn carriage. For eight to ten seconds after the woman and carriage disappear into the darkness, her voice remains strong and clear; then her singing stops abruptly in midsong. The rest is silence. The suggestion created by the interruption of the sound—and the engulfing darkness of much of the frame—is that she has been murdered.

As with any other technique, silence can be used in countless ways in countless contexts. Sometimes silence can be effective when words would be inadequate. A long silence occurs near the end of *Shall We Dance?* (1996) as the dance instructor slowly approaches her former student to ask him to dance before a large group. At that moment, pace and emotion are best served in silence.

More generally, silence can function as a pause in music or poetry does: as a break in the natural rhythm of life, a change that can be unsettling and make us eager, even nervous, to return to the sounds of life.

For an illustration of how the different components of a soundtrack can function within a movie, see the Close-Up section on pp. 186-87.

ADDITIONAL USES OF SOUND

As has been suggested, spoken words, sound effects, music, and silence may be used in countless creative ways within a film. Sound may also be used as a transition to foster continuity or promote discontinuity. In narrative films, sound may be used from an on-screen source or offscreen, as part of the story or not.

Transitions

One way sound designers direct viewer attention and promote continuity or discontinuity is by the type of sound transition they use between shots. Sound may be used to connect shots in many ways. Figures 4.9 to 4.13 illustrate five frequently used sound transitions.

Often the sound ends with the visuals of one shot and is replaced by new sound at the beginning of the next shot. The sound ending one shot may be similar to the sound beginning the next shot (if so, this transition is comparable to a visual **match cut**). Sometimes the sound of the first shot is quite unlike the sound beginning the next shot (something like a **jump cut**) (Figure 4.9).

match cut: A transition between two shots in which an object or movement (or both) at the end of one shot closely resembles (or is identical to) an object or movement (or both) at the beginning of the next shot.

jump cut: A transition between shots that causes a jarring or even shocking shift in space, time, or action.

During a sound dissolve, the first sound begins to fade out as the next sound fades in and overlaps the first sound before replacing it (Figure 4.10). Sound dissolves may be used to shift sound and mood gradually from one shot to the next and to promote continuity. Continuity may also be promoted when a continuous sound is used between two shots (Figure 4.11). Sometimes the same sound is used to connect three or more shots (Figure 4.12). If only music is used as a transition between scenes, the transition is often called a **bridge**. On rare occasions, the sound from the following shot occurs at the ending of the preceding shot (Figure 4.13).

Depending on their similarity or difference, the sounds between shots contribute to continuity or disruption. Usually, in **classical Hollywood cinema** the new sound in the new shot is different but not noticeably so, and

classical Hollywood cinema: Films that show one or more characters facing a succession of problems while trying to reach their goals and that tend to hide the manner of their making by using unobtrusive filmmaking techniques.

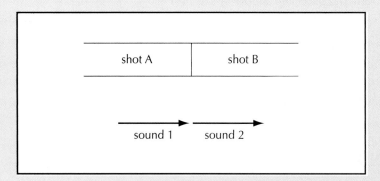

FIGURE 4.9 Sound ends with a shot then a new shot and new sound begin
A frequent sound transition between shots is for the first shot and its accompanying sound to end; then a new shot and its new sound begin. This transition can be used to promote continuity between shots or discontinuity.

If the sound of the first shot is even vaguely like the sound in the following shot, the transition seems continuous. An example of a similar, linking sound occurs in *Local Hero* (1983). A shot at an office ends with a woman office worker responding to the main character's request for a date: she simply says, "No." The next shot, in the main character's apartment, begins with him on the phone saying, "No, it's not. It's Mac." Although the speaker and tone of voice are different, the linking word *no* is the same.

If the sound of the earlier shot does not match the sound of the next shot, the transition is discontinuous, even startling. One shot late in *Citizen Kane* ends with the butler saying that he knew how to handle Kane, "like that time his wife left him." The next shot begins with a cockatoo shrieking and flying away. The result: surprise and discontinuity.

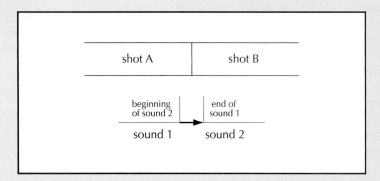

FIGURE 4.10 A sound dissolve
In a sound dissolve, the sound accompanying a shot fades out as the sound from the following shot fades in, momentarily overlapping it before replacing it. At the end of *Betrayal* (1983), a man and woman are about to begin an affair. As Jerry takes Emma's hand, the party music is replaced by more melancholy music in a sound dissolve: the next music gets louder, momentarily coexists with the party music, replaces it, and finally becomes louder still. The mood shifts gradually from festive to subdued.

FIGURE 4.11 The sound from one shot continues into the next shot
Fairly often, the sound from the ending of one shot carries over, perhaps diminished in volume, into the following shot. In *Schindler's List* (1993), a girl's hateful shouts of "Goodbye Jews!" in a shot in the street are heard three times at lower volume at the beginning of the next shot, which takes place inside a well-furnished residence that Schindler is taking over from a Jewish family.

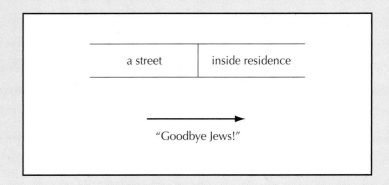

FIGURE 4.12 A sound used to connect multiple shots
Often a sound continues from one shot into the following shots. Approximately sixty-nine minutes into the classic western *High Noon* (1952), the town marshal is in his office writing his will because he has learned that the noon train is bringing a man planning to join three others to kill him. Immediately after the clock shows that it is noon, we see a shot of a chair and near the end of that shot, a train whistles abruptly and loudly with only two slight interruptions until the beginning of the seventh shot/scene (of the marshal's face); then the sound fades out quickly.

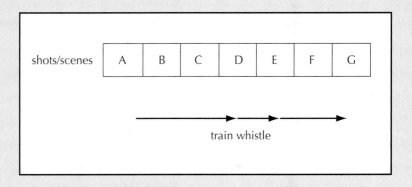

FIGURE 4.13 The sound for the second shot begins before the shot does
As a shot nears its conclusion, viewers may hear the sound from the following shot before they see its visuals. Early in *The War of the Roses* (1989), the sounds of rain, thunder, and wind can be heard. The wind sounds continue loudly during a brief visual fade-out, fade-in. In the next shot, which takes place in a different setting, it is a stormy day, and the sounds of rain and thunder can be heard. Similar sounds are used at the end of the earlier shot, during the brief transition, and at the beginning of the next shot to promote continuity.

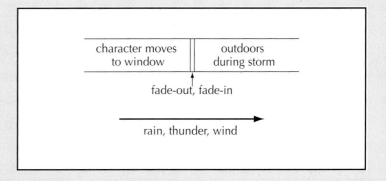

continuity is supported. Nonetheless, as with the editing of images, occasionally a discontinuous transition is used to surprise, amuse, or confuse viewers, as in the cockatoo example from *Citizen Kane* (see caption for Figure 4.9).

General Uses of Sound in Narrative Films

Table 4.2 illustrates sources and some possible functions of sound for narrative films. In most films, spoken words, occasional sound effects, and music that someone hums, whistles, sings, or plays all come from sources seen on the screen. On-screen sound in narrative films can also include a person's thoughts, memories, dreams, or fantasies, conveyed by the character's voice played over the action while the person is not directly speaking (Table 4.2A).

Sometimes sounds that are part of the story come from offscreen (Table 4.2B). In a few films, a **narrator** who is also a character in the film says

narrator: A character, person, or unidentifiable voice in a film that provides commentary about subjects in the film or outside it.

TABLE 4.2
General Uses of Sound in Narrative Films

	ON-SCREEN SOUND	OFFSCREEN SOUND
	A	**B**
▪ PART OF THE STORY (Sound derives from someone or something that is part of the story)	▪ INTERNAL Spoken words to convey thoughts, memories, dreams, or fantasies ▪ EXTERNAL Spoken words Sound effects Music	Spoken words Sound effects Music
	C	**D**
▪ NOT PART OF THE STORY (Sound derives from a source outside the story)	EXAMPLES ▪ Someone looks at the camera and says something that is not part of the story or says something that comments on the story ▪ The source of background music is visible, as in a scene in *Blazing Saddles* (Figure 4.14)	EXAMPLES ▪ Music that is not heard by those *in* the film but serves a function— for example, to intensify a mood ▪ Spoken words, often narration, by someone who is not in the story

something about a scene he or she is not in, as in *Double Indemnity* (1944) and *Citizen Kane*, or makes a few introductory comments in some scenes, as in *Menace II Society* (1993) and *The Virgin Suicides* (1999). Often, **offscreen** sound effects, such as ambient sound, are part of the story's environment. They may function as more than mere background noise. In *American Graffiti*, Curt and John are talking when a car revving its engine is heard off-screen. Curt says, "Hey, John. Someone new in town." We viewers need not see the car; hearing it is enough. Occasionally, we hear spoken words and music that are part of the narrative though we do not see their sources. It's even possible to hear the sounds of one scene as we see a later scene. Late in *Nelly and Monsieur Arnaud* (1995), we hear Arnaud's voice on a telephone imploring Nelly to come to him as we see her hurrying along a sidewalk in response to his call.

Sometimes—as in *Ferris Bueller's Day Off* (1986), *Just Another Girl on the I.R.T.* (1992), *Double Happiness* (1995), *High Fidelity* (2000), and *24 Hour Party People* (2002)—a character looks at the camera and says something that is not part of the story (Table 4.2C). Another example of a sound that is not integral to the story yet whose source is visible on-screen occurs in *Blazing Saddles* (1974, Figure 4.14). In classical Hollywood cinema, however, viewers rarely hear a sound that is not part of the story as they see its source.

Sounds that are not part of the narrative are more typically used off-screen (Table 4.2D). An example of this film convention is music that creates or reinforces a mood. For example, the screeching violins in both the 1960

FIGURE 4.14 Visible source of background music
As in many movies directed by Mel Brooks, *Blazing Saddles* (1974) sometimes makes viewers aware of movie conventions by presenting something unconventionally. Immediately before this point of *Blazing Saddles*, the main character is riding along on a horse as high-society big-band swing music plays in the background. Then the man rides up to the music's source: Count Basie and his band! *Warner Bros.*

narration: Commentary in a film about a subject in the film or some other topic, usually from someone offscreen.

and 1998 versions of *Psycho* tend to frighten viewers. Of course, the string section of an orchestra is not part of the story: viewers have no sense of a string orchestra holding a timely rehearsal in the Bates Motel. Another example of offscreen sound that is not part of the story is **narration** by someone outside the story, as in *Tom Jones*, *The Age of Innocence* (1993), and the opening of *Dr. Strangelove: Or, How I Learned to Stop Worrying and Love the Bomb* (1963).

Most often sounds are synchronized with their sources, as when spoken words match lip movements. But filmmakers may use **asynchronous sound**— a sound from a source on-screen that precedes or follows its source. And movie sounds usually sound like what we expect from their sources: a scream, for example, usually emanates from a frightened or an upset person. In Hitchcock's *The 39 Steps* (1935), though, the sound of a loud, onrushing train briefly seems to emanate from a woman's mouth (Figure 4.15). Other disjunctions between image and sound are possible. As Walter Murch has shown in his own work on film sound and has explained in his writings, "By choosing carefully what to eliminate, and then adding sounds that at first hearing seem to be somewhat at odds with the accompanying image, the film-maker can open up a perceptual vacuum into which the mind of the audience must inevitably rush" ("Sound Design" 247). A famous instance of

a)   b)

FIGURE 4.15 A sound from a surprising source
In *The 39 Steps* (1935), directed by Alfred Hitchcock, (a) a cleaning woman has discovered a body with a knife sticking out its back and opens her mouth and seems to scream. (b) In the next shot, viewers see a loud onrushing train and realize that its sound is the sound that seemed to come from the cleaning lady. Photo (a) is of the last frame of the shot; photo (b) is a frame from a half-second or so into the next shot. Frame enlargements. *Gaumont British; The Museum of Modern Art/Film Stills Archive*

sound briefly but not exactly corresponding with the image (created by Murch himself and later explained by him) occurs in a scene about 88½ minutes into *The Godfather*:

> The rumbling and piercing metallic scream just before Michael Corleone kills Solozzo in *The Godfather* is not linked directly to anything seen on screen and so the audience is made to wonder at least momentarily, if perhaps only subconsciously, "What is this?" The screech is from an elevated train rounding a sharp corner, so it is presumably coming from somewhere in the neighbourhood (the scene takes place in the Bronx). But precisely *because* it is so detached from the image, the metallic scream works as a clue to the state of Michael's mind at the moment—the critical moment before he commits his first murder and his life turns an irrevocable corner. It is all the more effective because Michael's face appears so calm and the sound is played so abnormally loud. This broadening tension between what we see and what we hear is brought to an abrupt end with the pistol shot that kills Solozzo: the distance between what we see and what we hear is suddenly collapsed at the moment that Michael's destiny is fixed. ("Sound Design" 249)

Today surround sound (360-degree sound) is available in theaters equipped with projectors capable of reading multiple soundtracks on the film and speakers in front of, on the sides of, and behind the audience. For such showings, sound can be used in new, more flexible ways. For example, viewers can hear the corresponding sounds as something seemingly approaches the audience and goes over or beside it. An airplane can be shown firing a machine gun as it approaches viewers and flies over them, and a split second after it is beyond the viewers' peripheral vision a booming explosion can be heard behind them. Nobody is going to remain uninvolved through that.

No aspect of film is so taken for granted as the soundtrack. Perhaps part of the reason we disregard sound is that even if we want to discuss it, we have a paltry vocabulary to do so. English and many other languages have many more words for visuals than for sounds, so to describe a sound we must often compare it to other, well-known sounds.

Viewers are seldom meant to notice the shadings of a trained voice, sound effects, music, and silence, but an effective soundtrack helps involve us in the film and amplifies our responses to it. Like **designers**, directors, cinematographers, and editors, sound designers can direct viewers' attention and powerfully influence how audiences respond. In movies the results usually seem true-to-life—and they are, in spirit—but they are also true to cinema, its illusions, and its artistry.

designer or **production designer:** The person responsible for the appearance of much of what is photographed in a movie, including architecture, locations, sets, costumes, makeup, and hairstyles.

CLOSE-UP: THE SOUNDTRACK IN A SCENE FROM *THE CONVERSATION*

Let us consider a scene from a film and see some of the ways the soundtrack may function. Figure 4.16 describes an excerpt that begins 18 minutes and 25 seconds into the film: the conclusion of one scene, a ninety-second scene in full, and the beginning of the following scene. The selection is from *The Conversation* (1974), whose soundtrack was done by a master of sound, Walter Murch. At the conclusion of the first scene, the main character, Harry Caul, a wiretapper, is seen working in his warehouse sound lab. In the following complete scene, he gets off a bus and makes a phone call to set up a meeting to deliver an audio tape to a client (see Figure 4.16).

In the complete, ninety-second scene, the soundtrack is used in varied, expressive ways. Dialogue is used approximately only half of the time. As is often the case in sound films, here the volume of dialogue is different than and more prominent than what it would be in a comparable life situation. As in many films, both the person calling and the person being called are heard clearly, even though we see the action from outside the phone booth. What is said is distinct, except for Harry's closing words. How the dialogue is said is clearly conveyed. Harry is hesitant and nervous; at the end of the conversation, he mumbles. By way of contrast, the man in the Director's Office sounds confident and not at all nervous.

As is usually the case in movie scenes, the sound effects are the least noticeable aspect of the track, and they are used selectively. Here, as elsewhere in movies, the effects are played at low volume and often along with music and dialogue or both. For the most part, the effects subtly support the sense of being at a particular place: sounds of the bus, street traffic, phone booth door closing, phone being dialed, and so on. As is often the case,

sounds off-frame enlarge the sense of a location. In this scene, the most interesting use of effects is the tapping on the glass of the phone booth. After Harry goes into the phone booth, we viewers may not notice a man approach from the left of the frame and stop behind the booth. The tapping sound—presumably the man tapping a coin against the glass of the phone booth because he's impatient to use the phone—is a reminder of his largely unseen presence and adds pressure to an already tense situation for Harry.

The music is used to support mood. Its tempo is slow and measured; its rhythms are consistent and not at all lively; its melody is repetitious and a bit melancholy or brooding. In ways difficult to put into words, the music seems appropriate for a character like Harry. For the most part, the music, not effects, accompanies the wordless action. The volume is varied for effect. As the dialogue with the man in the Director's Office gets under way, the music decreases in volume (easing itself out of our awareness) and stops after the voice says, "Director's Office." As in so many movie scenes, the music makes way for the most important aspect of this scene, the dialogue. The music is also used as a bridge from the end of the first scene to the beginning of the second. And at the end of the ninety-second scene, the music resumes and continues into the next scene, which takes place at a different location and a later time. In both cases, the music serves as a bridge between scenes, contributing to the continuity: one scene seems to flow into the next as the music does.

Reprinted with minor revisions from William H. Phillips, *Analyzing Films: A Practical Guide* (New York: Holt, Rinehart & Winston, 1985), 77–79.

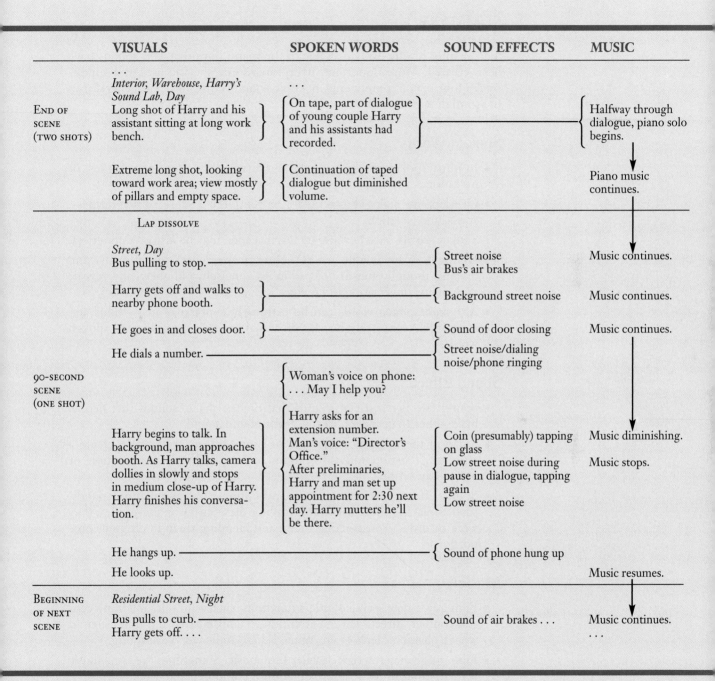

	VISUALS	SPOKEN WORDS	SOUND EFFECTS	MUSIC
END OF SCENE (TWO SHOTS)	*Interior, Warehouse, Harry's Sound Lab, Day* Long shot of Harry and his assistant sitting at long work bench.	On tape, part of dialogue of young couple Harry and his assistants had recorded.		Halfway through dialogue, piano solo begins.
	Extreme long shot, looking toward work area; view mostly of pillars and empty space.	Continuation of taped dialogue but diminished volume.		Piano music continues.
	LAP DISSOLVE			
	Street, Day Bus pulling to stop.		Street noise Bus's air brakes	Music continues.
	Harry gets off and walks to nearby phone booth.		Background street noise	Music continues.
	He goes in and closes door.		Sound of door closing	Music continues.
	He dials a number.		Street noise/dialing noise/phone ringing	
90-SECOND SCENE (ONE SHOT)		Woman's voice on phone: . . . May I help you?		
	Harry begins to talk. In background, man approaches booth. As Harry talks, camera dollies in slowly and stops in medium close-up of Harry. Harry finishes his conversation.	Harry asks for an extension number. Man's voice: "Director's Office." After preliminaries, Harry and man set up appointment for 2:30 next day. Harry mutters he'll be there.	Coin (presumably) tapping on glass Low street noise during pause in dialogue, tapping again Low street noise	Music diminishing. Music stops.
	He hangs up.		Sound of phone hung up	
	He looks up.			Music resumes.
BEGINNING OF NEXT SCENE	*Residential Street, Night* Bus pulls to curb. Harry gets off. . . .		Sound of air brakes . . .	Music continues. . . .

FIGURE 4.16 **Sound in an excerpt from** *The Conversation*

SUMMARY

The chapter briefly explains a few of the many ways that film sounds have been created. More important, it explores some specific uses of a soundtrack's four major components, possible sound transitions, and general uses of sound in narrative films.

Spoken Words

- In films, spoken words may take the form of dialogue, monologues, or narration.
- Overlapping dialogue can create or reinforce a sense of nervousness, stress, and isolation.
- Spoken words, such as those by Darth Vader, may be distorted for effect.
- Dialogue is invaluable for revealing a character's ideas, goals, and dreams, though often it does so more concisely, obliquely, and revealingly than conversation in life does.
- Although spoken words can be extremely expressive, many films and many film scenes rely heavily on visuals and use only limited spoken words.

Sound Effects

- Sound effects consist of sounds that objects make, sounds that people make other than spoken words, and ambient sound.
- Some of the many possible uses of sound effects are to help create a sense of a location, intensify a mood, enhance a humorous situation, or conceal an action.
- Sound effects specialists have many options in manipulating sounds, such as playing them backward, playing them faster or slower than they were recorded, constructing them, and blending them in different proportions.

Music

- Film music may serve countless functions, such as to mirror a film's central conflict, direct viewers' attention, establish place and time, suggest what a character feels or an animal is like, and cover weak acting.
- Film music may reference earlier film music. Sometimes the same music is used; other times an approximation is composed and used.
- In large-budget movies, sometimes the film music is selected with an eye to future recorded music sales.

Silence

- Possible uses of silence in films include during dreams, to suggest dying or death, or to interrupt the regular rhythm of life's sounds.

Transitions

- There are many possible ways to use sound between shots, such as to have the sound of the first shot end as the shot does.
- Sound transitions between shots are used to reinforce continuity or contribute to discontinuity.

General Uses of Sound in Narrative Films

- Sound in narrative films may come from on-screen or offscreen and may derive from a source in the story or outside the story.

Major Terms about Film Sound

Below, numbers in italics refer to the pages where the terms are explained. All terms are defined in more detail in the Illustrated Glossary beginning on p. 621.

ambient sound *178*	narration *184*	THX sound *161*
asynchronous sound *184*	offscreen *183*	Vitaphone *160*
bridge *180*	sound dissolve *165*	
Foley artist *171*	sound effect *168*	

QUESTIONS ABOUT FILM SOUND

The following questions are intended to help viewers understand the use of sound in a film and analyze their responses to it. Not all the questions are appropriate for every film. In thinking out, discussing, and writing responses to those questions most appropriate for the film being examined, be careful to stick with the issues the questions raise, to answer all parts of the questions, to explain the reasons for your answers, and to give specific examples from the film.

1. Where and why is offscreen sound used? Where is sound used to suggest the size of a location or the texture of the surfaces?
2. How frequently is dialogue used? Is the dialogue always distinct? Does it sometimes overlap? If so, with what consequences?
3. Where is the volume of the dialogue raised or lowered for effect?
4. Does the film use narration? If so, what functions does the narration serve?
5. Were any of the sound effects particularly important? If so, explain.

6. Consider the film's music.

   a. Where is music used? For what purposes? Is the music always subordinated to the rest of the film, or is it sometimes dominant? If the music is ever intrusive, explain where and with what consequences.

   b. What are the major melodies or tunes? Are they repeated? With or without variation?

   c. Is the music a part of the story itself, or is it played as complementary to the story (viewers hear the music, but the characters cannot)?

   d. Where does the music suggest a particular place or time or both?

   e. Where is music used to suggest what a character is feeling?

7. Is silence ever used in the film? If so, where and with what consequences?

8. Where is sound used between scenes to create a certain effect? What effect is created or supported?

9. Where is sound distorted? What does the distortion contribute?

10. Is sound ever used from a source offscreen? If so, explain its use.

11. Is any component of the sound ever "at odds with the accompanying image," as in the example of the screeching elevated train in *The Godfather*? If so, explain.

WORKS CITED

Coe, Brian. *The History of Movie Photography*. New York: Zoetrope, 1981.

Edman, Irwin. *Arts and the Man: A Short Introduction to Aesthetics*. New York: Norton, 1939.

Edwards, Mark. "Moving Sounds for Moving Pictures." *The Times* (U.K.) 23 April 2000. <http://www.the-times.co.uk>. Search on Back Issues.

Hall, Cecelia (executive sound director, Paramount Pictures). Telephone interview. 5 Aug. 1994.

Holden, Stephen. "Composers Show How to Make a Movie Sing." *New York Times* 9 July 1988: 12.

Lumet, Sidney. *Making Movies*. New York: Knopf, 1995.

"Making Godzilla Roar." *Morning Edition*. National Public Radio. 20 May 1998. <http://www.npr.org/ramfiles/980520.me.16.ram> (accessed 9 Feb. 2004).

Murch, Walter. "Sound Design: The Dancing Shadow." *Projections 4: Film-makers on Film-making*. Ed. John Boorman, Tom Luddy, David Thomson, and Walter Donohue. London: Faber and Faber, 1995: 237–51.

_____. "The Sound Designer." *Working Cinema: Learning from the Masters*. Ed. Roy Paul Madsen. Belmont, CA: Wadsworth, 1990.

Robinson, David. *The History of World Cinema*. New York: Stein, 1973.

Rydstrom, Gary. Audio Commentary. *A Bug's Life: Deluxe Edition* (DVD) 1999.
Serafine, Frank. "Audio Cinemagic." Lecture delivered at the Art Institute of Chicago.
     27 Apr. 1985.

FOR FURTHER READING

Brown, Royal S. *Overtones and Undertones: Reading Film Music*. Berkeley: U of California
     P, 1994. The book focuses "on how the interaction between a film and its score in-
     fluences our response to cinematic situations." Includes interviews with eight major
     film composers, including Miklós Rózsa, Bernard Herrmann, and Maurice Jarre. An
     appendix contains an outline of what to listen for and consider in a film score.
Film Score: The Art and Craft of Movie Music. Ed. Tony Thomas. Burbank, CA: Riverwood
     P, 1991. Includes a list of film scores for each composer featured.
Kalinak, Kathryn. *Settling the Score: Music and the Classical Hollywood Film*. Madison: U of
     Wisconsin P, 1992. History, theory, and analysis of music in classical Hollywood cin-
     ema plus an extensive bibliography.
Schelle, Michael. *The Score: Interviews with Film Composers*. Los Angeles: Silman-James,
     1999. Conversations with contemporary film composers of various styles, back-
     grounds, and positions in Hollywood.
Sound-on-Film: Interviews with Creators of Film Sound. Ed. Vincent LoBrutto. Westport,
     CT: Praeger, 1994. Includes glossary, filmographies, and bibliography.
The Sounds of Early Cinema. Ed. Richard Abel and Rick Altman. Bloomington: Indiana
     UP, 2001. The first book to examine the sounds that accompanied "silent" movies.
Thomas, Tony. *Music for the Movies*. 2nd ed. Los Angeles: Silman-James, 1997. A history
     of Hollywood film music with discussion of the lives, works, and influences of such
     film composers as Alfred Newman, Miklós Rózsa, Max Steiner, Bernard Herrmann,
     Aaron Copland, Elmer Bernstein, Jerry Goldsmith, and Lalo Schifrin.

Both an analysis of the soundtrack in an excerpt from the shower scene in Hitchcock's *Psycho* and the student essay "The Use of Sound in *Fatal Attraction*" can be found on the Web site for this book at <bedfordstmartins.com/phillips-film>.

A lengthy analysis of the expressiveness of the mise en scène, cinematography, editing, and sound in *The Third Man* can be found on the Web site for this book at <bedfordstmartins.com/phillips-film>.

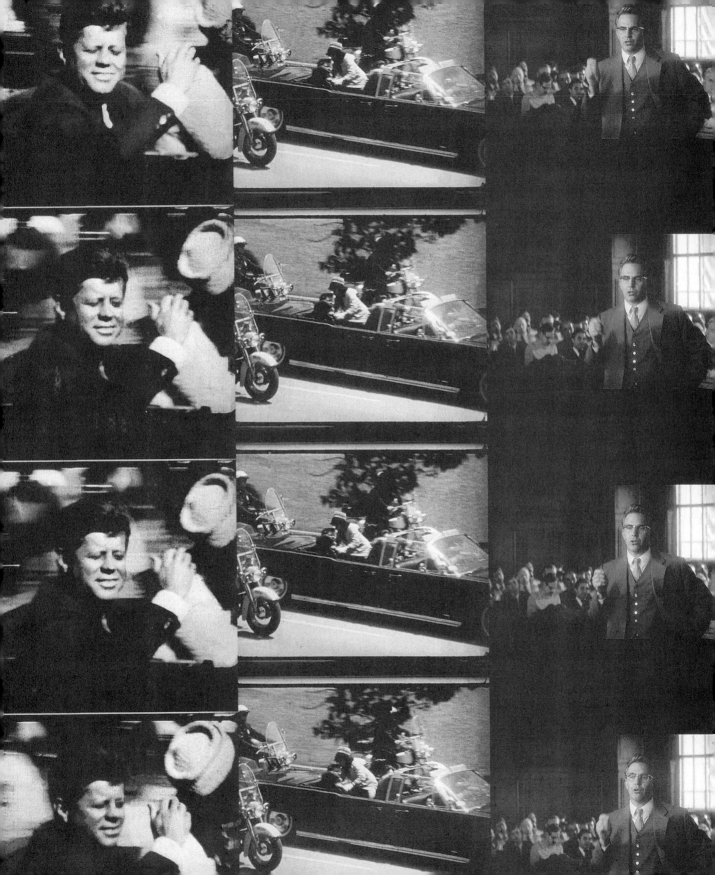

Part Two
THE FICTIONAL FILM

N EARLY SINCE THE BEGINNING OF PROJECTED FILMS in the 1890s, the fictional film has proven the most popular with audiences worldwide. By far. The fictional film has also garnered the most attention from critics. And many more studies and publications are devoted to the fictional film than any other type of film. The fictional film has attracted so much attention that we will examine it in some depth before turning our attention (in Part Three) to the variety of films that have been made. In Part Two, fictional film sources (such as history, fiction, and TV) and fictional film aspects (structure, treatment of time, and styles) are the focus.

◄ Typically, fictional films have multiple sources, as is illustrated here by frames from Oliver Stone's movie *JFK* (1991). The film includes actual historical footage of President and Mrs. Kennedy as they are being driven in a convertible that fateful 1963 day, re-created footage of the events of that same day in Dallas, and fictional characters partially based on actual people. *Warner Bros.*

Part Two
THE FICTIONAL FILM

CHAPTER 5

Sources for the Fictional Film

A FILM IS ONE OF MANY POSSIBLE KINDS of **texts,** something that people produce or modify to communicate meaning, such as a photograph, painting, newspaper article, or T-shirt message. Some theorists refer to the relationship of one text to another as **intertextual**, a term that literally means "between texts." Films are intertextual in an immense variety of creative ways: other texts that they use as sources include scripts, storyboards, written history, fiction, plays, TV, and other films. Intertextuality in films may take many forms, including adaptation, remake, allusion, parody, homage, sequel, and prequel.

Usually, a fictional film is based on a script. The script may be an original story, but often it is based on historical events, a fictional work (usually a novel), a play, a TV show or series, or other films. In this chapter, we focus on some of the most frequent sources for fictional films and on the process of transforming sources into films. In doing so, we will come to understand the film medium more completely—to understand, for example, some strengths and limitations of fictional films and their sources, the extensive connections that films have with other films and other types of texts, and the frequent influences of various cultures on a film.

Terms in **boldface** are defined in the Illustrated Glossary beginning on page 621.

text: Something that people produce or modify to communicate meaning. Examples are films, photographs, paintings, newspaper articles, operas, and T-shirts with a message.

intertextuality: The relation of one text (such as a film) to another text or texts (such as a journalistic article, a play, or another film).

SCREENPLAYS, SHOOTING SCRIPTS, AND STORYBOARDS

Written and graphic sources for a fictional film may take the form of a screenplay, shooting script, or storyboard.

Screenplays and Shooting Scripts

The **screenplay** is the earliest version of a script. It is written before filming begins and describes or supplies the **settings**, action, dialogue, and structure.

setting: The place where filmed action occurs.

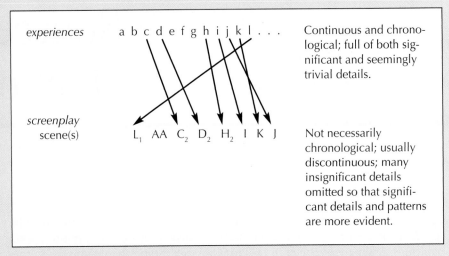

FIGURE 5.1 The making of a sample screenplay
In transforming experiences into scenes in a screenplay, the following may happen:

- Certain experiences may not be included in the script (a, b, e, f, and g).
- Experiences may be altered as they are transformed into scenes (c, d, and h become C_2, D_2, and H_2).
- Events may be rearranged (j and k become K and J).
- Experiences may be altered and transposed (l becomes L_1).
- New scenes without corresponding experiences in life may be made up (as in the case of AA).

Source: Adapted from Phillips (*Analyzing Films* 58).

scene: A section of a narrative that gives the impression of continuous action taking place in continuous time and space.

shot: An uninterrupted strip of exposed motion-picture film or videotape.

producer: A person in charge of the business and administrative aspects of making a film.

A **shooting script** is the version of the script used during filming. It includes changes made in the screenplay, usually breaks the **scenes** into **shots**, and normally includes instructions on camera placement and use.

In creating a screenplay, writers nearly always select from experiences (their own and experiences they imagine) and arrange them in an involving and meaningful order (Figure 5.1).

Table 5.1 illustrates the elements of a film that are usually the responsibility of the screenplay writer and those that are the contributions of others. In large productions, arrangements with the **producer**, director, and perhaps actors determine how closely the screenplay writer's wishes are followed. Usually all other aspects of a film—such as camera angles and transitions between shots—are the domain of the other filmmakers, such as the cinematographer and editor, usually under the guidance of the director. The screenplay writer's territory, and the territory of those shooting and editing the film, can be further explored by examining the last scene of *The Royal Tenenbaums* (2001). The left column in Table 5.2 reprints the scene

TABLE 5.1
Creative Territories for Making Fictional Films

THE WRITER'S TERRITORY

▪ SETTINGS: where and when the action takes place and generally what the settings look like

▪ SUBJECTS: the characters' actions and dialogues

▪ STRUCTURE: the selection and arrangement of dialogue (if any) and actions

▪ MEANINGS: what the film explains about its subjects in general terms or, more often, what it implies by showing subjects in particular situations

Source: Adapted from Phillips (*Writing Short Scripts*, 170).

THE TERRITORY OF PRODUCTION PERSONNEL

▪ CASTING AND PERFORMANCE: people, animals, or creatures selected to play the roles; behavior, gestures, tone of voice

▪ CINEMATOGRAPHY AND MISE EN SCÈNE: camera distances, camera angles, lenses, lighting, composition, and so forth

▪ EDITING: length and arrangement of shots; transitions between shots[a]

▪ MUSIC AND SOUND EFFECTS[a]

[a]Occasionally, the writer's directions for editing transitions, music, and sound effects are followed by the production personnel.

from the screenplay. The right column provides a description of the last scene in the finished film.

Note in the left column that the two screenplay writers for *The Royal Tenenbaums* indicate the setting (a cemetery and day) and something about what the setting looks like: snowy and darkening. They describe all the characters' actions, lowering the casket, firing the B.B. guns, and so forth, but they exclude dialogue from the scene. By indicating what happens and in what order, the screenplay writers determine the scene's structure. And by selecting setting and actions, they make it possible for readers to formulate a range of possible meanings the scene suggests.

The scene in the finished film, which consists of six shots and runs for 125 seconds, generally honors the scriptwriters' wishes but makes many changes as well. It is not a snowy, darkening day. During the time that the filmmakers had for filming the scene, the location probably was gray and drizzling. The actions in the film follow the script generally, but the film makes many changes. For example, the film shows six men lowering the casket, not seven, and it shows the seventh man (Pagoda) on the far end watching and then tossing in the flowers. The film also omits some details included in the script. For example, the film does not show Pagoda crying.

Sometimes the filmmakers added details. For example, the film includes the boys' spotted dog. He is a reminder of Royal's finest hour, when he saved the boys from an out-of-control car that killed the boys' dog. Royal quickly bought a new, spotted dog and gave it to the boys to help ease their pain at losing their first dog.

Nowhere in the script do the two screenplay writers stipulate which actors should be cast and how they should perform (one of the writers directed the film, and the other acted in it). Also, in this last scene and elsewhere in the script, the writers never indicate camera placement, camera movement, and composition. Nor do the scriptwriters indicate how many shots the scene should have and where to begin and end each shot. It was left to the production personnel to decide whether to include any **narration** in the last scene (they did), whether to include any music (they included two discontinuous excerpts), and whether to include sound effects (they did—for example, the firing B.B. guns).

narration: Commentary in a film about a subject in the film or some other topic, usually from someone offscreen.

Unless we have access to a version of the script that was written by the screenplay writers, we cannot know the writers' contributions to a film. In a large production company, many people—especially the producer, director, actors, and editors—may rewrite or edit parts of the script or insist on changes in it. In large, complicated productions, one or more "script doctors" may be hired to rewrite the script, sometimes again and again, and they often are uncredited. Comparison of a screenplay or shooting script with the finished film sometimes reveals the different contributions of the writer(s) and others, especially the director. We can see these relative contributions by comparing a scene from the shooting script for *The Third Man* (1949) with the comparable section of the finished film. In the film, Holly Martins has come to Vienna to work for an old friend, Harry Lime. Martins learns that Lime has been involved in stealing penicillin, diluting it, and selling it at an enormous profit. Late in the film Calloway, a British officer trying to enlist Martins's aid in trapping Lime, has brought Martins to a children's hospital. Two scenes from the shooting script are reprinted in the left column of Table 5.3.

Like the excerpt from the script for *The Royal Tenenbaums* reprinted in the left column of Table 5.2, this version of the script is written in the **master-scene format**, which often indicates the scene number, the setting, and the segment of the twenty-four-hour day (such as day, night, dawn, noon, late afternoon). The scriptwriter describes the action briefly and supplies all the dialogue, but does not indicate how the dialogue is to be delivered. The writer knew that well-written dialogue usually suggests its delivery and that the director and actors would probably have ignored overly specific directives.

In the right column, a description of the actual scene in the finished film indicates that the film is true to the script in showing only Martins's reactions to the children and not the patients themselves. But the film differs in several ways from the script, Table 5.3. The hallway and ward scenes in the shooting script have become one ward scene in the film—a wise decision because the script's hallway scene adds little to the story. The film also has far

the suffering that Lime's actions have spawned. The film also portrays a large ward full of Lime's victims; the script indicates victims in only six beds. The film shows many nurses busy tending the children; the script says nothing about the nurses' work. When we compare screenplays or shooting scripts with the corresponding films, we find that, as in the case of *The Third Man*, the film is usually more concise, less reliant on dialogue, and more visual.

Although we cannot say with certainty who is responsible for all the changes in this part of *The Third Man*, we can see roughly what the scriptwriter, Graham Greene, wrote and the final filmed product. Director Carol Reed probably deserves much credit for the changes from the script, which compress the action and present the information and moods more visually and more subtly.

Storyboards

A **storyboard** is a series of drawings (or occasionally photographs) of each shot (or sometimes part of a shot) of a planned film or video story, usually accompanied by brief descriptions or notes (Figure 5.2). Storyboards are the visual equivalent of a rough draft of a written story. They allow filmmakers to see how the finished film might look before the laborious and costly processes of filming and editing begin. Storyboards are useful for deciding how to divide the script into shots, determining how to arrange the shots (a sort of preediting), and deciding camera placement.

In animation, storyboarding is crucial because creating each frame of an animated film is usually especially time-consuming and expensive. Typically, once the storyboard for an animated film has been worked out in detail and the voices cast and recorded, the creation of individual frames begins.

INDIVIDUAL SOURCES

The history of cinema shows that just about any human subject can become the source of a fictional film. Possible, but infrequent, sources include nonfiction magazine articles (*Pushing Tin*, 1999, and *Isn't She Great*, 2000), video games (*Lara Croft: Tomb Raider*, 2001, and *Resident Evil*, 2002), comic books (*X-Men*, 2000, and *X2: X-Men United*, 2003), comic strips (the Peanuts films), series of short animated movies (*South Park: Bigger, Longer and Uncut*, 1999), musical albums (*Pink Floyd the Wall*, 1982), operas (*Carmen*, many times), and even (loosely) amusement park rides (*Pirates of the Caribbean: The Curse of the Black Pearl*, 2003). Although fictional films can have other sources, five of the most frequent ones are history, fiction, plays, TV, and other films. As is illustrated in this chapter's last section, a film often has a series of sources, and even films based on one major source inevitably have been influenced by additional sources.

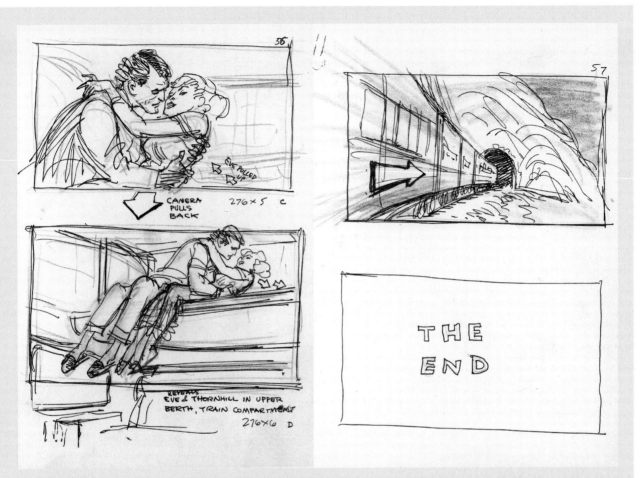

FIGURE 5.2 Sample storyboard
A storyboard is the visual equivalent of an outline for a story. Each panel represents an intended shot or part of a shot. Here are the final panels for Hitchcock's *North by Northwest* (1959). The first two represent the film's penultimate shot: the camera begins close to the two subjects and pulls back to reveal the surprising setting, the upper berth of a train compartment. The final shot is of the train speeding into a darkened tunnel. No part of a storyboard is binding on filmmakers; the panels are simply explorations of a film's possible shots. Hitchcock, however, worked out all of a movie's shots before filming began and rarely deviated from his plans once shooting was under way. *MGM; The Museum of Modern Art/Film Stills Archive*

An adaptation may be one of three basic types: loose (it retains only a few major aspects of the original—for example, only the title and one or two of its subjects); faithful (it imitates the subject and perhaps style of the original and captures its mood or spirit but with some changes); or literal (as nearly as possible, it re-creates the source). Literal adaptations are rare but most likely to be attempted when plays are adapted into films. Which type of adaptation is "best" is subject to debate. Some advocate literal adaptations, assuming that recreating the original as closely as possible is most important. At the opposite extreme, those who support loose adaptations believe that it's unimportant how closely a text adapts earlier texts.

History

Many fictional films, such as *Stand and Deliver* (1987) and *The Hurricane* (1999), are based on historical events. Often single historical events are the source for multiple, highly distinct film interpretations, as in the case of the sinking of the Titanic—*Saved from the Titanic* (1912), *Titanic* (1943), *Titanic* (1953), *A Night to Remember* (1958), and *Titanic* (1997). Usually movies based on historical events must attract large audiences to recoup the fortunes needed to make and market them. Consequently, filmmakers do not typically aim to teach their audiences traditional written historical accounts because they tend to be unengaging movies and therefore unprofitable. When a film deals with news or history, filmmakers usually omit, add, or change details to make the film more entertaining or to imply different **meanings**, or both. For centuries, novelists and playwrights, including Shakespeare, have done the same. (For a sample of the debate about the issues involved in one movie's interpretation of history, see pp. 204–06.)

meaning: An observation or a general statement about a subject.

Typically, fictional films based on history blend fiction and fact throughout. One example is *Stand and Deliver*, the story of a real Latino high school math teacher, Jaime Escalante, and one of his largely Latino classes. The film shows various barriers the students face, the methods the teacher uses, and the students' hard work. All this is presented in such a way that viewers are led to believe that the account is factual. In spirit, yes; in some details, no. For example, in the film the entire class seems to have to retake a test because authorities at a national testing service suspected cheating, but in fact only fourteen of the eighteen students had to take the test again. The film shows the students having only one day to review for the second test. The actual second test was administered several months later. Yet another example: as in nearly all fictional films, the movie character is livelier and more engaging than the real person (Figure 5.3).

The makers of *The Hurricane*—which shows the story of Rubin (Hurricane) Carter, a successful boxer

FIGURE 5.3 Actor and subject
Actor Edward James Olmos (left) as Jaime Escalante in *Stand and Deliver* (1987), with the real high school math teacher Jaime Escalante. Comparison of clips of the celluloid Escalante teaching with documentary footage of the real Escalante teaching illustrates that, as in most movies based on real people, the movie character seems more lively and engaging than the actual person. *American Playhouse; Warner Bros.*

JFK: Fact and Fiction

Someone assassinated President John F. Kennedy in Dallas, Texas, on 22 November 1963, and shortly afterward his accused murderer was himself murdered while in custody. Soon a flood of theories about who was behind the two murders surged forth. The Warren Commission, appointed by President Lyndon B. Johnson, investigated the matter at length and issued a report that failed to gain widespread acceptance. To this day, many people remain uncertain about the causes of Kennedy's death. Oliver Stone's *JFK* (1991) combines actual documentary footage, reconstructed documentary-like footage, and fictionalized versions of people involved to present one theory about the Kennedy assassination. However, it is very much a minority interpretation, one to which few or no published historians subscribe. Even before Stone's film came out in December 1991, a controversy about its merits broke out around the United States. Following are excerpts from the wide-ranging debate.

The following are excerpts from a seven-page statement by Jack Valenti, the president and chief executive of the Motion Picture Association of America and a former top aide to President Johnson, as reported in the national edition of the *New York Times*, 2 April 1992:

> Does any sane human being truly believe that President Johnson, the Warren Commission members, law-enforcement officers, C.I.A., F.B.I., assorted thugs, weirdos, Frisbee throwers, all conspired together as plotters in Garrison's wacky sighting? And then for almost 29 years nothing leaked? But you have to believe it if you think well of any part of this accusatory lunacy.
>
> In scene after scene Mr. Stone plasters together the half true and the totally false and from that he manufactures the plausible. No wonder that many

young people, gripped by the movie, leave the theater convinced they have been witness to the truth.

In much the same way, young German boys and girls in 1941 were mesmerized by Leni Riefenstahl's *Triumph of the Will*, in which Adolf Hitler was depicted as a newborn God. Both *J.F.K.* and *Triumph of the Will* are equally a propaganda masterpiece and equally a hoax. Mr. Stone and Leni Riefenstahl have another genetic linkage: neither of them carried a disclaimer on their film that its contents were mostly pure fiction.

This op-ed piece in the 7 March 1992 national edition of the *New York Times* was written by David W. Belin, a former counsel to the Warren Commission:

> What far right-wing extremists tried to persuade a majority of Americans to believe in the 1960's with their "Impeach Earl Warren" billboards, Hollywood has been able to achieve in the 1990's in its impeachment of the integrity of a great Chief Justice.
>
> Earl Warren is not the only victim. The Kennedy assassination is called a "coup d'etat," a "public execution" by elements of the C.I.A. and the Department of Defense, while President Lyndon B. Johnson is called an accessory after the fact—in other words, a murderer.
>
> When the film not only alleges conspiracy but names the guilty parties, it goes beyond just artistic license and entertainment. It crosses the threshold of slander and character assassination—a 1990's version of McCarthyism.

A letter from John Roberts in the 18 August 2000 issue of the *Chronicle of Higher Education* included the following:

> In his [Stone's] preposterous film *JFK*, the only unassailable fact presented in the movie is that Kennedy is dead. The numerous threads of Mr. Stone's paranoid

He's a District Attorney.

He will risk his life, the lives of his family, everything he holds dear

for the one thing he holds sacred . . . the truth.

KEVIN COSTNER

AN OLIVER STONE FILM

JFK

The Story that Won't Go Away

Poster for *JFK* (1991)
From this poster, potential viewers learn that the film will focus on one man's difficult and dangerous task in pursuing a noble goal, a frequent subject in popular American movies. Because of the placement and size of the lettering, certain groups of words receive more prominence than others. The largest lettering and the boldface is for *JFK* (the movie's name); the next largest lettering is for *Kevin Costner* (the name of the popular actor playing the main role). Also prominent is lettering for *The Story that Won't Go Away* (a reminder that the causes of the Kennedy assassination are still in dispute).

As the movie *JFK* does, the visuals on the right side of the poster combine fiction and fact—an image of the actor playing the main role combined with fragments of three historical images: a photograph of part of the motorcade shortly after President Kennedy was shot, a newspaper headline announcing Kennedy's assassination, and a photo of the accused assassin, Lee Harvey Oswald, holding a rifle. *Warner Bros.*

conspiracy theories can be held together only by his creating out of whole cloth a person who did not exist (Donald Sutherland's character) who breathlessly tells the hero (Kevin Costner) that "Yes, this assassination was a coup!" All of it was done to keep Kennedy from doing something he never intended to do in the first place—namely, get out of Vietnam. . . . Kennedy understood the logic of the cold war, the danger of authoritarianism, and the threat of passivity in the face of real oppression. Keep in mind, this is the man who wrote *Why England Slept*. He was not into appeasement.

Mr. Stone seems to think that this is a minor triviality. But it cuts to the core of his and others' conspir-

acy theories about the case. And without evidence to support the assertion that Kennedy was killed because he wanted to pull out of Vietnam, the conspiracy evaporates into thin air, whence Mr. Stone seems to have pulled it in the first place.

As film critic Roger Ebert, writing in the 20 December 1991 Chicago *Sun-Times*, saw it,

Stone's film is hypnotically watchable. Leaving aside all of its drama and emotion, it is a masterpiece of film assembly. The writing, the editing, the music, the photography, are all used here in a film of enormous complexity, to weave a persuasive tapestry out of an overwhelming mountain of evidence and testimony. Film students will examine this film in wonder in the years to come, astonished at how much information it contains, how many characters, how many interlocking flashbacks, what skillful interweaving of documentary and fictional footage. The film hurtles for 188 minutes through a sea of information and conjecture, and never falters and never confuses us. . . .

The achievement of the film is not that it answers the mystery of the Kennedy assassination, because it does not, or even that it vindicates Garrison, who is seen here as a man often whistling in the dark. Its achievement is that it tries to marshal the anger which ever since 1963 has been gnawing away on some dark shelf of the national psyche. John F. Kennedy was murdered. Lee Harvey Oswald could not have acted alone. Who acted with him? Who knew?

David Ansen, one of the film critics for *Newsweek*, wrote in the 23 December 1991 issue:

By turning Jim Garrison—a troubling, shoot-from-the-hip prosecutor whose credibility has been seriously questioned—into a mild-mannered, four-square Mr. Clean, Stone is asking for trouble. *JFK*'s Garrison is perhaps best viewed more as a movie convention than as a real man. Stone has always required a hero to worship, and he turns the D.A. into his own alter ego, a true believer tenaciously seeking higher truth. He equally idealizes Kennedy, seen as a shining symbol of hope and change, dedicated to pulling out of Vietnam and to ending the cold war.

But it is possible to remain skeptical of *JFK*'s Edenic notions of its heroes and still find this movie a remarkable, necessary provocation. Real political discourse has all but vanished from Hollywood filmmaking; above and beyond whether Stone's take on the assassination is right his film is a powerful, radical vision of America's drift toward covert government. What other filmmaker is even thinking about the uses and abuses of power?

Finally, historian Robert A. Rosenstone wrote in his 1995 book *Visions of the Past: The Challenge of Film to Our Idea of History* (123–24):

JFK, despite the many documentary-type elements that it contains, belongs to what is certainly the most popular type of film, the Hollywood—or mainstream—drama. This sort of film is marked, as cinema scholars have shown, by a number of characteristics, the chief being its desire to make us believe in that what we see in the theater is true. To this end, the mainstream film utilizes a specific sort of film language, a self-effacing, seamless language of shot, editing, and sound designed to make the screen seem no more than a window onto unmediated "reality."

Along with "realism," four other elements are crucial to an understanding [of] the mainstream historical film:

- Hollywood history is delivered in a story with beginning, middle, and end—a story that has a moral message, and one that is usually embodied in a progressive view of history.
- The story is closed, completed, and ultimately, simple. Alternative versions of the past are not shown; the *Rashomon* approach is never used in such works.
- History is a story of individuals—usually heroic individuals who do unusual things for the good of others, if not all humankind (ultimately, the audience).
- Historical issues are personalized, emotionalized, and dramatized—for film appeals to our feelings as a way of adding to our knowledge or affecting our beliefs.

Such elements go a long way toward explaining the shape of *JFK*. The story is not that of President Kennedy but of Jim Garrison, the heroic, embattled, uncorruptible investigator who wishes to make sense of JFK's assassination and its apparent coverup, not just for himself but for his country and its traditions—that is, for the audience, for us.

imprisoned for a triple murder but eventually freed—take great pains to make the film look historically accurate (Figure 5.4). The story is based on historical events about which there is disagreement. Before and after the film's opening in December 1999, reporters and attorneys involved in the original case painted a very different picture of the Carter case than the movie does.[1] The changes made seem to be the usual ones for movies based on history. Thus, for example, nine Canadians living on a commune become three Canadians doing some sort of work to end injustices in society. The detectives, prosecutors, witnesses, judges, and juries whose work led to two convictions of Carter become one racist police officer and two suspect witnesses. A trial, a conviction, nine months of liberty for Carter and John Artis (the other man arrested for the triple murder), a second trial, and a second conviction in the movie become one brief courtroom sentencing. In the film, Artis becomes a minor character while the young Lesra Martin, who worked with the Canadians on Carter's behalf, plays a major role.

Some actual events after Carter's second release from prison are at odds with the movie's concluding explanations about the main characters' fates. After his release from prison, Carter married one of the Canadians but eventually became disillusioned with her and the others of the commune and evidently remains alienated from them all. The film informs viewers before the movie's closing credits only that "Terry, Sam, and Lisa returned to Canada. Rubin Carter joined them there and makes his home in Toronto. He is the Executive Director of the Association in Defence of the Wrongly Convicted."

Like so many other movies based on historical events, *The Hurricane* illustrates all of the following points made by historian Robert Brent Toplin:

> Filmmakers must attend to the demands of drama and the challenges of working with incomplete evidence. In creating historical dramas they almost always need to collapse several historical figures into a few central characters to make a story understandable. Often they are pressed to simplify complex causes so that audiences will comprehend their movies' principal messages and not lose interest, and the dramatic medium often leads them to attribute changes in history to the

FIGURE 5.4 Re-creating the look of an earlier time and place
Like other commercial films based on historical events, the images in *The Hurricane* (1999) look authentic. Here actor Denzel Washington and others reenact a celebration after one of Rubin (Hurricane) Carter's boxing victories. The scene was filmed in black and white, as photographs of the time would have been, and everything else about the image, including the short haircuts, looks true to the story's time and place. Frame enlargement. *Beacon; Universal*

---

[1]For example, a former newspaper reporter who covered the case and is highly critical of the movie's accuracy has maintained a Web site (<www.graphicwitness.com/carter>) with links to many newspaper articles about the case.

actions of dynamic individuals rather than to impersonal forces. Cinematic historians often lack detailed evidence about situations in the past, so they invent dialogue and suggest impressions about the emotions and motivations of historic figures. Also, they suggest **closure** on a story, revealing few doubts, questions, or considerations of alternative possibilities. (10)

closure: A sense of coherence and completion at the end of a narrative.

A fictional film based on historical events always fictionalizes the material to a greater or lesser extent.

Some filmmakers and film distributors downplay the fictional elements of movies based on history—for example, by burying the disclaimer (if there is one) at the end of the film when only a few viewers remain in the theater. (Such disclaimers may be unreadable on home videotape versions.) In theatrical showings, both *Gladiator* (2000) and *The Hurricane* end with disclaimers that are on screen only a few seconds. Here is the disclaimer for *The Hurricane*: "While this picture is based upon a true story, some characters have been composited or invented, and a number of incidents fictionalized." "Some" and "a number of" conceal the extensiveness and nature of the changes made. After the prolonged controversy about the historical accuracy of *The Hurricane* when it was released in theaters, the video and DVD releases carry the disclaimer at the beginning and ending. Filmmakers may even hide their fiction by claiming factuality. *Fargo* (1996) begins as follows:

THIS IS A TRUE STORY.
The events depicted in this film took place in Minnesota in 1987.
At the request of the survivors, the names have been changed.
Out of respect for the dead, the rest has been told exactly as it occurred.

Some reviewers of *Fargo* were skeptical of the above claim, and an investigation by the *Minneapolis Star Tribune* failed to unearth any case like the one the movie depicts. A fictional film may even falsely imply at its conclusion that it has been factual. The 1994 Russian-French film *Burnt by the Sun* has an epilogue explaining the fates of the main characters, but the film's director and cowriter, Nikita Mikhalkov, has said that "he added the epilogue for dramatic effect and invented the characters himself" (Stanley B1).

Other fictional filmmakers enhance their films' semblance of actuality by including **documentary**-like material. *Schindler's List* (1993) includes **title cards** about actual events, and the main body of the movie concludes with documentary footage of survivors and their relatives honoring Schindler by placing stones on his grave. *JFK* (1991) begins with documentary footage of President Dwight D. Eisenhower warning of the powers of the military-industrial complex and includes frequent excerpts from historical films and TV newscasts. *Apollo 13* (1995) uses old TV clips, interviews, subtitles conveying factual information, and (concluding) narration to enhance the appearance of factuality.

documentary film: A film or video representation of actual (not imaginary) subjects.

title card: A card or thin sheet of clear plastic on which is written or printed information included in a film.

With a fictional film based on historical events, let the buyer beware: such a movie should be regarded primarily as a fictionalized entertainment that nearly always focuses more on enjoyable storytelling than on written accounts regarded as historical. In both *Stand and Deliver* and *The Hurricane*, for example, as in so many American movies, the two major goals of the films are to entertain and to give hope that individuals or small groups that work hard and persistently can eventually triumph over society's flaws.

> The student essay "Understanding the History of the 1870s West with *The Ballad of Little Jo*" can be found on the Web site for this book at <bedfordstmartins.com/phillips-film>.

> Many historical sources for films are cited in the first column of the chronology for 1895 to 2003 (see pp. 559–610).

Fiction

According to critic and **film theorist** Dudley Andrew, "Well over half of all commercial films have come from literary originals" (98). Two examples of fiction adapted to film illustrate what changes may be made when fiction is adapted into a film and what each medium is capable of.

The first example is *The Player*, the 1988 novel by Michael Tolkin and the 1992 film adaptation directed by Robert Altman. In their characters and **plots**, the novel and film have much in common. Both focus on a thirty-something Hollywood studio executive, Griffin Mill, whose job it is to listen to and pass judgment on pitches for possible movies (Figure 5.5). In both

film theorist: A person who formulates a general explanation of the film medium or a part of the medium.

plot: The structure or arrangement of a narrative's events.

FIGURE 5.5 Novel into film: *The Player* As in the 1988 source novel, in the film of *The Player* (1992), the main character, Griffin Mill, works for a Hollywood studio and initially confronts two major problems: the rumor that he may be replaced and a series of anonymous threatening messages from a writer who has submitted material for a possible film but has been rejected by Mill. Frame enlargement. *Avenue Pictures & Spelling Entertainment; Fine Line Features*

novel and film, Mill is romantically involved with Bonnie Sherow. In both, he seeks out a writer he thinks is sending him postcard threats, finds him at a screening of *The Bicycle Thief*, has drinks with him, and later that night, during a struggle, kills him. At the writer's funeral, Mill meets the writer's girlfriend, June, who soon becomes Mill's love interest. In both novel and film, both the studio head of security and the Pasadena police treat Mill as a suspect, but he is not identified in a police lineup and ends up with a job promotion and the love of the murdered writer's girlfriend.

Many changes were made in converting the novel to a script and then a film because the filmmakers chose to add, delete, or change details. In both novel and film, Mill continually hides his feelings from others and reins in his emotions, although in the book, at the conclusion of Chapter 14, when he fears arrest is imminent, he cries. Film critic Michael Wilmington points out that unlike the novel, the film surrounds the central character with a large and varied group: "Tolkin's novel was chilly, spare and lean: It zeroed right into Griffin's skull. Altman, predictably, has enriched the milieu and built up a huge community around the cipher at the center."

Because of other decisions made by the filmmakers, the novel and film differ in yet other ways. In the book, the screenwriter does not pitch his script as an independent film with unknown actors and a tragic ending. In the film, he does. In the novel (and the script), Mill and June go to a Mexican seaside resort for a weekend vacation. For the film, given the limited budget for making *The Player*, the filmmakers shifted the vacation from Mexico or a Mexico look-alike to a desert hideaway. In the novel, because of Mill's reluctance, Mill and June do not entirely consummate their relationship until the epilogue, which takes place six months later and implies that Mill and June are married, though with no clue that she is pregnant. In the film, Mill and June consummate their relationship at the conclusion of the romantic evening at a desert hideaway resort, and at the end of the story, one year later, Mill and June are living together. Though it is unclear if they are married, she is clearly pregnant. In the novel, Mill agrees to move to a different type of position with a different company before the head of the studio is ousted. Near the end of the film, Mill has mysteriously displaced the studio head. In the book's epilogue, the anonymous postcard writer quits scriptwriting, moves out of state, and sends Mill a letter of apology and $1,000 cash to pay for the car windows the writer had shot out while stalking Mill. In the film, he calls Mill and indirectly threatens to blackmail him.

The filmmakers also decided to change the female characters. In the book, June is an art director for Wells Fargo banks, and readers get to know her somewhat better than viewers get to know the cinematic June, though in both her attraction to Mill is more contrived than credible. Police detective Susan Avery is also a different character in the novel: for example, sometimes she is attracted to Mill and is impressed by his position and power. According to Altman, Whoopi Goldberg devised much of the tampon-twirling scene where she questions Mill in her office, and the film Avery, as Goldberg can be, is more confident, ironic, and forceful than the book's Avery. In the book, Bonnie Sherow works for a different studio and is less prominent than in the film. But because Cynthia Stevenson is a charming, skilled actor, the filmmakers gave the film Sherow more prominence and presented her in a more sympathetic light. The casting of Goldberg and Stevenson are examples of how casting influences characterization, a situation not uncommon in films, particularly Altman's, which tend to be more collaborative and improvisatory in their making than most films.

Some changes were made in converting the novel to a film because of different strengths of each medium. The most striking difference between the novel and the film is that the novel is driven by Mill's frequent thoughts and the film by dialogue, action, and expressive images. In the novel, readers have frequent access to Mill's thoughts and feelings. While on a vacation with June in Mexico, for example, Mill thinks: "He had made too many mistakes. He had lied to too many people. When the first card arrived, no, when the third card arrived, the card with the death threat, he should have gone straight to Walter Stuckel [head of studio security], straight to Levison [head of the studio], and showed it to them. He should have asked for help. He shouldn't have worried about the cards' effect on his job. And now it was too late to show the cards to anyone" (Tolkin 168). In the book, Mill is preoccupied with events that led up to the murder and with ways to avoid getting caught for his crime. Mill also thinks about the complex and unstable world of the movie industry. Throughout the book, Mill worries about how he appears to others. Since the film presents the characters' personalities through action and dialogue, we never learn what Mill ruminates about, and the **celluloid** Mill is far less reflective than the conjecture-obsessed creation in the book. Filmmakers can reveal a character's thoughts, usually by using narration, but most filmmakers and viewers believe that extensive use of narration is not an efficient use of the film medium, so filmmakers tend to use it selectively.

> **celluloid** (adj.): movie.

Now let's examine a passage of fiction and the corresponding section of a film based on the fiction. The fictional passage is from the end of Chapter 12 of *The Woman in the Dunes* (1964), Kobo Abé's Japanese novel about a man trapped in a large sand pit with a woman who lives there in a shack (left column, Table 5.4).

The comparable section of the film version consists of the conclusion of one shot and three additional shots, begins nearly thirty-five minutes into the film, and runs about forty-five seconds. A description appears in the right column of Table 5.4 (dialogue is from the film's subtitles).

There are many differences between the experience of reading the passage and seeing and hearing the corresponding section of the film. Some of the differences result from choices of the filmmakers. For example, the filmmakers chose to have the man laugh, catch himself, and become brusque, whereas in the book the man shrieks and the woman laughs.

TABLE 5.4
The Woman in the Dunes (novel) and *Woman in the Dunes* (film)

NOVEL EXCERPT	FILM EXCERPT
The woman sidled up to him. Her knees pressed against his hips. A stagnant smell of sun-heated water, coming from her mouth, nose, ears, armpits, her whole body, began to pervade the room around him. Slowly, hesitantly, she began to run her searing fingers up and down his spine. His body stiffened.	Shot 1. . . . *At the end of this lengthy shot, the woman, carrying a pan of water and a rag, approaches the man—who is lying on his back, naked from the waist up—and kneels beside him.*

The woman sidled up to him. Her knees pressed against his hips. A stagnant smell of sun-heated water, coming from her mouth, nose, ears, armpits, her whole body, began to pervade the room around him. Slowly, hesitantly, she began to run her searing fingers up and down his spine. His body stiffened.

Suddenly the fingers circled around to his side. The man let out a shriek.

"You're tickling!"

The woman laughed. She seemed to be teasing him, or else she was shy. It was too sudden; he could not pass judgment on the spur of the moment. What, really, was her intention? Had she done it on purpose or had her fingers slipped unintentionally? Until just a few minutes ago she had been blinking her eyes with all her might, trying to wake up. On the first night, too, he recalled, she had laughed in that strange voice when she had jabbed him in the side as she passed by. He wondered whether she meant anything in particular by such conduct.

Perhaps she did not really believe in his pretended illness and was testing her suspicions. That was a possibility. He couldn't relax his guard. Her charms were like some meat-eating plant, purposely equipped with the smell of sweet honey. First she would sow the seeds of scandal by bringing him to an act of passion, and then the chains of blackmail would bind him hand and foot. (Abé 90–91)

FILM EXCERPT

Shot 1. . . . *At the end of this lengthy shot, the woman, carrying a pan of water and a rag, approaches the man—who is lying on his back, naked from the waist up—and kneels beside him.*

WOMAN: How do you feel?

Shot 2. *The man turns his head slightly away from her and groans.*

MAN: Not too bad.

WOMAN: I'll wipe you down.

As she turns him on his side, he lets out more groans. The camera moves slightly to the left, and we see and hear her rinse and wring the rag in the metal pan; the camera moves right and we see her begin to wipe the man's back with the damp rag. She turns the rag over.

Shot 3. *Part of the man's back and side is visible. The camera follows the woman's hand as she slowly wipes near his side (see photo). With a finger, she thumps or tickles his side.*

Shot 4. *As we see the man's face and shoulders, he giggles then quickly turns his head back toward the woman.*

MAN (*angry and loud*): Stop it!

With a serious look on his face, he lowers his head and faces forward again.

WOMAN (*unseen*): It hurts?

MAN (*still serious*): Yes!

Source: Teshigahara Productions & Toho; Pathe Contemporary Films

Although filmmakers typically prune the dialogue they adapt from fiction, in this scene the filmmakers of *Woman in the Dunes* chose to supply slightly more dialogue than is in the novel.[2]

Many differences between the passage in Abé's novel and the corresponding section of the film, however, result from the limitations of film in comparison with fiction. The novel gives many of the man's thoughts, including a memory, but to render these mental states in a film might confuse viewers. Look again at the last two paragraphs reprinted from the book. How can film accurately convey what those words do? Without words, how can a filmmaker convey the simile and the two implied metaphors in the sentences "Her charms were like some meat-eating plant, purposely equipped with the smell of sweet honey. First she would sow the seeds of scandal by bringing him to an act of passion, and then the chains of blackmail would bind him hand and foot"? The figurative language cannot be entirely converted into visual images and sounds, including music. Similarly, neither images nor sounds can convey well the experiences of smell, taste, and feeling. Thus, "A stagnant smell of sun-heated water, coming from her mouth, nose, ears, armpits, her whole body, began to pervade the room around him" cannot be captured by film.

Other differences between the passage and the film result from the limitations of fiction in comparison with film. In forty-five seconds, the film gives viewers an excellent sense of place, shape, volume, textures, and sounds. For example, we can see the forms and sizes of the man and woman; we can see the texture of the man's skin; we hear his groans and the tone of voice of the man and woman. Most of these details are not rendered in the comparable passage of fiction. To do so would require enormous space and slow the story to a crawl, and even then the images in the reader's mind would be less precise than the images and sounds of the film. The movie camera can select actions and render them with clarity and force (as in the second shot where the camera moves left, then right); it can capture movements and gestures and their significance (such as the man's spontaneous laugh, followed by a quick suppression of it). Film can convincingly show places, real and imaginary. It can juxtapose images more quickly than the blink of an eye.

Film can present visual details such as faces, the viewing of which, as scientist and educator David Attenborough has said, is itself extraordinarily expressive:

> Letting others know how you feel is a basic part of communication. No creature in the world does so more eloquently than man, and no organ is more visually expressive than his face. Even in repose, the human face sends a message and

---

[2]The title of the English translation of the novel is *The Woman in the Dunes*. The title of the English translation of the film is *Woman in the Dunes*.

one that we tend to take for granted. Each face proclaims individual identity. In teams, recognition of other members is of great importance. A hunting dog in a pack proclaims its identity by its own personal smell. Primates, with their reduced sense of smell but their very acute vision, do it by the infinite variety of their faces. We have more separate muscles in our faces than any other animal. So we can move it in a variety of ways that no other animal can equal and not only convey mood but send precise signals. By the expression on our face, we can call people and send them away, ask questions and return answers without a word being spoken.

Adept actors can express mood and meaning with facial expressions and can contribute much more. Michael Cunningham, author of *The Hours* (1998), has written with admiration about what the main female actors contributed to the 2002 film adaptation of his novel: "Actors . . . this good can introduce details you can't convey on paper. If only because by writing them down, you'd render them too obvious. Actors have the incidental at their disposal. Ms. [Meryl] Streep's Clarissa is stunningly complex, in part because she creates a whole person out of movements, expressions and inflections. . . . And when she finally begins to lose her desperate composure, there's a moment, you miss it if you blink—when she literally loses her balance, tips over to the left, and immediately rights herself. If there's a way to do things like that on paper, I haven't found it" (1).

JONIK
USA

"In the book she dies."

FIGURE 5.6
Copyright 1989 by John Jonik, from Movies Movies Movies: An Entertainment of Great Film Cartoons, *edited by S. Gross*

Film can also capture well the nuances of sound and music. Prose is hard pressed to compete with cinema in presenting what can be seen and heard and in making us feel that we are at a particular place.

As we saw illustrated by *The Player*, fictional films that are based on novels or short stories rarely re-create the source fiction in its entirety. In film stories, passages of characters' thoughts, descriptions of characters' backgrounds, analysis by the author, and a more or less consistent point of view or means of perception are uncommon. The order of scenes may also be changed. Especially in popular movies, the ending of the source novel is often changed to a happier, more crowd-pleasing conclusion (Figure 5.6). Nor does the fictional film usually re-create all the characters and action of a novel. *Greed*—the 1925 American film classic, which is a literal adaptation of the novel *McTeague*—attempted to do so, but the initial version reportedly ran nine and a half hours. Such a length was quickly judged too long to be marketable because it could be screened only in two or three lengthy installments, whereas a two-hour film can be shown several times a day and thus can generate more revenue. Soon *Greed* was edited down to about two hours. Even *Tom Jones* (1963), which critics have praised for capturing the structure, **events**, and moods of the long, complicated source novel, omits characters and events.

Reading fiction and seeing a film are different experiences because each medium has its own techniques, strengths, and limitations. Perhaps the basic difference between fiction and film is that fiction requires its audience to visualize and subvocalize from printed words, whereas film presents images and sounds directly. People who enjoyed a novel are rarely satisfied with a film made from it because, in part, they visualize the characters and events as they read, and the film presents different visuals and sounds. Then, too, sometimes readers are disappointed that film adaptations do not include all of the novel's characters or plot.

Fiction and film are distinct media, with their own strengths and weaknesses. It is misleading to judge a film by how closely it re-creates the story one visualizes while reading. Instead, the film is something related yet new and separate, a creative expression in a different medium with its own resources and techniques. Likewise, whenever a novel or play is based on a film, it is unfair and misleading to evaluate the later work in another medium by how well it re-creates the source film. If one takes the view that a derivative creative fictional work should be judged by its fidelity to its source(s), then, for example, many of Shakespeare's plays, such as *Macbeth* and *Richard III*, would be judged deficient: they are not reliable history but make for effective theater.

Instead of evaluating a film by comparing it to its fictional source, it is more helpful to compare the film version with other, similar films (and to compare the fiction with other, similar fiction). However, a close comparison of a film and its fictional source can be instructive, revealing what creative decisions were made during the transformation, what the two forms share, and what is distinct to each.[3]

> For a sample student essay about a fictional work adapted into a film, see the Close-Up section of this chapter on pp. 240–41.

event: In a narrative or story, either an *action* by a character or person or a *happening* (a change brought about by a force other than a person or character).

---

[3]Some authors, such as Gabriel García Márquez and E. L. Doctorow, and some film scholars have written about the many general ways movies have influenced the ways fiction is now often written—for example, with little initial description of setting, sparse initial exposition, shorter scenes, and a faster pace. Movies have also been responsible for a type of fiction, *novelizations*—paperback novels that re-create and expand the plots of recent movies. By first appearing usually a few weeks before the movie first comes out, these books help publicize the movie, but they are written and published rapidly and are usually judged as inferior fiction when compared with other published fiction.

Plays

In the early years of cinema, many fictional films closely imitated plays. After all, plays had been around the Western world for more than two thousand years, and in the 1890s people on both sides of the footlights had a good sense of what a play was. For this reason, many early films look like awkwardly filmed theater (Figure 5.7). Gradually, though, film developed its own identity. Today, the two forms are still cousins but are not as close as they were in film's first few decades.

Basically, plays are the more verbal medium. If you listen to a recording of a play, you will notice that much of its moods and meanings are communicated by the lines of dialogue and their delivery. So expressive is the human voice that a trained actor can convey a world of information and feeling by pauses, volume, timbre, timing, and pronunciation.

Films, in contrast, tend to be more visual. Several times I have begun a film course by giving students a list of questions to answer about a film, such as "Who is the main character? What does he or she seem to want? What does that character's personality seem to be like? Where and when does the story take place?" Then I turn off the volume and show students the beginning of a British film few of them have seen. I show the film clip twice. After each showing, I ask students to jot notes in answer to my questions and about anything else they noticed in the clip. Then I collect and read the responses aloud. The results: students generally come close to what the film is

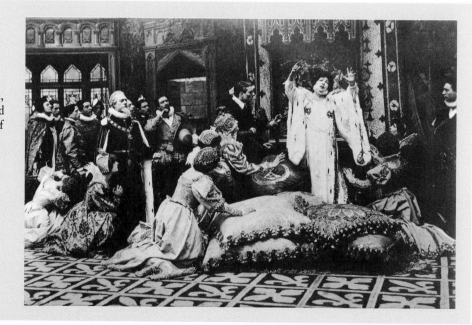

FIGURE 5.7 **Early film actors with theatrical backgrounds**
In the 1912 *Queen Elizabeth*, Sarah Bernhardt, one of the most famous actors of her era, played her part with the broad stylized gestures that actors of the day used so that they could be seen from distant seats in large theaters. Actors with theater experience had not yet learned to restrain their acting style for the movies. Frame enlargement. *The Museum of Modern Art/Film Stills Archive*

showing—with only its moving pictures. Films can convey so much information visually that the acclaimed 1924 silent German film *The Last Laugh* includes readable words only four times. Many movies—for example, *2001: A Space Odyssey* (1968) and Jane Campion's *The Piano* (1993)—have scenes with little or no dialogue or sign language. If you watch a foreign-language film with inadequate subtitles—and do not allow yourself to be distracted with thoughts about how annoying it is not to know all that is being said—you will understand a great deal from the film's visuals.

Some would argue that the essence of a play is at least one actor acting and reacting. Actors also interact with the audience. Experienced theater actors attest to how much an alert, responsive, and supportive audience contributes to their performance. Live acting differs markedly from the rehearsed, edited, larger-than-life performances shown from different distances and angles on the movie screen. The live actor is more nearly what we see in our lives outside the theater, someone who might even occasionally seem to look us in the eye, someone who makes imperfect delivery or has all-too-human movements. In small theaters where the audience is close to the stage, live acting may also seem more intimate.

Because of these basic differences between plays and films, certain changes tend to be made when a play is transformed into a film. Most filmmakers want to make a film, not simply record a performance of a play. A film version of a play tends to locate some of the scenes outdoors. This process is called "opening up" the play. With more scenes, it's not unusual for a film to have more characters than its source. The film derived from a play often prunes the play's dialogue and relies more on the visuals, music, and **sound effects**. And as we watch a film, we seem to get to sit in many seats and view the action from many distances and angles.

sound effect: A sound in film other than spoken words or music.

In staging a play, directors, actors, costumers, set designers, and others decide what words and actions to include, how to show the action and deliver the dialogue, how to costume the characters, and what the lighting and settings will be like. In the stage directions printed with their plays, some playwrights include details about how the plays should be staged. Other writers, such as Shakespeare, supply few such directions (perhaps in Shakespeare's case in part because he himself did not prepare his own plays for publication).

As we saw in the chapter on mise en scène, when a play is filmed, filmmakers make many of the same decisions that are made by people staging a play—about the selection of dialogue and actions, lighting, costuming, settings, and the like. However, filmmakers have many additional concerns, such as camera distances and angles, editing, and nearly always a more complex mixture of spoken words, sound effects, and music than is found in a staged play.

To see some of the differences between a play and one of its film adaptations, consider Shakespeare's *Richard III*, which was a play (probably first published in 1597) before it was a film (the version discussed below is the 1995

TABLE 5.5
Richard III: Scene 1 of the Play and the First 14 Scenes of the 1995 Film

[ ] = Dialogue deleted for the film. Boldface = dialogue added in the film. {   } = Additional information.

THE PLAY (first scene)

THE FILM
(first 14 scenes, 11 minutes, 34 seconds)

Act 1, Scene 1
London. A street.

Enter Richard, Duke of Gloucester, solus.

GLO. Now is the winter of our discontent
Made glorious summer by this sun of York,
And all the clouds that lowered upon our house
In the deep bosom of the ocean buried.
Now are our brows bound with victorious wreaths,
Our bruisèd arms hung up for monuments,
Our stern alarums changed to merry meetings,
Our dreadful marches to delightful measures.
Grim-visaged war hath smoothed his wrinkled front,
And now, instead of mounting barbèd steeds
To fright the souls of fearful adversaries,
He capers nimbly in a lady's chamber
To the lascivious pleasing of a lute.
But I, that am not shaped for sportive tricks,
Nor made to court an amorous looking-glass;
I, that am rudely stamped, [and want love's majesty
To strut before a wanton ambling nymph;
I, that am curtailed of this fair proportion,
Cheated of feature by dissembling nature,]
Deformed, unfinished, sent before my time
Into this breathing world, scarce half made up,
And that so lamely and unfashionable
That dogs bark at me as I halt by them—
Why, I, in this weak piping time of peace,
Have no delight to pass away the time,
Unless to spy my shadow in the sun
And descant on mine own deformity.
And therefore since I cannot prove a lover,
[To entertain these fair well-spoken days,]
I am determinèd to prove a villain
And hate the idle pleasures of these days.
Plots have I laid, [inductions dangerous,
By drunken prophecies, libels, and dreams,]
To set my brother Clarence and the King
In deadly hate the one against the other,

1. Field headquarters of King Henry VI's army at Tewkesbury. Richard kills the Prince of Wales and the prince's father, King Henry VI. Only dialogue in the scene: Son: "**Goodnight, your Majesty.**" King: "**Goodnight, son.**" Son: "**Father.**"

2. Richard is driven in an escorted car in London.

3. At the palace, young prince Edward playfully tries to avoid being dried after his bath.

4. Nurse to King Edward IV: "**Your Majesty.**" She gives him his medicine.

5. Clarence finishes developing some photos, grabs his coat and camera, and rushes off.

6. At the airport, Rivers gets off a plane and gives a stewardess his card.

7. Richard's motorcade arrives at the palace, and Richard gets out.

8. Richard addresses the Duchess of York as "**Mother,**" but she and her granddaughter, the young Elizabeth, pass by Richard without a word.

9. Clarence sets the camera timer and takes the York family photo.

   {Up to this point, the film has supplied information on three title cards and two superimposed title cards.}

10. At a party the Yorks throw to celebrate their victory over King Henry VI and the House of Lancaster, King Edward IV dances with his queen, Elizabeth. Richmond asks the young Elizabeth to dance. Buckingham and Richard greet each other warmly.

11. Outside, Rivers, the queen's brother, arrives by car; he gets out of the car and walks up the steps toward the party.

12. The queen dances with young Edward, her son and the heir to the throne. Rivers greets various people and dances with the queen and his young nephew Edward. Clarence is led away by several men. Richard steps up to the microphone and begins to speak {8 minutes, 47 seconds into the film}:

THE PLAY (continued)

[And if King Edward be as true and just
As I am subtle, false, and treacherous,
This day should Clarence closely be mewed up,
About a prophecy, which says that G
Of Edward's heirs the murderer shall be.
Dive, thoughts, down to my soul—here
    Clarence comes.]

Clarence enters, under guard. He is being taken
as a prisoner to the Tower. Richard acts surprised
and vows to help him.

After Clarence is led away, Richard, alone, reveals he plans to have Clarence killed.

Lord Hastings, who has recently been released
from imprisonment in the Tower himself, tells
Richard that King Edward IV is very ill.

Alone again, Richard reveals more about his
plans for Clarence and how Richard for tactical
reasons plans to marry Lady Anne, whose husband and father-in-law (King Henry VI) Richard
himself had killed.

THE FILM (continued)

Now is the winter of our discontent
Made glorious summer by this sun of York,
And all the clouds that lowered upon our house
In the deep bosom of the ocean buried.
Now are our brows bound with victorious wreaths,
Our bruisèd arms hung up for monuments,
Our stern alarums changed to merry meetings,
Our dreadful marches to delightful measures.
Grim-visaged war hath smoothed his wrinkled front,
And now, instead of mounting barbèd steeds
To fright the souls of fearful adversaries,
He 13. {Richard enters men's room} capers nimbly in a lady's
    chamber
To the lascivious pleasing of a lute.
But I, that am not shaped for sportive tricks,
Nor made to court an amorous looking-glass;
I, that am rudely stamped, [and want love's majesty
To strut before a wanton ambling nymph;
I, that am curtailed of this fair proportion,
Cheated of feature by dissembling nature,]
Deformed, {flushes urinal} unfinished, sent before my time
Into this breathing world, scarce half made up,
And that so lamely and unfashionable
That dogs bark at me as I halt by them—
Why, I, in this weak piping time of peace,
Have no delight to pass away the time,
Unless to espy my shadow in the sun
And descant on mine own deformity.
Why I can smile and murder while I smile
And wet my cheeks with artificial tears
And frame my face to all occasions.
And therefore since I cannot prove a lover,
[To entertain these fair well-spoken days,]
I am determinèd to prove a villain
And hate the idle pleasures of these days.
Plots have I laid {Richard leaves men's room} [inductions
    dangerous,
By drunken prophecies, libels, and dreams,]

14. {above a pier leading to a boat and some distance from it}
To set my brothers Clarence and [the] King **Edward**
In deadly hate the one against the other.
[And if King Edward be as true and just
As I am subtle, false, and treacherous,
This day should Clarence closely be mewed up,
About a prophecy, which says that G
Of Edward's heirs the murderer shall be.
Dive, thoughts, down to my soul—here Clarence comes.]

FIGURE 5.8 Main determinant of actions, consequences, and meanings
As in most Shakespearean film adaptations, in the 1995 version of *Richard III*, many changes were made between the play and film. The focus of the film, however, remains on Richard—his charm and political skills but also his utter ruthlessness (even to those who support him), his overreaching, and his fall from power—and finally, as in other Shakespearean dramas, the restoration of political order. *Lisa Katselas Paré and Stephen Bayly; United Artists*

production with Ian McKellen, Figure 5.8). Table 5.5 illustrates some of the similarities and differences between the play and the 1995 film version. In its fundamentals, the film adaptation remains faithful to the original play. The film's opening, for example, retains most of the play's dialogue; the personalities of the major characters are unchanged, and the focus stays on a disgruntled Richard setting in motion schemes to hurt others while advancing himself into a position of power.

Here, as in most plays transformed into films, there are many differences. The film shows actions only mentioned in the play—the murders of the Prince of Wales and his father, the king. As is usually the case when a play is compared with its corresponding film, the film version also has many more scenes and settings. In Shakespeare's play, the entire first scene takes place on a London street. The opening of the McKellen *Richard*, however, takes place in King Henry VI's field headquarters, on a London street, in the palace, at an airport, back at the palace, and near a docked boat. The film changes the setting of the play's opening soliloquy (which takes place on a London street) to two settings: before a large party and in a men's restroom. In the film, objects (car, airplane, palace, clothes) show the York family's wealth and power. Viewers may also notice that the uniforms and banners resemble those used by the Nazi regime in Germany, suggesting that York-ruled England is a fascist state. Unlike the play, the film uses five brief title cards to supply basic information about settings and situations. The film also has less dialogue than the play. During the film's first eight minutes and forty-seven seconds, only nine spoken words are heard (not counting the lyrics that a woman sings at the party). Of the play's forty-one-line first soliloquy, only thirty lines are used in the film plus three lines inserted from Act 3, Scene 2, of Shakespeare's *Henry VI, Part 3* (see the three consecutive lines in boldface in Table 5.5). As in nearly all films based on plays, the film relies more heavily on visuals than does the play.

Shakespeare's plays have been a deep and enduring well of inspiration for films. The stories have remained of interest to viewers, and Shakespeare's insights into human behavior are matched by perhaps only a few other writers in the history of Western literature. His language—though often difficult for modern audiences and in places obscure even to scholars who have dedicated their lives to its study—is often striking, apt, and memorable.

In transferring a play to the screen—especially Shakespeare's plays—filmmakers often take major liberties. Period, settings, costumes, and props may all be added or altered. Lines are nearly always pruned. The actors' gestures may suggest possible new interpretations. Consider the 2000 film *Hamlet*, with Ethan Hawke playing Hamlet. The setting is shifted from Denmark in approximately the year 1600 to New York City in 2000. Instead of scenes taking place in a castle at Elsinore, they are set in the Hotel Elsinore, a high-rise luxury hotel presumably near Times Square; a laundromat; a diner; and the Guggenheim Museum. In the action videos section in the neighborhood Blockbuster, Hamlet delivers part of his "To be, or not to be" soliloquy. Instead of traveling to England in a boat, Hamlet is transported via a jet. Costumes are not period clothing but what early twenty-first-century New Yorkers would wear. Props include the latest electronic gadgets, a pistol to supplement fencing foils, and a briefly glimpsed little rubber duck that Ophelia nearly returns to Hamlet along with his love letters. King Claudius is now a dapper new CEO of the Denmark Corp., although he is as smooth and treacherous as ever. Hamlet is an aspiring film/videomaker whose mousetrap to test the conscience of the king is not a play within the play but a film within the film. In this as in other *Hamlet*s, lines are pruned, characters are dropped, and whole scenes are eliminated. The performances also add new or at least unusual interpretive possibilities. The Laertes of this first filmic *Hamlet* of the new century, for example, seems to have a stronger than brotherly attachment to his sister Ophelia. She seems here more emotionally pained and more prone to serious instability than she does in many earlier productions. Gertrude seems to sense that the cup of wine Claudius offers Hamlet is poisoned and drinks from it anyway. The results are another *Hamlet*: same basic plot, same language—in what remains of Shakespeare's lines—but a *Hamlet* that the makers of the film doubtless hoped would attract and engage a new generation.

There are exceptions to the above generalizations about films and plays. Some films—*My Dinner with André* (1981), for example—have much in common with traditional plays: few scenes, much dialogue, and limited visuals. And some recent plays have much in common with films—scores of short scenes, many settings, and sparse dialogue.[4]

Television

Television has long been a source for movies, especially since the box office success of *The Addams Family* (1991). Since then, U.S. studios have made a slew of TV shows into movies, including *The Fugitive* (1993), *The Beverly Hillbillies* (1993), *The Flintstones* (1994), *Mission Impossible* (1996), *The Rugrats Movie* (1998), *The X-Files* (1998), *South Park: Bigger, Longer and Uncut* (1999), *Mission: Impossible 2* (2000), *Charlie's Angels* (2000), *Traffic* (2000), *I Spy* (2002), *Charlie's Angels: Full Throttle* (2003), and many others that were not box office or critical successes, such as *Lost in Space* (1998). TV has been a frequent source for the characters and plots of movies and the writers, actors, and directors who bring them to life on the big screen. Perhaps almost as often, TV borrows from films. It is a two-way street with heavy traffic. The mutual dependence of one medium on the other has become so commonplace that knowledge of the relationship of the two media deepens one's understanding of both.

The TV medium itself has also been a subject for films. Commercial television's proclivity to present a sanitized and artificial world was a subject of several late 1990s films. In *Pleasantville* (1998), David wishes that his life were more like the TV series *Pleasantville*, a re-creation of 1950s sitcoms

---

[4]In recent decades, films increasingly influence plays, in both the writing and the staging. Sometimes plays discuss or allude to films, which happens in *The Baltimore Waltz* (1990), a play that refers to the films *The Third Man* (1949), *Dr. Strangelove: Or, How I Learned to Stop Worrying and Love the Bomb* (1963), and *Wuthering Heights* (1939). Plays may also be structured as a film typically is. In general, recent plays consist of many more brief scenes than plays had before the arrival of cinema. *The Baltimore Waltz*, for example, has thirty scenes during its approximately eighty minutes of playing time. Often, staging is influenced by films. A 1996 production of *Four Dogs and a Bone* added video versions of imaginary film footage made during a day's work.

For many decades, Broadway supplied many of Hollywood's most successful musical films, such as *Oklahoma!*, *South Pacific*, *West Side Story*, *My Fair Lady*, *Chicago*, and many others. Now, that trend has somewhat reversed, as films become the sources of musical plays. Examples are *Sunset Boulevard*; *Victor/Victoria*; the MGM musicals *Singin' in the Rain*, *Meet Me in St. Louis*, and *Seven Brides for Seven Brothers*; the Disney hits *The Little Mermaid*, *Beauty and the Beast*, and *The Lion King*; *The Full Monty* (with an American setting); *The Producers*; and *Hairspray*. From time to time, films are still the basis of nonmusical plays, as with *The Graduate*, which has played in both New York and London. Plays may also be based on a movie topic or type. An example is *Action Movie: The Play—The Director's Cut*, a 1998 parody of action movies.

FIGURE 5.9 TV as source and subject for a film
In the scene from *Natural Born Killers* (1994) represented by this image fifty-five minutes and fifty-three seconds into the director's cut DVD, the main male character is finally caught by police officers, who give him a savage, prolonged beating as TV crews film the event. The scene is reminiscent of the widely publicized TV broadcasts of police officers beating Rodney King in Los Angeles. *Natural Born Killers* shows the story of two murderous lovers and their victims, most prominently law enforcement officers, prison guards, a prison warden (indirectly), and a TV tabloid journalist. The police officer/author who murders a prostitute, the warden who is twisted by hatred of the murdering couple, and the TV host of *American Maniacs* are also satirized—the TV tabloid journalist most of all for his self-promotion, thin veneer of self-control, pride, and pandering to the worst in human nature. The frequent music, garish saturated colors bathing entire scenes, fast cutting, occasional lack of continuity within scenes, inclusion of images from the couple's minds within scenes of the couple, and frequent use of Dutch angles all contribute to the hallucinatory or nightmarish quality of the film, which at times looks and sounds like a music video. Frame enlargement. *Regency; Warner Bros.*

such as (*The Adventures of*) *Ozzie and Harriet* (1952–1966) and *Leave It to Beaver* (1957–1963). Because David's family life and social life are frustrating, he is attracted to the stable and comforting lives he sees on the show. In this fictional world, it's always 72 degrees and sunny, divorce is nonexistent, there is no conflict, Mom is always home to make dinner and cookies, and one of the prettiest girls in school is eager to date David. Nevertheless, when he and his sister become trapped in the TV show as two black-and-white characters, David slowly realizes that the sanitized world of Pleasantville is artificial and constricting. While this fifties TV world is safe, it also precludes opportunity for individualism, creativity, and deeply felt emotions. Like the widely held view of the 1950s as a decade, Pleasantville is colorless and is characterized by a restricted range of options. *The Truman Show* (1998) provides much the same image of TV shows. The movie focuses on a character who eventually realizes his life in an idealized small town is controlled by a television producer and that his entire life is being broadcast for the benefit of a huge television audience. Like Disneyland, which itself is a creation of the 1950s, *Pleasantville* and *The Truman Show* present a world that is safe, sanitized, and reassuring—at least initially.

Movies often **satirize** television, as in *Network* (1976), which shows the extremes to which an unpopular fictional TV network will go to achieve higher ratings. The satire of tabloid TV coverage found in Oliver Stone's *Natural Born Killers* (1994) is similar though more biting (Figure 5.9). In that film, Wayne Gale, the host of a sensational TV tabloid show, *American Maniacs*, will do anything to get a story. The film satirizes the American public's love affair with violence—especially when it is largely used against authorities—by

satire: A representation that indirectly exposes and perhaps ridicules individual or group thinking or behavior for being foolish, evil, or stupid or for exhibiting some other shortcoming.

showing how ratings-hungry journalists turn two killers into international celebrities. Gale's behavior reveals the extremes to which a reporter will go to use sensational news to get spectacular ratings. The film also shows how a smug journalist loses control of himself, gets caught up in a prison escape, and shoots at prison guards, assuming he is safe because he holds the TV camera. One of the most prominent satiric targets in *Bamboozled* (2000) is the programming of commercial TV run by European Americans who do not understand African American culture(s) yet are eager to present tired, offensive racial **stereotypes** in the name of entertainment. The film also satirizes TV audiences who eagerly lap up the rancid old wine poured from new bottles (see Figure 10.11 on p. 483).

Two other sources for films, though rarely the main sources, are TV commercials and music videos. Commentator Maria Demopoulos points out that directors of music videos seek "to translate into film the ethos characteristic of the young demographic of the music: rebellion, defiance, individuality, teen angst. Music videos, by design, reflect a youth-driven agenda, distinguished by impermanence and disposability" (36). Often, these are the same subjects and outlook of teen movies. Demopoulos also points out that the techniques and ideas of TV commercials and music videos have influenced filmmakers and vice versa:

> The techniques and ideas behind these short formats have crossed over to **feature films**. Commercials and music videos have long served as a testing ground for visual styles migrating upward, and at the same time have spawned a new generation of directors. . . . Still, the influence flows both ways. Much of the raw material mined for music videos and commercials derives from films in the first place. The video-as-movie-adventure-epic, for instance, dates back to MTV's infancy with Duran Duran's video "Hungry Like the Wolf" ([directed by] Russell Mulcahy, [19]82). (35)

Commentators concur that the two short TV formats have influenced moviemaking most notably in editing. It seems likely that viewing both TV commercials, including movie **trailers**, and music videos has conditioned a new generation of viewers to process a succession of images more quickly than earlier generations. Because so many viewers have seen so many TV commercials and music videos, filmmakers have the option of doing less continuity editing and more editing by association, intuition, or accident, as in sections of *Natural Born Killers*.

TV has also borrowed from film. Television parodies of movies or parts of movies have a long history in the United States, going all the way back to TV's birth and providing subjects for performers like Milton Berle, Sid Caesar, Imogene Coca, and Carol Burnett and the show *Saturday Night Live*. A Thanksgiving episode of *South Park* (Episode 109, "Starvin' Marvin," 1997) provides another instance of TV borrowing from film. In that episode, an attack by vengeful turkeys is made even more amusing because it parodies the epic battle scenes in *Braveheart* (1995). Over the years, various popular

stereotype: A commonplace, simplified, and in some ways inaccurate representation (likeness of a subject created in a text).

feature (film): A fictional film that is at least sixty minutes long.

trailer: A brief compilation film made to advertise a movie or a video release.

movies, such as *M*A*S*H* (1970) and *Buffy the Vampire Slayer* (1992), have also led to TV series.

The relationship between the two media is sometimes complex. The successful transformation of the 1966–1969 *Star Trek* TV series into six films is an example of this mutual dependence. The first Star Trek movie, *Star Trek: The Motion Picture* (1979), reunited the television cast from the *U.S.S. Enterprise*; it was followed by five sequels and inspired a new television series. In the second TV series, crew members can walk onto the "holograph deck" of the *Enterprise* and enter simulated environments that are often inspired by films or are informed by film aesthetics.

Although television and film now provide innumerable sources for each other, they have not always coexisted amicably. When television appeared on the American national scene in force during the 1950s, its arrival coincided with a time when Hollywood was floundering. During the war years of 1941 to 1945 and the postwar years from 1946 to 1948, Hollywood experienced its most profitable period. During the war, weekly attendance was estimated at ninety million people, a number that was five times the weekly attendance number in the mid-1990s (Cook 442). This wartime boom for the movie industry, however, slowed in the late forties and early fifties as television viewing grew. By 1949, movie attendance had dropped from ninety million to seventy million. In the same year, there were one million television sets in the United States. By 1951, the number of sets had climbed to ten million, and by 1959, it had reached fifty million (Cook 459). For some years, television and film competed intensely for the same audience. Hollywood's initial reaction was to refuse to interact with television or even acknowledge its existence. Members of the Motion Picture Association of America would not lease or sell their films for broadcast until 1956, and many film **studios** refused to allow their stars to appear on television (Cook 459). Gradually and haltingly, movie studios got into TV production, and media conglomerates included movie and TV production components under one corporate umbrella. Today, TV and film have grown more comfortable with—or at least more resigned to—their marriage, though flashes of envy and condescension remain.

For more information on the development of TV and other mass media, see the third column of the chronology for 1895 to 2003 (see pp. 559-610).

Other Films

I'm often asked by younger filmmakers why do I need to look at old movies. . . . I'm always looking for something or someone that I can learn from. I tell the younger filmmakers and young students: do it like painters used to do, what painters do. Study the old masters. Enrich your palette. Expand the canvas. There is always so much more to learn.

—Martin Scorsese

a)   b)

FIGURE 5.10 A literal remake
(a) A frame from the 1960 *Psycho* shows Norman Bates in the parlor behind the motel office as he talks with the young woman who has recently checked into the motel. (b) A frame from the comparable shot in the 1998 remake, also called *Psycho*. Here as throughout the remake, the plot, mise en scène, camera work, editing, and soundtrack all closely or sometimes fairly closely re-create the original film.

Typically, new and more recognizable actors are employed for the remake, and if the original was in black and white, color is usually used instead, as it was in the 1998 *Psycho*. The remake of *Psycho*, which did not do well at the box office, illustrates that a literal remake of a famous movie will not necessarily attract large audiences. Frame enlargements. *Universal*

IMITATIONS

Filmmakers may imitate earlier films, either in part or (less commonly) in their entirety. Like an adaptation of any earlier text, an imitation may be one of three basic types: loose (it retains only a few major aspects of the original, such as only the title and one or two of its subjects); faithful (it imitates the subject and perhaps style of the original and captures its mood or spirit but with some changes); or literal (as nearly as possibly it re-creates the sources). Imitations of texts or, more often, parts of texts may take the form of a remake, an allusion, a parody, or an homage.

In a remake, the original film or part of a film is re-created but usually updated: changes are made in the hope that the remake will seem more appealing to current audiences. Remakes are attractive to producers because the original film usually made a lot of money and some of the public will remember it favorably and be curious to see a modern version of it. For economic reasons, then, remakes have been plentiful in Hollywood (Figure 5.10).

Loose remakes are plentiful. An example are the remakes of the classic American comedy *It Happened One Night* (1934), which has twice been remade in India as *Chori Chori* (1956) and *Dil Hai Ke Manta Nahin* (1991) but with changes:

> Whenever a Hollywood film is remade in India it has to be recast in the Indian mould, that is, emotions have to be overstated, song, dances and spectacle have to be added, family relationships have to be introduced if they do not exist in the original, traditional moral values such as dharma (duty) must be reiterated and female chastity must be eulogised. Only then will the film find success at the box office. (Kasbekar 412)

In their fast pace, frequent cliff-hanging action, and exotic costumes and locations, the *Star Wars* movies, *Indiana Jones* movies, and many other action movies can be seen as loose but high-budget remakes of **serials**, including the Flash Gordon serials and Buck Rogers serials (Figure 5.11).

In *What's Up, Tiger Lily?* (1966) Woody Allen remade only the soundtrack of a Japanese movie by deleting the original soundtrack and adding new dialogue, music, and sound effects to tell a very different, often amusing story about the complicated adventures of a Japanese James Bond–like secret agent, Phil Moscowitz. In various ways, the soundtrack reuses parts of many earlier texts. Two examples: viewers briefly hear voice imitations of such famous earlier movie stars as James Cagney and Peter Lorre, and occasionally the film includes clips of The Lovin' Spoonful performing songs that have nothing to do with the story.

serial: From the 1910s until the early 1950s, a low-budget action film divided into chapters or installments, one of which was shown each week in downtown and neighborhood movie theaters.

If you examine one of the reference books, CD-ROMs, or Web sites that describes and evaluates thousands of films, you may be surprised by how many hundreds and hundreds of them are remakes. A later film with the same title, however, does not guarantee that it is a remake because many titles are reused for a different story (both film stories and titles get recycled, but not necessarily together).

An **allusion** is a reference to an earlier text or part of one. Filmmakers may allude to an earlier text for various reasons—for example, "to acknowledge their own debt to other directors, to enrich their work with the themes and emotions associated with the earlier work, or simply as an ironic contrast to their own characters and situations" (Konigsberg 9). Allusions are also a way to share aspects of a culture. Occasionally, filmmakers make allusions to their own earlier films. In two scenes in *The Sure Thing* (1985), directed by Rob

FIGURE 5.11 A serial
From the teens of the twentieth century to the early 1950s, serials were shown in short weekly installments in neighborhood and downtown movie theaters. They featured extensive, fast-paced action; danger for the heroes; occasional episodes of tepid romance; and exotic villains, costumes, and settings. Seen here is a publicity still for one of the twelve episodes of the popular serial *Buck Rogers* (1939). Hero Buck Rogers, played by Larry (Buster) Crabbe, is seen in the center.
Universal; British Film Institute Stills, Posters and Designs

FIGURE 5.12 An allusion to a friend's earlier work
George Lucas directed *American Graffiti* (1973); his friend
Francis Coppola co-produced it. About 79¼ minutes into
the film and on a background movie marquee, the attentive viewer can briefly spot *Dementia 13*, the title of an
early Coppola film. If *American Graffiti* is not seen in letterbox format, the title on the marquee is excluded from
the image. Frame enlargement. *Francis Coppola and Gary
Kurtz; Universal*

Reiner, a poster for *This Is Spinal Tap* (1984), also directed by Reiner, is visible briefly in the background. In a scene in *Spaceballs* (1987), which was
produced and directed by Mel Brooks, a shelf on a spaceship contains
videotapes of films directed by Brooks! In *American Graffiti* (1973), director
George Lucas makes a sly allusion to an earlier film directed by the film's
co-producer (Figure 5.12). Such is human creativity that it is even possible
to make an allusion to a work that initially seems to have been made by
someone else but was in fact also made by the person
making the allusion. Pedro Almodóvar's *Talk to Her*
(2002) includes excerpts from an unusual black-and-
white silent film called "The Shrinking Lover," which
was in fact the creation of Almodóvar. One could label
such usages *mock allusions* (Figure 5.13).

FIGURE 5.13 A mock allusion
Beginning a little more than sixty-one minutes into
Pedro Almodóvar's *Talk to Her* (2002), the film includes excerpts from a black-and-white silent film that
Almodóvar himself created. In the film within the
film, the man had consumed an untested drug and
shrunk to the size seen here, but he and his lover remain devoted to each other. Frame enlargement.
Agustín Almodóvar; Sony Pictures Classics

More often, allusions are made by one filmmaker
to the work of earlier filmmakers. *Babe: Pig in the City*
(1998) includes frequent references to other texts as
amusing, enjoyable rewards for informed adult viewers
(Figure 5.14). And in both her personality and her
manner of speaking, the pink poodle in *Babe: Pig in the
City* is reminiscent of a major character in *A Streetcar
Named Desire*, both the play and first film adaptation
of it. In *Analyze This* (1999), the Billy Crystal character, a psychiatrist, has a dream that imitates shot by
shot the scene in *The Godfather* where two men attempt to assassinate the godfather as he is buying oranges from a street vendor, and his youngest son
fumbles his chance to protect his father. A scene about
eighty-five minutes into *American Pie* (1999) alludes to
the popular 1967 film *The Graduate*. The scene shows
a situation similar to one in the earlier film and includes an excerpt from "Mrs. Robinson," one of *The*

FIGURE 5.14 Allusion as a bonus
In *Babe: Pig in the City* (1998), the pit bull's manner of speaking and low, gravelly voice make him sound like a movie gangster. Critic Christopher Kelly points out a connection between the representation of the dog and *The Godfather* (1972): "the pit bull . . . sounds like Vito Corleone's long-lost pet" (42). In a speech recalling the making-an-offer-that-he-couldn't-refuse story in *The Godfather*, after Babe saves the pit bull's life, the dog steps forward and addresses the other animals: "I'd like to offer up a solution that I feel confident you'll all respond to. Whatever the pig says goes. Anyone hostile to the notion?"
Such an allusion is a source of amusement and pleasure for viewers with a broad knowledge of American culture but will pass unnoticed by those unfamiliar with the earlier texts. Frame enlargement. *A Kennedy Miller Film; Universal*

Graduate's best-known songs. In the scene, a virginal high school male is alone with the earthy mom of one of his classmates, and we sense that they are becoming attracted to each other as a few bars of the popular song are heard.

A **parody** is an amusing imitation of human behavior or of a more serious text, part of a text, or groups of texts. In a parody, viewers who know the subject that is being parodied recognize similarities yet see amusing differences. Parody may result from re-creating highly selected excerpts from the original story, as in "The Fifteen Minute Hamlet" (1996), which reenacts snippets of the original play (and delivers the lines at maximum speed). For example, as Laertes is dying, he is cut off in midsentence, and instead of the original "Exchange forgiveness with me noble Hamlet," we hear "Exchange forgiveness with me noble Ham." A feature film may be a pastiche of allusions and parodies. *Scary Movie* (2000) parodies the various *Scream* and *What You Did Last Summer* movies and parts of *The Exorcist* (1973), *The Blair Witch Project* (1999), *The Sixth Sense* (1999), *The Matrix* (1999), *The Usual Suspects* (1995), and others. *Not Another Teen Movie* (2001) parodies subjects and scenes from numerous (mostly) teen movies, including *The Breakfast Club* (1985) and other John Hughes movies, *Cruel Intentions* (1999), *American Pie* (1999), *Bring It On* (2000), *Never Been Kissed* (1999), and *American Beauty* (1999). A single movie is rarely the main subject of an entire movie parody, although the original *Star Wars* (1977) is an exception (Figure 5.15).

Films that parody a film **genre** or group of movies include *The Rocky Horror Picture Show* (1975), mainly a musical parody of classic horror movies like the 1931 *Frankenstein* (Figure 5.16). Other films that parody a genre or group of films include *Blazing Saddles* (1974), a parody of western films (see Figure 7.23 on p. 314); the Austin Powers movies, which parody James Bond movies; and "The Dove" (or "De Duva"), a 1968 film parody of several earnest films

genre ("ZHAHN ruh"): A commonly recognized group of fictional films that share characteristics both filmmakers and audiences recognize as making the films members of the same group.

FIGURE 5.15 Parodies of a film or films
Star Wars (1977) is parodied by "Hardware Wars" (1978).
Star Wars and other science fiction movies are parodied by
Spaceballs (1987). (a) A widely distributed image for *Star
Wars* shows (left to right) Chewbacca, Luke Skywalker, Obi-
Wan Kenobi, and Han Solo in Solo's Millennium Falcon.
(b) The image from "Hardware Wars," with its low-budget
setting (here a stripped-down "space vehicle" sporting dangling dice in the window), includes dim actors and a spaced-
out or nauseous Cookie Monster: left to right, Wookie
Monster, Fluke Starbucker, Augie "Ben" Doggie, and Ham
Salad. (c) Late in *Spaceballs*, this scene takes place inside a
recreational vehicle spacecraft: from left to right, Barf (who's
half man, half dog, and his own best friend), Dot Matrix (a
protective female robot with the voice of Joan Rivers),
Princess Vespa (the endangered damsel), and Lone Starr
(the heroic pilot).

How marvelous the powers of the human mind: while
watching both "Hardware Wars" and *Spaceballs*, many viewers immediately recognize similarities to *Star Wars* and
laugh at the differences. The compositions are the same, the
setting roughly the same, but the characters are amusingly
different. Parodies of the various *Star Wars* films and *Star
Wars* characters—such as "Star Wars Gangsta Rap," "Who
Wants to Marry Darth Maul?," "Trooper Clerks," and "Pink
Five"—and even of *Star Wars* films' trailers have been extremely popular on the Web. (a) *Lucasfilm Ltd.;* (b) *Michael
Wiese; Pyramid Film and Video, Santa Monica;* (c) *Mel Brooks;
MGM*

a)

b)

c)

by the Swedish director Ingmar Bergman. The more unamusing the original
subject being parodied is and the better the viewer knows it, the more amusing
the parody might be. Thus, to those who know well the early films directed by
Bergman, "The Dove" is especially amusing. The Swedish of the original
films becomes the mock Swedish of "The Dove," as when Death says, "All
dem peoples bin feelin my presenska zooner or latska," the English subtitle
reads, "Yes, all mankind feels my presence eventually." And "He must've
morten in da blacka" is translated as "He must have died at night."

Other films are parodies of documentary films. At first, these **mock
documentary** films (sometimes called *mock docs* or *mockumentaries*) may

FIGURE 5.16 A parody of a film genre
The Rocky Horror Picture Show (1975) is a parody mostly of horror films, especially various Frankenstein movies. (a) The Dr. Frankenstein–type character (center) is the "scientist" Dr. Frank N. Furter, a homosexual transvestite from the distant planet of Transylvania. His assistant, Riff Raff (left), at first looks and acts like Dr. Frankenstein's hunchback assistant of the 1931 *Frankenstein*. (b) Near the end of *The Rocky Horror Picture Show*, Riff Raff dresses (at least from the hips up) and acts as if he stepped out of a 1930s low-budget sci-fi serial or movie. *20th Century–Fox*

seem to be factual and to follow the **conventions** of documentary filmmaking, such as the use of interviews, subtitles, and handheld camera shots. Mock documentaries do not *mock* documentaries; however, they imitate them in playful, humorous ways. They are amusing fictional imitations using documentary filmmaking techniques. *This Is Spinal Tap* is purportedly a documentary about an inept, aging heavy-metal band (Figure 5.17). *Fear of a Black Hat* (1994) is supposedly a documentary film about the endless problems confronted by a hip-hop group, including troubles with various recording companies, rivalries with other hip-hop groups, and losing their managers to gunfire—six of them in a row! The film uses (and sometimes exaggerates) the techniques of **cinéma vérité**, such as handheld camera work, interviews, and surprising, supposedly even embarrassing developments for the film's subjects. *A Mighty Wind* (2003) uses such techniques as interviews, subtitles, excerpts from TV news programs, and clips from home movies to impart a documentary feel. But it's a completely fictional and wryly satirical film about a reunion concert of three 1960s folk music groups, each of which takes itself very seriously, though some viewers will immediately recognize professional movie actors in the cast, such as Bob Balaban and Paul Dooley, and know that the film is not a documentary.

convention: In films and other texts, a subject or technique that makers of texts and audiences have grown to accept as natural or typical in certain contexts.

FIGURE 5.17 **The mock documentary: a fictional film that parodies documentary films** *This Is Spinal Tap* (1984) imitates rock documentaries in amusing ways. The film has two main subjects. One is an imaginary earnest documentary filmmaker who interviews and supposedly films the heavy metal band, Spinal Tap. The other main subject is the aging and largely forgotten band itself, which "earned a distinguished place in rock history as one of England's loudest bands," and various people connected to the band, including its hapless manager and the girlfriend of one of the band members. *This Is Spinal Tap* uses the techniques of many documentaries—such as handheld camera work, clips from TV shows, subtitles, and interviews—to record the group members as they suffer one amusing setback after another. Once viewers figure out that *This Is Spinal Tap* is a parody of earnest rock documentary films, they can enjoy its creativity, playfulness, and humor. *Spinal Tap Prod.; Embassy Pictures, Inc.*

FIGURE 5.18 **Documentary or mock documentary?** In *20 Dates* (1998), the main subject, Myles, is on a date with Christian, who called herself a feminist ballerina. After he points out to her that a hidden movie camera has been photographing their date, Myles says "her reaction was disappointing—and surprisingly violent." In the next scene, viewers learn she had attacked him, necessitating twenty stitches in his hand, and was suing him for invasion of her civil rights (the second of his dates to file a lawsuit). Is *20 Dates* a documentary or an amusing mock documentary where a lot goes wrong for the main subject? Frame enlargement. *Phoenician Films; Fox Searchlight Pictures*

Occasionally, it is difficult to be certain if a film is a documentary or a mock documentary (Figure 5.18). Many reviewers interpreted *20 Dates* (1998) as a documentary with perhaps a few staged scenes. Other viewers, however, see the film as a mock documentary. By the end of the film, no viewer can say with certainty which parts are factual and which are fictional. However, so many things go wrong for Myles and the film has such a tidy happy ending (Myles succeeds in both his work and his love life), that the entire film or most of it may be a mock documentary or amusing fiction

TABLE 5.6
Part of an Homage

NEAR THE END OF *CASABLANCA* (1942)

. . .

RICK: I'm staying here with him [Renault] till the plane gets safely away.

ILSA: No, Richard, no! What happened to you? Last night we said —

RICK: Last night we said a great many things. You said I was to do the thinking for both of us. Well, I've done a lot of it since then and it all adds up to one thing. You're getting on that plane with Victor where you belong.

ILSA: But Richard, no, I—

RICK: Now you've got to listen to me. Do you have any idea what you'd have to look forward to if you stayed here? Nine chances out of ten we'd both wind up in a concentration camp. (looking off-screen) Isn't that true, Louis?

RENAULT: I'm afraid Major Strasser would insist.

ILSA: You're saying this only to make me go.

RICK: I'm saying it because it's true. Inside of us we both know you belong with Victor. You're part of his work. The thing that keeps him going. If that plane leaves the ground and you're not with him, you'll regret it.

ILSA: No.

RICK: Maybe not today, maybe not tomorrow, but soon, and for the rest of your life. . . .

Casablanca: Hal B. Wallis; Warner Bros. Play It Again, Sam: Arthur P. Jacobs; Paramount; British Film Institute Stills, Posters and Designs

NEAR THE END OF *PLAY IT AGAIN, SAM* (1972)

. . .

ALLAN [the character played by Woody Allen]: Linda, we have to call it quits.

LINDA: Yes, I know.

ALLAN: (shocked) Pardon me?

LINDA: Suddenly everything became very clear. And when I asked myself, do I really wanta break off my marriage? The answer is no. I love Dick. And although somebody as wonderful as you is very tempting, I can't imagine my life without'm.

ALLAN: You can't?

LINDA: He needs me, Allan. In some unexplainable way, I need him.

ALLAN: I know he needs you.

LINDA: This is the first time I've ever been affected by anyone besides Dick. I'm already in love with you. And unless I stop it now, I'll become too deeply involved to be able to go back to him. Oh, I don't regret a moment of what's happened because—what it's done for me is to reaffirm—my feelings for Dick.

ALLAN: Linda, I understand, really.

LINDA: Are you sure? You're not just saying that to make things easy?

ALLAN: No, I'm saying it because it's true. Inside of us, we both know you belong to Dick. You're part of his work. The thing that keeps him going. If that plane leaves the ground and you're not on it with him, you'll regret it. Maybe not today, maybe not tomorrow, but soon, and for the rest of your life.

LINDA: That's beautiful.

ALLAN: It's from *Casablanca*. I waited my whole life to say it. . . .

disguised as a documentary. In general, reviewers who interpreted the film as a documentary judged it negatively, whereas those who saw the film as a "mock doc" and were amused by it valued it more highly.

Unlike a parody, an **homage** is a tribute to a person or a text or part of one. It may be a respectful reference to or an affectionate re-creation of parts of an earlier film. An example occurs near the end of *Play It Again, Sam* (1972), which echoes part of the ending of *Casablanca* (1942), but the laughter is not at *Casablanca*'s expense but at Woody Allen's movie (Table 5.6). Homages may be verbal or visual or—as the example from *Play It Again, Sam* illustrates—both. Perhaps the films of Alfred Hitchcock have elicited the most homages. A British Film Institute booklet lists twenty selected homages to Hitchcock in such films as *High Anxiety* (1977), *Basic Instinct* (1992), and *Twelve Monkeys* (1995) (*Hitchcock* 14).

SEQUELS AND PREQUELS

Another source for a movie is a sequel. If a film is popular and later filmmakers see ways to continue the story and develop it, they may make a sequel. Because Hollywood sequels have proven generally profitable in recent years, more and more of them are getting made. Half of the top ten grossing films in the United States in 2001 were sequels. If the ending of a popular fictional film seems too final (the main character dies, for example), a sequel based on one of the main characters' offspring may be made, as in the sequel to *King Kong* (1933), *Son of Kong* (1933). Since 1997, the death of a protagonist no longer precludes a sequel. Thanks to cloning, the main character of the *Alien* movies was reconstructed from leftovers before the plot of *Alien Resurrection* (1997) begins.

Although sequels are often profitable, they usually disappoint viewers. Todd Berliner has studied sequels and concluded, "The almost inescapable failure of sequels results from the fact that, at the same time a sequel calls to mind the charismatic original, it also recalls its absence, fostering a futile, nostalgic desire to reexperience the original aesthetic moment as though it had never happened. . . . Sequels . . . can only *remind* us of the original film, and continually and conspicuously fail to reinvoke that initial pleasure" (109). Professor Berliner goes on to point out that the makers of a sequel usually try to compensate for the sequel's "sense of absence and loss" by supplying excessive amounts of whatever audiences seem to have enjoyed in the original, such as fast-paced action and violence (109).

Occasionally, a movie is the inspiration for a **prequel**: a movie that depicts some of the characters from a previous film at earlier stages of their lives. *Butch Cassidy and the Sundance Kid* appeared in 1969; in 1979, *Butch and Sundance: The Early Days* came out. More widely known examples are the three prequels to the original three *Star Wars* movies: *Star Wars: Episode I—The Phantom Menace* (1999), *Star Wars: Episode II: The Attack of the Clones* (2002), and *Star Wars: Episode III* (Figure 5.19). It's also possible but rare for a film to

a)   b)

FIGURE 5.19 A film and its prequels
As is well known, the second three *Star Wars* movies are prequels to the first three, and view-ers are introduced to the adult Darth Vader (a) in the first three films before meeting his younger self (b) as here in the first of the three prequels. *George Lucas; 20th Century–Fox*

be both a prequel and a sequel, as in the case of *The Godfather, Part II* (1974), which has related events involving the same characters that precede and fol-low the story of *The Godfather* (1972). Many other family trees are possible: *Nutty Professor II: The Klumps* (2000), for example, is a sequel to a remake.[5]

---

[5]Sometimes art is an important source for films. At various times in film history, painters and other visual artists have been especially prominent in making films. Two such periods were the 1920s in Europe and the 1950s and 1960s in the United States (pop art). Filmmak-ers have also long learned from painters, especially in the use of lighting, composition, color, and grain. Such filmmakers as Martin Scorsese in *The Last Temptation of Christ* (1988), Stan-ley Kubrick in *Barry Lyndon* (1975), Tony Richardson in *Tom Jones* (1963), Derek Jarman in *Caravaggio* (1986), Peter Greenaway in *The Cook, The Thief, His Wife and Her Lover* (1989), and Carlos Saura in *Goya in Bordeaux* (1999) have all imitated particular painters and some-times specific paintings. In recent years, some filmmakers have made artworks, including temporary museum exhibitions involving two or more arts (**installation art**), and increas-ingly museums of modern or contemporary art include film or video art combined with other media (see pp. 382–84).

MULTIPLE SOURCES

Although most fictional films derive mainly from history, fiction, a play, a TV show or series, or previous films, they inevitably have more complicated ancestries. Such is the case with *Cabaret* (1972). A story—"Sally Bowles" in the 1939 book *Goodbye to Berlin* by Christopher Isherwood—was the basis for the play *I Am a Camera*, which was filmed in 1955 and made into a Broadway musical, called *Cabaret*, in 1966. The film version of *Cabaret*, with Liza Minnelli and Joel Grey, appeared in 1972. *Music of the Heart* (1999) is based on the 1996 documentary film *Small Wonders*, which in turn was based on a published essay.

Even when a film seems to have one main source, lesser influences are at work. The film *Dangerous Liaisons* (1988), with a screenplay by Christopher Hampton, is based on Hampton's 1985 British play *Les liaisons dangereuses*, but that play in turn was based on the 1782 French novel of the same title, which had many other sources itself, including two earlier epistolary novels, one of them English (Duyfhuizen 46 and 47; see Table 5.7). Another influence on the 1782 French novel is the story of Don Juan in its many variations, including the popular 1665 Molière play, *Dom Juan ou le festin de Pierre*. The 1988 film, then, is the product of three countries: French and English sources influenced the 1782 French novel, which in turn influenced the 1985 English play, which in turn helped shape the 1988 French-English-U.S. film.

Many factors can complicate discussions of sources. In interviews, filmmakers often tell of being impressed by a technique or detail in one film and later using it while making an unrelated movie. In practice, although a film may be based primarily on one main source, it is also the product of the scriptwriters', directors', and actors' previous experiences. Sources for a creative work are varied and not always easily identifiable by audience or artist. After all, successful creative people spend most of their time and energy creating (and revising)—not reflecting on their sources. Then, too, few are probably aware of the full range and interdependence of their sources, their intertextuality.

Human creativity being limitless, the combination of sources may be even more original and complex than the examples examined so far (Figure 5.20). *Adaptation* (2002) is primarily about three characters whose names are identical to three real people, and the actions of the three movie characters are based closely on the lives of the three real people. The sources for the movie might be diagrammed as follows:

Before the movie was made:

Susan Orlean (person) and John Laroche (person) meet and interact.

Susan Orlean (person) writes a magazine article ("Orchard Fever") and a book (*The Orchid Thief*, 1999) about John Laroche (person).

Charlie Kaufman (person) writes the script for the movie *Adaptation* (2002).

TABLE 5.7
A Highly Selective Chronology of a Story's Versions

Clarissa (The History of Clarissa Harlowe) **(1747)** English novel of letters by Samuel Richardson.

Julie (Julie, ou la nouvelle Héloïse) **(1761)** French novel of letters by Jean-Jacques Rousseau.

Les liaisons dangereuses **(1782)** French novel by Choderlos de Laclos consisting of 175 letters by about a dozen characters.

According to Milos Forman, the director of *Valmont*, there were several stage adaptations of *Les liaisons dangereuses* in the nineteenth century and at least three stage adaptations in the twentieth century.

Les liaisons dangereuses **(1961)** French black-and-white, modern-dress film adaptation set in Paris and a Swiss ski resort, with Jeanne Moreau and Gerard Philipe as the two main characters who are married to each other and aware of each other's seductions. Directed by Roger Vadim. (106 minutes)

Les liaisons dangereuses **(1985)** British period play by Christopher Hampton, based fairly closely on the source novel with two former lovers still warily attracted to each other and scheming with and against each other as he seduces a very young woman and a pious married woman. The play enjoyed critical and commercial success in London and then New York.

Dangerous Liaisons **(1988)** American and British period film in color with Glenn Close and John Malkovich as former lovers. Direction by Stephen Frears and screenplay by Christopher Hampton, based closely on Hampton's own play, which in turn was "adapted from the novel" by Choderlos de Laclos. Compared with the play *Les liaisons dangereuses*, this film version captures more of the epistolary quality of the original novel by dramatizing some brief scenes that are only recounted in the play. (120 minutes)

Valmont **(1989)** French/U.S. period film with updated language, filmed in color on location in France with extensive attention to visual details. Stars: Annette Bening and Colin Firth; screenplay: Jean-Claude Carrière and Milos Forman; and direction: Forman. The film is based loosely on the French novel: the endings of the novel and film, for example, differ widely. Compared with other adaptations, *Valmont* also devotes much more time to fifteen-year-old Cecile, her innocence and social education. (137 minutes)

Cruel Intentions **(1999)** American film in color with Sarah Michelle Gellar and Ryan Phillippe as stepbrother and stepsister. The stepbrother seduces a willing young virgin and eventually an unwilling young virgin with whom he soon falls in love. Directed and scripted by Roger Kumble. Modern-dress version with young cast and characters set in New York City. The film's credits include the following: "Script suggested by the novel *Les liaisons dangereuses*." (97 minutes)

Note: Unavoidably, this table simplifies. For example, a later creative work will not be shaped equally by all previous influences, and later works are typically also influenced by sources outside the lineage represented here.

FIGURE 5.20 Multiple sources, creatively combined
The playful, satirical, and knowing *Adaptation* (2002) cuts back and forth in place and time between multiple fictional subjects. (a) Uptight nonfiction writer Susan Orlean forms a relationship with eccentric, self-taught exotic wildlife specialist John Laroche, whose life and ideas she recounts in her book, *The Orchid Thief*. Here Orlean follows Laroche during one of his expeditions into a swamp in search of special orchids. (b) Screenwriter Charlie Kaufman encounters persistent difficulties in adapting Orlean's book into a viable script for a movie. (c) Charlie's temperamentally opposite twin brother Donald (center frame) decides to try scriptwriting himself and by following commercial formulas enjoys rapid success. Here Charlie is shocked at Donald's declaration about and playful demonstration of how he would like to "push the bush" of his girlfriend (on the left). Frame enlargements. *Edward Saxon, Vincent Landay, and Jonathan Demme; Columbia*

a)

b)

c)

In the movie:

Susan Orlean (character) has already published her nonfiction book.

Susan Orlean (character) and John Laroche (character) meet and interact.

Charlie Kaufman (character) struggles to adapt the book into a movie script.

Charlie's twin brother, Donald Kaufman (character), takes up commercial scriptwriting and quickly achieves success.

FIGURE 5.21 Multiple cultural sources
This publicity still illustrates the opening shot of the Senegalese *Karmen Geï* (2001), a loose adaptation of Prosper Mer-
imée's novella that also served as the main source for Bizet's
1875 opera *Carmen*. The statuesque woman with the broad
smile soon dances with so much vitality and self-possession
that it helps her bewitch the beautiful female prison warden
(after they go to bed together, Karmen is allowed to slip out
of the prison later that night). Before this film, there had already been Bizet's opera and more than fifty film versions of
Carmen, but probably no bisexual Carmen and perhaps no
Carmen who so defiantly rebels against police authority and
so decisively wields power over various men. The languages
used in the film are French and Wolof (a language widely

used in Senegal). Unlike in the source novella and the Bizet opera, the setting is contemporary
Senegal, and the dancing and most of the music are indigenous (there are frequent jazz passages composed by the American David Murray). The script—by the film's Senegalese director Joseph Gaï Ramaka—has more differences than similarities to the original source novella.
France, the United States (Murray's jazz), and Senegal are sources for the film. *Courtesy of California Newsreel, San Francisco*

The sources of *Adaptation*, then, are multiple, complex, and creative: real
people and real experiences are adapted into versions of the real people and
their experiences.

The situation with sources can also get complicated when the sources
come from different times and different cultures. The 2001 Senegalese film
Karmen Geï (pronounced "gay")—which is a loose adaptation of Prosper Mer-
imée's 1847 French novella *Carmen*—can serve as an example (Figure 5.21).

Texts do not emerge out of only a single human imagination or a team of
people working on the same creative project at the same time: texts are always intertextual, always related to other texts, and always influenced by the
cultures that nurture them.

CLOSE-UP: "THE DEAD": NOVELLA TO FILM

by William Meyer

Contemporary film critics praise Tony Huston's adaptation of "The Dead" for its faithfulness to James Joyce's original text. Tim Pulleine calls the film "a close literary adaptation" (67). Richard Blake asserts that the adaptation is "extremely faithful to the text" (194–95). And Vincent Canby simply calls the film a "magnificent adaptation." However, despite its reputation for faithfulness, a careful analysis reveals that the film is unlike Joyce's novella in three major ways. First, the adaptation expands the scope of the original narrative by adding new scenes. Second, the adaptation deletes important contextual elements from its literary source. Finally, the adaptation modifies significant dramatic elements in the literary source.

Perhaps the most apparent difference between the film and its source is the addition of new scenes not found in the novella. For example, the opening scene of the film is shot from the **exterior** of the Morkans' home. It includes images of snow falling, carriages stopping, guests arriving, and people dancing. While the scene effectively establishes the social context and physical setting of the film, it does not appear in Joyce's novella. A second example is a scene in which Freddy Malins walks into a bathroom, washes his face, combs his hair, and relieves himself. The elements of this scene clearly reinforce Joyce's depiction of Malins as a disheveled drunkard, but the scene itself fails to appear in the literary source. While Huston's new scenes extend elements of the narrative introduced by Joyce, they are still invented. It seems clear that Tony Huston's addition of scenes to the screenplay supports Michael Klein's observation that the brevity of short stories provides scriptwriters with room for "imaginative expansion" (10).

A second major difference between the film and its literary source is the deletion of important contextual elements from the novella. For example, in the original text, we learn the context of Molly Ivors's relationship with Gabriel. "They were friends of many years' standing and their careers had been parallel, first at the University and then as teachers" (Joyce 204). This background information is deleted from the screenplay. Consequently, the audience never fully understands the professional and academic nature of their relationship. Another contextual element that is deleted from the film is a scene in which Gabriel becomes discontent with the party and wishes to leave the Morkans' home. In the novella, we learn that he walks to a window, taps his fingers on a windowpane, and stares outside (Joyce 208). Moreover, we learn that he wonders "how much more pleasant it would be there than at the supper-table" (Joyce 208). Because this scene is cut from the screenplay, viewers of the film cannot accurately gauge the depth of Gabriel's discontent. Therefore, they can never fully appreciate the emotional context in which his words and actions are expressed.

A third major difference between the film and the short story is the modification of significant dramatic elements in the original novella. For example, Molly Ivors's exit from the party is modified to clarify her political significance for contemporary audiences. In the novella, "Joyce allows his patriot to depart quietly, offering only that she does not choose to join the party for dinner" (Blake 194). However, in the film, Molly's exit is modified to include the lines "I'm off to a union meeting at Liberty Hall. A Republican meeting." Film critic Richard Blake argues that in the novella, "Her farewell is shot through with irony: 'Beannacht libh' (a blessing upon you all). The point would not be lost on the original readers, but for film audiences Huston must underline

240

Molly's political function in the story" (194). In this case, Huston's modification of the literary source effectively clarifies the political significance of an important dramatic element in the film.

By addition, deletion, and modification, Tony Huston created a screenplay adaptation that is different from its literary source. However, commentary by professional film critics seems to indicate that *different* does not necessarily mean unfaithful (Blake 194–95; Canby; Pulleine 67). Perhaps this is why Huston's adaptation of "The Dead" received so much critical praise. Such praise clearly underscores Huston's skill at weaving his way through what film critic Gabriel Miller calls the filmmaker's "dilemma of remaining faithful to the novel's spirit while realizing the necessity of altering its design" (xi).

Works Cited

Blake, Richard A. "The Living and the Dead." *America* 20 Feb. 1988: 194–95.

Canby, Vincent. "The Party's Over." *New York Times* 17 Dec. 1987, natl. ed.: C19.

Joyce, James. "The Dead." *The Portable James Joyce*. Ed. Harry Levin. New York: Viking, 1966. 190–242.

Klein, Michael. "Introduction: Film and Literature." *The English Novel and the Movies*. Ed. Michael Klein and Gillian Parker. New York: Ungar, 1981. 1–13.

Miller, Gabriel. *Screening the Novel*. New York: Ungar, 1980.

Pulleine, Tim. "A Memory of Galway." *Sight & Sound* Winter 1987/88: 67–68.

SUMMARY

A text is something that people produce or modify to communicate meaning. Fictional films are based on one or usually more texts. A fictional film may be based on a screenplay, which may be an original story but often is not. Frequently, a screenplay is based on historical events, a fictional work (usually a novel), a play, a TV show or series, or other films. Texts, including fictional films, are always intertextual, always influenced by earlier texts and by the culture(s) that helped bring them to light.

Screenplays, Shooting Scripts, and Storyboards

- Typically the screenplay writer determines the settings, subjects (action and dialogue), and structure of a fictional film and directly or indirectly many of its meanings.
- The shooting script is the version of the script used during filming. It includes changes made in the screenplay, usually breaks the scenes into shots, and normally includes instructions on camera placement and use.

■ Comparing a screenplay or shooting script with the finished film seldom reveals who contributed exactly what, but typically the film is more concise, less reliant on dialogue, and more visual than the script.

■ A storyboard is a series of drawings or photographs of each shot or part of a shot for a planned film or video story. It helps filmmakers visualize how the story might look and function before filming and editing begin.

Individual Sources

Nearly any subject can become the source of a fictional film, but five of the most frequently used sources are history, fiction, plays, television, and other films.

HISTORY

■ Fictional movies based on history inevitably omit, change, or fabricate some of the events.

■ In spite of the advertising claims and the documentary qualities of an historical movie, commercial fictional films based on history, such as *The Hurricane*, tend to give priority to drama and entertainment, not the accepted written historical accounts.

FICTION

■ Short stories, novellas, and novels are well suited to render a character's mental activity. Other strengths of fiction include descriptions of characters' backgrounds, analysis by the author, figurative language, and a more or less consistent point of view or means of perception.

■ Film is adept at presenting sights and sounds. It can also show the nuances of faces and the infinite flexibility and expressiveness of movement. It can render the human voice and music in much of their fullness. And through editing, it can condense the time needed to present significant events and transport viewers through time and space instantaneously.

■ People who admire a novel are usually disappointed with a film adaptation of it because as they read the novel, they visualize it and later usually find the filmmakers' visualization wrong. Then, too, a novel is usually too long and involved for a complete rendition on the screen; consequently, parts of it are omitted.

■ A film based on a fictional source should be understood as a film, not as adapted fiction.

Plays

- Plays, in general, are a verbal medium; films, a visual one. Plays filmed with minimal variations in the camera work and editing tend to be disappointing as films because they do not take advantage of film's capabilities.

- Fundamentally, plays rely on the give-and-take of audience and live performer, whereas films rely on the audience's responses to controlled moving images and usually a soundtrack.

Television

- Although initially American TV and film were in fierce competition and their makers refused to cooperate with each other, now the two media are intertwined and often borrow actors, writers, directors, characters, stories, and techniques from each other.

- Often film and TV represent each other critically, even satirically. Sometimes each medium uses the other medium as a source for parody.

Other Films

- Films are often based, at least in part, on earlier films or parts of them.

- A film may imitate earlier films in various ways. It may be a remake. A movie or part of one may include allusions (references) to earlier films, an amusing imitation of a more serious film (parody), or a respectful imitation of parts of an earlier film (homage).

- A movie may also be a sequel or, far less commonly, a prequel. It is even possible, though rare, for a film to be both.

Multiple Sources

- Texts are always intertextual, always related to earlier texts.

- Even when a film seems to have one main source, other influences, including the filmmakers' culture and other cultures, are at work.

Major Terms about Sources for the Fictional Film

Below, numbers in italics refer to the pages where the terms are explained. All terms are defined in more detail in the Illustrated Glossary beginning on p. 621.

allusion *227*	mock documentary *230*	serial *227*
homage *234*		shooting script *196*
intertextuality *195*	parody *229*	storyboard *201*
master-scene format *198*	prequel *234*	text *195*
	screenplay *195*	title card *208*

QUESTIONS ABOUT SOURCES FOR THE FICTIONAL FILM

The following questions are intended to help viewers understand sources for fictional films. Not all the questions are appropriate for every film. In thinking out, discussing, and writing responses to those questions most appropriate for the film being examined, be careful to stick with the issues the questions raise, to answer all parts of the questions, to explain the reasons for your answers, and to give specific examples from the film.

1. Is the film based on an original screenplay, or is it an adaptation? If the film is based on a screenplay that is accessible to you, what are the major differences between the screenplay and the finished film?

2. Is the film based on written historical accounts? If so, how closely does the film follow the earlier accounts? Where does the film make changes for dramatic effect? Where does it make changes unnecessarily?

3. Is the film based on fiction? If so, how closely does the film follow the source fiction? Where does the film make changes for dramatic effect? Where does it make changes unnecessarily?

4. Is the film based on a play? If so, how closely does the film follow the source? Where does the film make changes for dramatic effect? Where does it make changes unnecessarily?

5. Is the film based on a TV show or series? If so, how closely does the film follow the source? Where does the film make changes for dramatic effect? Where does it make changes unnecessarily?

6. Is the film based on other films? Does the film allude to, parody, or pay an homage to film(s)? Is the film a sequel or prequel?

7. Is the film based on multiple sources? If so, what are the main ones? Is the film the product of more than one society? If so, explain.

WORKS CITED

Abé, Kobo. *The Woman in the Dunes*. Trans. E. Dale Saunders. New York: Knopf, 1964.

Anderson, Wes, and Owen Wilson. *The Royal Tenenbaums*. London: Faber & Faber, 2001.

Andrew, Dudley. *Concepts in Film Theory*. New York: Oxford UP, 1984.

Attenborough, David. "The Compulsive Communicators." *Life on Earth*. Program 13. BBC Bristol. 1979. (The wording is from the television program, not the book based on the series.)

Berliner, Todd. "The Pleasures of Disappointment: Sequels and *The Godfather, Part II.*" *Journal of Film and Video* 53.2–3 (Summer/Fall 2001): 107–23.

Cook, David A. *A History of Narrative Film.* 3rd ed. New York: Norton, 1996.

Cunningham, Michael. "My Novel, the Movie: My Baby Reborn; *The Hours* Brought Elation, But Also Doubt." *New York Times* 19 Jan. 2003, late ed., 2:1.

Demopoulos, Maria. "Blink of an Eye: Filmmaking in the Age of Bullet Time." *Film Comment* 36.3 (May/June 2000): 34–39.

Duyfhuizen, Bernard. *Narratives of Transmission.* Rutherford, NJ: Fairleigh Dickinson UP, 1992.

Hitchcock. Ed. Nick James. London: British Film Institute, 1999.

Kasbekar, Asha. "An Introduction to Indian Cinema." In *An Introduction to Film Studies.* 2nd ed. Ed. Jill Nelmes. London: Routledge, 1999: 381–415.

Kelly, Christopher. "Toys in the Attic: The Unsung Pleasures (and Terrors) of *Babe: Pig in the City* and *Small Soldiers.*" *Film Quarterly* 53.4 (Summer 2000): 41–46.

Konigsberg, Ira. *The Complete Film Dictionary.* 2nd ed. New York: Penguin, 1997.

Phillips, William H. *Analyzing Films: A Practical Guide.* New York: Holt, Rinehart and Winston, 1985.

———. *Writing Short Scripts.* 2nd ed. Syracuse: Syracuse UP, 1999.

Scorsese, Martin (filmmaker). Commentary. "The Director as Smuggler." *A Personal Journey with Martin Scorsese through American Movies* (documentary film). 1995.

Stanley, Alessandra. "Surviving and Disturbing in Moscow." *New York Times* 21 Mar. 1995, natl. ed.: B1+.

The Third Man: A Film by Graham Greene and Carol Reed. New York: Simon, 1968.

Tolkin, Michael. *The Player: A Novel.* New York: Atlantic Monthly, 1988.

Toplin, Robert Brent. *History by Hollywood: The Use and Abuse of the American Past.* Urbana: U of Illinois P, 1996.

Wilmington, Michael. "Movies; On Location; The Rules of His Game; *The Player* Marks Altman's Return to Hollywood." *Los Angeles Times* 29 Sept. 1991, home ed., Calendar: 23+.

FOR FURTHER READING

Armes, Roy. *Action and Image: Dramatic Structure in Cinema.* Manchester, Eng.: Manchester UP, 1994. The first of the book's three parts, "Film as Drama," consists of four chapters: "Readings and Viewings," "Showing and Telling," "Text and Performance," and "Stage and Screen."

Based on a True Story: Latin American History at the Movies. Ed. Donald F. Stevens. Wilmington, DE: SR Books, 1997. Various essays on how films have represented Latin America from the late fifteenth century to the present.

Custen, George F. *Bio/Pics: How Hollywood Constructed Public History.* New Brunswick, NJ: Rutgers UP, 1992. Using a sample of over a hundred biographical films from 1927 to 1960, Custen argues that Hollywood created a virtually monochromatic view of history that was systematically distorted in regard to race, gender, nationality, and profession.

Film Adaptation. Ed. James Naremore. New Brunswick, NJ: Rutgers UP, 2000. An investigation of how cinema transforms stories from other sources, such as literature and history, into films. Contributors examine the process of adaptation in both theory and practice, discussing a wide variety of films.

Revisioning History: Film and the Construction of a New Past. Ed. Robert A. Rosenstone. Princeton: Princeton UP, 1995. Theoretical issues about films based on history.

Rosenstone, Robert A. *Visions of the Past: The Challenge of Film to Our Idea of History.* Cambridge: Harvard UP, 1995. Argues that history is a mode of thinking that can use "elements other than the written word" and that history can be done through films.

Tibbetts, John C., and James M. Welsh. *The Encyclopedia of Stage Plays into Film.* New York: Facts on Film, 2001. Three hundred entries classified in one of three sections: "Dramatic Adaptations," "Shakespearean Adaptations," and "Musical Adaptations."

———. *Novels into Film: The Encyclopedia of Movies Adapted from Books.* New York: Checkmark Books, 1999. More than 120 entries, each describing a novel and one or more of its film adaptations. Each entry concludes with a brief references section.

Toplin, Robert Brent. *Reel History: In Defense of Hollywood.* Lawrence: UP of Kansas, 2002. Using examples mainly from contemporary movies, Toplin argues that critics often do not recognize how fictional movies often convey important ideas and information about the past.

CHAPTER 6

Aspects of the Fictional Film

B Y DEFINITION, NARRATIVE ALWAYS RECOUNTS one or more events. . . . It does not simply mirror what happens; it explores and devises what can happen. . . . Narrative can thus shed light on individual fate or group destiny, the unity of a self or the nature of a collectivity. . . . [B]y marking off distinct moments in time and setting up relations among them, by discovering meaningful designs in temporal series, by establishing an end already partly contained in the beginning and a beginning already partly containing the end, by exhibiting the meaning of time and/or providing it with meaning, narrative deciphers time and indicates how to decipher it. In sum, narrative illuminates temporality and humans as temporal beings. (Prince 60)

A few years after the first motion pictures were created in the 1890s, the new medium was used to present short, entertaining fictional stories. Fictional films became so popular that during the late 1910s, **feature films** became commonplace, drew large audiences, served as an evening's or afternoon's major pastime, and supported a large and growing industry. Since then, people have remained captivated by fictional films, in part because they are endlessly fascinated by the causes and consequences of human behavior. As part of the opening **narration** of *Blood Simple* (1984, 2000) indicates, "Nothing comes with a guaranty. I don't care if you're the Pope of Rome, the President of the United States, or Man of the Year. Something can all go wrong." Often fictional films show how neither the characters nor the audience can anticipate how things "can all go wrong." In the animated film "T.R.A.N.S.I.T." (1997), a suitcase falling off the back of a sports car makes all the difference in the world (p. 395). Had it not fallen, the man would not have seen and become infatuated with the attractive woman, and none of the ensuing tragedies would have transpired. And as some stories show, developments can also be profound and far-reaching. In *A Simple Plan* (1998), movements by a wild animal and the decisions of three men result in unexpected complications and unanticipated grief. Near the beginning of the film, a fox runs across the path of a pickup truck with three men inside,

Terms in **boldface** are defined in the Illustrated Glossary beginning on page 621.

feature film: A fictional film that is at least sixty minutes long.

narration: Commentary in a film about a subject in the film or some other topic, usually by someone offscreen.

FIGURE 6.1 Action leading to complications
Early in *A Simple Plan* (1998), three men find a small crashed airplane covered by snow in the woods. Inside the plane are a dead pilot and a duffel bag full of money. Soon the three decide what to do with the money, and that decision leads to complications and more complications and eventually death for six characters. Frame enlargement. *Mutual Film Company; Paramount*

the driver swerves to miss the fox, and the truck hits a tree. After the accident, the three men pursue the fox, which leads to their discovery of a downed plane and a duffel bag containing $4.4 million. The decisions of the three very different men about what to do with this money lead to all sorts of unanticipated complications (Figure 6.1).

Most people are so drawn to narratives or stories that when they are confronted by any type of **text** with no obvious story, they still try to find one. As film archivist and critic Robert Rosen writes,

text: Something that people produce or modify to communicate meaning.

> Film and painting . . . display intriguing points of convergence, among them the inescapability of narrativizing spectators. Even in the face of totally nonrepresentational works, viewers have a powerful urge to uncover or invent narrative—a basic need to normalize the challenge of the unfamiliar by situating it in a comfortably recognizable sequence of events. (252)

In this chapter, we briefly consider narrative and fictional narrative and then examine some ways the fictional narrative film can handle structure, time, and style.

NARRATIVES

Unlike ordinary experience, which mixes the meaningful with the amorphous and random, a story's ingredients are selected for appropriateness to the story's intended effects, **meanings**, and structures. A story can therefore be almost free from redundancy, meaninglessness, and, especially, inexpressiveness. . . . Thus a story promises comprehensibility in a way that ordinary experience does not. (Eidsvik 61)

meaning: An observation or general statement about a subject.

"Narratives" or stories are commonplace in every society. We all produce them, enjoy them, and often learn from them directly or indirectly, yet explanation of what precisely constitutes a narrative is a complex, contentious issue in critical theory. For our purposes, **narrative** can be defined as "a **representation** of a series of unified **events** (happenings and actions) situated in one or more **settings**." The events may be arranged chronologically or nonchronologically and may be factual, fictional, or a blend of the two (Figure 6.2). As an example of narrative, consider the main events of the seventeen-minute wordless fictional film "The String Bean" (1962):

representation: A likeness of a subject created in a text.

setting: The place where a narrative's action occurs.

1. An old woman finds a discarded potted plant near her apartment building.
2. In her apartment, she discards the dead plant and plants in the pot a seed that she took from a package.
3. In her apartment, the plant grows to a certain size.
4. The woman transplants the plant to a park, where it thrives.
5. One day, she sees park caretakers uproot the plant and discard it. The woman takes pods from the discarded plant.
6. In her apartment, she takes seeds from a pod, plants them, places the pot outside on the sill, and looks on as rain begins to fall on the pot.

This narrative shows selected, chronologically arranged events in the life of one character. Viewers can usually figure out the relationship of later events to earlier ones: between the major units of the narrative (or **sequences**) numbered

sequence: A series of related consecutive scenes, perceived as a major unit of a narrative film, such as the Sicilian sequence in *The Godfather*.

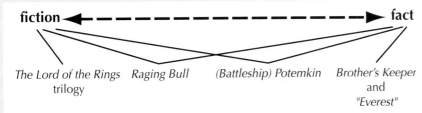

FIGURE 6.2 The continuum of narrative films
Some narrative films are completely fictional, but many blend fiction and fact. *The Lord of the Rings*: *The Fellowship of the Ring* (2001) and its two sequels are all completely fictional: as we watch them, we recognize no character as being based on an actual person and no actions re-creating real events. But *Raging Bull* (1980) is a fictional film that many viewers will recognize as partially factual: certain aspects of the celluloid Jake are the same as those of the real Jake La Motta, the famous boxer. Some narratives are more difficult to categorize. The Soviet classic (*Battleship*) *Potemkin* (1925) is a blend of fiction and fact, and though scholars usually categorize it as a fictional film, some consider it a narrative documentary. Even narrative documentary films are never entirely factual. For example, significant details might be omitted, or the order of some events changed in editing. Narrative films that blend fiction and fact and have as their subjects recent news or history are sometimes called *docudramas*, especially if they were originally made for TV.

3 and 4, viewers can infer that the woman transplants the plant to the park because she hopes it will grow even larger and healthier outdoors.

If the film showed only sequences 1 to 5, it would still be a narrative, though one with an unhappy ending, both for the woman and for those in the audience who identify with her. If the film showed only sequences 1 to 3, there would still be a narrative, though to many viewers it would be unsatisfactory because it would lack complications and resolution of them.

A narrative's events are unified in some manner. The following three **scenes** (selected and adapted from a short film discussed later in this chapter) are not clearly related:

scene: A section of a narrative that gives the impression of continuous action taking place in continuous time and space.

5. At a university, wary students accept flyers that Leon gives them and quickly discard them. Leon finds the discarded flyers.

4. At the *Los Angeles Times* building, Leon is unable to see his friend Keith to give him a copy of a news release.

1. In his basement apartment Leon, who is dressed as a priest, puts on a false mustache and leaves.

If a film showed only these scenes, viewers could detect no unity to the events and could make no sense of them. The film would not be a narrative.

Some films—such as many films directed by the French directors Jean-Luc Godard and Alain Resnais—make it difficult or impossible for viewers to perceive the unity of events. Other films—such as *Mr. Hulot's Holiday* (1953), *Nashville* (1975), *Short Cuts* (1993), and *Clerks* (1994)—are only loosely unified overall. Although individual scenes are unified and easy to follow, some scenes could be located elsewhere in the story with little consequence. Such films are said to have an **episodic plot**.[1]

A fictional film is a narrative that shows mostly or entirely imaginary events. The events are selected and arranged in some sort of meaningful order (structure). They are represented over time (chronologically or not). In addition, the events are represented in one or more styles. The rest of this chapter explores the basic components of the fictional film: structure, time, and style.

STRUCTURE

Structure, which some scholars and theorists call *form*, refers to the arrangement of the parts of a text. In a fictional film, the selection and order of events help viewers comprehend the story and strongly influence how they respond.

---

[1] Digital technology has made it possible to rearrange a film's parts. For example, "digital technology [was used] to shuffle audio and visual tracks, reassembling a different story on each viewing" of "City Hall 2.0" on the Web site *The Bit Screen: Films Made for the Internet* (Stables 5).

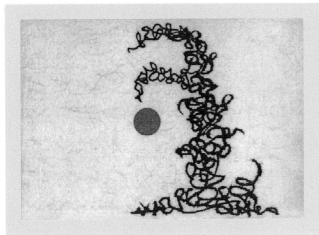

FIGURE 6.3 Shapes functioning as characters
Most fictional films include characters that are played by humans, but occasionally a character is played by something with human qualities. "The Dot and the Line: A Romance in Lower Mathematics" (1965) presents the story of a love triangle with a female dot and the two male lines that contend for her acceptance—a straight line and an ever-changing squiggle. Shown here are the dot and the squiggle cavorting or dancing. *Chuck Jones & Les Goldman, MGM; Turner Entertainment*

This section discusses the basic fictional structure (characters, goals, and conflicts); some functions of beginnings, middles, and endings; and the combination of different brief stories (plotlines) into a larger, more complex story.

Fictional films include at least one character, and that character is usually based on characteristics of actual people. It is even possible to base a character almost entirely on an actual person. *Being John Malkovich* (1999) includes the character John Malkovich, who seems to be exactly like the real John Malkovich (except for a peculiar portal inside his head). Occasionally, nonhuman characters—such as extraterrestrials, robots, zombies, ghosts, animals, and even abstract shapes—are portrayed as having human qualities (Figure 6.3). Fictional films show imaginary events, although filmmakers often re-create some actual events, film them, and combine them with the completely fictional events. It is even possible, though rare, to combine fictional events with **footage** of actual events, as in the scenes beginning 91¾ minutes into *Medium Cool* (1969) in which one character attends the actual 1968 Chicago Democratic National Convention as a reporter while on the streets outside the convention another character gets caught up in a demonstration and is threatened by tear gas and police violence. Similarly, the fictional *Chinese Box* (1998) includes some actual footage of the ceremony of Great Britain's return of Hong Kong to Chinese rule. The settings of narratives may be fictional, as in most science fiction stories, or they may be essentially factual, as in the **Italian neorealist** films or other movies filmed on largely unaltered **locations**.

Characters, Goals, Conflicts

Some generalizations about characters, goals, and conflicts apply to all fictional films regardless of length, but feature films and short films have some major differences. In this section, we first consider the qualities of fictional

footage: A length of exposed motion-picture film.

Italian neorealism: As a film movement in Italy during and after World War II, neorealist films are a mixture of imaginary and factual events usually located in real settings and showing ordinary characters caught up in difficult social and economic conditions.

location: Any place other than a film studio that is used for filming.

films regardless of length and later turn our attention to how characters, goals, and conflicts tend to be handled in the short film.

FEATURE FILMS AND SHORT FILMS

All fictional films share a number of characteristics. For instance, regardless of its length, a fictional narrative nearly always includes at least one character that wants something but has problems trying to obtain it (Figure 6.4). People are fascinated with characters that have trouble reaching their goals, in part because in such circumstances viewers learn about human nature or think they learn about how they might handle a similar situation. Perhaps viewers also sometimes enjoy seeing others struggling with problems. Whatever their motivations, viewers tend to be fascinated by how others behave in adverse situations and how their efforts affect them and others around them.

Typically, a main character's goals in a film are not immediately apparent, though one major goal becomes clear early in the film so that viewers do not lose interest. As a story progresses, sometimes a second goal emerges. In the French film *Ridicule* (1996), viewers soon learn that the main character wants the king's support for draining a swamp that breeds disease and kills peasants. In pursuing that goal, the man travels to the royal residence at Versailles, where he meets a worldly, calculating woman of the court. At about this time, he also meets an attractive, intelligent young woman. The story illustrates

FIGURE 6.4 The basics of narrative: character, goal(s), setbacks, and resolution
This graph for "The String Bean" (1962) illustrates how a central character seeks a goal (described at the top of the vertical axis), makes progress or encounters setbacks in reaching the goal, and then either succeeds or not. Similar graphs can help scriptwriters as they work on their scripts and film students as they study a plotline's structure. *Source: Phillips, 101 (© 1991 by William H. Phillips)*

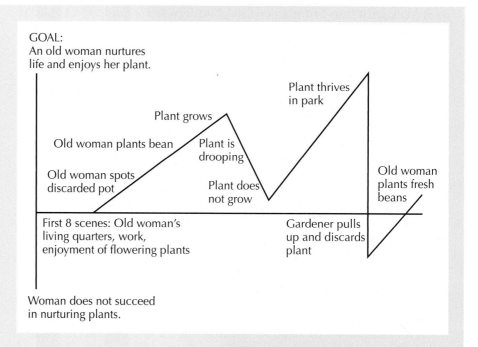

that by pursuing a second goal (winning the love of the young woman), the main character might fail in his first goal (draining the swamp) (Figure 6.5). Sometimes a story's main character fails to achieve either of two major goals. In *Citizen Kane* (1941), Charles Foster Kane has two major goals in his life— to win a woman's lasting love and to win the love of the populace, most notably by becoming governor. He fails to achieve either goal: his first wife leaves him after his affair with another woman becomes public, his second wife leaves him because of his self-centeredness and her isolation and boredom, and voters decline to send him to the governor's office.

In films with two or more major characters, the characters usually have different goals, at least initially; the result is conflict, with or without humor. Conflict largely without humor is prominent in many movies, including most war movies and westerns, whereas conflict with humor abounds in most romantic comedies, such as *It Happened One Night* (1934), *Bringing Up*

a)

b)

c)

FIGURE 6.5 Character, goals, conflicts
Nearly all of *Ridicule* (1996) takes place in 1783 France at a time when wit was king and ridicule could kill. (a) The main character is an engineer who seeks royal support to clear swamps and thus eradicate a fatal disease. (b) In pursuing his goal, he meets and becomes entangled with a calculating, worldly woman of the king's court, who helps him gain the king's ear. (c) At about the same time, the engineer becomes attracted to Mathilde, an intelligent, individualistic woman. After many complications, the man abandons the woman of the court, who arranges his downfall so that he fails to attain his initial goal. A concluding title card informs viewers that twelve years later the engineer and Mathilde succeed in draining the swamps. Frame enlargements. *Miramax Zoë*

FIGURE 6.6 **The three types of conflict**
The three main human subjects of *Jaws* (1975) are (left to right) the chief of police (Brody), a veteran fisherman (Quint), and a marine-life specialist (Hooper). During the film, each comes into conflict with each of the others. All three come into conflict with a great white shark. And Brody wants to accommodate the political leaders and businesspeople yet protect townspeople and tourists against shark attacks. In short, the film illustrates the three basic types of conflict possible in stories: people versus nature, people versus people, and a character conflicted in his or her thinking.
David Brown & Richard D. Zanuck; Universal

Baby (1938), *My Best Friend's Wedding* (1997), *Bridget Jones's Diary* (2001), and *Down with Love* (2003).

In pursuing goals, people inevitably encounter conflict or problems, in fiction as in life. In *Jaws* (1975), a huge killer shark is menacing swimmers who venture into the waters off an island that caters to summer tourists. The film exemplifies the three traditional types of conflict (Figure 6.6). At the film's end, however, the conflicts are resolved: the veteran fisherman Quint is destroyed by his shark adversary, but soon afterward the shark is destroyed; Hooper and Brody resolve their differences and later paddle back to the beach; and Brody no longer feels divided in his allegiances because the townspeople and tourists are no longer in danger. Often fictional stories take the form of two opposing characters or two opposing groups of characters (Figure 6.7).

classical Hollywood cinema: Films that show one or more characters facing a succession of problems while trying to reach their goals and that tend to hide the manner of their making.

In films of **classical Hollywood cinema**, regardless of their length, the main characters typically achieve all their major goals. If a feature film has only one major character, that character normally has more than one major goal. For example, in countless movies—such as *Rocky* (1976), *Top Gun* (1986), *The Mask* (1994), and *Mission: Impossible 2* (2000)—the central male character tries to succeed in love and work or some other major goal and does so. In many musicals, the main male character eventually wins the woman of his dreams and is instrumental in the successful staging of a show or making of a movie. In most movies, especially the popular ones, the major characters don't just succeed; they succeed against enormous odds. In *Stand and Deliver* (1987), an overworked high school math teacher in a Los Angeles barrio wins the respect of his students, who overcome their various prob-

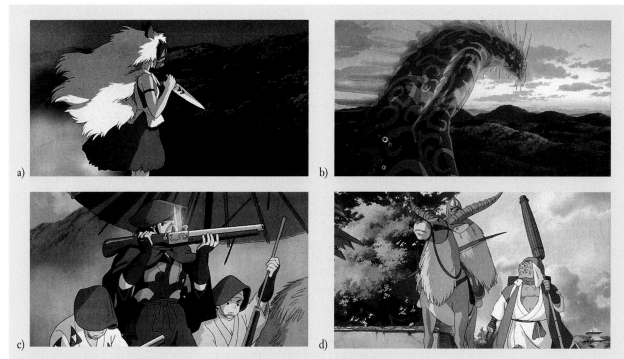

FIGURE 6.7 Two opposing forces in a fictional film
Hayao Miyazaki's anime (Japanese animated film) *Princess Mononoke* (1997) has a long, complicated story, but as in many fictional tales, two forces war with each other: those who seek to protect nature and those who seek to convert it for industrial uses. (a) Princess Mononoke or San—a young woman here seen wearing a mask—has been raised by wolf gods and lives with them. She is allied with wild animals and (b) forest spirits to defend the natural environment. (c) The other major force—a collaboration of Lady Eboshi (seen here), her ironworkers, and her soldiers—intends to industrialize nature. (d) Jigo (right) is yet another threat to nature: he and his men intend to take the great forest spirit's head back to the emperor, who believes it will gain him immortality. One major character belongs to neither warring group: Ashitaka (left), a brave young man who tries to mediate between the warring factions. Frame enlargements. *Studio Ghibli; Miramax*

lems at home, work diligently to pass the math Advanced Placement test, and pass the test a second time after being allowed only a few days to study. *Music of the Heart* (1999) is yet another movie in which the main character—a violin teacher in an East Harlem elementary school—endures setback after setback, including a husband who abandons her and their two sons; loss of income and resultant housing problems; resentment from fellow teachers and resistance from some parents; difficulties in handling her two sons, especially the older one, who misses his father; a boyfriend who is not interested in a long-term relationship; unending parking tickets because she never gets a parking space at work; and loss of her position and funds for her violin program, even after it becomes so successful that students have to enter a lottery for a chance at admittance. Early in the story, she decides to do without a social life and instead to focus on her two sons and her work. Like the stories of so many popular movies, her story shows that despite seemingly unending hurdles, one person who works hard can achieve a dream.

SHORT FICTIONAL FILMS

From 1895 to about 1906, all fictional films ran for less than sixty minutes, a frequent definition of the **short film**. Until the 1960s, short fictional films often accompanied a feature film in movie theater showings. Today, short films are seldom shown in theaters and are rarely available in video stores. They are shown at film festivals; by film societies, museums, and libraries; on some cable channels, including the Sundance Channel, the Independent Film Channel, and Turner Classic Movies; in various school and college courses; and on many Web sites. In addition, short films—such as the series of collections beginning with *Short 1* and continuing through at least *Short 11*—have been available on DVD. Helping make a short film is usually required of filmmaking students. Occasionally, short films attract attention at film festivals and lead to the funding for feature productions.

At its best, a short fictional film is not a truncated feature but a flexible and expressive form in its own right. Like a short story, its brevity can be an advantage: for example, compared with a feature film, a short film may be more compressed, demanding, and subtle. And since its budget is relatively small, its makers are under fewer financial pressures to conform to the usual Hollywood movie and are freer to be true to their vision. Let's examine briefly two sample short films.

"Leon's Case" (1982), which is twenty-five minutes long, shows the often amusing story of the idealistic Leon Bernstein, who resides in 1980s Los Angeles but still thinks of himself as a Vietnam War protester and a fugitive from the military draft. Accordingly, he still thinks and acts as he did two decades earlier. In trying to publicize his opposition to the U.S. military-industrial complex, Leon goes through the following steps:

1. In his basement apartment, Leon is dressed as a priest. He puts on a false mustache and leaves.

2. At the house of his friends Keith and Karen, Leon discusses his plans and hides his manuscript about his life resisting the war and the draft. His two friends offer him no direct support and sometimes ignore him.

3. At a duplicating shop, Leon has copies made of a press release and a flyer announcing a demonstration he plans to stage. The worker in the store, a former hippie, does not give Leon a "discount for the movement."

4. At the *Los Angeles Times* building, Leon is unable to see his friend Keith, who writes a real estate column, to give him a copy of a news release.

5. At a university, wary students accept Leon's flyers and quickly discard them. Leon finds the discarded flyers.

6. Leon has trouble gaining access to a lawyer he knows, and when he does, he learns the lawyer doesn't do resistance work anymore "'cause there's no resistance."

7. At a telephone booth, Leon calls the FBI to announce that his demonstration is being held the next day, but he learns that President Carter pardoned war resisters long ago.

8. Back at his apartment, Leon's friends give him a surprise party. He is uncomfortable and uncharacteristically speechless; his friends do not entirely support him in his cause.

9. The next day, Leon cuts his hair, puts on conventional clothing, goes to the Los Angeles airport, presumably chains himself to a bomber on display there, gets arrested, and appears on a local television news show: mission accomplished.

Like "Leon's Case," most short fictional films exhibit the characteristics of classical Hollywood cinema but have fewer major characters and fewer events. Most short fictional films have:

1. One or two major characters, who usually do not change goals or personality during the film;

2. A brief story time, usually a few days or less;

3. One goal, which the main character usually does not state explicitly but which viewers can figure out early in the film;

4. One or more obstacles or conflicts in trying to reach the goal but none of them very time-consuming;

5. Success or failure in reaching the goal.

A minority of short fictional films reject the conventions of classical Hollywood cinema. A good example is "The Other Side," a ten-minute 1966 black-and-white film from Belgium. The film is a **symbolic** story about masses of people in an unidentified town who are forced to keep their hands against the walls of buildings as they move slowly sideways. Eventually, some try to rebel but are gunned down. The film has no dialogue, no narration, and no music except during the opening credits and the final moments. The only sound effect is occasional machine-gun fire. "The Other Side" is a brief, complex, and somewhat ambiguous film that calls for multiple viewings, which are easier to manage with short films than with features.

symbol: Anything perceptible that has meaning beyond its usual meaning or function.

Conflict between characters is used in stories of classical Hollywood cinema to show what individual characters are like and to initiate and develop the plot. In "The Other Side," we see only one side of the conflict: we never learn about those suppressing the people in the street, nor do we know why they do so. The oppressors kill people one at a time and evidently kill no more than necessary to keep the others in line (literally and figuratively). The film shows that authorities shoot rebels. At the beginning of the film, it appears that they may also shoot nonrebels at random.

Unlike classical Hollywood cinema, "The Other Side" reveals little about individual characters. The film has no spoken words and no written language except the final "1966." "The Other Side" also lacks **close-ups** of faces, so viewers cannot infer what the characters are feeling. No one looks happy, yet no one looks angry either. In nearly all of the film, people move lethargically, like drugged inmates in an institution or animals in a zoo. The lack of emotion and interaction between characters are two of the film's most prominent features. The film focuses not on individual psychology but on political issues, force, and conformity.

As in most short films of classical Hollywood cinema, the main characters—here a mass of people—have a single main goal: freedom from oppression and conformity. Failing at that, they want to survive, even if that requires conformity, lack of interaction, and the absence of vitality. Unlike most films of classical Hollywood cinema, the characters fail to achieve their main goal, and the film ends as it began—except more bodies fill the street than in the beginning.[2]

Beginnings, Middles, and Endings

The beginning of a fictional film tends to involve viewers and to establish where and when the story starts. Many fictional films start with one or more shots of the setting before introducing the subjects. Soon after that, the story begins to unfold and leads viewers to anticipate and readjust to developments that take place before their eyes.

Typically, a fictional film's beginning uses minimal **exposition** (information about events that supposedly transpired before the beginning of the plot): too much exposition, especially at the beginning, tends to keep audiences uninvolved. Tellers of tales—whether in print, online, on the stage, or on the screen—typically use as little initial exposition as possible and feed their audiences tidbits of background information when needed as the story progresses.

Beginnings usually introduce the major characters and encourage viewers to infer their goals. The events of fictional films are so intertwined that often a character's need or desire at the story's beginning largely determines

close-up: An image in which the subject fills most of the frame and little of the surroundings is shown.

---

[2]Both the descriptions and analyses of "Leon's Case" and "The Other Side" are adapted from Phillips.

the story's ending. Early in *Finzan: A Dance for the Heroes* (1990), a man's desire to force his late brother's widow to marry him sets off a chain of actions and consequences (Figure 6.8). *The Maltese Falcon* (1941) also begins with characters seeking something, which leads to lots of complications and eventually a resolution (Figure 6.9).

The middle section of fictional feature films typically includes a series of obstacles that prevent or delay the main characters from achieving their goals. In the long central section of *Schindler's List* (1993), for example, Schindler tries to thwart the Nazis and help save as many Jews as possible, but in pursuing his goals, he faces setbacks, dangers, and delays. In dealing with the impediments to reaching their goals, the central characters in films reveal their natures and the consequences of their actions for them and others. Consider the structure of *Unforgiven* (1992). The film begins with acts of injustice both by a cowboy who slashes a woman's face and by the sheriff who cavalierly acts as law officer, jury, and judge. The large middle section of the film shows who will avenge the injustice against the woman, how they will do so, and what consequences their actions cause. The middle section of a fictional film also tests the filmmakers' inventiveness and skill in creating satisfying surprise and suspense and in using other ways to keep the audience involved with the story.

Narrative endings show the consequences of the major previous events. Filmmakers, however, sometimes include an ending that isn't well integrated with the rest of the story. Consider *Schindler's List*. Early in the film, Schindler is portrayed as a complex, multidimensional man—exploitative, philandering, and callous, yet shrewd, self-confident, powerful, and somewhat inexplicable. Later in the film, after he retrieves the Jewish women from the Auschwitz concentration camp, he

FIGURE 6.8 A character's initial need or desire causing consequences
Seen here is Nanyuma, the main character in *Finzan: A Dance for the Heroes* (Mali, 1990). Early in the film, Nanyuma's husband dies, and soon her husband's brother, the village idiot, wants to marry her. In pursuing that goal, he sets in motion most of the film's complications. The story ends with the man not getting what he wants: the widow evades the consummation of her forced marriage but only by exiling herself and her young son from her village and chancing an uncertain future. *Courtesy of California Newsreel, San Francisco*

FIGURE 6.9 Something sought at the beginning shaping the narrative's middle and ending
Early in *The Maltese Falcon* (1941), we learn that various characters seek the Maltese Falcon, which is a statuette thought to be valuable. The large middle section of the narrative shows the consequences of their trying to acquire it: it shows to what extremes people will go to acquire "the stuff that dreams are made of." Seen here is a still illustrating a scene late in the film when three of the seekers (on the right) think they have the long-sought fabled object within their grasps. *Hal B. Wallis; Warner Bros.–First National*

FIGURE 6.10 Ending shaped by the context of the production

Not One Less (1999) is the story of a resolute girl who is put in charge of a small rural Chinese primary school while the teacher is away for a month. The film shows the difficult conditions in which the children are taught—for example, a run-down schoolroom with only one piece of chalk per day, a pitted chalkboard, pitted walls, a leaky roof, no books, and an unqualified substitute teacher. Most of the story shows the conditions at the school and in a city in a credible way. To avoid censorship, however, the filmmakers show that those in positions of power were eventually helpful and compassionate and that the story ends happily. Frame enlargement. *Columbia Pictures Film Production Asia; Sony*

title card: A card or thin sheet of clear plastic on which is written or printed information included in a film.

seeks out his wife to be reconciled with her and presumably strays no more. Viewers learn that his factory workers build deliberately flawed armaments to sabotage the German war effort. Schindler urges the rabbi who works for him to prepare for the Sabbath and spends a lot of money sustaining his workers and bribing Reich officials. At the war's end, he credits his Jewish workers with saving themselves and persuades the armed camp guards to leave without harming the workers. Later, as the music swells, he breaks down and says that he squandered money and should have saved even more Jews; then he is quietly and lovingly enfolded by many of those he did save. By the end of the movie, the Schindler character has been reduced to a one-dimensional man, as the film tries too hard to make sure no one misses Schindler's admirable qualities. The movie ends not with modulated chords but a single repeated note. The ending may be emotionally satisfying for many viewers—and understandable, given the filmmakers' desire to honor Schindler—but it does not mesh with the film's earlier restraint and complexity.

Sometimes a film ends improbably because the filmmakers respond to political or societal pressures. The Chinese film *Not One Less* (1999) shows both the inadequate conditions of a rural Chinese primary school and the brusque or uncaring attitudes of the people that the main character meets in a Chinese city. But as the film nears its end, it morphs into a fairy tale. The thirteen-year-old girl who takes over the teaching while the adult teacher is away is suddenly rewarded in highly unlikely ways: a TV broadcast helps her locate the boy she went to the city to retrieve; a TV crew drives the boy and her back to their hometown while recording the happy developments; and the village receives gifts and money to rebuild the school and refurnish it. A final **title card** informs viewers that a million Chinese children drop school for work each year. The happy ending and inaccurate final title cards (the number of Chinese school dropouts is actually much higher) were included because the director (Zhang Yimou) had trouble with Chinese censorship in the past and feared that the authorities would object to too unfavorable a representation of life in contemporary China (Figure 6.10). Maybe other endings are wrong for their stories because filmmakers know how unpopular unhappy endings can be. Director Stanley Kubrick observed, "'Maybe the reason why people seem to find it harder to take unhappy endings in movies than in plays or novels is that a good movie engages you so heavily that you find an unhappy ending almost unbearable'" (quoted in Hohenadel).

Films with **closure** end by showing the consequences of events that viewers have become curious about. Closure supplies viewers with the answers and sense of completion that real life so often withholds. Films may also lack closure—that is, be open-ended: the film leaves the fate of a significant character or person uncertain or the causes or consequences of a significant event unknowable. Generally, films of classical Hollywood cinema have a sense of completion because mainstream audiences tend to dislike inconclusive or puzzling endings. The endings of **independent films**, however, are more likely to be open. Examples are *The Crying Game* (1992) and *L.A. Confidential* (1997). At the end of *The Crying Game*, viewers cannot know what Fergus and Dil's relationship will be. They can only review relevant events from the film and make an informed guess. In *L.A. Confidential*, the ending for one of the two main characters is open: viewers cannot know Ed Exley's fate. He has survived an attempt on his life and been awarded honors again. For now, Exley is aware that the police chief and the district attorney are using him to repair damage done to the image of the Los Angeles Police Department. But in the long run, can he trust the police chief and the DA, especially now that his colleague, a powerful ally, is leaving the police force?

independent film: Film made without support or input from the dominant, established film industry.

Plotlines

A **plotline** is a brief narrative—a series of related events situated in one or more settings—that usually involves a few characters or people. A plotline can function as a complete short narrative, as it typically does in a short film. A feature film, however, often has two or more plotlines. When a film consists of two or more plotlines, often one plotline is given more of the film's total time. Plotlines may be combined in countless creative ways and serve many different functions.

To compress a wide-ranging story into an endurable movie, plotlines can be consecutive yet have large gaps of story time between them. *2001: A Space Odyssey* (1968) contains the consecutive but not continuous plotlines of four groups: man-apes, scientists, a computer and two astronauts, and the starchild. *Being Human* (1994) has five plotlines (set, for example, in cave times, ancient Rome, and the modern era) with vast gaps of time between them.

Multiple alternating plotlines can be used to show relationships between different time periods. *The Godfather Part II* (1974) and *Heat and Dust* (1983) alternate between a narrative primarily about one character and a story set years earlier about a relative. *Intolerance* (1916), directed by D. W. Griffith, alternates four plotlines, each set in a different place and historical period: Babylon in 539 B.C., Judea toward the end of Christ's life, France in 1572, and the United States early in the twentieth century. As might be expected from a film with so complicated a structure, many viewers see little unity in the film and are confused about its purpose.

A film can alternate between simultaneous plotlines to heighten suspense. *Dr. Strangelove: Or, How I Learned to Stop Worrying and Love the Bomb* (1963) has three major simultaneous plotlines: at a U.S. Air Force base where the paranoid General Jack D. Ripper has ordered U.S. bombers to attack the Soviet Union; on a U.S. bomber on its way to bomb a target in the Soviet Union; and in the Pentagon war room, where the U.S. president, military commanders, and Dr. Strangelove, the leading scientist, try to call back the plane and prevent the catastrophe.

A film may have multiple plotlines, with fragments of those plotlines distributed among the film's main sections. The Mexican film *Amores Perros* (2000), which is set in contemporary Mexico City, has three major characters: Octavio, a teenager who is obsessed with his brother's young wife, Susana; Valeria, a successful model having an affair with Daniel, a married father; and El Chivo (the goat), a bearded former revolutionary and now occasional hit man who lives alone with his dogs and yearns for a relationship with his grown daughter Maru. The film begins with a car chase and auto accident, which is followed by three lengthy sections: "Octavio and Susana," "Daniel and Valeria," and "El Chivo and Maru." The first plotline includes most of the "Octavio and Susana" section, which starts a little more than three minutes into the film by flashing back weeks before the auto accident and then showing chronologically arranged scenes. The first plotline also includes some scenes that appear later in the film's third section. The second plotline consists of a few scenes that appear late in the first section and most of the second section, which begins at sixty-three minutes into the film and is mostly a series of chronologically arranged scenes beginning after the car accident and ending with Daniel and Valeria by their apartment window. The third plotline includes occasional scenes from the first two sections plus most of the "El Chivo and Maru" section, which begins at ninety-four minutes; flashes back to show events before the accident, the accident yet again, and developments after the accident; and ends at 149 minutes. (The third plotline also includes two scenes seemingly out of chronological order: Leonardo is seen in a bank and later in a scene saying he is going to the bank.)

The film's unusual structure demands that audiences be unusually attentive and thoughtful. Although it is sometimes impossible to know where some of the third section's events fit chronologically, that is not a barrier to coherence and comprehension. The cutting between events from the different plotlines gives viewers a sense of what different characters are doing before or after the accident or in some cases at about the same time. Since all three plotlines converge in the auto accident, the film's structure also demonstrates that entirely dissimilar characters may converge in unexpected ways and then experience profound consequences.

To show various aspects of a large group, plotlines may also be numerous, chronological, simultaneous, and sometimes intersecting. *Short Cuts* includes nine pairs of major characters plus six other important characters, but the film has so many groupings of characters that one cannot say there are nine plotlines. Different critics of the film have detected "nine interlocking narratives," "approximately ten stories," or "a dozen stories." There are at least ten (Figure 6.11). The film's multiple plotlines are arranged chronologically or simultaneously—the viewer cannot tell which—and each couple interacts

FIGURE 6.11 Multiple, simultaneous, and intersecting plotlines

Short Cuts (1993) has twenty-four major characters and many different groupings of them. For example, (a) Howard Finnigan (a TV news commentator) and his wife, Ann, have a son Casey who is hit by a car, walks home, falls asleep, lapses into a coma, and is treated in a hospital. Two other characters are seen in the film only in relation to the Finnigans: (b) Mr. Bitkower, a baker who as requested has made a special birthday cake for Casey, and (c) Howard's father, Paul, who unexpectedly appears at the hospital after years of alienation from his son. Other characters have lives in the film beyond their interactions with the Finnigans: (d) Doreen, a waitress, drives the car that Casey darted in front of; (e) Ralph Wyman is the physician in charge of Casey's care; and (f) Zoe is a disturbed cellist who lives next door to the Finnigans with her mother and is upset by news of the boy's fate. Frame enlargements. *Cary Brokaw; Fine Line Features*

with at least one other major character. With so many characters and intersecting plotlines in something as fleeting and onrushing as a film, however, a viewer may sometimes lose track of who is who. There is also a danger that with so many events some may be implausible (one murder seems insufficiently motivated and its "cover-up" highly unlikely). Nonetheless, a story

FIGURE 6.12 Multiple chronological plotlines that emphasize a group's situation
The many plotlines of the Iranian film *The Circle* (2000) do not reveal any character in depth and are not much developed as stories. In a prologue, a daughter is born, and it is suggested that the father's family will be bitterly disappointed that the child was not a male. Soon the camera is following three women released from prison early that morning. The publicity still seen here represents the first scene they are in, approximately five minutes into the film, desperately trying to place a telephone call that will bring some sort of help. The woman seen on the right is quickly rearrested. Sometime later, the other two disappear from the film as the camera moves on to another woman and her difficult situation, then another, and another, and another, until the film ends in a large dim prison cell, where we see again the initial trio of women and viewers learn that the woman who gave birth to a daughter during the film's opening credits had recently also been a prisoner in that same cell. The multiple plotlines illustrate the many limitations placed on women in contemporary Teheran. *Jafar Panahi; WinStar Cinema; British Film Institute Stills, Posters and Designs*

consisting of many intersecting plotlines can effectively present a panoramic view of a society or group. In *Short Cuts* as in *Nashville* (1975), *A Wedding* (1978), *The Player* (1992), and *Gosford Park* (2001), director Robert Altman and his collaborators are exploring how inclusive a narrative can be—both in terms of the number of characters and the various combinations of plotlines—yet remain unified enough and comprehensible enough to be a satisfying narrative. Like many Altman films, the Iranian film *The Circle* (2000) uses many plotlines to focus on a group, not the backgrounds, situations, and personalities of the individual characters (Figure 6.12).

Director Mike Figgis has also experimented with how inclusive a narrative can be in *Time Code* (2000), which also consists of multiple, chronological, simultaneous, and intersecting plotlines that present a panoramic view of a group, in this case an assortment of small-time independent Hollywood movie-makers and others with ties to them. But the film uses no editing. Instead, it shows simultaneous, often converging, uninterrupted plotlines on different quadrants (Figure 6.13). While viewing *Time Code*, the viewer probably watches the quadrant with the loudest or most distinct soundtrack. At other times, the viewer is less guided about which quadrants to observe and for how long. (Each viewer in effect edits the film and constructs a somewhat different story.) With more than twenty characters to keep track of, many visuals bombarding the viewer from four sources simultaneously, and sometimes more than one soundtrack competing for the viewer's attention, no viewer can completely reconstruct the plot after only one viewing. *Time Code* invites multiple

FIGURE 6.13 Four interconnected plotlines shown simultaneously
In *Time Code* (2000), action in one plotline occasionally intersects with action from another plotline, but viewers usually see four unedited plotlines simultaneously. *A Red Mullet Production; Screen Gems/Sony Pictures Entertainment Company*

viewings. However, like viewers struggling with the four alternating plotlines of *Intolerance*, many viewers may find trying to figure out the story of *Time Code* too demanding and frustrating to give the film a second chance.

Plotlines may be viewed consecutively even though they occur simultaneously. Jim Jarmusch's *Night on Earth* (1992) has five consecutive brief plotlines. Each is set in one of four different time zones, but each begins at the same moment in time: 7:07 p.m. in Los Angeles, 10:07 p.m. in New York, 4:07 a.m. in Paris and Rome, and 5:07 a.m. in Helsinki. Viewers are offered the rare opportunity to see what happens simultaneously at various places around the world (Figure 6.14).

Plotlines may be nonchronological and from many time periods, yet for all but one of the major characters they may intersect at one time and place, as in *The Joy Luck Club* (1993), which has eight major plotlines: for four middle-aged women born in China and for each woman's American-born grown daughter (Figure 6.15).

Ways to structure a narrative seem limitless. Plots may be extremely complicated yet entertaining and easy to follow, as in *Run Lola Run* (see the feature on pp. 268–69). The film begins and proceeds chronologically except for some brief flashbacks. From the time Lola begins to run, the story pro-

a)

b)

c)

d)

FIGURE 6.14 Multiple simultaneous plotlines
In *Night on Earth* (1992), each of the five uninterrupted and simultaneous plotlines involves a taxi driver and his or her fare,
and the stories take place (in order) in (a) Los Angeles, (b) New
York, (c) Paris, (d) Rome, and (e) Helsinki. In its use of simultaneous nonintersecting plotlines that are presented successively,
the film's structure is rare, perhaps even one of a kind. *Jim Jarmusch; Fine Line Features*

e)

FIGURE 6.15 Multiple interwoven plotlines
The Joy Luck Club (1993) tells the stories of four Chinese mothers and each mother's Chinese American daughter. The film illustrates how complex the combinations of multiple plotlines may be. In the months before the plot of *The Joy Luck Club* begins, Suyuan (on the left) has died, and Suyuan's middle-aged women friends (seen here) have written to friends and relatives in China to locate Suyuan's abandoned daughters, left behind as babies decades earlier during a war in China. The movie begins with a going-away party for Suyuan's daughter June (the second woman from the left), who plans to leave for China the next day to meet her two half-sisters. Most of the movie consists of flashbacks from the going-away party to each middle-aged woman's painful childhood or early adulthood in China, present-tense scenes from the party, and flashbacks to selected events from the lives of the four adult American daughters. The film concludes with June's arrival in China and her meeting with her two half-sisters. Except for Suyuan, all the other seven major characters meet at one place and time, the going-away party. *Wayne Wang, Amy Tan, Ronald Bass, Patrick Markey; Buena Vista*

gresses chronologically (with three scattered brief flashforwards) toward an ending. But the story begins again as Lola begins to run again; this time with a different three brief flashforwards and a very different ending. The film is still not over. The story begins a third time as Lola begins to run yet again and includes a brief flashforward as the story races to its conclusion.

TIME

Fictional films have three tenses: present, future, and past. Also to be considered is the amount of time it takes to show a film and the time span represented by a story.

Structure of *Run Lola Run*

EXPOSITION (11 MIN., 51 SEC.)

Crowd seen in fast motion. Actors are highlighted briefly. Bank guard kicks soccer ball high up in air. Film's title formed by masses of people. Opening credits over animation of Lola running. Photo I.D.s of characters and cast. Establishing shots. Inside Lola's apartment, she answers phone call from a desperate Manni. In black-and-white flashbacks, we see how Lola's moped was stolen and learn she could not pick up Manni after his criminal transaction. We also learn Manni had to get on a subway train, on which he left a bag with the money he was to deliver to his criminal boss, Ronnie. Lola has twenty minutes to reach Manni with DM 100,000 (at that time, nearly $60,000). She runs by a room in which her mother is on the phone. On the nearby TV, we see a cartoon Lola running toward stairs and down them.

I (22 min., 26 sec.)	II (20 min., 15 sec.)	III (20 min., 57 sec.)
■ Cartoon Lola runs by cartoon dog on the stairs.	■ Cartoon boy on stairs trips cartoon Lola, and she tumbles down stairs.	■ Cartoon Lola jumps over cartoon dog on stairs.
■ On sidewalk, Lola brushes against a woman pushing a baby stroller.	■ Running outside, she limps for a while.	■ Lola does not brush against the woman with a baby stroller.
■ Flashforward photos: authorities take the woman's baby; the woman steals a baby.	■ She bumps against the woman with the baby stroller.	■ Flashforward photos: the woman becomes a Jehovah's Witness.
■ Lola's father with his disgruntled mistress.	■ Flashforward photos: the woman wins a lottery.	■ On sidewalk, nuns do not part, so Lola runs into street and nearly hits cyclist.
■ On sidewalk, nuns part and allow Lola to run through their group.	■ On sidewalk, nuns part and allow Lola to run through their group.	■ Cyclist rides off and stops at a snack place; he offers to sell his cycle to the homeless man.
■ Nearby cyclist offers to sell Lola his bicycle.	■ Nearby cyclist offers to sell Lola his bicycle.	■ Lola runs into Mr. Meyer's car and ends up on its hood; the white car passes by. Lola runs off.
■ Flashforward photos: cyclist beaten up; courtship; marriage.	■ Flashforward photos: cyclist's unhappy fate.	■ Lola rounds a corner where we previously saw the homeless man walking with the bag of money.
■ Lola runs in front of Mr. Meyer's car (see Figure a).	■ Lola runs over hood of Mr. Meyer's car.	■ Homeless man cycling.
■ Meyer's car hits side of white car driving by.	■ Meyer's car hits side of white car driving by.	■ Lola's father learns that his mistress is pregnant and assumes the child is his. He hurriedly leaves his office as Lola runs toward his office.
■ Lola runs by the homeless man carrying Manni's bag of money.	■ Lola bumps into the homeless man carrying Manni's bag of money.	■ Lola's father gets in Meyer's car, and they drive off as Lola vainly shouts after them.
■ Mistress tells Lola's father that she is pregnant.	■ Lola runs by woman in bank hallway.	
■ Lola runs by woman in bank hallway.	■ In Lola's father's office, mistress has already told Lola's father that she is pregnant but not by him. . . . Lola calls the mistress a stupid cow. Lola's dad slaps Lola; she wrecks part of his office as the frightened mistress looks on.	
■ Flashforward photos of that woman's tragic fate.		

a)

b)

Run Lola Run (1998) consists of a prologue followed by three variations of the rest of the story. In the film, some actions are repeated with variation, such as (a) Lola and Mr. Meyer's car; in the first version she runs in front of it without being hit and (b) the red ambulance and the large plate glass window men are carrying across the street; in the second version, the ambulance shatters the glass. Frame enlargements. *Stefan Arndt; Sony Pictures Classic*

I (continued)	II (continued)	III (continued)

I (continued)

- Lola's dad escorts Lola out of his office and tells her he is not her birth father.
- Outside bank, Lola asks old woman the time of day.
- Red ambulance stops short of hitting large plate glass being carried across the street.
- Lola is a second too late, and Manni enters market and begins robbing it. Lola hits armed guard on back of head with a plastic bag of groceries and helps Manni with the robbery.
- Outside, they run as the song "What a difference a day makes" is heard on soundtrack.
- Police stop Lola and Manni and accidentally shoot Lola.
- Her dying thoughts: she asks Manni many questions related to his feelings for her.

II (continued)

- In bank hallway, Lola shouts at woman.
- Lola takes bank guard's pistol and takes her father hostage.
- Flashforward photos for woman in bank hallway: romantic happiness with male bank colleague.
- Bank guard places his hand near his heart as if the stress were causing him pain as Lola robs the bank.
- Lola tosses the gun aside then leaves the bank. Outside, police push Lola aside, assuming that someone else is trying to rob the bank. She runs away.
- Red ambulance runs through large plate glass being carried across the street (see Figure b).
- Lola arrives in time to stop Manni from robbing market, but looking straight ahead at Lola, he walks in front of ambulance.
- Manni's dying thoughts: Lola will soon forget him and find another lover.

III (continued)

- A blind woman by a phone booth helps Manni spot the homeless man who is cycling by. Manni chases him.
- The homeless man and Manni indirectly cause the car with Meyer and Lola's father to run into the white car after all. The man who stole Lola's moped runs into the back of the white car.
- Lola runs in front of a large truck and is nearly hit by it.
- She goes into a nearby casino and wins a lot of money.
- Manni pulls his gun on the homeless man on the cycle, gets back the bag of money, but gives homeless man the gun.
- After the red ambulance stops to avoid hitting the plate glass, Lola gets into the back of the ambulance. It contains the bank guard, who has a life-threatening heart problem. After Lola holds his hand, his heart recovers.
- At the intersection where she is supposed to meet Manni, Lola gets out of the ambulance.
- Down the block, Manni arrives in black car with Ronnie. All is OK between them.
- Manni kisses Lola briefly; then they walk away. Lola is carrying the sack of money. Freeze-frame. (75:48 total)

269

Present Time, Flashforwards, and Flashbacks

"Movies should have a beginning, a middle, and an end," harrumphed French Film Maker Georges Franju at a symposium some years back. "Certainly," replied [film director] Jean-Luc Godard. "But not necessarily in that order." (Corliss)

Most makers of narrative films agree with Franju and arrange scenes chronologically. But the earliest scenes of a film's story may occur late in the film or even at its ending, and the latest scenes of some other story may occur early in the narrative, as in *Heavenly Creatures* (1994). As we will see, these and countless other temporal arrangements of scenes are possible because of flashbacks and flashforwards.

flashforward: A shot, scene, or sequence—though usually only a shot or two—that interrupts a narrative to show events that happen in the future.

Only a few movies use chronological order with an occasional **flashforward**. *Easy Rider* (1969) is one of them. About 77¼ minutes into the film, the Captain America character is in a brothel; he looks up past a small statue toward a plaque that reads "Death only closes a man's reputation and determines it as good or bad." Next we see from a helicopter a one-second shot of something burning off to the side of a country road. In the brothel, Captain America looks down, and the action resumes. Does the **cutaway shot** suggest he vaguely glimpses the future, or are viewers meant to see the shot as a glimpse of the future, or is it meant to puzzle viewers because it doesn't fit in and make sense at the moment? Or does the shot function in two or more ways? Viewers cannot even recognize it as a flashforward unless they remember that one-second shot approximately sixteen minutes later as they see the end of the film, when Captain America is shot by a passing motorist and, in the film's last shot, his motorcycle is seen in flames off to the side of that country road. Occasionally during the opening credits, a flashforward shows events that are repeated well into a film, as in *My Life as a Dog* (1985), *GoodFellas* (1990), *Go* (1999), and *American Beauty* (1999).

cutaway (shot): A shot that briefly interrupts the visual representation of a subject to show something else.

Although flashforwards are usually mainly visual, they may be auditory. At the end of *Medium Cool*, 108¼ minutes into the film, the car radio announces a serious car accident that we witness nearly fifty seconds later. According to the French scholar Marc Vernet, this **technique** was used years earlier in Alain Robbe-Grillet's *L'immortelle* (1962): "We hear the sound of an accident at the beginning of the film even though that crash will occur later in the film" (92).

film technique: Any aspect of filmmaking, such as the use of sets, lighting, sound effects, music, or editing.

Flashforwards "can only be recognized retrospectively" (Chatman 64) and are demanding of viewers. They can be confusing and frustrating if the events shown are too far into the future or the flashforwards are frequent or lengthy. Perhaps because flashforwards let viewers glimpse consequences they do not yet anticipate or are not yet interested in, they are rarely used.

flashback: A shot or a few shots, a brief scene, or (rarely) a sequence that interrupts a narrative to show earlier events.

Flashbacks are much more common than flashforwards. Like flashforwards, they are nearly always visual or visual and auditory, but they may be exclusively auditory. In *The Night Porter* (1974), the main character returns home after fishing with another man and remembers the words that the other man speaks—seconds before the main character pushes the other man into the water to drown.

Often a flashback briefly interrupts a chronological progression of events to show what influenced a character earlier. Flashbacks may also be used at the end of a film to reveal causes of previously puzzling events, as in *Exotica* (1994). Near the end of that film, a flashback reveals how the discovery of a murdered girl affected an enigmatic young woman, and in the film's last two scenes a flashback to an even earlier time reveals more information about the enigmatic young woman's relationship to the troubled main male character. By withholding these revelations until the last scenes, which is what some theorists refer to as a "privileged" placement, the final scenes help clarify the whole. A flashback may also be used within a flashback, as when viewers learn who indeed shot Liberty Valance in *The Man Who Shot Liberty Valance* (1962) and as when viewers see scenes that two twelve-year-old characters (Vern and later Gordie) recount or remember in *Stand by Me* (1986).

In some films—such as the Italian classic *8½* (1963) and the Japanese classic *Rashomon* (1950)—it is sometimes difficult, sometimes impossible, to know if certain scenes are flashbacks to events that happened or are dreams, fantasies, or lies. In *8½*, a director tries to regain his creativity and confidence and finish a costly and complicated film while trying to cope with his wife, lover, producer, actors, and the press. That much of the narrative proceeds chronologically but is intercut with frequent scenes of the director's dreams, fantasies, or memories, although sometimes viewers cannot know which is which. In *Rashomon*, viewers cannot know which of four quite different accounts of a man's death and events leading up to it is the most reliable and which are self-serving lies. Both *8½* and *Rashomon* are not based on "the assumptions on which all conventional (Hollywood-style) film narrative is based, namely that the world is wholly decipherable, that people's motivations can be understood, that all events have clear causes and that the end of a fiction will offer us the chance to fuse all elements of the plot into a single coherent dramatic action" (Armes 103–04).

On rare occasions, a film is basically chronological but includes flashbacks and flashforwards, as in *Run Lola Run* (see the feature on pp. 268–69). *Don't Look Now* (1973) is also mostly chronological but sometimes uses flashbacks and occasional flashforwards. One memorable flashforward occurs when the main male character glimpses his wife on a passing boat with two other women, and all three are dressed in black. Near the film's ending viewers see some shots related to that earlier scene, but they are from the man's funeral procession in Venice. The flashforward earlier in the film reveals that the man is so psychic he could briefly see beyond his own life although he did not realize what he was seeing then. One movie narrative that jumps around in time extensively is *Slaughterhouse-Five* (1972). It uses many flashforwards and flashbacks, some of which are difficult to place in a chronological ordering of the events but seem appropriate because its central character has become "unstuck in time."

Chronological Time and Nonchronological Time

Plot is the selection and arrangement of a story's events. **Fabula** is the chronological reconstruction of all the events of a nonchronological plot. Both a plot and its corresponding fabula contain the same events, but the nonchronological arrangement of events changes focus, mood, and viewer interest—sometimes considerably.

Storytellers have used flashback at least since the time of Homer and his *Odyssey*, which begins in the middle, flashes back to the beginning, and then returns to where the first section left off and concludes the story. *Out of the Past* has basically the same structure (Figure 6.16). The plot begins not with the earliest event, when Jeff, the main character, is given the job of retrieving Kathie and thus is about to be sucked into a dangerous, uncertain life. Instead, it begins at a later stage, when he is seemingly free of his past and in love with a woman he can trust, so by the end of the film his loss of security and happiness is all the more poignant.

For another example of a nonchronological film's plot and fabula, see the Close-Up section on pp. 281–83.

So strong is the human proclivity to try to sort through events and make sense of them (that's perhaps the main reason most people are endlessly fascinated by narratives) that for most viewers, attempting to construct fabulas is irresistible. But as demonstrated by *Slaughterhouse-Five*, *Jacob's Ladder* (1990), *Lost Highway* (1997), *Mulholland Drive* (2001), and occasional other movies, constructing the fabula may be problematic because different attentive and thoughtful viewers will disagree about whether certain events are present, past, or future events or are only imagined (fantasized or dreamed). Then, too, some films, such as *Amores Perros*, are constructed so that making a complete fabula is impossible.

Both a description and brief analysis of the plot and fabula of *Citizen Kane* can be found on the Web site for this book at <bedfordstmartins.com /phillips-film>.

Running and Story Times

Running time is the amount of time it takes to view a film and includes opening and closing credits. Sometimes the credits accompany images of the film's subjects; sometimes they do not. Running times of features vary from one hour to nearly twenty-six hours for a TV series later shown in theaters

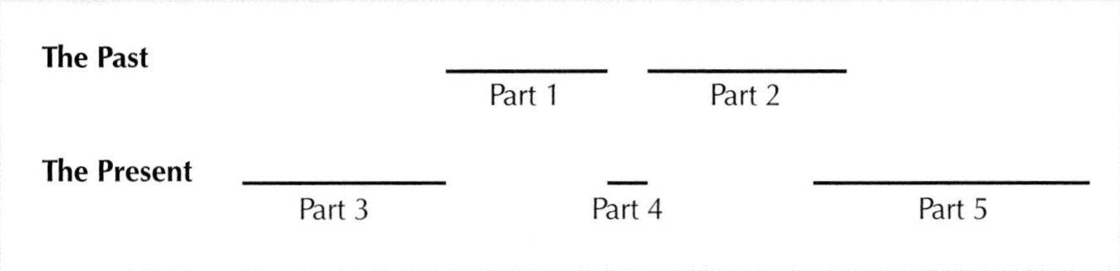

The Past

                           Part 1   Part 2

The Present

        Part 3   Part 4   Part 5

FIGURE 6.16 The plot and fabula of *Out of the Past* (1947)

THE PLOT = Parts 3, 1, 4, 2, 5:

1 minute into the film:

Part 3 Joe, Whit's assistant, arrives at Jeff's gas station and tells Jeff that Whit, a big-time gambler, wants to see him. . . . As Jeff and Ann, his girlfriend, drive to Whit's Lake Tahoe residence, Jeff begins to tell Ann about his past in New York where he and his partner Jack Fisher worked as "detectives."

12 minutes into the film:

Part 1 Whit gives Jeff the job of finding Kathie, who shot him and ran off with $40,000 of his money. . . . In Acapulco, Jeff locates Kathie—and promptly falls for her. . . . During Whit and Joe's surprise visit to Jeff in Acapulco, they learn nothing about Kathie's whereabouts and leave. Soon Jeff and Kathie do, too.

33½ minutes into the film:

Part 4 We are very briefly reminded that Jeff is still telling Ann about his past as they drive toward Lake Tahoe.

34 minutes into the film:

Part 2 Jeff and Kathie hide out in San Francisco but Fisher spots them and Jeff and Kathie split up. . . . As the couple is reunited, Fisher shows up and tries to blackmail them, but Kathie kills Fisher and drives off.

39½ minutes into the film:

Part 5 After Jeff finishes telling Ann about his past, they arrive at Whit's residence, and Ann drives off. Inside, Jeff sees that Kathie has returned to Whit. To repay Whit for his betrayal with Kathie, Jeff agrees to steal some papers from an attorney in San Francisco but is framed for the man's murder, which viewers learn later Joe committed. . . . Joe intends to shoot Jeff, but from below Jeff's helper hooks Joe with a fishing hook and pulls him to his death. . . . Jeff discovers that Kathie has killed Whit. She threatens to tell authorities that Jeff committed murders and makes it clear she intends to be in charge from now on. Jeff seems to agree with her but makes a telephone call. At a police roadblock, Kathie quickly realizes Jeff had called the police and shoots him, but she is shot and their car crashes. . . . Later Jeff's helper lies to Ann so she can more readily get on with her life with a man who has long loved her.

96 minutes into the film:

The End

THE FABULA = 1, 2, 3, 4, 5

(*Heimat II*, 1993) or seven hours for a film made for theatrical release (*Sátántangó*, 1993).[3]

Story time is the amount of time covered in a film's narrative or story. For example, if a film's earliest scene occurs on a Sunday and its latest scene takes place on the following Friday, the story time is six days. Beginning with some of the early short silent films, story time has nearly always been much longer than running time. As early as Georges Méliès's "A Trip to the Moon" (1902), story time stretched out over days but running time was only minutes (pp. 116–17). The story time of the Chinese film *To Live* (1994) is approximately twenty-five years (from "the 1940s" to "the 1960s" plus five or six more years); the running time is 129 minutes. The plot of *Women on the Verge of a Nervous Breakdown* (1988) begins one morning and ends approximately thirty-six hours later, on the evening of the following day; the film's running time is eighty-eight minutes.

In a few movies, the story time is approximately the same as the running time. For example, the story time of *High Noon* is about 102 minutes (from about 10:30 to 12:12), and the film's running time is 81½ minutes. The story time of *Nick of Time* (1995) is approximately ninety-five minutes (from noon until at least five minutes after the attempted assassination at 1:30), but the running time, excluding the opening credits, is only about eighty minutes. *Nick of Time* keeps story and running times approximately equal by sometimes condensing story time, sometimes expanding it. For example, the opening events supposedly take 480 seconds, but actually only 143 seconds pass. Conversely, the events shown in the film from precisely 1:28 to exactly 1:30 take not 120 seconds but 327. For both *High Noon* and *Nick of Time*, many critics and viewers have commented that their story times coincide with their running times. Almost. Examples of films in which running time and story time are identical are extremely rare, although, excluding its opening credits, *Time Code* is such a film.

On rare occasions, a film's story time is less than its running time. *Night on Earth* consists of five plotlines, each beginning at the same moment in time and each having a story time of thirty-five minutes. Although the film's story time is thirty-five minutes, its running time is 125 minutes. Another film with a story time less than its running time is "An Occurrence at Owl Creek Bridge" (1962), a story of a civilian facing being hanged from a rail-

---

[3]The longest film for theatrical release cannot be identified because many early films have not survived: there are no known copies of more than 70 percent of all feature films made before the 1920s or of about 50 percent of all American films made before 1950. Moreover, many films that have survived may be incomplete. In addition, before the late 1920s, not all projectors ran at the same speed. The French film *Travail* (1919) may have run eight hours. The 1925 *Les misérables* reputedly consisted of thirty-two 35 mm reels (each reel could be from thirteen to sixteen minutes long), so that movie might have run anywhere from seven to eight-and-a-half hours.

road bridge during the American Civil War. The film's story time is slightly more than ten minutes; its running time is almost twenty-eight minutes.

Nearly all fictional films are imprecise about how much time supposedly elapses between scenes. "The String Bean" (described on p. 249) shows an old woman finding a discarded plant, planting seeds, nurturing the new plant, finding it uprooted, then planting seeds from it, presumably to begin the cycle again. How much time passes between the time the woman first plants the seeds and one sprouts? How much time passes altogether in the film? What is the story time: one month, two months, three? This imprecision is not a weakness of the film but a characteristic of fictional films, which are generally less specific about their story time than fiction or published plays.

Filmmakers can present many events selected from a brief story time, as in *High Noon*, or relatively few events taken from a long story time, as in *2001*, which depicts highly selective events from 4 million B.C. to beyond our sense of time. Storytellers may even repeat the same block of story time and segments within it—for example, a twenty-four-hour period and various minutes within it—over and over, though with many variations in the events during each repetition of the time. That was done for parts of a day in *Groundhog Day* (1993). Repetition is also used in the three versions of the sequence that shows Lola running to save her boyfriend in *Run Lola Run*.

STYLE

Style is another term that has different meanings for different critics and theorists. In this book, *style* refers to the way a text, such as a film, represents its subjects. Possible styles include farce, black comedy, fantasy, **realism**, abstract, magic realism, **socialist realism**, and parody. A style may be used in any kind of film. For example, a parody (an amusing imitation of human behavior or of a text, part of a text, or texts) may be used in any **genre** or type of fictional film. A western or horror film, for instance, may include a parody, or an entire film may be a parody. This chapter does not present an exhaustive discussion of film styles, but some styles, such as parody and socialist realism, are discussed elsewhere in the book. What follows illustrates only two of the most challenging styles for beginning film students: black comedy and magic realism.

Some writers, filmmakers, and other weavers of tales have tacitly asked viewers to consider the possible humor in subjects often considered inappropriate for comedy, such as warfare, cannibalism, murder, death, and illness. Such a narrative style is usually called black humor or **black comedy**. Often black comedy is used in **satires**. After its first fifteen minutes or so, *Citizen Ruth* (1996) satirizes the extreme behavior of both anti-abortion groups and abortion rights groups, daring choices as the main subjects of a comedy. *Happiness* (1998) also has flashes of black humor (Figure 6.17).

realism: Representation in a text that is widely believed to render its subjects accurately.

socialist realism: A Soviet doctrine and style in force from the mid-1930s to the 1980s that decreed that Soviet texts, including films, must promote communism and the working class.

satire: A representation that indirectly exposes and perhaps ridicules individual or group thinking or behavior for being foolish, evil, or stupid or for having some other shortcoming.

FIGURE 6.17 Black humor within a serious situation
Initially, the opening scene of *Happiness* (1998) shows a serious subject being treated in the usual serious way. The story's first shot is of a concerned young woman's face; then appears the man's anguished look. We viewers soon figure out that she has just told him that she doesn't want to date him anymore. Later, he cries briefly and blows his nose into his cloth napkin. Later still, he asks if she is sure, and when she replies without hesitation that she is, he asks "Is it someone else?" and she responds without malice, "No. It's just you." For many viewers, this part of the scene is unexpectedly humorous, and sometimes in this film, viewers don't know whether they should laugh or feel for the emotional pain being witnessed. As elsewhere in *Happiness*, the first scene shows amusing moments in situations not normally considered humorous. In black comedy, certain moments may amuse some viewers but offend or shock others. Frame enlargement. *Good Machine/Killer Films; Good Machine International*

pace: A viewer's sense that a subject (such as narrative developments or factual information) is being presented rapidly or slowly.

In plot summary, black comedies rarely sound amusing because they often involve violence, death, or at least extreme emotional or physical pain. To make them work, their makers must handle **pace** and mood masterfully. Typically, black comedies amuse some viewers and shock or offend others. In *Female Trouble* (1974), the main character has so many problems—some of them outrageous or at least startling—that some viewers are offended; some are amused; and still others are by turns offended and amused (Figure 6.18).

Comedy involves pain—such as embarrassment, confusion, a fall—for someone else, but successful makers of comedies know where and how to mute or distance the pain. Because the sounds of someone being hit or hitting the floor in the new sound films could be alarming and disconcerting to audiences in the late 1920s or early 1930s, the comedy team of Laurel and Hardy exaggerated those sounds to achieve comic results. *Eating Raoul* (1982) downplays the pain of several murders in a number of ways. For one thing, the soundtrack contributes to the film's amusing results. The weapon of choice is usually a large cast-iron frying pan, and the sound effect of it hitting a head (which viewers hear often) is never squishy, squirting, bone crushing, or snapping. For another thing, the killings are never messy and never seen close-up. We never see blood or sense that the victims suffer: one minute they are alive; a few seconds later they are still and breathless (Figure 6.19). Makers of black comedies dare to include more pain than some viewers are used to seeing in comedies. Depending on the filmmakers' skill in anticipating viewers' responses and on the viewers' backgrounds and tastes, black comedies may amuse or offend.

Another style used since World War II, mainly in fiction, is **magic realism**—wildly improbable or impossible events in an otherwise realistic narrative. Most of *Erendira* (1982)—based on a script by a master of literary

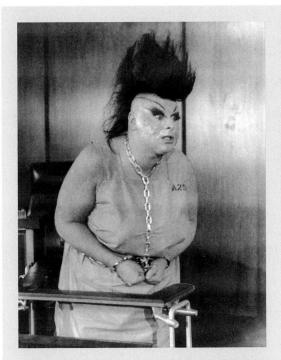

FIGURE 6.18 A black comedy that may amuse or offend
John Waters's *Female Trouble* (1974) shows the story of Dawn Davenport (played by Divine/Dave Lochary), a woman whose problems start in her high school days, especially after her parents fail to give her "cha-cha heels" for Christmas. Approximately nine minutes into the film, she throws a tantrum, overturns the Christmas tree onto her mother, and runs away. Nearly everything that could go wrong in a woman's life goes wrong in Dawn's. For example, she is raped and ends up with an uncontrollable child, who years later is nearly raped by the same man. Her face is scarred when her former husband's aunt throws acid at her. After many complications, Dawn is tried for kidnapping and multiple murders. For some viewers, *Female Trouble* is mostly offensive; for others, it is fairly consistently amusing. *Copyright 1974 by New Line Productions, Inc. All rights reserved. Photo by Bruce Moore. Photo appears courtesy of New Line Productions, Inc., New York City*

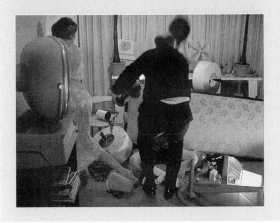

FIGURE 6.19 De-emphasizing pain and emphasizing humor
Eating Raoul (1982), a black comedy classic, includes many killings, but viewers never see one close up. One way of hiding the deed is by interposing something or someone between the victim and the camera. Here, nearly thirty-six minutes into the film, the man wielding the large iron skillet bonks a victim who is sitting on the floor. At least twice, the victim is in another room, and viewers hear only the familiar bonking sound made by the skillet presumably hitting yet another head. Frame enlargement. *20th Century–Fox International Classics & Quartet/Films Incorporated*

magic realism, the Colombian writer Gabriel García Márquez—is rendered in a realistic style. But the film also has many scenes incorporating magic realism. In one series of scenes that begins 87½ minutes into the film, the cruel grandmother consumes an enormous amount of rat poison mixed into a birthday cake and collapses onto her bed. After she starts to revive, the young man who has poisoned her observes, "Incredible! She's tougher than an elephant! There

FIGURE 6.20 Magic realism as symbol
Most of the story of *Like Water for Chocolate* (1992) is plausible or realistic. At times, however, the film includes magical events. Here, approximately forty-seven minutes into the film, is the beginning of a shot that eventually shows that Tita is trailing a shawl nearly half as long as an American football field presumably because of the enormous cold she has been feeling. Frame enlargement. *Alfonso Arau; Miramax*

was enough poison to kill a million rats!" The next morning, the grandmother wakes up, smiles, then says to her granddaughter Erendira, "God bless you, child. I hadn't slept that well since I was 15! I had a beautiful dream of love." The only ill effect from her previous night's dessert is that her hair is falling out, which amuses her. The episode is unreal or magical (and in this case, symbolic to some viewers): no one could survive so huge a dosage of poison or would react with amusement as her hair falls out.

In the 1992 film *Like Water for Chocolate*, the scrumptious food that Tita prepares causes those who eat it to feel as she felt when she prepared it—for example, sad or lustful. Some of the film's magic realism is unrelated to food (Figure 6.20). Examples of magic realism appear in the French film *Amélie* (*Le fabuleux destin d'Amélie Poulain*, 2001)—talking photographs, a winking statue, and approximately 106 minutes into the film Amélie's disappointed face and her body **morphing** into water that splashes onto the floor when the man she is attracted to doesn't see the note she has written for him. A film may use magic realism only occasionally. In *Trainspotting* (1996), a film that is overwhelmingly gritty and realistic, one of the most memorable scenes is rendered as magic realism (Figure 6.21).

A film may use one style sporadically, as in *Fargo*, which mixes black comedy with unamusing realism. Or as a fictional film unwinds, it may increasingly emphasize one style more than another. At first, the Italian film *Life Is Beautiful* (1998), like so many crowd-pleasing movies, blends fantasy and realism as a man courts a woman amusingly and romantically. Later, disquieting signs of fascism and anti-Semitism begin to emerge, and the film turns darker, literally and figuratively. In the last part of the film, which is set in a Nazi concentration camp, the style is somewhat grittier and more realistic than it was at the film's beginning (Figure 6.22).

Styles can strongly influence how viewers react to a film. If viewers refuse to go along with the magic realism of *Erendira* or *Like Water for Chocolate*, they will miss much of the pleasure of interacting with the film on its own terms. Likewise, if viewers beginning to watch the famous **experimental film**

experimental film: A film that rejects the conventions of mainstream movies and explores the possibilities of the film medium.

FIGURE 6.21 Magic realism as central symbol

In *Trainspotting* (1996), a young man addicted to drugs has hidden two suppositories of illegal drugs in the back of his pants. Urgently, he goes to a public toilet. After relieving himself, he realizes the suppositories have fallen into the toilet. Then, almost ten minutes into the film, the magic realism begins: (a) he plunges into the toilet, (b) swims down through clear water past a large spiked mine to the bottom, (c) snatches up the two suppositories, turns to swim back up, and says something unintelligible. (d) He tosses out the suppositories of drugs, emerges from the toilet, and spits out some water. These actions are impossible in actuality, but they symbolically and memorably show to what depths a person hooked on drugs might descend—and, the presence of the mine suggests, the dangers in doing so. Frame enlargements. *Channel Four Films, A Figment Film; Miramax Films*

"Un chien andalou" (1928) expect the usual mixture of realism and fantasy so prevalent in Hollywood movies, they will remain uninvolved and disappointed. Viewers who quickly recognize that "Un chien andalou" consists of a series of discontinuous dreamlike scenes are much more likely to become intrigued by the film and enjoy it. If audiences are watching a film that uses a style that they have not previously seen, such as magic realism, they need to figure out the film's style quickly and give the film a chance to do what it can do within the parameters it has set out for itself. If viewers know nothing about the film's style and cannot figure it out quickly or if they refuse to play along with a style they do know (for example, if they decline to be amused by a parody), they will sit glumly and hope for a different style and a different film—in vain.

a)

b)

c)

FIGURE 6.22 Shifting the mix of styles as a film progresses
(a) The initial sequences of *Life Is Beautiful* (1998), in which a man courts a woman in 1939 Italy, blend realism and (romantic) fantasy. (b) Gradually the political situation worsens. This frame from near the end of the film's first half shows the subject somewhat more realistically: Guido has rescued the woman he has been courting from her stuffy fiancé, and they have ridden off on the horse owned by Guido's Jewish uncle, but the horse has been painted what translates as "Attention, Jewish horse"—an indication of rising anti-Semitism. (c) In Nazi Germany, where the family is imprisoned, the horrors of the Nazi camp are kept largely in the background, though some realistic details are shown. Here, Guido, as seen by his son peering out of a rectangular opening, is seen dressed as a woman. He has been caught by a Nazi guard and is being marched away. Even then, Guido has the presence of mind to look in the direction of his hidden son (toward the camera), wink at him, and exaggerate his walking to make the boy think that this development is only part of the game that Guido has convinced his son the entire camp is playing. Through a gradual shift of emphasis, the scenes in the concentration camp have somewhat less fantasy material than the scenes at the film's beginning. Frame enlargements. *Cecchi Gori Group; Miramax*

CLOSE-UP: THE PLOT AND FABULA OF *PULP FICTION* (1994)

The plot for *Pulp Fiction* includes many deviations from a straight chronology (see the plot and fabula outlined below). For one thing, unlike nearly all fictional films, the film's plot includes repeated actions and parallel actions. In the plot, Jules (the Samuel L. Jackson character) is prominent at both the beginning and ending. In the fabula, he does not appear in the last two major sections, though for many viewers he is probably the film's most complex and intriguing character. The nonchronological plot of *Pulp Fiction* makes possible a more exciting and engaging beginning (the beginning of a robbery) than a chronological arrangement of all the film's events (two guys talking in a car). The plot also results in a less upbeat ending: at the end of the film's plot, we know that death lurks around the corner for Vincent; at the end of the fabula, Butch picks up his girlfriend, and they drive off. The plot's last scene also allows viewers to experience the unusual situation of learning what happens before and after the film's first scene. Because the plot shows two versions of the action in the grill and revisits the apartment where men get killed, we can better understand the context of actions we saw earlier and the perspectives of different characters at the same place: for example, the film first focuses entirely on Ringo and Honey Bunny at the grill and the second time at the grill focuses on the couple, Vincent, and especially Jules. The plot for *Pulp Fiction* is so intricate that few viewers can completely reconstruct the fabula after only one showing. Its plot is much more demanding of the audience than its fabula, and for some viewers the film's complex structure is both a challenge and a pleasure.

THE PLOT OF *PULP FICTION*

B.2. In a grill, Ringo and Honey Bunny talk about robbery; Ringo calls out "Garçon" to the waitress. Ringo and Honey Bunny talk

FIGURE 6.23 Butch with his boss Marsellus
Here, almost twenty-three minutes into *Pulp Fiction* (1994), Butch is considering Marsellus's implied request that he accept a large sum of money and throw an upcoming boxing match. Frame enlargement. *Lawrence Bender; Miramax.*

some more; then they decide to rob the grill and its customers, pull out their guns, and shout that it's a holdup.

[Opening Credits]

A.1. Vincent and Jules in car. The two arrive at a building. When they are about to go inside an apartment, it's 7:22 a.m. Inside, they confront two men who had been trying to get away with an attaché case containing something valuable and belonging to the two men's "business partner," Marsellus. Jules and Vincent locate the attaché case and kill the two men.

Title card: "Vincent Vega & Marsellus Wallace's Wife"

C. At Marsellus's business, Marsellus tells Butch, a prize fighter, that Butch's best times are past and offers him an envelope full of money (Figure 6.23). After Butch accepts it, Marsellus tells him he's to take a dive in his upcoming boxing match. Vincent and Jules arrive with the attaché case. Marsellus calls to Vincent and embraces him.

D.   Vincent buys powerful heroin, shoots up, and (now night) goes to take out Marsellus's wife, Mia, as Marsellus had asked him to do while he is away. Vincent and Mia go out, then return to her and Marsellus's place, where she overdoses on drugs and almost dies. . . .

E.   Before his fight, Butch dreams about receiving a watch originally acquired by his great-grandfather.

Title card: "The Gold Watch"

Butch wins the fight and escapes. Vincent and Marsellus's bartender (Paul) report about the search for Butch to Marsellus, who is furious. Butch joins his lover, Fabienne, then the next morning returns to his apartment, fetches his watch, and kills Vincent. At a nearby stoplight, Butch "runs into Marsellus" and tries to kill him; then Marsellus tries to kill Butch (Figure 6.24). Both enter a pawnshop and are captured and tied up. Marsellus is sexually assaulted; Butch saves him, takes the motorcycle of one of their captors, and picks up Fabienne.

Title card: "The Bonnie Situation"

A.1. (parallel to part of A.1 at beginning of film). A man in the next room hears Jules speaking immediately before the second of the two murders seen near the film's beginning. Repeating the end of A.1 at the beginning of the film, Jules and Vincent shoot the second man.

A.2. The man from the next room bursts into the room that Jules and Vincent enter at the beginning of the film, shoots at them, but misses; they kill him (see Figure 3.21 on p. 139). Jules thinks it's a miracle he wasn't killed. In car, Jules says he is going to retire.

Vincent accidentally kills their own accomplice (Marvin), thereby splattering blood all over the car and the two men. At Jimmie's house, Jules and Vincent seek help (it's 8:00 a.m.). Calls are made, and at 8:50 Mr. Wolf arrives to supervise the cleanup before Jimmie's wife, Bonnie, will arrive home from work at about 9:30. At Monster Joe's Used Auto Parts, Mr. Wolf has presumably made arrangements for the elimination of the car with the accomplice's body in the trunk. Vincent and Jules decide to go for breakfast.

B.1. At a grill, Jules again tells Vincent that he plans to quit the business and "walk the earth."

B.2. (repeat of a line from near the beginning of the film). Ringo calls out "Garçon."

B.2. (parallel to the time at the beginning of the film between the time Ringo calls "Garçon" and Ringo and Honey Bunny begin the robbery). Jules and Vincent talk some more; then Vincent leaves to go to the restroom.

B.2. (repeat of the end of B.2 at film's beginning). Ringo and Honey Bunny pull their guns and begin the holdup.

B.3. After many complications, Ringo and Honey Bunny complete the robbery and leave; soon afterward Vincent and Jules leave (Jules still has the attaché case he plans to deliver to Marsellus).

THE FABULA OF *PULP FICTION*

A.   Vincent and Jules in car. The two arrive at an apartment building. When they are about to enter an apartment, it's 7:22 a.m. Inside, they confront two men who had been trying to get away with something valuable belonging to Marsellus. Jules and Vincent retrieve an attaché case full of Marsellus's valuables and kill the two men. The man from the next room bursts into the room and shoots at

FIGURE 6.24 Marsellus resolved to kill Butch
Approximately ninety-five minutes into *Pulp Fiction* (1994), Butch has used his car to run into Marsellus and try to kill him. In response, Marsellus whips out a large gun and is soon shooting at Butch. Frame enlargement. *Lawrence Bender; Miramax.*

Vincent and Jules but misses; they kill him. Jules thinks it's a miracle he wasn't killed. In car, Jules says he is going to retire. Vincent accidentally kills their own accomplice (Marvin), thereby splattering blood all over the car and the two men. At Jimmie's house, Jules and Vincent seek help (it's 8:00 a.m.). Calls are made, and at 8:50 Mr. Wolf arrives to supervise the cleanup before Jimmie's wife, Bonnie, will arrive home from work at about 9:30. At Monster Joe's auto wreckers, the clean car with the assistant's body in the trunk is left. Vincent and Jules decide to go for breakfast.

B. At a grill, Jules again tells Vincent that he plans to quit the business and "walk the earth." Ringo and Honey Bunny talk about robbery; Ringo calls out "Garçon" to the waitress. Ringo and Honey Bunny talk some more as Vincent and Jules talk, and Vincent leaves to go to the restroom. Ringo and Honey Bunny decide to rob the grill and its customers, pull out their guns, and shout

that it's a holdup. After many complications, Ringo and Honey Bunny complete the robbery and leave; soon afterward Vincent and Jules leave (Jules still has Marsellus's valuables in the attaché case).

C. At Marsellus's business, Marsellus is telling Butch, a prize fighter, that Butch's best times are past and gives him an envelope full of money. After Butch accepts it, Marsellus tells him he's to take a dive in his upcoming boxing match. Vincent and Jules arrive with the attaché case. Marsellus calls to Vincent and embraces him.

D. Vincent buys powerful heroin, shoots up, and (now night) goes to pick up Marsellus's wife, Mia, as Marsellus had asked him to do while he is away. Vincent and Mia go out, then return to her and Marsellus's place, where she overdoses on drugs and almost dies. . . .

E. Before his fight, Butch dreams about a watch originally acquired by his great-grandfather. Butch wins the fight and escapes. Vincent and Marsellus's bartender (Paul) report about the search for Butch to Marsellus, who is furious. Butch joins his lover, Fabienne, then the next morning returns to his apartment, fetches his watch, and kills Vincent. At a nearby stoplight, Butch "runs into Marsellus" and tries to kill him; then Marsellus tries to kill Butch. Both enter a pawnshop and are captured and tied up. Marsellus is sexually assaulted; Butch saves him, takes the motorcycle of one of their captors, and picks up Fabienne.

SUMMARY

This chapter explains briefly what a narrative is and then examines major aspects of the fictional film: structure, time, and style.

Narratives

- A narrative—in film and in other texts—may be defined as a representation of a series of unified events (represented actions and happenings) that are situated in one or more settings.

- A narrative may be factual or fictional or a blend of the two. It may be chronological or nonchronological.

Structure

- A fictional film is a narrative film including at least one character (imaginary person) and largely or entirely imaginary events; its settings may be factual or imaginary.

- In fictional films, usually the major characters have one or more goals but face problems in trying to reach them.

- Short fictional films typically have only one or two major characters that do not change much during the film's brief story time. The major characters of a short fictional film usually have a goal or goals, have obstacles to overcome, and succeed or fail in reaching the goal.

- Typically, the beginning of a fictional film does not supply much exposition, although it usually establishes where and when the story begins. It also attempts to involve audiences in the story.

- Among other functions, the middle section of a film shows how the central characters deal with problems that impede progress toward their goals and reveals how happenings and the characters' actions affect them and others.

- The ending of a fictional film usually shows the consequences of major previous events. In stories with closure, by the end of the narrative the consequences of previous major events are shown or clearly implied. Most films of classical Hollywood cinema have closure, but many other narrative films do not.

- A plotline is a brief narrative focused on a few characters or people that could function on its own as a separate (usually very brief) story. Typically, short films have only one plotline, and feature films have multiple plotlines.

- In feature films, many combinations of plotlines are possible. For example, plotlines can be consecutive but with large gaps of story time between them, can alternate between different time periods, or can be chronological and simultaneous and occasionally intersect.

Time

- Flashforwards are used only occasionally in fictional films, usually to suggest a premonition or inevitability. Flashbacks are often used and can serve many different purposes, such as showing how a character's past has influenced the character or continues to trouble the character. On rare occasions, fictional films combine present-tense action with flashforwards and flashbacks.
- A fabula is the mental reconstruction in chronological order of all the events in a nonchronological plot. Although a nonchronological plot contains the same events as its corresponding fabula, the plot creates different emphases and causes different responses in viewers.
- How much time is represented in a fictional film (story time) is usually unspecified and difficult to determine, but story time nearly always far exceeds the film's running time.

Style

- A style is the way that subjects are represented in a text, such as a film. A film may use a style only occasionally or throughout.
- If viewers know nothing about a film's style, such as black comedy, and cannot figure it out quickly, the film will probably not engage them. If viewers know about the film's style yet refuse to accept it, they will also likely fail to become engaged by the film.

Major Terms about Aspects of the Fictional Film

Below, numbers in italics refer to the pages where the terms are explained. All terms are defined in more detail in the Illustrated Glossary beginning on p. 621.

QUESTIONS ABOUT ASPECTS OF THE FICTIONAL FILM

The following questions are intended to help viewers understand possible sources for a fictional film. Not all the questions are appropriate for every film. In thinking out, discussing, and writing responses to those questions most appropriate for the film being examined, be careful to stick with the issues the questions raise, to answer all parts of the questions, to explain the reasons for your answers, and to give specific examples from the film.

1. Is the narrative fictional, factual, or a blend of the two? How do you know?
2. What are the main characters' goals?

   a. What are the major conflicts? How are they resolved?

   b. Do any of the characters have internal conflicts (such as uncertainty, conflicting values or duties, or guilt)?

   c. Are the film's most important conflicts between sharply distinguished good and evil, or are the most important conflicts more complex and subtle?

3. Consider the film's structure.

   a. What are the film's sequences (major groups of scenes)?

   b. Does the film have a chronological or nonchronological structure? What are the advantages of the choice?

   c. If the film has a nonchronological plot, what is its fabula?

   d. Does the film have more than one major plotline? If so, how are the different major plotlines related?

   e. Does the film have closure? Explain.

4. In what sequences is the story time longer than the running time? Conversely, and much less commonly, in what sequences is the running time longer than the story time?
5. What styles are used? What do they contribute to the film?

WORKS CITED

Armes, Roy. *Action and Image: Dramatic Structure in Cinema*. Manchester: Manchester UP, 1994.

Chatman, Seymour. *Story and Discourse: Narrative Structure in Fiction and Film*. Ithaca: Cornell UP, 1978.

Corliss, Richard. Review of *Continental Divide*, directed by Michael Apted. *Time* 14 Sept. 1981: 90.

Eidsvik, Charles. *Cineliteracy: Film among the Arts*. New York: Random, 1978.

Hohenadel, Kristin. "'Happily Ever After' Fading Fast from Film." *New York Times* 13 Jan. 2002 (late ed.) 2:13. <http://www.nytimes.com/2002/01/13/movies/13HOHE.html>.

Phillips, William H. *Writing Short Scripts*. Syracuse: Syracuse UP, 1991.

Prince, Gerald. *Dictionary of Narratology*. Lincoln: U of Nebraska P, 1987.

Rosen, Robert. "Notes on Painting and Film." *Art and Film since 1945: Hall of Mirrors*. Ed. Kerry Brougher. Los Angeles: Museum of Contemporary Art, 1996.

Stables, Kate. "Zap the Gerbil, Blend the Frog." *Sight and Sound* 10.1 (NS) (Jan. 2000): 5.

Vernet, Marc. "Cinema and Narration." *Aesthetics of Film*. Trans. and rev. Richard Neupert. Austin: U of Texas P, 1992.

FOR FURTHER READING

Hayward, Susan. *Cinema Studies: The Key Concepts*. 2nd ed. London: Routledge, 2000. Especially pertinent to the study of the fictional film are the entries *flashback, form/content, narrative, sequencing/sequence, setting,* and *space and time/spatial and temporal continuity*.

Mamber, Stephen. "Simultaneity and Overlap in Stanley Kubrick's *The Killing*." *Postmodern Culture* 8:2 (Jan. 1998). <http://muse.jhu.edu/journals/pmc/v008/8.2mamber.html>. One of several essays in this special issue on film, Mamber's essay incorporates various graphics to illustrate the complexity and achievements of the film's structure.

Phillips, William H. *Writing Short Scripts*. 2nd ed. Syracuse: Syracuse UP, 1999. Includes three unproduced scripts for short films, detailed descriptions of two award-winning short films, discussions of the general characteristics of the short script and short film, and partial credits and brief descriptions for many short films.

Raskin, Richard. *The Art of the Short Fiction Film: A Shot by Shot Study of Nine Modern Classics*. Jefferson, NC: McFarland, 2002. Each film has a chapter of its own, including a shot-by-shot reproduction of the film with a frame enlargement for every shot. In most cases, an interview with the director and an original screenplay and storyboard are included.

Stam, Robert, Robert Burgoyne, and Sandy Flitterman-Lewis. "Film-Narratology." *New Vocabularies in Film Semiotics: Structuralism, Post-structuralism and Beyond*. London: Routledge, 1992. Part 3, 69–122. Theoretical issues about narrative for the advanced student.

Part Three
THE VARIETY OF FILMS

Now that we have studied the expressiveness of film techniques and the sources and basic components of the mostly widely viewed type of film, the fictional film, we consider completed films. Part Three discusses some of the many types of live-action fictional films and the alternatives to them: documentary, experimental, hybrid, and animated films.

There are many reasons to consider the broad diversity of films. Considering the sources, techniques, and type of a film can help us relate it to other films and understand it more clearly. Examining a variety of films also helps us understand the film medium more fully: the properties, techniques, forms, and purposes of different films. Understanding that the film medium is far more inclusive and diverse than what is found on the screens of the nearest multiplex, in the neighboring video store, on movie channels, and in music videos helps us avoid simplifying and overgeneralizing about the film medium. A film, for example, does not always last 80 to 180 minutes and convey a story. Indeed, a film does not even necessarily aspire to coherence, completeness, and popularity. As the following two chapters demonstrate, film has been and is much more.

◄*Witchcraft through the Ages* (*Häxan*)—which was directed by Benjamin Christensen and made in Sweden in 1922—illustrates how varied a film can be and how problematic it can be to classify one. *Witchcraft through the Ages* combines elements of narrative and nonnarrative documentary with experimental film and of realism with surrealism as it re-creates and illustrates a variety of historical and contemporary manifestations of witchcraft and witch hunting. The film abounds with information for students of witchcraft and memorable expressive images for students of film. Seen here is one of the film's most famous and most striking images: a re-creation of part of a witches' Sabbath as the lascivious bearded Satan leans over a woman who is reaching up to embrace him and surrender herself to him. *Svensk Filmindustri; The Museum of Modern Art/Film Stills Archive*

CHAPTER 7

Types of Fictional Films

FICTIONAL FILMS ARE NUMEROUS, POPULAR, AND ENDURING. Perhaps that is why critics, scholars, and others often try to classify them (Figure 7.1). Seeing similarities and patterns in films helps viewers place a film in context and understand it more completely. Considering some of the types of fictional films also helps viewers understand the properties and potentials of the film medium.

Documentary, experimental, and hybrid films are major alternatives to fictional films, but these groupings of films are so large that they are treated in the next chapter. Here we examine a few of the most frequently used ways to group fictional films: classical Hollywood cinema (throughout the world the most popular and influential type of fictional film) and some alternatives to it: Italian neorealist cinema, French new wave cinema, independent films, Bollywood, Hong Kong cinema, and Dogme 95. Although

Terms in **boldface** are defined in the Illustrated Glossary beginning on page 621.

documentary film: A film or video representation of actual (not imaginary) subjects. A documentary film may or may not present a story (be a narrative film).

experimental film: A film that rejects the conventions of mainstream movies and explores the possibilities of the film medium.

hybrid film: A film that is not exclusively fictional, documentary, or experimental but instead shares characteristics of two or all three of the major film types.

FIGURE 7.1

various groupings of films are discussed in this chapter and Chapter 8, it is important to remember that filmmakers are not ruled by formulas or books. Instead, they may be influenced by such matters as intuition, creativity, cinema traditions, demographic patterns (such as the percentage of teens who attend movies), and box office potential. As a consequence and increasingly so in recent years, some films are not exclusively one type.

CLASSICAL HOLLYWOOD CINEMA

> The film experience resembles a fun house attraction, a wild ride, the itinerary of which has been calculated in advance but is unknown to the spectator. By spurts and stops, twists and roller coaster plunges, we are taken through a dark passage, alert and anxious, yet confident we shall return satisfied and unharmed. (Andrew 144)

Film scholars have explored many ways of grouping fictional films. David Bordwell, Janet Staiger, and Kristin Thompson studied representative American films across the years to see if they could discover recurrent **conventions**. In their influential book *The Classical Hollywood Cinema: Film Style and Mode of Production to 1960* and in other publications, Bordwell, Staiger, and Thompson argue that most American **feature films**—and indeed most movies worldwide—share certain qualities that are explained below.

Characteristics of Classical Hollywood Cinema

According to Bordwell, Staiger, and Thompson (1–84), **classical Hollywood cinema** tends to have the following characteristics:

1. The story is set mainly in a present, external world and is seen largely from outside the action, although **point-of-view shots**, memories, fantasies, dreams, or other mental states are sometimes included.
2. The film focuses on one character or a few distinct individuals.
3. The main characters have a goal or a few goals.
4. In trying to attain their goals, the main characters must confront antagonists or a series of problems.
5. The film has **closure**—a sense of resolution or completion at the end of a **narrative**—and often the main characters succeed in reaching their goals (happy endings).
6. The emphasis is on clear causes and effects of actions: what **events** happen and why they happen are clear and unambiguous.
7. The film uses unobtrusive **filmmaking techniques**.

convention: In films and other texts, a subject or a technique that makers of texts and audiences have grown to accept as natural or typical in certain contexts.

feature film: A fictional film that is at least sixty minutes long.

point-of-view shot: Camera placement at the approximate position of a character or person (or occasionally an animal) that gives a view similar to what that subject would see.

narrative: A representation of a series of unified consecutive events situated in one or more settings.

event: In a narrative or story, either an *action* by a character or person or a *happening* (a change brought about by a force other than a person or character).

Bordwell, Staiger, and Thompson argue that in American films of recent decades, "the classical paradigm continues to flourish, partly by absorbing current topics of interest and partly by perpetuating seventy-year-old assumptions about what a film is and does" (372). They also point out that many foreign films exemplify the traits of classical Hollywood cinema. Recent examples are *Shall We Dance?* (1996) from Japan (see Figure 1.1 on p. 12) and *Not One Less* (1999) from China.

So pervasive are the basic story components of classical Hollywood cinema that they also shape animated narratives. *Antz* (1998) is the story of a male ant seeking to win a society's most highly prized female while in the end attempting to save his society from a deadly outside threat. Throughout the story, the protagonist confronts a series of problems, but the story ends with closure and a happy ending as the main character, who was initially full of self-doubts, achieves his goals and gains his society's adulation (Figure 7.2b).

a)    b)

FIGURE 7.2   Classical Hollywood cinema: two examples
So widespread is classical Hollywood cinema that most fictional films, including foreign films and animated stories, exhibit its characteristics. (a) The Chinese film *Not One Less* (1999) and (b) the animated feature *Antz* (1998) are examples. Both stories are set in the present world and are largely seen from outside the action. Both movies show only a few distinct characters and focus on one character. In *Not One Less*, the young girl has been hired to keep order in a small, rural school and to deter students from dropping out. In pursuing her goals, the girl faces a series of problems. In *Antz*, a male ant called Zee has two goals: to win the princess and later to thwart the mass extermination of the ant colony. In pursuing his goals Zee confronts a succession of problems. Both films have closure: they leave no major unanswered questions and no uncertainty as to what happened and why. Like most movies of the classical Hollywood cinema, the endings are happy for those in the audience they intend to please. Finally, both *Not One Less* and *Antz* avoid distracting filmmaking techniques. (a) Frame enlargement. *Columbia Pictures Film Production Asia; Sony;* (b) Frame enlargement. *PDI; DreamWorks Pictures*

So widely seen is classical Hollywood cinema that it has influenced virtually all narrative films: filmmakers either imitate characteristics of classical Hollywood cinema or purposely ignore its conventions.

Film Genres: Related Films

> What genre does is recognize that the audience [watches] any one film within a context of other films, both those they have personally seen and those they have heard about or seen represented in other media outlets. . . . In general, the function of genre is to make films comprehensible and more or less familiar. (Turner 97)

Action, war, western, comedy, science fiction, horror, mystery/suspense, drama, family, and children. Sound familiar? These major categories are commonly used for ease of marketing in video stores. Many other films are seen as part of a group, including adaptations of literature (for example, movies based on the novels of Jane Austen or the plays of Shakespeare), road movies, urban comedies, and ethnic films. Filmmakers, film critics, film scholars, and film viewers all think of films in terms of categories, although for different reasons.

Most films of the classical Hollywood cinema are **genre** films or members of a widely recognized group of films. Exactly what constitutes a film genre (or type) and which films belong to a genre are subject to much debate. For our purposes, we can think of film genres as commonly recognized groups of fictional films—such as the western, musical, romantic comedy, detective, gangster, science fiction, horror, and war—with shared characteristics accepted by both filmmakers and audiences. It is difficult to be more precise than that because the criteria for one genre differ from those for another genre, and different critics and scholars define particular genres in somewhat different ways. Westerns, at least the traditional ones, tend to share the same basic conflict (civilization versus the wilderness) and usually the same **setting** (sparsely settled regions—often frontiers—west of the Mississippi River, in northern Mexico, or in the Canadian Rockies). All detective films share the same basic story: the uncovering of causes (who did what when, and why). But musicals share nothing more than frequent, recurring interludes of music during a story.

setting: The place where filmed action occurs.

Filmmakers and experienced film viewers share a sense of what constitutes a particular genre at a particular time and place. Filmmakers can follow the traditions of the genre and thus reassure audiences; reject the genre's conventions and thereby amuse, shock, or disturb viewers; or in some ways reassure audiences but in other ways reject some of the genre conventions. Genres may evolve when social attitudes change. Many westerns before World War II depicted Native Americans in negative ways that encouraged European Americans to continue to think of themselves as superior. An example can be seen in the comedy western *My Little Chickadee* with W. C. Fields and Mae West (1940), which consistently depicts American Indians in

stereotypical ways and as the butt of tired jokes. But as times and attitudes have changed, later westerns such as *Little Big Man* (1970) and *Dances with Wolves* (1990) show Native Americans in a sympathetic light, in fact sometimes more favorably than they do the European American settlers. Even more recently, the first feature movie made by and about Native Americans, *Smoke Signals* (1998), does much to dispel stereotypes about American Indians—for example, that they are stoic and humorless (Figure 7.3). Makers of genre films inevitably are influenced by previous films of the same genre. They either imitate earlier films, reject the genre's fundamentals, or follow the genre in some ways and change it in others. Let's consider three of the most enduring genres: the western, film noir, and the musical.

The Western

Since "The Great Train Robbery" (1903), many viewers have enjoyed western films (Figure 7.4). Westerns have proven so popular that they have been made in many countries, including Italy, Mexico, Spain, and East Germany. "Between 1965 and 1983, the East German studio . . . produced 14 westerns. **Shot** on **location** in Yugoslavia, Czechoslovakia, Romania, Bulgaria, the Soviet Union, and Cuba, and usually starring a hulking former physical-education instructor . . . , these so-called *Indianerfilme* are as clumsy and predictable as many of Hollywood's cowboy films. There is one notable distinction: in East German westerns, the American Indians are always the good guys" (Shulman), fighting "wars of liberation against the capitalists" (Barton Byg, quoted in Ingalls).

Typically the setting of a western film is the United States plains, the Rockies, the Northwest, the Southwest, northern Mexico, or perhaps the Canadian Rockies, and some **shots** usually linger on the vastness, openness, beauty, or menace of the terrain (Plate 21 in Chapter 2). The focus of traditional westerns is people who stand for law and order, for settling and taming the West (often territories before they become states), and for bringing the civilization of the eastern United States or Europe to the recently populated West (often women perform this last function). The transformations so often celebrated in westerns can be seen in an excerpt from *Bend of the River* (1952), where a settler says, "We'll use the trees that nature has given us. Cut a clearing in the wilderness.

FIGURE 7.3   Dispelling stereotypes
Although traditional westerns helped perpetuate demeaning stereotypes about American Indians, later westerns and non-westerns such as *Smoke Signals* (1998) present a different picture. The first feature-length movie made by and about American Indians, *Smoke Signals* repeatedly undercuts the stereotype that Native Americans lack humor (with or without a satirical bite). Here Thomas, on the left, and Victor are talking to two Indian women who gave them a ride:

FIRST WOMAN: Ain't you guys got your passports?

THOMAS: Passports?

FIRST WOMAN (with mock seriousness): Yah. You're leaving the rez and going to a whole different country, cousin.

THOMAS (seriously): But it's the United States.

SECOND WOMAN: Damn right it is. That's as foreign as it gets. Hope you two got your vaccinations.
(The women laugh.)

Frame enlargement. *Larry Estes & Scott M. Rosenfelt; Miramax*

shot (verb): Filmed.

shot (noun): An uninterrupted strip of exposed motion-picture film or videotape that represents a subject during an uninterrupted segment of time.

FIGURE 7.4   **An early western**
"The Great Train Robbery" (1903)—which Charles Musser claims was "the most commercially successful film of the pre-nickelodeon era, perhaps of any film prior to *The Birth of a Nation* (1915)" (18)—includes what was to become the basic story of many western films: a threat to civilization (outlaws committing a crime) and the eventual reestablishment of order (outlaws getting killed and the stolen goods regained). Frame enlargement. *Edison; The Museum of Modern Art/Film Stills Archive*

We'll put in roads. . . . Then we'll build our homes. . . . There'll be a meeting house, a church. We'll have a school. Then we'll put down seedlings." To achieve the traditional western's goals, those who represent civilization usually have showdowns and shootouts with one or more of the following: Native Americans, Mexicans, and the men who wear black hats. Makers of westerns work variations, slight or major, on the generic western.

Most westerns directed by John Ford are generic but not without complexities, subtleties, and surprises, including music, dancing, and humor. In many respects Ford's *My Darling Clementine* (1946) reenacts the generic western story. The film's basic conflict involves the attempt of Wyatt Earp and his brothers to establish order in a town (which includes reining in the ill, troubled, and dangerous Doc Holliday) and bringing the murderers of their eighteen-year-old brother to justice. Another important conflict is between Chihuahua—the sensual, emotional Mexican saloon singer—and Clementine, the less sensual, more emotionally restrained Boston nurse. By the end of the film, a drunken, unruly Native American has been silenced and disappears from the movie; a crooked professional gambler has been run out of town; and a traveling actor has recited Shakespeare, the quintessence of British culture. The town's first church has been dedicated, and an outdoor dance held as American flags blow in the breeze; Chihuahua, the dishonest and unfaithful Mexican beauty, has died; and Clementine—the restrained, churchgoing easterner—plans to stay and teach school. Most significantly, two of the four Earp brothers survive. They are leaving, although Wyatt may return to Clementine. He has achieved what he set out to do: see that the evil ones are brought to justice (though at the cost of brothers and sons killed) and order is established in the town. Civilization as many European Americans might think of it is coming to the dusty desert community of 1882 Tombstone, Arizona (Figure 7.5).

Sometimes viewers enjoy having their expectations gratified by a conventional genre film. Other times viewers enjoy seeing major variations on a genre. Since about 1950, most westerns have been **revisionist**: they ignore or challenge the fundamental traditions of the western film. Films may be revisionist because the times change and the films reflect those changes or because the filmmakers deliberately reject major conventions of the genre. For some films, such as Robert Altman's *McCabe and Mrs. Miller* (1971), both causes of revisionism are at work. Fifties revisionist westerns include *Broken Arrow* (1950), which depicts Native Americans at least as sympathetically as the European American settlers; *High Noon* (1952), which attacks the cowardly behavior of townspeople afraid of or sympathetic to those in black hats; and *The Searchers* (1956), which shows the human cost of pursuing vengeance long-term (Figure 7.6).

The early sixties also saw various revisionist westerns. John Ford's *The Man Who Shot Liberty Valance* (1962) exhibits major creative variations of the western. Here the agent of civilization is a man of the law, in this case a lawyer who doubles as a teacher of English and civics, but the film shows that without the power conferred by skill in using a gun, the agent of law and order is helpless in the face of a bullying murderer. *The Man Who Shot Liberty Valance* also shows that legend masks the truth, in this case of the real hero's bravery and integrity. From late in 1963 to the end of the sixties, the United States experienced massive domestic upheaval: political and racial assassinations; an increasingly unpopular war in Vietnam; growing

FIGURE 7.5   Generic western
Although *My Darling Clementine* (1946) surprises viewers with its low-keyed Marshal Earp, a complex Doc Holliday, and the lack of closure to the budding Wyatt Earp–Clementine Carter romance, the film is a generic western. In this frame enlargement from the film's last shot, Earp is seen riding away from Clementine toward the wilderness, Monument Valley. Most of the basics of westerns such as *Shane* and *The Searchers* are contained within this image: the wilderness, the promise of domesticity, and a man's tug of allegiance between these two forces. Frame enlargement. *Samuel G. Engel; 20th Century–Fox*

FIGURE 7.6 A 1950s revisionist western
The Searchers (1956), directed by John Ford from a script by Frank Nugent, begins in 1868 with Ethan Edwards (on the right) arriving unexpectedly at his brother's ranch in Texas. Here we see Ethan shortly after the reunion with his brother, nephew, two nieces, and sister-in-law, Martha. Ethan proves to be a complex hero, more complex and flawed and even mysterious than any seen in westerns before and few if any since. He has many of the typical western hero's qualities—including knowledge of a Native Indian culture, skill with guns and horses, bravery, self-sacrifice, and perseverance. Such details as the tender way Martha hangs up Ethan's coat hint that the two share deep though undefined feelings: he seems worthy of an admirable woman's love. However, Ethan becomes consumed by vengeance and murderous rage and is doomed to remain an outsider. The film's memorable last shot shows him with his mission finally accomplished but forgotten and ignored by a family and outside the door leading into a home. When he turns and slowly walks away, the door closes on his image in the windy wilderness, and darkness fills the screen. In *The Searchers* the main agent of European American civilization is deeply flawed and without a place in an enclave in the wild, without a place to hang his coat or have it hung. *C. V. Whitney; Warner Bros.*

FIGURE 7.7 Western showing the end of an era
The Wild Bunch (1969), which is set in 1913, begins and ends with prolonged and elevated levels of violence never before seen in a western. This publicity still represents action near the end of the film when four of the wild bunch are on their way to try to free a Mexican colleague regardless of the considerable danger to themselves. "While early modern Westerns tended to deal with stories from the period of pioneering and the beginning of settlement, Westerns of the 60s and 70s more often centered around the end of the West, the passing of its heroic and mythical age and its entry into the modern world of cities and technology.... By the time of *The Wild Bunch* ... [director Sam] Peckinpah's aging bandits confronted a modern world of machinery [including machine-guns and automobiles], militarism and social revolution which destroyed them" (Cawelti 7). *Phil Feldman; Warner Bros.*

demonstrations against the war; and civil rights unrest, violence, and demonstrations. Many viewers of the late 1960s who had become disillusioned with the federal government and others in power identified with the violent outlaws of *The Wild Bunch* (1969) who try to cope during the sunset of an era (Figure 7.7).

Like a number of late 1960s American movies, *McCabe and Mrs. Miller* implies criticism of the power structure. The film has an inhospitable, rough-hewn setting rarely seen in western films (Figure 7.8). The two central characters are not settlers bringing the usual socially acceptable goods or services to the untamed West. Mrs. Miller is a practical, intelligent opium-smoking prostitute and madam who has goals and a clear sense of how to achieve them. McCabe is a card shark-businessman-pimp who ignores Mrs. Miller's sound advice, lacks the confidence and power he initially seems to have, and is too naïve to see when to cut a deal with those with power. Near the end of the film the townspeople are more concerned with saving the burning church, which they had ignored and will likely continue to ignore, than with helping McCabe in his deadly confrontation with three murderous thugs sent by an acquisitive corporation. As scholar John H. Lenihan points out, the film implies that "the future of America lay not with the individual but with the corrupt and indomitable corporation" (164).

FIGURE 7.8 **Revisionist representation of western settings** Nearly three minutes into *McCabe and Mrs. Miller* (1971), on a cold, rainy day, McCabe arrives at a saloon/hotel in the remote western town where most of the story takes place. Unlike most earlier westerns, *McCabe and Mrs. Miller* was filmed on location and teems with the messiness of life. Even the film's weather is untraditional for westerns: except for a few shots, it is persistently gloomy and the color is desaturated throughout. The film shows lots of mud, rain, gray skies, fallen snow, light snowing, and near the end heavy snowing. Throughout most of the exterior scenes, there is also a howling wind, which is the first sound viewers hear in the film, occurring even before the story begins behind the Warner Bros. logo, and is loudest at the film's end. Frame enlargement. *David Foster & Mitchell Brower; Warner Bros.*

In the 1980s and into the 1990s, some critics were writing about the death of the western. Then came *Unforgiven* (1992), which set off another wave of revisionist westerns. The setting and subject of *Unforgiven* make it instantly recognizable as a western, but for those who have seen many westerns, the film has many surprises. The major antagonist is not a Native American, a Mexican, or an evil cowboy but the sheriff himself; he's so brutal that the townspeople are both embarrassed and afraid when he starts (literally) kicking someone around. The film's killings, which are committed in the name of justice, are based on rumor and dubious moral grounds and are messy, excruciating, and in one instance protracted. Perhaps most surprisingly, the hero is not a macho cowboy. He is an aging pig farmer aching to forget his past and to be left alone and longing for his deceased wife, who helped him give up alcohol and helped civilize him. Furthermore, the hero has a nagging conscience: he regrets murders he committed years before.

a)   b)

FIGURE 7.9 A feminist revisionist western

In *The Ballad of Little Jo* (1993), (a) Josephine Monaghan is first seen dressed much as she is here, but carrying a suitcase and protecting her head from the sun with a parasol. Viewers eventually learn that she has had a baby out of wedlock and been exiled by her family. (b) In the West, men menace her—she is nearly raped—so to avoid further danger and abuse, Josephine becomes Jo by inflicting a scar on her cheek, dressing as a man, and gradually learning how to act as one. Unlike most westerns, *The Ballad of Little Jo* shows both the limited options available to nineteenth-century American women and the civilizing influences that a woman doing men's work could bring to the wild West. *PolyGram Filmed Entertainment; Fine Line Features*

Other nineties westerns explored the possibilities of subjects usually pushed to the sides or backgrounds of movie screens, such as single women, African American males, and female prostitutes. *The Ballad of Little Jo* (1993) shows the trials, triumphs, and civilizing effects (such as compassion) of a woman in the man's world of 1870s Montana territory (Figure 7.9). Another western that focuses on a group usually on the periphery of westerns, if included at all, is *Posse* (1993); most of its main characters are African American (Figure 7.10). *Bad Girls* (1994) also focuses on characters normally peripheral in the conventional western (Figure 7.11). Yet another option available to makers of western films is to blend components of the old western with elements of the new West (Figure 7.12).

In recent years, critics yet again revived talk about the death of the western. Though not numerous, they still get made. Only time will tell whether the western is now largely corralled, but given its long and active history, that is unlikely.

FIGURE 7.10 An African American revisionist western
Posse (1993)—which focuses on five African Americans and one European American—gives a contemporary African American perspective on a group rarely seen in mainstream westerns, even in recent years. In *Posse*, blacks do not face opposition from the usual western antagonists, such as Native Americans, Mexicans, or an assortment of obvious outlaws. Instead, they have to contend with the white power structure. The posse's major antagonists are two European Americans: a cruel, corrupt army officer and his motley band of Spanish-American War veterans eager to steal war booty from the "posse" while exacting revenge, and a racist, greedy, power-hungry sheriff and his followers who years earlier had killed blacks with impunity. It is not clear if the white sheriff and his followers constitute the local version of the KKK or if that is a separate group, but the KKK is also a threat. Another problem for the African American community is that the black marshal of an all-black town has naïvely struck an illegal business deal with the racist white sheriff and fails to oppose him when the sheriff treats blacks unjustly. *PolyGram Filmed Entertainment; Gramercy Pictures*

FIGURE 7.11 Taming the wild West
Throughout *Bad Girls* (1994) the four major female characters fight back against any injustice. Initially, they are prostitutes wronged by men's laws, but when provoked, they outsmart, outride, and outshoot the men. Early in the film one of them catches up with a runaway horse-drawn carriage, jumps into it, and reins it to a halt. Among their many accomplishments as a group are rescuing one of their own from being hanged, killing four armed outlaws, and evading two detectives on their trail. While they are at it, two of them also win the love of two attractive young men. In their own fashion, they help tame the West. *Ruddy Morgan Productions; 20th Century–Fox*

a)

b)

FIGURE 7.12 Prominent love lives in a revisionist western
Most of *The Hi-Lo Country* (1998) is set in New Mexico shortly after World War II has ended, but traditional western elements remain. (a) A dramatic poker game is played about forty-four minutes into the film, and the usual whiskey drinking and fistfights transpire. In other scenes, cowboys on horses tend cattle. The story includes a greedy cattle baron (the big guy nobody much likes) and others who oppose him and are determined to make a living the old way, on desolate land in a difficult climate.

On the other hand, *The Hi-Lo Country* does not always look like a western. Motorized vehicles—jeeps, trucks, and cars—go racing around stirring up the plentiful dust. Some of the pistols are of twentieth-century vintage. Most of all, the film spends a lot of time on relationships. Two young men who are best friends are attracted to a married woman. (b) Here, in a scene approximately seventy-nine minutes into the film where the two lovers are seen beyond a campfire on the left of the frame, as elsewhere in the film, we learn more about the two men's love lives than was ever conceivable in earlier westerns. Finally, in yet another departure from the traditional western, the two men are so close that some viewers will wonder if they have stronger feelings for each other than either one has for the married woman. Frame enlargements. *De Fina-Cappa & PolyGram Filmed Entertainment; Gramercy*

FILM NOIR

film movement: A group of films sharing innovative styles or subjects (or both) that emerges from the same country or region over a period of a few years and that is in opposition to the dominant cinema(s) of the time.

style: The way subjects are represented in a text, such as a film.

scene: A section of a narrative that gives the impression of continuous action taking place in continuous time and space.

This large body of films, flourishing in America in the period 1941–58 [from *The Maltese Falcon* to *Touch of Evil*], generally focuses on urban crime and corruption, and on sudden upwellings of violence in a culture whose fabric seems to be unraveling. Because of these typical concerns, the film noir seems fundamentally about violations: vice, corruption, unrestrained desire, and, most fundamental of all, abrogation of the American dream's most basic promises—of hope, prosperity, and safety from persecution. (Telotte 2)

Film noir ("film nwahr") is a partial translation of *cinéma noir* (black or dark cinema), a term first used by some French critics to describe a group of American films made during and after World War II. Different critics and scholars define *film noir* as a genre, "sub-genre of the crime thriller or gangster movie," **movement,** "quasigeneric category," "fluid concept," mode, mood, **style,** visual style, or "stylistic and narrative tendency." But here and in other sources, film noir stands for a film genre whose films tend to have frequent **scenes** with dark, shadowy (**low-key**) **lighting** and many night scenes (Figure 7.13). Other characteristics of film noir are urban settings and characters who are motivated by selfishness, greed, cruelty, and ambition and are willing to lie, frame, double-cross, and kill or have killed (Figure 7.14). Often films noirs

low-key lighting: Lighting with predominant dark tones, often deep dark tones.

FIGURE 7.13 Film noir lighting and darkness

This still closely approximates the last shot of *The Big Combo* (1955), cinematography by John Alton, who later wrote a book on cinematography, *Painting with Light*. In his introduction to a reprinting of that book, Todd McCarthy writes, "In fashioning the nocturnal world inhabited by noir's desperate characters, Alton was ever consistent and imaginative in forging his signature, illuminating scenes with single lamps, slanted and fragmented beams and pools of light, all separated by intense darkness in which the source of all fear could fester and finally thrive. . . . Often, the light would just manage to catch the rim of a hat, the edge of a gun, the smoke from a cigarette. Actors' faces, normally the object of any cameraman's most ardent attention, were often invisible or obscured, with characters from *T-Men* to, perhaps most memorably, *The Big Combo* playing out their fates in silhouette against a witheringly blank, impassive background. . . . [In *The Big Combo*] Alton pushed his impulse toward severe black-and-white contrasts and silhouetting of characters to the limit. . . . And the final shot, with the figures of a man and woman outlined . . . against a foggy nightscape and illuminated by a single beacon [beyond the fog and midway between the man's head and the woman's], makes one of the quintessentially anti-sentimental noir statements about the place of humanity in the existential void" (x, xxix). *Sidney Harmon; Allied Artists*

a)

b)

FIGURE 7.14 Film noir classic

Some critics regard *Touch of Evil* (1958) as the last of the classic films noirs. The film has all the characteristics of film noir, including (a) many scenes with dark, shadowy (low-key) lighting (here a man and his shadow follow another man and his shadow) and (b) as the central character a police detective (on the left) who's shrewd, driven, complex, and flawed. Frame enlargements. *Albert Zugsmith; Universal*

a)

b)

c)

FIGURE 7.15 Various faces of a femme fatale
Rita Hayworth as the femme fatale in *The Lady from Shanghai* (1948). (a) She is on a boat deck singing, and her song lures the main male character up to the deck; she's a Circe. (b) The background reminds viewers she doesn't obey laws. (c) By the end of the film, she has pulled a gun on her husband and is ready to kill him in a fun house full of mirrors. She does, but the film was released in 1948 and was subject to the production code, so she does not go unpunished. Frame enlargements. *Orson Welles; Columbia*

are fatalistic, and the main characters seem doomed to fail. *Detour* (1945), for example, includes such lines as "Until then, I'd done things my way, but from then on something else stepped in and shunted me off to a different destination than the one I had picked for myself" and "That's life. Whichever way you turn, Fate sticks out a foot to trip you." Films noirs tend to exhibit embittered or cynical moods and to be compressed and convoluted, as in *Double Indemnity* (1944), which begins and ends in the present and has five **flashbacks**, and *Out of the Past* (1947), which also includes flashbacks (see Figure 6.16 on p. 273).

Because these films were made when the American production code was strongly enforced (see pp. 430-32), characters who commit crimes are eventually punished. By the end of *Murder, My Sweet* (1944), for example, the three who commit murder have murdered each other; by the end of *The Lady from Shanghai* (1948), the three lethal characters have also killed each other. Near the end of *Force of Evil* (1948), the three major criminal characters confront one another in a dark room; two are shot; then the third calls the police and says he'll be turning himself in.

Often films noirs feature a femme fatale, invariably an attractive, young, worldly woman who thinks and acts quickly and is verbally adroit, manipulative, evasive, sexy, dangerous, perhaps even lethal, especially to men who succumb to her wiles and charms— and many do. In *The Lady from Shanghai* the femme fatale is a Circe who figuratively enchains her husband's business partner and nearly lures the film's central character to his doom (Figure 7.15). In *Out of the Past*, the femme fatale is so dangerous that when another woman character says of her, "She can't be all bad. No one is," the Robert Mitchum character, who is no innocent yet succumbs to her more than once, replies, "Well, she comes the closest" (Figure 7.16).

The changing role of women in 1940s American society influenced film noir. During World War II, women were urged to take over factory jobs traditionally held by men, and millions did. After the war, the men returned and displaced the women workers, often unceremoniously. The self-sufficiency many women showed during the war doubtless threatened many men, perhaps including those involved in making films noirs. "A large number of the postwar noir thrillers are concerned to some degree with the problems represented by women who seek satisfaction and self-definition outside the traditional contexts of marriage and family" (Krutnik 61).

Films noirs can be understood as in part a reaction against the brightly lit **studio** entertainment films of the 1930s. The look of films noirs was also influenced by German and Austrian immigrant filmmakers attuned to

a)   b)

FIGURE 7.16 A girlfriend and her femme fatale rival

(a) Jeff, played by Robert Mitchum, is the main character in *Out of the Past* (1947). Early in the film, we see him with his girlfriend Ann, played by Virginia Huston. (b) Later in the film, we learn of Jeff's earlier involvement with Kathie, the Jane Greer character, who like most femmes fatales in films noirs, is young, worldly, attractive, calculating, resourceful, and charming when need be, and she almost always gets her way with men, including Jeff.

In Nicholas Christopher's reading, Ann is "antiseptic, static, sexually repressed, socially rather dull, she lives with her parents and works as a schoolteacher; she want to marry and have kids and never leave her hometown. Should we be surprised that when reunited with Kathie, who is freewheeling, worldly, intellectually (if criminally) active, dangerous, and highly sexed, Jeff finds it so easy to fall back under her spell?" (198–99). *Warren Duff; RKO General Pictures*

expressionism: A style of art, literature, drama, and film used to represent not external reality in a believable way but emotions in striking, stylized ways.

mise en scène: An image's setting, subject (usually people or characters), and composition (the arrangement of setting and subjects within the frame).

expressionistic lighting and **mise en scène**. Then, too, it is likely that the urban painting of such American artists as Edward Hopper influenced the look of film noir: "When Abraham Polonsky, the director of *Force of Evil*, was dissatisfied with the look his cinematographer . . . was getting, he took him to an exhibition of Hopper's paintings at a Greenwich Village gallery and said, 'This is how I want the picture to look.' And it did: full of black windows, looming shadows, and rich pools of light pouring from recessed doorways and steep stairwells" (Christopher 15).

The detective fiction of such writers as Raymond Chandler, Dashiell Hammett, and James M. Cain was a major influence and provided sources for some of the major scripts. Films noirs reject the nationalistic films of World War II and reflect the unsettled postwar times, the disorientation and lack of clear identity many experienced after surviving the severe economic depression of the 1930s, and the massive casualties, genocide, torture, and atomic clouds of World War II.

Many film scholars see the 1941 version of *The Maltese Falcon* as the first film noir, and although that film has most of the characteristics outlined here, it is not nearly as dark and shadowed as many later films noirs. In addition, as critic and scholar Foster Hirsch points out, various earlier films have elements of film noir (12–13). Undisputed major films noirs include *Double Indemnity*; *Murder, My Sweet*; *Detour*; *The Big Sleep* (1946); *Out of the Past*; *The Lady from Shanghai*; *Force of Evil*; *Criss Cross*; *The Asphalt Jungle* (1950); *The Big Combo* (1955); and *Touch of Evil*.

Many later American color films are film noir or have been influenced by it—such as *The Long Goodbye* (1973); *Chinatown* (1974, Figure 7.17); *Body Heat* (1981); *Pulp Fiction* (1994); *Devil in a Blue Dress* (1995); *Fargo* (1996); and *L.A. Confidential* (1997, Figure 7.18). There has even been a rare black-and-white film noir. The 2001 *The Man Who Wasn't There*, which is set within the period of classic films noirs, 1949, is immersed in darkness and shadows, and features an unassuming, ambitious main character who seems anything but in charge of his own fate. Some French films—such as *Breathless* (1959), *Shoot the Piano Player* (1960), and *Alphaville* (1965)—have also been labeled film noir or influenced by it. Critics also speak of certain British crime

FIGURE 7.17 A night scene in a modern film noir
Approximately 42½ minutes into *Chinatown* (1974), Detective Jake Gittes (left) is about to get his nose cut by two thugs hired to guard secrets in the night. In its night scenes filled with mystery, danger, and violence and in its lying, duplicitous, and murderous antagonists, *Chinatown* is a film noir in color. Like so many films noirs, it also includes interiors with the shadows of venetian blinds against the walls. Frame enlargement. *Long Road Productions; Paramount*

films as Brit noir. An example is a British-Irish-German-French co-production, *Croupier* (1998)—a twisted tale set in a nocturnal city. The story includes crime, intrigue, lies, betrayal, and a beautiful, worldly, mysterious, duplicitous, and potentially dangerous woman. Writing in 1998, Hirsch summarizes noir's subjects, evolution, and enduring appeal:

> The private-investigation quest; crimes of passion and profit; stories involving masquerade, amnesia, split identity, and double and triple crosses continue to be the genre's abiding concerns. . . . Noir endures, but, inevitably, not in the same way as forty and fifty years ago. Like any genre that survives, it has had to adapt; and as a set of narrative patterns, a repertoire of images, a nucleus of character types, it has proven remarkably elastic. Against the odds, and after several premature obituaries, noir is a mainstay of commercial narrative filmmaking. (14, 320)

Film noir is not restricted to one period (1941–1958) or to one country (the United States). It is not a movement restricted to a place and time but a genre that has been adapted to different times and places and has continuing appeal.

FIGURE 7.18 Continuing popularity of film noir
Films noirs continue to be made. By anyone's definition of the term, *L.A. Confidential* (1997) is film noir or, more precisely, film noir in color. As in many films noirs, in *L.A. Confidential* light and shadows from partially opened venetian blinds illuminate several interior scenes, as here about 35½ minutes into the film. A meeting of Los Angeles police detectives has been called to announce the discovery of multiple murders, including the killing of a recently discharged police detective. Part of the continuing appeal of films noirs is that they reinforce the widespread public perception that those in authority, perhaps especially the police, are not to be trusted because they act as if they are above the law. Frame enlargement. *Regency; Warner Bros.*

THE MUSICAL

Musicals come in an enormous variety, but essentially, a musical features some combination of intermittent instrumental music, singing, and dancing in combination with a narrative or story. The musical genre has existed since the introduction of movie sound technology in the late 1920s. The term *musical* came into use in the early 1930s to describe such films (Altman 32), which constituted one of Hollywood's most prestigious genres throughout the era of the studio system, commanding impressive resources and attracting large audiences. Many of the Academy Awards for Best Picture have gone to musicals, including *Broadway Melody* (1929), *An American in Paris* (1951), *West Side Story* (1962), *My Fair Lady* (1964), *The Sound of Music* (1965), and *Chicago* (2002). *The Wizard of Oz* has been a staple of American culture since it first lit up screens in 1939. Two of the most endearing and enduring cult movies are musicals, *The Rocky Horror Picture Show* (1975) and the "*Sing-a-Long Sound of Music*" (see p. 470). For many years, the musical held the place in American cinema now occupied by action films: many were big-budget extravaganzas

FIGURE 7.19 Musicals celebrating the human body
Like sporting events and yoga, musicals celebrate the human body
by showing its flexibility, balance, strength, and grace. Here, a
dancer seen for less than a second 4¼ minutes into *Chicago* (2002)
whirls her legs around with superior flexibility, range, and ease.
The shot celebrates human sexuality, a frequent aspect of musicals.
The dancer's well proportioned body is neither cloaked nor hidden
in the shadows, nor is she wearing panty hose and clogs! From her
high heels and up, she is adorned in ways many societies consider
both enhancing and celebratory of female sexual allure. Frame enlargement. *Miramax*

aimed at a mass audience, appealing on the level of visual spectacle, and emphasizing the strength, speed, flexibility, grace, and expressiveness of the human body (Figure 7.19 and Plate 17 in Chapter 2). In addition to visual
spectacle, musicals showcase the expressiveness of instrumental music, the
human body moving in sync with music, and the range and nuance of emotion possible with the singing voice.

Hollywood is the best-known source for musicals but hardly the world's
only one. Film industries in the Middle East, Latin America, Europe, and
South Asia have made musicals part of their output. India is the most prolific
producer of musicals, which are made in many different languages. Most Indian films have many musical numbers and the "playback singers," who are
major Indian pop stars and attract audiences in their own right, sing the
songs as the actors lip-sync along (see also the section on Bollywood later in
this chapter beginning on p. 327).

The origins of the American musical genre are diverse. European influences include opera and operetta, whereas American sources include vaudeville, minstrel shows, burlesque, and the Broadway stage. Most musicals are
live action, but many are animation or a blend of live action and animation.
As it has evolved, the musical has not been limited by setting, subject, or
style. Some musicals are set in the past, others in the present; some aim for
realism, others for fantasy or a blend of realism and fantasy. A musical may
be a tragic romance set in an urban world of ethnic mistrust (*West Side Story*)
or a fairy tale with a happy ending (*Snow White and the Seven Dwarfs*, 1937,
see Figure 8.34 on p. 390). A musical might be set during the era of rising
Nazi power (*Cabaret*, 1972). A musical might very well include a story of
courtship: the man pursuing the initially reluctant female (Figure 7.20a). A
musical could be a genial gangster **parody** and **homage** with a cast with the
average age of twelve (Figure 7.20b). It may be a remake (of an opera, for example) and have an all African American cast, though its sources do not
(*Carmen Jones*, 1954). A musical may be an animated satire of recent events
and trends (*South Park: Bigger, Longer and Uncut*, 1999) or a parody of a

homage: A tribute in a text to
a person, other text (such as a
film), or part of a text.

a)

b)

c)

d)

FIGURE 7.20 The scope of the musical

Musicals may be live action or animation or a blend of the two. They may strive for realism or fantasy or both. They may be set anywhere and show any story. These four films suggest some of the vast range of the musical. (a) Seen here about ninety-three minutes into *Top Hat* (1935), the Fred Astaire and Ginger Rogers characters dance "The Piccolino" in (Hollywood-made) Venice, Italy. The story of *Top Hat* is about courtship and prolonged comic misunderstandings that can alienate a couple. (b) *Bugsy Malone* (1976) is a British gangster musical, small time. Everything is scaled down, from the sets to the pedal-powered cars to the characters themselves in this film that parodies prohibition-era gangster movies. Here one gang is about to try to take over a rival speakeasy with their splurge guns that shoot only blobs of white stuff. (c) *The Nightmare before Christmas* (1993) is an animated film about what happens when the characters of Halloween Town take charge of Christ-

mas Eve events at Christmas Town. Before that, Jack, the leader of Halloween Town, uses readings, science, and then math to try to figure out the secrets of Christmas. Here nearly twenty-nine minutes into the movie, Jack is trying out a formula for Christmas that factors in "Sandy Claws." (d) *Hedwig and the Angry Inch* (2001) combines live action and animation and has wry standup comedy, music, and a story told in action and songs. The film shows the story of a put-upon transsexual seeking success, respect, recompense, and love. Here Hedwig performs before an initially unsuspecting and then largely unappreciative audience, customers at one of a chain of "Bilgewater's" seafood restaurants (think of a Red Lobster restaurant with a maritime disasters motif). (a) *Pandro S. Berman; RKO* (b) *Alan Marshall; Carlton International;* (c) Frame enlargement. *Tim Burton and Denise Di Novi; Walt Disney; Touchstone;* (d) *Killer Films & New Line Cinema; British Film Institute Stills, Posters and Designs*

movie genre (*The Rocky Horror Picture Show*, see Figure 5.16 on p. 231). Alternatively, it may be an animated film that entertains both children and adults (Figure 7.20c). A musical may set some of the numbers within the mind of a character and **cross-cut** between what is happening in the story and what the character is fantasizing about (*Chicago*). It may even be about an East German youth who suffers a botched sex change operation and thereafter dresses and functions as a female seeking artistic acclaim, gender acceptance, unity, and love (Figure 7.20d). As this sampling suggests, the possible settings and subjects for the musical are limitless.

In the first few decades of the American film musical, the dominant style of music was popular standards, with melody and harmony deriving from the European tradition. The most respected talents in American popular music in those years were as much the songwriters as the performers. Irving Berlin, George and Ira Gershwin, Jerome Kern, Cole Porter, and Richard Rodgers wrote scores of songs that are still often heard today. Many of these were written for Hollywood musicals, including Gershwin's "They Can't Take That Away from Me" (*Shall We Dance*, 1937), Kern's "The Way You Look Tonight" (*Swing Time*, 1936), Porter's "I've Got You under My Skin" (*Born to Dance*, 1936), and Berlin's "Cheek to Cheek" (*Top Hat*, 1935) and "White Christmas" (*Holiday Inn*, 1942).

While musicals in the traditional popular music style of earlier decades were still made into the 1960s, beginning in the 1950s, American film musicals adopted other musical styles. During this time, popular music changed drastically. Musical influences were less European and more American: folk, western swing, jazz, and especially rock and roll and the blues. Films starring Elvis Presley, such as *Love Me Tender* (1956) and *Jailhouse Rock* (1957), draw on these new musical sources. These films started appearing in the mid-1950s and continued at a pace of more than one a year through the end of the 1960s. In the 1970s, *The Wiz* (1978), *Nashville* (1975), and both *Saturday Night Fever* (1977) and *Grease* (1978) worked African American pop, country, and disco (respectively) into the genre. In more recent examples of the genre, no single musical style dominates. Films are made in various different musical idioms and sometimes even an eclectic mix of styles within a single film. *Hedwig and the Angry Inch* features original punk rock. *Dancer in the Dark* (2000) uses Björk's original songs, in her inimitable alternative techno-rock sound, whereas *Chicago*, based on a 1975 stage musical, has John Kander and Fred Ebb's retro, Jazz Age tunes. *Moulin Rouge* (2001), which uses mostly existing compositions for its score, contains a grab bag of hit pop songs of the past few decades but only one number, "Diamonds Are a Girl's Best Friend," from the popular standards era.

In musicals, filmmaking techniques are also varied. Some musicals use a long-shot/long-take camera style that emphasizes the uninterrupted performances of the leads. The athletic Gene Kelly could dance seemingly effortlessly for long fragments of time (see Figure 1.5 on p. 14). So could Fred

Astaire, who insisted on minimal editing. In *Swing Time*, the Astaire and Rogers numbers are made up of mostly extremely lengthy shots that necessitated lengthy rehearsals. For example, the penultimate shot of "Never Gonna Dance" runs 150 seconds and reportedly required 48 **takes**. In contrast, other musicals inject energy by using frenetic choreography (as frequently in Bob Fosse musicals), abrupt camera movements, and fast-**paced** editing, a style familiar from TV commercials and music videos. The most extreme cases are *Moulin Rouge* and *Chicago*, in which some scenes have such **fast cutting** that one's eyes can scarcely take in the mise en scène.

take: A version of a shot.

From the 1930s into the 1950s, many musicals were "backstage" or "show" musicals or backscreen musicals, stories about the production of a play or film. In these films, including *42nd Street* (1933), the musical numbers are motivated as rehearsals or performances.

Other backstage or backscreen musicals, however, include numbers that have nothing to do with rehearsals or performances. Examples are the early numbers in *The Band Wagon* (1953), such as "By Myself," which Astaire sings approximately six minutes into the film, and "Dancing in the Dark" (59½ minutes), which shows the Astaire character and the Cyd Charisse character testing whether they can overcome their different dancing styles and dance together. Can they ever! In contrast, the movie's diverse concluding numbers are part of the show the characters are putting on, for instance, "Louisiana Hayride" (86 minutes) and "Triplets" (91 minutes, see Figure 1.6 on p. 15).

However the songs are worked into a backstage or backscreen musical, the characters are show business performers who sing and dance for a living. The plot centers on mounting a successful production, with the main characters encountering obstacles along the way. Typically, the lead performers in the show are also a male-female couple whose relationship succeeds in parallel to the success of the production. If the female does not initially reciprocate the male's romantic interest, he uses song, dance, or song and dance together to court her, and eventually they achieve harmony and grace, musically and emotionally—as in *Singin' in the Rain* (1952).

In contrast to the backstage or backscreen musicals, other musicals have been described as "straight," meaning that all their numbers are sung without the motivating device of a play or film within the film. In a straight musical, the numbers seem to arise spontaneously. *Meet Me in St. Louis* (1944)—which is set in 1903 to 1904 St. Louis, a time when horse-drawn carriages share the streets with "horseless carriages"—works its music into the film through such situations as characters singing at the piano, traipsing through the house, saying goodnight, and riding on a trolley. An example of the integration of narrative events and music (as well as an example of the power of music to bring the family together) is the number "You and I" approximately seventy-seven minutes into the film. Minutes before, the father had announced to the assembled family that they would all be moving from St. Louis to New York. The reactions are shock, hurt, and resentment. Everyone

FIGURE 7.21 A straight musical
During the opening of Disney's animated feature *The Lion King* (1994), animals from far and wide make their way to at first we know not where. Soon we learn their destination: a presentation ceremony for Simba, the lion toddler who will one day be the lion king. This opening action is accompanied by the song "Circle of Life," which immediately suggests the African setting and also conveys messages—that life is abundant and varied, that different creatures react to life differently and fare differently, and that life is ongoing. Almost fifteen minutes into the film, Simba's song "I Just Can't Wait to Be King" helps convey his excitement at the prospect of the freedom and power before him (he's "brushing up on looking down"). The songs of *The Lion King* reinforce setting, characterizations, plot development, meaning, or mood. Frame enlargement. *Walt Disney; Buena Vista*

leaves the room except the mother and father. Soon the mood shifts a bit, and she sits down and starts playing the piano. As he joins in singing and the mother joins him during a repetition of the chorus, all the other family members drawn by the music return and resume where they had left off before the disruptive paternal announcement. In this scene, as throughout the film, the ways in which the musical numbers are worked into the narrative are less contrived than the show-within-a-show backstagers. A more recent example of a straight musical is Disney's *The Lion King* (1994, Figure 7.21).

Numbers may serve to express meanings, support characterizations, or advance actions. In Bob Fosse's *All That Jazz* (1979), for example, the songs and dances help reveal the personality and situation of the driven, creative, yet self-destructive central character. Beginning about 69½ minutes into *Chicago*, "Mr. Cellophane" highlights the nonassertive personality of the John C. Reilly character, whereas ten minutes later in the film, "Razzle Dazzle" shows Billy Flynn's circus/flimflam/magical courtroom strategies perhaps more completely than any other aspect of the film.

In contrast, numbers may be poorly motivated, superfluous to the action, or too spectacular and elaborate to justify in the narrative. The "revue" films of the late 1920s and early 1930s, for example, had only a minimal plot, and the comical or musical numbers stand largely on their own (Neale 105). The plot seems like little more than an excuse to mount a series of production numbers.

Some musicals have numbers that are motivated and others that are not, as in the musicals of the first full decade of the filmed musical, the 1930s, including three 1933 Warner Bros. movies with choreography by Busby Berkeley: *42nd Street*, *Gold Diggers of 1933* (see Figure 9.14a on p. 428), and *Footlight Parade*. The last named shows the story of a Broadway producer who after the coming of talking pictures decides to produce live musical numbers and stage one of them before the showing of a feature film. The first part of *Footlight Parade* shows how he gets the idea and how he goes about realizing it; the story also involves two possible romances. The movie ends with three long, involved production numbers supposedly staged before a live audience in a theater, but the numbers are so elaborate and sometimes **filmic** (such as the underwater shots of swimmers) that they could never be staged, let alone seen, in a real theater (Figure 7.22). In these and other early musicals, the

filmic: Characteristic of the film medium or appropriate to it.

FIGURE 7.22 Musical with some motivated numbers, some not The number "By a Waterfall"—the second of three Busby Berkeley mini-musicals concluding *Footlight Parade* (1933)—begins approximately seventy-eight minutes into the film and runs nearly eleven minutes. The publicity still seen here shows most of the number's first set, which includes five long water slides. The number has a second set: a huge swimming pool in which scores and scores of young women cavort and form various changing symmetrical formations often seen from a high angle or a bird's-eye view, the latter angle resulting in shifting kaleidoscopic patterns. Unlike some of the earlier numbers in this film, "By a Waterfall" is too large-scale and too filmic to be mounted in a theater and seen by a theatrical audience. *Warner Bros.*

scale of some of their numbers exceeds their narrative function, or the numbers are too filmic to be credible in a theatrical context.

In recent years, the musical has been enjoying a new popularity, in large part because of the continued success of animated musicals, the cult favorites *Rocky Horror Picture Show* and "Sing-a-Long *Sound of Music*," and the popularity of recent musicals such as *Hedwig and the Angry Inch* and the Academy Award–winning *Chicago*. The coming years may see a continuing revival of the musical—or they may not. Like all genres, the musical is subject to changing times and interests, evolution, and cycles of prominence and eclipse.

Occasionally a film is a parody of a genre: an amusing imitation of traditional films in the genre. Examples of parodies of westerns are Paul Bartel's *Lust in the Dust* (1985) and Mel Brooks's *Blazing Saddles* (1974, Figure 7.23). In another western parody, a supremely poised ("cool") fighter for hire arrives in a town torn by two greedy, violent, warring factions. Amused by the shortcomings of both groups, he plays one against the other and partially orchestrates their eventual mutual destruction. Though greatly outnumbered, he also kills some of each group and then strides away. The story re-creates many elements of the western, such as *High Noon* and *Shane* (1953), but

FIGURE 7.23 **A parody of westerns**
The bad (and dense) guys rein up to pay the toll for the Governor William J. Le Petomane Thruway 79½ minutes into *Blazing Saddles* (1974). Here, as elsewhere in the film, the subjects (cowboys) and settings (the nineteenth-century American West) are those of the traditional western, but such actions as building a railroad, saving a town from corruption, and brawling in a saloon are exaggerated and mocked. As illustrated here, often *Blazing Saddles* also knowingly includes details from twentieth-century life. *Crossbow; Warner Bros.*

satire: A representation that indirectly exposes and perhaps ridicules individual or group thinking or behavior for being foolish, evil, or stupid or for exhibiting some other shortcoming.

much of its characterization and action is rendered humorously, even **satirically**. The country and film: Japan and *Yojimbo* (*The Bodyguard*) (1961).[1]

Many filmmakers combine elements of two or more genres. Occasionally, they do so in only part of a film (Figure 7.24). Elements of horror films are combined with those of westerns in *Curse of the Undead* (1959) and *Billy the Kid vs. Dracula* (1965, Figure 7.25). The French new wave film *Shoot the Piano Player* mixes crime, romance, and slapstick comedy. Some films written and directed by David Cronenberg, including *Scanners* (1981) and *eXistenZ* (1999), combine horror and science fiction; so do *Alien* (1979) and its sequels (Figure 7.26). *Blade Runner* (1982, revised and rereleased in 1991) combines visual and story elements of film noir, characters typical of a horror film (a Dr. Frankenstein type and his dangerous yet finally pitiable creation), and a decayed futuristic science fiction setting. All three *Matrix* movies can also be seen as a combination of elements from three genres (Figure 7.27). Director Jim Jarmusch has called his own *Ghost Dog: The Way of the Samurai* (1999) a "gangster samurai hip-hop eastern western." Although a blending of genres can be inventive, refreshing, and fun, sometimes these combined genre films

---

[1]For a comparison and contrast of *Yojimbo* and *High Noon*, see Alan P. Barr, "Exquisite Comedy and the Dimensions of Heroism, Akira Kurosawa's *Yojimbo*," *Massachusetts Review* 16 (1975): 158–68. *Yojimbo* was remade in Italy as the first of the so-called spaghetti westerns, Sergio Leone's *A Fistful of Dollars* (1964), and later remade in the United States as a story of an outsider and two rival groups of gangsters in a prohibition-era Texas town in *Last Man Standing* (1996) starring Bruce Willis.

FIGURE 7.24 Combining genres in part of a film
"Girl Hunt: A Murder Mystery in Jazz," a stylish jazz and dance number that begins ninety-five minutes into the musical *The Band Wagon* (1953) and runs 11½ minutes, combines elements of film noir with the musical. The number begins at night in an unidentified city where the main character, a detective played by Fred Astaire, is soon trying to solve a murder. During his investigation, he finds himself in an underworld nightspot where all the men carry guns and resent his presence. The other two major characters of "Girl Hunt" are danced by Cyd Charisse, here as a brunette dressed in red and playing the femme fatale and elsewhere as a blonde dressed in white and playing the innocent in need of help. *Arthur Freed; Loew's Incorporated*

FIGURE 7.25 A vampire western
In this publicity still for *Billy the Kid vs. Dracula* (1965), a vampire in western clothes and in a western setting menaces a beautiful woman. "The text [is] endowed with a strong degree of logical coherence, largely through a kind of process of condensation, whereby elements common to both genres [horror and western] . . . receive heavy emphasis. A key site of such condensation is the film's lead player, [John] Carradine, being an iconographic figure for both the horror and western genres, having played both numerous poverty-row vampires and numerous western character roles. . . . His nineteenth-century costume, the horse-drawn carriages he often travels in, and the cave-turned-silver mine he sleeps in all seem appropriate to both the western and the horror film" (Knee 145). *Circle Productions; Embassy Pictures*

yield ludicrous results, as in *Plan 9 from Outer Space* (1959, see Figure 9.18 on p. 440), which mixes "science fiction" and "horror" with its story of aliens resurrecting the dead.

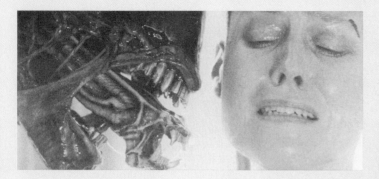

FIGURE 7.26 Horror stories in science fiction settings

As so often happens in the *Alien* movies, in *Alien*[3] (1992) people cut off from others are destroyed by a swift, voracious, and unrelenting monster. Here the Sigourney Weaver character is once again in mortal danger from an alien, but she survives this encounter halfway into *Alien*[3] because of a surprising condition viewers learn about later. Like the other *Alien* movies, *Alien*[3] combines the horror film components of shadows, disturbing sounds, unsettling music, and a lurking monster with a futuristic science fiction setting. *20th Century–Fox*

FIGURE 7.27 Sci-fi, action, kung-fu movie

The Matrix (1999) blends elements of science fiction, action, and kung-fu movies. (a) Neo, the Keanu Reeves character, tries to dodge bullets that he and we viewers can more or less see, an image one might expect in a science fiction movie. (b) The Laurence Fishburne character leaps out of a building on the right as Neo, who is tethered to a helicopter, jumps toward him. Such exciting actions are not of this world but of the world of action movies. (c) The Carrie-Anne Moss character does a somewhat slow-motion cartwheel off a wall (on the left) as bullets and stone chips fly all around her. Many acrobatic movements here and elsewhere are reminiscent of kung-fu movies. The filmmakers had seen many Hong Kong action movies, and the major cast members were trained for months with a system of wires used to support them. Frame enlargements. *Joel Silver; Warner Bros.*

a)

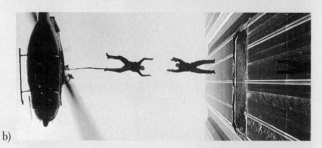

b)

c)

OTHER CINEMAS

There are many influential groups of fictional films other than classical Hollywood cinema, but space and limited accessibility to certain groups of films allow us to consider only a few of them: Italian neorealist cinema, French new wave cinema, European and American independent cinemas, Bollywood, Hong Kong cinema, and Dogme 95. We consider them in the order in which they first elicited attention in film studies.

Critics and scholars sometimes group films into movements—groups of films sharing innovative styles or subjects (or both) that emerge from the same country or region over a period of a few years and that are in opposition to the dominant cinema(s) of the time. Two widely studied film movements are Italian neorealist cinema and French new wave cinema.

Italian Neorealist Cinema

> Along with [Luchino] Visconti, such other directors as Roberto Rossellini and Vittorio De Sica strove to create a film art of authenticity. . . . Feeling that reality could better be conveyed through created situations than through the direct recording of actual events, they employed a synthesis of documentary and studio techniques, merging actual situations with a scripted story line. The essentials of neorealist films were the use of nonprofessional actors, authentic settings, naturalistic lighting, simple direction, and natural dialogue. (Phillips 686)

In *The Bicycle Thief* (a.k.a. *Bicycle Thieves*, 1948), a long-term unemployed family man finally gets a job pasting up movie posters but soon loses his bicycle to a thief and his accomplices and faces the loss of his job if he cannot retrieve the bicycle by Monday morning. Most of the film is devoted to showing the man and his young son searching for the bicycle in various parts of Rome and the mostly difficult conditions under which different people live. *The Bicycle Thief* exhibits the characteristics of Italian **neorealism**: heavy but not exclusive use of nonprofessional actors (in the three major roles), mostly unaltered location settings, and a chronological story. Generally, the film uses unobtrusive filmmaking techniques: few **close-ups**, **wipes** that are about as inconspicuous as an editor could make them, and little or no supplemental lighting (Figure 7.28). Its dialogue is natural, not rhetorical, and includes a range of dialects.

close-up: An image in which the subject fills most of the frame and little of the surroundings is shown.

wipe: A transition between shots, usually between scenes, in which it appears that one shot is pushed off the screen by the next shot.

For an outline of the scenes of *The Bicycle Thief*, see the Web site for this book: <bedfordstmartins.com/phillips-film>.

In addition to *The Bicycle Thief*, other important neorealist films include *Open City* (1945), *Shoeshine* (1946), and *Umberto D.* (1952). *Open City* shows

FIGURE 7.28 The Italian neorealist film *The Bicycle Thief* (1948)
This photograph illustrates how Italian neorealistic film-makers use real people, actual locations, and little or no supplemental lighting. The seated woman is an untrained actor playing the part of a fortune-teller. Like other neo-realist films, *The Bicycle Thief* deals with ordinary, believ-able characters—often played by nonactors—caught up in difficult social and economic conditions. The main character and his son (the actors playing those two cen-tral characters are seen on the right side of the photo-graph) have come to see the fortune-teller in hopes she can give the man information that will help him regain the stolen bicycle he needs to retain his desperately needed, recently acquired job. *PDS-ENIC; The Museum of Modern Art/Film Stills Archive*

Catholics (especially a humane and compassionate priest), Communists, and others working together to resist the brutal Nazi occupation of Rome and exposes the myth of German superiority. A year later, *Shoeshine* showed two boys, who are best friends, trying to survive in the streets of Nazi-occupied Rome but getting into trouble and suffering arrest, prison, reform school, and mutual betrayal. *Umberto D.* is the story of an old pensioner increasingly distraught because he is behind in his payments to his wealthy, uncaring landlady; he is comforted only by his dog and to a lesser extent by his land-lady's young, pregnant, unmarried servant (Figure 7.29).

The characters in neorealist films are ordinary and believable, but they are not probed for their psychological complexities. Instead, the focus is on characters caught up in the difficult conditions of Italy during and after World War II, such as poverty and unemployment. Generally, these films failed to make money in Italy because audiences found them depressing, an affront to national pride, and not diverting enough. They fared better at for-eign box offices, especially in the United States.

The movement began in Italy during World War II and largely died out there by the early 1950s. It was a product of the economic and social condi-tions of the times. In part, neorealism was also a reaction to prewar and wartime Italian cinema that often presented idealized images of fascist Italy, studio-made comedies, and costume histories.

Neorealism did not set out mainly to be an alternative to classical Holly-wood cinema; indeed, in its clear linear plots and unobtrusive filmmaking techniques, neorealism is similar to it. However, in its frequent use of non-professional actors, unadorned location settings, simplified lighting, natural dialogue, concern for the social and economic problems of everyday people,

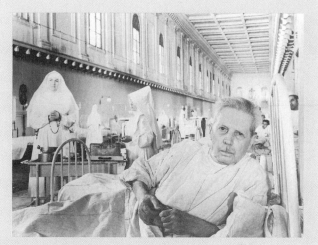

FIGURE 7.29 The Italian neorealist film *Umberto D.* (1952)

In *Umberto D.*, a childless retired civil servant is struggling to live in Rome on his limited pension. Here—approximately forty-one minutes into the film—the man is in a hospital or clinic where he has learned he has appendicitis but will not be operated on. He doesn't seem to feel ill but is nonetheless hoping he will be allowed to stay a few extra days so he can save some precious money. Like *The Bicycle Thief, Umberto D.* exhibits the characteristics of Italian neorealist films: mostly nonprofessional actors (the man playing Umberto was a university professor without previous acting experience), location filming (as in the scene depicted here), and a chronological story. The film uses few close-ups and generally unobtrusive filmmaking techniques (although its music is sometimes prominent).

The everyday people in the story are in no way glamorized or idealized. Like *The Bicycle Thief, Umberto D.* shows believable characters trying to cope with difficult social and economic circumstances. In addition, as scholar and author Roy Armes concludes, the film operates "as social study and meditation on solitude, as a critique of bourgeois rapacity [the landlady] and a defence of bourgeois dignity [the old pensioner], as stark tragedy and warmly human story" (*Patterns* 163). *Rizzoli-De Sica-Amato; British Film Institute Stills, Posters and Designs*

and credible unhappy endings, neorealism was an alternative to the studio-made classical Hollywood cinema of its time.

Neorealist films influenced some later films—such as the early films directed by acclaimed Italian directors Federico Fellini and Michelangelo Antonioni, French new wave directors (see below), the Bengali filmmaker Satyajit Ray, and some American directors working after World War II, such as Nicholas Ray, Elia Kazan, Jules Dassin, Joseph Losey, Robert Rossen, and Edward Dmytryk (Cook 438). Other films—such as *Salt of the Earth* (1954), which shows poor zinc miners and their families trying to cope during a prolonged labor strike—have strong resemblances to Italian neorealist films (Figure 7.30). In recent years, many of the most cineliterate film critics have pointed out the neorealistic qualities of some recent Iranian films and how other films are at least partially neorealistic. An example is David Riker's *The City* (*La ciudad*, 1999), which was filmed in black and white and consists of four vignettes showing the difficult economic conditions of Latin American immigrants in New York. The film is neorealistic in its subject, location shooting, nonprofessional actors, documentary quality, and unresolved endings.

Since the 1950s, students of Italian neorealist films have come to see their artifice more clearly. Nonetheless, the stories and contexts of neorealist films continue to fascinate and engage film students and film scholars.

FIGURE 7.30 American neorealist-like film
Salt of the Earth (1954) shows zinc miners in New Mexico striking to gain a safe and fair deal from the callous big-business mine owners, who control the district attorney, the sheriff, and the sheriff's deputies. First, the men, mostly Mexican Americans, go on strike. When their efforts seem to be at a dead end, gradually the women become involved in the strike. Eventually, some of the women leaders are arrested illegally and jailed, including the film's narrator and main character, seen here in jail giving up her baby to its father (on the left) so he can see that it gets its formula.

Like Italian neorealist films, *Salt of the Earth* was shot on location on a low budget. Except for the woman shown here, a Mexican cinema star, and a few other professionals (including the actor who plays the sheriff, on the right), the large cast is nonprofessional. Like Italian neorealist films, *Salt of the Earth* uses mostly unobtrusive filmmaking techniques, blends fact and fiction, and focuses on the difficult social and economic conditions under which poor workers try to survive with some dignity. The film is unlike neorealism in its overt messages, its use of a narrator who explains many of the story's important points, and its hopeful ending. It is no accident that the film's central character is named "Esperanza," which means hope. *Paul Jarrico; Independent Productions Corp. and The International Union of Mine, Mill and Smelter Workers; The Museum of Modern Art/Film Stills Archive*

French New Wave Cinema

New wave films were a diverse group of French fictional films made in the late 1950s and early 1960s as a reaction to the carefully scripted products of the French film industry and as explorations of more current subjects sometimes rendered with untraditional techniques.

> The New Wave—however we define it—captures the surface texture of French life in a fresh way, if only because the low budgets with which most young directors work initially necessitate a certain contemporary flavour lacking in the 1951–57 period, when the characteristic works were . . . period reconstructions. The newcomers had no money to build elaborate **sets**, pay for costumes or employ star names: they shot on location, with reduced crews and fresh young performers. But this contemporary flavour was not accompanied by any real social or political concern. . . . The post-1958 feature film industry . . . remains essentially a Parisian cinema, dealing with middle-class problems in middle-class terms, and above all concerned with the "eternal" issues of human emotions and relationships. (Armes, *French* 169, 170)

The films of the new wave were made by such directors as François Truffaut, Jean-Luc Godard, Claude Chabrol, and, to a lesser extent, Eric

set: A constructed setting where action is filmed.

Rohmer and Jacques Rivette.[2] Most new wave directors had watched many films at the Cinémathèque
Française (French national film archive) and various
film clubs and had written about films and the film
medium in the journal *Cahiers du cinéma*. In their
writings they advocated that directors should have
control over all creative stages of production and
criticized traditional French films, especially those of
the preceding decade. Before the new wave, French
movies—as typified by the famous 1945 film *Children of Paradise*—tended to be period pieces and
more literary than filmic (Figure 7.31). New wave directors argued that such films gave too much control
to writers at the expense of directors.

New wave films are often imbued with a knowledge of earlier films, especially American genre films,
and even more so are marked by unpredictable plot
developments and the independent spirit of their directors. Jeanne Moreau, whose independent and
openly sexual characters embody quintessential qualities of new wave films, said that the new wave way of
making films freed up actors:

> In other films I made . . . the lighting was so compli-
> cated. There were shadows on one side and another
> light on the other side, so, really, when you are in close-
> ups you are in a corset. It was impossible to move.
> That's what the new wave was about, that absolute free-
> dom. The light was made in such a way that you could
> move and do whatever you wanted, like in real life.

Like a type of documentary filmmaking evolving
in France at about the same time (**cinéma vérité**), new
wave films were set in the present or recent past and were often shot on location
with portable handheld cameras and sound equipment, **faster film stock**, and
new, more portable lighting equipment. Sometimes they include surprising or
whimsical moments, perhaps the product of improvisation while filming.

New wave cinema may also include homages or tributes to earlier films or
parts of them (Figure 7.32). A homage results when visual details from the two
main characters in Charlie Chaplin's *The Kid* (1921) are re-created in *Jules and
Jim* (1961, Figure 7.33).

FIGURE 7.31 French film before the new wave
In the theatrical and literate *Children of Paradise* (*Les en-
fants du paradis*) (1945), one of the main characters is a
mime (left). As a costume film and period piece that was
shaped more by the script than the direction, *Children of
Paradise* was the type of film the French new wave directors rebelled against in their publications and their filmmaking. *S. N. Pathé Cinéma*

cinéma vérité: A type and
style of documentary filmmaking developed in France during
the early 1960s whose aim was
to capture events as they happened.

fast film stock: Film stock that
requires relatively little light for
capturing images.

---

[2]As Susan Hayward points out in her *Cinema Studies: The Key Concepts* (2nd ed., 2000), Agnès
Varda's 1954 film *La Pointe Courte* is a forerunner of French new wave cinema (146).

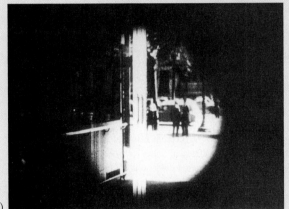

FIGURE 7.32 **Homages to another actor and to an earlier transition in film**
In the French film *Breathless* (1959), the main character, Michel, sometimes pays homage to American actor Humphrey Bogart. For example, in various scenes Michel runs his thumb across his lips and back as Bogart did in many films. In the last three shots of the scene represented here viewers see (a) a lobby card (photograph advertising a movie) of Bogart and (b) a shot of Michel rubbing his thumb across his lips. (c) The scene ends with another homage: an iris-out, a popular optical effect used in silent films. Frame enlargements. *SNC; New Yorker Films*

cutaway: A shot that briefly interrupts the visual representation of a subject to show something else.

jump cut: A transition between shots that causes a jarring or even shocking shift in space, time, or action.

New wave films abound in editing rarely used in classical Hollywood cinema. Sometimes the results are surprising and whimsical. In *Shoot the Piano Player*, a gangster says to a boy he is kidnapping, "I swear it on my old lady's head. May she die if I lie." In a **cutaway**, a woman old enough to be his mother moves her hand toward her chest, falls down backward, and briefly kicks her legs straight up in the air. In the next scene, the boy says, "Then I believe you," and the gangster replies, "Didn't I tell you so?" And the film resumes its story. *Breathless* sometimes uses **jump cuts**, as in the scene where Michel shoots the motorcycle police officer; as edited, the scene is a little disorienting and confusing (see Figure 3.16 on p. 135). Jump cuts are also used in a later scene where Michel and Patricia are talking in a moving car and between shots the background changes in inexplicable ways. There is continuity in the conversation in the foreground (continuity of action and time) but discontinuity of settings in the background. In *The 400 Blows*

a)   b)

FIGURE 7.33 A source and a French new wave homage
(a) The two main characters in *The Kid* (1921): Charlie Chaplin as the tramp and Jackie Coogan as the abandoned boy the tramp is raising. (b) An homage from one filmmaker (François Truffaut) to another (Chaplin): in this publicity still we see Jeanne Moreau as she appears in a brief section of Truffaut's *Jules and Jim* (1961): her shoes and mustache are reminiscent of Charlie Chaplin's in *The Kid*; her cap and sweater are like the boy's. (a) *Charlie Chaplin; First National;* (b) *Marcel Berbert; Les Films du Carrosse*

(1959), two boys emerge from a movie theater and start running; then their movement blends into a blurred horizontal image (**swish pan**) that ends by blending with the boys arriving at another movie theater. In one brief scene of *Shoot the Piano Player*, Charlie and Léna are in bed; as she talks to him, five times the scene alternates with even briefer shots of them together in bed at some other time. Quite unconventionally, each of these five cutaway shots is preceded and followed by a rapid **lap dissolve**: as the first shot fades out, the next shot fades in, momentarily overlapping it before replacing it.

swish pan: The blurred images that result from pivoting a movie camera horizontally too rapidly during filming.

European Independent Films

Neorealism and new wave cinema are not the only European alternatives to classical Hollywood cinema. Various films since the 1960s directed by European directors working outside of the commercial mainstream—such as Jean-Luc

Godard and François Truffaut (throughout their careers, not merely during their earlier new wave years), Ingmar Bergman, Federico Fellini, Michelangelo Antonioni, and Luis Buñuel—are also alternatives to classical Hollywood cinema. Sometimes these films are called "art cinema," but it is more descriptive to refer to them as "European **independent films**." Perhaps the easiest way to begin considering these films is to compare and contrast their features with the features of classical Hollywood cinema (see the list on p. 292):

1. The characters' memories, fantasies, dreams, and other mental states are rendered much more often than in classical Hollywood cinema. Such films are more likely to be fragmented and are more likely to shift quickly and without explanation between different states of consciousness.

2. As in classical Hollywood cinema, the films focus on only one or a few distinct characters.

3. Often the main characters' goals are unclear or shifting. Often the characters are ambivalent and hard to figure out (as in most films directed by Antonioni).

4. The main characters confront various antagonists or a series of problems, but the antagonists and problems are not always as evident (for example, as obviously evil) or as simple as in classical Hollywood cinema.

5. Often the films lack closure and have unresolved **plotlines**, and the protagonists do not succeed in reaching a goal (the endings are more likely to be true to life than the endings of most commercial American movies of the time).

6. The emphasis is not as emphatically on clear causes and effects of actions; ambiguity may be pervasive; and sometimes the narratives are **episodic**: scenes could be shifted without changing the film substantially, as in films directed and cowritten by Jacques Tati.

7. As in classical Hollywood cinema, filmmaking techniques tend to be unobtrusive, but European independent films are more likely to have authorial **narration**.

8. European independent films have additional features. They are more likely than classical Hollywood cinema to be **self-reflexive**, to be in part about the film medium or filmmaking or to interrupt the viewers' involvement to draw attention to themselves as films. Ingmar Bergman's *Persona* (1966) is highly self-reflexive: on one level, it is about the nature of film and film presentation. At one point, for example, the story is interrupted with a **title card** reading "One moment please while we change **reels**," and after a **fade-out**, we see briefly only blackness and hear silence before a rapid **fade-in** introduces the next scene.

European independent films are also likely to stress relationships between people and to have a pace and intensity that approximate those of nor-

plotline: A narrative or series of related events usually involving only a few characters or people and capable of functioning on its own as a story.

narration: Commentary in a film about a subject in the film or some other topic, usually from someone offscreen.

self-reflexive: Characteristic of a text, such as a novel or film, to refer to or comment on itself as a text or as a medium.

fade-out: Optical effect in which the image changes by degrees from illumination to darkness (usually black).

fade-in: Optical effect in which the image changes by degrees from darkness (usually black) to illumination.

FIGURE 7.34 European independent film
Guido, the main character of *8½* (1963), is a film director who often evades the many problems in his personal and professional lives by escaping into fantasies and memories. After his wife berates him as a liar, he retreats into two fantasies: a fantasy of his wife and mistress getting along fabulously and a fantasy of a harem staffed by important women in his life. After the women in his harem temporarily rebel, he takes up a whip (seen here about 100 minutes into the film) and quickly restores an order pleasing and reassuring to himself—but then it is *Guido's* fantasy. The frequent transitions from present-tense reality to fantasy or dream or memory are a feature more common in European independent films of the 1960s than in films of the classical Hollywood cinema. *Angelo Rizzoli; Kino International*

mal human experience, whereas the films of classical Hollywood cinema are more likely to emphasize physical action and to have a pace and intensity exceeding normal experience. The European independent cinema is also more likely to be explicit about sexuality, whereas classical Hollywood cinema is more likely to be explicit about violence.

Finally, films directed by independent European directors are much less likely to be genre films than are the films of classical Hollywood cinema. *Run Lola Run* (1998) and *Amélie* (2001), for example, are not recognizable as any genre.

Although few films have all the characteristics described above, all European independent films have many of them. The Italian film *8½* (1963)—which was directed by Federico Fellini and is partly autobiographical (Fellini himself had completed eight films before directing *8½*)—exemplifies all the major features of European independent cinema. It focuses on the story of Guido, an exhausted movie director besieged with doubts and fears about the film he is trying to complete and beset with problems with his wife and his mistress, his producer and actors, and the press (Figure 7.34).

For an outline of the sequences of *8½*, see the Web site for this book: <bedfordstmartins.com/phillips-film>.

American Independent Cinema

American independent films since the 1960s, which tend to be relatively low budget and focus on personal relationships, originate outside the Hollywood studios and are made all over the United States, not only in southern California. Because of their low budgets, American independent films are usually made without costly directors, writers, and stars (or with personnel willing to work for a relatively small salary, a percentage of the profits, or both). An example is *Just Another Girl on the I.R.T.* (1992), which is a candid film about a bright seventeen-year-old African American living in Brooklyn who plans to go to college but gets pregnant. The movie concludes with a title card reading "A Film Hollywood Dared Not Do."

Funding for an American independent film may come from one of a variety of sources or, more often, a combination of sources, such as a series of maxed-out credit cards, relatives, friends, investor groups, grants, semi-independent film companies such as Fine Line, Canadian-based companies, and European TV firms. In recent years, cable TV networks such as HBO, Showtime, TNT, A&E, Lifetime, USA Networks, Independent Film Channel, and others have helped to finance and then show independent films; later some of those films are shown in theaters. However, many independent films are never accepted at film festivals, and most of them that get shown never get distribution. In fact, such is the competition and marketplace that most independent films are never shown in theaters.

So varied are American independent films that it is difficult to generalize about their subjects and techniques, as we can about neorealist films, new wave cinema, and European independent films. With lower budgets, independent films need not draw huge crowds to turn a profit, and the filmmakers are freer to take on a controversial subject or a subject of limited interest, so independent films tend to be more varied, less formulaic, and more individualistic than films of the classical Hollywood cinema. They are more likely, for instance, to deal with a controversial subject without showing audiences what they want to see and to include an unhappy ending if the story has been building toward it.

Independent films such as *Night of the Living Dead* (1968), *Blood Simple* (1984, revised and rereleased in 2000), *Daughters of the Dust* (1991), *El Mariachi* (1993), and *Memento* (2000) have won awards or been nominated for awards and often secured a distributor at one of the major film festivals such as Cannes, New York, or Sundance. Many independent films garner excellent reviews and critics' awards, like those given by the National Society of Film Critics, a group of writers for major U.S. newspapers and magazines.

Independent filmmakers have two major cooperating organizations: the Association of Independent Video and Filmmakers (AIVF) and Independent Feature Project (IFP). Both groups foster independent filmmakers and promote the independent film. Each organization also publishes a magazine:

AIVF publishes *The Independent Film & Video Monthly* and IFP publishes *Filmmaker*. Each year since 1986, members of Independent Feature Project/ West, one of four branches of IFP, have gained publicity for independent films by giving Independent Spirit Awards. Best feature awards for 1990 to 2003 have gone (in order) to *The Grifters, Rambling Rose, The Player, Short Cuts, Pulp Fiction, Leaving Las Vegas, Fargo, The Apostle, Gods and Monsters, Election, Crouching Tiger, Hidden Dragon, Memento, Far from Heaven,* and *Lost in Translation*.

Two cable channels devoted solely to the independent film—the Independent Film Channel (since 1995) and the Sundance Channel (since 1996)— have also been important in promoting independent films, including fictional shorts and documentaries, from countries throughout the world.

Bollywood[3]

In 2001, the epic-length film *Lagaan (Tax)* depicted the mythic formation of the first all-Indian cricket team under British colonial rule. After playing to packed theaters around the world, the film was nominated for an Academy Award. For some viewers, this surprising mix of sports, romance, history, and music was their first exposure to a Hindi film, a form that has nonetheless entertained one of the world's largest film audiences and been one of Hollywood's only popular rivals for decades. (Previously, if Western viewers saw Indian films, they were likely directed by the Bengali master Satyajit Ray, whose realist narratives were widely viewed only by an intellectual elite within India.) Also in 2001, the star-filled family melodrama *Kabhi Khushi Kabhie Gham (Sometimes Happiness, Sometimes Sadness)* ranked in the American top-ten box-office charts, though few non-South Asians were aware of the film's sell-out run in North American theaters.

For South Asian audiences, *Lagaan* dealt with a fresh topic through a familiar formula established by the Hindi-language popular cinema produced in Bombay (now officially Mumbai) or "**Bollywood**," a term that some use affectionately and others reject as derisive and condescending. While India actually produces popular films in many languages, including the major south Indian languages of Tamil and Telegu, and at times has supported a vibrant art or "parallel" cinema, popular Hindi cinema plays a dominant role in South Asia, similar to Hollywood's impact throughout much of the world. Hindi cinema has also consistently allowed Indian audiences to resist American cinema, unlike most other cultures where Hollywood overwhelms local productions. Hindi cinema also has a long history of exhibition outside of India, especially in China, the Soviet Union, Africa, and the Middle East. It

[3]Thanks to Corey Creekmur of the University of Iowa for helping me with the following two sections.

is the world's largest popular cinema, producing hundreds of films annually, though it remains largely unknown among mainstream North American and European audiences.

The term "Bollywood" is usually applied to recent films, but Hindi cinema extends back into the silent period. The father of Indian cinema, D. G. Phalke, began making films based on Hindu myths in 1913, and by the 1930s a vibrant film industry built around a Hollywood-style studio system was active. World War II, India's independence movement, and the 1947 Partition of India (creating the Muslim nation of Pakistan) somewhat derailed the film industry, but by the 1950s, Bombay was producing films that invoked India's ancient culture and mythology while exploring the nation's contemporary identity: Hindu epics were dramatized in "mythologicals," while contemporary issues were treated in films termed "socials."

Popular Hindi cinema resembles classical Hollywood in its reliance on melodramatic narratives and a prominent star system but is distinctive for its reliance on "picturized" film songs, which are a prominent element of virtually all Indian films (contributing to their approximately three-hour **running time**). Moreover, the songs, often with poetic lyrics, are not performed by the stars on screen but by prominent "playback singers" whose voices are often more famous than the actors they dub. Among these legendary singers, Lata Mangeshkar has provided the musical voice of Indian actresses for almost fifty years and is one of the world's most prolific recording artists. Hindi film songs are a common feature of everyday life throughout South Asia: they are heard constantly on radio and television and sung at parties, festivals, and weddings. Often seen as unnecessary intrusions by Western viewers, film songs are central to the appeal of Hindi films to their audiences: a film without hit songs is rarely successful at the box office, and film songs are fondly recalled long after many movies are forgotten.

Bollywood is also a star-driven cinema, and film heroes and heroines (as they are called) are the objects of adoration as well as endless gossip in India's many glossy movie magazines. Films are often tailored to the images and talents of their stars, who remain consistent in their character types. No Hindi star has been more prominent than Amitabh Bachchan (Figure 7.35). Recent, more boyish and fashionable male stars are extremely popular, but so far no Hindi star has matched Bachchan's impact on audiences.

FIGURE 7.35 Bollywood star
Amitabh Bachchan, whose key roles during India's 1975 to 1977 Emergency (when Prime Minister Indira Gandhi restricted civil rights) defined him as an "angry young man" for a generation of fans. His role in the blockbuster *Sholay* (*Flames*, 1975) contributed to the film's legendary status, and his prominent "dialogs" can be quoted by loyal fans. Here he is seen in *Major Saab* (1998). In 2000, Bachchan was voted the greatest star of the concluding millennium in a British poll, a result that shocked only those previously unaware of perhaps the world's most popular film star.

Since a half dozen songs are a common feature of films that also include action, romance, drama, and comedy, critics have identified contemporary Hindi cinema as a "masala" or spicy mix of ingredients. More so than Hollywood movies, Bollywood films typically combine and juxtapose diverse elements for audiences seeking a feast rather than a single flavor or two or three. Subplots and digressions are common since Hindi films rarely strive for the seamless story of Hollywood films.

While commonly dismissed as superficial entertainment, controversial recent films such as *Bombay* (1995) and *Gadar* (*Mayhem*, 2001) have explored "communal" (Hindu-Muslim) violence in India's recent history, whereas blockbuster family films like *Dilwale Dulhania Le Jayenge* (*The Lover Wins the Bride*, 1996) and *Hum Aapke Hain Koun . . . !* (*Who Am I to You?*, 1994) consider the dynamics of romance in a culture that both celebrates and increasingly questions arranged marriages. At the same time, violent gangster films such as *Satya* (*Truth*, 1998) and *Company* (2002) compete for audiences with slapstick comedies like *Hero No. 1* (1997).

Recently, independent films produced by South Asian filmmakers in North America and Britain have examined the Indian diaspora, the global movement of people who leave India and develop hybrid cultures abroad. Directors such as Mira Nair, in *Mississippi Masala* (1992) and *Monsoon Wedding* (2002), and Gurinder Chadha, in *Bhaji on the Beach* (1993) and *Bend It Like Beckham* (2002), rely on popular Hindi films for **allusions** and affectionate parody, even though the international audience for these films may not recognize those sources. At the same time, hints of Bollywood have shown up in innovative films such as *Moulin Rouge* and *Ghost World* (both 2001). On the whole, however, Western viewers are just beginning to acquaint themselves with a cinema enjoyed by close to a billion people around the globe.

allusion: A reference in a text to a person, earlier event, or text or part of a text.

In summary, as a popular cinema influenced by Western models, Bollywood relies on many of the same elements as classical Hollywood cinema, including goal-driven protagonists and a star system that places popular actors in familiar roles. But Bollywood films also draw on classical Indian forms to mix together moods and narrative forms that Hollywood isolates. Bollywood films often combine action, romance, and comedy and most notably feature elaborate song sequences using the voices of famous offscreen (or "playback") singers. Though made for popular audiences, Bollywood films are also highly self-referential and stylistically playful, breaking the rules of cinematic realism even as they involve audiences in highly emotional family melodramas.

Hong Kong Cinema

Ang Lee's *Crouching Tiger, Hidden Dragon* (2000) introduced millions of viewers to a new kind of action film and to actors Chow Yun Fat and Michelle Yeoh. The hit film was a big-budget homage to the immensely popular 1980s and 1990s movies produced in Hong Kong and starred two of that cinema's superstars. By the time *Crouching Tiger* was released, films produced in the former British colony had redefined action films worldwide. In fact, the increased demand for spectacular action in Hollywood films in recent decades suggests a belated response to Hong Kong's challenge.

Hong Kong cinema refers to the commercial film industry produced (by the 1980s) in the local Cantonese dialect, as distinguished from the Taiwanese New Cinema and films produced in official Mandarin Chinese in the People's Republic of China. Popular Chinese films were produced in Shanghai before the Communist takeover in 1949, when commercial filmmaking shifted to Hong Kong. But the first Chinese movies to reach an international audience were the kung-fu or martial arts (*wuxia pian*) films produced in Hong Kong, especially those featuring the charismatic Bruce Lee, including *The Big Boss* (1971) and the international co-production *Enter the Dragon* (1973). After Lee's untimely death in 1973, the vogue for such films dwindled, but a decade later a new, reinvigorated cinema emerged from a generation of filmmakers informed by the cosmopolitan values of the highly industrialized British colony as well as Chinese tradition. After attracting local viewers and a cult audience in the West, this cinema would influence filmmakers around the world.

Although Hong Kong continued to produce films in a range of genres, including comedies and romances, its most popular and influential films emphasize dynamic action, either in martial arts competition or urban gun battles. In groundbreaking films such as *Peking Opera Blues* (1985) and *Once Upon a Time in China* (1990), Director Tsui Hark staged wildly inventive fight scenes, often relying on the "wire work" that allowed his warriors to defy gravity. (Hong Kong's stunts do not adhere to the realism Western viewers often expect.) John Woo's "heroic bloodshed" films, beginning with *A Better Tomorrow* (1985) and including *The Killer* (1989) and *Hard-Boiled* (1991), all starred the suave Chow Yun Fat and stunned audiences with their highly stylized violence and operatic emotions (Figure 7.36). At the same time, the actor-director Jackie Chan became a superstar by combining his kinetic martial arts skills with ingenious comic stunts (sometimes reminiscent of the stunts of the

FIGURE 7.36 Hong Kong action cinema
The Killer (1989), which was written and directed by John Woo several years before he made his first U.S. movie, was filmed in Hong Kong. It stars Chow Yun Fat as Jeff (his name in the English language version), an ace hitman with a conscience, sense of style, and strong convictions about friendship and honor. Although *The Killer* includes numerous chases on foot, in boats, and in a variety of motorized vehicles and more than a few loud, fast-paced, stylized killings (one observer counted 120!), it also has three male characters developed in some depth, especially Jeff. As Inspector Li, one of the other three main male leads, says of him, "He looks determined without being ruthless. . . . He doesn't look like a killer. He comes across so calm, acts like he has a dream, eyes filled with passion." As seen here, about forty-four minutes into the film, Jeff looks to be in a bad way, but he's actually testing the honor and friendship of the man holding that humongous gun. *Tsui Hark; Film Workshop Co., Ltd.*

FIGURE 7.37 Jackie Chan's Hong Kong cinema
In *Police Story* (a.k.a. *Jackie Chan's Police Force*, 1985), Chan directs the film, functions as the stunt coordinator and fight choreographer, and plays the main role of Kevin, an honorable Hong Kong police officer beset with challenges. In pursuit of a drug baron, Kevin had taken a woman's umbrella, chased a speeding bus, hooked onto the back of it, and here, about 10¾ minutes into the film, is briefly dragged along. Soon he pulls himself up, gets into the speeding bus, fights off the drug baron's henchmen, and arrests the man. The action is typical of Jackie Chan's inventiveness and athleticism. *Police Story* also includes an abundance of cartoonish violence, situations where damage and danger multiply, people fight fiercely and long, yet no one seems to suffer any pain that the audience would take seriously. The film's frequent verbal and physical humor, often at Kevin's expense, illustrates the dictum that comedy is a man in trouble. Kevin has girlfriend problems (she wrongly assumes that he is unfaithful) and work difficulties (he even kidnaps the police superintendent at gunpoint). And although Kevin is shown to be capable of extraordinary agility, strength, and gracefulness, he is often amusingly awkward with people and objects.
Raymond Chow; Paragon Films

silent-era superstars Charlie Chaplin and Buster Keaton) in films like *Project A* (1982) and *Police Story* (1985, Figure 7.37).

Hong Kong films are not just characterized by the action on screen but by their relentless stylistic energy. Quickly paced, the films can leave audiences breathless. The films often switch moods suddenly, from high tragedy to low comedy, and display a playful visual style through an accumulation of bizarre angles, distorted close-ups, and jarring perspectives, such as the point of view of a bullet leaving a gun and passing through a body in Ringo Lam's *Full Contact* (1992). Hong Kong films are also full of allusions to and parodies of previous films, rewarding loyal fans with the sort of self-reflexivity often associated with art cinema rather than popular entertainment. The lush sounds of local Canto-pop music also link the films to Hong Kong's youth culture, and many of the stars of Hong Kong films also have careers as popular singers.

Contemporary Hong Kong cinema clearly shows Hollywood's influence, especially in its reliance on streamlined plots and conventional genres such as comedies and gangster films. But in drawing on more traditional Chinese elements, such as martial arts and Chinese opera, Hong Kong action films often feature highly stylized action, achieved through rapid editing, surprising camera positions, and the dynamic choreography of actors and camera movement. Hong Kong films thus seek to startle, amuse, and jolt audiences, often at the expense of believability.

Along with outrageous comedies and blood-drenched gangster sagas, Hong Kong has allowed for the production of more subtle films, such as Clara Law's *Song of the Exile* (1990) and Stanley Kwan's *Center Stage* (a.k.a. *Actress*, 1989), starring Maggie Cheung as the actual 1930s Shanghai star Ruan Lingyu. Hong Kong's most distinctive filmmaker is perhaps Wong Kar-Wai, whose portraits of urban ennui in *Chungking Express* (1994) and *In the Mood for Love* (2000) reduce narrative to a minimum while featuring restrained performances (achieved through improvisation with actors), lush images, and inventive soundtracks. His distinctive technique of blurring images (developed with cinematographer Christopher Doyle) makes his films resemble modern paintings as much as photographic images.

Following the end of Great Britain's ninety-nine-year lease on Hong Kong in 1997, the return of sovereignty to China, and a severe economic recession in 1999, Hong Kong cinema has scaled back. Many of its most prominent figures—including stars Jackie Chan, Jet Li, and Chow Yun Fat and director John Woo—have established careers in the United States, though for many fans their Hollywood films haven't matched the quality of their earlier work. Meanwhile, the influence of Hong Kong cinema is evident in films ranging from the Hollywood sci-fi action kung-fu film *The Matrix* (1999, Figure 7.27c) to the French art film *Irma Vep* (1996), starring Maggie Cheung as herself. Retaining some independence as a commercial cinema, recent Hong Kong films are again exploring their simultaneously Chinese and international identities in stories that allude to recent history and politics. Despite fears that Hong Kong's popular cinema would disappear under China's administration of the island, creative work continues to appear.

Dogme 95

Like Italian neorealist films and French new wave cinema, the **Dogme 95** movement's films take relations between well-developed characters as their principal subject, but unlike neorealism, Dogme 95 films ignore, for the most part, the larger economic and social relations of their characters. In contrast to most film movements, which are named and described *after* they exist, Dogme 95 began in the spring of 1995 when two Danish film directors tried to lay out what a film movement needed to do. Lars von Trier and Thomas Vinterberg co-wrote the "Dogme 95 Manifesto" and its accompanying "Vow of Chastity" (for the Vow, see the feature on p. 333) and then invited two other Danish directors—Soren Kragh-Jacobsen and Kristian Levring—to join the movement. Only then did each director produce a Dogme 95 film. However, membership was not limited to the four founders;

Dogme 95's The Vow of Chastity

"I swear to submit to the following set of rules drawn up and confirmed by DOGME 95:

1. Shooting must be done on location. Props and sets must not be brought in (if a particular prop is necessary for the story, a location must be chosen where this prop is to be found).

2. The sound must never be produced apart from the images or vice versa. (Music must not be used unless it occurs where the scene is being shot).

3. The camera must be hand-held. Any movement or immobility attainable in the hand is permitted. (The film must not take place where the camera is standing; shooting must take place where the film takes place).

4. The film must be in colour. Special lighting is not acceptable. (If there is too little light for exposure the scene must be cut or a single lamp be attached to the camera).

5. Optical work and filters are forbidden.

6. The film must not contain superficial action. (Murders, weapons, etc. must not occur.)

7. Temporal and geographical alienation are forbidden. (That is to say that the film takes place here and now.)

8. Genre movies are not acceptable.

9. The film format must be Academy 35 mm.

10. The director must not be credited.

11. Furthermore I swear as a director to refrain from personal taste! I am no longer an artist. I swear to refrain from creating a "work", as I regard the instant as more important than the whole. My supreme goal is to force the truth out of my characters and settings. I swear to do so by all the means available and at the cost of any good taste and any aesthetic considerations.

Thus I make my VOW OF CHASTITY."

Copenhagen, Monday 13 March 1995

On behalf of **DOGME 95**

Lars von Trier   Thomas Vinterberg

Source: <www.dogme95.dk/the_vow/vow.html>

anyone was welcome to produce a film in accordance with the Vow of Chastity rules, apply for a Dogme 95 certificate, and, if granted, advertise the Dogme 95 certification (Figure 7.38). Filmmakers were also under no obligation to make only Dogme 95 movies.

FIGURE 7.38 Dogme 95
Films that earned the Dogme 95 seal could advertise their certification, as here on this poster for *Mifune* (a.k.a. *Mifune's Last Song*, 1999), the third film to earn the Dogme 95 seal. The film's opening credits also indicate that *Mifune* is the third Dogme film. In the commentary on the DVD version, the director often discusses following the rules of the Vow of Chastity. There were challenges: the need to fudge on a detail occasionally, working with only available light, and recording the sound while filming in 16 mm. Overall, though, he says in effect that working within the rules was not a big problem. *Birgitte Hald* and *Morten Kaufmann; Sony Pictures Classic*

ideology: The influential underlying social and political beliefs of a society or social group.

For von Trier and Vinterberg, the problem with contemporary filmmaking—not just Danish but Hollywood film—is its overproduced nature. In place of examinations of the "truths" of the "inner lives" of characters, contemporary film offers "illusions" built of special effects, lighting, genre formulas, and soundtracks. Rejecting what they understood as a superficial and basically meaningless cinema that is highly dependent on current (expensive) technology, the Dogme 95 "brethren" (as they called themselves) attempted to substitute a much simpler aesthetic (in fact, the Vow of Chastity forbids any aesthetic at all) that allowed the narrative and characters to express a film's "truths." The movement's filmmakers claimed that film should represent, as realistically as possible, how people interact with one another. Consequently, the rules of the Vow of Chastity forbid the use of, among other distracting filmic devices, studio shooting, "superficial action, . . . murders, weapons, etc.," "sound . . . produced apart from the images," and genre movies. The Dogme 95 aesthetic, or anti-aesthetic, also suggests an **ideology**: Filmmaking has become the province of trained and well-financed professionals and needs to be "liberated" and returned to the people. As the group's manifesto makes clear, because of improvements in digital video and its low costs, "today a technological storm is raging, the result of which will be the ultimate democratization of the cinema. For the first time, anyone can make movies," and the Dogme 95 brethren saw that their job was to help advance this democratization.

Because many of the thirty-three official Dogme films received only limited distribution and have not been transferred to video or DVD, most are difficult to locate and view. However, several are readily available in the United States and give a sense of the movement. Thomas Vinterberg's *The Celebration* (*Festen*, 1998) shows a family reunion on the occasion of the family patriarch's sixtieth birthday, developing several of the characters in great depth. The elder son announces that he and his sister were sexually abused as children; the assembled family, guests, and employees react to this infor-

FIGURE 7.39 Dogme 95 1
Seen here in the family wine cellar nearly forty-three minutes into *The Celebration* (1998) are the two main forces in the first Dogme 95 film: the sixty-year-old family patriarch and the son who has recently announced before the assembled guests that the father sexually molested both him and his twin sister when they were children. As was done throughout the film, this scene was shot on videotape with a small handheld camera and available light; later the footage was edited and transferred to 35 mm film for theatrical showings. During the making of *The Celebration*, the filmmakers followed most of the rules of the Vow of Chastity. Frame enlargement. *Birgitte Hald; October Films*

mation; and the father grapples with the son's accusations (Figure 7.39). The film's representation of the social relations between fully developed, complicated characters illustrates Dogme 95's success at encouraging directors to create credible characters who relate to one another in plausible plots. Similarly, Lars von Trier's *The Idiots* (1998) shows a collective of young men and women experimenting with communal living and "spazzing," pretending to be mentally challenged to point up the frigidity of bourgeois Danish life. Both these films were shot using digital video (although this is not a Dogme 95 requirement), which gives them the look of home movies or documentaries. Using numerous digital video cameras, sometimes attached to a character's glasses or positioned near a ceiling, Harmony Korine directed the first U.S. Dogme film, *Julien Donkey Boy* (1999), which offers viewers glimpses of what life is like for Julien, a schizophrenic.

In addition to producing a series of intimate plot- and character-driven films, Dogme 95 can be credited with making some filmmakers more mindful of their craft. While many directors have felt affronted by the Vow of Chastity's rules and various commentators have thought that the rules were merely an attention-seeking ruse, the rules might be understood as a provocation. Perhaps the point is less to obey them perfectly (and not even the four founders have done so) than to think about why and when they need to be followed or broken. Understood this way, the Vow is not a set of strictures but a call for filmmakers to take responsibility for their aesthetic and economic choices. After all, it is not difficult to imagine an unspoken set of Hollywood film "rules": "Special effects are mandatory." "Some of the shooting must be done in a studio." "The soundtrack must be saleable when separated from the film's images." And so forth. The Dogme 95 Vow suggests that these "rules" need to be questioned.

As a formal movement, Dogme 95 existed for seven years, by which point thirty-three movies had been officially certified as Dogme films. In 2002, the Dogmesecretariat (the business end of Dogme 95 that maintains its Web site and archive) announced that Dogme 95 had almost acquired genre status and therefore was disbanding as an organization. But the secretariat's press release announces, "In case you do desire to make a Dogmefilm, you are free to do so; you do not need to apply for a certificate anymore." The press release adds that the Vow was meant to inspire filmmakers, not to be a brand name or copyright.

As the Dogmesecretariat notes, in spite of themselves, the Dogme 95 directors established an aesthetic. Even an anti-aesthetic that consistently avoids using any mechanical means of moving the camera during filming or using supplementary lights is recognizable as an aesthetic of sorts. The Dogme 95 aesthetic became characterized more by the filmic instruments of production and techniques that its followers refused to use than by those that they did use. Dogme 95 made it possible for some low-budget films without slick production values, such as Lone Scherfig's *Italian for Beginners* (2000), to gain some distribution among art houses in the United States and abroad. In addition, the movement's attempt to shift more people across the divide between consumers and producers was, and can still be, a revivifying force in cinema.

Classical Hollywood cinema is so much a part of the world that most of us were born into and grew up in that many viewers do not easily adapt to other cinemas; initially other films seem odd and perhaps too demanding. But in seeing more of these films, studying them, and learning about the contexts in which they are created, many viewers come to enjoy and appreciate them and to broaden their understanding of the possibilities and achievements of the fictional film.

CLOSE-UP: *OUT OF THE PAST* AS FILM NOIR

by Zach Finch

Out of the Past (1947) has a complicated plot. If you have not seen the film recently, please study Figures 6.16 (on p. 273) and 7.16 before you read the following essay.

Out of the Past (1947) exhibits many characteristics of film noir, such as dark, shadowy cinematography; urban settings; complex and flawed main male characters; a complex, flawed femme fatale; and a protagonist who is a loner and emotionally restrained.

Dark lighting and prominent shadows permeate many films noirs. *Out of the Past* is no exception. Films noirs focus on the darker side of human nature, and the cinematography is appropriately dark. In *Out of the Past*, the darkness of the San Francisco scenes contrasts with the bright lighting of the exterior scenes in Mexico and the exteriors of the small California town where Jeff lives. In Mexico, Jeff says of Kathie, the film's femme fatale, "I never saw her in the daytime. She seemed to live by night." The dark lighting is appropriate for dark dealings such as double-crossing, revenge, and murder.

In *Somewhere in the Night: Film Noir and the American City*, Nicholas Christopher points out similarities between the city setting of a film noir and Greek mythology's labyrinth. In Greek mythology, Theseus enters the labyrinth, attempts to reach the center, but finds that the way is impossibly hard with many traps, twists, turns, and confusing passageways. Similarly, the protagonist of a film noir tries to find his way through the city's figurative twists and turns, and the barriers of deception and double-crossing that he encounters are reminiscent of an actual labyrinth. Often the protagonist is caught in this labyrinth only to

discover that it has no center and that he is playing a small role in a game he understands only slightly (7–8). In *Out of the Past*, San Francisco serves as the labyrinth that Jeff returns to after leaving his previous life in the dark of San Francisco for a quiet, brightly illuminated, small-town existence. Early in the film, a former colleague recognizes Jeff pumping gas, and Jeff is soon forced to reenter a dark world. When Ann, Jeff's small-town girlfriend, accompanies him to Whit's home and drives away, Jeff must confront the consequences of his past by himself: find his way through a dark, treacherous big-city labyrinth and then cope with Whit and Kathie.

In film noir, the main male players are complex and flawed. Their motivations tend to be greed, self-interest, and ambition. These motivations fuel threats of blackmail, double-crossing, and convoluted plots. In *Out of the Past*, Whit hires Jeff to find Kathie and bring her back; however, when he finds her in Acapulco, he decides to keep her for himself. When Jeff and Kathie return from Mexico and go to California, Jeff's old partner tries to blackmail the couple. Whit is obviously flawed too: he is a tax cheat who employs dense, thuggish hit men like Joe and plans to frame Jeff for a murder.

The noir femme fatale is also complex and flawed. Her power lies in her cold, calculating intellect and her sexual appeal to men. Even if the protagonist knows that she is bad news, her sexual allure and guile are usually too much for him. When Jeff finds Kathie in Mexico, he is instantly enchanted by her even though he knows that she has recently tried to kill Whit. The femme fatale sees the protagonist as a means to achieve her goals. Early in the film, Kathie uses Jeff to distance herself from Whit. Throughout the film, she deceives both Jeff and Whit. She lies to cover

337

up her own crimes and switches sides without blinking. During a moment of clarity, Jeff says she's like a leaf that is blown by the wind from one gutter to another. Should the femme fatale's powers of persuasion fail her, she may resort to violence. Before she is finished, Kathie, who has outbursts of temper, shoots and kills three men.

The loner and "tough guy" protagonist of a film noir is another major characteristic of the genre. These characters are generally men in their thirties or forties. Like Jeff, they are almost always unmarried. Jeff has a partner but seems to not particularly like or respect him, and Jeff is seen always working alone and spending a lot of time alone. There is no indication he has friends or family other than Ann and perhaps the young man who works for him. The typical film noir protagonist also reins in his emotions and exudes a "tough guy" image. Jeff rarely shows anything more than a poker face and rarely confides his private thoughts or feelings to anyone, so his personal thoughts and emotions remain shrouded in mystery.

In these and other ways, *Out of the Past* remains an illuminating example of film noir.

Works Consulted

Christopher, Nicholas. *Somewhere in the Night: Film Noir and the American City*. New York: Holt, 1998.

Phillips, William H. *Film: An Introduction*. 2nd ed. New York: Bedford/St. Martin's, 2002.

SUMMARY

Most fictional films, including foreign films and animated stories, exhibit the major characteristics of classical Hollywood cinema. Alternatives to classical Hollywood cinema include Italian neorealist cinema, French new wave cinema, European and American independent films from the 1960s to the present, Bollywood, Hong Kong cinema, and Dogme 95 films.

Classical Hollywood Cinema

- Throughout the world, classical Hollywood cinema has been the most influential group of fictional films in history.
- Such films show one or more individualized characters with clear goals who face a series of problems in reaching them; these films stress continuity and the clear causes and effects of actions; and they tend to use unobtrusive filmmaking techniques.
- A film genre is a commonly recognized group of fictional films that share characteristics both filmmakers and audiences recognize as making the films members of the same general group.
- Three widely studied film genres are the western, film noir, and the musical. Traditionally the western features civilization versus the wilderness

and is set west of the Mississippi River, in northern Mexico, or in the Canadian Rockies.

- Films noirs include scenes with low illumination, convoluted plots, and complex, flawed characters caught up in crime.

- Musicals are widely various, but they always give prominence to intermittent music and often also dance, and they are unrestricted in the type of music used and the setting and the subjects of their stories.

- A genre film may be traditional or revisionist. Most westerns made since about 1950, for example, are revisionist and vary widely from the traditional western.

- Occasionally, a film is a parody of a genre. A film may also be a combination of two or more genres, such as horror and science fiction or western and musical.

Other Cinemas

- Other fictional films—such as Italian neorealist films, French new wave cinema, the European independent cinema since the 1960s, many American independent films since the 1960s, Bollywood, Hong Kong cinema, and Dogme 95 films—offer alternatives to classical Hollywood cinema.

- Neorealism was a film movement in Italy during and after World War II. Neorealist films, which are a mixture of scripted and actual situations, are located for the most part in real settings and show ordinary and believable characters caught up in difficult social and economic conditions, such as poverty and unemployment. The endings of neorealist films tend to be unhappy.

- New wave films were a diverse group of French fictional films made in the late 1950s and early 1960s in reaction to the carefully scripted products of the French film industry and as explorations of more current subjects sometimes rendered with untraditional filmmaking techniques.

- Since the 1960s, films directed by such Europeans as Ingmar Bergman, Federico Fellini, Michelangelo Antonioni, and Luis Buñuel are also alternatives to classical Hollywood cinema. These films are likely to have a pace and intensity that approximate those of normal human experience. Compared to the films of the classical Hollywood cinema, they are more likely to be explicit about sexuality than violence, are less likely to belong to a genre, and are more likely to be self-reflexive.

- American independent fictional films since the late 1960s are made all over the United States, not just in southern California; have lower budgets than their Hollywood counterparts; are free of Hollywood studio creative control; and tend to be more varied and less formulaic than the movies of classical Hollywood cinema.

- Bollywood (India's Hindi-language popular cinema) is the most prominent component of the world's largest film industry. Bollywood films typically offer a full mix of drama, action, comedy, and romance, with prominent, dubbed songs an especially vital element. Often rooted in Indian mythology while exploiting current trends, Bollywood films display India's balance of tradition and modern life, often through highly melodramatic plots involving multigenerational families. Like Hollywood in its heyday, Bollywood films rely on a star system that features favorite actors in familiar roles.

- As a popular cinema, Hong Kong films resemble Hollywood movies in their reliance on character-driven and goal-oriented plots, as well as familiar genres and stars. But Hong Kong films also draw on traditional Chinese elements, such as martial arts, and often rely on a highly kinetic style that breaks the bounds of realism. Hong Kong cinema's over-the-top action scenes and sudden shifts into low comedy seek to startle and jolt viewers rather than represent a convincing reality.

- Danish filmmakers founded the Dogme 95 film movement, which lasted from 1995 until 2002. Dogme 95 directors more or less attempted to obey a set of rules, called the Vow of Chastity, which encouraged them to produce relatively inexpensive films that concentrated on relations between people instead of elaborate special effects, supplemental lighting, fantastic plots, and genre conventions. The ideological aim of the movement was to help return filmmaking "to the people" by lowering its costs.

Major Terms about Types of Fictional Films

Below, numbers in italics refer to the pages where the terms are explained. All terms are defined in more detail in the Illustrated Glossary beginning on p. 621.

Bollywood *327*
classical Hollywood
    cinema *292*
Dogme 95 *332*
feature film *292*

film movement *302*
film noir *302*
French new wave
    320
genre *294*

independent film
    323, 326
Italian neorealism
    317
revisionist *297*

QUESTIONS ABOUT TYPES OF FICTIONAL FILMS

The following questions are intended to help viewers understand some of the many types of fictional films. Not all the questions are appropriate for every film. In thinking out, discussing, and writing responses to those questions most appropriate for the film being examined, be careful to stick with the issues the questions raise, to answer all parts of the questions, to explain the reasons for your answers, and to give specific examples from the film.

1. If the film is fictional, how may it be further classified—as classical Hollywood cinema or in some ways an alternative to it? Why do you say so?

2. If the film is a genre film—such as a western, musical, or horror film— consider the following questions:

   a. What major similarities and differences does the film have with earlier films of the same genre?

   b. Is the film revisionist? If so, explain in what ways.

   c. Is the film traditional of its genre in some ways but untraditional in others? If so, explain.

   d. Is the film a parody of earlier films of the same genre? In what ways does it imitate earlier films of the same genre? In what ways does it treat the subject(s) humorously? What conventions of the genre does the parody make fun of?

   e. Is the film a combination of genres? If so, explain which genres and which features of them the film incorporates.

3. If the film is an alternative to classical Hollywood cinema—for example, Italian neorealism, Bollywood, or Dogme 95—consider the following questions:

   a. In what major ways is the film like classical Hollywood cinema, and in what major ways is it unlike classical Hollywood cinema?

   b. In what major ways is the film like and unlike earlier examples of the same type of alternative to classical Hollywood cinema?

WORKS CITED

Altman, Rick. *Film/Genre*. London: British Film Institute, 1999.

Andrew, Dudley. *Concepts in Film Theory*. New York: Oxford UP, 1984.

Armes, Roy. *French Cinema*. New York: Oxford UP, 1985.

———. *Patterns of Realism: A Study of Italian Neo-Realist Cinema*. Cranbury, NJ: Barnes, 1971.

Bordwell, David, Janet Staiger, and Kristin Thompson. *The Classical Hollywood Cinema: Film Style and Mode of Production to 1960*. New York: Columbia UP, 1985.

Cawelti, John. "(Post)Modern Westerns." *Paradoxa* 4.9 (1998): 3–28.

Christopher, Nicholas. *Somewhere in the Night: Film Noir and the American City*. New York: Holt, 1998.

Cook, David A. *A History of Narrative Film*. 3rd ed. New York: Norton, 1996.

Hirsch, Foster. *Detours and Lost Highways: A Map of Neo-Noir*. New York: Limelight, 1999.

Ingalls, Zoë. "Notes from Academe." *Chronicle of Higher Education* 12 Nov. 1999: B2.

Knee, Adam. "The Compound Genre Film: *Billy the Kid versus Dracula* Meets *The Harvey Girls*." *Intertextuality in Literature and Film: Selected Papers from the Thirteenth Florida State University Conference on Literature and Film*. Ed. Elaine D. Cancalon and Antoine Spacagna. Gainesville: UP of Florida, 1994. 141–56.

Krutnik, Frank. *In a Lonely Street: Film Noir, Genre, Masculinity*. New York: Routledge, 1991.

Lenihan, John H. *Showdown: Confronting Modern America in the Western Film*. Urbana: U of Illinois P, 1980.

McCarthy, Todd. Introduction. In John Alton, *Painting with Light*. Berkeley: U of California P, 1995.

Moreau, Jeanne. Interview. *Morning Edition*. National Public Radio. 11 Mar. 1994.

Musser, Charles. "The Innovators 1900–1910." *Sight and Sound* 9.3 (NS) (March 1999): 16–18.

Neale, Steve. *Genre and Hollywood*. London: Routledge, 2000.

Phillips, William H. "Neorealist Cinema." *Benét's Reader's Encyclopedia*. 3rd ed. Ed. Katherine Baker Siepmann. New York: Harper, 1987.

Shulman, Ken. "From a Vanished Country, a Viewable Cold-War Archive." *New York Times* 26 Oct. 1997, Arts and Leisure Sec. *New York Times on the Web* at <http://www.nytimes.com>. Click on Archives.

Telotte, J. P. *Voices in the Dark: The Narrative Patterns of Film Noir*. Urbana: U of Illinois P, 1989.

Turner, Graeme. *Film as Social Practice*. 3rd ed. London: Routledge, 1999.

FOR FURTHER READING

Altman, Rick. *The American Film Musical*. Bloomington: Indiana UP, 1999. Nine chapters on theory of genre analysis, dual-focus narrative, structure, style, genre history, fairy tale musicals, show musicals, folk musicals, and genre and culture.

Bordwell, David. *Planet Hong Kong: Popular Culture and the Art of Entertainment*. Cambridge, MA: Harvard UP, 2000. An appreciative and detailed analysis of the form and style of Hong Kong cinema.

Coyne, Michael. *The Crowded Prairie: American National Identity in the Hollywood Western*. London: Tauris, 1997. Close analysis of westerns as a source for exploring American concerns—such as miscegenation, dysfunctional family structures, McCarthyism, civil rights, Vietnam, and receding frontiers—during the period from 1939 to 1976.

Dickos, Andrew. *Street with No Name: A History of the Classic American Film Noir*. Lexington: UP of Kentucky, 2002. The book's subtitle describes its subject.

Film Genre Reader II. Ed. Barry Keith Grant. Austin: U of Texas P, 1995. A wide variety of essays by a variety of film scholars. Includes bibliographic references.

Film Genre 2000: New Critical Essays. Ed. Wheeler Winston Dixon. Albany: State U of New York P, 2000. Essays by film scholars on American genres since 1990 and on the influences of new technologies and market forces on genre filmmaking.

Gopalan, Lalitha. *Cinema of Interruptions: Action Genres in Contemporary Indian Cinema*. London: British Film Institute, 2002. Close **readings** of specific films and filmmakers, emphasizing interactions between Indian narrative forms and international genres such as the gangster film.

Hollywood Musicals, The Film Reader. Ed. Steven Cohan. New York: Routledge, 2002. Each of the book's sections explores a central issue of the musical, including the musical's significance as a genre, the musical's own particular representation of sexual difference, and the displacement of race in Hollywood's representations of entertainment.

Kabir, Nasreen Munni. *Bollywood: The Indian Cinema Story*. London: Channel 4 Books, 2001. An introductory overview based on interviews with industry insiders.

Larkin, Colin. *The Virgin Encyclopedia of Stage and Film Musicals*. London: Virgin, 1999. A 680-page one-volume encyclopedia covering both American and British musicals that traces the history of the genre from Busby Berkeley to Andrew Lloyd Webber.

Levy, Emanuel. *Cinema of Outsiders: The Rise of American Independent Film*. New York: New York UP, 1999. On the major cycles in the indie film movement from the late 1970s to 1999, including regional cinema, the New York school of film, African American, Asian American, gay and lesbian, and movies made by women.

Miles, Adrian. "*Singin' in the Rain*: A Hypertextual Reading." *Postmodern Culture* 8:2 (Jan. 1998). <http://muse.jhu.edu/journals/pmc/v008/8.2miles.html>. One of several essays in this special issue on film, Miles's work consists of his written analysis of the film's "You Were Meant for Me" song and dance sequence, which Miles divides into parts, each of which has links to other parts. The site also has links to the parts of the movie's "You Were Meant for Me" sequence.

Neupert, Richard. *A History of the French New Wave Cinema*. Madison: U of Wisconsin P, 2003. Captures the dramatic impact these films made on their release, closely examining such famous movies as *The 400 Blows* and *Breathless* as well as many less studied films.

Pierson, John. *Spike, Mike, Slackers and Dykes: A Guided Tour across a Decade of American Independent Cinema*. New York: Miramax/Hyperion, 1995. An introduction to American independent films from 1984 to 1994 by someone involved in their making and marketing. Appendix I lists all American independent features from late 1984 to 1993.

Prats, Armando José. *Invisible Natives: Myth and Identity in the American Western*. Ithaca, NY: Cornell UP, 2002. A study of the representation of Native Americans in the western film since the genre's beginnings. Certain films—such as *Stagecoach*, *The Searchers*, and *Dances with Wolves*—are discussed at length.

Silver, Alain, and James Ursini. *The Noir Style*. Woodstock, NY: Overlook Press, 1999. The book includes close readings of its many black-and-white stills from noir films. Chapter titles: Out of the Past, Night and the City, Deadly Is the Female, The Dark Mirror, The Reckless Moment, Night Has a Thousand Eyes, and Neo-Noir.

Stokes, Lisa Odham, and Michael Hoover. *City on Fire: Hong Kong Cinema*. New York: Verso, 1999. A study of Hong Kong cinema emphasizing social and political contexts.

Teo, Stephen. *Hong Kong Cinema: The Extra Dimensions*. London: British Film Institute, 1997. A history of Hong Kong cinema up to 1997, with full filmographies for major figures.

Thompson, Kristin. *Storytelling in the New Hollywood: Understanding Classical Narrative Technique*. Cambridge, MA: Harvard UP, 1999. Argues that Hollywood's storytelling techniques are still used to make complex, clear, entertaining movies that are based on the narrative system used by earlier generations of Hollywood filmmakers.

Virdi, Jyotika. *The Cinematic ImagiNation: Indian Popular Films as Social History*. New Brunswick, NJ: Rutgers UP, 2003. A study of post-independence cinema in terms of nationality with particular attention to representations of gender and sexuality.

Westerns: Films through History. Ed. Janet Walker. New York: Routledge, 2001. Leading scholars unpack the ways in which westerns have embellished, mythologized, and erased past events. Essays also explore how the genre addresses key issues of biography, authenticity, race, and representation.

CHAPTER 8

Alternatives to Live-Action Fictional Films

I N THE PREVIOUS THREE CHAPTERS we considered the fictional film, which has overwhelmingly dominated viewer and critical attention almost since the birth of motion pictures. This chapter considers four alternatives to the live-action fictional film: documentary, experimental, hybrid, and animated films.

Terms in **boldface** are defined in the Illustrated Glossary beginning on page 621.

DOCUMENTARY FILMS

> Documentaries, which are more or less films about reality, are actually not considered by most people to be real films, but Hollywood films, which usually have an extremely high fantasy quotient, are considered to be real.
> —Ross McElwee's narration in his documentary *Six O'Clock News* (1997)

Every summer since 1988, Public Television's series *Point of View* (or *P.O.V.*) has shown a series of documentaries. Cable television networks have financed and shown many documentaries, including films on the History and Discovery channels and the series of films by Errol Morris on Bravo's 2000 *First Person*. Film festivals are swamped with submissions of documentary films, many of them later praised as among the highlights of the festival. The Full Frame Documentary Film Festival, the Hot Spring Documentary Film Festival, and the Yamagata (Japan) Documentary Film Festival, for example, are all devoted exclusively to the documentary. Magazines such as *Dox* focus on the documentary film. *International Documentary* is published by the International Documentary Association, which also champions the documentary film on its Web site <www.documentary.org>. Many books are being written about the subject. College and university courses are devoted to it. And students in introduction to film courses often rate such documentary films as *The Thin Blue Line* (1988), *Hearts of Darkness: A Filmmaker's Apocalypse* (1991), *Visions of Light* (1992), *Hoop Dreams* (1994), *The Celluloid*

Closet (1996), *Fast, Cheap & Out of Control* (1997), *Buena Vista Social Club* (1999), and others among their course favorites. More than ever, documentary films are being made, seen, promoted, studied, and enjoyed.

Those of us who have seen a wide variety of documentaries have a pretty good sense of what they are, but because of their immense variety, coming up with a precise definition of *documentary* is difficult. A **documentary film** might be defined as a film or video **representation** of actual (not imaginary) subjects. Documentary filmmakers select what subjects to film and under what conditions (or they select from existing **footage** or combine footage they **shot** with already filmed footage); sometimes they stage or re-create situations; and they nearly always edit the resultant footage. As we see illustrated below, "Documentaries adopt no fixed inventory of techniques, address no one set of issues [or subjects], display no single set of forms or styles" (Nichols 21). Documentary films are sometimes referred to as *nonfiction films*. I prefer the older and more widely understood term *documentary films* because *nonfiction films* identifies this group of films not by what they are but what they are not (they are not fiction) and because *nonfiction film* suggests that this type of film is the opposite of fictional films, whereas some documentaries have much in common with fictional films.

representation: A likeness of a subject created in a text.

footage: A length of exposed motion-picture film.

Goals

Documentaries are made for various reasons. Four of the most frequent ones are to inform, entertain, criticize, and celebrate.

All documentaries inform. Viewers watching *The Thin Blue Line* learn or are reminded about the circumstances of a man wrongly imprisoned for murdering a Dallas police officer and about the man who probably committed the crime. Viewers watching *Standing in the Shadows of Motown* (2002) can learn about the role a group of unheralded backup musicians played in many popular recordings from an earlier era.

Documentaries are also nearly always meant to entertain; most filmmakers know that they must hold viewer interest if they are to achieve any other goals. Thus, for *The Thin Blue Line*, director Errol Morris made sure that the images, music, editing, interviews, and the investigative story that unfolds all work together to rivet audience attention.

A sizable number of documentaries are made mainly to criticize. These films are made out of the filmmakers' conviction that something is wrong and should be improved. An example is *Justifiable Homicide* (2001), which informs viewers about the killings of two Puerto Rican youths by two New York City police detectives. The film explains why the two young men and the police were where they were at the time of the shootings, the twelve-to-eight vote by a Bronx grand jury that the killings were "justifiable homicide," the subsequent investigation by the city Civilian Complaint Review Board, a report and demonstration by a representative for an independent pathologist, justifications for the police action by a police official and Mayor Rudolph Giuliani, the finding of the Civilian Complaint Review Board that the police detectives had used unnecessary and unjustified force in the shooting deaths, and the police commissioner's prompt dismissal of that report. The film also shows the parents' responses to the death of one of the young men; other people's frustration and anger over police killings of loved ones; the grief, abiding love, and dedication of the mother of one of the slain youths; and her role in the establishment of the group Parents Against Police Brutality. More than anything else, the film criticizes members of the New York City Police Department and Mayor Giuliani.

By way of contrast, some documentary films celebrate a subject, presenting it in a way that viewers can appreciate or admire. Examples include most of the films directed by Les Blank, perhaps especially those focusing on music or food, such as in "Marc and Ann" (1991), which celebrates Cajun music, and "Garlic Is as Good as Ten Mothers" (1980). Other examples of laudatory documentaries include *Marcello Mastroianni . . . I Remember* (1999), about a famed Italian film actor; "A Great Day in Harlem" (1994), which pays tribute to many great American jazz musicians; and *The Life and Times of Hank Greenberg* (2000), which extols the personality and achievements of the first American Jew to become a major league baseball star.

Although a documentary may have *one* major goal, it usually achieves more than one goal. We saw above how *Justifiable Homicide* primarily criticizes the actions and reactions of some NYPD officers and city officials. The film has additional less prominent goals. It informs about the context of a police shooting, entertains with its investigative structure (what led to the two deaths and why), and celebrates the strength of two parents, especially the wife. *Amandla! Revolution in Four-Part Harmony* (2002) also achieves more than one goal: it informs about and criticizes apartheid, the system of brutal, sometimes lethal racial segregation and discrimination formerly enforced in South Africa. The film also celebrates the music, spirit, vivacity, community, persistence, dignity, and eventual triumph of (mostly black) South Africans who opposed apartheid.

Subjects and Sources

Documentary films can be about any subject—for example, human behavior (including human creativity or any aspect of history), animal behavior, plant life, or any other aspect of science.

Capturing the Friedmans (2003) illustrates that one subject of a documentary film can be the limitations of memories. The film is about the Friedman family—a father, a mother, and three sons—torn by charges that the father and youngest son sexually abused many young boys. The film includes interviews with a wide range of people, including all members of the family except the middle son (who declined to be interviewed), detectives, lawyers, the judge involved in the case, an author who had earlier written about the case, the father's brother, various people who might have been victims, and a few parents. Different people remember things differently, and nearly everyone is contradicted by something someone else says. Occasionally an interviewee contradicts him- or herself. And at various times, it seems possible that various interviewees are in denial or do not remember certain events because they are simply too painful to dredge up. At the end of the film, the viewer may have questions and more questions about the extent of the guilt and the fairness of the investigation, convictions, and sentences. Fascinating, yes. But what happened? What is the truth? In interviews, the film's director, Andrew Jarecki, who did exhaustive research on his subject, has said that he will leave it to viewers to decide for themselves. As he said, "Our memories evolve over time to suit our needs and . . . you can't trust a memory to be just this static thing you can trust" (Jarecki). What, then, of the many documentaries that rely so heavily on the memories of so many interviewees?

Occasionally, one subject of a documentary is its maker. An example would be *Stevie* (2002), which is mainly about a young man who had been born out of wedlock, beaten by his mother, given up by her after she remarried, and eventually placed in various juvenile centers and foster homes, in some of which he was beaten and raped. The adult Stevie is understandably emotionally guarded. He is also given to substance abuse and outbursts of anger and violence and is eventually tried and sentenced for sexually abusing an eight-year-old female cousin. Also prominent in the film is its primary maker, Steve James, who served as a Big Brother while Stevie was a youth but moved away and did not stay in touch as promised. Ten years after their last contact, James visited Stevie (as the camera films the encounter) and gradually became involved in his troubled adult life. He sometimes wondered aloud off camera about his proper role in Stevie's life. This and other documentary films raise ethical questions about their making. To what extent should the filmmaker become involved with the subject? Is it right for the filmmaker to influence the subject's life? Should the filmmaker's fundamental allegiance be to the welfare of the subject or the good of the film?

A documentary film may be drawn from any combination of sources as long as the representation is primarily factual or informative. In creating a documentary film, filmmakers may film new material, staged or not. In re-creating subjects, they may try to capture the look and sounds of the original as closely as possible, or they may choose to stylize the representation, for example with **soft lighting** or different colors. They may use existing footage exclusively, incorporate existing footage into footage they **shot**, or use exclusively the new footage they shot. As we see below, they also may use other sources for information—including fragments of radio broadcasts, audio recordings in any of their permutations, still photographs, paintings, signs, and maps. They often add **narration**, interviews, or **title cards**—or a combination of two or all three. They may add sound effects or music—or both. Typically, documentary filmmakers do a lot of filming, which the availability of digital cameras makes easier and more economical than ever. And typically, due to the amount of footage they shoot, documentarians do ex-

soft lighting: Light that somewhat obscures surface details and creates shadows that are soft-edged.

narration: Commentary in a film about a subject in the film or some other topic, usually from someone offscreen.

title card: A card or thin sheet of clear plastic on which is written or printed information included in a film.

tensive editing: selecting their **shots** and arranging them into some sort of unified whole. The possible sources—and combinations of them—are endless, for human creativity knows no bounds.

As with fictional films, one possible source for a documentary is an earlier film. Jill Godmilow's "What Farocki Taught" (1998) is a close remake of Harun Farocki's 1969 German documentary entitled "Inextinguishable Fire," which is about Dow Chemical's development of napalm B during the war in Vietnam. The remake, which is in color and in English, re-creates the original black-and-white film shot-for-shot, often superimposing shots from the original (complete with subtitles) with newly staged sections. "What Farocki Taught" challenges spectators to question conventional approaches to documentary while enabling a version of Farocki's film to receive the American screening it was denied on release.

Normally sequels are fictional films, but a documentary film may also be a sequel. An example is "Pets or Meat: The Return to Flint" (1993)—Michael Moore's follow-up to his **satirical** documentary *Roger & Me* (1989)—which shows what happened to some of the people featured in the earlier film and even more sharply satirizes its subjects. Another sequel to a documentary is *Best Man* (1998); this follow-up to the award-winning *Best Boy* (1979) shows how the gentle, mentally impaired subject of the earlier film is faring nearly twenty years later. An even more recent documentary sequel is Agnès Varda's *The Gleaners and I: Two Years Later* (2002), which is a follow-up to her *The Gleaners and I* (2000).

Nonnarrative and Narrative

Most documentary films tell no **narrative**: a representation of a series of unified events situated in one or more settings. These **nonnarrative documentaries** include most scientific films, many TV documentaries on social conditions, industrial films (which present information about a company or industry), training films, promotional films, and many TV advertisements. Most nonnarrative documentary films either make an argument or present a variety of information usually organized into categories.

An example of a nonnarrative documentary film is *Fast, Cheap & Out of Control*, which conveys a wide variety of information by alternating among four thoughtful and articulate men who discuss their occupations (Figure 8.1). A very different nonnarrative documentary, which also conveys a wealth of information, is Jonas Mekas's *As I Was Moving ahead Occasionally I Saw Brief Glimpses of Beauty* (2001), which consists of more than four hours of edited home movies divided into twelve chapters arranged in no discernible order within the chapters or between them. The film is nonnarrative because it is impossible to mentally reconstruct all its many fragmented subjects and **events** into a whole. As Mekas narrates early in the film, he was not sure where the pieces of his life went, so he edited intuitively (Figure 8.2).

shot: An uninterrupted strip of exposed motion-picture film or videotape that represents a subject during an uninterrupted segment of time.

satire: A representation that indirectly exposes and perhaps ridicules individual or group thinking or behavior for being foolish, evil, or stupid or for exhibiting some other shortcoming.

nonnarrative documentary: A film or video that uses no narrative or story in its representation of mainly actual (not imaginary) subjects.

event: In a narrative or story, either an *action* by a character or person or a *happening* (a change brought about by a force other than a person or character).

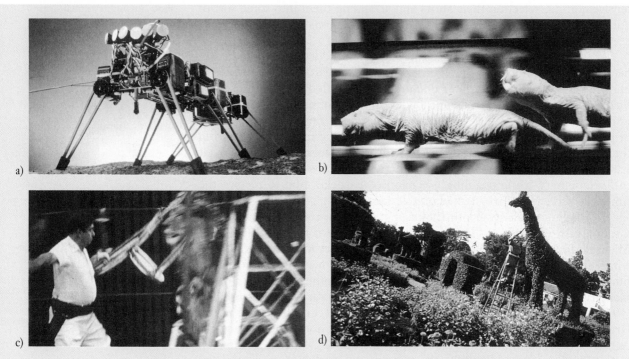

FIGURE 8.1 A nonnarrative documentary film with multiple subjects
Fast, Cheap & Out of Control (1997) alternates among four main subjects, four men and the occupations that they pursue: (a) making robots shaped approximately as insects, (b) studying mole-rats, (c) taming wild animals, and (d) doing topiary gardening that features plants shaped like large animals. The film presents information about its four major subjects and ideas related to each of them yet implies meanings transcending its parts. Critic Richard Corliss wrote that the film "is a funny, thrilling tribute to people's urge to find play and profundity in the work they do." Karen Jaehne has written, "In the final sequence, we witness the lion tamer retiring and passing his baton to a kinder, gentler tamer who sticks her head in the lion's mouth. Then footage from *Darkest Africa* shows the lost city collapsing, a volcano spewing, and our hero [Clyde] Beatty scrambling for his life, before we return to the brave new world of a robot on lunar terrain, as the circus elephants depart. We see a storm looming over Green Animals, and George the gardener with his shears in his hand holding an umbrella against the raging elements. This bleak conclusion reminds us of the evanescence of human existence: not much survives. Creativity is our only consolation" (46). As commentator Peter Applebome sees it, "Mr. Morris's films . . . are about . . . epistemology—the nature of knowledge: what things are and what they seem to be, how people know what they think they know, and do they really know it or just think they know it?" (c–d) Frame enlargements. *Errol Morris; Sony Pictures Classics*

narrator: A character, a person, or an unidentifiable voice in a film that provides commentary about subjects in the film or outside it, or both.

Other nonnarrative documentary films make an argument, as in the very brief "Television, the Drug of the Nation" (1992). The phrase "Television, the drug of a nation, breeding ignorance and feeding radiation" is heard repeatedly in the film. The rap **narrator** also claims that commercial TV is the

FIGURE 8.2 A nonnarrative documentary of edited home movies
As I Was Moving ahead Occasionally I Saw Brief Glimpses of Beauty (2001)—which is made up of thousands of shots, many of them superimposed—has as its subjects the beauty and joy of children, nature, animals (especially cats), the seasons, New York City, and friends. In addition, the filmmaker narrates occasional observations about his subjects. Some of the film's techniques—portable, sometimes shaky camera; zoom shots; swish pans; superimpositions; fast cutting with many shots in only a vague context; fast motion; out-of-focus images; and overexposed and underexposed images—all help suggest the whirlwind abundance of life's everyday and sometimes beautiful or joyous experiences. The film also suggests the difficulty of arranging memories into a meaningful whole and the inevitability of living in our own constructed worlds that nonetheless seem real to us. Frame enlargement. *Jonas Mekas; Anthology Film Archives*

reason so few Americans read books and the reason most Americans think "Central America means Kansas." The narrator adds, "A child watches fifteen hundred murders [on TV] before he's twelve years old, and then we wonder why we've created a Jason generation." The film's chaotic but mesmerizing visuals suggest that TV is dizzying, fragmented, highly manipulative, addictive, and dangerous to our health. "Television, the Drug of the Nation" conveys information but mainly makes an argument: (commercial) TV is detrimental to American life.

Often a nonnarrative documentary film uses editing to praise or criticize; it may **cut** from one shot to the next to criticize, as is often done in *Hearts and Minds*, a 1974 film about U.S. involvement in Vietnam. About sixty-one minutes into the film, an enraged high school football coach in a locker room shouts at and hits some of his players. The players are then seen in part of a football game, and an injured player is shown in pain. Next, President Johnson (whom viewers may equate with the out-of-control coach) declares that the United States will win (the war in Vietnam). The following footage shows some of the chaos and destruction of a massive surprise counterattack by North Vietnamese fighters against U.S. and South Vietnamese forces, which abruptly casts into doubt when and how the war in Vietnam will finally end. Elsewhere the film again uses editing to suggest guilt by association. At the conclusion of the film, 107¼ minutes in, a shot of countless freshly dug, empty Vietnamese graves accompanied by sounds of moaning and crying is followed by shots in the United States of various patriotic parades and demonstrations, including marching soldiers, a flag-waving spectator, marching boys in military uniform, and a formation of police riding motorcycles.

cut (verb): To change from one shot to the following shot seemingly instantaneously.

The suggestion (though not evidence) is that pain and suffering in a foreign country are caused by a regimented, patriotic, and militaristic American society.

A small percentage of documentary films present a narrative or story. **Narrative documentary** films are largely true narratives: a series of unified factual events in one or more settings. But as the figure called *The Continuum of Narrative Films* illustrates, many narratives combine fiction and fact in different proportions (see Figure 6.2 on p. 249).

Like the fictional film, the narrative documentary features someone with a goal or goals. In *The Farmer's Wife* (1999), a farmer and his wife work extremely hard to try to save their farm and their marriage. In *Brother's Keeper* (1992), the main person filmed has been accused of suffocating a brother suffering from ill health and wants to avoid being convicted (Figure 8.3). *Lost in La Mancha* (2002) shows film director Terry Gilliam trying to complete filming of *The Man Who Killed Don Quixote*.

Like fictional films, narrative documentaries may not represent events chronologically. *The Gate of Heavenly Peace* (1995) focuses on the historical occurrences leading up to the 1989 military crackdown on student demonstrators in Tiananmen Square in China and its aftermath, but from time to time the film also includes historical background footage, some dating as far back as 1919.

Narrative documentaries are never simply narratives. They also include supporting artifacts and informative language. Consider *Burden of Dreams* (1982), a film by Les Blank, which shows what happened during the filming

FIGURE 8.3 **A narrative documentary**
Seen here are three of the Ward brothers, who are featured in the narrative documentary *Brother's Keeper* (1992). As in most stories, the main person has a goal but has trouble reaching it. Delbert (on the right) wants to avoid conviction for the smothering death of one of his ill brothers, but impediments include Delbert's signed confession, damaging testimony given by another brother, and a prosecution tactic discovered before the trial. *Photo by Joe Berlinger; Courtesy of Creative Thinking International, New York City*

of the movie *Fitzcarraldo* (1982). Viewers can easily figure out the order of events in *Burden of Dreams* and see how they are connected. The scenes are even arranged chronologically, from November 1979 to November 1981. The film concentrates on the people making *Fitzcarraldo*, although occasionally the main story is interrupted so that various details of the Amazon jungle (such as the size, speed, and dexterity of ants) and the lives of the natives of the region can be explained (Figure 8.4). The narrative is also punctuated with frequent interviews, especially with Werner Herzog, the director of *Fitzcarraldo*. *Burden of Dreams* doesn't lack unity, but like most narratives, whether fictional or documentary, it includes more than a story.

Like nonnarrative documentary films, narrative documentary films may use editing to criticize or praise a person or idea. Consider the opening of *Triumph of the Will* (1935). Leni Riefenstahl made the film to document and celebrate a huge Nazi party conference. It opens with aerial shots of clouds, church spires and the tops of other buildings, an airplane flying above a city, the shadow of the airplane speeding over the ground of the city below, and troops marching in formation. On the ground, many shots of excited crowds alternate with the plane landing and pulling to a stop, followed by the emergence of Adolf Hitler and Joseph Goebbels, the Nazi minister of propaganda. In the next **sequence**, shots alternate between the large and excited crowds on the sides of the streets and Hitler standing in a moving car and saluting with a stiff arm. Thus in the film's opening scenes, Hitler is associated with power, speed, grace, and the adoration of the masses.

Narrative documentary films often have only one **plotline**, but like fictional films they may have two or more. *Hoop Dreams* has two plotlines, each about an inner-city youth who hopes to play in the National Basketball Association (Figure 8.5). "The Heck with Hollywood!" (1991) alternates three narratives of filmmakers who are trying to market their films outside the Hollywood network: a young man, a young woman, and three young men. Most of *Pumping Iron* (1976) consists of five plotlines: the background and training of two bodybuilders and their competition for the 1975 Mr. Universe title and the background, training, and competition of three men, including Arnold Schwarzenegger, for the 1975 Mr. Olympia title.

Occasionally it is difficult to categorize a documentary film as nonnarrative or narrative, as is the case with one of the first feature-length documentaries,

FIGURE 8.4 **A secondary subject in a narrative documentary film**
The problems in filming the movie *Fitzcarraldo* (1982) are the primary subject of the narrative documentary *Burden of Dreams* (1982). One of the film's secondary subjects is the lifestyles of the Amazon Indians, seen here, including how they bathe, wash clothes, weave, cook, and play games. *Photo by Maureen Gosling; Courtesy of Flower Films, El Cerrito, California*

sequence: A series of related consecutive scenes, perceived as a major unit of a narrative film.

plotline: A narrative or series of related events usually involving only a few characters or people and capable of functioning on its own as a story.

FIGURE 8.5 Multiple plotlines in a narrative documentary *Hoop Dreams* (1994) shows the stories of two inner-city young men who dream of playing in the National Basketball Association: Arthur Agee (a) and William Gates (b). The film represents parts of their lives from their days in junior high to the beginning of college. Although the two stories occasionally intersect (the two commuted to the same high school for a while, and their paths cross occasionally after one of them goes to a different school), basically this narrative documentary alternates between their two stories. *KTCA-TV & Kartemquin Films; Fine Line Features*

a)

b)

structure: The arrangement of the parts of a whole text.

location: Any place other than a film studio that is used for filming.

film technique: Any aspect of filmmaking, such as the use of sets, lighting, sound effects, music, or editing.

Nanook of the North (1922, restored 1976; Figure 8.6a). There is little clear-cut unity to the film's sections (many could be switched without consequences for viewers), yet the Inuits' lives are presented more or less chronologically (from a summer to a winter). Although the film's skimpy story is loosely **structured** and the film presents information as much as it shows a story, many critics think of *Nanook* as a narrative.

Whether narrative or not, a documentary film has most or all of the following characteristics: mediated reality, real people instead of actors, **location** shooting, artifacts and informative language, and a wide range of **techniques**.

a)

b)

FIGURE 8.6 Narrative or nonnarrative documentary
Nanook of the North (1922, restored 1976), a famous early documentary film, reveals important aspects of Inuit life, especially getting food and surviving a harsh environment. Through the film's various parts, viewers learn how Nanook, a Canadian Inuit, and his family live: for example, by (a) spearing fish, using a kayak, trading, hunting walrus, traveling, building an igloo, hunting seal, and preparing for a storm. The film's emphasis seems to be as much on presenting different types of information as in telling a story. (b) Director Robert Flaherty took many liberties with his subjects, a small group of Canadian Inuits, including asking them to restage or modify their behavior or the world they live in. For example, Flaherty found that the igloos were too small and too dim for him to fit in his bulky 35 mm camera and tripod and to provide enough light to film, so he had the Inuits build a larger igloo without a top. (a) Frame enlargement. *Revillon Frères; The Museum of Modern Art/Circulating Film Library*

Mediated Reality

Documentary films are mediated reality: they are selected, filmed, and edited representations. A documentary film may *seem* to represent reality objectively, but it cannot. Consider Frederick Wiseman's *Belfast, Maine* (1999), which has a **running time** of slightly over four hours and shows different aspects of life in and near the seacoast town of Belfast, Maine (such as a social worker picking lice out of a woman's hair and a high school English teacher lecturing on *Moby Dick*). The film has no narration, no interviews, no title cards, no music that does not derive from a source shown in the film. The opening title card does not cue viewers about the film to come. In plain lettering, it simply announces the title: Belfast, Maine.

At first glance, the filmmakers seem to have only selected the subjects, filmed them, and selected the footage to include. However, in constructing the film, the filmmakers made many significant decisions that influenced the outcome and viewers' responses to the film. For example, the filmmakers selected

running time: The time that elapses when a film is projected.

which subjects to film and which to ignore. They selected the time of year in which to film (autumn) and often the time of day (many shots were filmed in the morning hours or in the late afternoon, when objects outdoors are bathed in flattering soft light). They decided how many shots would be of locations without people, which shots would be of run-down or even polluted areas, and which would not. For each shot, they decided camera location, distance from subject, and lens. They decided how long to hold a shot, when to use a zoom lens (only very rarely in this film), and when to move the camera during a shot (also rarely).

Later, the filmmakers decided which shots to include and their duration, the order of shots, and the transitions between them (one black screen of a few seconds, otherwise only **cuts**). During fourteen months of editing, 110 hours of footage was fashioned into a four-hour film. Probably during editing whole sections that had been filmed were dropped. Often a section begins with one or two **establishing shots**, frequently including a building's identifying sign; sometimes an identifying sign is seen in a section's concluding shot. During the editing, decisions were also made about where to include **reaction shots** and how often, as during a lawyer's presentation to the Belfast city council. The filmmakers decided the order and duration of each major section and the **pacing** of the parts and of the whole film. In addition, they decided what sounds would be prominent (the many sounds of motorized vehicles, for example, remind viewers that even in this small town and surrounding area, motorized vehicles are an integral part of life). The filmmakers also decided to occasionally use sound from a source before we viewers see the source and to carry over a sound from one location into the following one. Thus, even documentary films that might seem simply presentations of reality are actually complicated mediations of reality. They are not objective, indisputable truths. Rather, they are one group's selections, recordings, manipulations, and representations.

Another example of the selectivity involved in making a documentary can be seen in *Marcello Mastroianni . . . I Remember*. The film focuses on the Italian actor's stage and film acting, his films, his travels and thoughts about various cities, and his work with different directors. Mastroianni himself supplies all the narration. The film includes no interviews with family, friends, or filmmaking colleagues and little information about his adult personality. Unaddressed are many questions: Was Mastroianni difficult to work with? Was he aloof in his personal life? Was he as modest and charming **offscreen** as in interviews and in his narration of the documentary? What was his identity when he was not making a movie? Was he ever married? Who was the mother of his daughter? Was he close to his daughter? The director and editor of the film, Mastroianni's companion of more than two decades, decided to focus on his films and filmmaking and largely avoid his personal life and any perspective other than his and hers. Another example of a highly selective documentary is *The Kid Stays in the Picture* (2002),

cut (noun): A transition between shots, made by splicing or joining the end of one shot to the beginning of the following shot.

establishing shot: A shot, usually a long shot or extreme long shot, used at the beginning of a scene to show where and sometimes when the events that are to follow take place.

reaction shot: A shot, usually of a face, that shows someone or occasionally an animal presumably reacting to an event.

pace: A viewer's sense of a subject (such as narrative developments or factual information) being presented rapidly or slowly.

offscreen: The area beyond the frame line; also can mean life outside the movies.

which is about the movie producer Robert Evans. The film is based on Evans's book of the same title and includes narration by Evans and interviews only with him.

Other documentarians make changes in a film's subject before filming it (Figure 8.6b). A similar situation arose in the filming of *Crumb* (1994). An interviewer on the Sundance Channel observed that a large wall cabinet full of 78 rpm records in director Terry Zwigoff's house looked a lot like Crumb's record cabinet. Zwigoff responded, "We actually shot fake scenes in this room where he's [Crumb's] sitting here with, like, a drawing board and we moved this lamp that used to be in his house over here, and this [indicating Zwigoff's record cabinet] is the background. We faked it for his house because we didn't want to drive back up there." Near the beginning of cinema, in "The Execution of Mary, Queen of Scots" (1895), the filmmakers substituted a dummy for the person enacting Queen Mary immediately before the beheading. Since then, countless documentary filmmakers have staged actions or re-created them or in other ways changed details about the way things were. An entire film may be a recreation, as was the case with a German and Swiss film, *The Saltmen of Tibet* (1997), which shows a story illustrating a ritualistic pilgrimage that had been discontinued before the film was made. Like fiction makers, for various reasons—including to save time and money or to show something judged important in an engaging way—documentary makers sometimes fudge the details.

Some filmmakers change the order of presentation through editing. A title card at the beginning of *Dead Birds* (1963), a film about the lifestyles of similar warring New Guinea tribes, states that the film

> is a true story composed from footage of actual events photographed. . . . No scene was directed and no role was created. The people in the film merely did what they had done before we came and, for those who are not dead, as they do now that we have left.

Yet the director Robert Gardner later wrote that the film has "compressions of time which exclude vast portions of actuality. There are events made parallel in time which occurred sequentially" (346–47).

Real People

When the subject is human behavior, the documentary film nearly always uses ordinary people, not actors. For example, *Hoop Dreams* features two real youths and their families. *Capturing the Friedmans* includes all but one member of the Friedman family, detectives, lawyers, a judge, an author, an adult brother, various people who might have been victims, and a few parents. All these people were people being themselves; no one was creating representations of them for the film. Only rarely do documentaries use actors. Charlie Sheen plays a judge in Emile De Antonio's *In the King of Prussia* (1983); actors reenact some minor roles in *The Thin Blue Line*; and actors play all the roles in the many re-created scenes of *Thirty-Two Short Films about Glenn Gould* (1993).

Location Shooting

Documentary films are usually filmed on location. In the late 1950s, location shooting became common with the development of lighter and more mobile cameras and sound recording equipment. Recent years have seen the development of digital equipment that is even more portable and versatile and produces even better quality, and many documentaries are now shot on location with a lightweight digital video camera. More than ever it is possible for one or two people to go practically anywhere and film and record sound unobtrusively. If the opportunity for a theatrical release arises later, the video can be transferred to 35 mm film, as was done for *Buena Vista Social Club*, *The Original Kings of Comedy* (2000), *Startup.com* (2001), and other films.

Occasionally documentary films are not filmed entirely on location. Les Blank told me that his "Gap-Toothed Women" (1987) was shot largely within his own studio instead of in the homes or workplaces of his subjects. Other exceptions: Errol Morris shot parts of *The Thin Blue Line* in New York City, not Texas, and he filmed the interviews for *A Brief History of Time* (1992) and *Fast, Cheap & Out of Control* in a studio.

Artifacts and Informative Language

Artifacts used to make documentaries include other films (including newsreels), TV shows, photographs, and objects a person has made or owned. Sometimes only one type of artifact or a few types of artifacts are used in a documentary film. *The Atomic Cafe* (1982)—which is about the arrival of nuclear weapons and some of the U.S. government's subsequent responses—consists entirely of excerpts from commercial and government media. *Point of Order* (1963), by Emile De Antonio, is a ninety-seven-minute **compilation film** made mostly from 188 hours of TV footage of the 1954 Army-McCarthy hearings.

compilation film: A film made by editing together clips from other films.

Often a documentary film includes informative language: narration (or title cards or subtitles), interviews, signs, even headstones, or a combination of sources (Figure 8.7). The words of songs may also function as narration or commentary on the film's subjects, as they do throughout Les Blank's "Chulas Fronteras" (1976), a film about Chicano experiences and the centrality of music in Chicano lives. Until the early 1960s, documentary films relied heavily on all-knowing narrators, in part because the equipment then available made it cumbersome to film and to record synchronous sound on loca-

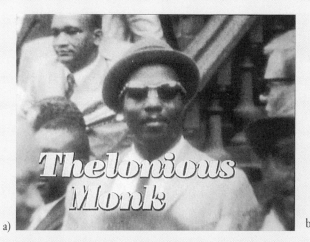
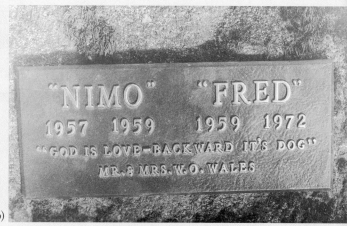

a)   b)

FIGURE 8.7 **Informative language in a documentary film**
Informative language used in documentary films may appear in various forms. (a) Often, subtitles
are used to convey information, as here in "A Great Day in Harlem" (1994) to identify a jazz
great. (b) Here informative language is used in a pet cemetery on a headstone honoring departed
dogs in Errol Morris's first documentary film, *Gates of Heaven* (1978). (a) Frame enlargement. *Jean
Bach; Castle Hill Productions;* (b) *Errol Morris; New Yorker Films*

tion. Most recent documentary films use interviews more often than narration or use interviews alone, in part because of the availability of more
portable filmmaking equipment and in part because of the widespread belief
that no one person or narrator can do justice to a subject's complexity. Some
films, such as those directed by Frederick Wiseman, use neither narration
nor interviews. And a few—such as *The Wonderful, Horrible Life of Leni
Riefenstahl* (1993) and the British *Up* series of documentaries, such as *42 Up*
(1999)—use both.

Artifacts and informative language help persuade viewers of the accuracy
of a film's representations. They may be incorporated into a film in countless
creative ways. In the third part of Ken Burns's *Baseball* (1994), we see a photograph of the exterior of a building, presumably where a grand jury is meeting, and a photograph of a man's face looking toward the camera. As we see
these photographs, we hear a gavel banging, the usual sounds of people inside a room, and voices of two actors reenacting a prosecutor posing questions about the throwing of the 1919 World Series and Chicago White Sox
player "Shoeless" Joe Jackson responding to them. After the offscreen re-
created testimony has finished, we are allowed about four seconds to continue to scrutinize the photograph of Joe Jackson in silence. Other
documentaries that include artifacts and informative language are represented in Figures 8.8 and 8.9.

FIGURE 8.8 **Artifacts and language in a documentary film**
"The Match That Started My Fire" (1991) by Cathy Cook includes supporting artifacts (including existing film clips) and informative language (off-camera accounts by women). In the shot represented here, artifact is combined with informative language: a woman twirls around and around as a woman's voice recounts how as a girl she would sometimes wear a certain type of skirt to school and spin around and around for her pleasure and the boys'. *Photo by Cathy Cook, dancer: Heidi Heistad; Women Make Movies, New York; Film-makers' Cooperative, New York*

FIGURE 8.9 **Multiple sources in a documentary film**
Carmen Miranda: Bananas Is My Business (1994) is a film directed by a Brazilian woman about one of her compatriots, Carmen Miranda, who was first a popular singer and movie star in Brazil and later a star in American musical movies and TV. The film shows Miranda initially closely identified with her Brazilian roots but eventually alienated from them by her transforming experiences with American media, which presented her progressively as exotic, stereotypical, and a self-parody and a subject of parody by others. She was torn between two different cultures; demoralized by depression, drugs, and an abusive marriage; and dead by 1955 at age forty-six.

To convey a broad range of information and perspectives, the film uses a wide range of sources. Artifacts shown include a Carmen Miranda paper doll, a Miranda puppet, small Miranda models, a self-portrait painting, many photos, and calendar pages for different days rapidly floating toward and past the camera. Other artifacts used to convey information and perspectives include reenactments of Miranda's death by a heart attack and of one of the documentary director's dreams, clips from movies including Miranda, clips that parody her, an excerpt from a movie trailer, home movies, and clips from a travelogue about Brazil, newsreels, and TV shows. Informative language used includes newspaper headlines, program notes, Miranda's handwriting, narration (by the director and others), interviews, an excerpt from a song, and a fragment of a radio broadcast to the people of Brazil. Amassing so many sources and such a wide range of them and editing the film were massive endeavors. *Helena Solberg and David Meyer; Women Make Movies, New York*

Wide Range of Techniques

As with fictional filmmaking, technology influences techniques used in documentary filmmaking and the results achieved. In the late 1950s and early 1960s, development of 16 mm **fast film**, handheld 16 mm cameras with a **zoom lens**, and portable sound packs gave filmmakers much greater mobility and flexibility (Figure 8.10). In the United States, filmmakers using portable equipment developed **direct cinema**, a type of documentary filmmaking in which the film is shot on location with minimal planning. The aim of such films is not so much to prove a point but to explore a subject. An exchange between an interviewer for the film journal *Cineaste* and the filmmaker Frederick Wiseman, who is one of the main practitioners of direct cinema, highlights that purpose:

> *CINEASTE*: And your film [*Welfare*, 1975] doesn't generalize, at all. Nor does it attempt to suggest any possible solutions or answers. That stance characterizes all of your films.
> *WISEMAN*: That's right. I don't know the answers. I'm interested in the complexities and ambiguities of our experience. (Lucia 9)

Makers of direct cinema attempt to win their subjects' trust and to minimize interference with their lives; consequently, they often use the **long take** and the zoom lens so they may film their subjects from afar or close up without the camera distracting them.

fast film (stock): Film stock that requires relatively little light for capturing images.

zoom lens: A camera lens that can be adjusted by degrees during a shot so that the size of the subject and the size of the area being filmed both change.

long take: A shot of long duration. Not to be confused with **long shot**.

FIGURE 8.10 The portability of direct cinema equipment
To film the onstage and offstage action of a three-day outdoor concert attended by an estimated 400,000 people, one or two cameras would have been inadequate. Fortunately, by the time of the Woodstock concert in 1969, documentary filmmakers could use portable 16 mm cameras and lightweight, largely unobtrusive magnetic tape recorders. In this photograph can be seen two of the many cameras (left and extreme left) used in making the documentary *Woodstock* (1970). Some of the cameras were propped on the stage itself; some were mounted on tripods; some were handheld. *A Wadleigh-Maurice, Ltd. Production; Warner Bros.*

FIGURE 8.11 Documentarians as observers and participants
Although *Divorce Iranian Style* (1998) is mostly cinéma vérité, occasional narration is used to fill gaps in the information that viewers need to follow the situations, including occasional questions from the filmmakers to their subjects. Late in the documentary, the filmmakers are unwittingly and briefly transformed from observers and recorders to participants when the divorce court judge turns to the filmmakers and asks if they saw the woman depicted here tear the judge's court order as her husband alleged. After the filmmakers reply that they did not, the judge rescinds his order that the woman be held in detention for a day, although she is still under order to turn over custody of her child, shown here, to her previous husband. *Kim Longinotto and Ziba Mir-Hosseini; Women Make Movies, New York*

take: A version of a shot.

An example of direct cinema is Michael Wadleigh's *Woodstock* (1970), which shows action on- and offstage at a huge open-air concert in upstate New York. This film and others of direct cinema often have technical imperfections: the camera operator sometimes does not refocus on a new subject as quickly as movie viewers are used to seeing. The camera work might occasionally be wobbly; sometimes the dialogue is indistinct; and at times the film might be too dark or too light. To some viewers these imperfections only strengthen the film's credibility. They can imagine that the film is not a slick, manipulated representation—as, for example, *Triumph of the Will* is—but more nearly a representation of actions as they happened. Nonetheless, as we saw with *Belfast, Maine*, direct cinema entails its own, perhaps less obvious, manipulations. For instance, the camera operator chooses what to film and how to film it, and the editor chooses what shots to include and in what context.

At about the same time as direct cinema emerged and using the same type of equipment, a similar type of documentary filmmaking, **cinéma vérité**, developed in France, although during filming, French filmmakers were likely to ask questions of their subjects and talk with them, as in the later cinéma vérité film *Divorce Iranian Style* (1998, Figure 8.11).

Since the late 1990s, documentarians' much wider use of digital video has made possible much longer **takes**, fewer interruptions while filming, and greater portability and thus greater access to subjects. The smaller, more portable equipment may also make the filming less noticeable and intrusive. Perhaps most significantly, because digital equipment is relatively inexpensive, it has opened up documentary filmmaking to many who before could not afford to make documentaries.

At the other extreme of direct cinema and cinéma vérité, some documentary films look and sound as polished and professionally made as fictional films with a large budget. In *Brother's Keeper*, the filmmakers do more than simply record one scene after another, cut some dead time, and present the results—far from it, as is seen in an excerpt that begins a little more than forty-five minutes into the film (Table 8.1). In scene 1, the man says in effect

TABLE 8.1
Ten Consecutive Scenes from *Brother's Keeper*

SCENE NUMBER	LENGTH SECONDS	DESCRIPTION
1	28	A man in a truck says he now thinks Delbert probably did murder his brother, Bill, to put him out of his misery, "like you would a sick cat or something like that."
2	12	Voice of the man from the previous scene continues as he says of the four Ward brothers, "They've been damn good boys" and we see one of Delbert's brothers lying on the ground. Then we see a cat sniffing a dead cat.
3	24	An official (a subtitle earlier identified him as Captain Loszynski of the New York State Police) justifies the use of question and answer in interrogation.
4	7	Long shot of a man unloading bales of hay from a conveyor belt as we hear a voice asking the beginning of a question: "Were you befuddled in any way on the sixth of June. . . ."
5	7	Close-up of Delbert. The off-frame voice finishes the question begun in scene 4, and Delbert answers no. In response to a follow-up question, Delbert admits he doesn't know what *befuddled* means.
6	17	Another official (a subtitle earlier identified him as Investigator Cosnett) explains that Delbert understood his rights (when he was brought in for questioning).
7	4	Long shot of the man shown in scene 4 now covering bales of hay with a tarp as a voice is heard asking a question.
8	17	Delbert answers the question from the previous scene. On request, he demonstrates on the man beside him (much earlier in the film identified in a subtitle as Harry Thurston/Friend) how officials said Delbert suffocated his brother.
9	20	Another official (identified in a subtitle as Investigator Killough) says that Delbert has changed his story and that on the night of his interrogation Delbert put his hand over his own mouth to demonstrate "how he did it."
10	65	Shots of foggy farmland and Delbert as we hear the voice of Delbert and presumably the voice of the prosecutor asking whether Delbert understood what he was signing (his confession) and if he had been forced to sign it. Throughout this scene, music is heard, except just before the end when it quickly fades out.

parallel editing: Editing that alternates between two or more events, often suggesting that the events are related to each other or are occurring simultaneously.

fast cutting: Editing characterized by frequent brief shots.

swish pan: Blurred images that result from pivoting a movie camera horizontally too rapidly during filming.

high angle: A view of a subject from above.

cutaway (shot): A shot that briefly interrupts the representation of a subject to show something else.

that Delbert probably put his brother out of his misery as one would a sick cat. In the next scene, viewers see a Ward brother, then a dead cat: the second scene hints at the validity of the point expressed in the first. **Parallel editing** is used to contrast the state police's picture of Delbert with the one viewers see. In scenes 2, 4, 7, and 10, offscreen sound is used, the second and third times from a questioner in the following scene. In the tenth scene, farm animal sounds and music add to the mood, as do the shots of farm life. Throughout the film the cinematography and editing are as accomplished as those of many features.

Some documentary films use yet other techniques. *Unzipped* (1995) includes frequent wobbly handheld shots plus **fast cutting**, **swish pans**, and even **fast motion**—all of which contribute to an out-of-control, dizzying effect. *The Thin Blue Line* uses some extremely **high-angle** shots; **slow motion**; lighting and color that are dramatic rather than strictly functional (note the warm-colored light on and behind the prisoner being interviewed); and imaginary and repeated re-creations filmed years after the actions depicted (Figure 8.12). The film also uses parallel editing; unexpected **cutaway shots**; movie clips, some only obliquely related to the subject at hand; and a striking score by Philip Glass. As Errol Morris, the director of *The Thin Blue Line*, acknowledged, his film **style** is the polar opposite of Frederick Wiseman's (Bates 17). Yet both styles strike audiences as credible.

FIGURE 8.12 **Re-created scene in *The Thin Blue Line* (1988)**
Here and elsewhere, the film uses re-creations to show different people's versions of the same event, the killing of a Dallas police officer. As director Errol Morris pointed out in a TV interview, it is up to viewers to decide which version of the murder is most probable. *BFI; Third Floor; American Playhouse*

The first and last moving images of Harvey Milk in *The Times of Harvey Milk* (1984) are in slow motion. In both cases, viewers see a man who was charismatic and full of energy rendered as graceful yet drained of his natural vitality. Allie Light's *Dialogues with Madwomen* (1994), which is about the experiences and perspectives of seven northern California women who have suffered from mental illness, consists largely of alternating interviews with the women. During each interview, we see brief clips related to what the speaker is describing. Sometimes these cutaway shots reenact what is being described—for example, children rummaging through trashcans in search of food. Such cutaways are sometimes redundant and too literal to evoke emotional truth. More often, however, the cutaways are **symbolic** and evocative. For example, at one point as we hear a woman explaining what a tyrant her father was, we see a man in a nondescript **setting** gesturing as if directing traffic and walking forward in slow motion. This cutaway is made even more unsettling because it is the **negative** of a black-and-white shot and the man's face looks light, indistinct, and inscrutable. (For an example of a negative image, see Figure 8.13a.)

Finally, like fictional and experimental films, documentary films may be **self-reflexive**. Brief sections of Ross McElwee's *Time Indefinite* (1993) include a darkened screen or the tail **leader** (after the **reel** of film in the camera had run out) or occasional humorous, deliberately wobbly handheld

negative: Excluding reversal film, film that has been exposed and developed.

self-reflexive: Characteristic of a text, such as a novel or film, to refer to or comment on itself as a text or as a medium.

leader: Clear or opaque motion-picture film of any color that usually precedes and concludes a reel of film.

reel: A metal or plastic spool to hold film.

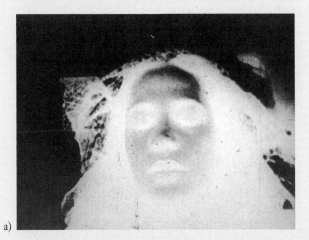 

a)   b)

FIGURE 8.13 A negative image and a positive image of it
Only the concluding shots of Maya Deren's experimental film "Ritual in Transfigured Time" (1946) are negative images. (a) This frame is from the film's last shot and is of a woman as she sinks deeper and deeper into some water and presumably is dying. (b) This image, which does not appear in the finished film, is a positive print of the same negative. Frame enlargements. *Maya Deren; The Museum of Modern Art/Circulating Film Library*

FIGURE 8.14 Self-reflexiveness in a documentary
This still illustrates the beginning of the famous experimental documentary *Man with a Movie Camera* (made in the Soviet Union in 1929). Seen here is a split-screen image (two images are joined at approximately the feet of the camera operator): a camera operator and a camera mounted on a tripod are seemingly standing on top of a very large-scale early movie camera. Here and throughout the film, viewers see various aspects of filmmaking and film exhibition: cameras, tripods, camera operator, lenses, editing table and editor, theater, audiences, projector, and a film being projected. To a degree perhaps unprecedented in documentary film, *Man with a Movie Camera* is self-reflexive. *VUFKU; Kino International; British Film Institute Stills, Posters and Designs*

FIGURE 8.15 Film itself as a subject of a documentary film
Decasia (2001) is a compilation film consisting almost entirely of excerpts from decaying black-and-white nitrate films and a relentless musical score. "'I wasn't just looking for instances of decayed film,' [the filmmaker Bill] Morrison recalls of his two-year excavation. 'Rather, I was seeking out instances of decay set against a narrative backdrop, for example, of valiant struggle, or thwarted love, or birth, or submersion, or rescue, or one of the other themes I was trying to interweave. And never complete decay: I was always seeking out instances where the image was still putting up a struggle, fighting off the inexorability of its demise but not yet having succumbed. And things could get very frustrating. Sometimes I'd come upon instances of spectacular decay but the underlying image was of no particular interest. Worse was when there was a great evocative image but no decay'" (Weschler). On one level, the film is about all those films made before the early 1950s and their inevitable losing battle against decay, distortion, and demise. *Decasia* shows the many ways nitrate footage can decay: it can blister, blotch, buckle, smear, and spot. When projected, it may flicker between light and darkness, clarity and obscurity. It may show decay in only one part of the frame or obliterate everything and appear as only swirling abstract images. On another level, critics have detected other implied meanings in the film. For example, some see *Decasia* as an ongoing but losing battle between life/form/clarity and death/chaos/obscurity. One critic sees it as "a cinematic ghost story. Spectral figures emerge from a mist caused by deterioration of the unstable nitrate film, but given that the images were captured, in some cases, nearly 100 years ago, there's an eerie certainty that the people we see are long dead. It's like watching phantoms from the beginning of film history" (Ide). Here, in a shot that begins about 35¼ minutes into the film, a boxer seems to punch at something unseen. It's probably a punching bag, but the boxer seems to hit into a void. He punches away seemingly without making any headway, an aggressive Sisyphus for the chemical/mechanical times of celluloid movies. Frame enlargement. *From* Decasia, *directed by Bill Morrison, courtesy of Hypnotic Pictures; distributed on DVD by Plexifilm, New York; original source material:* Ritchie Trains, Fox Movietone Newsreel outtake, *archived at the University of South Carolina Newsfilm Library*

shots. One of the earliest and most famous (experimental) documentaries is replete with self-reflexive details, Dziga Vertov's *Man with a Movie Camera* (1929). The film includes many shots showing the major components of both filmmaking and film exhibition (Figure 8.14). A more recent example of a self-reflexive documentary is *Decasia* (2001), which is about processing nitrate motion-picture film and its eventual decay (Figure 8.15).

Like fictional filmmakers, documentarians have countless options in choice of subjects, structure, techniques, and styles and thus enormous influence over the films they create. Some documentary films show a story; many others do not. All documentary films purport to be factual. Unless viewers lose faith in the credibility of the filmmakers or know of contradictory information from other sources, they accept such films as true or as a credible representation of their subjects.

An original extensive interview with documentary filmmaker Errol Morris can be found on the Web site for this book: <bedfordstmartins.com /phillips-film>.

EXPERIMENTAL FILMS

The experience [of studying experimental films] provides us with the opportunity (an opportunity much of our training has taught us to resist) to come to a clearer, more complete understanding of what the cinematic experience actually can be, and what—for all the pleasure and inspiration it may give us—the conventional movie experience is *not*. (MacDonald 2)

Scott MacDonald is a scholar of the experimental film; he and other scholars believe, as I do, that studying experimental films deepens one's understanding of the film medium. Indeed, as experimental filmmaker and theorist Edward Small demonstrates in his book *Direct Theory: Experimental Film/Video as Major Genre*, restricting one's study to fictional films limits one's understanding of the film medium.

The enormous variety of films often labeled *experimental* makes it difficult to define them. Films I consider as *experimental* have been referred to as *avant-garde*, *underground*, *personal*, or *independent*. All five terms reveal something of the nature of such films while also hinting at the inadequacy of any one term. Whenever you encounter *experimental films* in this book, think of films that may explore the possibilities of the film medium, may have been ahead of their times, are out of the mainstream, rely heavily on self-expression, and remain largely free of the limitations placed on commercial movies.

Experimental Films versus Mainstream Movies

convention: In films and other texts, a subject or a technique that makers of texts and audiences have grown to accept as natural or typical in certain contexts.

classical Hollywood cinema: Films that show one or more characters facing a succession of problems while trying to reach their goals and that tend to hide the manner of their making by using unobtrusive filmmaking techniques.

Before we examine the experimental film in detail, let's contrast experimental films with movies seen in theaters. **Experimental films** always reject the **conventions** of mainstream films and explore the film medium—for example, the filmmakers may scratch or paint the film itself. Often a major impulse of experimental filmmakers is to rebel against what movies are and what they stand for. Experimental filmmaker, teacher, and author Stan Brakhage argues: "Everything we have been taught about art and the world itself separates us from a profound, true vision of the world. We are straitjacketed by myriad conventions that prevent us from really seeing our world. So it is with the filmmakers" (Peterson 4).

Movies reflect or imply the dominant, usually unexamined fundamental beliefs of a society, its **ideology**—for example, its belief that hard work results in success and that one individual can make a difference in the outcome of major developments. Experimental films, however, tend to question the dominant ideology, including a society's political assumptions and sexual mores. Various experimental films of the 1960s—such as Kenneth Anger's "Scorpio Rising" (1963), Barbara Rubin's "Christmas on Earth" (1963), Andy Warhol's "Couch" (made in 1964 but unreleased), and Carolee Schneemann's "Fuses" (1964–1967)—represent sexuality explicitly (Figure 8.16). Since the sixties, some experimental films have dealt even more openly with sexuality. Autobiographical films or visual diaries—by Carolee Schneemann, George Kuchar, Robert Huot, Stan Brakhage, and others—show what we never see in mainstream films: the everyday and the intimate. For example, in separate films, George Kuchar, Robert Huot, and others have shown themselves masturbating.

FIGURE 8.16 Experimental film defying sexual mores "Fuses" (1964–1967) shows filmmaker Carolee Schneemann and her lover enjoying each other sexually in ways unimaginable in commercial American movies of the time. As film scholar Wheeler Winston Dixon has written, "this film . . . celebrates the beauty of the female and male body without shame or censorship, with a freedom at once casual and (to some viewers) terrifying" (141). In this frame, as elsewhere, the film uses techniques that momentarily obscure the brief but explicit views of lovemaking: markings from having been baked, deliberate scratches, out-of-focus shots, superimpositions, unexpected camera angles, fast cutting, and darkness and ambiguity. Frame enlargement. *Anthology Film Archives*

Experimental films contrast with movies in other ways. Often they can be made by one person or a few people; commercial movies are the products of large groups of specialists. Experimental films can be made on a low budget with inexpensive equipment, such as a super-8 film camera or a video camera; commercial movies typically require large budgets and are often made with the latest equipment. Because experimental filmmakers may not seek input from others or face time or budget constraints, there is a danger that the result may be overly long, self-indulgent, and boring—at least for the viewers.

Experimental films frustrate expectations of viewers brought up on **classical Hollywood cinema** and often aim to startle, if not shock. For example, in its dreamlike association of scenes, "Un chien andalou" (1928) has no coherent narrative (Figure 8.17). The film's director, Luis Buñuel, later wrote that "Un chien andalou" "has no intention of attracting nor pleasing the spectator; indeed, on the contrary, it attacks him, to the degree that he belongs to a society with which **surrealism** is at war" (30).

Sources and Subjects

Experimental filmmakers have vast reservoirs of possible sources at their disposal.

Frequently they use the most recent advances in filmmaking, or they apply advances in other forms of human expression to experimental films. For example, once **anamorphic lenses** were developed, some experimental filmmakers explored their use. As computer graphics evolved, experimental filmmakers explored their uses. Once video became less cumbersome and less costly (and **film stock** and developing film became more expensive), many artists and experimental filmmakers rushed to experiment with video's creative possibilities.

FIGURE 8.17 Lack of continuity in an experimental film Throughout "Un chien andalou" (1928), directed by Luis Buñuel, the film rejects narrative conventions and often surprises or shocks viewers. For example, the film ends with a shot of the main couple walking along a beach, followed by a title card "In the Spring," which is followed by a brief shot of the couple as seen here, buried in sand and presumably dead. To the end, the film rejects coherent narrative and surprises or shocks viewers. Frame enlargement. *Luis Buñuel; The Museum of Modern Art/Circulating Film Library*

Other experimental filmmakers take a variety of footage—TV ads and old movie footage, for example—and reedit it to create compilation films that surprise, entertain, and often "take a critical stance toward the culture that supplies their imagery" (Peterson 11). Bruce Conner's first film, a twelve-minute work entitled "A Movie" (1958), includes disparate footage from "cowboy and Indian" and submarine adventure movies, newsreels, documentaries, so-called girlie movies (which feature nude or scantily dressed young women posing for the camera), various types of leader including black leader, and title cards (Figure 8.18). "A Movie" is the antithesis of classical Hollywood cinema. It "is a series of middles and connections, a film without a beginning, with titles and credits broken up and interspersed in the middle; rather than an ending, there is a respite—the film runs down, exhausted" (Mellencamp 192). In its incorporation of leader and its untraditional placement of title cards, "A Movie" is self-reflexive: it refers to its own status as a film. And it continuously thwarts audience expectations. It includes "The End" title card early in the film and more than once but not at the end of the film; the opening title cards are repeated at various points in the film; and the film has rousing music to accompany many images of accidents and disasters (auto, motorcycle, and plane

surrealism: A movement in 1920s and 1930s European art, drama, literature, and film in which an attempt was made to portray or interpret the workings of the subconscious mind as manifested in dreams.

anamorphic lens: A lens that squeezes a wide image onto a film frame in the camera, making everything look tall and thin. On a projector, an anamorphic lens expands the image, returning it to its original wide shape.

film stock: Unexposed and unprocessed motion-picture film.

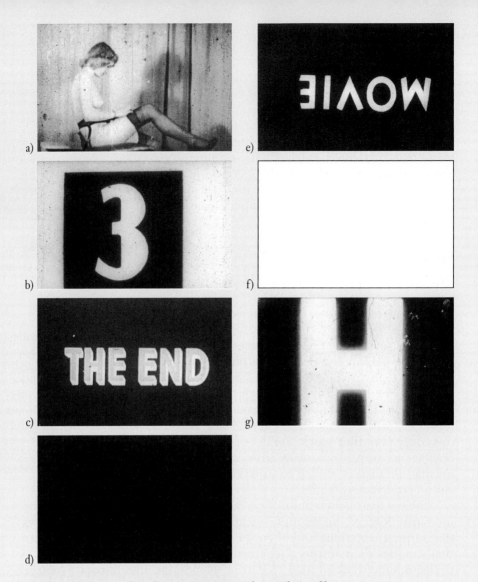

FIGURE 8.18 Sixteen shots from an experimental compilation film
Early in Bruce Conner's "A Movie" (1958) occur the following seven brief consecutive shots: (a) A woman taking off a nylon stocking. (b) A frame from a section of Academy leader, the numbered piece of opaque film that normally appears at the beginning of a reel to protect the film from damage and to help the projectionist know when the film is about to begin but used here by Conner after his film is under way. (c) The first but not last time the title card "The End" appears. (d) Some black frames. (e) Part of the film's title but here upside down. (f) One of four clear frames, which when projected results in a split second of bright white light. (g) An "H," which will be followed by "E," "A," and "D," letters that are also included in Academy leaders.

The film announces that it will differ from classical Hollywood movies in many fundamental ways. No story is begun, let alone developed. In fact, it is difficult to see how the shots are related. Some of the apparatus of cinema—especially the Academy leader—is shown rather than hidden from viewers as it normally is. Some images are inverted. Parts of the film are blank, either black or

h)

i)

j)

k)

l)

m)

n)

o)

p)

white. And parts of the film are placed out of order: for example, "The End" title card appears early in the film, though it does not appear at the conclusion.

Later in "A Movie" occur the following six shots (h–m): a submarine officer looking into a periscope, a woman dressed in a bikini posing for the camera, the officer giving an order, a hand pushing a mechanism forward, a torpedo being fired from a submarine, and a nuclear explosion. Here the editing creates sexually playful or ominous results: the suggestion that the submarine's phallic-shaped projectile fired at the sexy woman results in a nuclear explosion.

The film ends with the following three shots (n–p): a scuba diver descends into an opening in a sunken ship, some black frames, and the surface of the water seen from below with shimmering sunlight on the surface. During these concluding shots, the music swells to a resolution, though the corresponding visuals convey no sense of unity or completion. There is not even a "The End" title card.

As these images illustrate, "A Movie" lacks the usual continuity of "movies" and conveys no narrative. In fact, except for its violence and sex, occasional shots of exotic locales (East Asia and Africa), fast cutting, and jaunty music, "A Movie" has little in common with the usual entertaining feature films commonly referred to as "movies." The title of Conner's film is tinged with irony. Frame enlargements. *Bruce Conner; Anthology Film Archives*

FIGURE 8.19 Excerpts from existing films to create a new film
In "Meeting Two Queens," shots from the movies of Greta Garbo (left) and shots from the movies of Marlene Dietrich (right) are combined to suggest that the two stars interact and eventually become lovers. The film is organized into a dozen or so silent film–style vignettes (a few include music), and each is preceded by a title card indicating the location or situation. Sample vignette titles are "The library," "The telephone," "The dialogue" (in which superimpositions and a split screen make it appear that the two actors interact), and "The alcove" (in which the editing makes it appear that the two stars face each other and begin to undress). Frame enlargement. *Cecilia Barriga; Women Make Movies, New York*

meaning: An observation or a general statement about a subject.

crashes; sinking ships; a dirigible on fire; the mushroom cloud of an atomic blast; falling bridges; and the like).

Another example of experimental filmmakers fashioning excerpts from existing films into a film with new situations and new **meanings** is Chilean video artist Cecilia Barriga's "Meeting Two Queens" (a.k.a. "Meeting of Two Queens," 1991, Figure 8.19).

Experimental filmmakers may take not only snippets from various existing films but also whole films, especially films no longer protected by copyright law, and fashion them into their own film. In "Keaton's Cops" (1991), Ken Jacobs shows only the bottom fourth or fifth of each **frame** of Buster Keaton's classic silent film "Cops" (1922). In Jacobs's version we can see a subject in its entirety only rarely—for example, when Keaton falls down. Throughout the film, viewers see many feet (and horses' hooves) but not facial expressions. Nevertheless, if one has seen Keaton's "Cops," even years earlier, one may follow the story in Jacobs's version fairly well; such is the expressiveness of **mise en scène** and movement that only a partial view evokes much of what happens in the whole of the film. A viewer who has never seen "Cops" might be more available to Jacobs's aim:

frame: A separate, individual photograph on a strip of motion-picture film.

mise en scène: An image's setting, subject (usually people or characters), and composition (the arrangement of setting and subjects within the frame).

reading: Interpretation of a text.

> My intention is to interfere with narrative coherence and sense. To deny it, so as to release the mind for a while from story and the structuring of incident (compelling as it is in Keaton's masterly development). My filming, only showing the bottom fifth of Keaton's black-and-white screen-world, limits us to the periphery of story. Moves us, from the easy **reading** of an illustrated text, towards active seeing. Reduced information means we now must struggle to identify objects and places and, in particular, spaces. A broad tonal area remains flat, clings to the screen, until impacted upon by a recognizable object: Keaton smashes into it, and so it's a wall, diagonal to the screen . . . or a foot steps on it

or a wheel rolls across it and it's a road! We become conscious of a painterly screen alive with many shapes in many tones, at the same time that we notice objects and activities (Keaton sets his comedy in some actual street traffic) normally kept from mind by the moviestar-centered moviestory.

Experimental filmmakers may use entire films in many other creative ways. For "Intolerance (Abridged)" (1971), Stan Lawder took D. W. Griffith's *Intolerance* (1916), which runs over two hours, copied every twenty-sixth frame twice, and left only those frames in the finished film, thus reducing that film's running time by a factor of thirteen. During a screening, most of the title cards are unreadable, but so expressive are the film's images that much of its story, structure, mise en scène, editing, and camera work flash through the onrush of images. At an opposite extreme, in 1993, video artist Douglas Gordon transformed Hitchcock's *Psycho* (1960) into *24 Hour Psycho*. He created the new film by projecting *Psycho* not at the usual twenty-four frames per second but at two frames per second, thus stretching the film's running time from almost two hours to twenty-four hours. As a result, the film showing eliminates all sound, movement, and variations in pace but makes possible greater viewer awareness of each frame's mise en scène and cinematography. In effect, Gordon transformed the movie into a long series of still photographs.

Like lyric poems, experimental films explore an immense variety of subjects usually avoided in narrative. One subject is the possible combinations

FIGURE 8.20 Exploring ways to combine shifting abstract forms and music
Here, the acclaimed Canadian filmmaker Norman McLaren paints on clear 35 mm film in making part of "Begone Dull Care" (1949), a 7½-minute abstract film with a soundtrack of jazz played by the Oscar Peterson Trio. "After the score was recorded, McLaren and Evelyn Lambart began working on the visual material. . . . They painted long strips of film jointly and separately, then they would view the freshly painted strips (after drying) through a Moviola [editing/viewing machine] with the music. Many times they would paint five or six variations for one section of music, then select the one which went best with the music" (Richard 70). *Norman McLaren and Evelyn Lambart; National Film Board of Canada*

of abstract forms and music, as in Evelyn Lambart and Norman McLaren's "Begone Dull Care" (1949, Figure 8.20).

Another subject for experimental films is the scope and limitations of mental activities, as in "(nostalgia)" (1971, Figure 8.21). An experimental film may also explore the scope of human perception and cognition, as in J. J. Murphy's "Print Generation" (1974). The film consists of 3,002 shots: fifty generations of sixty shots plus two title cards. A generation is a copy, so the second generation of a shot is not quite as distinct as the first, and the third generation is a copy of a copy and is even less clear. Before the fiftieth generation of a shot, its content is unrecognizable. (The same thing happens with a photocopy machine if you make a copy, then a copy of the copy, and so forth for a total of fifty generations.) The film begins with the forty-ninth generation of each of sixty shots; these images are a series of abstract patterns of indistinct lights against a reddish background, such as in Figure 8.22a. Gradually viewers figure out that the film is made up of many brief full-color shots of the same duration (one second each) and can discern more and more of the subjects of other shots until, near the middle of the film, almost all of the subjects are recognizable (Figure 8.22b–h). However, it's impossible to see much of a connection between the sixty shots, so by somewhere near the film's middle, viewers conclude that the sixty shots do not constitute a story.

After a title card, "Print Generation/(A-WIND)/JJ Murphy/©1973–74," the images begin to return gradually to the abstract patterns seen at the film's beginning. The film ends with the fiftieth generation of each shot and a second title card, "Print Generation/(B-WIND)/JJ Murphy/©1973–74." Overall as the film progresses from abstract patterns to recognizable subjects and back to abstract patterns, an opposite action is happening on the soundtrack: sounds of ocean waves gradually become unrecognizable, then after the middle title card again gradually become recognizable.

In experiencing "Print Generation," viewers constantly watch, listen, and think as they try to perceive the film's subjects, see a unity to the shots, and make some meaning from the film's 3,002 shots. On one level, the film is about the changes that occur to images as more and more generations are made from them: beneath recognizable film images are increasingly abstract patterns, and underneath a full-color film image is less and less color until only red remains (the bottom layer of color **emulsion**). "Print Generation" is also about the limitations of perception, visual and auditory, and cognition: as more and more distortion is introduced into the representation of the subjects, viewers are limited as to what they can perceive and understand. On the most general level, the film shows that from chaos, signs of life emerge and just as quickly return to chaos. Murphy could have structured the film so that it began with recognizable subjects that gradually decompose and later regenerate into the original images. Such a structure would suggest a different, more upbeat meaning: life may decompose into unrecognizable parts and just as quickly regenerate itself.

emulsion: A clear gelatin substance containing a thin layer of tiny light-sensitive particles (grains) that make up a photographic image.

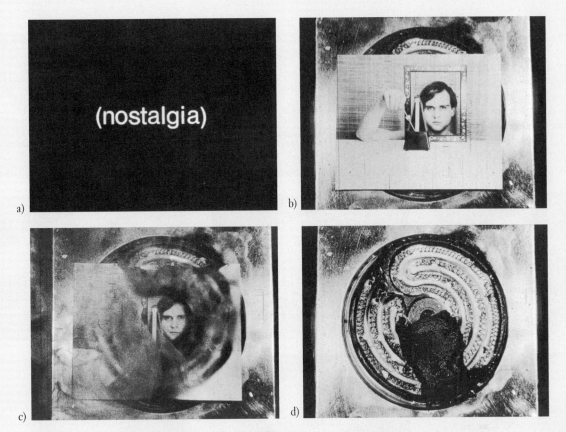

a)   b)   c)   d)

FIGURE 8.21 The limits of memory and other subjects
Hollis Frampton's experimental film "(nostalgia)" (1971) begins with (a) the title card and the simultaneous narration: "These are recollections of a dozen still photographs I made several years ago." Each of the following shots shows (b) a bird's-eye view of a photograph and (c) the photograph slowly catching fire on top of a hot plate and completely combusting as a narrator gives background and brief commentary about the *next* photograph viewers will see. After the narration accompanying each photo ends, in one to two minutes of silence we see (d) ashes slowly twisting on the hot plate. The film's last shot includes narration for a photo we viewers never get to see (even at the film's beginning) about which the narrator concludes, "What I believe I see recorded in that speck of film fills me with such fear, such utter dread and loathing, that I think I shall never dare to make another photograph. Here it is. Look at it. Do you see what I see?" Then the image goes black. The film is constructed to prevent viewers from experiencing synchronized image and sound throughout and suggests the difficulty of linking memory to the appropriate image, the transitory quality of images, and the impossibility of capturing and holding on to the past. Frame enlargements. *Hollis Frampton; Film-makers' Cooperative, New York*

FIGURE 8.22 Perception and cognition as subjects
Eight spaced frame enlargements from different generations of the same one-second shot illustrate the gradual increased resolution of an image during the first half of J. J. Murphy's "Print Generation" (1974). Frame enlargements. *J. J. Murphy; Film-makers' Co-operative, New York*

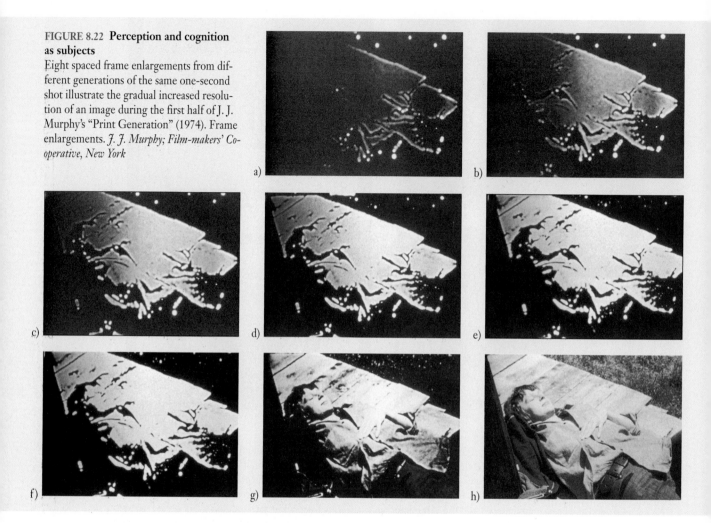

Filmmaking Techniques

filmic: Characteristic of the film medium or appropriate to it.

zoom: To use a zoom lens on a movie or video camera to cause the image of the subject to either increase in size as the area being filmed seems to decrease (zoom in) or to decrease in size as the area being filmed seems to increase (zoom out).

Experimental filmmakers tend to use traditional techniques in new ways. As critic Patrick S. Smith points out, Andy Warhol's films from 1963 to 1968 use well-known **filmic** techniques in ways rarely used by mainstream films. During that period, Warhol's films feature an unmoving camera; shots sometimes thirty or more minutes long; strobe cuts (used only in the later films), which result in a few white frames and a loud "bloop" sound at the beginning of each shot; and arbitrary **zooming**. Warhol reportedly also welcomed accidents during filming; when one occurred, he would keep filming. Warhol's films "remove the viewer's psychological identification with the performers by means of various interruptions or sustained viewpoints, so that one may notice qualities normally obscured by the perceptions of everyday existence or by the traditional condensations of narrative form" (Smith 150).

Experimental filmmakers tend to explore film techniques. They may superimpose a readable **text** over a moving image, present parts of the film upside down (Figure 8.18e), or use double or triple exposure. Experimental filmmakers may scratch, paint, dye, or bake an exposed and processed film. An entire film may be made without a camera: the film consists of images scratched or painted directly onto film or leader plus perhaps a soundtrack (Figure 8.20). For part of an untitled black-and-white film made by George Kuchar and his college film class, Kuchar gave each student actor "white eyebrows, lipstick, etc., on a face that was painted black." Then the footage of the black-faced actors was processed and the processed negative included with the rest of the finished film. Kuchar later

FIGURE 8.23 Untraditional filmmaking techniques, traditional subject
Using an optical printer to make multiple images of two dancers in "Pas de deux" (1968), Norman McLaren combines music with the expressiveness of human movement during the ritual of male and female courtship. The setting is nil; form, movement, and music are all. *Norman McLaren; National Film Board of Canada*

wrote, "It all worked out OK except that their teeth appeared black whenever they smiled. This made for a rather horrifying and funny effect as we were shooting glamour shots of the rather attractive cast." In "Pas de deux" (a.k.a. "Duo," 1968), Norman McLaren uses two dancers dressed in white against a black background and on a black floor, opposing bright light from each side of the frame, and frequent flowing multiple images made with an **optical printer**. In slow-motion dance the film shows the isolation, courtship, and union of male and female with novelty, grace, and feeling (Figure 8.23).

Other Characteristics of Experimental Films[1]

Experimental films rarely show a narrative: a representation of a series of unified events situated in one or more settings. If one initially seems to do so, viewers soon realize they cannot find the unity that stories offer. The

text: Something that people produce or modify to communicate meaning.

optical printer: A device consisting of a movie camera and one or more projectors used to reproduce images or parts of images from already processed film.

---

[1]In the following section I have used some of the same phrases as Edward Small did in his book *Direct Theory: Experimental Film/Video as Major Genre*, but I have added, combined, and renamed characteristics and supplied my own examples.

FIGURE 8.24 Events but no narrative
"Wavelength" (1967) has only four brief actions: 1. At the beginning of the film two men carry in a bookcase accompanied by a woman who indicates where to leave it; the men set the bookcase down, and all three leave. 2. Later, two women enter the room and go to the far side, where one turns on a radio that plays part of a song and the other closes a window. Soon one woman leaves, and the other woman turns off the radio and leaves. 3. After a variety of breaking sounds and footsteps are heard offscreen, a man slowly walks into the room and collapses. 4. Later a woman enters the frame, looks toward where the man had fallen, goes to the phone, and calls someone. The woman says that she thinks the man is dead, asks what to do, and asks the person on the other end of the phone to come over. She hangs up the phone and leaves. These limited actions are glimpsed during a seemingly continuous zoom shot, from wide-angle to close-up of a photograph of waves on the back wall, but like nearly all actions in experimental films, they do not add up to a coherent story. *Michael Snow; The Museum of Modern Art/Film Stills Archive*

forty-five-minute film "Wavelength" (1967) initially seems to show a story, but viewers eventually realize it does not (Figure 8.24). Instead, "The long journey across the loft . . . deliver[s] the audience to the absolute nemesis of the conventional cinema: to a still photograph viewed in silence for several minutes" (MacDonald 36). Like "Un chien andalou," at first "Meshes of the Afternoon" seems as if it is going to have a narrative—we see the same character in consecutive scenes—but narrative continuity soon breaks down (Figure 8.25). Another experimental film that is the antithesis of traditional narrative motion pictures is *Blue* (1993), which was directed by Derek Jarman and is not to be confused with another film of the same title directed by

FIGURE 8.25 Lack of narrative in an experimental film
Alexander Hammid and Maya Deren's "Meshes of the Afternoon" (1943) focuses on one character and various events but lacks narrative continuity and coherence. These ten frame enlargements illustrate five consecutive but discontinuous shots that begin slightly more than nine minutes into the film. First shot (a–c): The woman (Deren herself) looks down and off-frame; the camera pans left and viewers see what she was seeing: a knife and then herself sleeping. Second shot (d): Now near a window, she looks down, perhaps at herself sleeping. Third shot (e–f): Outside and below, a woman—whom viewers had seen earlier dressed in black and with a mirror instead of a face—rushes away, carrying a large plastic flower. Later in the shot, Deren runs after her. Fourth shot (g–h): The mysterious woman is in the distant background walking rapidly, rounding a corner, and going out of sight. Deren is running toward the mysterious woman but is even farther behind her than toward the end of the previous shot; Deren stops and walks off to the left of the frame. Fifth shot (i–j): Deren is again seen at the window; later in the shot she takes a key from her mouth. Like "Un chien andalou" (see Figure 8.17), "Meshes" seems dreamlike and ambiguously symbolic. Frame enlargements. *Maya Deren; Film-makers' Cooperative, New York*

FIGURE 8.26 Experimental film as antithesis to movies
Empire (1964)—an eight-hour experimental film by Andy
Warhol consisting solely of a view of the Empire State Building as seen from the same position—is the antithesis of traditional films. It has no human subject, no perceptible variation
in its subject, little noticeable movement from moment to moment, and no variation in filmmaking techniques. Furthermore, its pace is *so* slow it gives viewers extremely little
information during its very lengthy duration, except that outdoor lighting changes gradually over time. Frame enlargement. *Andy Warhol Foundation*

Krzysztof Kieslowski. Jarman's film, his last,
shows no moving pictures conveying a story but
seventy-six minutes of unvarying solid blue light.
The soundtrack of *Blue* does not help convey a
story or group of related stories. Instead, it uses
fragments of narration (both prosaic and poetic)
and other voices, sound effects, and music to reveal some of Jarman's thoughts, observations,
memories, and feelings as his eyesight is failing,
his body is wasting away, and he is dying of
AIDS.[2] Andy Warhol's *Empire* (1964), which consists of eight seemingly uninterrupted hours of a
view of the Empire State Building from the same
camera position, also comes close to static images, especially in the short term (Figure 8.26).

Experimental films also often draw attention to themselves as films or to the film medium itself. As we have seen, both fictional and
documentary films may be self-reflexive, but experimental films are even more likely to be so.
For example, they may show the camera filming
part of what will be included in the final version
of the film or include a film's opening leader.
They may show the parts of a projector as it is
projecting a film. They may make motion-
picture film itself the main subject of a film, as
Owen Land did in "Film in which there appear
sprocket holes, edge lettering, dirt particles, etc." (1965–66). (For another
film about the physical properties of films, see Figure 8.15.)

Film Apparatus and the Experimental Film

As a traditional film or video is made, the camera, film or videotape, lenses,
and so on are used in fundamentally conventional ways. For example, the
camera is used to film consecutive frames, not every other one or every third
one. When a conventional film or video is shown, its components—film-
projector-screen or videotape-video player-monitor—also tend to be used
in the usual ways. For example, traditionally the same lens is used throughout a film showing. Many experimental films, though, change one or more
of the basic components of making and exhibiting a film or video. A film is

---

[2]For the text of *Blue*, see Derek Jarman, *Blue: Text of a Film* (Woodstock, NY: Overlook Press,
1994). For the CD of the film's complete soundtrack (along with a printed transcript), hear
(and perhaps read) *Blue: A Film by Derek Jarman*, Mute/Elektra Nonesuch 79337-2, perhaps
while staring at something completely blue.

TABLE 8.2
Film Apparatus and the Experimental Film: A Few of the Visual Possibilities*

APPARATUS	TRADITIONAL USES	EXPERIMENTAL USES
PRODUCTION		
▌Camera	Filming at the same speed within each shot	Using distorting camera lens(es)
		Filming at variable speeds
		Filming, cranking back, and filming again to produce multiple exposures
▌Film	Recording consecutive fragments of space, time, or, most often, both on consecutive frames	Recording mostly clear frames, perhaps resulting in a strobe effect
		Painting
		Scratching
▌Editing	Coordinating multiple shots, usually through continuity editing	Rejecting editing by making a film consisting of one shot
		Avoiding continuity
		Making a compilation film, a film made up of clips from other films
EXHIBITION		
▌Projector	Running at an unvarying speed of 24 or 25 frames per second for modern sound film	Projecting the images upside down, backward, or both
	Using no distorting projector lens(es) other than possibly anamorphic	Causing multiple images, superimposed images, or both through multiple versions
		Projecting through some intervening substance, such as a full fish tank
▌Finished film	Depicting consecutive fragments of time, action, or both	Depicting discontinuous fragments of time, action, or both
▌Screen	Using a flat or concave, white, reflective, rectangular, uniform surface for projected film	Using a person's body or an inanimate object, such as a shirt or milk jug, for projected film
▌Theater	Allowing audience members to be in full sight of other audience members	Shutting off audience members from each other by erecting panels between seats

*A comparable table could be made for video production and exhibition consisting of video camera, videotape, player, and monitor, or video camera, tape, player-projector, and screen.

normally projected onto a flat, white, reflective, rectangular screen or wall, but it need not be so. During the opening night of the 1996 Los Angeles exhibition on the relationship of film and art since 1945, a film was projected onto a woman's bare chest, and throughout the exhibition different films were projected onto objects such as a bucket of milk and a spinning fan. In another part of the exhibit, a video projector suspended above an unmade bed projected a video image of a reclining man onto the bed. Table 8.2 lists the basic components of the film apparatuses and some conventional and unconventional ways in which filmmakers may use them.

Categories of Experimental Films

Experimental films have been categorized different ways by different scholars. Sometimes they are divided into "representational" and "abstract." In representational experimental films, the subjects are recognizable as people and real objects, as in "Un chien andalou" (see Figure 8.17). In **abstract films**, the subjects are unrecognizable, as in "Begone Dull Care" (see Figure 8.20). In a more sophisticated classification, film theorist James Peterson divides American experimental films since World War II into three "open and flexible grouping[s]": poetic, minimal, and assemblage (especially compilations of footage) (10). Edward Small divides experimental film and video into five categories: European avant-garde, American avant-garde, American underground, expanded cinema, and minimalist-structuralist (81). So boundless is human imagination, however, that two or three or five categories often prove inadequate, and many experimental films elude clear-cut classification.

Experimental Films and Other Arts

Since the 1970s, some films or videos have been combined with other visual objects and arts and shown in museums, usually museums of modern or contemporary art. Such ensemble artworks are called **installation art**. An example is Jeff Wall's "Eviction Struggle" (1988), which combines a fluorescent-lit transparency (about 13½ feet wide and 7½ feet tall) on one side of a gallery wall with nine **close-up** or **medium close-up** video excerpts of the same struggle and reactions to it on the other side of the wall (Figure 8.27). One version of the installation *Bordering on Fiction: Chantal Akerman's "D'Est"* (1995) consisted of a showing of *D'Est* (*From the East*, 1993), which is Akerman's feature-length documentary, in one museum gallery; video clips from it on multiple monitors in the next gallery; and in a third gallery a single video monitor and the filmmaker's recorded voice from yet another source reading a passage in Hebrew from the Bible and a selection from her own writings about the film. "Viewed in its entirety, *Bordering on Fiction: Chantal Akerman's 'D'Est'* engages in a deconstructive tour of the production process, working back from the completed feature film to the individual shot segments of which it is constructed and, in the end, back to language

a)

b)

FIGURE 8.27 Installation art: photography and video
Jeff Wall's installation "Eviction Struggle," which was made in British Columbia in 1988, has two sides. (a) On one side of an art gallery wall is a large still photograph showing two officers struggling with a man (to the right of the car parked at an angle to the sidewalk), a woman rushing from the direction of a house toward them, and various other people in the neighborhood watching the conflict. (b) The other side of "Eviction Struggle" consists of nine nineteen-inch video monitors showing brief close-up and medium close-up clips enacting some of the situations seen in the huge photograph. The three monitors on the left and the two monitors on the right side of the wall show people looking at the struggle. The four central monitors show, from left to right, an officer, the struggling man, another officer, and a woman running toward the men. By looking at the large image and then the nine video monitors (or vice versa), viewers can compare the expressiveness of the photograph's mise en scène with the expressiveness of video clips of the same subject. The nine monitors also allow viewers to function as editors in that they will select the order, duration, and repetition, if any, of the clips seen. The installation gives viewers the opportunity to compare and contrast two different representations of the same subject and to consider the expressiveness and limitations of still photography and video. *Collection: Ydessa Hendeles Art Foundation, Toronto*

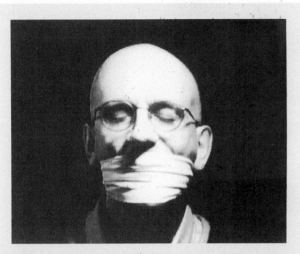

FIGURE 8.28 Installation of ten videos
"Hall of Whispers" is one of five parts of Bill Viola's installation art *Buried Secrets* (1995). "'Hall of Whispers' consists of a
series of ten video projections, five each on the long facing
walls of a dark corridor. This black-and-white gauntlet consists
of the life-size heads of men and women who have been bound
and gagged [as here]. Eyes shut, they struggle against tightly-
wrapped cloth bandages but their efforts to speak prove futile;
only muffled sounds escape into the room.... 'Hall of Whispers' announces . . . the difficulty, if not impossibility, of communication and the importance of protecting secrets. This can
be read on a political level since the figures so clearly conjure
images of tortured prisoners in a police state. But so literal an
interpretation misses their ambiguity and the wider possibilities of meaning" (Boyle 9). *Bill Viola.* Hall of Whispers *(1995)
(detail). Video/sound installation. Collection of the artist. Photo: Kira
Perov*

itself" (*Bordering* 9). For a third example of installation art, see Figure 8.28.

One of the biggest problems facing the student of experimental films is getting to see them,
especially if one does not live near a museum of
modern or contemporary art or near a large city
offering a wide range of film showings. Video
stores rarely carry them. (For that matter, some
experimental filmmakers will not allow their
films to be transferred to videotape.) To date, cable channels are of limited help, although the
Sundance Channel and the Independent Film
Channel sometimes show them. Some libraries
have a few of the classic titles or may be able to
get them for you through interlibrary loan.
Some university film series show them from time
to time. For videos and DVDs, both Facets Multimedia in Chicago and TLA Video in Philadelphia and New York have some titles or collections of short experimental films. More titles
are appearing on DVD, including the DVD
series of award-winning short films called
"Short" (Short 1, Short 2, and so forth). Searches
on the Web will help you locate films by such
filmmakers as Bruce Conner and Stan Brakhage.
By Brakhage: An Anthology (2003) is a two-DVD
set that includes twenty-six Brakhage films. On
the Web, the first site to visit is Flicker at
<www.hi-beam.net>. Included is a wide array of
information about experimental films and filmmakers and many useful links, including some to
film clips and short films. As Flicker's home
page asserts, "Here you will find films and videos that transgress the boundaries of the traditional viewing experience, challenge notions of physical perception and provide cutting edge alternatives to the media information
technocracy."

HYBRID FILMS

Most films are clearly one of the three major film types: fiction, documentary, or experimental. Viewers watching any of the *Star Wars*–related films,
for example, never think of them as anything other than fiction, and viewers
of *Hoop Dreams* see the film strictly as a documentary. A number of films,

however, are more difficult to categorize. A film that shares characteristics of two or all three of the major film types can be called a **hybrid film**.

Combinations of experimental and documentary are unheard of in classical Hollywood cinema but appear from time to time in **independent films** from various nations. Andy Warhol's *Sleep* (1963), which shows only a man sleeping for nearly five and a half hours, can be labeled experimental documentary. *Sleep* is a documentary film—it shows its subject factually—yet it is so unconventional as to be experimental (so long, so uneventful, so unvaried, so unengaging).

"You Take Care Now" (1989) by Ann Marie Fleming is an experimental narrative documentary. The film uses a blank screen, a wobbly camera that causes blurred images, repeated close-ups of a live bird's head surrounded by animated lines and patterns, the head of a man jumping up into the frame briefly and repeatedly (the camera is aimed above his head), an extreme close-up of a man's mouth as he presumably shouts curses as viewers hear a dog barking, snow on a TV screen, an out-of-focus night shot, and many other techniques to help convey the disorientation and physical and psychological pain of being raped and on another occasion being hit by one car and run over by another. The film's female narrator recounts two brief, presumably factual stories and provides whatever context and continuity the film has; the visuals show little of the stories and instead create or reinforce moods.

Experimental documentaries are also made by the Iranian American filmmaker Shirin Neshat. In "Turbulent" (1998), two black-and-white videos are projected on opposite sides of a room as viewers sit against either of the two remaining walls. In one of the videos, "a veiled woman waits by a microphone before an empty auditorium. In the other, a bearded man dressed in a white shirt and dark pants, like the men who fill the audience before him, sings a classical Persian song . . . about divine love. . . . When the man has finished, the woman begins. Her wordless song . . . is a primal emotional language, poised uncertainly between love and lament, bliss and pain. The camera swirls around her as her face contorts with the rhythmic, guttural cries emerging from her body" (Camhi 151). The many differences between the man and woman—the ways they are dressed, their audience (or lack of one), the subjects of their songs, the manner of their singing, their lack of interaction with each other—along with the ways they are filmed (she with a moving, exploratory camera; he with a stationary one) and the way they are seen, on opposite walls, all reinforce the meaning that the man and woman reside in a world where women are not allowed to sing in public (Figure 8.29).

A film may be a blend of fiction and documentary. As Figure 6.2 (on p. 249) illustrates, occasional films, such as (*Battleship*) *Potemkin* (1925), are classified as fiction or as documentary because they have characteristics of both types. It is even possible for parts of a film to be fictional and other parts of the same film to be documentary. Such a rare combination is found in Su Friedrich's *Hide and Seek* (1996), which **cross-cuts** between (1) a short fictional film set in the 1960s about a twelve-year-old girl beginning puberty

independent film: Film made without support or input from the dominant, established film industry.

a)

FIGURE 8.29(a) Hybrid film: experimental and documentary
During a showing of "Turbulent" (1998), footage of a man singing a traditional song presumably in contemporary Iran is shown on one wall of a room as on the opposite wall the woman seen on p. 387 waits. *Shirin Neshat, "Turbulent," video still, © 1998 Shirin Neshat, Courtesy Barbara Gladstone*

FIGURE 8.30 A nonnarrative fake documentary
While watching *Slacker* (1990), the viewer might initially think that the film is a documentary made by a highly mobile camera crew that recorded a few subjects briefly (often a one-sided conversation or monologue), picked up a new small group of people and followed them, and repeated this pattern throughout the film. After a certain point, it is clear the film shows no coherent narrative, so the viewer might conclude that the film is a nonnarrative documentary. As the film unspools even further, the viewer might start to suspect that the film is not a documentary after all (for one thing, some episodes seem too contrived to be entirely credible). The concluding credits include the "writer" (the same person as the producer and director) and someone in charge of casting. The film is a nonnarrative fake documentary.

Here the character on the left, identified in the closing credits as "Been on the moon

since the 50s," has attached himself to the young man on the right and has been walking along with him while spouting a stream of unorthodox theories. He claims, for example, that the United States first got to the moon in the 1950s by using anti-gravity technology stolen from the Nazis after the end of World War II. This episode begins 13¼ minutes into the film and runs for a little more than five minutes. As in the film's other episodes, the episode represented here looks and sounds like part of a narrative documentary. But the film's episodes are only loosely related (people out of the mainstream, the same twenty-four hours or so, and the same city). Richard Linklater—the film's producer, writer, and director—has not presented a story but re-created a society of mostly youthful outsiders, eccentrics, and loners in Austin, Texas, at the end of the 1980s. *Richard Linklater; Orion Classics*

FIGURE 8.29(b) **Hybrid film: experimental and documentary**
During a showing of "Turbulent" (1998), after the man seen on p. 386 finishes singing a traditional Iranian song and waits, footage of an Iranian woman singing an untraditional song is seen on the opposite wall. *Shirin Neshat, "Turbulent," video still, © 1998 Shirin Neshat, Courtesy Barbara Gladstone*

b)

and more attracted to girls than boys, (2a) documentary interviews of adult lesbians recounting some of their childhood feelings and experiences, and (2b) various documentary artifacts, such as photographs of lesbians when they were young girls, clips from movies, and archival footage from home movies and educational films, including the kinds of sex education films used in schools at that time.

On rare occasions, a film may be either a **fake documentary** or a **mock documentary**. Both kinds of film are made with documentary techniques (such as interviews, handheld camera shots, subtitles), but they are not documentaries. As viewers watch the entire fake documentary, they interpret it as factual (sometimes the film's closing credits reveal that the film is not factual after all). A fake documentary does not necessarily show a fictional story (Figure 8.30). Most fake documentaries, however, do, as is the case with *The Blair Witch Project* (1999, Figure 8.31). As is explained in Chapter 5, a mock documentary is a fictional film that at first seems to be a documentary, but most viewers quickly catch on that the film is fictional and an extended joke.

Films, especially independent films, may also combine elements of fiction and experimental. *The Cabinet of Dr. Caligari* (1919) is a fictional film with both a mise en scène and a preoccupation with a disturbed mental state more often found in experimental films. Another fictional film incorporating experimental aspects is Bergman's *Persona* (1966, Figure 8.32). The film shows the fictional story of two women. Parts of the film, however, include material extraneous to the **plot** and repetition rarely found in a fictional film: self-reflexive shots of motion-picture

In October of 1994, three student filmmakers disappeared in the woods near Burkittsville, Maryland while shooting a documentary.

A year later their footage was found.

FIGURE 8.31 **A narrative fake documentary**
One of the many ways that *The Blair Witch Project* (1999) gives the impression of factuality is its use of informative title cards, which are often used in films to convey factual information. In fact, *The Blair Witch Project* is the product of the imaginations and work of some film students at the University of Central Florida. Frame enlargement. *Haxan Entertainment; Artisan Entertainment*

plot: The structure or arrangement of a narrative's events.

FIGURE 8.32 Hybrid film: experimental and fictional
The two main characters of *Persona* (1966) are a nurse, Alma (left), and her patient, Elisabeth (right), a famous actor who suddenly has become mute and withdrawn. As this publicity still suggests, at times the two characters seem to change roles. At other times, as when a shot shows the halves of the two faces seemingly fused into one, they seem to blend into one another. In these and many other ways, *Persona* blends a fictional story and experimental filmmaking. *Ingmar Bergman; The Museum of Modern Art/Film Stills Archive*

FIGURE 8.33 A hybrid of fiction, documentary, and experimental
(a) A view through a fisheye lens of the main character seemingly dangling above sidewalks about 47¼ minutes into *David Holzman's Diary* (1968). In this frame, he is about to reach up and turn off the camera. This and other shots are characteristic of experimental films; in fact, it's hard to see how this shot fits into the story of this hybrid film. (b) This frame enlargement from 58¼ minutes into the film illustrates the film's occasional self-reflexiveness by showing most of the apparatus used to make the film: left to right, the main character's portable reel-to-reel audio tape recorder, rewinds and 16 mm reels, and a 16 mm editor/viewer, and above them and reflected in the mirror, a tripod holding a 16 mm camera. Elsewhere in the film, viewers see shots of the zoom lens presumably used in filming *David Holzman's Diary* and the portable tape recorder and the accompanying microphone. Frame enlargements. *Jim McBride; Direct Cinema Ltd.; The Museum of Modern Art/Film Stills Archive*

a)

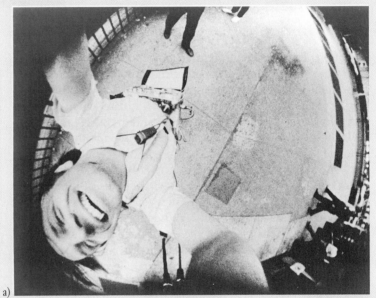

b)

cameras, projectors, and 35 mm film that do not fit into the plot; accusations by Alma as we see Elisabeth; and the same accusations by Elisabeth as we see Alma. *Persona* also includes a lengthy shot that begins badly out of focus and soon comes into focus.

An occasional film exhibits characteristics of all three major types of films, as in *David Holzman's Diary* (1968). Initially, the film seems to be a narrative documentary with experimental aspects, such as the self-reflexive shots of the equipment used during filming and editing; shots of the dark screen accompanied by narration; a galloping succession of shots supposedly representing one frame from each shot of an evening's worth of TV; and a shot looking down on the top of "David Holzman's" head (Figure 8.33). When the end credits reveal that the film was scripted and acted and is not factual, the viewer can understand that the film is fictional with documentary and experimental components.

Critics and scholars sometimes disagree about how to classify a film. Some film specialists see *Female Trouble* (1974) and other early films directed by John Waters as experimental fiction, whereas others believe that they are fictional films done in a particular style, **black comedy** (see Figures 6.18 and 6.19 on pp. 277). Such disagreements involve judgment calls and sometimes different uses of terms, and informed and thoughtful people will inevitably categorize some films differently. Filmmakers' imaginations and creativity outrun critics' and scholars' classifications.

black comedy: A narrative style that shows the humorous possibilities of subjects often considered off limits to comedy, such as warfare, murder, death, and illness.

ANIMATION

Beginning for films made in 2001, the Academy of Motion Picture Arts and Sciences added the category of Best Animated Feature Film to its list of annual awards. Some of the biggest money-makers of recent years, particularly *The Lion King* (1994) and *Finding Nemo* (2003), are animated. Big-name actors such as Robin Williams, Billy Crystal, Mike Myers, Eddie Murphy, and Cameron Diaz are increasingly willing or even eager to do the voices for animated features. Especially since Robin Williams did the voice for the genie in *Aladdin* (1992), many feature-length animated films include **parodies** and **allusions** that adult viewers enjoy (see Figure 5.14 on p. 229). In addition, the scripts for *Toy Story* (1995), *Antz* (1998), *Finding Nemo*, and others are so carefully written, revised, and polished that the stories delight both children and adults. Japanese animation (anime) has grown in popularity and can now occasionally be seen in American theaters (see Figure 6.7 on p. 255); it has also strongly influenced video games. Films such as *Natural Born Killers* (1994), *Run Lola Run* (1998), *Amélie* (2001), *Hedwig and the Angry Inch* (2001), *Frida* (2002), *Bowling for Columbine* (2002), *Kill Bill: Vol. 1* (2003), and others include animated segments. Steven Spielberg's *Catch Me If You Can* (2002) begins with a highly praised animated title sequence. Film festivals are inundated with submissions for the animated film categories. Ever since the success of *The Simpsons* in

parody: An amusing imitation of human behavior or of a more serious text, part of a text, or groups of texts, often to ridicule or criticize.

allusion: A reference in a text to a person, an event, or a text or part of a text. Unlike an homage or a parody, an allusion does not convey clear-cut admiration or amusing derision.

FIGURE 8.34 Animation of flat (two-dimensional) subjects
Snow White and the Seven Dwarfs (1937), which was Disney's first feature-length animated film, is an example of the animation of flat subjects, in this case colored drawings. Here, 81¼ minutes into the film, Snow White has received that kiss, has revived with her composure intact, and is about to depart with her prince and go away to live happily ever after. Frame enlargement from the rereleased 1987 widescreen version (achieved by those rereleasing the film by cropping a little off the top and bottom of all the images). *Walt Disney*

animation: The process of photographing or creating a series of individual images with visual variations from one frame to the next so that later a showing of the series of still images can give the appearance of movement.

1989, more and more animated television shows have been running on cable networks. *The Simpsons, SpongeBob SquarePants, King of the Hill, Beavis and Butt-head*, and others are all hits. The Cartoon Network has been on the air since 1992, and one of its late-night animated shows has sometimes beat Jay Leno and David Letterman in the ratings. Popular animated TV shows, such as Nickelodeon's *Rugrats*, have been adapted into movies. Like the *Star Wars*, James Bond, Austin Powers, and other movie franchises, some animated movies have commercial tie-ins, such as toys, video games, and fast foods. Short animated films, many of them parodies, are commonplace on the Web. Animation is studied in various types of college courses, including in many introduction to film courses, and many articles and books are being published on the subject. In short, in recent years, increasing numbers of animated films are being made, seen, enjoyed, and studied.

Animation is not a type of film (as are fictional, documentary, and experimental) or a combination of types of films (as is the hybrid film). Rather, it is a technique for making a film or part of a film. Animation is used in fictional films, documentary films (though extended use of animation in documentaries is rare), and experimental films. Occasionally—as in *Mary Poppins* (1964), *Jurassic Park* (1993), *Stuart Little* (1999), and *Stuart Little 2* (2002)—animation is combined with live action, thereby joining imaginary worlds with more familiar ones.

To "animate" means to bring to life. Both flat (two-dimensional) and plastic (three-dimensional) subjects may be animated. One of the most frequent sources of animation is a series of drawings (Figure 8.34). Other flat subjects that may be animated include paintings;[3] photographs; paper cutouts with hinged and movable body parts; computer graphics images; and drawings, scratchings, or paint applied directly on the film itself (see Figure 8.20). Plastic objects that may be animated include people in rigid poses, clay, and plasticine, a synthetic material used as a substitute for clay (Figure 8.35).

In **stop-motion cinematography**, a two-dimensional or three-dimensional subject, such as a drawing or a puppet, is filmed for a frame or two;

---

[3]Experimental animator Robert Breer paints on individual 4-by-6-inch cards. After he has completed a number of consecutive cards, he flips through them to see how that section will look and move. Next, he redoes, omits, adds to, rearranges. Once he is happy with the results, he photographs each finished frame.

FIGURE 8.35 Animation of plastic (three-dimensional) subjects
In the Wallace and Gromit short animated films, Wallace is "the daft, loquacious inventor and [Gromit is his] silent, long-suffering dog" (Canemaker). In this scene from "A Close Shave" (1995), Gromit and Wallace have discovered a hungry lamb in their kitchen. Worse yet, the lamb is gnawing on Gromit's bone. In an e-mail to me, Rich Aardman of Aardman Animations (production company) wrote that the plasticine model of Wallace is about ten inches high and the model of Gromit is approximately eight inches high. *Aardman; The Museum of Modern Art/Film Stills Archive*

a)

b)

c)

d)

FIGURE 8.36 Stop-motion animation
(a) Producer Tim Burton with some puppets used in making *Tim Burton's The Nightmare before Christmas* (1993). In the movie, each holiday has its own place and own set of characters. Jack, the leader of Halloween Town, discovers Christmas Town and thinks it could be improved. Soon, Halloween Town characters are dispatched to kidnap "Sandy Claws," and Jack as Santa Claus returns to Christmas Town on Christmas. He leaves toys he thinks the children will enjoy, but instead they frighten the children and their parents.

During filming, usually the puppets or parts of them and perhaps parts of the setting were moved slightly between exposures, and twenty-four separate images were exposed for each second of finished film. The images (b–d), which appear 55¼ minutes into the film, are three equally spaced but not consecutive frames that reveal a young boy showing his parents a Christmas present that Jack left. The parents react by shuddering. (In a later scene, we see that they have passed out from shock!) (b–d) Frame enlargements. *Tim Burton and Denise Di Novi; Walt Disney; Touchstone*

FIGURE 8.37 Stop-motion cinematography for continuous motion and pixillated motion

(a) Stop-motion animation is usually used to create the illusion of smooth, continuous movement, as it is throughout Disney's classic *Snow White and the Seven Dwarfs* (1937). Note that in the five contiguous frames seen here, which appear thirty-six minutes into the film, there are only minor differences between the frames. In stop-motion animation that creates the illusion of continuous movement, sometimes it is difficult to detect any changes in two neighboring frames. To detect differences between two frames, one might have to compare two frames that are separated by several other frames. (b) Stop-motion cinematography can also be used to pixillate subjects. These five consecutive frames from the experimental fictional film "Neighbours" (1952) illustrate pixillation, which is animation that shows subjects moving continuously or discontinuously in ways impossible in the real world. Because there are major changes from frame to frame, here, nearly 2½ minutes into the film, the two competing neighbors circle each other rapidly (note how much ground they cover in five frames or only about one-fifth of a second). Frame enlargements. (a) Frames from the rereleased 1987 widescreen version (achieved by those rereleasing the film by cropping a little off the top and bottom of all the images). *Walt Disney;* (b) *National Film Board of Canada; The Museum of Modern Art/Film Stills Archive*

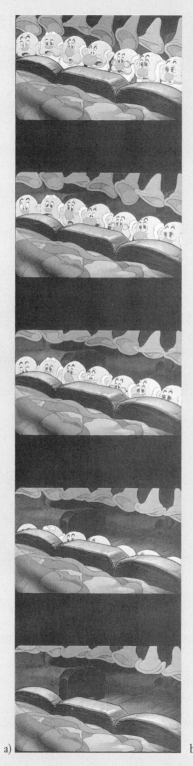

a)

b)

then usually something in the image is changed, one or two more frames are filmed, and so on (Figure 8.36). Stop-motion cinematography is normally used to show continuous movement, and when it is, the process is time-consuming and costly (Figure 8.37a). It may, however, be used to show other types of movement. Bill Plympton, for example, creates only six different drawings for a second of film because he prefers to create moving images that twitch and wiggle, not move with life's fluidity. Sometimes the choice to create noncontinuous animation is not aesthetic but economic. Some traditional animators, including more than an occasional student animator, may use only six or so frames per second because time or budget is severely limited.

Pixillation is a type of animation that shows living subjects or inanimate objects (or both) moving in ways impossible to show in live action: by showing certain continuous movements that are impossible in the real world or discontinuous (jumpy) movements. Pixillation may be achieved by using stop-motion cinematography or, less often, by selecting some frames from shots already filmed, copying the frames selected, and then projecting the results. Pixillated movement is now also possible with computer animation. Examples of pixillation from Norman McLaren's "Neighbours" (1952) are a person sliding smoothly in circles across a level lawn while balanced on one foot and two men circling each other in a jumpy, speeded-up manner (Figure 8.37b). Pixillation may be used for various purposes. "One is to manipulate time, as in 'Neighbours' (the quick building of the fence). Another . . . is to create a caricature by altering the tempo of human action, in other words, by creating . . . exaggerated movements to distort human behavior, as in . . . 'Neighbours' (the violence emphasized in the fight scene)" (Richard 37).

Animation is not always created by photographing a series of images or objects. One may animate without a camera. One way is to scratch or paint onto the individual frames of film, or, as Stan Brakhage and others have done, to affix small objects to the film stock and copy the film (Figure 8.38). Increasingly, animation is done with computers. In some computer-assisted animation, penciled drawings are scanned into the computer. Next, the computer is used to choose and assign

FIGURE 8.38 Film made without a camera
To make "Mothlight" (1963), a four-minute silent film, Stan Brakhage pasted pieces of moth wings, grass, seeds, leaves, and flowers on clear 16 mm film then copied the results. Frame enlargements. *Courtesy of Stan Brakhage*

393

colors to areas of the image, ink and paint the images, set the characters against a background, add "camera movements," match the image to the soundtrack, and transfer the finished product to either film, videotape, or DVD. It is now also possible to do the animation completely within the computer or with a group of people working on computers and transfer the results to film. And it is possible—indeed, now commonplace—to combine traditional animation with computer animation while making a film.

The Web has become a major source for producing and viewing short animation in part because of the availability of an easy-to-use software program called Flash animation. Some of this animation is interactive: for example, the user can manipulate the mouse to change the direction of an animated character or control the story's pace. Much Web-based animation is clearly drawn and the sound is appropriate, but the animation is without fluid movement; the skin tones are flat and unvaried; and the faces are restricted to a narrow range of expression. Like the movie **serials** that used to be shown in weekly installments in neighborhood movie theaters, some animated stories on the Web are divided into episodes of a few minutes, each except the last ending in a dangerous or unresolved situation for the main character. Again, like some of the old serials, some Web series feature a (male or female) superhero triumphing over a series of dangers. In spite of its technical limitations, the Web is proving to be a place for animators to develop their skills and in some cases to attract attention and funding for more ambitious projects.

An animated film may be as accomplished in its visuals, soundtrack, and narrative as live-action fictional films. "T.R.A.N.S.I.T." (1997) exemplifies how subtle, sophisticated, and engaging a short animated film can be (see feature on p. 395). Although only twelve minutes long, the film shows the complicated story of a love triangle, an attempted murder, and two murders. The film's seven sequences are arranged in reverse chronological order, so viewers need to be particularly attentive to the film's plot to figure out the chronological arrangement of the events, the **fabula**. Viewers are rewarded with each repeat viewing of this carefully made film as the characterization and plot and the subtleties in the filmmaking (such as the symbolism of the strawberries, selective use of red, and the appropriateness and expressiveness of the music) become more evident.

Animation can allow viewers to see and experience from a new perspective. In "The Fly" (1980), we see the countryside and the inside of a large country home entirely from the point of view of a fly. We see, hear, and to some extent experience the flying and stopping, flying and stopping. Near the end, we also hear footsteps and the sounds of a person swatting at the fly and finally see through a blur a collection of mounted insects as the fly's life and the film end together.

Compared with live-action filming, animation has many other advantages. It provides filmmakers greater control of mise en scène: they control all aspects of settings, subjects, and composition. Perhaps especially significant

serial: From the 1910s until the early 1950s, a low-budget action film divided into chapters or installments, one of which was shown each week in downtown and neighborhood movie theaters.

"T.R.A.N.S.I.T." (1997): A Description

a. Live action. Suitcase presumably floating. Opening title card superimposed. Travel labels on suitcase. Last label shown (in French): "SS L'AMERIQUE DU SUD."

1. Ship in ocean. Hole of ship: men stoking furnace. On deck: rich passengers passing their time (Plate 29). Newspaper headline: "Oil Tycoon Murdered in Egypt. Wall Street in Turmoil." Oscar (we learn his name at the end of the film) comes onto the deck. One arm is in a sling; his head is bandaged. He carries the heavy leather suitcase seen at beginning of the film. All activities on deck stop momentarily. Oscar walks across a shuffleboard game in progress. From the back of the ship he throws the suitcase overboard. It floats away from the ship. Lap dissolve to the suitcase covered with travel labels.

2. Orient Express train. Night. Map: Venezia (Venice) → Verona → Milano. Emily (we learn her name at the end of the film) opens a train window and a suitcase with travel labels. She takes a red cloth from it and tosses it (and the gun inside it) out the window into water below. Oscar, with a bandaged head, is on a plane within sight of the train. The plane passes the train. Oscar waiting at Paris train station. Train arrives. He gets on, enters a compartment, seems to kill Emily, then sits with his head in his hands.

3. Venice. Large luxurious hotel. Emily and Oscar in bed. She has a black eye and a bruised mouth (Plate 30). She gets up, gets a gun, and shoots at Oscar twice. Emily leaving hotel as a Charlie Chaplin movie being shown outside is finishing. Carrying the suitcase, she gets into a gondola. Oscar, bloodied, staggers out onto the balcony of the hotel room.

4. Egypt. Desert near pyramids. Guide, Emily, and the tycoon. Emily ignores guide's gesture to help her down off her camel and instead accepts the tycoon's help. The guide is enraged. Tycoon starts to kiss Emily. Guide stabs tycoon with a knife and is revealed to be Oscar. He slaps Emily in the face. Using his own garment, Oscar covers up the tycoon. Emily has a black eye.

5. St. Tropez (France). Emily and Oscar picnic. She feeds him a strawberry and eats one herself. The juice bleeds down her chin. They kiss. Nearby a sports car is parked.

6. Baden Baden (Germany) resort. Men's steam room. Tycoon getting a massage. In casino, Oscar wins at roulette (Plate 31). Emily stands near tycoon and smiles in Oscar's direction. In Oscar's hotel room, Emily rubs fresh strawberries on his body and indicates her sexual availability. At dawn, she returns to the room where the tycoon is sleeping, kisses him lightly, and slips into her bed.

7. Emily and the tycoon drive through the countryside. City street: suitcase falls out of the back of the car (same one as in sequence 5). Oscar picks it up and hands it to Emily. She kisses a card advertising a hotel (where the couple will be staying) and gives it to Oscar. He's a handsome though unshaven butcher in a bloody apron and has a pregnant wife and two small children.

b. Live action with animated effects. The suitcase full of travel labels floating in the ocean and superimposed title cards about Emily Buckingham Parker, who was last seen boarding the Orient Express in Venice in 1928. A shark swims nearby, then the suitcase sinks abruptly and a faint red (Emily's blood) briefly stains the sea. Title cards tell about Oscar Bleek's later successful new life in Argentina.

The plot = a, 1–7, b
The fabula = 7, 6, 5, 4, 3, 2, 1, a, b

morphing: The alteration of a film image by degrees through the use of sophisticated computer software and multiple advanced computers.

are the wider range of character movements and the **morphing** of subjects possible in animation. Animation makes possible the impossible, such as a man metamorphosing (or morphing) into a beast and back into a man, dinosaurs roaming the earth 65 million years ago (*Dinosaur*, 2000), or remnants of the human race scattered about the universe because alien invaders destroyed earth in the thirty-first century (*Titan A.E.*, 2000). As many scenes in animated movies demonstrate—the death of Bambi's mother in *Bambi* (1942), the terror of the evil witch in *Sleeping Beauty* (1959), the death of Mufasa in *The Lion King* (1994), and the reunion of father and son in *Finding Nemo*—animation can also call forth strong emotional viewer responses from both children and adults. Perhaps because animation is seen as less threatening or less serious than live-action films and other texts, it can get away with being raunchier, more subversive, sharper in its social critiques, or even politically incorrect—or all four—as is illustrated, for example, by *The Simpsons* and some of the other animated TV shows and by *South Park: Bigger, Longer and Uncut* (1999).

designer: The person responsible for the appearance of much of what is photographed in a movie, including architecture, locations, sets, costumes, makeup, and hairstyles.

Animation can create characters that are as memorable as people: for years throughout the world, Mickey Mouse was as popular as any movie star. (Perhaps as computer animation grows more and more powerful and subtle, one day animated stars will rival flesh-and-blood stars and even partially displace them.) No wonder animation so animates animators: they can play **designer**, casting director, director, and editor; they can show entire stories from otherwise impossible points of view; they can create life, set it in motion, act out what they wish, and decide the precise moment the life fades out or the image cuts to black. Such are its powers and expressiveness that "[a]nimation can defy the laws of gravity, contest our perceived view of space and time, and endow lifeless things with dynamic vibrant properties. . . . Animation can change the world and create magical effects, but most importantly, it can interrogate previous representations of 'reality' and reinterpret how 'reality' might be understood" (Wells 214).

CLOSE-UP: *HEARTS OF DARKNESS: A FILMMAKER'S APOCALYPSE* AS A NARRATIVE DOCUMENTARY FILM

Hearts of Darkness: A Filmmaker's Apocalypse is a ninety-six-minute narrative documentary written and directed by Fax Bahr with George Hickenlooper. The 1991 film shows some of the background and planning for the making of the 1979 version of *Apocalypse Now* and many of the problems director Francis Coppola and his crew faced as they filmed his fictional Vietnam War epic in the Philippines.

In many ways, *Hearts of Darkness* shows a classic story of one man facing tests of both character and nature as he tries to realize his vision. The film is like classical Hollywood cinema in its focus on a distinct individual with goals, a succession of problems that the individual faces in reaching them, clear cause-and-effect relationships, closure, and unobtrusive filmmaking techniques. *Hearts of Darkness* is also an example of an independent film made outside the Hollywood system; it was made on a low budget for the Showtime cable network and later shown in theaters.

NARRATIVE COMPONENTS

Hearts of Darkness begins at the Cannes Film Festival in May 1979; soon flashes back to the large, mostly chronological, middle section; then returns briefly to the 1979 Cannes Film Festival and events after it. The film's structure can be represented as B, A, C, although the huge middle section is not always arranged chronologically.

Francis Coppola is the main person in the story of *Hearts of Darkness*, and his goal is transparent: to finish filming an effective story within a reasonable time and at an endurable cost. In attempting to achieve his goal, he is beset with problem after problem—after problem. Some of Coppola's troubles, it could be argued, were of his own making, such as too often trusting to chance developments.

Hearts of Darkness shows the three types of conflict: people versus people, people versus nature, and conflict within a person. The cast was one major source of conflict between people. After Coppola replaced Harvey Keitel with Martin Sheen, many scenes had to be reshot. Later, Sheen's heart attack created additional delays and expense. As with many U.S. soldiers late in the Vietnam War, some actors in *Apocalypse Now*, most conspicuously Dennis Hopper and Sam Bottoms, consumed drugs copiously. Marlon Brando's slowness in getting into the role caused a major oblique conflict as well.

Coppola was also forced to struggle with nature when a typhoon hit the Philippines and halted production. The American technology that Coppola brought to the Philippines was no match for the storm that destroyed sets and disrupted the production for two months. Both Sheen and Coppola suffered from conflict within themselves: Sheen during filming of the hotel room scene and Coppola from time to time as he despaired about being able to finish the Herculean task involving himself and many others.

Hearts of Darkness has yet other narrative components. Like most successful stories, its beginning intrigues the audience, in this case by emphasizing that the production was plagued with problems. In the film's opening shots, at a Cannes Film Festival news conference, Coppola says,

> My film is not about Vietnam. It *is* Vietnam. It's what it was really like. It was crazy. And the way we made it was very much like the way the Americans were in Vietnam. We were in the jungle. There were too many of us. We had access to too much money, too much equipment, and little by little we went insane.

397

a)   b)

FIGURE 8.39 Editing to comment on a subject obliquely
(a) Filipino boys have been playing with a toy sailboat seen here immediately after it topples over.
(b) The next shot is of Coppola talking about building projects inevitably going over budget. The juxtaposition of images suggests that Coppola is like a boy with a toy that is not entirely under control and
ends up in an accident. The juxtapositioning of the two shots is sly but expressive. Frame enlargements.
George Zaloom and Les Mayfield; New Yorker Films

The film continues by supplying additional background, including information about Coppola's
despair about being able to conclude *Apocalypse
Now* successfully. The large middle section presents problems for Coppola and his company that
were vexing to them but are of interest to viewers
of *Hearts of Darkness*. The ending of *Hearts of
Darkness* has closure, a sense of wholeness and
completion, implying that eventually the obstacles
were overcome and the film became a commercial
and critical success.

Like some other narrative documentary films,
such as *Hoop Dreams*, *Hearts of Darkness* has two
plotlines: Coppola facing problems while filming
and in far less detail Coppola facing personal problems (stress, collapse, depression, suicidal impulses,
and infidelity). Unlike Eleanor Coppola's book
called *Notes*, which she wrote during the production of *Apocalypse Now*, *Hearts of Darkness* does not
include information about Coppola's infidelity during the filming and the subsequent major though
temporary disruption of their marriage (210–12).

Using a structure not uncommon in narrative
documentaries, *Hearts of Darkness* presents its tale
out of order. The film's middle section is a huge
flashback that itself is not arranged entirely
chronologically. And like nearly all narratives,
Hearts of Darkness is often vague about when cer-

tain actions occurred and how much time it took
for some of them to transpire. In common with the
treatment of time in nearly all narrative films, the
film's story time (approximately four years) far exceeds its running time (ninety-six minutes). Finally,
like nearly all documentaries, the dominant style of
Hearts of Darkness is **realism**: representation in a
text that is widely believed to render its subjects accurately.

DOCUMENTARY ASPECTS

Documentaries are mediated reality: the selection
and arrangement of information. As in the construction of many other documentaries, *Hearts of
Darkness* entailed an enormous amount of selecting
and arranging. When the makers of *Hearts of Darkness* were selecting excerpts from earlier texts—
such as clips from *Apocalypse Now* and from
Eleanor Coppola's footage—they were presenting
a mediated reality based on an earlier mediated
reality.

Hearts of Darkness illustrates yet other recurrent features of the documentary film. It uses real
people being themselves. The excerpts from
Eleanor Coppola's footage show people doing
what they do in their work and in their spare time,
not (presumably) posing for her camera. Like so

a) b)

FIGURE 8.40 Interviewee in late 1970s and more than a decade later
(a) Dennis Hopper being interviewed during the making of *Apocalypse Now*. (b) The next shot is of Hopper being interviewed during the making of *Hearts of Darkness*. In the later interview he says that at the time of the filming of *Apocalypse Now* his acting career was "not in the greatest shape." Frame enlargements. *George Zaloom and Les Mayfield; New Yorker Films*

many other documentaries, *Hearts of Darkness* was filmed on location where the subjects live and work—in this case, mostly in the Philippines.

As has been explained, various documentary films—such as those by Frederick Wiseman and those of Errol Morris—use quite different filmmaking techniques. Sometimes a wide variety of techniques are used within the same documentary

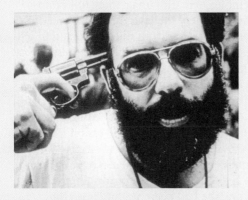

FIGURE 8.41 Darkness and despair
Coppola with darkened eyes, depressed and despairing during the late stages of trying to finish *Apocalypse Now* successfully. So anguished had he become that he had been considering what sickness he could contract to get himself off the hook or even how he could commit suicide. Frame enlargement. *George Zaloom and Les Mayfield; New Yorker Films*

film. As a few examples illustrate, *Hearts of Darkness* uses a fairly wide range of techniques. The film cuts from Filipino boys to Coppola himself to suggest a point (Figure 8.39). Editing is also used to show how much someone has changed when the film occasionally juxtaposes shots of an actor then and now (Figure 8.40). Another particularly expressive example of filmmaking occurs when the camera moves in on one of Coppola's darkened eyes; after a fade-out and fade-in, the camera moves away from his eye, and viewers see Coppola holding a pistol to his head (Figure 8.41). Then too, music original to *Hearts of Darkness* is used effectively to support the film's moods and meanings.

Hearts of Darkness: A Filmmaker's Apocalypse illustrates some of the possibilities of both narratives and documentaries. In showing the trials and eventual triumph of an individual and his associates, the film informs and entertains. Like other narrative documentaries, *Hearts of Darkness* also gives viewers the opportunity to ponder the unexpected, sometimes far-reaching consequences of actual decisions and actions.

Work Cited

Coppola, Eleanor. *Notes*. New York: Simon and Schuster, 1979.

CLOSE-UP: "UN CHIEN ANDALOU" (1928) AS AN EXPERIMENTAL FILM

With the seventeen-minute film "Un chien andalou," director Luis Buñuel and to a lesser extent artist Salvador Dali made the most famous experimental film in the history of Western cinema.

Unlike traditional movies, many individual shots of "Un chien andalou" contain puzzling mise en scène. Perhaps the most perplexing and most famous/notorious shots are the following: A young man has been sexually aroused and fondled a young woman, but then she runs away from him in the room and threatens to hit him with a tennis racket. Next, inexplicably the man seems to think it will be a good idea to pull on two ropes that now lie on the floor, though neither he nor the viewer knows what they are attached to. Excerpts from the script give some sense of the burden he is about to shoulder:

> The man slings the ropes over his shoulders [about 7¼ minutes into the film] and, making a tremendous effort, begins pulling a mysterious cargo towards the young woman. . . . Visible on each rope near his shoulders are a cork mat and a melon. Seen from behind, the full load is now visible. On two huge grand pianos lie the carcasses of two donkeys, badly ripped and decaying. . . . Close-up of a donkey's head hanging down over the keyboard of one of the pianos. The eye which is visible has been gouged out. . . . Two priests are lying . . . [on their backs] and allowing themselves to be pulled along [by the ropes]; they . . . look completely relaxed. (Buñuel 108–9)

How is the viewer to make much sense of such bizarre actions and all the disparate subjects that the young man pulls as he tries to reach the young woman?

As was illustrated in Chapter 3, "Un chien andalou" also contains many examples of surprising, sometimes even shocking combinations of shots.

Early in the film, wispy clouds float past the moon followed by a shot showing a straight razor supposedly slicing through the docile woman's eye (see Figure 3.15 on p. 133). The film ends with a shot of a couple walking romantically on the beach to the accompaniment of tango music then shows the film's final title card, "In the Spring," followed by a shot of the man and the woman buried up to their chests in sand, immobile and presumably dead (see Figure 8.17). As so often in this untraditional film, shots encourage certain expectations that are thwarted by the following shot: the shots of both the two walking romantically along the beach and the title card "In the Spring" are followed by the film's startling final image of immobility, barrenness, decay, and death.

It is not just that the film surprises or shocks by its editing. Like dreams, which "Un chien andalou" closely resembles, one film image may follow another in ways that defy the laws of science and our sense of time and space. From the time that the first man (played by Buñuel himself) sharpens a straight razor to the time that he supposedly cuts the woman's eye, he has changed shirts. Most filmmakers take pains to avoid such inconsistencies, but they abound in "Un chien andalou." Almost six minutes into the 1960 version (the version with music approved by Buñuel), a young woman (in his script, Buñuel refers to her as an androgynous person) stands in the street with her arms upraised, and the striped box she had been holding is on the ground nearby. In the next shot (a **jump cut**), she is hugging the box to her chest, and a split second later a car that had been hurling toward her hits her. Given the speed of the approaching car and its distance from the woman, not enough time has elapsed for her to have picked up the box. As the script describes it, in the ropes-corks-melons-donkeys-priests-pianos shots, the two priests are initially shown "lying back and allowing themselves to be pulled along; they . . . look completely relaxed" (109). A few seconds later, the priests "look terrified" (109). Besides the change in mood between the two shots, there is also a change of actors: the man on the left in the first shot is on the right in the second shot; the man on the right in the first shot is played by a different man in the second shot. Here's a final example of the defiance of the laws of time and space: when a stranger wearing a hat throws out a window the small pieces of feminine clothing that a man on a bicycle had been wearing, it is nighttime inside the room and daytime outside.

"Un chien andalou" is not a fictional film: it is not a narrative that shows mostly or entirely imaginary events selected and arranged in some sort of meaningful order and represented chronologically or not. "Un chien andalou" is not a documentary: a film or video representation of actual (not imaginary) subjects. In its puzzling mise en scène, surprising juxtapositions of shots, and perplexing dreamlike representation of space and time, "Un chien andalou" is an experimental film that consistently rejects traditional movies and the coherence of a story; puzzles, surprises, shocks, and provokes viewers; and defies systematic interpretation.

Work Cited

Buñuel, Luis. *"L'age d'or" and "Un chien andalou": Films by Luis Buñuel*. Trans. Marianne Alexandre. New York: Simon and Schuster, 1968.

SUMMARY

Although live-action fictional films have been by far the most popular films in the history of world cinema, there are other major types of films: documentary, experimental, and hybrid. Animation, which is not a type of film, is a filmmaking technique used in all the major types of films.

Documentary Films

- Whether narrative or not, a documentary film or video is a filmed (and usually edited) representation of actual (not imaginary) subjects.
- Most documentary films present no narrative or story. The information in many nonnarrative documentary films is organized into groups or categories. Some nonnarrative documentary films attempt to praise or criticize a subject, as in *Hearts and Minds*.
- Narrative documentary films present stories that are largely factual, but like fictional films they are never simply a succession of related events. For example, they may also linger on settings or interrupt the narrative for interviews.
- Documentary films always present a version of mediated reality: they are a selected, perhaps staged, filmed, and edited representation of their subjects.

- Typically, documentary films depict occurrences where they happened and use no actors.

- Documentary films usually include supporting artifacts—such as photographs or old film clips—and informative language, such as narration or interviews, or both.

- As *Woodstock* and *The Thin Blue Line* illustrate, documentarians may use an enormous variety of film techniques.

Experimental Films

- Because experimental films are so various, no one term—*experimental, underground, avant-garde, personal,* or *independent*—adequately captures their complexity and scope.

- Unlike commercial movies, experimental films often radically reject the conventions of earlier films and explore the possibilities of the film medium.

- Unlike commercial movies, experimental films tend to rebel against a society's ideology (the influential and usually unexamined underlying social and political beliefs of a society or social group).

- Experimental filmmakers may work alone and tend to be largely free of censorship.

- Experimental filmmakers may explore the use of recent technological advances in communications (such as personal computers and the Web), use existing films or parts of them in a changed form, or focus on other subjects rarely explored in fictional or documentary films, such as the limits of memory.

- Often experimental films use traditional filmmaking techniques in new ways, as in "Wavelength."

- Experimental films are usually highly visual (and not very verbal) and often self-reflexive.

- Often experimental filmmakers change one or more components of filmmaking and film exhibition—for example, by projecting a film onto a hanging shirt.

- Experimental films may be divided into representational and abstract; poetic, minimal, and assemblage; or in other ways. Because of their individuality and enormous variety, however, experimental films are difficult to classify.

- Installation art, which is usually displayed in museums of modern or contemporary art, often incorporates film or video into an ensemble or environment of arts and objects.

Hybrid Films

▪ Although most films are exclusively fictional, documentary, or experimental, some films are hybrids: films that share characteristics of two or all three of the major film types. For example, *The Cabinet of Dr. Caligari*, though mainly fictional, also has characteristics of experimental films, and Andy Warhol's *Sleep* is an experimental documentary.

Animation

▪ Animation is a technique that may be used in making any type of film. It may be of flat or plastic subjects, and it may be made with or without a computer.

▪ Compared with live action, animation has many advantages. For example, animators have total control over the mise en scène, can show viewers new perspectives (such as the point of view of a fly), can make possible the otherwise impossible (such as characters moving in ways not possible outside movie theaters), and can show the morphing of objects.

▪ Perhaps because animation is seen as less threatening or less serious than live-action films and other texts, its makers have fewer restrictions than creators of other kinds of texts and can more easily get away with being raunchier, more subversive, sharper in their social critiques, or even politically incorrect—or all four.

Major Terms about Alternatives to Live-Action Fictional Films

Below, numbers in italics refer to the pages where the terms are explained. All terms are defined in more detail in the Illustrated Glossary beginning on p. 621.

abstract film *382*
animation *389*
cinéma vérité *362*
compilation film *358*
direct cinema *361*
documentary film *345*

experimental film *367*
fake documentary *387*
hybrid film *384*
installation art *382*
mediated reality *355*
narrative documentary film *352*

nonnarrative documentary film *349*
pixillation *393*
stop-motion cinematography *390*
surrealism *369*

QUESTIONS ABOUT ALTERNATIVES TO LIVE-ACTION FICTIONAL FILMS

The following questions are intended to help viewers understand some of the many alternatives to live-action fictional films. Not all the questions are appropriate for every film. In thinking out, discussing, and writing responses to those questions most appropriate for the film being examined, be careful to stick with the issues the questions raise, to answer all parts of the questions, to explain the reasons for your answers, and to give specific examples from the film.

1. Is the film an alternative to live-action fictional films? If so, explain why you think it is.

2. a. If the film is a documentary, is it narrative or nonnarrative? Why do you say so?

   b. What major types of sources are used?

   c. Is editing used to criticize or praise a subject? If so, explain.

   d. What major choices did the filmmakers make that affect the meanings and impact of the film? How would some different choices result in different meanings and a different impact?

3. a. If the film is experimental, in what ways is it unlike classical Hollywood cinema?

   b. For the experimental film, what are the major types of sources (such as earlier films or the filmmaker's imagination)?

   c. In what ways does the film surprise or frustrate you, or both?

4. If the film is a hybrid, what major types are combined? What expectations did you have early in the film, and how were you surprised as the film progressed?

5. If the film is animation, what does the animation make possible that would be extremely difficult or impossible to achieve with live action?

WORKS CITED

Applebome, Peter. "A Taste for the Eccentric, Marginal and Dangerous." *New York Times on the Web* 26 Dec. 1999.

Bates, Peter. "Truth Not Guaranteed: An Interview with Errol Morris." *Cineaste* 17.1 (1989): 16–17.

Blank, Les, independent filmmaker. Telephone interview. April 1995.

Bordering on Fiction: Chantal Akerman's "D'Est." Minneapolis: Walker Art Center, 1995.

Boyle, Deirdre. "Post-traumatic Shock: Bill Viola's Recent Work." *Afterimage* Sept./Oct. 1996: 9–11.

Breer, Robert. Showing and Lecture. "Breer on Breer: The Films of Robert Breer." Walker Art Center, Minneapolis. 25 Feb. 2000.

Buñuel, Luis. "Notes on the Making of 'Un Chien Andalou.'" *Art in Cinema*. Ed. Frank Stauffacher. 1947. New York: Arno, 1968. 29–30.

Camhi, Leslie. "Lifting the Veil." *ARTnews* 99.2 (Feb. 2000): 148–51.

Canemaker, John. "Chickens Fleeing on Feet Made of Clay." *New York Times on the Web* 30 April 2000. <http://www.nytimes.com/library/film/043000sum-chicken.html>.

Corliss, Richard. "Take This Job and Love It." *Time* 27 Oct. 1997: 111.

Dixon, Wheeler Winston. *The Exploding Eye: A Re-Visionary History of 1960s American Experimental Cinema*. Albany: State U of New York P, 1997.

Gardner, Robert. "Chronicles of the Human Experience: *Dead Birds*." *Nonfiction Film Theory and Criticism*. Ed. Richard Meran Barsam. New York: Dutton, 1976. 342–48.

Ide, Wendy. "Decasia." [London] *Times on Line* 2 Oct. 2003. <http://www.timesonline .co.uk/printFriendly/0,,1-8087-837939,00.html>.

Jacobs, Ken, independent filmmaker. Letter to the author. January 1998.

Jaehne, Karen. Review of *Fast, Cheap & Out of Control*. *Film Quarterly* 52.3 (Spring 1999): 43–47.

Jarecki, Andrew. Interview. *Fresh Air*. National Public Radio. 24 June 2003.

Kuchar, George, independent filmmaker and author. Letter to the author. January 1998.

Lucia, Cynthia. "Revisiting *High School*: An Interview with Frederick Wiseman." *Cineaste* 20.4 (Oct. 1994): 5–11.

MacDonald, Scott. *Avant-Garde Film: Motion Studies*. New York: Cambridge UP, 1993.

Mellencamp, Patricia. *Indiscretions: Avant-Garde Film, Video, and Feminism*. Bloomington: Indiana UP, 1990.

Nichols, Bill. *Introduction to Documentary*. Bloomington: Indiana UP, 2001.

Peterson, James. *Dreams of Chaos, Visions of Order: Understanding the American Avant-Garde Cinema*. Detroit: Wayne State UP, 1994.

Richard, Valliere T. *Norman McLaren, Manipulator of Movement: The National Film Board Years, 1947–1967*. Newark, DE: U of Delaware P, 1982.

Small, Edward S. *Direct Theory: Experimental Film/Video as Major Genre*. Carbondale: Southern Illinois UP, 1994.

Smith, Patrick S. *Andy Warhol's Art and Films*. Ann Arbor, MI: UMI, 1986.

Wells, Paul. "Animation: Forms and Meanings." *An Introduction to Film Studies*. 3rd ed. Ed. Jill Nelmes. London: Routledge, 2003: 213–38.

Weschler, Lawrence. "Sublime Decay." *New York Times* (late ed.) 22 Dec. 2002: 6.44.

FOR FURTHER READING

The Animated Film Collector's Guide. Ed. David Kilmer. Bloomington: Indiana UP, 1998. Lists nearly three thousand animated films and their video and laser disc sources. Included are many hard-to-find films, as well as a listing of more than two hundred films that have won major prizes at animation festivals or placed in animation polls.

Barnouw, Erick. *Documentary: A History of the Non-Fiction Film*. 2nd rev. ed. New York: Oxford UP, 1993. A concise illustrated history plus an extensive bibliography.

Barsam, Richard M. *Nonfiction Film: A Critical History*. Rev. and expanded ed. Bloomington: Indiana UP, 1992. Part One (1820–1933): Foundations of the Nonfiction Film; Part Two (1933–1939): Documentary Films to Change the World; Part Three (1939–1945): Nonfiction Films for World War II; Part Four (1945–1960): Nonfiction Films after World War II; Part Five (1960–1985): Continuing Traditions and New Directions.

Bendazzi, Giannalberto. *Cartoons: One Hundred Years of Cinema Animation*. Bloomington: Indiana UP, 1994. A comprehensive and detailed history and critique of film animation. Includes ninety-five color plates and comprehensive indexes of names and titles.

Borowiec, Piotr. *Animated Short Films: A Critical Index to Theatrical Cartoons*. Lanham, MD: Scarecrow, 1998. Five sections: a brief history of animated short films, reviews of over eighteen hundred cartoons, director index, chronological index of cartoons from 1906 to 1997, and four- and five-star reviews.

Bruzzi, Stella. *New Documentary: A Critical Introduction*. London: Routledge, 2000. Provides a comprehensive account of the last two decades of documentary filmmaking in the United States, Great Britain, and Europe. The book also explores how issues of gender identity, queer theory, performance, "race," and spectatorship are important to an understanding of contemporary documentary.

Canyon Cinema Film/Video Catalog No. 8. San Francisco: Canyon Cinema, 2000. Descriptions of available films and videos. Especially valuable for information on the experimental.

Clements, Jonathan, and Helen McCarthy. *The Anime Encyclopedia: A Guide to Japanese Animation since 1917*. Berkeley: Stone Bridge P, 2001. More than two thousand short entries that describe and evaluate anime films—including *Astro Boy*, *Princess Mononoke*, *Akira*, *Giant Robo*, *Pokémon*, and *Sailor Moon*—plus entries on directors, writers, animators, composers, and studios.

Collecting Visible Evidence. Ed. Jane M. Gaines and Michael Renov. Minneapolis: U of Minnesota P, 1999. Sixteen essays by various film scholars for the advanced introductory student.

Documenting the Documentary: Close Readings of Film and Video. Ed. Barry Keith Grant and Jeannette Sloniowski. Detroit: Wayne State UP, 1998. Essays by twenty-seven film scholars; each essay is focused on one or two major films.

Experimental Cinema: The Film Reader. Ed. Wheeler Winston Dixon and Gwendolyn Audrey Foster. New York: Routledge, 2002. Four parts: Origins of the American Avant-Garde Cinema, 1920–1959; The 1960s Experimental Explosion; Structuralism in the 1970s; and Alternative Cinemas, 1980–2000.

Film-makers' Cooperative Catalogue No. 7 and *Film-makers' Cooperative Catalogue No. 7 Supplement*. New York: Film-makers' Cooperative, 1989, 1993. Descriptions of films and videos available through the co-op, arranged alphabetically by filmmaker. Especially valuable for information on experimental films.

James, David E. *Allegories of Cinema: American Film in the Sixties*. Princeton: Princeton UP, 1989. Survey of American experimental cinema of the 1960s and its various cultural contexts.

Jenkins, Bruce. "Explosion in a Film Factory: The Cinema of Bruce Conner." *2000 BC: The Bruce Conner Story Part II*. Minneapolis: Walker Art Center, 1999. 184–223. Background and analysis of the films; includes many frame enlargements, some in color.

MacDonald, Scott. *A Critical Cinema: Interviews with Independent Filmmakers*. Berkeley: U of California P, 1988. Introductory essay followed by a short essay on the life and films of each of seventeen experimental filmmakers and an interview with each.

———. *A Critical Cinema 2: Interviews with Independent Filmmakers*. Berkeley: U of California P, 1992. Fifteen more interviews plus three interviews each focusing on a film.

———. *A Critical Cinema 3: Interviews with Independent Filmmakers*. Berkeley: U of California P, 1997. Includes an overview for each interviewee, interviews with experimental filmmakers from many nations, film/videographies, and bibliographies.

———. *Screen Writings: Scripts and Texts by Independent Filmmakers*. Berkeley: U of California P, 1995. Includes introduction and a script for or a partial description of a wide variety of experimental films. Also includes nearly a hundred stills, most of them frame enlargements; distribution sources; and a bibliography.

O'Pray, Michael. *Avant-Garde Film: Forms, Themes, and Passions*. London: Wallflower Press, 2003. A 144-page general introduction and history for the student.

Rees, A. L. *A History of Experimental Film and Video*. London: British Film Institute, 1999. A history of avant-garde film and video ranging from Cézanne and Dada, via Cocteau, Brakhage, and Le Grice, to the new wave of British video artists in the 1990s.

Rothman, William. *Documentary Film Classics*. Cambridge: Cambridge UP, 1997. Detailed analyses, supported with many frame enlargements, of some major documentary films, such as *Nanook of the North*, *Chronicle of a Summer*, and *Don't Look Back*.

Wells, Paul. *Understanding Animation*. New York: Routledge, 1998. Includes history and theory. Discusses such issues as representations of race and gender, "Disneyesque hyper-realism," and animation and audience research.

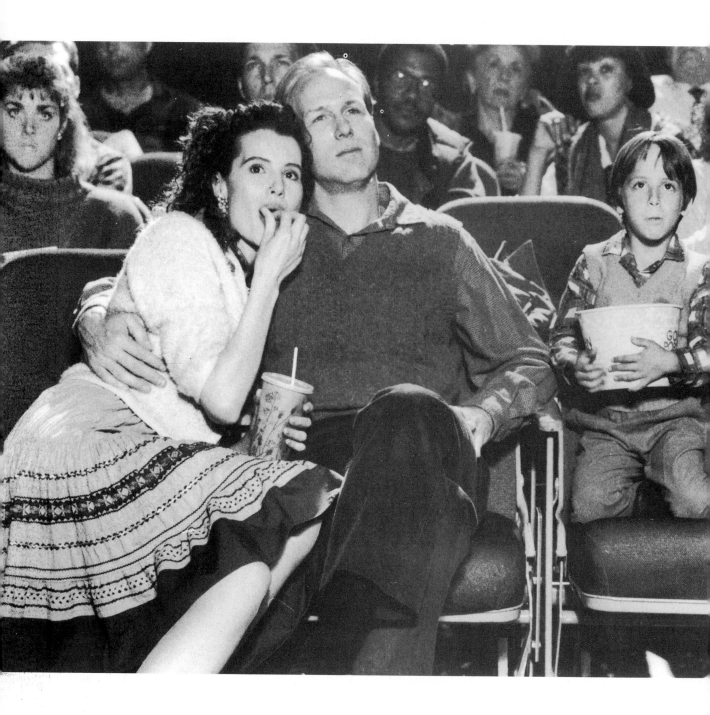

Part Four
UNDERSTANDING FILMS

W E HAVE CONSIDERED the impact of various filmmaking techniques, the sources and other aspects of the fictional film, and the variety of films. Part Four considers some of the ways viewers can come to understand a film. In Chapter 9, we examine how knowledge of a film's contexts helps viewers understand a film more completely. Where and how a film is made, where it is seen, and who sees it all influence filmmakers and in turn their films and viewer responses to the films. Chapter 10 considers some of the many complex ways viewers think about a film. For example, as viewers see a film, they form expectations and hypotheses and readjust them as the film progresses. As viewers see a film and as they think about it afterward, they also usually try to make general sense of it—to figure out some of its meanings. Viewers are sometimes told some meanings by the film itself, and they often make meanings in various ways, including explaining the general implications of the story or the significance of a symbol. Chapter 10 examines these and other issues, including some of the ways the formulations of meanings are influenced by the viewer's background and other circumstances.

◄ If a film succeeds in capturing the viewers' interest, viewers react emotionally and mentally, including formulating and reformulating expectations and figuring out some of the film's general significance or meanings. As illustrated here in a scene from *The Accidental Tourist* (1988), usually film viewing is also communal. *Warner Bros.*

CHAPTER 9

Understanding Films
through Contexts

CONTEXT IS WHAT PEOPLE USE to make sense of new information. An unfamiliar word can make sense in a sentence. An unfamiliar place can have meaning on a map. An isolated event can be significant in the context of history. Context turns information into knowledge. It's the difference between a warehouse and a museum. (Herz 1999)

Terms in **boldface** are defined in the Illustrated Glossary beginning on page 621.

We have all heard of people who were upset that their statements were "taken out of context" and thus their meaning distorted and misunderstood. Conversely, any statement examined in its contexts is more likely to be understood. As this chapter illustrates, knowledge of the conditions that precede and surround the making of a film, of the film version seen, and of the conditions under which the film is viewed—its contexts—helps viewers understand a film more completely. The influences can be schematized as follows:

contexts in which a film is made → filmmakers → film → viewer responses

film version seen → viewer responses

contexts in which a film is seen → filmmakers → film → viewer responses

There are so many possible contexts for a film that it would take a sizable book to begin to explore them fully. The first part of this chapter—contexts in which a film has been made—introduces five types of contexts: society and politics, censorship, artistic conventions, financial constraints, and technological developments. Generally, these contexts are presented from the most abstract to the most concrete—from ideas, such as societal attitudes, to practical realities, such as money and filmmaking equipment. The second part of the chapter—the film version seen—explores the ways in which a film may be available in different versions. The third part of the chapter—contexts in which a film has been seen—describes how viewing environment and audience can influence filmmakers, the films they make, and viewer responses to the films.

CONTEXTS IN WHICH A FILM HAS BEEN MADE

A film does not begin when the house lights dim and the projector begins to send dancing lights through the darkness or when we turn on the TV and pop a disc into the DVD player. What has happened before a film was made and sometimes what is going on while the film is being made influence how the finished film begins, how it all unwinds, and eventually how viewers respond to it.

Let's consider three examples of how knowledge of the contexts of a film's making can help the viewer better understand the film. Before you are shown a 1920s Soviet film in a course or a film series, someone may stand before the audience and explain the political climate in the Soviet Union at the time the film was made. As a result, when you watch the film, you understand why it focuses not on a few individuals but on large groups. Imagine that before you see *Fatal Attraction*, you learn that shortly before the film appeared in 1987, the AIDS epidemic had led to mass media warnings about the dangers of unprotected sex. You also learn that in the 1980s, growing numbers of American men felt threatened by successful, financially independent, career-minded, sexually active single women. When you see *Fatal Attraction*, you notice that the film shows horrible consequences after a married man has unprotected sex with a single career woman, and you notice that the movie's career woman is shown unsympathetically. You now understand how societal attitudes at the time of the film's making can influence its content. Finally, imagine that you see *The World of Apu*, a 1958 film from India, and think it curious that the young married couple never kiss,

FIGURE 9.1 Showing affection in a 1950s film from India
Kissing was not allowed in Indian films in the 1950s, so loving feelings had to be conveyed in other ways. About 54½ minutes into *The World of Apu* (1958) a new wife gives her husband a look that blends love and concern. Frame enlargement. *Satyajit Ray; Edward Harrison*

though they are clearly in love. Later you learn that censorship regulations for Indian films of that time prohibited kissing, so the couple's affection had to be conveyed by other means (Figure 9.1). In these and countless other situations, knowing something about when and under what conditions a film was made helps viewers better understand the film.

Both filmmakers and film exhibitors often consider how much of a film's context their audiences are likely to know. Most filmmakers assume that audiences know something about the context of the film's story. If audiences may not, filmmakers often include background information in the film itself. **Title cards** give tidbits of historical information throughout *Schindler's List* (1993). The opening two title cards in *Das Boot*, or *The Boat* (1981, 1997), inform viewers that "the battle for control of the Atlantic is turning against the Germans" as the story begins in the autumn of 1941 and that of the 40,000 German sailors who "served on U-boats during World War II, 30,000 never returned." Television channels that focus on old movies, such as Turner Classic Movies, also usually include a brief introduction to each film explaining at least a little of the film's contexts.

title card: A card or thin sheet of clear plastic on which is written or printed information included in a film.

Once viewers understand that filmmakers work under forces that restrict how they can represent political, religious, or sexual subjects, viewers are less likely to misjudge how a film represents these three subjects. Viewers who know when and where a film was made and under what conditions are also more likely to notice when filmmakers follow conventions and when they depart from them. They are more likely to understand how the film's budget precludes certain options and how the available filmmaking technology and the audio and visual presentations of competing media and electronic entertainments may influence the film.

Society and Politics and Representations

There are always limits to what filmmakers can show and how they show it. Various forces help determine the choice of subjects and then the scope, depth, and manner in which the subjects are shown. Two such powerful influences on how texts represent their subjects are social and political attitudes. For many years now, various film scholars have studied the **representation** of a recurring subject in movies—such as gender roles, sex, social class, ethnic group, race, religion, and national identity—to better understand what those re-presentations reveal about the filmmakers' beliefs and values and those of their society. Consequently, as some of the entries in the For Further Reading section of this chapter illustrate, there are many books on the cinematic representations of Native Americans, African Americans, Asians and Asian Americans, Arabs, women, gays, and many other groups. Studies of representation may be about subjects in mainstream cinema or about **independent films** and **experimental films**, where representations are more likely to be less traditional and more individualistic.

representation: A likeness of a subject created in a text.

independent film: Film made without support or input from the dominant, established film industry.

experimental film: A film that rejects the conventions of mainstream movies and explores the possibilities of the film medium.

FIGURE 9.2 Advertising for a 1940s movie that hints at a character's homosexuality
This photo approximates a few brief images from 24 minutes 25 seconds into *The Maltese Falcon* (1941) and hints at the Peter Lorre character's homosexuality—the umbrella handle near his mouth—the explicit representation or mention of which was forbidden by the U.S. production code then in effect. *Hal B. Wallis; Warner Bros.–First National*

REPRESENTATIONS OF HOMOSEXUALITY IN FILM

Societal attitudes may exert powerful influences on filmmakers, especially those who hope their films are seen by large audiences. For example, dominant attitudes about homosexuality influence whether, when, and how homosexuals are represented in films. Because so many people disapproved of homosexuality from the birth of cinema in the 1890s until the production code was more stringently enforced beginning in 1934, gay characters in American movies were nearly always represented as laughable. After the production code placed restrictions on filmmakers (see the feature on pp. 430–32), from 1934 into the 1960s homosexual characters were seldom identified openly. In *The Maltese Falcon* (1941), for example, several characters are homosexual though the film does not make their homosexuality explicit (Figure 9.2). *Rebel without a Cause* (1955), *Tea and Sympathy* (1956), *Cat on a Hot Tin Roof* (1958), *Suddenly Last Summer* (1959), and many other American films of the production code era refer to homosexuality only obliquely.

As attitudes in Western societies have changed, so has the representation of gays in films. In his book *The Celluloid Closet: Homosexuality in the Movies*, Vito Russo says that the first positive images of gays in commercial cinema appear in two 1961 British movies, *A Taste of Honey* and *Victim* (126–33). In *A Taste of Honey*, a sensitive homosexual friend cares for the main character, an unwed pregnant teenager. In *Victim*, a British movie star, Dirk Bogarde, plays a man who admits to his desire for another man; some of the film's "character portrayals are relatively sympathetic, given the era and social climate in which the film was made" (Jones 321–22).

After the U.S. film industry abandoned the production code and instituted a rating system in 1968, more adult subjects, including homosexuality, began to appear on movie screens. *The Boys in the Band* (1970), which was originally a 1968 Mart Crowley off-Broadway play, was the first American commercial movie featuring a cast of gay characters (Figure 9.3). Probably because the film and play are products of the 1960s and their audiences included many straight people, the film does a lot of explaining. For example, it explains how a married man (Hank) could finally realize that he was more gay than straight. The film also shows that gay people wrestle with many of the same issues as straight people. Larry and Hank, for example, quarrel about fidelity: Larry wants the right to have an occasional fling, whereas his lover, Hank, wants them both to be monogamous. Although the play and the film

FIGURE 9.3 Various aspects of 1960s gay life
The Boys in the Band (1970) focuses on eight gay or bisexual male characters and one heterosexual male character who may have tried homosexuality while in college. The film was the first widely distributed U.S. movie featuring gays and shows a wide range of gay behavior, much of it stereotypical and negative but some of it playful, silly, funny, and fun as in the dancing seen here early in the evening of a birthday party, before the outdoor and indoor storms begin. Frame enlargement. *A Leo Productions, Ltd. Production; National General Pictures*

a)

b)

FIGURE 9.4 Mainstream film with star playing a bisexual
In *Dog Day Afternoon* (1975), Al Pacino, fresh from his critical and popular successes in the first two *Godfather* films, plays Sonny, a bisexual who is married and has two children but has undertaken a concurrent marriage to his "darling wife, Leon." Here, about 115 minutes into the film, Sonny—who viewers eventually learn attempted to rob the bank to finance Leon's sex change operation—is seen having a long talk with Leon (a). As the lover Leon, who feels as if he is a woman trapped in a man's body and whose intimate relationship with Sonny has resulted in a storm of dangerous, conflicting emotions, Chris Sarandon won an Oscar nomination as best supporting actor (b). Frame enlargements. *Warner Bros.*

were initially seen as groundbreaking, with the beginning of the gay liberation movement in the late 1960s, many gays disavowed them as dated; they also criticized them for highlighting negative images of gays: characters that are often catty, venomously witty, self-involved, self-loathing, and alcohol and drug dependent. In recent years, however, some critics see the play and film as largely accurate representations of American gay life in the pre-gay-lib times of enforced secrecy and repression. In *Dog Day Afternoon* (1975), Al Pacino was perhaps the first major movie star who had played only heterosexual characters to act the role of a bisexual, and he did so credibly and without inviting ridicule or condescension. The film also includes a persuasive performance by Chris Sarandon as the Pacino character's lover (Figure 9.4).

Even with the coming of the ratings system, more than a few movies trod well-worn paths and showed gays as miserable, depressed, suicidal, danger-

FIGURE 9.5 Tolerance of sexual and gender preferences
The Crying Game (1992)—featuring an Irish Republican Army volunteer (left) and a hairdresser who is a transgenderist—questions whether sexual and gender preferences are the only considerations in a close relationship. The film, which was a critical and popular success, treats its complex characters sympathetically in ways inconceivable in earlier eras. *Palace; Channel 4; Miramax*

FIGURE 9.6 Stereotypical yet complex and sympathetic gay character
The Cuban film *Strawberry and Chocolate* (1993) can be seen as mainly the story of a growing friendship in spite of the two men's many fundamental differences. Here, the two are seen approximately 45½ minutes into the film. The main character, Diego (left) is a gay photographer who is religious and critical of Cuban governmental policies. The other main character, named David (right), is a heterosexual though initially virginal university student from an impoverished village background who is not religious and basically supports the Castro government. Gradually, Diego teaches David a greater awareness of the power of the arts and increases his tolerance toward those who have been labeled as different. The film devotes much time to Diego's homosexuality, though since the film is a product of 1990s Cuba, no homosexual contact is shown. Often the actor playing Diego plays the part broadly and amusingly, with a full range of belongings, dress, tastes, gestures, and manners thought typical of gays. But because of some details in the script and the often nuanced performance of the main actor, Diego can be subtle, amusing, engaging, complicated, and sympathetic. Furthermore, he is articulate, intelligent, talented, and brave in speaking out for more tolerance and artistic diversity in Cuba, yet proudly Cuban as well. Frame enlargement. *Cuban Institute of the Arts and Film Industry; Robert Redford and Miramax Films*

ous, or laughable. In *la cage aux folles* (1978), its sequels, and its remake as *The Birdcage* (1996), gay characters have pivotal roles, though they and the situations they end up in are **stereotypical**, amusing, and nonthreatening to heterosexual audiences. In many other films since the 1960s, however, gay characters are seen in less stereotypical, more complex roles, as in *Longtime Companion* (1990) and *Philadelphia* (1993). The huge commercial success of *The Crying Game* (1992) was a barometer of changing social tolerance in matters of gender and sexual orientation (Figure 9.5). From then on, films with credible gay characters became commonplace in American cinema, and even societies that have attempted mightily to repress homosexuality, such as Castro's Cuba, brought forth an occasional film sympathetic to gays (Figure 9.6).

stereotype A commonplace, simplified, and in some ways inaccurate representation (likeness of a subject created in a text).

REPRESENTATIONS OF AFRICAN AMERICANS IN FILM

For years, film scholars have studied celluloid representations of various races and ethnic groups. Race and ethnicity are complex subjects. Indeed there is much disagreement about what constitutes a "race," and many think that race is only an evolving social construct of no scientific validity. I have space to introduce the subjects only briefly, so I restrict the following discussion to a few observations about U.S. movies that include African Americans and movies that include Latin Americans or Latinos.

In early "silent" films, the parts of Africans and African Americans (and Native Americans) were usually acted by European Americans, who often wore crude makeup. In keeping with widespread beliefs in European American society of the time, African Americans were usually represented as simple-minded and faithful slaves or servants or as lazy, corrupt, or lecherous. All these stereotypes are displayed in the 1915 classic *The Birth of a Nation*. During the following decades, these negative stereotypes endured in U.S. movies. They were also perpetuated in minstrel shows: live variety shows of songs, dances, jokes, and skits, usually performed by white actors in blackface (for some vivid examples of minstrel shows, see Spike Lee's 2000 film *Bamboozled*, Figure 10.11 on p. 483). And these stereotypes were kept alive in various stereotypical objects, including bric-a-brac (also prominent in *Bamboozled*) and lawn ornaments.

Studies show that in earlier eras, as now, American blacks were avid movie-goers. After *The Birth of a Nation* and until the late 1940s, some low-budget films were made by American blacks, most notably Oscar Micheaux, who were frustrated because they could rarely see recognizable let alone positive images of themselves on the big screens. Most of these films were shown in (mainly big city) movie theaters catering to black audiences or late at night in theaters catering to white audiences.

From the beginning of U.S. cinema until recent years, mainstream movies rarely showed African American life outside crime-infested big-city ghettoes. *Nothing but a Man* (1964) credibly shows an African American man

FIGURE 9.7 **Credible representation of some African American lives**
Nothing but a Man (1964) has been much praised for the two main characters' humanity and dignity and for the film's credible, restrained representation of its volatile subjects. *DuArt; New Video Group, New York City*

event: In a narrative or story, either an *action* by a character or person or a *happening* (a change brought about by a force other than a person or character).

blaxploitation (film): A U.S. film movement from 1971 to 1975 or 1976 consisting of low-budget movies usually made by African American filmmakers, with black characters for black audiences.

in the 1960s South trying to get and hold a job that allows him some dignity, marrying outside his class, attempting to relate to an aloof father, trying to decide whether to take responsibility for a boy who may be his son, and coping with prejudice against African Americans (Figure 9.7). Other noteworthy exceptions are Spike Lee's *She's Gotta Have It* (1986), which is about an attractive independent woman and her three competing lovers, and *Do the Right Thing* (1989), which is set in a recognizable city neighborhood and shows believable characters and **events** (see Figures 1.48 and 1.57 on pp. 47 and 52).

Sweet Sweetback's Baad Asssss Song (1971)—which was "dedicated to all the Brothers and Sisters who had enough of the Man" and is considered to be the first of the so-called **blaxploitation** movies—focuses on police brutality against the Los Angeles African American community and exalts the sexual potency and the resilience of an African American male. The film spoke to black frustrations, determination, and pride and proved wildly popular with black audiences. Other blaxploitation movies—*Shaft* (the original, 1971 version) and perhaps 200 more films for, (largely) by, and about American blacks during the following few years—along with many U.S. movies of the 1980s and 1990s featuring African American characters, such as *Boyz N the Hood* (1991) and *New Jack City* (1991), mainly show American blacks caught up in violent crime in inner cities.

For various reasons, probably including more and more American whites' halting but gradual acceptance of American blacks into the mainstream, in recent years, a wider range of black people (in documentaries such as Marlon T. Riggs's 1995 film *Black is . . . Black ain't*) and credible black (mostly male) characters (in fictional films) have been seen more often on the big screen. As the film critic A. O. Scott has observed,

For many years, . . . the movies have largely treated black people as . . . clowns and criminals and as agents for the moral advancement of white people. . . . But there have been, in the past few years, a steady stream of movies . . . that decline to view black life primarily as a set of social problems to be addressed, or to assume that the most important thing about black people is how white people perceive them. A string of successful romantic comedies . . . have followed in the tradition of [Spike Lee's] *She's Gotta Have It*, addressing the complicated love lives of ambitious African-American professionals. . . . Also evident in . . . movies [such as two 2002 films, *Barbershop* and *Drumline*] . . . whose main characters arise from a blue-collar, urban milieu is an unsentimental and affectionate sense of community and tradition, . . . individual pluck and discipline, . . . and an ideal of excellence and commitment passed on from one generation to the next.

REPRESENTATIONS OF LATIN AMERICANS AND LATINOS IN FILM

Various film scholars—such as Rosa Linda Fregoso, Charles Ramírez Berg, and Chon Noriega—and some **documentary films**—most prominently *The Bronze Screen: 100 Years of the Latino Image in Hollywood* (2002)—have explored the representations of Latin Americans and Latinos in American movies.[1] A brief history of the representation of Latinos in U.S. films reveals similarities to the history of the representation of African Americans in U.S. movies.

documentary film: A film or video representation of actual (not imaginary) subjects.

Early celluloid Latinos and Latin Americans were usually minor roles or negative role models. In the earliest U.S. movies, for example, the Mexican man was, as the writers of *The Bronze Screen* term him, "Hollywood's First Bad Guy." In countless westerns, Mexican American and Mexican males were portrayed (sometimes by European American actors) as crude, ignorant, lazy, and vicious (Figure 9.8). To advance their acting careers, some Latinas—such as Dolores Del Rio, Rita Hayworth (see Figure 7.15 on p. 304), and Raquel Welch—dyed their hair a lighter color. Others—including Rita Hayworth, who was originally named Margarita Cansino—changed their names. Countless minor Latino and Latin American roles and even some major ones were mainly stereotypes, such as the hot-blooded Latin male lover, the immoral woman, the lazy and ignorant Mexican, and the "greaser" (an insulting term for a Latin American, especially a lower class Mexican). The reasons for these pervasive simplified and mostly demeaning cinematic representations may be partially understood in context. "In the United States, especially in the Southwest, Manifest Destiny meant taking

---

[1]*Latin American* usually stands for a citizen of the Spanish Caribbean, Mexico, or a country in Central or South America. *Latino* signifies people of Latin American descent—such as Puerto Ricans, Guatemalans, and Peruvians—living in the United States. And *Chicano*, as Charles Ramírez Berg explains, "is a term made popular by the Mexican American civil rights movement in the 1960s and 1970s; as an ethnic self-identifying label, it implied pride as well as activism and oppositional politics. . . . Our children, however, tend to prefer the term 'Mexican American'" (6).

FIGURE 9.8 Stereotypical representation of Mexicans in a U.S. movie
Much of the story of *The Wild Bunch* (1969) is set in Mexico, which the film sometimes represents as stereotypically idyllic: both the worry-free village of nurture, comfort, and pleasure and the army camp with its abundance of women who are all young, beautiful, and available. At other times, the film represents Mexico as stereotypically hellish: the army men of all ranks are crass and cruel. For example, as a form of celebration for the soldiers, their girlfriends, and boys, the man seen here, a loyal member of the wild bunch, has been dragged face down in the dust on a rope pulled by a car as the men and women drink whiskey, smile, and laugh. *Phil Feldman; Warner Bros.*

land from Mexico, displacing Mexican landowners, subjugating . . . Texans, New Mexicans, and Californians of Mexican heritage . . . , and exploiting them as cheap and expendable labor. In order to rationalize the expansionist goals . . . , Latinos [and Latin Americans] . . . needed to be shown as lesser beings. Movie stereotyping of Latinos [and Latin Americans], therefore, has been and continues to be part of an American imperialistic discourse about who should rule the hemisphere" (Berg 4–5).

As is the case with representations of African Americans in movies, in recent years a wider range of believable Latino and Latin American characters have been appearing in movies, though this is more true of males than females. More films about Latinos, such as *Real Women Have Curves* (2002), are being made by Latinos. And now a number of the most prominent stars—such as Jennifer Lopez, Salma Hayek, Antonio Banderas, and Benicio del Toro—are Latino/a. Nonetheless, from time to time, studies point out that the percentages of Latinos in mainstream movies and TV are still disproportionately low.

As we have seen, where and when a film was made (and by whom) strongly influences whether gays, African Americans, and Latinos and Latin Americans are included at all and, if they are, how they are represented. As studies by other film scholars cited in the For Further Reading at the end of this chapter demonstrate, the same is true of representations in mainstream movies of other minority groups, such as American Indians, Asians and Asian Americans, and Arabs and Arab Americans.

As times change, so do representations of subjects, including stories that continue to speak to audiences and so get made and remade and remade. Consider the **celluloid** Tarzan, whose characters, story, and concerns vary according to time and place of production (Figure 9.9).

Political developments—especially as reported in the mass media—influence what topics people are concerned about and how they think about them. In turn, political concerns affect the choice of subjects represented in many forms of human expression, including films.

celluloid: Synonym for *movie,* as in "celluloid heroes."

Consider the situation in the United States shortly after the end of World War II, with the Soviet Union's rise in power. With heavy media coverage of those political developments, many Americans began to worry about Communist infiltration of American institutions. As part of its activities, in 1947 the House Committee on Un-American Activities (HUAC, as the committee was often imprecisely called) held hearings in Hollywood to investigate Communist infiltration of the film industry. Some filmmakers— either from the conviction that the committee's actions infringed on their constitutional rights or because they had been Communist Party members (or both)—refused to cooperate with the committee. Ten filmmakers, mostly screenwriters, dubbed the "Hollywood Ten," were eventually sentenced to prison for contempt of Congress. In 1951, HUAC held a second round of hearings on Communist influence in Hollywood, and more than three hundred Hollywood filmmakers either confessed to past membership in the Communist Party or were accused by witnesses of having been members. Until well into the 1960s, most of those people were blacklisted and could not find work in the American film industry.[2]

The atmosphere of fear and distrust caused enormous upheaval in the industry. Some filmmakers found other work; some moved abroad to find film work; others worked in the American film industry under assumed names. Freedom of expression was curtailed for all who worked in the film industry at the time, not just for those who were accused of being Communists. Filmmakers shied away from controversial projects, especially those with political subjects. Some films commented indirectly on the political climate of the time. For example, some observers see parallels between those who refused to cooperate with HUAC and the town marshal in the western *High Noon* (1952); both acted on their principles and refused to give in to intimidating forces. Some critics see parallels between *The Invasion of the Body Snatchers* (1956) and its times. The film shows a cautionary story about the gradual, unobtrusive invasion of alien life forms that take on the appearance of people but not their emotions and then replace the people. To some critics, the film is symptomatic of the menace and passivity of the era.

In every period, political climate influences the choice and representation of subjects. Another example is seen during the cold war period, from the late 1940s to the 1980s. Such American movies as *Red Dawn* (1984),

---

[2]Professor Jon Lewis argues that the blacklist was less a result of ideology and more a consequence of economic forces: "The blacklist was a first step in a larger transformation of the film industry from its roots in entrepreneurial capital to a more corporatist, conglomerate mode. . . . [The blacklist] encouraged studio owners to develop and adopt a corporate model more suited to a future new Hollywood" (5).

FIGURE 9.9 Different societies, different Tarzans

(a) American Edgar Rice Burrough's novel *Tarzan of the Apes* (1912) was first adapted, in most of its essentials, into an American film of the same title six years later. The first Tarzan movie is set in what for 1918 American audiences must have been exotic locales and features plenty of action, including attacks by a variety of wild animals. *Tarzan of the Apes* stars a boy playing Tarzan at a youthful age and the portly Elmo Lincoln as the strong but not particularly graceful adult Tarzan, who never swings through trees—perhaps for fear of cracking tree branches. Typical of the film's racial insensitivity is the title card stating that before Jane, Tarzan had never seen a woman, although earlier in the film viewers saw him looking at African women. The film consistently shows that Tarzan is much more at home with apes than with native Africans and reflects the fear and distrust so many European Americans of the time felt about people with dark skins. (b) *Tarzan: The Ape Man* (1932) stars former Olympic swimming champion Johnny Weissmuller and Maureen O'Sullivan. This *Tarzan* gives no explanation how Tarzan happened to be living in the jungle with wild animals. The film can be seen as Depression-era escapist fare featuring exotic locales, lots of action, condescending stereotypes of Africa and Africans aplenty, a love triangle of two men pursuing the same woman, a crowd-pleasing resolution, and little interest in such issues as race, colonialism, and identity.

(c) *Greystoke: The Legend of Tarzan, Lord of the Apes* (1984) was an international though largely British production. The story alternates between western Africa and Scotland, as it focuses on the loneliness and loss of being caught between two worlds, two families: "lord of the apes" and earl of Greystoke. The film also shows the artifice and shortcomings of civilized society, and "civilized" man's exploitation of the African environment and callous treatment of its wildlife. As Kenneth M. Cameron writes, the film was "heavily weighted . . . toward environmental concern—the Green Party version of Tarzan— . . . [and] examined the great apes, particularly, in far more detail and with far more sympathy than other Tarzan pictures" (166).

(d) Disney's *Tarzan* (1999) is curiously void of Africans and, as so many Disney films do, exalts the glories of nature and the worth of an outsider. Here a handsome, athletic Tarzan moves through trees as youths do when they surf or skateboard. Like the 1984 *Greystoke*, Disney's *Tarzan* also shows "civilized" men's cruelty and their callous and exploitative treatment of animals. The film also deals with such subjects as the outsider, family, assimilation, and identity—issues generally of more concern to the late twentieth century than to early in the century when Tarzan came to light. Unlike *Greystoke* but in keeping with the Disney tradition, the film is often amusing and concludes with romantic love triumphant. (a) *The Museum of Modern Art/Film Stills Archive; (b) Bernard H. Hyman; MGM; (c) Hugh Hudson and Stanley S. Canter; Warner Bros.; (d) Frame enlargement. Bonnie Arnold and Christopher Chase; Walt Disney Pictures*

which shows Soviets and Cubans invading a small Colorado town, and *Rambo: First Blood Part II* (1985) depict Soviets as untrustworthy and treacherous. *Rocky IV* (1985) also reflects the political mood of the times through two boxing matches between representatives of the Soviet Union and the United States, and it is unsurprising which political system the movie cham-

pions (Figure 9.10). *Rocky IV* and other cold war–era movies exalt Americans and encourage nationalism while denigrating Soviets and the Soviet system. In contrast, since the breakup of the Soviet Union in 1992 and the increased cooperation between Russia and the United States in the 1990s and beyond, few such anti-Russian American movies have been forthcoming.

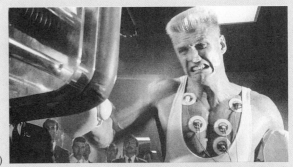

a)   b)

FIGURE 9.10 The cold war in a boxing ring

Rocky IV (1985) culminates in a boxing match between Rocky and his Goliath Soviet opponent, Ivan Drago. It's not giving away a surprise ending to reveal that Rocky prevails. He does so for a combination of reasons. In part, Rocky wins because *Rocky IV* is an American movie made during the cold war. Although the film is draped in national flags and the last image before the ending credits is of Rocky with a U.S. flag above him, Rocky's victory is also a victory for the old ways of doing things. (a) Rocky trains in nature with nature's objects (rocks, mountains, snow, logs) and simple country tools (sled, ax, block and tackle, rope, yoke, cart, and saw). (b) Drago uses all the most advanced computerized exercise equipment and is injected with drugs. Here he is being measured for the force of his punch and his bodily functions, such as the performance of his heart. Rocky is advised by a trainer with years of experience with professional boxing. Drago is trained by a cadre of state-employed scientists and a trainer with no professional experience in boxing. Other factors contribute to Rocky's victory. He keeps getting back up and going at Drago, and he is not burdened by arrogance. He also prays and he fights for others, including his late friend Apollo Creed. By the twelfth round, even the initially hostile Soviet crowd begins chanting "Rocky!" "Rocky!" "Rocky!" Of course, Rocky has earned the loving support of his wife and young son. (Are there any emotional buttons this film does not push?) Before the final round, a Soviet official berates Drago, who announces that he fights to win—for himself. Drago is then alone and on the doorstep of defeat. Frame enlargements. *Robert Chartoff and Irwin Winkler; United Artists*

Censorship

Censorship is closely related to societal attitudes and political climate. From the beginning of cinema, some people have been concerned about the possible harm inflicted on *others* who see certain behavior, especially sex and violence, or who are exposed to certain ideas, particularly religious and political ones. Different societies address these concerns in different ways.

Some societies forbid the making of certain films. Iranian movies, most of which are funded by the government, forbid criticism of the Iranian Islamic government and all religions. In Iranian films women must be shown in headscarf and long coat. Forbidden are **close-ups** of women, makeup, kissing, handholding, and eye contact between men and women. To ensure

close-up: An image in which the subject fills most of the frame and little of the surroundings is shown.

compliance with these and other guidelines, the government imposes multiple stages of censorship, beginning with the approval of the script.

In Vietnam, a censor is always present during filming, as one was during the filming of *Three Seasons* (1999). If the censor sees or hears anything questionable, the filmmakers must make changes on the spot or come to an agreement with the official. In China, filmmakers are not supposed to make sexy films, films that criticize the government explicitly or implicitly, or depressing films with sad endings. If filmmakers shoot their film without first getting the script approved and a permit, they face the likelihood of a stiff fine and exclusion from the large Chinese market. *Xiu Xiu: The Sent Down Girl* (1998), which Joan Chen filmed on the sly in a remote Western Chinese province, is a film suffering this fate, as is the more widely seen *Farewell My Concubine* (1993). Chinese control over movies is far reaching. *Postman* (1995)—which is not to be confused with the Italian film *Il Postino (The Postman)* of the same year or Kevin Costner's *The Postman* (1997)—touches on adultery, prostitution, homosexuality, and drug use. Even before its completion, its director was banned from making further films.

Sometimes government authorities may halt a production, as was the fate of the Soviet filmmaker Sergei Eisenstein, who was forced both to abandon *Bezhin Meadow* in 1937 and to repudiate it publicly. Eisenstein ran into trouble with *Bezhin Meadow* and most of his later films because he did not follow the general guidelines of **socialist realism**. This Soviet doctrine and **style**, which was in force from the mid-1930s to the 1980s (until the Gorbachev era), decreed that all creative works—including music, artworks, and films—must promote socialism, Communism, and thus the proletariat or working people. Soviet creative works were not to imply approval of Western ideas and lifestyles or even ambivalence toward them. Under socialist realism, creative works were supposed to be "realistic" (actually an idealized representation of the working class) and readily accessible to mass audiences. Styles judged innovative or arty were taboo. Works that were judged to fall short of the standards of socialist realism were labeled "decadent," "bourgeois," "capitalistic," or "formalist," and at times in the 1930s and 1940s the Soviet dictator Stalin himself made that judgment. At a minimum their makers were publicly rebuked; some met other, more painful fates. For fifty years socialist realism severely restricted the subjects and styles of Soviet artists, not just such filmmakers as Sergei Eisenstein and Lev Kuleshov but also the composers Dmitri Shostakovich and Sergei Prokofiev, writer Isaac Babel, theater director Vsevolod Meyerhold, and many others. Unlike the United States, the Soviet Union (and many other countries) censored its own films because of their unflattering representation of the country.

In the United States, early films were sometimes censored by state or city boards (Figure 9.11). By the early 1930s, many American viewers found many popular American movies offensive. Whereas some viewers seemed especially upset by violence and sex, others swarmed to such popular gangster films as

a)

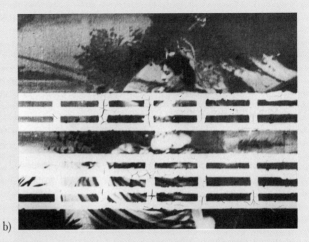

b)

FIGURE 9.11 Early, local censorship
(a) An 1897 American film, "Fatima's Dance," shows a woman dancing provocatively (shimmying and bumping), at least by the standards of the day. (b) Some exhibitors showed a censored version of "Fatima's Dance" with scratched emulsion obscuring much of her body. Frame enlargements. *The Museum of Modern Art/Film Stills Archive*

FIGURE 9.12 Mae West's sexuality in pre–production code movies
In *I'm No Angel* (1933)—which was written by Mae West and included a youthful Cary Grant (seen here)—West wears her usual variety of revealing and often glamorous clothes. She plays a single woman who is quick-witted, resourceful, confident, attractive to many men, and nearly always fully in control of situations with men. Although she is skimpy with her displays of affection and usually turns away from the men's attempted embraces and kisses, she often looks at men directly (not obliquely), wears tight and revealing clothing, and sings suggestively as she gently sways her hips. Even today, the Mae West characters are sometimes still quoted for such well-timed witty double entendres as, "When I'm good, I'm very good, but when I'm bad, I'm better." By today's standards, the Mae West characters in her early 1930s movies are campy and suggestive, even quaintly so, not carnal, and certainly not as one Hearst newspaper editorial of the time proclaimed a "menace to . . . the American Family." To many 1930s U.S. audiences, she was sexual, assertive, unrepentant, and shocking, and her movies have been blamed as partially responsible for stricter enforcement of the production code. *William LeBaron; Paramount*

Little Caesar (1930), *The Public Enemy* (1931), and *Scarface* (1932) and films featuring unrepentant, sexually assertive women, especially those played by Mae West (Figure 9.12). Of West's impact, scholar Ramona Curry writes:

> Unlike most other Hollywood movies of the 1930s, West's films do not suggest that morality or questions of taste dictate female sexual behavior. Instead, West's films and star image present female sexual allure as a commodity that women themselves can control and benefit from. . . . West's movie image exposed contradictions in the well-established American capitalist practice of simultaneously exploiting and repressing female sexuality as a commodity under men's control. (28)

Rather than face government interference, in 1930 American film producers and distributors set up a written production code, a self-regulatory system of acceptable speech and behavior in films (see the feature on pp. 430–32). In 1934, the code was revised and from then on more strenuously enforced. Until 1968, all movies to be shown in the United States were supposed to be submitted to the Production Code Administration for a seal of approval. The production code restricted the explicit or attractive representation of vast areas of human experience—such as illegal drugs, illicit sex, scenes of passion, prostitution, miscegenation, childbirth, and obscene and profane speech (Figure 9.13). From 1934 to 1968, to earn the seal of approval American films had to be suitable for audiences of all ages, including young children. Some of the differences between films made before and after the code was enforced are evident in stills for *Gold Diggers of 1933* and *Gold Diggers of 1937* (Figure 9.14).

Enforcement of the code often undermined a story's plausibility or logic, sometimes even resulting in incoherence. *The Big Sleep* (1946) is confusing because it omits nearly all references to the sex and drugs so prominent in the source novel by Raymond Chandler. As critic Frank Krutnik shows, enforcement of the code in a romantic scene involving the two main characters in *Out of the Past* (1947) created confusion:

FIGURE 9.13 A visualization of production code–era cinematic no-no's
Paramount Studio's Whitey Schafer photographed this 1940 staged photograph to illustrate subjects forbidden by the production code: a police officer killed, a gun pointing at someone, an automatic machine gun, the inside of a woman's thigh, lacey lingerie, a partially exposed breast, narcotics (the syringe on the table), alcoholic drinks, and gambling (note the clever prominence of the deadly ace of spades in the lower right-hand corner). *A. L. (Whitey) Schafer; Courtesy of The Academy of Motion Picture Arts and Sciences*

FIGURE 9.14 **Pre-1934 movies and post-1934 movies**
(a) From the "Pettin' in the Park" musical number in *Gold Diggers of 1933* (1933). After the production code was applied to all movies from 1934 until the 1960s, such glimpses of sexuality were forbidden in U.S. movies. (b) A few years after the production code was fully in effect, *Gold Diggers of 1937* (1936) represents men and women as innocent (dressed in white), childlike (small in comparison to the chairs), and unerotic (covered up and sitting, not partially uncovered and lying down as in the 1933 film). The language of *Gold Diggers of 1937* is also less suggestive than that of *Gold Diggers of 1933*, and in the later film, words such as "pettin'" or "petting" are nowhere to be heard.
(a) *Jack L. Warner; Warner Bros.;* (b) *Hal B. Wallis; Warner Bros.–First National*

a)

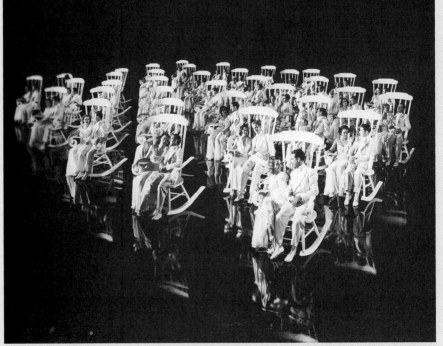

b)

The couple run through the rain to the beach-house, laughing like carefree young lovers. When they arrive there, Kathie dries his hair, and Jeff does the same for her. He kisses her on the back of the neck and then [about twenty-seven minutes into the film] tosses away the towel, which knocks the lamp over. When the light goes out, there is a swirl of music, and the camera then **tracks** towards the door, which blows open in the wind. There is then a cut to the outside, with the camera continuing its forward-tracking. This leading away from the scene, together with the reprisal of the film's love-theme and the dousing of the light, suggests that Jeff and Kathie are making love. However, the film cuts back to the inside of the beach-house: Jeff closes the door, and Kathie takes a record off the gramophone. There is a marked, seemingly post-coital change in their attitudes. However, although the slow forward-tracking of the camera has implied that intercourse takes place, the cut back to the inside, and the continuity of Jeff shutting the door after it has blown open, suggest that there has been no time-lapse. Sex is thus both firmly suggested and disavowed. (246)

track (verb): To film while the camera is being moved around.

The code is also responsible for more than one implausible ending, such as in *Detour* (1945). That film was initially refused a seal of approval because it ended with the main character, who had inadvertently killed someone, free and walking along a road. To gain a seal, a short scene was appended: the police drive up, stop, pick up the man, and drive off, as he narrates, "Someday a car will stop to pick me up that I never thumbed. Yes. Fate or some mysterious force can put the finger on you or me for no good reason at all." In this case, the not so "mysterious force" was the production code.

As more and more films were released without a seal in the 1950s and 1960s, it became harder and harder to enforce the code. As film historian and scholar Robert Sklar explains:

The tendency in motion-picture production and exhibition had always been to get away with as much risqué and socially disreputable behavior as the vigilance of censors would allow and economic necessity dictated. For nearly two decades after 1934, the Production Code Administration had maintained stringent control over Hollywood productions, and rising box-office figures through 1946 seemed to confirm that clean family entertainment was the road to prosperity. But as families found their clean entertainment on the TV screen, there was a natural impulse in the movie trade to revert to shock and titillation. (294)

In 1953, the American film *The Moon Is Blue* was refused a seal because it treated seduction and adultery comically, and its distributor, United Artists, resigned from the producers' association and released the film on its own without a seal. Later in the 1950s and in the 1960s, such European films as the French *And God Created Woman* (1956) were more candid sexually than American films and were shown without a seal of approval in art theaters in large cities throughout the United States (Figure 9.15).

Excerpts from *The Production Code of the Motion Picture Producers and Directors of America, Inc., 1930–1934**

PREAMBLE

Motion picture producers recognize the high trust and confidence which have been placed in them by the people of the world and which have made motion pictures a universal form of entertainment.

They recognize their responsibility to the public because of this trust and because entertainment and art are important influences in the life of a nation.

Hence, though regarding motion pictures primarily as entertainment without any explicit purpose of teaching or propaganda, they know that the motion picture within its own field of entertainment may be directly responsible for spiritual or moral progress, for higher types of social life, and for much correct thinking. . . .

On their part, they ask from the public and from public leaders a sympathetic understanding of their purposes and problems and a spirit of cooperation that will allow them the freedom and opportunity necessary to bring the motion picture to a still higher level of wholesome entertainment for all the people.

GENERAL PRINCIPLES

1. No picture shall be produced which will lower the moral standards of those who see it. Hence the sympathy of the audience shall never be thrown to the side of crime, wrongdoing, evil or sin.

2. Correct standards of life, subject only to the requirements of drama and entertainment, shall be presented. . . .

    I. CRIMES AGAINST THE LAW

    These shall never be presented in such a way as to throw sympathy with the crime as against law and justice or to inspire others with a desire for imitation.

    1. Murder
        a) The technique of murder must be presented in a way that will not inspire imitation.
        b) Brutal killings are not to be presented in detail.
        c) Revenge in modern times shall not be justified. . . .

    II. SEX

    The sanctity of the institution of marriage and the home shall be upheld. Pictures shall not infer that low forms of sex relationship are the accepted or common thing.

    1. Adultery and illicit sex, sometimes necessary plot material, must not be explicitly treated or justified, or presented attractively.

    2. Scenes of passion
        a) These should not be introduced except where they are definitely essential to the plot.
        b) Excessive and lustful kissing, lustful embraces, suggestive postures and gestures are not to be shown.
        c) In general, passion should be treated in such manner as not to stimulate the lower and baser emotions.

    3. Seduction or rape
        a) These should never be more than suggested, and then only when essential for the plot. They must never be shown by explicit method.
        b) They are never the proper subject for comedy.

*Approximately 40% of the Code is excerpted here.

430

4. Sex perversion or any inference to it is forbidden. . . .

6. Miscegenation (sex relationship between the white and black races) is forbidden. . . .

III. VULGARITY

The treatment of low, disgusting, unpleasant, though not necessarily evil, subjects should be guided always by the dictates of good taste and a proper regard for the sensibilities of the audience.

IV. OBSCENITY

Obscenity in word, gesture, reference, song, joke, or by suggestion . . . is forbidden.

V. PROFANITY

Pointed profanity and every other profane or vulgar expression, however used, is forbidden.

No approval by the Production Code Administration shall be given to the use of words and phrases in motion pictures including, but not limited to, the following: . . . broad (applied to a woman); . . . God, Lord, Jesus, Christ (unless used reverently); . . . fanny; fairy (in a vulgar sense); finger (the); . . . hot (applied to a woman); . . . louse; lousy; . . . nerts; nuts (except when meaning crazy); pansy; . . . slut (applied to a woman); S.O.B.; son-of-a; tart; . . . traveling salesman and farmer's daughter jokes; whore; damn. . . .

The Production Code Administration may take cognizance of the fact that the following words and phrases are obviously offensive to the patrons of motion pictures in the United States and more particularly to the patrons of motion pictures in foreign countries: Chink, Dago, Frog, Greaser, Hunkie, Kike, Nigger, Spig, Wop, Yid. . . .

VIII. RELIGION

1. No film or episode may throw ridicule on any religious faith.

2. Ministers of religion in their character as ministers of religion should not be used as comic characters or as villains. . . .

REASONS SUPPORTING PREAMBLE OF CODE

. . . The moral importance of entertainment is something which has been universally recognized. It enters intimately into the lives of men and women and affects them closely; it occupies their minds and affections during leisure hours; and ultimately touches the whole of their lives. A man may be judged by his standard of entertainment as easily as by the standard of his work. . . .

3.D. The latitude given to film material cannot, in consequence, be as wide as the latitude given to book material. In addition:

a) A book describes; a film vividly presents. One presents on a cold page; the other by apparently living people.

b) A book reaches the mind through words merely; a film reaches the eyes and ears through the reproduction of actual events.

c) The reaction of a reader to a book depends largely on the keenness of the reader's imagination; the reaction to a film depends on the vividness of presentation.

Hence many things which might be described or presented in a book could not possibly be presented in a film. . . .

F. Everything possible in a play is not possible in a film:

a) Because of the larger audience of the film, and its consequential mixed character. Psychologically, the larger the audience, the lower the moral mass resistance to suggestion.

b) Because through light, enlargement of character, presentation, scenic emphasis, etc., the screen story is brought closer to the audience than the play.

c) The enthusiasm for and interest in the film actors and actresses, developed beyond anything of the sort in history, makes the audience largely sympathetic toward the characters they portray and the stories in which they figure. Hence the audience is more ready to confuse actor and actress and the characters they portray, and it is most receptive of the emotions and ideals presented by their favorite stars.

G. Small communities, remote from sophistication and from the hardening process which often takes place in the ethical and moral standards of groups in larger cities, are easily and readily reached by any sort of film. . . .

In general, the mobility, popularity, accessibility, emotional appeal, vividness, straightforward presentation of fact in the film make for more intimate contact with a larger audience and for greater emotional appeal.

Hence the larger moral responsibilities of the motion pictures.

FIGURE 9.15 Sexual frankness in 1950s and 1960s European films
Some European films of the 1950s and 1960s were more candid in their representations of sexuality than American films of the time and were shown without the production code seal of approval in mostly big-city American theaters. Here, 19½ minutes into Ingmar Bergman's *The Silence* (1963), one of the two main characters is seen reacting as she masturbates, an act that is unmistakably suggested. Elsewhere, the other main character sees a couple having sexual intercourse in the back of a movie theater. In both instances, the representations of sexuality would have been inconceivable in American movies of the time because of the force of the production code. The inclusion of such scenes made these European films more appealing to many American viewers and distributors and probably contributed to the abandonment a few years later of the U.S. production code and adoption of a ratings system that permitted more adult films for adult audiences. Frame enlargement. *Allan Ekelund; Svensk Filmindustri; Embassy*

Finally in 1968, the U.S. production code was replaced with a rating system loosely modeled on the British rating system. The American ratings have been modified several times since then. (For an explanation of the current American ratings, see Figure 9.16.) Studios that belong to the Motion Picture Association of America are required to submit finished films for a

What Everyone Should Know About The Movie Rating System.

GENERAL AUDIENCES

Nothing that would offend parents for viewing by children.

G GENERAL AUDIENCES
All Ages Admitted

PARENTAL GUIDANCE SUGGESTED

Parents urged to give "parental guidance." May contain some material parents might not like for their young children.

PG PARENTAL GUIDANCE SUGGESTED
SOME MATERIAL MAY NOT BE SUITABLE FOR CHILDREN

PARENTS STRONGLY CAUTIONED

PG-13

Parents are urged to be cautious. Some material may be inappropriate for pre-teenagers.

PG-13 PARENTS STRONGLY CAUTIONED
Some Material May Be Inappropriate for Children Under 13

RESTRICTED

R

Contains some adult material. Parents are urged to learn more about the film before taking their young children with them.

R RESTRICTED
UNDER 17 REQUIRES ACCOMPANYING PARENT OR ADULT GUARDIAN

NO CHILDREN UNDER 17 ADMITTED

NC-17

Patently adult. Children are not admitted.

NC-17 NO CHILDREN UNDER 17 ADMITTED

FIGURE 9.16 The current U.S. movie rating classifications Before the latest change in the ratings system in 1990, both sexually explicit films and serious films unable to win an R rating were given an X, which meant that many theaters would not show them, many newspapers would not advertise them, and many video stores carrying current releases would not carry them. The NC-17 rating was devised for films that are made primarily to present their subjects with candor and not to stimulate sexual arousal. Since the inception of the NC-17 rating, the Motion Picture Association of America no longer assigns films an X rating. Few sexually explicit films were ever submitted for a rating anyway. © *Motion Picture Association of America, Encino, Calif.*

rating. Independent film companies, which operate outside Hollywood control, are not. Advertisements and theaters are to display the rating so viewers will know what to expect, and theaters are supposed to exclude certain age groups from films with certain ratings. Although both the industry and public generally approve of the system, it is a source of persistent problems and persistent complaints. The ratings board continues to tend to be much harsher on films with sexual content than films with violence. Children under seventeen are often admitted or find ways to get into R-rated films. And the NC-17 rating, which was intended to remove the pornographic stigma from frank but serious representations of sexual subjects, is a failure. Films released with the NC-17 rating are shut out of many theaters and advertising venues, and films so rated, such as *Requiem for a Dream* (2000) and *Bully* (2001), are often released by the distributor without a rating. Because of dissatisfaction with the rating system, from time to time alternatives to it emerge.[3]

Censorship forces assume various guises. In many countries, filmmakers often face pressures, perhaps contractual obligations, to delete parts of a film before its release so that the film can receive a more commercially viable rating (in the United States, an R rating). American studios that release videotape versions may also face pressure from Blockbuster Video, with the commercial clout of its approximately 5,000 U.S. outlets, to reedit films and omit some of the violence, sex, and obscene language because Blockbuster will not carry films rated NC-17 or X. Even after a film has been rated and released in the U.S. market, it may be subjected to inconspicuous forms of censorship. On cable, for example, Turner Classic Movies has shown altered versions. Even such unrated tame films as *L'Avventura* (1960) and such PG-rated movies as *Tootsie* (1982) may be preceded with the announcement "This feature has been edited due to content."

Knowing something about the restrictions on filmmakers and film distributors helps viewers understand and judge films more accurately and fairly. Such knowledge may help one understand, for example, why *Detour* stumbles to its conclusion and why two films that share the same general subject and are only a few years apart are so different (see Figure 9.14).

---

[3]Since September 1995, an agency of the United States Catholic Conference has run a movie review line (800-311-4CCC) that provides brief reviews of films currently in theaters and a family video of the week. For six or so films each week, callers can hear explanations for the USCC's classification (A-I = general patronage; A-II = adults and adolescents; A-III = adults; A-IV = adults only and with reservations; and O = morally offensive) and the Motion Picture Association of America rating for the same films. Callers also hear a brief description and evaluation of the film. Full and brief movie reviews and an archive of USCC movie reviews are also available on the Web at <usccb.org/movies/index.htm>.

Artistic Conventions

Subject: Things you learn at the movies

- It does not matter if you are heavily outnumbered in a fight involving martial arts. Your enemies will wait patiently to attack you one by one and will dance around in a threatening manner until you have knocked out their predecessors.
- Once applied, lipstick will never rub off—even while scuba diving.
- In war it is impossible to die unless you make the mistake of showing someone a picture of your sweetheart back home.
- A man will show no pain while taking the most ferocious beating but will wince when a woman tries to clean his wounds.
- If staying in a haunted house, women should investigate any strange noises alone and while wearing their most revealing underwear.
- If you decide to start dancing in the street, everyone you meet will know all the steps.

(from an uncredited list circulated widely on the Internet)

Different types of movies have their own set of conventions. Hong Kong action movies feature behavior that to the novice viewer may initially seem odd. In John Woo's *The Killer* (1989), for example, the many bad guys won't die unless their gunshot wounds are numerous, even if they are from close range. The aggressive hordes can also appear oddly considerate by not attacking in unison and thereby overwhelming the beleaguered hero. Sometimes it seems as if they simply bide their time offscreen until it is their turn to rush forward and get slaughtered. In **Bollywood** movies it is a convention that musical numbers are included frequently and in places that surprise viewers who have not seen a lot of Bollywood movies. In *The Legend of Bhagat Singh* (2002), for example, "The action simply stops for a few minutes as the characters burst into song, tablas and sitars throb on the soundtrack and dancing choruses materialize out of nowhere. The political-historical nature of *Bhagat Singh* forces the filmmakers to curtail some of the more extreme tendencies of the Bollywood musical, but there are still plenty of startling moments: jailed hunger strikers breaking into song as they are beaten, and the hero and his two closest comrades smiling broadly and singing lustily of the glory of self-sacrifice as they march to the gallows" (Kehr). Filmgoers raised on Bollywood films probably do not pay much attention to these conventions, but an audience unfamiliar with singing prison inmates may find these interludes surprising. Music in movies from the Western world has its own conventions. For example, as yet another cowboy dressed in black enters yet another saloon, the music changes from a major to a minor key, but audiences in the West don't notice the shift because they've heard it done this way in many other westerns (Figure 9.17). Like the examples cited above, this use of music in movies is a **convention**: a subject or technique that both makers of texts and audiences have grown to accept as natural or typical in certain contexts. Most movies are permeated with conventions. Consider dialogue, for example:

Bollywood: Extremely popular Hindi-language movies made in India that usually feature complicated plots, large casts of mostly uncomplicated characters, frequent extravagant musical interludes, and often happy endings.

"Bad guy comin' in, Arnie! . . . Minor key!"

FIGURE 9.17 **A musical convention in movies**
The Far Side © 1992 Farworks, Inc. *Used by permission of Universal Press Syndicate. All rights reserved.*

Does anyone believe that when police show up at a bank heist, the criminals say coolly, "We got company"? And has a real police detective ever said to a reticent witness, "You and I are going downtown for a little chat"? At no point in my life has anyone used these words with me: "I hope so, Todd. I hope so." In fact, I hardly ever hear anyone use my name at all in conversation. It would sound peculiar, yet in movies it happens all the time, and it sounds perfectly natural. Movie dialogue obeys its own customs. We accept it according to the terms of the cinema, not of reality. (Berliner 3)

Some conventions—such as showdowns and shootouts in westerns and telephone conversations in which one speaker is shown but both are heard—endure for decades. If used too often or for too long, conventions may become boring or in other ways ineffective, as has happened with tremolo stringed instruments used to accompany suspenseful moments. Conventions may also fall out of favor but later be rediscovered. An example is the reintroduction of a variety of **techniques**, such as **iris shots**, **iris-in** shots, and **iris-out** shots, by the directors of **French new wave** films (see Figure 7.32c on p. 322). Another example is the reintroduction by *Star Wars* (1977) of **wipes**—a transition in which it appears that one image pushes off the preceding image as it replaces it (see Figure 3.9 on p. 126). Yet other conventions—such as the introduction of memories by an undulation of the image—simply disappear for long stretches of film history (and may be revived).

Iconoclastic filmmakers often draw attention to filmmaking conventions by flouting them. Mel Brooks is one such filmmaker. In *High Anxiety* (1977), for example, the camera moves toward French doors through which viewers can see people sitting at a formal dinner. The camera moves forward and forward until it loudly shatters a glass pane, and the dinner party stares at it; after a brief pause, the camera begins to retreat. In the last scene of the same film, the camera pulls back from its subjects rapidly, and viewers hear a cam-

iris shot: Shot in which part of the frame is masked or obscured, often leaving the remaining image in a circular or an oval shape.

French new wave (cinema): A movement made up of a diverse group of French fictional films made in the late 1950s and early 1960s in reaction to the carefully scripted products of the French film industry and as explorations of more current subjects sometimes rendered with untraditional techniques.

era operator warn, "We're going too fast. We're going to hit the wall." Almost instantaneously they do, noisily, and make a gaping hole in it. As the camera continues to retreat, the other man says, "Never mind. Keep moving back. Maybe no one will notice." Gliding exploratory camera work is a conventional technique most viewers take for granted. But most viewers have probably neither seen a camera operator have an accident nor considered when, how, and why camera movement is used.

A film may also be unconventional in its subjects. In the conventional western **genre**, for example, the protagonist is a European American male, and his antagonists are American Indians, Mexicans, or European American male outlaws. In American westerns since World War II, the protagonist may be female (*The Ballad of Little Jo*, 1993, and *Bad Girls*, 1994), African American (*Posse*, 1993), or European American and Mexican outlaws (*The Wild Bunch*, 1969). On the other side, the antagonists may be European American males, as throughout Jim Jarmusch's *Dead Man* (1995). The antagonist may be a law enforcement officer (*Unforgiven*, 1992, and *Posse*). European American outlaw antagonists may even be supported by the inaction of the townspeople (*High Noon*).

Some breaks with conventions—such as having an actor step out of character to speak directly to the audience, which is used throughout *High Fidelity* (2000)—never catch on with other filmmakers. Other breaks with conventions seem odd initially but are imitated by other filmmakers and eventually become conventions themselves. One example is the use of **slow motion** to represent violence. When *Bonnie and Clyde* (1967) used slow motion in a violent scene, many viewers commented on its use and found it distracting. But soon other movies, including those directed by Sam Peckinpah, followed the practice. It became widespread and, through repetition, now seems natural to many viewers. As with other texts, the unconventional can become conventional through repetition.

Unconventional filmmakers help us see that conventions are arbitrary: they do not have inevitable and unchanging meanings or significance. For instance, a **lap dissolve**—in which one image fades out as the next image fades in, momentarily overlaps it, and replaces it—does not have to mean "now the **setting** changes," though it usually does in films of recent decades. In films before the 1930s, lap dissolves are occasionally used within a scene (see Figure 3.8 on p. 125). Filmmaking practices take on widely understood meanings or associations through repeated use in similar contexts. For instance, if enough filmmakers use lap dissolves to suggest that the action now shifts to another setting, viewers learn that new meaning (similarly, we learn the meanings of most words by hearing or reading them in context, not by hearing or reading definitions).

When we examine **filmic** conventions, we start to see how widespread, expressive, and influential they are. Conventions influence how a film is made and in turn how viewers respond. Conventions are like teachers and clergy: although most people take them for granted most of the time, they strongly influence succeeding generations.

genre: A group of fictional films that share enough similarities that both filmmakers and audiences recognize the films as members of the same group.

slow motion: Motion in which the action on the screen is slower that its real-life counterpart.

setting: The place where filmed action occurs.

filmic: Characteristic of the film medium or appropriate to it, such as parallel editing.

Financial Constraints

> Lot of times just your schedule, your budget determines how you're going to do things. (Altman)

The budget for a film influences the choice of equipment, personnel available, settings, time that can be devoted to making the film, and promotion and distribution. Consider the situation of Terry Zwigoff, the director of the acclaimed documentary *Crumb* (1994), whose lack of money restricted what he could film and influenced how he filmed it:

> I just didn't have any film to use. It was horrible. I'd be in this situation with great stuff happening, and I'd have to allot myself two rolls of film instead of ten. And it was also what forced me to prompt and to stage and to manipulate a lot of things—you just couldn't wait for them to happen naturally with that kind of budget. (Katz 38)

feature (film): A fictional film that is at least sixty minutes long.

location: Any place other than a film studio that is used for filming.

Big **feature films** are terrifically expensive to make and market. A movie with stars, special effects, lots of action filmed at foreign **locations**, and widespread advertisements requires a budget in the tens of millions of dollars, perhaps even more than $100 million.[4] To attract enough viewers to earn back all the expenses in making and marketing the film and make a profit, such a movie has to be entertaining to huge audiences. In other words, once a big-budget deal is fashioned—for example, for *Pearl Harbor* (2001)—or the making of the film proves much more costly than it was budgeted for—as with *Titanic* (1997)—the filmmakers are under a lot of pressure to deliver a movie with some proven popular characteristics. Popular components are chases, fights, explosions, spectacular sights, romantic or sexual attraction and interaction, a youthful heartthrob, captivating music, and a happy ending. Filmmakers responsible for making a movie with a big budget are also under pressure to avoid generally unpopular subjects, such as religion, and unconventional styles, such as **magic realism**.

magic realism: A style in which occasional wildly improbable or impossible events are included in an otherwise realistic story.

Many movies are not just movies. They are mines for other products to be marketed by other components of the media conglomerate that includes the company that made or distributed the movie in the first place. Consider *Austin Powers: The Spy Who Shagged Me* (1999), which is distributed in the United States by New Line Cinema, which had been taken over by Ted

---

[4]Two sources on the breakdown of expenses of movies are found in Art Linson, "The $75 Million Difference," *New York Times Magazine* 16 Nov. 1997: 88, 89, and "Bills, Bills, Bills" in *The Los Angeles Calendar* (*on line*) 20 Dec. 1998. The *L.A. Times* article lists "the typical costs associated with producing a major Hollywood studio movie," including "Sound equipment: $1,800 a week," "Ferrari Daytona: $850 to $1,000 a day," "Rattlesnake: $400 a day," and "50-caliber machine-gun blanks: $3 each." The article is available (by purchase) through the archives at <www.latimes.com>.

Turner, who in turn agreed to a merger with Time Warner. The *Austin Powers* movies, in other words, are now the property of Time Warner. As one commentator explained shortly before the film's initial release,

> Within weeks, Warner Brothers retail stores and Spenser Gifts stores across the country will roll out a plethora of merchandise from snazzy nightshirts to the Austin Powers Swedish Penis Enlarger ("the perfect gift for Dad on Father's Day!"). TBS and TNT, two cable networks owned by Time Warner, will feature wall-to-wall promotion of the movie. *Entertainment Weekly*, the glossy magazine owned by Time Warner, is set to have an Austin Powers cover.
>
> Warner Records will release the soundtrack album, which includes a single, "Beautiful Stranger," by Madonna, whose label, Maverick Records, is also a Warner subsidiary. And by now, Warner Books has probably delivered to stores the first of its no doubt multiple printings of *The Austin Powers Encyclopedia*.
>
> There's more. The home video, due out in the fall [of 1999], will be sold by Time Warner's sales force; early next year there will be an animated series by HBO, a Time Warner subsidiary. . . .
>
> There may also be a theme park tie-in with Six Flags Great Adventure, which was sold recently by Time Warner but retains a licensing agreement with the company. (Hass)

For an independent film without stars, special effects, and exotic locations, the budget will be far less. "Digital video has dramatically lowered the barriers to feature film-making. For aspiring film-makers who don't have $200,000 to shoot on 35 mm, or $50,000 for 16 mm, it's an affordable alternative. Instead of spending years searching for financing, film-makers can devote their time to improving the script, rehearsing the actors and shooting the best possible movie. When their film is finished, they can decide if it is good enough to launch their careers. If not, they can make another feature for a few thousand dollars, learning from their mistakes. . . . DV is shifting power from financiers to film-makers, who no longer need their money, permission or approval" (Broderick 7). With a smaller budget, the return need not be huge to cover all the expenses and turn a profit. Independent filmmakers—such as John Sayles, Jim Jarmusch, Charles Burnett, Ang Lee, Julie Dash, and Robert Rodriguez—are freer to fashion a film more to their liking, such as one with a controversial or offbeat subject or perhaps an ending that lacks **closure** or a happy fate for characters that viewers identify with. As one director indicated, a low budget can have yet other advantages: "I've always found that not having a lot of money was a tremendous source of strength. It forces you back onto your wits, your intelligence, your imagination and gives you a sort of defiance, which is very invigorating" (Stephen Frears, quoted in Burlingame). However, as illustrated in *Plan 9 from Outer Space* (1959), budgets may be so restricted as to cause curious results (Figure 9.18).

Today, for a short film or video, the budget can be so small that many filmmakers can afford to shoot and edit until they get nearly exactly the results

closure: A sense of coherence and completion at the end of a narrative.

FIGURE 9.18 Low budget, curious results
The budget for Ed Wood's *Plan 9 from Outer Space* (1959) was minimal. When actor Bela Lugosi died early in the filming, another actor was brought in to take over the part. Rather than reshoot Lugosi's scenes, Wood had the new actor cover his face, presumably so no one would notice Lugosi's absence! The results are laughable. *Edward D. Wood, Jr.; Reynolds Pictures, Inc.*

microcinema: A program of untraditional short videos that may be shown on the Internet or in a casual atmosphere such as a coffeehouse, or that may be purchased on videotape or DVD.

film stock: Unexposed and unprocessed motion-picture film.

they want. Because makers of short films do not require a large audience, they have enormous freedom to express themselves on film. And on the Internet and through **microcinema** or **kino** screenings, they can reach audiences with similar interests because there is "a certain hunger, particularly in younger people, for films that aren't formulaic, that express something more personal, honest or quirky than what you could see at the local cineplex or even at an independent film festival like Sundance" (Shuster).

Technological Developments

Although new technology makes possible effects that were previously impossible, advances in filmmaking technology are not without their costs and sometimes limitations. In the late 1920s and early 1930s, films began to be made with sound synchronized with the image, but because the microphones picked up the camera noise during filming, the cameras were placed in soundproof rooms, and camera movement in dialogue scenes largely came to a halt (Figure 9.19). Such films tended to be unmoving and overwhelmed by dialogue.[5]

New technology can also affect the types of movies that get made. In the late 1920s, for example, the introduction of **film stock** that contained a soundtrack made possible new types of films but ended some old types:

Sound . . . made possible a bringing together into one unit elements of vaudeville with filmed images which previously had been two disparate entertainment forms in silent cinema spectacles. In the case of Hollywood this produced a new genre—the musical. However, it also put an end to other generic types, such as

---

[5]*Singin' in the Rain*—a 1952 American musical film whose story is set in the late 1920s—includes fairly accurate, humorous scenes demonstrating some of the problems encountered in filming early sound films while recording the sound (beginning about 51⅓ minutes into the film) and keeping the records in synch with the projected images (beginning 58¼ minutes into the film).

FIGURE 9.19 The coming of sound
In the early months of sound on films, in the late 1920s, the camera was entombed in a small soundproof room so the microphones on the set would not pick up the sounds of a running camera. Seen here is director Alfred Hitchcock on the set of the first British sound film, *Blackmail* (1929), the star of the movie, and behind the window, the camera operator and camera. Such an arrangement ended the mobility of the camera during shots. The chalked message below the window reads "Please keep away from front of CAMERA." *British Film Institute Stills, Posters and Designs*

the gestural, slapstick comedy associated with Chaplin and Keaton. Conversely, it created a new type of comedy: the fast repartee comedy with snappy dialogue (as with the Marx Brothers and W. C. Fields) and screwball comedy—usually based on the "battle between the sexes." (Hayward 333)

Competition from other media may also spur the movie industry to develop technology that makes movies more appealing to consumers. For example, when box office revenues began to decline in the United States in the late 1940s with the growth of small-screen black-and-white television, the film industry countered with greater use of color films and a variety of other new technologies. One of the most spectacular was the **Cinerama** process introduced in 1952, which used three projectors and seven-**track** stereo sound (Figure 9.20a). Because of the onrushing images on both sides of the curved screen, the system proved most effective for action shots, such as of **point-of-view shots** of roller-coaster rides or running the rapids, but during quieter moments, viewers were often at least partially aware of the three side-by-side images demarcated by two somewhat fuzzy lines (not visible in the scale model shown here). Then, too, close-ups were out of the question because no one wanted to see parts of someone's face simultaneously in more than one of the three projected images. For these and other reasons, Cinerama had a lifespan of only a few years. Because of the growing popularity of TV, the film industry even tried to lure customers into theaters with a few 3-D movies such as *Bwana Devil* (1952), with lions and spears seemingly hurling toward the audience, and *Dial M for Murder* (1954), a suspenseful movie about a man plotting his wife's murder (Figure 9.20b). By the end of the 1950s, Hollywood was presenting large and occasionally the widest of wide-screen images ever shown commercially in the United States (Ultra-Panavision), as in the critical

track (noun): A film soundtrack, a narrow band on the film that contains recorded optical, magnetic, or digital sound.

point-of-view shot: Camera placement at the approximate position of a character or person (or occasionally an animal) that gives a view similar to what that subject would see.

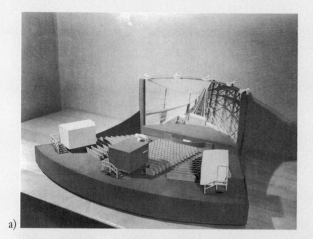

a)

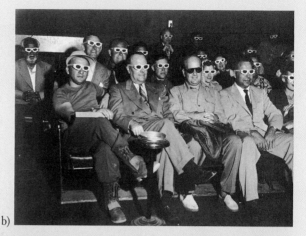

b)

c)

FIGURE 9.20 **Competing with the popular new medium, TV**
During the 1950s, moviemakers and movie exhibitors introduced new technologies in filmmaking and film exhibition to try to lure customers away from their new, small, and increasingly popular black-and-white TV sets. Three of the technologies of the 1950s and 1960s are illustrated here. (a) Cinerama (a scale model) was a wide-screen format created by the use of three cameras during filming and three projectors during screenings. (b) 3-D movies required that viewers wear simple, lightweight special glasses. A few such American movies were made and marketed between 1952 and 1954. (c) Huge and super wide-screen images were the era's most successful and enduring technological answer to TV. When shown in the theaters, *Ben-Hur* (1959), seen here, had an aspect ratio of 2.75:1, meaning the image's width was nearly three times greater than its height. (a–c) *The Museum of Modern Art/Film Stills Archive*

and popular success, *Ben-Hur* (1959, Figure 9.20c).

Ever since the 1990s, computers have been used to create effects with a verisimilitude previously impossible in live-action films. For example, computers can be used to change moving parts of images. For **morphing**, a transformation of one shape into another, sophisticated software can make something seem to transform into something else. In *Terminator 2: Judgment Day* (1991), for example, a cyborg transforms itself from a pool of liquid into its usual appearance as a man and at another time from its usual appearance into what looks like a police officer (see Figure 2.56 on p. 103).

Computers have many other uses for filmmakers. Digital manipulation can be used to eliminate part of a subject, such as part of a character's legs in *Forrest Gump* (1994). Computers were used to combine images to show Forrest Gump meeting and mingling with Presidents Nixon and Kennedy and to show characters in *Contact* (1997) interacting with President Clinton.[6] With computers, people can be placed in any setting, whether in an actual location or on a set constructed of building materials or of photographs stored in a computer. In *Contact*, for instance, computers were used to move images of President Clinton from one place to another. Perhaps most impressively of all, computers can be used to create **virtual realities**—computer-generated worlds with changing imaginary environments and virtual people who can interact and change shape (be morphed) as in *The Lawnmower Man* (1992, Figure 9.21). Virtual realities and other filmmaking effects possible only through computers were also used even more extensively and impressively in *The Matrix* and its successors (1999, see Figure 7.27 on p. 316).

FIGURE 9.21 Computers used to depict virtual reality in movies
For *The Lawnmower Man* (1992), computers were used to create scenes of virtual reality, a computer-generated artificial world complete with changing imaginary environment and virtual people who interact with their environment and each other. At one point in *The Lawnmower Man*, a man and a woman in an advanced laboratory don virtual-reality headgear then see and seem to experience themselves as is shown here, as virtual people who change shape. Here the cybercouple are demonstrating in a new way the unifying force of love. *Gimel Everett; New Line Cinema*

---

[6]"Through the Eyes of Forrest Gump" (1994), a documentary/promotional film, shows how the shot of Forrest meeting President Kennedy was a composite of altered **footage** of the president meeting with a football team in the White House and a shot of Forrest shaking hands with the air against a blue background. The film also explains how computers were used in the scenes of Lieutenant Dan without his legs, Forrest's championship Ping-Pong match, and that floating feather.

The coming of high-definition video (HDV) has also had a major impact on the ways movies can be filmed and shown. With celluloid, the length of a shot was limited by the amount of film the camera could hold, and for 35 mm film that usually meant ten to fifteen minutes, depending on the speed of filming. With videotape, a single shot can now run hours. For some time now, because of improvements in the quality of HD video images, it is now possible to film on HDV, edit the footage digitally, then transfer the results to 35 mm film for theatrical showings, as in *Time Code* (2000), which consists of four shots, each ninety-seven minutes long and seen simultaneously on a quadrant of the same movie screen (see Figure 6.13 on p. 265). *Russian Ark* (2002), which was also shot on HDV and runs ninety-six minutes, consists of a single shot made with a highly mobile camera, just outside and mostly inside the vast Hermitage Museum in St. Petersburg, Russia. In these and other films, HDV allows filmmakers to experiment with lengthy shots and to edit less or not at all.

It is not just visuals that have changed with the times. More recently, in the face of competition from cable and satellite, videotape, laser discs, DVDs, and CDs, theaters have countered yet again with superior multitrack digital sound systems: DTS (Digital Theater Sound), SDDS (Sony Dynamic Digital Sound), and DDS (Dolby Digital Sound) (Figure 4.3 on p. 162).

THE FILM VERSION SEEN[7]

The images in the original copies of the 1919 German movie *The Cabinet of Dr. Caligari* were crystal clear since the movie was filmed and projected on **nitrate** stock (Figure 9.22). The movie was not in color, but each scene was **tinted**. A live orchestra played a score especially selected for the film and coordinated with it, excerpts from some of the most avant-garde composers of the day. The man who compiled and adapted the music for the U.S. premiere later writes:

> In the phantasmagorical scheme of *Dr. Caligari* people move and live in a world out of joint. The cracked country is dotted with grotesque houses, skinny twisted trees, enormously steep and rutted pathways. . . . The key principle of this sprawling architecture and wild terrain is, distortion. With that steadily in mind . . . [the conductor and I] built up the score. We went to Schönberg, Debussy, Stravinsky, Prokofieff [sic], Richard Strauss for thematic material. We assembled our themes, assigned characteristic ideas to the principals of the play, and then proceeded to distort the music. The music had, as it were, to be made eligible for citizenship in a nightmare country. (S. L. Rothafel, quoted in Rogers 359)

Today, many people do not have a chance to see *The Cabinet of Dr. Caligari* in a 35 mm tinted print accompanied by a live orchestra. Instead, many see a videotape or a 16 mm print. Such a version contains the same shots as

nitrate: Short for cellulose nitrate, film stock used until the early 1950s that could produce high-quality images that were subject to decomposition and combustion.

tinting: The process of dyeing a film with color.

---

[7]Adapted from Chapter 11 of William H. Phillips, *Analyzing Films: A Practical Guide* (New York: Holt, Rinehart & Winston, 1985).

FIGURE 9.22 Showings in movie palaces
When *The Cabinet of Dr. Caligari* (1919) had its U.S. premiere at a New York movie palace in 1921, the images looked something like this: large and clear, with the angular expressionistic sets clearly visible as they were intended to be. Frame enlargement. *Decla-Bioscop; The Museum of Modern Art/Circulating Film Library*

the original. But it is a copy of a copy of a copy of a copy and so on and has a general fuzziness and a lot of contrast: black and white and not many shades of gray. In such a version it is hard to make out some details. Most videotape versions, 16 mm film prints, and even some DVD versions have no tinting. Many versions have no music or maybe only a piano score. Compared with the original version of the film, most of these more recent versions are harder to follow and harder to get caught up in. Same title as that earlier film, but not the same film. Different version, different responses.

For those who want to see films as they were originally meant to be seen, DVDs can be a wonder and blessing. But DVDs have not solved all the problems with film versions. For *Lawrence of Arabia*, the films of Stanley Kubrick, *Casablanca* (1942), *Unforgiven*, and many others, the original DVD releases did not do justice to the original film versions, and those titles and many others have been or will be re-released in improved DVD versions. Many other substandard DVDs remain on the market. And currently many films are available only in a substandard DVD version or VHS—or, like *The Last Emperor* (1987), are currently available only in a substandard DVD version *and* VHS.

The film version seen may be different than the original film in many ways. Probably the following are the most significant: its shape, resolution and brightness, color, sound, dubbing and subtitles, and length.

Shape

Inside the can of the first **reel** of the French film *Grand Illusion* (1937) was found the following letter from the director to the projectionist:

reel: One thousand feet of 35 mm motion-picture film stored on a metal spool.

frame (noun): The borders of the projected film, TV set, or monitor.

Dear Sir,

This appeal is from one technician to another. You're going to show my *Grand Illusion*.

This film is still in good shape despite its age: twenty-two years. But it still has a few characteristics that were in style in 1936. One of these is that it is designed for an aspect ratio of l.33 x 1. I have composed each image to fill up this surface and leave no empty space. I have arranged details both at the top and the bottom of the **frame**. By projecting my film on a screen of enlarged dimensions, you would risk eliminating these details that I feel are important and also cutting off part of the heads of the actors, which seems to me unaesthetic.

I ask you to help me to present my work under the best conditions—that is to say, on a screen with dimensions that will suit it.

Thanks in advance.

Regards,
Jean Renoir[8]

wide-screen: A film format with an aspect ratio noticeably greater than 1.33:1 (a shape wider than that of an analog TV screen).

crop: To trim or block out one or more parts of an image.

Renoir had reason to be concerned: since the introduction of various **wide-screen** formats in the 1950s, some films that were not filmed in a wide-screen format have been shown in wide-screen by the use of an inappropriate **aperture plate** (a rectangular metal plate that determines the shape and area of the light emitted from the projector). Renoir was concerned that the projectionist would use a wide-screen aperture plate that would give his film more of a wide, modern look at the expense of **cropping** some of the top and bottom of the image.

Showings of pre-1950s films with a wide-screen aperture plate occur. A more frequent problem is showing wide-screen films in less than their original widths (see Figure 1.29d on p. 36). When so much of the sides of an image are cropped, the results can be misleading. Late in the Italian film (*The*) *Red Desert* (1964), for example, the characters are scattered across the wide frame and facing in different directions (see Figure 1.30 on p. 37). If less than the original aspect ratio is shown and the viewer loses a sense of distances between characters, the sense of estrangement and rootlessness is decreased. Indeed, some of the characters are cut right out of the picture. In some films, characters may be diminished by a nose, an ear, or another body part. Also distorted are films conveying the expanse of a locale, whether it is a meadow or outer space.

Resolution and Brightness

The version seen may also differ from the theatrical release print in its **resolution** (or sharpness) and its brightness. The kind of film stock, the projection light, the speed and focus of the lens(es) through which light is projected, the reflective qualities of the screen, the quality of the videotape,

---

[8]Jean Renoir, *La Grande Illusion: Decoupage integrale* (Paris: Edition du seuil/Avant-scene, 1971), 6. This letter was translated and brought to my attention by Fred Simeral.

and the quality of the video player and monitor all help determine the image's sharpness and brightness.

Consider what happens to resolution and brightness when *Citizen Kane* (1941) and *Psycho* (1960) are shown on videotape on a television set or monitor. The 35 mm release prints of those two films have sharp, bright images. But when they are shown on an analog TV or monitor, the results are **grainy** (since video images have less definition than film images). The lighting is without subtle shades of gray, and in shadowed areas details tend to get lost because TV has less range of tones than film; thus, many details in night scenes are especially difficult to see. As a consequence, many analog television viewers are likely to miss such details as Susan Alexander's doll (see Figure 10.7 on p. 479), the whiskey bottle Kane finds in her bookcase in Xanadu after she leaves him (109½ minutes into the film), and the fleeting triple superimposition of the last shot of *Psycho* (see Figure 3.14 on p. 132). These details are also scarcely noticeable in some 16 mm prints that are too many generations removed from the release print because those versions may have **high contrast** and be grainy. They blur detail. We can see this loss of detail if we compare two images from black-and-white films: Figure 10.7 on p. 479, which had to be made from a 16 mm print many generations from the release print, and Figure 9.22, which is a photograph of a frame from an earlier-generation 35 mm print.

grainy: Having rough visual texture.

high contrast: Photographic image with few gradations between the darkest and lightest parts of the image.

Color

Several factors determine the color quality of film versions we see. Some early "silent" films were hand-colored (each frame was painted different colors with small brushes) or tinted (usually whole scenes were dyed a particular color). Today, viewers rarely have an opportunity to see such prints. Also, prints of color films, including those for theatrical release, may vary in quality since most are mass produced. And the color of many older film prints, especially for many films made since 1949, fades and shifts; usually they become reddish. In these instances, the moods and meanings that the color originally conveyed are altered.

With the aid of computers, some black-and-white films on videotape have been colorized: years after the films were made, the blacks, whites, and grays are replaced with colors. Even in the best of circumstances, color film is an approximation of the color we see in life, and colorized images are only desaturated approximations of color film. Furthermore, the colorized colors are not chosen by directors, costumers, or set **designers** but by video technicians whose judgment in choosing colors is often questionable, especially for films made many years ago and perhaps in a different culture. As a consequence, they may choose a color that draws undue attention to an unimportant part of the image or that underplays the importance of its subject. To people who tend to dislike black-and-white films, colorization has appeal. But to film scholars, film teachers, and filmmakers, perhaps especially directors, the process is offensive. Director John Huston, after watching seven minutes of the colorized version of his own *The Maltese Falcon* (1941)—he could stand no more—said, "It's not color any more than pouring tablespoons of sugar water over a roast constitutes flavoring."

Sound

There were few truly silent film showings because even the earliest films were shown with some kind of musical accompaniment to cover the noises of the projectors and audience and to support continuity and mood. Before the adoption of the soundtrack along the film's edge, exhibitors often chose the music and sound effects and supervised their presentations (see Figure 4.1 on p. 160). But discovering the original music and sound effects or even the kind of original music and sound effects is impossible for early films. And some re-releases include distracting, inappropriate music and sound effects. Some of Charlie Chaplin's early short films have suffered this fate.

There is also a danger that the soundtrack on a videotape release inadequately re-creates a multitrack soundtrack. Even if one sees and hears a multitrack DVD, without a home theater or at least a multispeaker system, much of the original soundtrack goes unheard, and the contribution of the sound to the overall film experience is lessened.

Dubbing and Subtitles

Many people prefer dubbed prints to subtitles, but dubbing also presents problems. The major drawback of dubbed prints—in which the voices of the original foreign performers are replaced by the voices of native performers speaking translated dialogue—is that spoken translated words can never be totally synchronized with the original foreign-language lip movements. Another disadvantage is that spoken words can be dropped or added by the distributors. In some dubbed prints, the entire soundtrack is redone, and many of the nuances of the original spoken words, sound effects, and music are lost. In many dubbed prints, only the spoken words are changed; the effects and music tracks are the same as in the original.

Nearly all filmgoers are aware of the problems with subtitles in foreign-language films, especially in older films, but there is no simple and completely satisfactory solution. Prints with a complete and accurate translation could be costly to make, and for many films a complete set of subtitles would turn the audience into readers more than viewers.

Length

One last major aspect of the film version seen—perhaps the most troublesome and significant aspect as far as film analysis is concerned—is the length of the film.

After a film has been released theatrically, it occasionally is issued in a longer version. Examples include *American Graffiti* (1973) and *Close Encounters of the Third Kind* (1977). Some films shown on network television have been stretched out by adding **outtakes** (rejected footage), perhaps while trimming some of the original footage. One of the most notable instances would be the more complete TV version of *The Godfather* (1972) and *The Godfather, Part II* (1974).

A film may be shortened after its original release. Films of one culture are often shocking or unsettling to people of a different culture, especially in sexual and political matters; thus, many U.S. films have been altered when shown abroad. To hold down production costs and increase the chances that a film will be widely seen, producers and studios have sometimes intervened to shorten a film. In some cases, though—and the classic American silent film *Greed* (1925) is a glaring example—much of the original film is lost. (In these cases, whether or not the original would be judged superior by current standards is unknowable.[9])

Some large TV stations and some video distributors speed up films so that an odd-length movie will fit into the available time slot. An audio pitch corrector is also used to compensate for the higher pitch when the film is projected at a faster speed. Thus a two-hour and ten-minute film may be projected at a faster speed as the pitch is corrected so it is not noticeably too high, and the film will fit onto a two-hour videotape. Perhaps in extreme cases, an astute viewer's sense of pace could be altered by this process.

In conclusion, often the changes made after a film is released are of little consequence to viewer responses to the film. However, sometimes the changes made after a film is released are significant, especially in the following ways:

- **Shape of Projected Image** If altered drastically, the original compositions are changed significantly. Whole characters may not be visible in some shots.

- **Resolution and Brightness** If blurred and dulled, significant details cannot be seen.

- **Color** The color may be unlike the original color. It may even have changed so much that it is distracting. The moods the color was meant to create or support may be distorted or lost.

- **Sound** Sound effects and music for "silent" films are often omitted altogether, or if supplied, they may be inappropriate and distracting. An original multitrack soundtrack cannot be heard in a later monophonic

---

[9]Usually **cutting continuity scripts** fail to discuss the source or reliability of the film version described. For example, the introductory page of Theodore Huff's 1961 shot analysis of *The Birth of a Nation* says that it is "based on a 16 mm print of the original 12-reel version, circa 1939" but gives no explanation of the relationship of the print described to the 1915 versions. For another example, the Simon and Schuster script of *M* says nothing about the numerous different versions of that classic German film.

cutting continuity script: A script that describes a finished film.

version or on a monophonic home or classroom system.

- **Translations** Translations in the subtitles or dubbing may be incomplete or inaccurate. They may contain distracting errors in spelling or syntax.
- **Length** Not all of the original shots may be included. Shots may be shortened. On the other hand, new material may have been included (as in some TV broadcasts, occasional theatrical re-releases, and DVDs).

Often other versions, perhaps quite different versions, of the same title exist, especially for older films. In significant ways, the film you are analyzing may not be the film your readers or listeners saw, and a film you read about may not really be the film you have seen.

CONTEXTS IN WHICH A FILM HAS BEEN SEEN

Imagine that it is March 1921 and you are approaching the Capitol Theater in New York City, a huge theater used for live shows and movies. As you near the theater from the outside and as you enter it, you can tell at once that this is no ordinary theater. In the lobby and in the theater itself, you see evidence of wealth, exoticism, and excess everywhere. Inside the theater it looks something like what we see inside a somewhat later theater (see Figure 9.24b). The U.S. premiere of the German movie *The Cabinet of Dr. Caligari* is about to take place. The audience sits in cushioned seats as comfortable as those found in an upscale theater or opera house, the house lights dim, and a beam of bright light emerges from behind and high overhead and instantly fills up the huge screen as a live orchestra plays a score especially commissioned for this film. Now imagine another showing of the same title, a showing much easier to imagine. In a classroom, a class sees a videotape or 16 mm print of *Caligari*. During this showing, the setting is nothing special. It is certainly no picture palace. For one thing, there is more light in the room than in a movie house. After a while, you occasionally become aware that the seats are not very comfortable, and from time to time outside noises intrude into your awareness. Compared with that 1921 theatrical showing, this showing is harder to follow and harder to get caught up in.

Nickelodeons

What have been some of the main viewing environments, and how have they indirectly influenced filmmakers and the films they made? During the second decade of motion pictures (from about 1905 to 1915), most movies were seen in nickelodeons. Their interiors tended to be plain and functional, not

a)

b)

c)

FIGURE 9.23 **Contexts in which a film has been seen: nickelodeons**

(a) Nickelodeons were small storefront movie theaters popular in the United States from roughly 1905 to 1915. It is estimated that by 1910 there were already 10,000 of them, and most towns and urban neighborhoods had at least one. They were inexpensive to attend, accessible (though initially thought not very respectable), yet small and modest in environment and presentation. In the early years, their programs of short films lasted from twenty to thirty minutes. Seen here is the Cascade Theatre in New Castle, Pennsylvania, which was purchased by the Warner family in 1903. Sam Warner, seen on the left, sang to the audience during reel changes and intermissions, as was the usual practice in nickelodeons, and later was one of the four brothers who founded Warner Brothers Pictures. The small signs visible in this photograph include the information that the shows were "Refined Entertainment for ladies, gentlemen, and children," which assured would-be patrons that *this* theater was respectable. Other signs indicate that the pictures were changed twice a week; admission was always five cents; and performances were continuous. (b) An unidentified 1913 nickelodeon with mostly male audience members; male uniformed usher standing in the aisle; unpadded wooden chairs; a framed white sheet serving as the screen; and no ventilation. Swanky it was not. (c) A sample sign hung in some nickelodeons. (a) *The Museum of Modern Art/Film Stills Archive;* (b) *Unidentified U.S. trade magazine; Courtesy Bison Archives, Hollywood, California;* (c) *Unknown source*

very decorative or even comfortable (Figure 9.23). The audiences consisted of perhaps a hundred or two, initially mostly recent immigrants and working-class viewers, many with only a shaky command of English. Nearly always, some form of musical accompaniment was provided, at least a piano or a piano and drums. More than a few nickelodeons provided "lecturers" to explain the films as they ran. As the nickelodeons grew popular, they quickly became part of the neighborhood scenery. Eileen Bowser's account of Indianapolis nickelodeons in 1908 is illustrative of the situation:

> There were twenty-one nickelodeons and three ten-cent theaters in 1908, only three years after the first nickelodeon had appeared there. Each nickelodeon in this city gave a show consisting of one reel of film, which might contain two or three different subjects, and an illustrated song, with the show taking twenty to twenty-five minutes—"except when there is a crowd waiting, then it is speeded up to 15 to 17 minutes." The shows in Indianapolis were open from nine in the morning till eleven at night, which allowed about twenty to thirty shows each day. If you could afford ten cents, you could go to one of the three high-class theaters and get an evening of three or four reels of pictures with live entertainment consisting of illustrated songs, vaudeville acts, and slide lecturers lasting from one to one-and-a-half hours. By 1911, the number had increased to seventy-six motion-picture theaters alone, not including regular theaters that changed over to movies during the summer. However, only fifteen of the movie houses remained downtown in 1911, because of the high rents. (6)

Going to the nickelodeon was a modest experience easily accessible to the masses. Given the multiethnic and mostly uneducated audiences of the time, the limitations of the technology, and the nickelodeons' Spartan accommodations, early filmmakers made short and mostly intellectually undemanding films that they hoped would be entertaining and popular.

Movie Theaters: Then and Now

As movie-going grew as a business in the United States and elsewhere, beginning around 1914 and continuing into the early 1930s, movie palaces were erected in various American cities, mostly in downtowns (Figure 9.24a and b): "The greatest of silent picture palaces was unquestionably the Roxy in New York, the 6,214 seat 'cathedral of the motion picture.'. . . Patrons who were not intimidated by a trip under the massive, five-story tall rotunda faced a squadron of ushers drilled by a retired Marine Corps captain. The statuary, the carpeting, the mural decorations, all worked together to create an effect of overwhelming grandeur, but the frame had grown far more important than any picture" (Koszarski 23, 25). Also adding to the experience was a large pipe organ (often a Wurlitzer) used to accompany the films and fill the interludes. Compared with nickelodeons, the movie palaces cost more, attracted wealthier customers, and showed longer and more involved programs (including live variety acts). Such an environment encouraged moviegoers to think of movies and their venues as bigger than life, since the images and sounds were bigger and more involving than ever. The opulent and often exotic settings reflected by theater names such as the Egyptian, the Chinese, the Aztec, Loew's Paradise, and the Kings also nurtured the feeling that movie-going was an escape into a new world, a world of soft lights and music

a)

b)

c)

FIGURE 9.24 Contexts in which a film has been seen: movie theaters, ornate and plain

(a) A movie palace, the Brooklyn Paramount Theatre in 1928, eleven stories high. When the Paramount Theatre opened on Flatbush Avenue in Brooklyn late in 1928, it was the second-largest theater in New York City. Part of the sign on the side of the building says "Brooklyn Paramount Theatre, the last word in beauty, comfort, luxury, and entertainment." (b) Inside were 4,100 plush upholstered seats that in the back of the theater required the main floor and five levels above it to accommodate them all; a huge, exotic, ornate stage setting; and thick decorated curtains that opened up to a bright, shimmering world as the movie began. Tickets ranged from approximately twenty-five cents to $1.25 depending on when one went and where one sat. For years, the theater was used to show either movies or various live shows, such as rock 'n' roll stage shows. It was last used to show a movie in 1962. Like most of the ornate American movie palaces built in the teens, 1920s, and 1930s, it has not survived intact. Eventually, parts of the building were incorporated into a building that is part of Long Island University. Now a gym floor covers the original stage and orchestra seating, and the auditorium's much-admired blue recessed dome is situated above a basketball court. *Sic transit gloria mundi.*

(c) A huge screen in an IMAX theater. Although this screen is not as large as those for 3-D IMAX theaters, which are the equivalent of eight stories high, it extends beyond most viewers' peripheral vision. While watching a film in such a theater, viewers looking straight ahead see only the image and are caught up in it. (a–b) *The Museum of Modern Art/Film Stills Archive;* (c) *Courtesy of IMAX Corporation*

453

throughout the theater and huge moving images up on the screen. Such theaters could function as an opiate against the unreliable world outside. Venue, in short, could strongly affect viewer anticipation and response. Note the order in which the Brooklyn Paramount Theatre of 1928 touted its qualities: its "beauty, comfort, luxury, and entertainment" (Figure 9.24a). More than at any other time in movie history, the place where the movies were shown could be more exciting, more special than the movies themselves.

Something of the same experience was recaptured in the 1970s with the coming of IMAX (Image MAXimization) theaters and films (Figure 9.24c). Like movie palaces, IMAX theaters seem special partly because they are generally available only in large cities. Like movie palaces, IMAX theaters provide the biggest image and sometimes the most enveloping sound available. Some IMAX theaters also provide the most satisfying 3-D experience yet achieved in movie history. Unlike the movie palaces, however, IMAX theaters in name and decoration are plain and functional. The system's screen can be up to approximately eight stories high and a hundred or so feet wide. For 3-D IMAX, viewers wear special glasses, and a subject in the extreme foreground can appear to be in the viewer's face or to move to the side of the viewer's head. The sense of three dimensionality is so convincing, it's hard not to duck—or at least flinch—as objects seem to hurl toward the audience or as the camera skims over the top of terrain. While viewing "Alaska: Spirit of the Wild" (1997) and many other IMAX films in three dimensions in an Omnimax theater with its huge dome screen, viewers may feel queasy while seemingly looking straight down as an airplane flies over a vast territory. With no noticeable distortion, the accompanying multitrack digital sound system can vibrate the viewers' feet, armrests, and seats.

Although IMAX films have proven effective for short documentaries, it is not yet certain how amenable the system is to feature-length **narrative** films. IMAX cameras are noisy, heavy, bulky, and hard to move around quickly and fluidly (no **Steadicam** shots here!), so IMAX films do not have as much movement as many theatrical movies. Gigantic close-ups of faces can look grotesque or at least strange. Films not made with IMAX cameras but converted to IMAX and re-released in IMAX theaters—such as *Apollo 13* (1995; 2002 in IMAX) and *The Matrix Reloaded: The Imax Experience* (2003)—have had mixed results. Even those re-releases that have undergone a special digital remastering (DMR) have suffered in spots from increased graininess. Some computer animated shots are less credible because the images from 35 mm have been blown up to fill the much larger IMAX frames (see Figure 2.2b & d on pp. 63 and 65), and then those IMAX frames are projected to fill up the huge IMAX screen. Then, too, some viewers have found watching a feature on an IMAX screen is a bit of an eyestrain. How widespread IMAX theaters become will be determined, as are all technological developments, by economic imperatives: to what extent filmgoers are willing to pay for an expensive product made with the new technology.

narrative: A representation of a series of unified events situated in one or more settings.

Steadicam: A lightweight and portable mount for holding a movie camera that provides for relatively steady camera movements during handheld shots.

Home Viewing

Many people now see more movies at home than in theaters. Since the 1960s, many filmmakers have known that their films would eventually be shown on TV screens, so they have filmed with **spherical lenses** and **framed** their images with two screen shapes in mind: the wide-screen film shape most often used in theaters (1.85:1) and the shape of an analog TV screen (1.33:1) (see Figure 1.31 on p. 38). Some filmmakers mindful of later TV audiences use fewer **long shots** and more close-ups than they would otherwise because the details of a long shot tend to get lost on analog TV; for the same reason, they might use more light. Since home viewing equipment can be relatively low-priced and access to some form of the films and to refreshments much less expensive than in movie theaters, home viewing has vastly expanded the number of viewers. Viewers typically respond differently to a film seen at home than they do to one seen in a movie theater. Home presentation has many advantages over a theatrical showing—control over speed of presentation, continuity of presentation, replay, volume, tone, color, contrast, and so forth—but it has many potential shortcomings as well. Home viewers may miss a visual or audio subtlety because it is difficult or impossible to discern (see, for example, Figure 10.7 on p. 479). Then, too, viewers are often more distracted and less caught up in the images and sounds at home than they are in a theater.

Although many predicted a major drop in movie attendance with the growth of home videotape, movies via satellite, DVDs, home theaters, and the Internet, theater attendance remains robust. It is likely to stay so because movie theaters can always provide technology and an environment that no home can match. In the latest development, many new movie theaters have extremely large screens and stadium seating. In such theaters, viewers can see the entire screen regardless of who sits in front of them; seats can be as large and comfortable as first-class seats on an airplane, and there is no danger from your neighbors' elbows. The sound is also superior to any home system. Some of these theaters have seen attendance jump 300 percent. As of this writing, digital projection—with its ability to project large, sharp, unfaded, unscratched, and unwavering images—seems likely to gain in use in theaters. In short, movies shown in up-to-date theaters will always be superior in environment, image, and sound to movies shown at home.

Many contexts for films are included in this book's chronology for 1895 to 2003, which includes columns on major world events, the arts, mass media, and films and videos (pp. 559-612).

Now that we have explored some of the factors that influence the making of films, the film version seen, and the exhibition and viewing of films, we turn our attention in the next chapter to how viewers interact with the films themselves, including the meanings they find in them.

spherical lens: A lens used in cinematography that transmits the image to the film in the camera without squeezing or compressing the image.

frame (verb): To position the camera in such a way that the subjects are kept within the borders of the image.

long shot: A shot in which the subject may be seen in its entirety and much of its surroundings is visible.

CLOSE-UP: HOMOSEXUALITY IN *THE MALTESE FALCON*: THE NOVEL, THE PRODUCTION CODE, AND THE 1941 MOVIE

In the excerpts we examine here, which appear early in the novel and 1941 movie, Effie—the secretary who works in the detective office of Sam Spade and his partner—enters Spade's office. See Table 9.1.

As we can see implied by the excerpts from the novel and film, in both fiction and film, gays were represented stereotypically. When one studies the historical contexts of the time that *The Maltese Falcon* first appeared (1941) and learns about the widespread beliefs and values of the time (in part, as implied by the production code), one can better understand the film's restraint in representing the characters' homosexuality. We can also see that

TABLE 9.1

Homosexuality in *The Maltese Falcon*: The Novel, the Production Code, and the 1941 Movie

LATE IN CHAPTER 4 OF THE NOVEL	THE PRODUCTION CODE AND THE SCRIPT	THE 1941 MOVIE
The girl returned with an engraved card—*Mr. Joel Cairo*. "This guy is queer," she said. "In with him, then, darling," said Spade. Mr. Joel Cairo was a small-boned dark man of medium height. His hair was black and smooth and very glossy. His features were Levantine [characteristic of countries of the Eastern Mediterranean]. A square-cut ruby, its sides paralleled by four baguette diamonds, gleamed against the deep green of his cravat. His black coat, cut tight to narrow shoulders, flared a little over slightly plump hips. His trousers fitted his round legs more snugly than was the current fashion. The uppers of his patent-leather shoes were hidden by fawn spats. He held a black derby hat in	The production code is not specific about homosexuality, but the public of the time overwhelmingly disapproved of it, and enforcers of the production code always disapproved of it. Presumably those enforcing the code thought that the following two principles applied to homosexuality: General Principles . . . 2. Correct standards of life . . . shall be presented. . . . II. 4. Sex perversion or any inference to it is forbidden. The script that Warner Bros. submitted for approval has not been published, but historian Rudy Behlmer has researched the matter and reports, "As was the custom, the temporary script was sent automatically for approval to the	Approximately 23¼ minutes into the movie, Spade is talking on the phone as Effie enters his office carrying something in her hand before her. She hands Spade a business card. Spade finishes his call and hangs up. He takes the card from Effie, detects a fragrance, and smells the card. Effie says, "Gardenia," as she raises her eyebrows slightly. Spade replies, "Quick, darling, in with him!" Effie walks to the office door, opens it and says, "Will you come in, Mr. Cairo?" Cairo walks into the room. He has dark, curly hair and is dressed in a dark suit and wears a bow tie. In one hand he carries an expensive umbrella with a straight handle, white gloves, and a dark hat.

the filmmakers found ways to get by the strictures of the code by subtly suggesting Cairo's homosexuality: for example, the way he dresses, his scented calling card, and, most of all, the inclusion of that umbrella, which is not referred to in the scene in the book. The umbrella's handle can be seen as a phallic symbol that Cairo gently handles and more than once nearly touches with his lips. We can also see that the production code was more restrictive than laws covering the publication and circulation of books because, as the production code states, it was believed at the time that films had the potential to affect behavior more so than did books (see Reasons Supporting Preamble of Code, section 3.D, on p. 431).

Work Cited

Behlmer, Rudy. *America's Favorite Movies: Behind the Scenes*. New York: Ungar, 1982.

LATE IN CHAPTER 4 OF THE NOVEL

a chamois-gloved hand and came towards Spade with short, mincing, bobbing steps. The fragrance of *chypre* came with him.

Spade inclined his head at his visitor and then at a chair, saying: "Sit down, Mr. Cairo."

Cairo bowed elaborately over his hat, said, "I thank you," in a high-pitched thin voice and sat down. He sat down primly, crossing his ankles, placing his hat on his knees, and began to draw off his yellow gloves.

Spade rocked back in his chair and asked: "Now what can I do for you, Mr. Cairo?"

THE PRODUCTION CODE AND THE SCRIPT

Production Code Administration, the film industry's self-regulatory body. Joseph I. Breen wrote back to Jack L. Warner that while the basic story was acceptable under the code, there were certain objectionable details. . . . Regarding the character subsequently played by Peter Lorre, the letter stated that 'we cannot approve the characterization of Cairo as a pansy as indicated by the lavender perfume, high-pitched voice, and other accouterments'" (136–37).

THE 1941 MOVIE

Spade says, "Will you sit down, Mr. Cairo?" . . .

Approximately twenty-five seconds later Mr. Cairo looks at his umbrella and turns it over in his hands as he talks with Spade. In two later shots, Cairo's lips almost touch the tip of the umbrella handle (Figure 9.2).

SUMMARY

This chapter introduces five types of contexts in which a film has been made. The second part considers how the film version seen might differ from other later versions and from the original version. The last part of the chapter briefly illustrates how the contexts in which the film is seen (theater and audience) can also influence filmmakers, the films they make, and viewer responses to the films.

Contexts in Which a Film Has Been Made

Filmmakers are subject to many influences, such as widespread attitudes in a society, censorship, filmic conventions, financing, and technological developments. Viewers who know about these and other contexts of a film can understand the film more completely.

SOCIETY AND POLITICS

- Societal attitudes influence how filmmakers represent a subject. For example, before the late 1960s, American movies generally represented homosexuals not at all or only obliquely and stereotypically.
- As studies of the representations of African Americans, Latinos, and Latin Americans demonstrate, representation reflects the beliefs and values of the times, and as those change, so do the representations.
- As is illustrated by some Tarzan movies, other subjects, such as certain popular stories, also change as societal attitudes do.
- The political climate strongly affects how much freedom of expression filmmakers have and what political outlooks are likely to be explained or implied in their films.

CENSORSHIP

- Censorship (written or implied) strongly influences the content of films.
- In the United States from 1934 into the 1960s, most films were censored by an agency set up by the film producers and distributors to ensure that movies were suitable for viewers of all ages.
- Often governments ban or censor a film as it is being made or after it is completed.
- In many societies a rating system is devised that allows for a wide latitude of subjects and treatments but restricts some films to certain age groups.

ARTISTIC CONVENTIONS

- Filmic conventions are representations or techniques that both filmmakers and audiences have grown to accept as natural or typical.

- Filmmakers may follow conventional practices. Or they may reject them, as in many westerns made since World War II.
- Conventions may fall out of favor, and unconventional practices may catch on and become conventional.
- Filmmaking conventions do not have inevitable and fixed meanings; usage, which varies over time, establishes their meanings.

FINANCIAL CONSTRAINTS

- Since the amount of money available to filmmakers helps determine equipment, personnel available, settings, time to film, and distribution, financing is a crucial influence on the making of films.
- Generally, the greater the finances needed to make and promote a film, the greater the pressures to make a movie with such popular characteristics as chases, fights, explosions and other spectacular sights, romance or sex, and a happy ending.
- In general, the smaller the budget, the greater control filmmakers have over their work, and the more individualistic it is likely to be.

TECHNOLOGICAL DEVELOPMENTS

- New filmmaking technology may influence the types of films that are made.
- Advances in the technology of competing mass media and electronic entertainments, such as television, may influence the techniques filmmakers use, settings, and actions presented as well as the type of film exhibition used.
- Computers are now used to achieve effects with a verisimilitude previously impossible in live-action films, such as to change moving parts of the image, eliminate parts of a subject, combine images, place subjects in new settings, and even create a virtual reality.

The Film Version Seen

Sometimes the changes between the film as originally shown and as later viewed are significant, especially in the following ways:

- **Shape of Projected Image**   If altered drastically, the original compositions and corresponding meanings and moods are changed significantly.
- **Resolution and Brightness**   If blurred and dulled, significant details cannot be seen.
- **Color**   The color may be unlike the original color. It may even have changed so much that it is distracting. The moods that the color was meant to create or support may be distorted or lost.

- **Sound**   Sound effects and music for "silent" films are often omitted or if supplied may be inappropriate and distracting. The original multi-track soundtrack cannot be heard in a later monophonic version or on a monophonic home or classroom system.
- **Translations**   Dubbing and subtitles may be incomplete or inaccurate. They may contain distracting errors in spelling or syntax.
- **Length**   Not all of the original shots may be included. On the other hand, new material may have been included (as in some TV broadcasts, occasional theatrical re-releases, and DVDs).

Contexts in Which a Film Has Been Seen

- The size, design, comfort, and accessibility of the viewing environment along with the types of audiences attending the showings can affect the types of movies made and in turn how viewers respond to them.

Major Terms about Understanding Films through Contexts

Below, numbers in italics refer to the pages where the terms are explained. All terms are defined in more detail in the Illustrated Glossary beginning on p. 621.

blaxploitation *418*	filmic *437*	representation *413*
convention *435*	microcinema *440*	socialist realism *425*

QUESTIONS ABOUT UNDERSTANDING FILMS THROUGH CONTEXTS

The following questions are intended to help viewers understand films through their contexts. Not all the questions are appropriate for every film. In thinking out, discussing, and writing responses to those questions most appropriate for the film being examined, be careful to stick with the issues the questions raise, to answer all parts of the questions, to explain the reasons for your answers, and to give specific examples from the film.

1. When and where was the film made? How do the times and place(s) of its making affect how the film turned out? For example, did the political climate or widespread societal attitudes of the time preclude or restrict certain subjects or treatments?

2. What does the film convey to you about a group it represents, such as African Americans, Latinos, or Arabs? In what ways is that representation a product of the place and time that the film was made?

3. What were the censorship regulations in place during the making of the film? In what ways do those regulations limit the film's content or treatment or both?

4. Does the film follow filmic conventions, or is it unconventional in its techniques and content?

5. Is the film a big-budget action film aimed at large audiences, a more modestly budgeted independent film, an inexpensive documentary or experimental film, or some other type of film? In what ways did the film's budget affect the outcome of the film?

6. How does the film technology available when the film was made affect how the film turned out?

7. Did the version of the film you saw differ significantly from the original showings in any of the following ways: shape of projected image, resolution and brightness, color, soundtrack, dubbing and translations of subtitles, and length? If so, how do those differences affect your experience in seeing the film?

8. What was the environment in which you saw the film, and how did the environment affect your responses to the film?

WORKS CITED

Altman, Robert. Audio Commentary. *The Player* (DVD). New Line Home Video, 1997.

Berg, Charles Ramírez. *Latino Images in Film: Stereotypes, Subversion, Resistance*. Austin: U of Texas P, 2002.

Berliner, Todd. "Hollywood Movie Dialogue and the 'Real Realism' of John Cassavetes." *Film Quarterly* 52.3 (Spring 1999): 2–16.

Bowser, Eileen. *The Transformation of Cinema, 1907–1915*. New York: Scribner's, 1990.

Broderick, Peter. "DIY = DVC." *Mediawatch '99*. Supplement to *Sight and Sound* 9.3 (March 1999): 6–9.

Burlingame, Jon. "Only What Grabs Him." *Los Angeles Times* 23 Sept. 2001: F6.

Cameron, Kenneth M. *Africa on Film: Beyond Black and White*. New York: Continuum, 1994.

Curry, Ramona. *Too Much of a Good Thing: Mae West as Cultural Icon*. Minneapolis: U of Minnesota P, 1996.

Hass, Nancy. "It's Synergy, Baby. Groovy! Yeah!" *New York Times on the Web* 2 May 1999 <http://www.nytimes.com/library/film/050299film-sequel-synergy.html>.

Hayward, Susan. *Cinema Studies: The Key Concepts*. 2nd ed. London: Routledge, 2000.

Herz, J. C. "What Is Art? That Can Mostly Depend on the Context." *New York Times on the Web* 11 March 1999 <http://www.nytimes.com/library/tech/99/03/circuits/articles/11game.html>.

Huff, Theodore. *A Shot Analysis of D. W. Griffith's* The Birth of a Nation. [New York]: Museum of Modern Art, Film Library, 1961.

Jones, Chris. "Lesbian and Gay Cinema." *An Introduction to Film Studies*. 2nd ed. Ed. Jill Nelmes. London: Routledge, 1999. 307–44.

Katz, Susan Bullington. "A Conversation with Terry Zwigoff." *The Journal* [Writers Guild of America, West] Feb. 1996: 36–40.

Kehr, Dave. "Gandhi Is Eclipsed by Another Indian Hero." *New York Times on the Web* 10 June 2002 <http://query.nytimes.com/gst/fullpage.html?res=9B01E2DE103DF933A2 5755C0A9649C8B63>.

Koszarski, Richard. *An Evening's Entertainment: The Age of the Silent Feature Picture, 1915–1928*. New York: Scribner's, 1990.

Krutnik, Frank. *In a Lonely Street: Film Noir, Genre, Masculinity*. London: Routledge, 1991.

Lewis, Jon. "'We Do Not Ask You to Condone This': How the Blacklist Saved Hollywood." *Cinema Journal* 39.2 (Winter 2000): 3–30.

M: A Film by Fritz Lang. English translation and description of action by Nicholas Garnham. New York: Simon and Schuster, 1968.

Rogers, Bernard. "Comes Stravinsky to the Film Theater." *Musical America* 33.25 (16 April 1921): 5. Reprinted in George C. Pratt. *Spellbound in Darkness: A History of the Silent Film*. Greenwich, Conn.: New York Graphic Society, 1966. 359.

Russo, Vito. *The Celluloid Closet: Homosexuality in the Movies*. Rev. ed. New York: Harper, 1987.

Scott, A. O. "Blacks Being Themselves, Not Symbols." *New York Times* 19 Jan. 2003, Late Edition-Final: Sec. 2, p. 10.

Shuster, Robert. "A No-Budget Production." *Los Angeles Times* 2 Sept. 2001: F8.

Sklar, Robert. *Movie-Made America: A Cultural History of American Movies*. Rev. and updated. New York: Random, 1994.

FOR FURTHER READING

Chicanos/Latinos in the Movies: A Bibliography of Materials in the UC Berkeley Library. On the Web at <lib.berkeley.edu/MRC/LatinoBib.html>. Approximately forty pages' worth of information organized into four parts: reference sources, books/videos, journal and newspaper articles, and articles and books on individual films. Some of the entries are annotated.

Dyer, Richard. *Now You See It*. New York: Routledge, 1990. An examination of gay and lesbian films from 1919 to 1980.

Entertaining America: Jews, Movies, and Broadcasting. Ed. J. Hoberman and Jeffrey Shandler. Princeton: Princeton UP, 2003. About prominent Jews in U.S. entertainment and the changing representations of Jews in American movies, radio, and TV—for example, in the multiple movie versions of *The Jazz Singer*.

The Ethnic Eye: Latino Media Arts. Ed. Chon A. Noriega and Ana M. López. Minneapolis: U of Minnesota P, 1996. Examines the range of Latino media arts, from independent feature production to documentary to experimental video. The essays explore the work of Chicano, Puerto Rican, Cuban American, and Latino film and video artists.

History of the American Cinema. 10 vols. Ed. Charles Harpole. New York: Scribner's, 1990–2003. The University of California Press also publishes these volumes in paperback.

Balio, Tino. *Grand Design: Hollywood as a Modern Business Enterprise, 1930-1939*. New York: Scribner's, 1993.

Bowser, Eileen. *The Transformation of Cinema, 1907-1915*. New York: Scribner's, 1990.

Cook, David A. *Lost Illusions: American Cinema in the Shadow of Watergate and Vietnam, 1970–1979*. New York: Scribner's, 2000.

Crafton, Donald C. *The Talkies: American Cinema's Transition to Sound, 1926–1931*. New York: Scribner's, 1997.

Koszarski, Richard. *An Evening's Entertainment: The Age of the Silent Feature Picture, 1915–1928*. New York: Scribner's, 1990.

Lev, Peter. *The Fifties: Transforming the Screen, 1950–1959*. New York: Scribner's, 2003.

Monaco, Paul. *The Sixties, 1960-1969*. New York: Scribner's, 2001.

Musser, Charles. *The Emergence of Cinema: The American Screen to 1907*. New York: Scribner's, 1990.

Prince, Stephen. *A New Pot of Gold: Hollywood under the Electronic Rainbow, 1980–1989*. New York: Scribner's, 2000.

Schatz, Thomas. *Boom and Bust: The American Cinema in the 1940s*. New York: Scribner's, 1997.

Hollywood's Indian: The Portrayal of the Native American in Film. Ed. Peter C. Rollins and John E. O'Connor. Lexington: UP of Kentucky, 1998. Essays exploring the changing representations of Native Americans in American movies.

Mediating Two Worlds: Cinematic Encounters in the Americas. Ed. John King, Ana M. López, and Manuel Alvarado. London: BFI, 1993. Includes López's article "Are All Latins from Manhattan?"

Screening Asian Americans. Ed. Peter X. Feng. New Brunswick, NJ: Rutgers UP, 2002. Explores Asian American cinematic representations historically and socially. Includes consideration of Asian American documentary, experimental, and fictional films and a wide range of ethnicities.

Shaheen, Jack. *Reel Bad Arabs: How Hollywood Vilifies a People*. New York: Olive Branch Press, 2001. An account of the persistent and prolonged vilification of Arab peoples in mainstream Western movies. The book shows how the image of the "dirty Arab" has reemerged over the last thirty years, even as other groups have more or less successfully fought to eliminate the use of racist stereotypes.

Singer, Beverly R. *Wiping the War Paint off the Lens: Native American Film and Video*. Minneapolis: U of Minnesota P, 2001. Traces the history of Native American experiences as subjects, actors, and creators since the 1970s and develops a critical framework for approaching Native work. The book's approach is both cultural and personal and provides both historical views and close textual readings.

Sklar, Robert. *Film: An International History of the Medium*. 2nd ed. Upper Saddle River, NJ: Prentice, 2002. Includes brief chronologies with columns for film, arts and sciences, and world events; bibliography; glossary; filmography; and an extensive assortment of photographs.

Thompson, Kristin, and David Bordwell. *Film History: An Introduction*. 2nd ed. Boston: McGraw, 2003. A comprehensive, one-volume survey.

Turner, Graeme. *Film as Social Practice*. 3rd ed. London: Routledge, 1999. A textbook that explains how movies can be understood not merely as artistic creations but as "representational forms and social practices of popular culture."

Wyatt, Justin. *High Concept: Movies and Marketing in Hollywood*. Austin: U of Texas P, 1995. An examination of the historical, institutional, and economic forces that influence the making of popular movies. Includes discussion of the functions of advertising, market research, film structure, and casting.

CHAPTER 10

Thinking about Films

Terms in **boldface** are defined in the Illustrated Glossary beginning on page 621.

narrative: A representation of a series of unified events situated in one or more settings.

AS WE SEE A FILM AND THINK ABOUT IT AFTERWARD, we respond in many complex ways. We respond to the film's sensuousness, its visual and aural appeals, and its beauty or ugliness. For example, we may respond to a scene featuring a sunset that is irrelevant to a **narrative** but beautiful and life-affirming. We respond emotionally to a film, sometimes powerfully; thus many viewers cry more often in movie theaters than they do outside them. And we respond to a film by thinking about it during and after the showing. There is scarcely space to explore all these responses in a mere chapter. Instead, this chapter focuses on some of the major ways viewers think about a film. Critics and scholars have explored this aspect the most thoroughly, and it is so far the best understood. In addition, it is the aspect most useful to the beginning student in understanding and appreciating the film medium.

There are two components of thinking about films to be explored in this chapter: the viewers' expectations and hypotheses that continuously change as the film proceeds and the tendency of films to supply some explicit meanings and the viewer to create implicit meanings. The chapter also considers how explicit and implicit meanings may be symptomatic of the society in which the film was made and how the implicit meanings that viewers formulate are not universal but reflect various influences.

EXPECTATIONS AND INTERACTIONS

When I first showed *Smoke Signals* in Spokane to a largely Indian audience, we had to reshow it immediately because everyone had been talking so much and laughing so much. But when I showed it at the Nantucket Film Festival [in Massachusetts], it was very quiet during the showing. There was some laughter, but I don't think they saw the humor in it. There was certainly none of the raucous laughter of Indian groups watching the film. (Alexie)

If viewers are told beforehand that they are going to see a film entitled "Bambi Meets Godzilla" (1969), they begin to formulate expectations about the film. Some laugh at the mere mention of the title. When I asked students to write down their expectations for the film based on its title, some guessed that they were about to see a romance. As one wrote, "I expect a beautiful woman to be meeting some big, rugged guy." Others hypothesized a David and Goliath story: "Bambi is smarter than Godzilla and outwits him in the end." One student expected "a giant lizard chasing a baby deer around Tokyo." Various others expected Godzilla to fight Bambi: "I expect a gruesome tale of violence and bloodsport between two very different adversaries." Godzilla has a history of violence though Bambi does not, so right away we viewers are surprised by the matchup. If viewers know something about film history, they might assume that "Bambi Meets Godzilla" is about two modes of filmmaking: Disney's high-budget color animation and the low-budget, black-and-white Japanese action films of the 1950s and 1960s. Before a film begins, even based on only a title, we viewers begin formulating expectations and hypotheses.

As "Bambi Meets Godzilla" begins, soothing music accompanies the basic animation of Bambi's grazing. Nothing happens for a while except from time to time Bambi stops grazing to look upward as more and more opening credits roll by. We viewers soon notice that Marv Newland did all the work on the film, including the "choreography" and "Bambi's wardrobe."

Soon Godzilla's foot abruptly flattens Bambi as the sound shifts from the flute and strings music to a loud discordant chord (played on a piano?) that gradually starts fading out. Next, "the end" is **superimposed** and erased backward quickly a letter at a time, and we realize that the film has not met the viewers' usual expectation that a film show at least some of its story *after* the opening credits. Guess what? The film is still not over. There is yet another credit: "We gratefully acknowledge the city of Tokyo for their help in obtaining Godzilla for this film." While Godzilla's foot remains unmoving on the film's hapless costar, its toenails extend straight out then go limp and hang downward again, which is another unexpected and puzzling development in the plot. Has Godzilla experienced excitement followed by release? Is it merely twitchy or stretching or tired? Viewers cannot know the cause of the toenail movement or its significance. Finally, the image and chord fade out together as this ninety-second film ends.

The film's title and opening image create certain expectations, but viewers are quickly surprised and amused. Few viewers will correctly anticipate the resulting developments: the timing and manner of Bambi's demise and the mysterious reaction of Godzilla's toenails. Nor are viewers likely to expect the prominence of the credits and their whimsy. The minimal story (Bambi eats; Bambi meets Godzilla; Godzilla remains standing and unmoving except for some toenails) happens behind the credits. Rarely have credits and a filmmaker's ego so (knowingly and amusingly) been used to compete with story.

Because human creativity is boundless, films may elicit countless viewer expectations and interactions. For example, a film may repeat itself in an

superimposition: Two or more images photographed or printed on top of each other.

endless loop, thwarting viewers' expectations of a completed narrative. Canadian Rodney Graham's "Vexation Island" (1997) is set on a small tropical island with a prominent coconut palm tree, green vegetation, a pristine beach, and aqua blue water. A buccaneer with a small wooden keg under his neck is stretched out on his back near a large coconut palm tree, seemingly asleep though he seems to have a wound on his forehead. Nearby are a parrot and another small wooden keg (color plate 32 in Chapter 2). After the parrot squawks, the man slowly opens his eyes and slowly stands up. While standing, he looks around briefly, spots the coconut palm tree, and starts to shake its trunk. A coconut comes loose, falls, and hits him on the forehead, and he falls backward. He ends up in the same position he was in near the film's beginning, passed out and with one of those small wooden kegs under his neck. In the last shot, the coconut rolls to the edge of the water where a wave carries it offscreen. The film then begins again and repeats itself indefinitely.

wide-screen: Film format with an aspect ratio noticeably greater than 1.33:1 (a shape wider than that of an analog TV screen).

resolution: The degree of detail visible in an image.

Because of the film's **wide-screen** images, high-quality color, detailed **resolution**, sound, **setting** (tropical island with a prominent coconut palm), and subject (lone buccaneer), viewers may initially expect that yet another castaway movie is in the offing. Soon, they may infer that the man is shipwrecked (seemingly isolated tropical island, those small wooden kegs, and the bruise on his forehead). But by the end of this nine-minute wordless film, viewers realize that the man is likely the victim not of a shipwreck but of a world that continuously frustrates his desires and any type of progress. Like Sisyphus—the character from Greek legend who was doomed to endlessly push a boulder up a hill only to watch it roll back down, follow it, and push it up again—he seems doomed to relive a repetitive, uneventful, and thwarted existence. Viewers may realize that the film also frustrates their desires for a story with a sense of development and resolution. After all, viewers tend to expect a story to begin, develop, and end.

celluloid: Synonym for *movie*, as in "celluloid heroes."

Normally, before we see a film, we know something about it. Usually we know its title, and that alone may conjure up visions to come, as we saw above in the case of "Bambi Meets Godzilla" and as when we see a film called *Tarzan*. Most viewers have seen at least one **celluloid** Tarzan story or read a Tarzan story and thus would expect a tale about a man brought up in the wild and isolated from Western civilization until some of its emissaries intrude into his world (see Figure 9.9 on pp. 422–23). If the movie we are to see has popular actors, we may know something about at least one of them. We may know something about the director and something about the types of films he or she tends to direct. We may have heard or seen a review or talked with a friend who's seen the film. We might even know the **genre**, or basic type of film, we are to see, such as western, musical, science fiction, horror, or detective. If so, we will expect the film to conform to at least the basics of the genre. For example, if we are going to see a 1950s western, we expect to see a lawful man, usually of European descent, challenged by lawless European American men, Mexicans, or Native Americans. Normally, too, genres set parameters to a narrative: what is possible, what is not. Thus, if we know we are going to see a western, we do not expect alien invaders sixty minutes into the film, nor do we at any time expect the woman who works in the dancehall to dance the *salsa* or *merengue*.

Our expectations may be shaped by other factors. The film's rating may lead us to expect sex and violence. Or we may have seen a **trailer**; we may have seen a printed advertisement, visited the film's site on the Internet, read Internet reviews of a test screening of the film, seen the film promoted on a cable channel, or seen toy spin-offs or other product tie-ins, all of which created expectations—sometimes false ones. Consider a poster for *High Sierra* (1941) and one for *The Maltese Falcon* (1941, Figure 10.1). Although the

trailer: A brief compilation film shown to advertise a movie or a video release.

a)

b)

FIGURE 10.1 Publicity shaping expectations
(a) A publicity still for *High Sierra*, a movie that first appeared early in 1941 featuring Humphrey Bogart as a criminal. (b) A poster advertising *The Maltese Falcon*, which appeared later in 1941. From the second poster, would-be viewers might expect to see Bogart reprise his role as a criminal because he looks like the criminal character he played in *High Sierra*. Note, for example, that his haircut is the same one he had in the earlier movie and that a vaguely defined shirt has been drawn in beneath his head. Because Bogart holds a smoking gun in the poster for *The Maltese Falcon*, we might expect him to fire a gun in that film (he does not). And we might expect Mary Astor to sport a fancy hairdo and wear glamorous, revealing evening clothing. Wrong again. *Warner Bros.–First National*

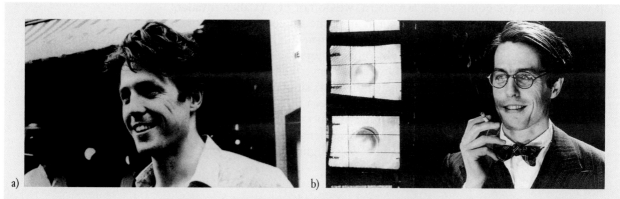

FIGURE 10.2 Publicity, expectations, and viewer responses
(a) In *Four Weddings and a Funeral* (1994), Hugh Grant plays a boyish, reserved, charming, yet nervous and bumbling heterosexual. (b) In *An Awfully Big Adventure* (1995), Grant plays a sarcastic gay director of a local theatrical company with whom an impressionable sixteen-year-old girl becomes infatuated. Before the film was publicized, its director warned that if *An Awfully Big Adventure* were marketed as the new film from the star and director of *Four Weddings and a Funeral*, "they'll kill it stone dead. . . . All the effort this time should go to altering expectations" (Maslin 11). (a) *Duncan Kenworthy; Gramercy Pictures;* (b) *Hilary Heath and Philip Hinchcliffe; Fine Line Features*

poster for *The Maltese Falcon* is misleading, it probably did not hurt the film at the box office; but advertising that creates fundamentally false expectations can hurt a film's chances for commercial success. Advertising for a movie that is released shortly after an immensely popular film but features the star in a very different role can be especially perilous (Figure 10.2). Then, too, a distributor may carry a film that garners excellent reviews but never find an effective way to market the film. In such cases, distributors occasionally try to promote the film again at a later time—and again fail to attract large audiences. That was the experience of Warner Bros. in trying to market *A Little Princess* (1995) and Paramount in trying to market *Wonder Boys* (2000). Often the advertising for a film arouses interest and creates reasonable expectations, as was done by a famous poster for *Persona* suggesting a mystery about the film's dual subjects (1966, Figure 10.3).

From all these and other sources, we enter the theater or approach the video store rental counter with expectations: to be amused, amazed, mystified, inspired, aroused, frightened, or something else. Once the film begins, its music or visuals or both start to influence the viewer's expectations. Theatrical showings of *West Side Story* (1961) and *Lawrence of Arabia* (1962, 1989), for example, begin with a design or blank screen and an overture of the film's music, thus giving a sampling of the music and moods to come. Much more often, music and moving images are used in tandem near the film's beginning. Consider the opening seconds of the superhero action movie *Spawn* (1997). First we see and hear a fiery explosion and briefly hear a (church?) bell ring faintly in the background. Sounds of wind and a chorus holding long notes are heard as we see a fiery round tunnel (seen later in the film as a gateway to hell). Then the **narrator** intones, "The battle between heaven and hell has waged eternal, their armies fueled by souls harvested on earth." Shortly after the beginning of the narration, a flying white dove is seen against the fiery background; then a bright white, round shape like the sun is seen behind the fire. Even without the narrator's exposition, the film immediately encourages the viewer to expect the central conflict of the story to come: fire and destruction versus light and peace. As a narrative film progresses, we also interact with it as readers interact with a written **text**:

text: Something that people produce or modify to communicate meaning.

The literary text may be conceived of as a dynamic system of gaps. A reader who wishes . . . to . . . reconstruct . . . the fictive world and action [that a text] projects is necessarily compelled to pose and answer, throughout the reading-process, such questions as, What is happening or has happened, and why? What is the connection between this **event** and the previous ones? What is the motivation of this or that character? To what extent does the logic of cause and effect correspond to that of everyday life? and so on. Most of the answers to these questions, however, are not provided explicitly, fully and authoritatively (let alone immediately) by the text but must be worked out by the reader himself on the basis of the implicit guidance it affords. . . . Some [gaps] can . . . be filled in almost automatically, while others require conscious and laborious consideration; some can be filled in fully and definitely, others only partially and tentatively; some by a single [hypothesis], others by several (different, conflicting, or even mutually exclusive) hypotheses. (Sternberg 50)

Throughout a narrative film we ask and try to answer a series of questions and fill in the gaps with our own inferences and hypotheses. Without the attentive eyes and ears

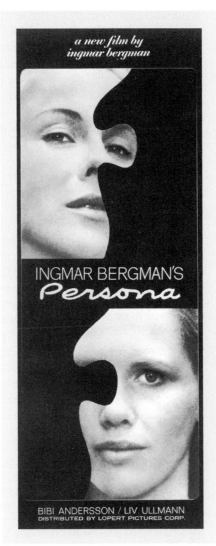

FIGURE 10.3 Publicity fostering appropriate expectations
This poster for Ingmar Bergman's *Persona* (1966) fosters appropriate viewer expectations and does so almost exclusively by its visuals. The poster's subject is two women seen close up but not seen in their entirety. If joined together, the two images would not show two complete faces but part of the first face overlapping the second and part of the second overlapping the first. *Persona* is about two women who are as closely associated as the parts of a puzzle. The film is concerned with the women's psychology and uses many close-ups of faces, and both that subject and that technique are characteristic of many films directed by Bergman. In short, the poster suggests that *Persona* is a Bergman film about women—this one about two incomplete women who are parts of a puzzle that do not fit together naturally. *Ingmar Bergman; United Artists*

and active minds of the viewing audience, the film is incomplete—mere changing images and sounds. Viewers are not simply receptacles of a cascade of audio and visual information but collaborators and players with a wondrous, elaborate mechanism.

If the film is to hold our attention, it must arouse viewer interest fairly quickly and from time to time renew that interest. In narrative films, story developments encourage us to consider possible consequences. We will get involved and be satisfied or frustrated in part by how well the film lives up to our changing expectations. We like to be manipulated, up to a point. People who enjoy horror films, for example, want to feel the tiny hairs on the back of their necks tingle—or at least they don't mind if they do. But viewers normally also crave variety, surprise, suspense, and some mental challenges. By the film's ending they like to think that they understand the film, more or less anticipated the major developments, or at least now see how developments could follow from earlier events, and viewers like to see unity and meaning in it all. There is much to experience in one viewing; later viewings of the same film usually reveal additional complexities, subtleties, meanings, and hidden meanings or ambiguities. In analyzing a film, many viewers find it useful to consider many of the issues relating to expectations and interactions, including consistency, plausibility, predictability, surprise, and suspense.

For a few movies, seeing them again and again has become a more interactive and more communal experience than the usual film showing. The most popular of these cult favorites are *The Rocky Horror Picture Show* (1975) in the United States and elsewhere and *The Sound of Music* (1965), which was first shown in the sing-along mode in the United Kingdom and later on tour as *Sing-a-Long Sound of Music* in Canada, the United States, Australia, and other countries. Audiences know these cult films thoroughly and sing their songs at full volume in the theater. During these showings, the films themselves create no surprises, but the film audiences do: for instance, audience members volunteer supplementary sound effects, wisecracks, and cheers, hisses, boos, and other sounds. During *The Rocky Horror Picture Show* they may also throw objects at the screen or squirt water pistols.[1] A more recent example of a film with devoted fans who enjoy repeated viewings and audience participation is *Hedwig and the Angry Inch* (2001, see Figure 7.20d on p. 309).

Digital video makes possible new types of audience-film interactions. For example, a Canadian filmmaker made a short movie about himself seeking and telephoning the girl with whom at age twelve he had had his first dance,

---

[1]The two-disc DVD of *The Rocky Horror Picture Show* has options that allow viewers to periodically see an audience's reactions to a showing of *Rocky Horror* and that encourage viewer participation, and the film's Web site, <Rockyhorror.com>, includes a variety of information, including what props to bring to a showing (for example, rice) and how to use the props during a showing. For a vivid account of *Sing-a-Long Sound of Music* showings in London, including sample wisecracks, see Kevin Murphy's *A Year at the Movies: One Man's Filmgoing Odyssey* (69–70).

telling the woman he was now a filmmaker, and inviting her to a showing of his movies. At a certain point during the showing of his film that showed the filmmaker searching for the girl and telephoning her, he had the projectionist stop the video when the screen read "Marie-France, Where are you?" The audience began chanting her name. She stood up. He brought her before the audience of five hundred and asked the projectionist to resume showing the video. As it showed "two teenagers dancing in the dancehall of the high school, . . . he took Marie-France by the hand and said let's dance." And they did, as many others in the audience joined them in dancing ("Behind").

Digital filmmaking for theaters and the Internet also makes possible yet other alternatives to the usual interplay of expectations and interactions. *Time Code* (2000), which consists of four simultaneous uninterrupted **plotlines** shown on the quadrants of the movie screen (see Figure 6.13 on p. 265), requires viewers to decide which story line to interact with and for how long. And Internet films such as Amy Talkington's four-minute "The New Arrival" (2000) allow viewers to use the computer mouse to pan left or right around a 360-degree **filmic** world with potential action or significant details in every direction. In these and other films that are made possible by developments in technology, the viewer has choices about where to interact with the story and for how long.

plotline: A narrative or series of related events usually involving only a few characters or people and capable of functioning on its own as a story.

filmic: Characteristic of the film medium or appropriate to it.

TYPES OF MEANINGS

> They watch moving shadows in dark caves together. Human females enjoy stories about one person dying slowly. The males prefer stories of many people dying quickly. (extraterrestrial narrator in *The Mating Habits of the Earthbound Human*, 1999)

We see a film; we think about it afterward; often we discuss it with others. Sometimes we read about others' thoughts about the film. Often we generalize about the film or an aspect of it. We may say, for example, that it glorifies violence or shows that wrongdoers end up suffering themselves. When we generalize about a subject, such as a film or an aspect of one, we are making **meanings**; we are explaining in general terms what we see as significant. It is crucial to remember that identifying a subject is not the same as explaining a meaning. A subject may be identified in one word or a short phrase. To explain a meaning requires at least one sentence. For example, one subject of the western *Unforgiven* (1992) is *killing*. One of the film's meanings is that *killing a man may be difficult for a person to do*. In a fictional film, meanings are usually a viewer's generalizations about the characters' situations, personalities, ideas, and behavior. In a **documentary film**, meanings tend to be generalizations about the subjects **represented** in the film (for an example, see Figure 8.1 on p. 350). In an **experimental film**, meanings are typically generalizations viewers make about film **conventions**, the

documentary film: A film or video representation of actual (not imaginary) subjects.

representation: A likeness of a subject created in a text.

experimental film: A film that rejects the conventions of mainstream movies and explores the possibilities of the film medium.

convention: In films and other texts, a subject or technique that makers of texts and audiences have grown to accept as natural or typical in certain contexts.

experimental film's untraditional representation of its subjects, or the properties of the film medium itself (for example, see Figure 8.22 on p. 376).

Meaning may be divided into three types. An explicit meaning is a general verbal observation in a text (such as a film) about one or more of its subjects. An implicit meaning is a generalization that viewers infer about a text or a subject in a text. A symptomatic meaning is a generalization about a text or part of a text that is characteristic of the society that nurtured the film.[2]

Explicit Meanings

title card: A card or thin sheet of clear plastic on which is written or printed information included in a film.

Explicit meanings are general observations included in a text about one or more of its subjects. In silent films, they may be conveyed by a subtitle or a **title card**. A sound film may use these forms of language and many other forms, such as a narrator, dialogue, or a monologue.

In silent films, examples of explicit meaning are commonplace. A title card of the classic American film *Greed* (1925) reads: "First . . . chance had brought them face to face; now . . . mysterious instincts, as ungovernable as the winds of the heavens, were knitting their lives together." Another explicit meaning is found in a title card early in *Sunrise* (1927):

> For wherever the sun rises and sets . . .
> in the city's turmoil
> or
> under the open sky on the farm,
> life is much the same:
> sometimes bitter, sometimes sweet.

Yet another explicit meaning in a film from the silent era occurs at the end of the classic German film *Metropolis* (1926): "Without the heart there can be no understanding between the hands and the mind."

Explicit meanings are less common in fictional sound films than in fictional silent films, but they are by no means rare. In *Unforgiven*, the Clint Eastwood character, William Munny, sometimes generalizes about one of the film's subjects, such as violence and killing. Approximately 108⅔ minutes into the film, for example, he says, "It's a hell of a thing killing a man. You take away all he's got and all he's ever gonna have." In narrative films, explicit meanings are generally not crucial to the plot. Munny's general statement, for example, could have been omitted without affecting the story. If an explicit meaning is short and well phrased, it may be memorable, as is the case of what Uncle Ben tells Peter Parker 35¾ minutes into *Spider-Man* (2002), "With great power comes great responsibility."

---

[2]For the terms *explicit meaning, implicit meaning,* and *symptomatic meaning,* I am indebted to David Bordwell's *Making Meaning: Inference and Rhetoric in the Interpretation of Cinema.*

A film's title may also reveal an explicit meaning. An animated film called "Technological Threat" (1988) shows that office workers may be replaced by more efficient anthropomorphic machines. There is also an explicit meaning in the title *Fatal Attraction* (1987): an attraction can be fatal or at least detrimental. A title may also misrepresent a story or understate a meaning. Mike Leigh's *Life Is Sweet* (1990)—about a husband and wife and their two very different grown twin daughters and three male friends—shows both sweetness and considerable emotional pain and could more accurately be characterized as bittersweet.

An explicit meaning is not necessarily comprehensive or persuasive; it is certainly not the final word on any subject. At the end of the original *King Kong* (1933), for example, one character says of Kong's fate, "It was beauty killed the beast." Many critics find that blame misplaced and the interpretation simplistic. If a fictional or experimental film explains meanings too often or if the meanings are already apparent to viewers but they are told what meanings are intended, viewers may be annoyed that they were not allowed to discover the significance for themselves. General statements are commonplace, however, in documentary films, usually in the form of a narrator, interviews, subtitles, or title cards.

Implicit Meanings

An **implicit meaning** is a generalization that a viewer or reader makes about a text (such as a film) or subject in a text. For example, an implicit meaning may be a viewer's generalization about an implication of a narrative or the significance of a symbol. In this section, we see how viewers can use awareness of cinematic **techniques**, symbols, satire, and narratives or stories to develop implicit meanings.

film technique: Any aspect of filmmaking, such as the use of sets, lighting, sound effects, music, or editing.

CINEMATIC TECHNIQUES

As is explained and illustrated throughout Part One of this book, the arrangement of the subjects within the **frame** (**composition**), the lenses, lighting, camera distances and angles, sound mix, and many other aspects of filmmaking may all affect what meanings audiences detect.

Consider a **shot** from about 39¾ minutes into the original *Psycho* (1960) that shows a man sitting in a room (Figure 10.4). Setting, lighting, camera angle, and composition all help suggest that the human subject is strange, if not dangerous. How different the mood and meaning would be if the setting had been a knotty pine back wall with only a large frame containing a print of mountains, the lighting bright and even, the camera at an **eye-level angle**, and the man in the center of the frame. Then the man would not seem strange and certainly not dangerous.

Editing also influences meanings. As explained and illustrated in the section called Juxtapositions in Chapter 3, a shot can develop or undercut

shot (noun): An uninterrupted strip of exposed motion-picture film or videotape that represents a subject during an uninterrupted segment of time.

edit: To select and arrange the processed segments of photographed motion-picture film or videotape.

FIGURE 10.4 Mise en scène and cinematography creating meaning
In a scene from the original *Psycho* (1960), a young woman has a conversation with the motel manager in a room behind the motel office. In the shot represented here—one of a dozen taken from the same camera position—setting, lighting, camera angle, and composition help create meaning. The illuminated stuffed bird seen above the painting of the nude woman is disquieting, as if the bird is poised to attack the woman below it. The painting behind the man is of a naked woman seemingly menaced by two men. Hard light illuminates parts of the setting (notice the sharp edges of the owl's shadow), and there are areas of darkness and shadows. Then, too, most of the light illuminates that large menacing stuffed bird and the side of the man's face. The hard lighting does nothing to soften the image or enhance its appeal. The camera angle is from below the subject and from off to one side (the dark side); viewers do not see the man eye to eye. In addition, he is positioned way off to the right side of the frame with only the large stuffed birds and the paintings of mostly naked (vulnerable?) women to balance out the composition. Altogether the techniques used suggest that for the woman the man is talking with the situation is uncomfortable, perhaps even dangerous. Frame enlargement. *Alfred Hitchcock; Universal*

fast cutting: Editing characterized by frequent brief shots.

montage: A series of brief shots used to represent a condensation of subjects and time.

the meaning(s) of the preceding shot. Superimposition and **fast cutting** can also create meanings. The forty-two-second **montage** of Susan's opera career that begins almost 94⅔ minutes into *Citizen Kane* (1941) conveys an enormous amount of information, including the consequences of a man forcing a woman to do what she is ill equipped and reluctant to do.

For descriptions of the opera montage in *Citizen Kane*, see the Web site for this book: <bedfordstmartins.com/phillips-film>.

Sounds that are selected, modified, and combined can also create or change meaning. During the 1987 Academy Awards ceremony, a clip from *The Sound of Music* showed Julie Andrews running through a meadow as viewers heard not the original soundtrack but sounds of an airplane engine and machine-gun fire. Because of the sounds, viewers incorrectly (and humorously) inferred that she was under attack. In *What's Up, Tiger Lily?* (1966), Woody Allen took a Japanese movie and redubbed it. With the new soundtrack, the cast of characters now includes Phil Moscowitz, a type of James Bond character, Wing Fat, and the sisters Terri and Suki Yaki, and the action centers on rivals trying to acquire a famous egg salad recipe. Overlap-

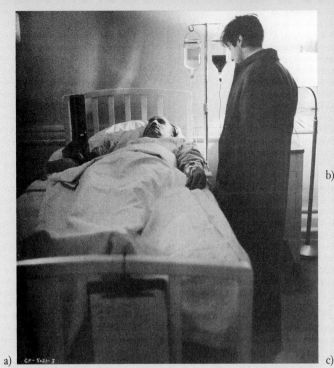

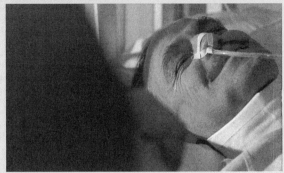

a) CF- 5·21- 3   b)   c)

FIGURE 10.5 Obvious and subtle use of film techniques
(a) This publicity still for *The Godfather* (1972) shows an image that was posed for the benefit of a still photographer and was used in publicizing the film but does not appear in it. (b–c) Frames from the last two shots of the same scene, which begins approximately 65¼ minutes into the film, show the scene's subdued lighting, two expressive faces, restrained acting, and in the scene's last shot the complex feelings conjured up by actor Marlon Brando's slight smile and a tear near his right eye. The film's mise en scène subtly suggests a love, respect, and affection not captured by the publicity still's greater camera distance from the subjects, brighter lighting, and greater emphasis on the setting than the faces of the two human subjects. (b–c) Frame enlargements. *The Coppola Company; Paramount*

ping dialogue—as in some films directed by Orson Welles and some directed by Robert Altman—suggests how people may talk *at* but not *to* or *with* each other. **Scenes** with this use of sound suggest that people may be together physically but isolated emotionally or spiritually.

Meaning in films, then, is always created or modified by the techniques of cinema, though it is important to remember that a technique's meaning can depend on the place and time the film was made. As we saw in Chapter 3, in previous years filmmakers tended to use **lap dissolves** to delete insignificant action and time within a scene. Later in the history of cinema, lap dissolves usually mean that the action is changing to a different setting or a later time or both.

The subtle use of cinematic techniques may have more impact than an obvious one because viewers are forced to imagine what happens and help create meaning (Figure 10.5).

scene: A section of a narrative that gives the impression of continuous action taking place in continuous time and space.

lap dissolve: A transition between shots in which one shot begins to fade out as the next shot fades in, overlapping the first shot before replacing it.

Some viewers believe that erotic situations are sexier if restraint is used in the representation. Sometimes a look can carry more erotic charge than caressing or kissing. And often the images that viewers imagine are more erotic than images on a screen. Novelist Leslie Epstein recounts that for her, "Perhaps the most erotic scene in all the sixties occurs in *Persona*. . . . Bibi Andersson tells the half-catatonic Liv Ullmann about the time she and a friend had been lying on a beach [sunbathing nude]. . . . Nothing [much] moves but the one actress's lips and the other's eyes" (289). About 28⅔ minutes into the film, the Bibi Andersson character's account begins as follows:

> Suddenly I saw two figures leaping about on the rocks above us who kept hiding and peeking. "There are two boys looking at us," I said to the girl. Her name was Katarina. "Let them look," she said, turning over on her back. It was such a strange feeling. I just lay there with my bottom in the air not a bit embarrassed. I felt very calm. Wasn't it funny? And Katarina was beside me with her big breasts and thighs. She just lay there giggling to herself. Then I saw that the boys had come closer and were staring at us. They were awfully young. Then the bolder of the two came over and squatted down beside Katarina and pretended to be busy with his foot and started to poke between his toes. I . . . I felt all funny. Suddenly I heard Katarina say: "Come here a minute." Then she helped him off with his jeans and shirt. Then he was on top of her. She showed him how and held him by his fanny. The other boy sat on the rock watching. I heard Katarina whisper and laugh. The boy's face was close to mine. It was all flushed and puffy. I turned over and said: "Won't you come to me too?" And Katarina said: "Yes, go to her now." So he left her and fell roughly on top of me and grabbed one of my breasts. It was over for me almost at once.

If the film instead showed a **flashback** of what happened, that part of the film would be less erotic for some viewers because instead of hearing once and briefly that the two boys were "awfully young," viewers would continuously see how young they are, and that would be troubling for some viewers who would interpret the scene as being about adults seducing children. For many viewers, then, the restrained representation in *Persona* is more erotic than a more explicit rendition.

Near the end of Fellini's *8½* (1963) is another example of less is more. After Guido, a distraught film director, has hidden under a table at his nightmarish press conference and pulled a pistol from his pocket (almost 127 minutes into the film), we see a scene consisting of only one shot: Guido's mother on a beach turning and calling offscreen "Guido. Guido. Where are you running, you low-life?" We first see her in **medium shot**, but as she stops running and begins to call out, the camera seems to race away from her, and we end up seeing her in **extreme long shot**, her face no longer discernible. In the next shot, we see Guido under the table again, hear a gunshot, and see his head drop. In the six or so seconds before Guido's fantasized death, we experience not the expected rush of images and sounds from

medium shot: Shot in which the subject and surroundings are given about equal importance.

extreme long shot: A shot in which the subject appears to be far from the camera.

Guido's life but one brief, spare, evocative scene. We do not even see Guido. We see only his mother being annoyed with him because he is evidently running away. By the end of the scene, Guido is presumably gone (in more than one sense), and she has shrunk in size and importance. The scene displays great restraint. Much more time, many more images, a much richer soundtrack could have been used, but the muse whispered to the director Federico Fellini, "Federico, less is more." For many viewers, it is off-putting for movies to explain their ideas, so teachers and books implore future scriptwriters to "show, don't tell": don't tell viewers anything that can be shown instead or has already been shown.

Finally, we can see how less can be more by considering another film that sometimes chooses to show less than it could (Figure 10.6).

FIGURE 10.6 Less is more
In *The Lord of the Rings: The Fellowship of the Ring* (2001), viewers learn that Sauron gave each of nine great kings a ring of power. "Blinded by their greed, they took them without question [and] one by one have fallen into darkness." They now are "Ringwraiths," neither living nor dead, and slaves to Sauron. Wearing black hoods and traveling on horseback, the nine can feel the presence of the ring and perpetually seek the one who carries it. Nearly always their faces remain unseen, which is doubly appropriate because they have no individuality and because human-shaped creatures without faces (the unknown) can be more frightening than men with faces (the known). Less is more. Frame enlargement. *New Line Cinema & WingNut Films; New Line Cinema*

Subtle technique is not without risks. If the image or sound is too faint or too fleeting or both, or if viewers are otherwise engaged, they may miss a significant detail, even on many later re-viewings. An example of excessive subtlety is from *Citizen Kane*. After Susan's disastrous opera career, Kane insists she persevere. Then comes the famous opera montage and the aftermath of Susan's suicide attempt. Just before Susan revives, one can hear an instrumental version of a fragment of an aria that Susan had struggled with during a singing lesson earlier in the narrative (86 minutes, 28 seconds). After Susan's revival, the music plays faintly for about fifty seconds as she tells Kane she couldn't make him understand how she felt and how the audience simply didn't want her. As Kane says, "That's when you've got to fight 'em," the music stops.

The music is in a minor key and sounds as if it's coming from a faraway calliope, the kind of instrument you may have heard played on merry-go-rounds. The music is a subtle reminder of Susan's disastrous singing career: she was as ill-suited for singing opera as that calliope was to render an aria. However, the music after Susan's suicide attempt is so faint that few viewers ever hear it. It is so faint that I heard it only after many viewings over the years and then only on a laser videodisc version (no projector noise to contend with). Even after I told a class about the music and played the laser disc version for them, some did not hear it. Like so much of *Citizen Kane*, it's a brilliant touch, but, as occasionally happens in the film, it is too subtle.[3]

Another example of filmmakers being too subtle occurs early in another widely admired film, *The Searchers* (1956). Ethan Edwards hates Comanches because early in the film they kill his brother, Aaron, two of Aaron's three children, and, most important, Aaron's wife, for whom Ethan has special feelings (the film is restrained in suggesting why and how deeply). Understandably, critics seem not to have noticed that Comanches had also killed Ethan's mother. When Comanches are about to attack Aaron Edwards and his family, Aaron and his wife send their little daughter Debbie to hide by her grandmother's grave. Before Debbie sits in front of the tombstone, at about 20⅔ minutes into the film for six video frames (out of thirty per second) the following is legible:

> Here lies
> Mary Jane Edwards
> killed by
> Comanches
> May 12, 1852
> A good wife and mother
> In her 41st year.

If viewers noticed this detail, they could better understand Ethan's feelings about Comanches and his obsession to retrieve from them his sole surviving relative, his niece Debbie. But how many viewers read the tombstone since they have only a fifth of a second to do so?

Like all who hope to communicate effectively, regardless of the medium, filmmakers are challenged to have a clear sense of their audiences and not to insult them by being too obvious or lose them by being so subtle that audiences have no chance of getting the point, even during later re-viewings. For those who make texts, it is a judgment call, sometimes wisely made, sometimes not.

In these examples and elsewhere, the filmmakers may have known how demanding they were being when they used these subtle techniques. Perhaps filmmakers include them for those in the audience who are especially observant. Perhaps they include such subtleties for those who see the film more than once, as rewards for the faithful. Perhaps they include such touches for their own pleasure in being creative and sly. Then, too, possibly the filmmakers were unaware of how demanding they were being and simply goofed, which is possible even in otherwise brilliantly made films.

Sometimes viewers miss the significance of a technique because they watch a videotape version. Prints of films shown in commercial theaters usu-

---

[3]On the Criterion CAV laser disc version of *Citizen Kane*, the music can be heard on side 4, frames 20,200 and following. If the volume is turned way up, the music is also audible about 96 minutes, 57 seconds into the DVD version.

a) b)

FIGURE 10.7 Subtle visual clue

In *Citizen Kane* (1941), (a) Kane's second wife, Susan, owns a doll seen on the bed in her room 104⅓ minutes into the film, on the day she walks out of her marriage (the doll is also visible 108½ minutes into the film). Even though the doll is large and prominent in the frame the first time viewers can see it, many viewers do not notice it, let alone consider its possible function. (Like the doll, Susan has been mainly another pretty plaything; the doll being on Susan's bed could be symbolic.) (b) Even more subtle is the last appearance of Susan's doll, visible only for a few seconds 115⅗ minutes into the film, amid the vast collection of objects from Kane's life, revealing that even though Susan left Kane and he then tore up her room in anger, he kept her doll (he also kept her glass paperweight, which he holds at the moment of his death). Seeing that doll among all that other stuff whose fate is soon to be a fiery furnace is extremely difficult on a videotape shown on any analog TV or monitor or during any broadcast to an analog TV. Frame enlargements. *Orson Welles; RKO General Pictures*

ally have detailed images. But when films are shown on an analog television set, the results are somewhat blurred and **grainy** (since video images have less definition than film images). The lighting is without subtle shades (**high contrast**), and in shadowed areas details tend to get lost because analog TV has far less range of tones than film; thus, many details in dark scenes are especially difficult to see. That is why films with many dark scenes—such as *The Third Man* (1949), the *Godfather* films, some of the *Batman* films since the late 1980s, and most **films noirs**—are frustrating to watch on analog television or videotape. Even in well-lit scenes, viewers watching on analog TV are likely to miss such significant details as the fleeting triple superimposition of the last shot of *Psycho* (see Figure 3.14 on p. 132). On analog TV it is also difficult to spot significant details in *Citizen Kane*, including the whiskey bottle Kane finds in the bookcase of Susan's room (109½ minutes) and her doll (Figure 10.7).

SYMBOLS

A **symbol** is anything perceptible in a text that has significance or meaning beyond its usual meaning or function. Every society has certain universally accepted symbols: each society invests certain sounds and sights with widely

grainy: Having rough visual texture.

high contrast: Photographic image with few gradations between the darkest and lightest parts of the image.

film noir: A type of film first made in the United States during and after World War II, characterized by frequent scenes with dark, shadowy (low-key) lighting; (usually) urban settings; characters motivated by selfishness, greed, cruelty, ambition, and lust; and characters willing to lie, frame, double-cross, and kill or have others killed.

understood meanings. In many societies, for example, a red traffic light symbolizes that people approaching it should stop. Painters, writers, filmmakers, and others who create imaginative texts may also create symbols (not always consciously). Depending on contexts, a sound, word (including a name), color, or representation of an object, action, or person may function as a symbol. Viewers (or readers) do not perceive a symbol as merely performing its usual functions; they see it as also conveying meaning.

In *The Godfather* (1972), *The Godfather Part II* (1974), and *The Godfather Part III* (1990), doors or doorways do not always function simply as connections between rooms: they are sometimes symbols. In the last two shots of *The Godfather*, Michael's wife, Kay, sees him through an open door in his office surrounded by three of his men. One of them kisses Michael's hand and says "Don Corleone"—meaning that Michael is now the head of the Corleone family and its criminal business. The second man kisses Michael's hand, and at nearly the same time, the third man goes to the door and closes it. The film's final action obliterates Kay from Michael's and our view and, more important, blocks both Kay and the audience from further views of Michael's criminal life. Here, the door symbolizes how criminal activities must be carried on out of sight. Nearly 186 minutes into *The Godfather Part II*, Michael finds Kay, who is now estranged from him, sneaking a visit to their two children at the Corleone estate. After a tense, wordless, face-to-face confrontation of about thirty seconds—and many viewers may find that to be an enormous amount of silence in a film with dialogue—Michael shuts the door in Kay's uncertain, then pained face. About 122½ minutes into *The Godfather Part III*, it seems that Kay is about to be reconciled with Michael, and they are holding hands. A man knocks on and opens twin doors leading into the room. In the background a woman is weeping. The man backs into the other room as Michael approaches him and asks what's wrong. The man tells Michael that a long-term associate has been shot. As Michael and the man talk, Kay moves sideways to see Michael and the man better, bends slightly sideways, and moves forward to see and hear more clearly. Still with his back to Kay, Michael has put his hand on the man's arm, thereby evidently indicating to him to move sideways; they do so, in effect making it harder for Kay to see and hear. (Probably Michael thinks Kay would be trying to learn what is going on.) We hear Kay's voice saying, "It never ends." After watching for a few more moments, she turns and walks out of the frame, no reconciliation after all. In all three movies, the door or doorway symbolizes the barrier that has come between Michael and his wife and reinforces an important meaning of the *Godfather* films: involvement in crime precludes spousal intimacy and trust.

The *Godfather* movies are rich in symbols. Another one occurs in *The Godfather* at the beginning and ending of the scene where Luca Brasi (Vito's faithful henchman) is strangled to death, and the camera looks into the bar through a glass window with fish etched on it (41⅔ and 43½ minutes into the film). Later, dead fish wrapped in Brasi's bulletproof vest are delivered to the Corleone compound, and a character explains that it is a Sicilian message

FIGURE 10.8 Symbolic mise en scène

This image from about seventy-five minutes into *Gangs of New York* (2002) suggests the possible fate of recent immigrants, Irish males fresh off the boat in New York who have been immediately accepted as U.S. citizens and immediately drafted and put into Northern uniforms to fight in the War between the States. Here new soldiers are being lined up and loaded onto a ship that will take them to battle as coffins are being unloaded and lined up on the wharf. The image symbolizes the possible fate of the new recruits and perhaps suggests that the authorities were unconcerned about the possible morale problems that the coffins might cause in new soldiers who see the results of their predecessors' efforts. Frame enlargement. *Miramax*

a)

b)

FIGURE 10.9 Symbol concluding a documentary

Crumb (1994), which was filmed in color, is about the life, work, and family of the satirical U.S. cartoonist Robert Crumb. (a) The penultimate shot in the documentary is of Charles, Robert's talented but suicidal brother, pulling down a window covering and darkening the room, followed by a rapid fade-out to black. (b) The film's final shot, a title card of white on black, informs us of Charles's fate; then the sentence in white fades out and leaves the screen black and blank. Frame enlargements. *Superior Pictures and Sony Pictures Classics; Sony Pictures Classics*

that Luca "sleeps with the fishes" (is dead). Then viewers may realize that the etched fish seen briefly in the foreground as Luca is strangled functions as a symbol, not just a decorative component of the **mise en scène**.

A symbol may be conveyed by the mise en scène of one carefully selected shot (Figure 10.8).

Symbols may also be used in some experimental films and documentaries. The documentary *Crumb* (1994), for example, concludes with a shot of a man lowering a window covering and a title card announcing the man's suicide the year after he was filmed. The shutting out of light may symbolize the man's death (Figure 10.9). The possibility of death may be symbolized in

mise en scène: An image's setting, subject (usually people or characters), and composition (the arrangement of setting and subjects within the frame).

fade-out: Optical effect in which an image changes by degrees from illumination to darkness.

footage: A length of exposed motion-picture film.

irony: A statement, an event, or a situation involving an incongruity or a discrepancy between appearance and reality.

parody: A representation that amusingly imitates human behavior or a more serious text, part of a text, or groups of texts, often to ridicule or criticize.

black comedy: A narrative style that shows the humorous possibilities of subjects often considered off-limits to comedy, such as warfare, murder, death, and illness.

many ways. In the documentary *Theremin: An Electronic Odyssey* (1995), a **freeze frame** and **fade-out** are used to suggest that someone has died. After viewers learn that Leon Theremin was kidnapped in the United States by KGB agents and spirited back to the Soviet Union and that investigations failed to turn up any leads, we are told that some American friends feared he was dead. Next we see **footage** of him as a young man with a young woman. In extreme slow motion they advance toward the camera; she moves off-frame to the left, and he remains on the extreme right side of the frame and is now seen in freeze frame. The shot concludes with a slow fade-out.

Because so few viewers of *The Godfather* are likely to know the significance of the Sicilian message about sleeping with fish, that symbol is explained. However, if we examine how symbols are used in films, we will notice that like other vehicles of meaning they usually go unexplained and are subject to different interpretations. Objects functioning as symbols are usually shown more than once, are placed in prominent positions, are seen in important parts of the film, or are used under a combination of these conditions.

SATIRE

Satire is a representation of an individual or group that indirectly exposes and perhaps ridicules the subjects for being foolish, evil, or stupid or for having some other shortcoming. Makers of satire often use **irony**, exaggeration, **parody**, **black comedy**, or other means to amuse but even more often to chide, inform, or reform. The mood of a satire may range widely from gentle and good-natured to scathing and bitter or somewhere in between. The meanings conveyed by satire are normally implicit, so it is up to readers or viewers to figure out what behavior is satirized and what in general is implied about it. Let's consider some of the uses of satire in four films.

The Life of Brian (1979) is Monty Python's take on the times of Jesus' last days on earth and on the hapless Brian, who was born in a neighboring manger on the same night as Jesus. As envisioned by the film, the time was one of competing would-be prophets. For example, about 45⅔ minutes into the film, one man prophesies, "And the young shall not know where lieth the things possessed by their fathers that their fathers put there only just the night before—about eight o'clock," which can be understood as satirizing or making fun of the trivial and unnecessary specificity of some prophesies. The film satirizes various aspects of human behavior, perhaps none more prominently than desperation to find a savior (Figure 10.10).

FIGURE 10.10 Satire of group behavior
In Monty Python's *The Life of Brian* (1979), a crowd quickly convinces itself that the unlucky Brian, who is a contemporary of Jesus, is the messiah and has gathered outside his window. Nearly sixty-seven minutes into the film, he tells them, however, "You don't need to follow anybody. You've got to think for yourself. You're all individuals," to which they respond in unison, "Yes, we're all individuals." This part of the film satirizes both the tendency of crowds to pressure their members to think alike and the human desperation to fashion a messiah from the flimsiest of evidence. Frame enlargement. *John Goldstone; Warner Bros.*

In Spike Lee's *Bamboozled* (2000), Pierre Delacroix, an African American TV writer, proposes a TV minstrel show made up of offensive African American **stereotypes** that he assumes will be a disastrous failure and get himself fired from a job he loathes (if he quits, he would be hit with a lawsuit and lose a lot of money). But the show quickly becomes a hit. Part of the film's satire is conveyed by parody, as in the imitations of minstrel shows and, about 68½ minutes into the film, of two TV advertisements. The spots for "Da Bomb ½ gal. malt liquor"—which is "125% pure"—and "Timmi Hill-nigger 125% authentic ghetto [pronounced GEE toe] active wear"—that comes complete with the bullet holes—are satirical imitations of TV ads and inner-city African American stereotypes.

Bamboozled has multiple targets of satire. The black TV writer Pierre Delacroix and his boss the white TV executive, Dunwitty, are most often caught in the satirist's crosshairs (Figure 10.11). The film satirizes many other targets, including African American TV shows with large writing staffs but no blacks; Dunwitty's superiors, unseen TV executives, who quickly

FIGURE 10.11 The two major characters satirized
In Spike Lee's highly satirical *Bamboozled* (2000), the two characters most often satirized are (a) Pierre Delacroix, a college-educated African American TV writer who overestimates the tastes of American TV audiences and suffers the consequences. After his deliberately racist minstrel (variety) show becomes an unexpected hit, he enjoys his success. (b) The other major character most often satirized is Delacroix's superior, Thomas Dunwitty (background, center), a white man who is married to a black woman and whose office is full of African art and large photographs of African American sports stars. Dunwitty thinks he has so fully appropriated a black identity that he tells Delacroix, "Brother, man. I'm blacker than you." Soon, however, Dunwitty shows his true color (and it is not black) by quickly embracing Delacroix's proposed show, replete with many of the oldest, most offensive stereotypes of African Americans: a plantation setting; two "ignorant, dull-witted, lazy, and unlucky" headliners; a tall, deep-voiced emcee who looks like a black Abraham Lincoln dressed in the parts of an American flag; a troupe of dancing stereotypes, including Jungle Bunny and Aunt Jemima; and a small group of musicians called the Alabama Porch Monkeys, who are dressed in prison outfits, wear shackles, and carry a ball and chain. All the minstrel performers wear blackface. The most important character that the film does not satirize is Delacroix's assistant, Sloan, who asks her boss probing questions, warns of consequences, and occasionally objects to the goings-on. As in (a), Sloan is often seen concerned and skeptical about Delacroix's plans and behavior. Frame enlargements. *A Forty Acres and a Mule Filmworks; New Line Cinema*

a)

b)

greenlight the minstrel show; American TV audiences composed of various ethnicities, races, and ages who soon ape the new minstrel show; and TV critics who hail the show with such superlatives as "earthshaking." The film has yet other satiric targets, including the misguided gangster-rap group the Mau Maus and some New York City police officers, who seem to be exclusively white, shoot first and ask later, and kill all the dark-skinned people but spare the one person who looks white.

The Life of Brian and *Bamboozled* are primarily satires. But satire may be a secondary concern of any text that has human behavior as its subject. The musical *Chicago* (2002) can serve as an example. Like *Bamboozled*, it has multiple objects of satire. Perhaps most prominent are its implicit criticisms of the public, journalists, and the Chicago justice system. The populace is satirized for getting caught up in the latest murder case and then quickly forgetting about it when the next dramatic example comes along. And people are shown to get excessively caught up in the latest fad, whether it is wearing a hair style like a notorious murder suspect, buying dolls in her image, or purchasing her underwear at inflated prices. Journalists are shown to almost literally stampede to get the latest coverage of each case where a woman murders a man. They are also repeatedly manipulated by the defense lawyer, Billy Flynn, perhaps most memorably in "The Press Conference Rag" ("We Both Reached for the Gun") (forty-six minutes), where the reporters are seen in the background as puppets and toward the end of the number Flynn pulls their strings and they dance to his tune. The justice system comes in for other criticisms. Life in jail is oiled by bribes. The most successful attorney is entirely motivated by greed and pride (of winning every case) and is not above using distracting courtroom antics and tampering with evidence. The film shows that you can murder someone, bribe jail officials, hire an expensive lawyer, tell lies (about a pregnancy), and walk away free. But those who lack money, such as the Hungarian woman who seems to be innocent, can end up on the wrong end of a hanging rope. That description may make the film sound grim, but the characters and their actions are exaggerated perhaps to the point of caricature, and the film's satire is mostly genial (least so in the fate of the Hungarian woman), so the film's satire does not upset or outrage viewers but amuses them.

Normally satire is used in fictional films. It can readily be used in experimental films or hybrid films, such as "Neighbours" (1952, see Figure 8.37b on p. 392), which satirizes men's proclivity to become violent over a trivial matter, but it is rarely used in documentary films. Exceptions are the films of Michael Moore, such as *Roger & Me* (1989), *The Big One* (1998), and *Bowling for Columbine* (2002). Like all documentaries, Moore's films represent actual, not imaginary, subjects. Like many documentaries, they also imply criticism of their subjects. But unlike other documentaries, Moore's films often suggest criticism by using satire. Consider an excerpt from *Bowling for Columbine* (2002, Table 10.1). The combination of the images and narration suggests a number of satiric points, most prominently that it is as typical for

---

TABLE 10.1
Shots 2–15 of *Bowling for Columbine* (2002)

The visuals are accompanied by an instrumental version of "The Battle Hymn of the Republic" and the calm narration of Michael Moore.

VISUALS (the shots)	**NARRATION**
A shot made using **time-lapse cinematography** of the sun rising behind the Washington Monument, an aerial shot of a town full of trees, a helicopter shot of a wheat field, shots of a farmer and milkman doing their morning work, a shot of bombed-out buildings, shots of a man leaving for a morning walk, an elementary school teacher shepherding her students in a hallway, a **zoom-in** shot of a building with mountains in the background, a bowling ball missing the remaining nine pins, a scantily clad muscular young woman posing with a large automatic rifle, and an encircling aerial shot of the Statue of Liberty's head and shoulders.	"It was the morning of April 20th, 1999. And it was pretty much like any other morning in America. The farmer did his chores. The milkman made his deliveries. The President bombed another country whose name we couldn't pronounce. Out in Fargo, North Dakota, Carey McWilliams went on his morning walk. Back in Michigan, Mrs. Hughes welcomed her students for another day of school. And out in a little town in Colorado two boys went bowling at six in the morning. Yes, it was a typical day in the United States of America."

the American president to order the bombing of other countries, even obscure ones, as it is for the farmer and milkman to do their routine work, a man to go on a morning walk, and a teacher to tend her flock of students. As part of these snapshots of American life, the next shots imply that it is typical for two boys to go bowling at six o'clock in the morning, but we viewers may wonder about this example, especially since it is a school day (we learn later that the two boys referred to were the ones who committed the Columbine High School massacre). The juxtaposition of the bowling (supposedly by the two unseen boys) with the following shot of the scantily clad woman with the large assault rifle might be ominous. And the juxtaposition of that armed woman with the Statue of Liberty links two divergent aspects of America: armed (and represented as sexy) and pacific (and platonic). As the film unfolds and viewers come to understand the film's subjects even more clearly, they can better understand the satiric implication of the concluding shots of this early part of the film: America encompasses the possibility of both gun violence (even by a woman) and the promise of refuge from the problems of the world. Here and throughout the film, Michael Moore does not come out directly and voice his criticisms; instead, he uses satire to imply them.

The Life of Brian, Bamboozled, Chicago, Bowling for Columbine, and many other texts exaggerate and in other ways distort the representations of their

realism: Representation in a text that is widely believed to render its subjects accurately.

subjects. Satires are less concerned with attempting to show true-to-life representations of subjects than with obliquely revealing the shortcomings of human behavior. Consequently, satiric works should not be judged by the standards of **realism** but by their effectiveness in exposing human folly.

FIGURE 10.12 Residences symbolizing different situations and different personalities
(a) In *Fight Club* (1999), the Edward Norton character's condo "on the fifteenth floor of a filing cabinet for widows and young professionals" is full of furnishings in desaturated colors, clean, uncluttered, modern, and very consumerist. He narrates, "Like so many others, I had become a slave to the Ikea nesting instinct." Here, 5¼ minutes into the film, part of his condo is seen with labeling from a catalog superimposed. (b) In contrast, the Brad Pitt character's residence, part of which is seen here about 59¼ minutes into the film, was actually built to satisfy the needs of the film. It is a dark, old, abandoned house without anything beyond the basics, often without even the basics: "The stairs were ready to collapse. . . . Nothing worked. Turning on one light meant another light in the house went out. . . . Every time it rained, we had to kill the power. . . . Rain trickled down through the plaster and the light fixtures. . . . Everywhere were rusted nails to snag your elbow on." Frame enlargements. *Ross Grayson Bell, Ceán Chaffin, and Art Linson; 20th Century–Fox*

NARRATIVES: MEANINGS AND UNCERTAIN MEANINGS

Viewers also detect implicit meanings in narratives. Sometimes they notice general qualities of settings, such as the beauty but danger of nature in *Never Cry Wolf* (1983), a thoughtful adventure film set in rural Alaska. In *Never Cry Wolf*, *Lawrence of Arabia*, *McCabe and Mrs. Miller* (1971), *Deliverance* (1972), *The Matrix* (1999), and many other films, setting affects how events unfold and helps reveal character and meaning. Settings are often used to reveal an occupant's personality or situation and to compare and contrast characters. One character's residence, for example, may be very different than another's, as in *Fight Club* (1999, Figure 10.12).

More often, viewers detect significance in human behavior, the subject of narratives. Consider *The Last Emperor* (1987). Its subject is the life of the last Chinese emperor, from childhood to old age. One plausible meaning of the narrative is that someone who seems to have every comfort and material good may suffer from loneliness. In *Waiting to Exhale* (1995), the main subjects are four single African American women and, secondarily, the men in their lives. Two of the film's narrative meanings are that men tend to disappoint the women and that the friendships of other women sustain them (Figure 10.13). Behavior also suggests meanings in *Divine Secrets of the Ya-Ya Sisterhood* (2002), whose subjects are the relationships between three generations of women and their daughters. What does the film imply about the general behavior of its subjects? One of the film's many possible implicit meanings is that a mother can sometimes show love to a daughter yet, because of her own uncured psychological damage, hurt the daughter emotionally and thereby make her reluctant to marry and have children of her own. Viewers also find meanings in narratives about living creatures with human quali-

FIGURE 10.13 Women's strengths
Waiting to Exhale (1995) shows four admirable women finding comfort in their friendships with one another as two of the four are treated badly by married men and later reject them; one eventually wins the neighborhood Prince Charming; and one is dumped by her husband but eventually wins the respect and love of a sensitive, noble man and a hefty divorce settlement from her husband. Frame enlargement. *Ezra Swerdlow and Deborah Schindler; 20th Century–Fox*

ties, such as extraterrestrials wanting to go home or the animals in *Homeward Bound: The Incredible Journey* (1993) and many other films.

Like countless other film stories, "The String Bean" (1962), which is described on p. 249, shows a realistic story. The settings are believable, and every event in it could have happened: an old woman who lives alone works at sewing purses and enjoys nurturing a bean plant. Many other movies are not realistic: they include settings or events that, given current human understanding, could not exist or occur. These nonrealistic or fantasy movies can be divided into two types. In one type, the unrealistic settings or events, or both, are soon obvious to viewers. Examples are *Godzilla* (1998), *The Matrix*, and *Crouching Tiger, Hidden Dragon* (2000). In *Crouching Tiger*, for example, the settings are realistic, but many events are not. As is conventional in other Asian martial arts movies, four of the main characters in *Crouching Tiger* have the discipline, training, focus, and mental attitude to be able to fly through the air, fall great distances without harm, spiral upward through the air, skip up walls, bound over rooftops, and fight unbelievably long and well.

The second group of fantasy films consists of films whose unrealistic aspects are not immediately apparent. These films include settings that audiences have no trouble believing in and situations that seem possible, but on reflection viewers realize that some of the events and often the resolution of the main characters' problems are more wish fulfillment than plausible outcomes. These movies look true to life, but their events are not always true to life. They often attract audiences by incorporating enjoyable and reassuring fantasies in a mostly "realistic" story. An example is *Stand by Me* (1986), popular with many teens and young adults (Figure 10.14). The movie's settings look authentic enough, and so do many of the main characters' actions, such as their bickering, insulting, and bonding. But as in so many movies, more dangerous and exciting events are packed into a short time than most of us ever experience outside movie theaters (Figure 10.14b), as when one of the young boys has to point a gun at the older gang's leader to persuade the gang to leave the boys alone—this from characters from a small town in 1959! Sometimes the boy who tends to act as

FIGURE 10.14 Realism and fantasy blended

Stand by Me (1986) is about four boys who are unhappy at home and are united in part by the indifference or hostility of adults. (a) The boys are happy to go off on an adventure together because adults consistently mistreat them. One boy's father, we are told, held the boy's ear "to a stove and almost burned it off." Another boy's father gets drunk and beats his son. A third father, grieving over an older son whom he favored, alternates between indifference and criticism of his surviving son. We learn nothing about the father of the fourth boy (second from left), but by implication perhaps he has been ineffective, too, because his son is insecure, awkward, and the target of much laughter. Other adults disappoint the youths. Even a woman teacher betrayed one of the boys. After he stole milk money and turned it over to her, she used the money to buy a new skirt and allowed the boy to suffer expulsion and a blotted reputation. (b) As in many popular movies, somewhat unrealistically many dangers are packed into the film's brief story time. An example is when the boys are threatened by an onrushing train (presumably driven by yet another mean male adult), which doesn't brake and nearly runs down two of the boys on a bridge high above water. (c) One of the three examples in the movie where a boy cries in front of at least one of the other boys and is comforted by a playmate, perhaps not an entirely credible situation given the age of the boys and the peer pressure they are under. *Bruce A. Evans, Raynold Gideon, and Andrew Scheinman; Columbia*

a)

b)

c)

the leader (on the left in Figure 10.14c) acts like a surrogate father, displaying wisdom and compassion well beyond his years. Most of the film's events considered individually are believable. However, the movie has so many events showing the dangers of adult males and the safety and reassurance of a small gang of young boys in so brief a **story time** (not even forty-eight hours, excluding the brief scenes of the adult Richard Dreyfuss character) that its story and the meanings implied by the story are not completely plausible.

story time: The amount of time represented in a film's narrative or story.

There are many other popular movies that seem realistic *while* you watch them, but you realize later that they incorporate quite implausible or even impossible events. *Double Jeopardy* (1999), which focuses on a woman who proves to be extraordinary, has a fairly high fantasy quotient and is in the tradition of Hitchcockian thrillers of a wronged person trying to set things right before the law catches up and intervenes (Figure 10.15). Much more often—both abroad and in the United States—films show males reenacting popular male fantasies. Several films directed by Alfred Hitchcock—such as *The 39 Steps* (1935), *Saboteur* (1942), and *North by Northwest* (1959)—show a man displaying his resourcefulness, bravery, and appeal to women and eventually clearing himself of the wrongdoing he was falsely accused of early in the story by helping bring the guilty ones to justice. *The Bourne Identity* (2002) enacts similar popular male fantasies by showing a man displaying resourcefulness, bravery, poise, and his appeal to women as he works his way out of his initial predicament. At the beginning of the film, the Matt Damon character has become an amnesiac and does not know who he is or why dangerous U.S. and European agents pursue him. While attempting to avoid authorities, find safety, and clear up matters, Bourne hooks up with an attractive woman who is attracted to him and willing to try to help him.

The Bourne Identity is yet another movie extolling the physical and mental powers and the sexual allure of an individual male, perhaps the most recurrent meaning in recent years of popular American movies. The producers of action movies, including the James Bond movies, have raked in truckloads of money by showing countless boys and men

FIGURE 10.15 Even more fantasy blended with realism
Double Jeopardy (1999) is a thriller about Libby, the Ashley Judd character. She is falsely imprisoned for murdering her husband, who has framed her for his supposed murder and disappeared with their young son and another woman. After six years in prison, Libby—seen here a little more than 93½ minutes into the film in a final meeting with that errant husband—shows poise, intelligence, resourcefulness, and athletic skill and grace. Some of the movie's scenes are rendered as more fantasy than realism. For example, when Libby and her parole officer are trapped in a car that has run off a ferry and is submerged and sinking, Libby takes the man's gun, swims to the surface, struggles with the parole officer who surfaces near her, hits him in the head with his gun, then swims to shore and escapes. Much later, when she regains consciousness while imprisoned in a coffin, she uses a lighter and that gun again to shoot off the coffin's locks and escape. Although the movie received mostly middling to poor reviews, it was popular with many viewers, especially women, and during its first two weeks grossed nearly $50 million at the U.S. box office. Frame enlargement. *Leonard Goldberg; Paramount*

a)

b)

FIGURE 10.16 Female characters as romantically desirable
(a) During this scene almost ninety minutes into *Gone with the Wind* (1939), many women viewers identify with Scarlett O'Hara and imagine being in Rhett Butler's/Clark Gable's arms and having his full attention. For years, American women viewers voted Clark Gable the most appealing of all male movie stars. (b) In the French new wave classic *Jules and Jim* (1961), two men, who are best friends, are in love with the same woman, and she determines the nature of her relationships with them and other men. As in many movies, a woman attracts the romantic attentions of more than one male and has power over them. (a) Frame enlargement. *Metro-Goldwyn-Mayer; Selznick International;* (b) *Films du Carrosse; Janus Films*

what they enjoy imagining themselves doing: dispatching tough guys and attracting an assortment of ravishing available women. In the late 1990s, a number of American movies enacted popular male adolescent fantasies. *There's Something about Mary* (1998), *Antz* (1998), *A Bug's Life* (1998), *American Pie* (1999), and *The Waterboy* (1998) all show geeky or insecure young males eventually winning an attractive female, quite implausibly. Most sexually explicit films enact common heterosexual male erotic fantasies: the women are attractive, available, subservient, and numerous; the men virile, usually dominant, and eventually unmistakably sexually satisfied.

Fantasies show life as audiences wish it to be. These films are not so much mirrors of life outside theaters as fun-house mirrors that briefly entertain viewers, often by showing them characters and situations that they can identify with and that make them feel heroic, powerful, or rich. Countless movies show characters who are romantically desirable (Figure 10.16) or sexy (Figure 10.17).

Movies may also play on viewers' fears and nightmares. Because many people distrust technology and the people who create and monitor it, movies such as *2001: A Space Odyssey* (1968), *Westworld* (1973), and *Jurassic Park* (1993) and its sequels show technology or scientists failing but non-scientists ultimately triumphing. Sometimes humans fail. *The Forbin Project* (1969, a.k.a. *Colossus: The Forbin Project*) cautions that if humans put complete trust in technology, it can become a Frankenstein monster that eventually dominates its creator. The *Matrix* trilogy carries the threat of supercomputers even further. Sometime in the twenty-first century, computers with artificial intelligence have created a new race of machines that use a form of fusion and human bodies that are grown and harvested as fuel to run the matrix, which is "a computer-generated dream world, built to keep . . . [humans] under control." As different technologies capture public awareness, as biotechnology and bioterrorism have in recent years, their possible harmful consequences become film subjects, such as the rage virus plague of *28 Days Later* (2003).

FIGURE 10.17 **Commonplace female and male sexual fantasies**
(a) As in many movies, in *Splendor* (1999), one woman attracts two very different men at the same time, but unlike most movies, she loves both of them and makes love to both of them, at first separately but soon together. Not entirely plausibly, this romantic comedy represents some of the possible problems and rewards of a long-term sexual and domestic threesome. (b) In many films, TV shows, and advertisements, images of two or more women attracted to one man are commonplace, as in this poster for the 1963 British movie *Tom Jones*. Note that four of the women look up to Tom Jones (and everything else in the image is below his head, hands, and arms); four have their mouths open, and all five of these bosomy women are touching one of his legs or a hip. Perhaps the woman on her back is looking at his crotch. Many viewers enjoy such images and the suggestion that one man can have so much appeal, pleasure, and power: he is encircled by attractive, adoring women. In the image, he is happy, and his virility is suggested by the vaguely drawn open shirt, that sword near his left hip, and his left knee touching the inside of an exposed knee of one of his admirers. (a) *Gregg Araki; Samuel Goldwyn; British Film Institute Stills, Posters and Designs;* (b) *British Film Institute Stills, Posters and Designs*

Some stories are told in such a way that the stories themselves or some aspect of them are open to two or more plausible interpretations of their meanings. They are **ambiguous**. An example is from a master of ambiguity, playwright and scriptwriter Harold Pinter. In *Betrayal* (1983), Jerry, a friend of a husband and wife who are having a party, confronts the wife in her own bedroom. After his passionate declaration of love, she calmly replies, "My husband is at the other side of that door." Does she mean "I'm not interested, and my husband may overhear you, and there could be trouble," or "I could be interested, but this is a poor time and place," or some other meaning? We cannot be certain. When the husband in *Betrayal* learns that his wife has been having an affair with his friend Jerry, he tells her that he has always rather liked Jerry better than her and that maybe he should have had an affair with Jerry himself. Does the husband mean it, or does he say it to hurt his wife, or both? In the play and film versions of *Betrayal* and many other contemporary texts, the intended meanings remain unknowable.

Sometimes an ambiguity may be peripheral to a narrative's main concerns. An example is the three brief references to the young girl's father in Jane Campion's *The Piano* (1993). The first time, the girl tells two women and her mother that her father was a German composer, but her mother is annoyed with that comment and quickly quiets her. Later, when the mother is not around, one of the two women asks the girl where her parents got married; the girl responds with a tale about the wedding ceremony, sees the disbelieving look on her listener's face, admits it was a lie, then names a location where they got married. Soon she also claims her father was killed by lightning (as we see a brief animated drawing of a man catch fire and burn up) and simultaneously her mother struck dumb. The woman seems to accept this last account. In a later scene, the mother nods to her daughter in agreement that the girl's father was a teacher, and in reply to the girl's question why they didn't marry she signs, "He became frightened and stopped listening."

What's to be made of all this? Probably the father was a teacher who would not marry the woman. Beyond that, it gets less certain. Perhaps the mother doesn't want the girl talking about the father (less chance of a slip-up about the girl's illegitimacy). Perhaps when the girl is asked about her father, she is afraid of revealing that her father never married her mother, so she tends to lie about him or to kill him off in her accounts so she won't have to talk about him anymore (or perhaps because she is angry at him for not marrying her mother). All the information about the father is presented so fleetingly and obliquely that his status is ambiguous, but audiences will probably not be troubled by the ambiguity, especially because the issue is touched on only briefly and is peripheral to the story's main concerns.

In other narratives, ambiguity is central. In *Reversal of Fortune* (1990), viewers cannot know whether the main character, Claus von Bülow, attempted to murder his wife or she attempted suicide. Near the end of the narrative, the defense lawyer has come to believe that the wife attempted suicide. His female assistant concludes that Claus tried to kill her. Various scenes focusing on Claus drip with ambiguity, perhaps none more tantalizingly than the one in which he tells the defense lawyer, Dershowitz, the circumstances of finding his wife passed out on the bathroom floor. Next, Dershowitz and

Claus arrive at Claus's chauffeur-driven car, and, 85 minutes 25 seconds into the film, Claus starts to get in:

DERSHOWITZ: Yeah, but is it the truth?
CLAUS (*annoyed*): Of course.
DERSHOWITZ: But not the whole truth.
CLAUS (*more annoyed*): I don't know the whole truth. I don't know what happened to her.

[*Claus finishes getting into the car's backseat.*]

DERSHOWITZ: Wish I didn't believe you. You know it's very hard to trust someone you don't understand.

[*As Dershowitz pauses, Claus, his face now largely obscured by a shadow, turns to look at Dershowitz.*]

DERSHOWITZ (*continuing*): You're a very strange man.

[*Claus's face is still partially covered by a shadow.*]

CLAUS: You have no idea [Figure 10.18].

Ambiguity is also central in *To Sleep with Anger* (1990). We viewers cannot be certain about much of anything related to the visitor in the film—his past actions, his motives, and the full extent of his influence on later developments—but after he comes to visit a family, the host family's problems multiply, as symbolically their well-kept backyard falls into disrepair and disorder (Figure 10.19).

Ambiguity may result when audiences are uncertain whether a major event occurred. In *Contact* (1997), there is uncertainty whether the main character's vast journey happened. Eyewitnesses and multiple cameras lead viewers to believe that it did not, but her video camera had nearly eighteen hours of elapsed tape, which is impossible to account for scientifically, and the main skeptic about the trip is untrustworthy (Figure 10.20). In *Reversal of Fortune*, *To Sleep with Anger*, *Contact*, and many other films and other texts of recent years, ambiguity is deliberate: key information is suggestive but also vague and indecisive or missing altogether.

FIGURE 10.18 Ambiguous statement, ambiguous character
At the end of a scene from *Reversal of Fortune* (1990), Claus responds to the observation that he is a very strange man with "You have no idea," then pulls the car door closed. His face is quickly obscured by the black car window as almost simultaneously his chauffeur begins to back the car out of the driveway. As in other scenes in the film, here we cannot be certain of Claus's meaning. Perhaps he means "I've done even worse than you can imagine," "You'll never get to know me well," or some other meaning. His meaning is elusive and because of that shadow on his face perhaps ominous. Viewers cannot be certain of Claus's nature either. Perhaps he has tried to kill his wife. Perhaps he has killed others, as is rumored elsewhere in the film. Maybe he has engaged in deviant sexual behavior, as is also commented on elsewhere in the film. *Reversal of Fortune* is permeated with ambiguity. Frame enlargement. *Edward R. Pressman and Oliver Stone; Warner Bros.*

FIGURE 10.19 Ambiguous main character
In *To Sleep with Anger* (1990), the character played by Danny Glover is hard to figure out—what he has done and what he is up to—but his visit to old friends is soon followed by one family problem after another. *SVS Films, Inc.; Samuel Goldwyn Co.*

FIGURE 10.20 Source contributing to ambiguity
In *Contact* (1997), James Woods plays a national security adviser and a prominent member of a presidential investigative committee who is quick to formulate theories and who comes across as anything but fair or scientific. Woods has a history of playing disreputable characters; for example, shortly before he acted in *Contact*, he played a racist murderer in *Ghosts of Mississippi* (1996). Ephraim Katz has written that Woods is "equally able to project villainousness or moral ambiguity" (1481). The skepticism voiced by the Woods character in *Contact* would be more credible if the role had been played by someone known for trustworthy characters, such as Tom Hanks. Frame enlargement. *Steve Starkey and Robert Zemeckis; Warner Bros.*

Symptomatic Meanings: World → Film → Viewers

As we saw in Chapter 9, widespread attitudes or beliefs at the time and place a film is made may influence how filmmakers represent their subjects. It is not surprising, then, that a film's meanings, whether explicit or implicit, may be symptomatic of the society out of which the film emerged. A **symptomatic meaning** is a generalization about a text or part of one that is characteristic of the society that nurtured the film.

Some meanings of *Unforgiven* are unthinkable in earlier westerns but coincide with popular beliefs in early 1990s America when *Unforgiven* was made, especially the wrongness of many men's violent and unjust treatment of women and the cruel and unlawful behavior of some law enforcement officials. On the latter score, the film shows that upholders of the law may themselves lose control: the town sheriff is so sadistic that when he becomes violent, the townspeople seem embarrassed by his excesses. It's police brutality, 1880s style. The videotape of part of the Rodney King beating by Los Angeles police officers was shown repeatedly on American TV nearly a year and a half before *Unforgiven* was first released in August 1992. That videotape excerpt increased public awareness of potential police brutality and perhaps influenced some viewers' reactions to the film's sheriff, maybe especially late in *Unforgiven* when the sheriff beats and tortures a black man so mercilessly that he dies.

Yet other films are symptomatic of the social and political conditions of the specific country that nurtured them. In addition to showing the story of two teenage boys and their sexually charged road trip with a young married woman in present-day Mexico, the Mexican film *Y Tu Mamá También* (2001) repeatedly shows both the advantages enjoyed by the wealthy and powerful and the disadvantages endured by the poor and powerless. The film's wealthy and powerful include the President of Mexico; his Harvard-trained economist who is Mexico's Secretary of State; that official's son, Tenoch, who lives in guarded luxury and will be going to the university to study economics (as his father did); and, to a lesser extent, Luisa, a Spaniard who has married an academic writer. In contrast, the poor and powerless face major disadvantages. They have to guard against being exploited by the rich (years earlier Tenoch's father had been linked to a scandal involving selling contaminated food to the poor). About 7¼ minutes into the film, viewers learn that a bricklayer who had moved to the city to find work avoided using a poorly located pedestrian crosswalk because using it would require him to walk an extra two miles to work, that he was killed by a speeding bus, and that his body went unidentified and unclaimed in the city morgue for four days. Approximately 80½ minutes into the film, viewers learn that a fisherman and his family will be forced out of their home in a nature preserve so an exclusive hotel can be built there and that the fisherman will eventually end up working as a janitor at the same hotel.

A story may even be symptomatic of the concerns and beliefs of a specific group and thus be remade with variations over the decades. Consider how since the first showings of *The Jazz Singer* in 1927 various *Jazz Singer* movies and TV shows have resonated with different generations of American Jews. The story shows a young man, the son of Jewish immigrants, torn between the wishes of his father, a cantor (someone who sings hymns in Jewish services), and his own drive to succeed as a singer in the secular world. J. Hoberman and Jeffrey Shandler—who are the curators of the exhibition "Entertaining America: Jews, Movies and Broadcasting" and the authors of a book with the same title—propose that *The Jazz Singer* is the "'key' Jewish narrative in twentieth-century American Jewish culture. They suggest that it symbolized the archetypal clashes between sacred and secular, tradition and modernity, ghettoization and assimilation, minority and mass culture and that it compellingly addressed a generation seeking identity in a world not of its fathers" (Glueck).[4]

A film may be symptomatic of a nation's ideals, as the following examples from two Japanese films illustrate. In *The Seven Samurai* (1954), the

---

[4]For evidence of the many, varied manifestations of *The Jazz Singer* in twentieth-century American culture, see J. Hoberman's "The Jazz Singer: A Chronology" (Hoberman and Shandler 84–92).

a)   b)

FIGURE 10.21 Japanese and Western influences
Shall We Dance? (1996) shows the story of a modern-day office worker in Tokyo who takes up ballroom dancing, a somewhat disreputable activity in the eyes of many Japanese.
(a) Some scenes of the movie show behavior accepted as part of Japanese culture since the end of World War II: office workers in crowded commuter trains and offices, for example. (b) The movie also includes Western behavior not yet widely considered acceptable and Japanese, such as ballroom dancing lessons and competitions. As a whole, the movie is symptomatic of the changing face of Japanese society and the resistance to accept (yet fascination with) Western behavior. Frame enlargements. *Shôji Masui and Yuji Ogata; Miramax*

samurai's defense of the farmers depends on coordinated, unified action; thus, when the individualistic Toshiro Mifune character goes off on his own and captures one of the brigands' rifles, the samurai leader reprimands him. The idea reinforced throughout the film that in unity there is strength is deeply symptomatic of Japanese society.

Shall We Dance?—a 1996 Japanese film—was enormously popular in its home country. It was also a critical success there, capturing thirteen of the Japanese equivalents of the Academy Awards. Probably part of the film's appeal to the Japanese is that many of its characters exhibit the mixed feelings the Japanese populace has toward Western lifestyles and values.

On the one hand, many Japanese cling to the values of the past, as is made clear by nearly all of the opening narration of the film version shown in the United States:

> In Japan, ballroom dance is regarded with much suspicion. In a country where married couples don't go out arm in arm, much less say "I love you" out loud intuitive understanding is everything. The idea that a husband and wife should embrace and dance in front of others is beyond embarrassing. However to go out dancing with someone else would be misunderstood and prove more shameful. Nonetheless, even for Japanese people, there is a secret wonder about the joys that dance can bring.

In *Shall We Dance?*, the Japanese office worker and his exuberant, disguised coworker hide their unusual extracurricular activity from their fellow workers to avoid their disapproval (Figure 10.21a). The main character feels compelled to hide his dance lessons from even his wife. Dancehalls had been considered questionable in Japan ever since the 1920s because men could buy alcoholic drinks and pay to dance with women who worked there. Even dance lessons were suspect. According to the film's director, Masayuki Suo, "Until recently, [dance] classes remained off-limits to people under 18" (Johnston 7).

On the other hand, *Shall We Dance?* shows the Japanese "secret wonder" about popular Western culture (Figure 10.21b). The influences of British and American cultures are especially strong. The film draws on the British tradition of ballroom dance competition. Part of the film is set in Blackpool, England, and while witnessing the Blackpool competition as a child, one of the dance instructors in *Shall We Dance?* had been inspired to become a dancer. American popular culture is also an influence. "Shall We Dance?" is not only the film's title but also the last line of the film's dialogue (in English) and the name of the famous waltz that is heard several times in the film, including at its conclusion. That popular waltz (and song) derives from the Rodgers and Hammerstein stage musical *The King and I* (1951) and a film adaptation, *The King and I* (1956), both of which are also in part about differences between East and West. The film version of *The King and I* also inspired one of the dance instructors in *Shall We Dance?* to become a dancer.

With its characters' widespread adherence to traditional values yet attraction to popular Western culture, *Shall We Dance?* is symptomatic of 1996 Japanese society. The movie shows that dancing can bring pleasurable release from the boring, tiring, repetitive routines of the modern urban industrial world. To oversimplify a bit: the film shows that it can be beneficial for the earnest, hard-working Japanese to relax sometimes. The film is so in tune with its people and times that it attracted large audiences and in turn greatly spurred the growth of dance class enrollments and the acceptance of ballroom dancing in Japan.

In contrast to the emphasis on the group in Japanese films and the films of many other countries in Asia and Africa, the emphasis in American films and other films from Western countries is much more typically on one person. Symptomatic of that view are the following claims from the advertising for the action movie *Tears of the Sun* (2003): "The lives of many rest in the courage of a few" and "He was trained to follow orders. He became a hero by defying them." The film attempts to speak to the audience's desire to witness the virtues of a few who fight against great odds for a noble purpose, in this case the rescue of civilians from a fictionalized war-torn Nigeria. Like so many popular movies, *Gladiator* (2000) demonstrates the extraordinary potential power of a dedicated, hardworking individual, even against staggering odds (Figure 10.22). The main character, Maximus—a Roman general chosen by the emperor Marcus Aurelius to be his successor—escapes execution, survives as a slave, and excels as a gladiator. Even in the one scene that best shows the value of the group effort—the combat in which the gladiators coordinate their efforts and together defeat the opposing forces—one person

FIGURE 10.22 Triumph of individualism as symptomatic of many Western societies
Like so many popular movies from Western societies, *Gladiator* (2000) extols the potential power of an individual, even in the face of tremendous adversity. Such movies excite large audiences and reassure them that one person can make a difference. Such a belief is a deeply ingrained component of American ideology. Here is seen the individual of the moment, actor Russell Crowe as Maximus, a general reduced to a gladiator trying to get his own personal vengeance and to set right the wrongs of the Roman power structure. Frame enlargement. *A Douglas Wick Production; DreamWorks; Universal*

(Maximus) organizes and rallies the others. Eventually, Maximus fulfills the wishes of Marcus Aurelius, ends the tyranny of the dictatorial successor (Marcus Aurelius's son Commodus), returns power to the Roman Senate and the people, avenges the murder of his wife and young son, and retains the love of Marcus Aurelius's beautiful and shrewd daughter (Lucilla). In his endeavors Maximus has the loyalty and help of others: Lucilla, Roman senators, Cicero (Maximus's assistant), and his own army, but the attempted coup against Commodus fails, and it is up to *one* man to make all the difference. Although Maximus is chained, imprisoned, and unfairly wounded by Commodus before their battle, Maximus kills Commodus in the final showdown. Unlike the stories of many societies, *Gladiator* celebrates individuality, but then individuality and the freedom to make significant choices are integral to American and some other Western countries' sense of themselves, whether or not

ideology: The influential underlying social and political beliefs of a society or social group.

members of those societies are conscious of the pervasiveness and force of those **ideological** beliefs. For many viewers, these stories not only embody a society's beliefs but also inspire and reassure the society's members.

For examples of different viewers' thoughts about one film, see the Close-Up on pp. 508-10.

INFLUENCES ON THE WAYS PEOPLE THINK ABOUT FILMS

The scene between Mr. Crothers and the boy [in Stanley Kubrick's *The Shining* (1980)] . . . showed how Kubrick was intent on giving little pieces of information visually, frequently reinforcing it by showing the same things several times. "He always said that you had to make sure the audience understood key pieces of information to follow the story, and that to do that you had to repeat it several times, but without being too obvious about it," Ms. [Nicole] Kidman said. "Here, in this scene, look at how there is this rack of knives hanging in the background over the boy's head. It's very ominous, all these knives poised over his head. And it's important because it not only shows that the boy is in danger, but one of those very knives is used later in the story when . . . [the boy's mother] takes it to protect herself from her husband." (Nicole Kidman and Rick Lyman 220)

The above passage is just one of many in a book of interviews that illustrate time and again how experienced filmmakers notice the significance of details that other viewers may not notice. The same principle is at work for people's responses to a film: depending on various factors, different people seeing the same film will have some different responses.

Knowledge of the Film or a Subject in the Film

Before or after we see a film, we may know something about it or one of its subjects that influences how we think about the film. We may have already seen many films of the same genre. For example, perhaps over the years we have seen many science fiction films, so when we see a sci-fi film we have never seen before or a mixed genre film that includes science fiction, such as *The Matrix*, we respond to it by comparing and contrasting it to sci-fi films we have seen in the past. Before or after seeing a film, or perhaps before *and* after a film viewing, we might read reviews, and something in them becomes part of our way of thinking about the film. We may have read the source novel and thus thought about the film in ways someone who had not read the novel would (see the Fiction section of Chapter 5).

Reading a cutting continuity script before or, more likely, after we have seen the film can also influence our understanding of a film. The **cutting continuity (script)** is a description of a finished film. It indicates each setting and describes major events and any dialogue. It may include descriptions of camera distances, camera angles, camera movements, transitions between scenes, and indications of where music is heard. A few cutting continuity scripts even number each shot and indicate how long each one is.

Below is a partial excerpt (shot numbers and shot lengths are omitted) from a cutting continuity script for *Citizen Kane* that describes two consecutive scenes. ("EXT" stands for **exterior**, a scene filmed outside; "CU" stands for **close-up**; "MS" for medium shot.)

> EXT. HOUSE CU—mother holding Charles—snow falling—music playing—she talks [to her husband]
>
> MOTHER
>
> . . . he's going to be brought up where you can't get at him.
>
> Camera moves down to Charles's face as he stares up to left.
>
> *Lap Dissolve*
>
> EXT. HOUSE MS—sled in snow—snow falling—train whistle heard—music playing
>
> *Lap Dissolve*
>
> (*The Citizen Kane Book*, 333–34)

close-up: An image in which the subject fills most of the frame and little of the surroundings is shown.

The cutting continuity for *Citizen Kane* is more detailed than many published cutting continuity scripts. For each shot, it includes length, location, description

cut (noun): The most common transition between shots, made by splicing or joining the end of one shot to the beginning of the following shot.

dubbing: Replacing certain sounds in a film after the film has been shot—for example, substituting native speaking voices for the original voices of a foreign-language film.

of setting and action, dialogue, camera distances (such as close-up), and transition to the next shot if it is not a **cut** (for example, lap dissolve).

Cutting continuity scripts may include some subjective interpretation and cannot convey the editing, sounds, moving images, and audience involvement that contribute to the experience of seeing a film. Most viewers find that reading any type of script before seeing a film is tedious because the script itself is neither literary nor filmic. Many scripts, too, are carelessly published and abound in factual errors.

Nevertheless, reading a cutting continuity script can help one understand and appreciate a film more completely. Cutting continuity scripts usually provide more complete, accurate, and legible translations for foreign language films than are given in the film subtitles or **dubbing**. The script can also refresh the viewer's memory of the film and reveal details and patterns not noticed when watching it. In the example cited above, perhaps reading the description of these two scenes makes the reader more aware of the costs to young Charles of being forced to leave his home: his mother's love and protection and the joys of play (the sled readers had earlier read about him enjoying). Reading the descriptions of the two scenes might also make the reader more appreciative of the filmmakers' skill, economy, and subtlety in suggesting the feelings of loss and melancholy.[5]

The viewer's thinking about a film may also be influenced by her or his knowledge of gender issues. **Gender** means a person's sex-related identity as exhibited by various aspects of appearance (including clothing, cosmetics, and hairstyles) and behavior (including conversational styles and body language). A person's gender is usually called feminine, masculine, or mixed. Gender can also be thought of as the evolving cultural roles that a society associates with each of the two main sexes. (Whether gender characteristics are determined by biology or culture or both continues to be a subject of debate.) *Gender* has been distinguished from both *sex*, which means the biological or physical characteristics of men and women (male, female, or intersexed), and *sexual orientation* (straight, lesbian or gay, or bisexual).

Those interested in gender issues have explored, for example, the many ways that gender, sex, and sexual orientation may interface in one person, including issues related to the *androgyne* (person who creates an ambiguous gender presentation by adopting characteristics of both main genders) and

screenplay: The earliest version of a script, a script written before filming begins.

shooting script: The version of the script used by the filmmakers during filming.

---

[5]Some commercial publishers (in the United States and foreign countries, especially France) publish film scripts. Some university presses publish them, too, sometimes with an editor's introduction, notes on changes between different versions of the script, interviews, and film reviews and commentaries. Since 1995, the magazine *Scenario* has published mostly recent scripts, including some short scripts. Film scripts show up on the Web. Occasionally, they are included on DVDs. Some bookstores with large collections of film books (and some Web sources) sell unbound, unpublished scripts, mostly from recent years. Regardless of the source, often there is no indication whether the script is a **screenplay**, **shooting script**, or cutting continuity script.

FIGURE 10.23 Gender as a film subject
Boys Don't Cry (1999), which is closely based on actual events, is about a 1990s Nebraska biological female (Teena Brandon) who, as seen here looking into a mirror about 2½ minutes into the film, changes genders by beginning to dress and act as a straight male (Brandon Teena). At first, Brandon is more successful socially than Teena had been, being accepted into a new (dysfunctional) extended family that includes the beautiful Lana and the unstable John, who is a former convict obsessed with Lana. Brandon is also successful in winning the love of Lana and retaining it even after she learns that Brandon is anatomically female. But insurmountable problems multiply for Brandon, including numerous past and present run-ins with the law, a web of lies that hurts or infuriates others, John's jealousy about Brandon's success with Lana, and prejudice against Brandon's transgender choice and new identity. Frame enlargement. *A Killer Films/Hart-Sharp Entertainment Production; Independent Film Channel; Fox Searchlight*

the *crossdresser* (a.k.a. *transvestite*, a person, often a straight, who enjoys occasionally wearing clothes identified with the opposite gender). Gender issues are also paramount in the case of the *transgenderist* (a person who lives either part-time or full-time as a gender opposite to anatomical sex). Examples would be a man dressing and living as a woman, like one of the main characters in *The Crying Game* (1992, see Figure 9.5 on p. 416), and a female who dresses as a male and learns to act like one in *The Ballad of Little Jo* (1993, see Figure 7.9 on p. 300). Some movies—such as *Dog Day Afternoon* (1975, see Figure 9.4b on p. 415 and *Hedwig and the Angry Inch* (see Figure 7.20d on p. 309)—include a *transsexual* (a person who feels he or she has the internal gender identity of one sex and the body of another). Transsexuals may feel a persistent discomfort about their gender intense enough to cause them to seek to change sex by undergoing therapy, crossdressing, taking hormones, and in some cases finally undergoing genital reassignment surgery.

Gender has long been a subject in film studies, where, for example, the possible influence of films in forming and perpetuating gender images and stereotypes has been much debated since some 1970s feminist thinkers raised the issue, and gender is increasingly a subject in movies such as *The Crying Game*, *The Ballad of Little Jo*, *Orlando*, *The Adventures of Priscilla, Queen of the Desert* (1994), *Different for Girls* (1996), *Ma vie en rose* (1997), *Fight Club*, *Hedwig and the Angry Inch*, and *Osama* (2003). Two other examples of films in which gender issues are prominent are the documentary *The Brandon Teena Story* (1998) and the fictionalized representation of Brandon Teena's last days, *Boys Don't Cry* (1999, Figure 10.23). These and other films can be examined for the characters' gender identity (innate sense of maleness or femaleness or both) and gender dysphoria (the discomfort characterized by a feeling of incongruity with the gender assigned at birth). Films can also be examined for the characters' gender presentation (the ways individuals express their gender identity to others, such as in choice of clothing), the wide range of gender expression by women (from butch to femme), and the narrower range of gender expression deemed acceptable in males. As in *Boys Don't Cry*, another possible subject is the reactions of other people to the transgendered, an umbrella term that now stands for all the different types of people whose gender identity and expression do not correspond with social or cultural norms and the expectations of their genetic sex.[6]

Constructed Identities

> Cultural artifacts are not containers with immanent meanings, . . . variations among interpretations have historical bases for their differences, and . . . differences and change are . . . due to social, political, and economic conditions, as well as to constructed identities such as gender, sexual preference, race, ethnicity, class, and nationality. (Staiger xi)

Many factors can influence the meanings that a viewer formulates, such as the viewer's social class, religious and political beliefs, sexual orientation, age and experience, and theories applied in analyzing texts. Let's consider four examples: the viewer's age and experience, political beliefs, sexual orientation, and application of critical approaches.

Perhaps you and one of your parents saw a film together, discussed it afterward, then decided that you had not seen the same film! The differences in age and experiences (and thus your different priorities) led you to focus on different subjects in the film or to interpret the significance of certain aspects of the film differently. Maybe you were moved by the loss of love and life while watching *Titanic* (1997), whereas a man from a family of U.S. Navy personnel was deeply moved by a different aspect of the film: the captain losing his ship. Scenes from *Barbershop* (2002) resulted in different interpretations, depending in part on the viewer's age and experiences (Figure 10.24). Reverends Jesse Jackson and Al Sharpton were so offended by this scene and others that they "demanded an apology and called on MGM to remove the scenes from future releases" ("*Barbershop*"). Months later, Rosa Parks refused to attend the NAACP Image Awards because it was being hosted by Cedric the Entertainer. In contrast, most younger viewers took the film's criticisms

---

[6]For definitions of sex- and gender-related terms and explanations of the concepts, various sources are helpful including Alan McKee's entry "Gender" on pp. 190–94 of the *Critical Dictionary of Film and Television Theory*, a book described in the For Further Reading at the end of this chapter, and Web sites such as <gendertalk.com/tgism/tgism.shtml> and <itpeople.org /glossary.php>.

in stride. According to Professor Todd Boyd, "The younger generation has always been 'instructed to pay appropriate homage' to the civil rights movement. . . . But 'they've created their own icons.'" Boyd continues, "I would suggest Tupac . . . and Biggie . . . are maybe more important to the hip-hop generation than Rosa Parks and Martin Luther King" ("*Barbershop*").

Viewers' political views may also influence how they interpret a film. When *Titanic* was first screened, many American viewers and reviewers focused on the film's special effects and its psychological aspects, particularly its initial celebration of human achievement and its later scenes of courtship, love, and loss. The movie was and still is enormously popular in China, too— but for different reasons. The Chinese are more focused on the film's social classes and particularly admire Jack (the Leonardo DiCaprio character) as a no-

FIGURE 10.24 Interpretations influenced by age and experience of viewer
In a scene that begins 54½ minutes into *Barbershop* (2002), the barber played by Cedric the Entertainer belittles the contribution to civil rights made by Rosa Parks. Perhaps he does so to be contrary to the previous speaker who praised some 1960s civil rights champions. Perhaps he does so to playfully taunt his listeners. Or perhaps he speaks out of ignorance. Whatever the barber's motivation(s), his criticisms provoke both laughter and uniform dissent from his fellow characters in the scene. Frame enlargement. *George Tillman Jr.; MGM*

ble working-class man. At the time of the film's release in China, even the Chinese premier lauded the film for promoting "the correct class viewpoint because the hero Jack is a lower class figure" (Hessler). Because North Korea also holds a different political **ideology** than the United States, after the release of the James Bond film *Die Another Day* (2002), which has scenes of capture and torture set in North Korea, the official North Korean response was not that of the typical U.S. viewer. The North Koreans attacked both the film and its country of origin. The official Korean Central News Agency called the film a "'dirty and cursed burlesque' . . . [and] 'a deliberate and premeditated act of mocking at and insulting the Korean nation' . . . and shows that the United States is 'the root cause of all disasters and misfortune of the Korean nation,' 'an empire of evil' and 'the headquarters that spreads abnormality, degeneration, violence and fin-de-siècle corrupt sex culture'" (Presse).

Some film scholars have studied how the viewer's sexual orientation influences interpretations of certain films. Elizabeth Ellsworth studied *Personal Best* (1982) and describes its narrative as follows:

> *Personal Best* is . . . about two women athletes, Chris Cahill (Mariel Hemingway) and Tory Skinner (Patrice Donnelly), who meet at the 1976 Olympic Track Trials and become friends and lovers. They live together for three years, but after their male coach places them in direct competition with each other for a place

on the Olympic Pentathlon team and hints that Tory is deliberately sabotaging Chris's training progress, they break up. Chris has an affair with a male Olympic swimmer, Denny. The two women meet again at the 1980 Olympic Track Trials. They reaffirm their friendship after Chris sacrifices her own chance to place first in the trials by bumming out [wearing out] the lead runner early in the race so that Tory can place in the 800 meter event. Both women win a place in the 1980 Olympic team. (56)

Ellsworth studied reviews from both mainstream and lesbian publications. Her findings?

> Dominant reviewers consistently . . . [focused on] competition, coming of age, goal seeking. . . . [By way of contrast,] most lesbian feminist reviewers ignored large sections of narrative material focusing on heterosexual romance. . . . Some redefined "main characters" and "supporting characters" in order to elevate Patrice Donnelly as the film's star despite the publicity's promotion of Mariel Hemingway as star and the relative length of screen time each character occupied. Lesbian feminist reviewers consistently referred to Patrice Donnelly's performance as convincingly "lesbian" and pleasurable to identify with, reinterpreting Donnelly as the appropriate "object of desire" against the pressbook's [publicity's] and dominant media reviews' contextualization of Mariel Hemingway as appropriate object of heterosexual desire. (53, 54)

In their interpretations of the film, lesbian feminist reviewers, however, go only so far: they "stopped short of rearranging the film's chronological order, severing or rearranging cause-effect relationships in the narrative and changing who does what in the narrative" (55).[7]

As film gained in popularity and status throughout the twentieth century, different people with different backgrounds and different ways of thinking developed different **critical approaches**, which are related ideas on how to interpret texts.

To help explain and analyze an individual film or group of films, a viewer might use concepts or ideas from one version of one critical approach or different concepts from different critical approaches. For example, a viewer with knowledge of Marxist theory (and Soviet ideology) could point out that Eisenstein's classic film (*Battleship*) *Potemkin* (1925) extols the masses in their struggles with the ruling class. Thus, the ship's officers are represented as cruel and indifferent to the sailors' plight (Figure 10.25). Like the ship's officers, the ship's priest also indirectly supports the oppressive status quo. A Marxist critical approach helps one understand why *Potemkin* has no individual heroes because it celebrates the masses, not the individual.

---

[7]For further illustrations of how sexual orientation may affect viewer responses to a film, including interpretations of meanings, see the documentary films *The Celluloid Closet* (1996) and "Jodie: An Icon" (1998) and the book *Flaming Classics: Queering the Film Canon* by Alexander Doty.

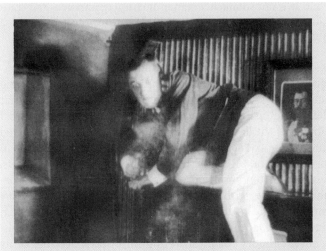

FIGURE 10.25 Film interpreted as Marxist story
Eisenstein's (*Battleship*) *Potemkin* (1925) is set during the 1905 uprisings in Russia. Sailors on the *Potemkin* are so mistreated by their officers that they eventually revolt. Seen here is one of the Russian naval officers atop a piano firing a pistol at the rebelling sailors. In the background and on the right can be glimpsed a photograph of the reigning tsar, a reminder that the naval officer is part of the tsarist power structure oppressing the workers. Frame enlargement. *Goskino; The Museum of Modern Art/ Circulating Film Library*

Many types of critical approaches have been used to interpret films. Formalist criticism, neoformalist criticism, and cognitive film theory all focus on the text and viewers' responses to qualities perceived in the work. Other approaches focus more on the relationship between the text and the world beyond it. Such contextual approaches include Marxist criticism, psychoanalytic criticism, feminist criticism, genre criticism, cultural studies, reception theory (which examines how historical conditions affect how groups interpret texts at different times and in different places), queer theory, and auteur theory.

Let us consider a critical approach that is very limited in its scope yet has nonetheless probably been more widely used than any other—**auteur theory**, the belief that some filmmakers, usually directors, function as the dominant creators of films and that the auteur's films embody recurrent **structures**, techniques, and meanings. Let's look at an example of auteur theory applied to film analysis. By examining closely the films directed by Howard Hawks, critic Robin Wood helps his readers understand aspects of one film in the context of other Hawksian movies. Of the main woman character in the western *Rio Bravo* (1959), Wood writes,

> Feathers is the product of the union of her basic "type"—the saloon girl—and the Hawks woman, sturdy and independent yet sensitive and vulnerable, the equal of any man yet not in the least masculine. The tension between background (convention) and foreground (actual character) is nowhere more evident. We are very far here from the brash "entertainer" with a heart of gold who dies (more often than not) stopping a bullet intended for the hero. Angie Dickinson's marvelous performance gives us the perfect embodiment of the Hawksian woman, intelligent, resilient, and responsive. There is a continual sense of a woman who really grasps what is important to her. One is struck by the . . . beauty of a living individual responding spontaneously to every situation from a

structure: The arrangement of the parts of a whole text.

secure centre of self. It is not so much a matter of characterisation as the communication of a life-quality (a much rarer thing). What one most loves about Hawks, finally, is the aliveness of so many of his people. (42)

All applications of critical approaches have their advantages and limitations. The auteur approach works best with directors who exercise strong creative control, such as Hawks, Stanley Kubrick, Alfred Hitchcock, Ingmar Bergman, and Federico Fellini. Many movies, however—especially most American **studio** movies of the 1930s, 1940s, and 1950s and most animated feature films—are more the product of a studio or production company than any individual. Thus during the big studio era from the 1920s to the 1950s, Warner Bros. movies were often about current social problems, such as organized urban crime during the prohibition era, and were presented in a way that viewers thought of as true to life. MGM movies tended to be lighter, both literally and figuratively, and include the upbeat, big-budget musicals. In recent years, the auteur theory for interpreting films has lost some of its popularity because critics and scholars have decided that the qualities shared by films of the same auteur are not the only aspects to be considered in interpreting films and not always clearly only the auteur's contributions (see the last section of the Introduction, pp. 5–6). Then, too, since the birth of the auteur theory, **film theorists** have come to emphasize contexts other than additional films directed by the same person. Many film theorists now stress the types of contexts discussed in Chapter 9—for example, societal attitudes, political climate, and changes in filmmaking or media technology—as factors shaping a film's subjects and **style** and downplay the contributions of individual filmmakers.[8]

film theorist: A person who formulates a general explanation of the film medium or a part of the medium.

style: The way that subjects are represented in a text, such as a film.

Because so many factors affect how viewers interpret films and other texts, meanings are not universal. This view is confirmed by scholar Barbara Klinger's study of the changing critical reception to films directed by Douglas Sirk—such as *Magnificent Obsession* (1954), *All That Heaven Allows* (1955), *Written on the Wind* (1957), *Tarnished Angels* (1958), and *Imitation of Life* (1959). Klinger discovered that different groups interpreting a text during the same time period—what others such as Stanley Fish call *interpretive communities*—produce different meanings. Academic critics, for example, are likely to see many of the same or similar meanings, whereas review jour-

---

[8]For more information about the auteur theory and other applications of critical approaches that are used in some film journals and some film courses, see J. Dudley Andrew's *The Major Film Theories: An Introduction*; Tim Bywater and Thomas Sobchack's *An Introduction to Film Criticism: Major Critical Approaches to Narrative Film*; Gerald Mast, Marshall Cohen, and Leo Braudy's *Film Theory and Criticism: Introductory Readings*; Bill Nichols, ed., *Movies and Methods* vols. 1–2; R. Barton Palmer's *Introduction to the Cinematic Text: Methods and Approaches*; Robert Lapsley and Michael Westlake's *Film Theory: An Introduction*; Robert Stam's *Film Theory: An Introduction*; and John Hill and Pamela Church Gibson's *Film Studies: Critical Approaches*.

nalists of the same time period and culture are likely to see other meanings. Klinger also found that more recent reviewers interpret Sirk's movies quite differently than did the reviewers in the 1950s; her findings illustrate that within the same interpretive community, people working at different times produce different meanings. After examining films directed by Sirk and reactions to them over a nearly forty-year period by different groups, Klinger concludes: "There has been nothing stable about the meaning of his melodramas; they have been subject at every cultural turn to the particular *use* to which various institutions and social circumstances put them. In this process, meaning itself becomes something we cannot determine 'once and for all' but a volatile, essentially *cultural* phenomenon that shifts with the winds of time" (159). Even among viewers with similar backgrounds and similar outlooks who are living at the same time, there are some variations in meanings. And even the same person experiencing the same text years later—whether *King Kong* or *King Lear*—usually sees different meanings.

Although there are always varying interpretations of the same film, not all interpretations are based on salient textual details and are persuasively argued. For all films a wide range of meanings is plausible, but some meanings are indefensible. If a viewer does not think carefully about the interpretation and support an explanation of it with examples from the film—and in the case of symptomatic meanings, with information about conditions beyond the film (contexts)—the meanings seen may be merely unsubstantiated opinions. In short, what is most illuminating and persuasive to readers and listeners are reasoned and supported arguments, not mere statements of beliefs.

In developing meanings and explaining them to others, viewers, readers, and listeners clarify their own understanding and communicate it, both deep-rooted human needs. Interpretations of meaning may not only illuminate films but also reveal both the interpreters—for example, their backgrounds, assumptions, priorities, or the critical approaches they favor—and the historical time in which the text is being interpreted. Understanding meanings and how they are derived can help viewers realize when a film tries to unduly manipulate them—as in propagandistic films—or when a film demeans a gender choice, ethnic group, religion, or nation. In societies where citizens need to be informed, critical of orthodoxy, and tolerant of the diversity of people, ideas, and lifestyles, viewers benefit from training in discovering and questioning meanings in films and other texts.

CLOSE-UP: THINKING ABOUT *THE TRUMAN SHOW*

FIGURE 10.26 **Setting in *The Truman Show*** (1998)
Truman Burbank lives out his life in the picture-perfect
Seahaven, a gigantic enclosed TV studio. As seen here on a TV
screen, Seahaven is incredibly clean, orderly, and light. Frame
enlargement. *Scott Rudin Productions and Paramount; Paramount*

The Truman Show is about Truman Burbank, a
young man who is unaware that he has lived his entire life on a gigantic television soundstage as the
subject of a long-running, enormously popular TV
show. As the story unfolds, Truman begins to question his life and rebel. These passages demonstrate
some of the different types of responses possible.

EXPECTATIONS AND INTERACTIONS

The film starts out with a burst of information, running the delicious risk of disorienting us by providing
more data than we can quite absorb. Its first shot is a
tight close-up of a man in a beret who looks directly
at the camera and goes to the heart of the matter.
"We've become bored with watching actors giving us

phony emotions. We're tired of pyrotechnics and special effects. While the world he inhabits is in some respects counterfeit, there is nothing faked about
Truman. No script, no cue cards. It isn't always
Shakespeare, but it's genuine. It's a life."

The speaker is Christof (Ed Harris), later
described as the "televisionary" who created
The Truman Show. . . .

. . . The film is savvy enough to dole out the ram-
ifications and specifics of Truman's situation in artfully
spaced doses. Only in bits and pieces do we find out
the true dimension of what has been done to Truman,
how it has all been managed. —Kenneth Turan

EXPLICIT MEANINGS

There are only a few explicit meanings. Christof explains that "we accept the reality of the world with
which we're presented," and he explains several explicit meanings near the end of the film, as when he
says to Truman, "You were real. That's what made you
so good to watch." —William H. Phillips

IMPLICIT MEANINGS

Cinematic Techniques

From the outset there's something strange about the
place: The squeaky-clean tract houses could have been
designed by Disney [Figure 10.26], the sunsets are so
beautiful they're weird, and the town's inhabitants
seem larger than life, as if they are characters, even
caricatures.

Seahaven is a surreal version of America as America wishes it once was: paradise without the serpent.
—Richard Rayner

Film noir . . . fifty years later . . . looks mannered, and
we find no realism worthy of our trust. Every depiction of us needs to be ironic, cool, untouched by conviction or belief. . . . And as we looked for an image

that embodied our detachment, our disaffection, we found it in the high-key, undifferentiated gloss of television—a look for those who have given up on the Holy Ghost of believing what they see.

Half a century after the ascendancy of film noir, a new genre may be emerging. Call it film blanc, film lumiere, film fluorescent, film flash, or film deadpan. I like the latter two because they convey the instantaneous oneness of a kind of photography that bombs us with light just to get a picture. It's the kind of light that exists, like climate, on most TV sets and shows: a one-dimensional lighting scheme without depth, shaping, or character; a flood of light that lets you film without having to pause; a light that, with only a little heightening, seems surreal, mad, glaring, and unsettling.

The Truman Show is bathed in such light. What makes this so intriguing is the way it plays off our dependence on and loathing of TV—as if TV had become the base level of visible existence.

—David Thomson

FIGURE 10.27 Symbolic name in *The Truman Show* (1998) Christof, the god of Truman's world, whose name rings of *Christ* and who commands the sun to rise and set, the sea to churn and calm. Frame enlargement. *Scott Rudin Productions and Paramount; Paramount*

Symbols

In a deft, ironic touch, even Truman Burbank's name simultaneously evokes both reality (true-man) and unreality (Burbank, Calif., of course, home to many a TV and movie studio). —Michael O'Sullivan

Christof [Figure 10.27] symbolizes a strong-willed TV director-writer with an increasingly unpredictable subject, father figure to a rebellious son, tyrant whose police force helps keep the subject ignorant and in line, and god who restricts his subject's free will, nearly kills him, and finally implores him to continue in his role. —William H. Phillips

Narrative Meanings

The Truman Show is a crowd pleaser that caters to our horror of totalitarianism, our love of personal freedom, our belief—justified or deluded—that knowledge is a powerful tool and that access to information is a God-given right. I'm not sure if the movie is more disturbing because Truman is a prisoner or because he has been lied to. —Barbara Shulgasser

Pic trades in issues of personal liberty vs. authoritarian control, safe happiness vs. the excitement of chaos, manufactured emotions, the penetration of media to the point where privacy vanishes, and the fascination of fabricated images over plain sight. —Todd McCarthy

For me, *The Truman Show* was about reality and television, but also about deception and trust, and control and ethics, and voyeurism, and movie-watching, and corporate involvement in our daily lives. —Lise Carrigg

We're asked to believe that it took Truman 30 years to realize he was being watched—that he hadn't noticed in all that time that everyone else in his life was performing, colluding to protect his innocence.

It's an outrageous conceit, but once we've surrendered disbelief (and what great fable doesn't require such a leap?), *The Truman Show* has a lot to say about the way we live—about voyeurism and lockstep consumerism, about media surveillance and lack of privacy. —Edward Guthmann

The captive of TV isn't Truman, it's the audience. Us. And our love of that captivity, the gobbling of shows—fictional drama or news or sports or politics, but always shows—engulfs us. We used to go to theaters and films; now . . . TV comes to our homes, entwines us. . . . The shows don't have to be dramatic. . . . They need only be shows, life outside transmitted to the TV screen inside.　　　　　—Stanley Kauffmann

Truman is living the universal fantasy, in a disease-, disaster-, war- and stress-free environment whose minute-to-minute geniality is beamed on Prozac waves into homes around the world, calming the poor, the elderly, the lonely and the working classes with images of a life running its course in paradise.
　　　　　—Jack Matthews

Its premise is a legitimate one: the shock and violent internal crisis undergone by an individual beginning to see his world for the first time, *really* see it, really see *through* it. A smiling face might suddenly suggest hidden malice, a cozy street complacency and even suffocation. This is not paranoia, but the beginning of knowledge.　　　　　—David Walsh

SYMPTOMATIC MEANINGS

Would anyone care to guess how many TV shows routinely violate the privacy of ordinary people—often by invitation? Add up the day-time talk tabloids, then factor in all the cops-in-action shows, the seemingly endless supply of the world's funniest home videos. What does this tell us about ourselves, and how we choose to spend our time?

　　　At a certain level, this is the central question in . . . *The Truman Show*.　　　　　—Stephan Magcosta

The accelerating blurring of news and entertainment, of real and simulated violence, of authentic history and landscape with screen and theme-park fictionalizations: they're all part of Truman's all too eerily familiar world. So is the passivity of an audience that, as Bill Gates has promised, will someday never have to leave its armchairs.　　　　　—Frank Rich

WORKS CITED

Carrigg, Lise. "Lise Reviews *The Truman Show*." 5 August 1998. <www.girlson.com/film/navigation /loader.asp?story-http%3A%2F%2Fwww>.

Guthmann, Edward. "Remote Control Jim Carrey Is a Born TV Star in *The Truman Show*." *San Francisco Chronicle* 5 June 1998: C1.

Kauffmann, Stanley. "Caught in the Act." *New Republic* 29 June 1998: 22.

Magcosta, Stephan. "Must-See TV: *The Truman Show*." 18 July 1998. <seattlesquare.com /pandemonium/featurestext/TheTrumanShow .htm>.

Matthews, Jack. "He Doesn't Know His World's a Stage." 18 July 1998. <www.newsday.com /movies/rnmxz0d3.htm>.

McCarthy, Todd. "The Truman Show." 18 July 1998. <www.variety.com/filmrev/ cfralso.asp?recordID=1117477427>.

O'Sullivan, Michael. "*Truman*: A Surreally Big Show." *Washington Post* 5 June 1998, Weekend: N58.

Rayner, Richard. "The Truman Show." *Harper's Bazaar* June 1998: 92.

Rich, Frank. "Prime Time Live." *New York Times* 23 May 1998, national ed.: A25.

Shulgasser, Barbara. "Carrey Rings True in *The Truman Show*." *San Francisco Examiner* 5 June 1998. 27 May 2001. <www.sfgate.com/cgi-bin /article.cgi?file=/examiner/archive/1998/06/05 /WEEKEND8781.dtl>.

Thomson, David. "The Truman Show." *Esquire* May 1998: 46.

Turan, Kenneth. "His Show of Shows." *Los Angeles Times* 5 June 1998, Calendar: F1.

Walsh, David. "*The Truman Show*: Further Signs of Life in Hollywood." World Socialist Web Site 15 June 1998. 27 May 2001. <wsws.org /arts/1998/jun1998/tru-j15.shtml>.

SUMMARY

This chapter introduces some of the major ways that viewers think about films. They form expectations and hypotheses and modify them as a film proceeds. Some films include explicit meanings, and viewers usually formulate implicit meanings. Those explicit and implicit meanings may be symptomatic of the society that nurtured the film's making. The implicit meanings every viewer formulates are not universal and are shaped by many factors, including knowledge of the film gained from sources other than the film itself and various other factors such as the viewer's political values and sexual orientation.

Expectations and Interactions

- As viewers watch a film, they interact with it, forming expectations, responding to clues set forth, guessing, readjusting their hypotheses, and consequently experiencing puzzlement or clarity and feeling excitement and pleasure or disappointment or boredom or some other response.

Types of Meanings

- As used in this book, *meaning* is a generalization about a subject.
- Unless a film includes some direct statement explaining its meanings, meanings are not inherent in a film. Mentally active people formulate most meanings.

EXPLICIT MEANINGS

- Explicit meanings are generalizations included in a text about one or more of its subjects. They are included more often in documentary films than in fictional films or experimental films.
- Fictional films that often include explicit meanings are frequently thought of as flawed in Western societies because generally modern audiences in the West expect movies to show, not tell or explain, their meanings.
- An explicit meaning is not necessarily comprehensive or persuasive, and it is not the definitive word on any of the film's subjects.

IMPLICIT MEANINGS

- An implicit meaning is a generalization that a viewer or reader makes about a text (such as a film) or a subject in a text.
- As Part One of this book shows, a film's mise en scène, cinematography, editing, and sound can suggest or reinforce meanings.

- A technique may be used subtly and viewers required to be especially attentive in discovering its significance. However, a technique's significance may go unnoticed if it is too subtle for the intended audience or if the version obscures important details.

- Filmmakers and other makers of texts may create symbols: anything perceptible in a text that has significance beyond its usual meaning or function. Usually symbols go unexplained within a film, and viewers interpret them variously, although not all interpretations are equally persuasive.

- Satire is a representation of an individual or group that indirectly exposes and perhaps ridicules the human subjects for being foolish, evil, or stupid or for having some other shortcoming. Satire suggests meaning indirectly, so it is up to readers or viewers to figure out what in general is being implied about the subject. Satires are not basically realistic but distorted representations of human folly.

- Narrative itself is a major source of implicit meanings because viewers often infer general implications from the story. For example, popular movies often present improbable though reassuring stories that show people overcoming overwhelming adversity and achieving their goals. (To formulate implicit meanings in a nonnarrative documentary film, viewers generalize about the film's representation of its factual subjects.)

- A narrative or some aspect of it may be ambiguous: it is open to two or more plausible interpretations perhaps because it withholds significant information or provides conflicting information.

SYMPTOMATIC MEANINGS: WORLD → FILM → VIEWERS

- Knowledge of the society where the film was made helps viewers discover symptomatic meanings: generalizations about a text or part of a text that are characteristic of the society that nurtured the film. For example, popular American movies are permeated with the symptomatic meaning that dedicated, industrious individuals can influence the outcome of important events. This meaning stated or implied in so many American movies is symptomatic of much of American society.

Influences on the Ways People Think about Films

- The meanings a person perceives in a text may be influenced by many factors, such as the viewer's knowledge of the film learned elsewhere and the viewer's various constructed identities, such as political views, sexual orientation, and ways of analyzing texts (critical approaches).

- Meanings are to some extent relative to time and place, but not all interpretations are well thought out and persuasive.

Major Terms about Thinking about Films

Below, numbers in italics refer to the pages where the terms are explained. All terms are defined in more detail in the Illustrated Glossary beginning on p. 621.

ambiguity *491*
auteur theory *505*
critical approach *504*
cutting continuity script *499*
explicit meaning *472*

film theorist *506*
gender *500*
ideology *503*
implicit meaning *473*
interpretive community *506*
irony *482*

reading (definition 3) *515*
representation *471*
satire *482*
symbol *479*
symptomatic meaning *494*
trailer *467*

QUESTIONS ABOUT THINKING ABOUT FILMS

The following questions are intended to help viewers understand ways to think about films. Not all the questions are appropriate for every film. In thinking out, discussing, and writing responses to those questions most appropriate for the film being examined, be careful to stick with the issues the questions raise, to answer all parts of the questions, to explain the reasons for your answers, and to give specific examples from the film.

1. What were your expectations before the film began? What developments in the film required you to readjust your expectations and hypotheses as the film was shown?

2. Does the film include any explicit meanings? If so, what are they? Are they necessary, or could viewers have figured out those meanings on their own?

3. Where do cinematic techniques help suggest or reinforce implicit meanings?

4. Does the film sometimes use techniques subtly and require attentive viewers and listeners? If so, where and with what consequences?

5. Is the film sometimes too subtle? If so, explain. If you were to see the film in a different format or version, what subtle techniques could be difficult or impossible to notice?

6. Does the film have any symbols? What do they mean or suggest? Why do you say so?

7. Which, if any, behavior or attitudes are satirized or made fun of? How strongly implied is the disapproval? Is the satire obvious or subtle? Why do you say so?

8. What implicit meanings does the narrative itself suggest?

9. What fantasies does the film embody? Does the film blend elements of realism and fantasy? If so, explain.

10. Is any aspect of the film ambiguous? If so, explain.

11. If you know the conditions that were prevalent at the time and place the film was made, do you detect any symptomatic meanings in the film?

12. How might knowledge of the source novel influence your thinking about the film?

13. How might a reading of the continuity cutting script for the film influence your thinking about the film?

14. How might a viewer's knowledge of gender issues influence the viewer's thinking about the film? Why do you say so?

15. How might a person's sexual orientation, political persuasion, nationality, or application of a critical approach influence that person's interpretation of the film? Why do you say so?

WORKS CITED

Alexie, Sherman (author, and scriptwriter of *Smoke Signals*). Telephone interview. 13 June 2000.

"*Barbershop* Controversy Boils Over." *The Associated Press* 28 Sept. 2002.

"Behind the Silver Screen." To the Best of Our Knowledge. *Wisconsin Public Radio.* 22 Dec. 2002.

Bordwell, David. *Making Meaning: Inference and Rhetoric in the Interpretation of Cinema.* Cambridge: Harvard UP, 1989.

The Citizen Kane *Book: Raising Kane, by Pauline Kael. The Shooting Script, by Herman J. Mankiewicz and Orson Welles, and the Cutting Continuity of the Completed Film.* Boston: Little, Brown, 1971.

Ellsworth, Elizabeth. "Illicit Pleasures: Feminist Spectators and *Personal Best.*" *Wide Angle* 8.2 (1986): 45–56. Reprinted in *Issues in Feminist Film Criticism.* Ed. Patricia Erens. Bloomington: Indiana UP, 1990.

Epstein, Leslie. "The Movie on the Whorehouse Wall/*The Devil in Miss Jones.*" *The Movie That Changed My Life.* Ed. David Rosenberg. New York: Viking, 1991.

Glueck, Grace. "How Jews Shaped Show Business, and Vice Versa." *New York Times on the Web* 28 Feb. 2003, late ed.–final: E44. <http://query.nytimes.com/gst/fullpage.html?res=9F00EEDA123CF93BA15751C0A9659C8B63>.

Hessler, Peter. Interview. *Fresh Air.* National Public Radio. 5 Feb. 2001.

Hoberman, J., and Jeffrey Shandler, eds. *Entertaining America: Jews, Movies, and Broadcasting.* Princeton: Princeton UP, 2003.

Johnston, Sheila. "Interview: Masayuki Suo." *The Observer* (England) 10 May 1998: 7+.

Katz, Ephraim. *The Film Encyclopedia*. 4th ed. Rev. Fred Klein and Ronald Dean Nolen. New York: HarperResource, 2001.

Kidman, Nicole, and Rick Lyman. "Nicole Kidman on *The Shining*." *Watching Movies: The Biggest Names in Cinema Talk about the Films That Matter Most*. New York: Times Books, 2003.

Klinger, Barbara. *Melodrama and Meaning: History, Culture, and the Films of Douglas Sirk*. Bloomington: Indiana UP, 1994.

Maslin, Janet. "Is It Unexpected? Is It Strange? It's Here." *New York Times* 28 Jan. 1995, nat. ed.: 11.

Murphy, Kevin. *A Year at the Movies: One Man's Filmgoing Odyssey*. New York: Harper-Collins, 2002.

Presse, Agence-France. "North Korea Denounces James Bond Film." *New York Times on the Web* 15 Dec. 2002. <http://www.nytimes.com/2002/12/15/international/asia/15KORE.html>.

Staiger, Janet. *Interpreting Films: Studies in the Historical Reception of American Cinema*. Princeton: Princeton UP, 1992.

Sternberg, Meir. *Expositional Modes and Temporal Ordering in Fiction*. Baltimore: Johns Hopkins UP, 1978.

Wood, Robin. *Howard Hawks*. Garden City, NY: Doubleday, 1968.

FOR FURTHER READING

Although film theory helps us understand the film medium more completely, some writings are frustrating for students to read because of their involved sentence structure and the writers' heavy use of jargon. The books listed below, however, should prove accessible to many beginning film students.

Andrew, J. Dudley. *The Major Film Theories: An Introduction*. New York: Oxford UP, 1976. Includes an explanation of what film theory entails and a discussion of major film theories: early theorists, realist film theory, and contemporary French film theory.

Approaches to Popular Film. Ed. Joanne Hollows and Mark Janncovich. Manchester, Eng.: Manchester UP, 1995. Eight essays on different critical approaches for doing film analyses.

Bennett, Tony, and Janet Wollacott. *Bond and Beyond: The Political Career of a Popular Hero*. New York: Methuen, 1987. A study of the James Bond novels and films (to the late 1980s) showing in part how they have been **read** or interpreted differently at different times and different places.

BFI Film Classics and *BFI Modern Classics*. London: BFI. Two series of short books published by the British Film Institute, each devoted to one film and written by a film critic, film scholar, or novelist. Sample *BFI Film Classics* titles examine *Belle de Jour*, *Blackmail*, *Bonnie and Clyde*, *The Blue Angel*, *Pather Panchali*, and *Vertigo*. Sample titles in the *BFI Modern Classics* series are *Blade Runner*, *Blue Velvet*, *L.A. Confidential*, *Eyes Wide Shut*, *Do the Right Thing*, and *Trainspotting*.

Bywater, Tim, and Thomas Sobchack. *Introduction to Film Criticism: Major Critical Approaches to Narrative Film*. New York: Longman, 1989. Includes discussions of major ways to analyze films; sample student papers; a chronology of film reviewing, criticism, and theory; and a glossary.

Cambridge Film Handbooks. Ed. Andrew Horton. Cambridge: Cambridge UP. A series of books, each focused on one film from a variety of theoretical, critical, and contextual perspectives and consisting of essays by film scholars and critics, a filmography, and a bibliography. Sample titles are *Bonnie and Clyde*, *Persona*, *The Wild Bunch*, *The Discreet Charm of the Bourgeoisie*, *Sherlock Jr.*, *Tokyo Story*, *Do the Right Thing*, and the *Godfather* trilogy.

Carson, Diane, Linda Dittmar, and Janice R. Welsch, eds. *Multiple Voices in Feminist Film Criticism*. Minneapolis: U of Minnesota P, 1994. A collection of mostly theoretical essays, most for the advanced student.

Close Viewings: An Anthology of New Film Criticism. Ed. Peter Lehman. Tallahassee: Florida State UP, 1990. Part 1 emphasizes formal analysis; Part 2, cultural analysis; Part 3, an essay, applies many forms of criticism to one film, *The Searchers*.

Critical Dictionary of Film and Television Theory. Ed. Roberta Pearson and Philip Simpson. New York: Routledge, 2001. Includes over 400 entries from 500 to 3,000 words each. Sample entries are for *continuity editing*, *film noir*, *mise en scène*, *narrative*, and *western*. Also included are suggestions for further reading, cross-references, and an index.

Doty, Alexander. *Flaming Classics: Queering the Film Canon*. New York: Routledge, 2000. The author argues against the assumption that only explicitly gay films are subject to gay readings and examines six classic films for their gay potential.

The Film Cultures Reader. Ed. Graeme Turner. New York, London: Routledge, 2002. Focuses on film as a social and cultural practice and on the relationship between cinema and popular culture. Six thematic sections: Understanding Film, Technology, Film Industries, Meanings and Pleasures, Identities, and Audiences and Consumption.

Film Theory Goes to the Movies: Cultural Analysis of Contemporary Film. Ed. Jim Collins, Hilary Radner, and Ava Preacher Collins. New York: Routledge, 1993. Interpretations of popular American movies in terms of issues in current film theories.

Greenberg, Harvey Roy. *Screen Memories: Hollywood Cinema on the Psychoanalytic Couch*. New York: Columbia UP, 1993. Film criticism from a psychoanalytic perspective.

Lane, Christina. *Feminist Hollywood: From* Born in Flames *to* Point Break. Detroit: Wayne State UP, 2000. Includes original interviews with women directors and close analyses of their films.

Litch, Mary. *Philosophy through Film*. New York: Routledge, 2002. Nine chapters organized into four parts: Knowledge and Truth; Minds, Bodies and Persons; Ethics and Moral Responsibility; and Philosophy, Religion and the Meaning of Life.

Lyden, John C. *Film as Religion: Myths, Morals, and Rituals*. New York: New York UP, 2003. In Part One, the book explains generally and in Part Two demonstrates specifically how film can convey beliefs and values and have ritual power to provide emotional catharsis.

Miles, Margaret R. *Seeing and Believing: Religion and Values in the Movies*. Boston: Beacon, 1996. Examines what popular films of the 1980s and 1990s say and suggest about religion and values. Essays are divided into two parts: Religion in Popular Film and Race, Gender, Sexuality, and Class in Popular Film.

The Political Companion to American Film. Ed. Gary Crowdus. Chicago: Lake View, 1994. Includes essays on filmmakers, genres, racial and ethnic representations, and social characterizations (such as politicians). Many essays discuss the implicit and symptomatic political meanings (broadly defined) of specific films. Includes a short bibliography after most of the essays.

Powers, Stephen, David J. Rothman, and Stanley Rothman. *Hollywood's America: Social and Political Themes in Motion Pictures.* Boulder, CO: Westview, 1996. The book combines an "extensive systematic content analysis . . . of social and political themes in [popular] motion pictures from 1946 to the present with the most detailed study ever conducted of the political views and personalities of a random sample of leaders in the motion picture industry." Includes many tables presenting the results of the research and an appendix entitled The Poverty of Film Theory.

Salt, Barry. *Film Style and Technology: History and Analysis.* 2nd ed. London: Starword, 1992. Both a critique of much of current film theory and a history of film technology and analysis of its impact on film style.

Sprengnether, Madelon. *Crying at the Movies: A Film Memoir.* Saint Paul, MN: Graywolf Press, 2002. In each chapter, the author describes a film, her emotional reactions to it, the parallels to her life, and the understanding of herself that she gained.

Tan, Ed S. *Emotion and the Structure of Narrative Film: Film as an Emotion Machine.* Mahwah, NJ: Erlbaum, 1996. A theoretical study of a largely neglected subject with emphasis on the traditional feature film. Sample chapter titles: The Psychological Functions of Film Viewing; Thematic Structures and Interest; and Character Structures, Empathy, and Interest.

Trosman, Harry. *Contemporary Psychoanalysis and Masterworks of Art and Film.* New York: New York UP, 1996. Demonstrates how classical and contemporary psychoanalytic thought can be used to enrich one's understanding and appreciation of paintings and of films such as *Citizen Kane*, *Vertigo*, and *8½*.

Other materials illustrating ways to understand films can be found on the Web site for this book: <bedfordstmartins.com/phillips-film>.

APPENDICES

Close-Up on *The Player*: A Sample Film Analysis

T
O HELP YOU UNDERSTAND SOME OF THE SCOPE OF THE FILM medium and how individual films can function, this book breaks films down into elements and addresses them one at a time—for example, one chapter on cinematography and one on contexts for films. Of course, when a film is shown, the cinematography and all the other elements function simultaneously and ideally complement one another to produce a unified effect. This Close-Up applies many of the book's concepts to a single film and serves as a partial summary and review of the book. The goal is to help you appreciate ways to use some of the book's concepts in your own film analyses and in your explorations of the film medium. As with any analysis of one film, this Close-Up cannot address every aspect of this book or of the film under study, nor can any one film exemplify all the aspects of cinema. The medium is far too encompassing for any film to serve that function.

The film chosen is *The Player*, which came out in 1992 and was written by Michael Tolkin and directed by Robert Altman. This film was selected because it is often used in introductory film courses; is readily available on videotape, laser disc, and DVD; is fun to watch; and exemplifies many aspects of interest to filmmakers, film critics, and film scholars. Also, *The Player* is a movie about the Hollywood movie industry, filled with references to earlier films and observations about the Hollywood studio system.

DESCRIPTION

If you have not seen *The Player* recently or will not be seeing it, please read the following description at least twice.

The film is set in modern Hollywood and focuses on a film studio executive named Griffin Mill whose job entails listening to and approving brief

FIGURE A.1 Main character's initial love interest
Early in the film viewers see that Griffin Mill is romantically involved with a co-worker, Bonnie Sherow. Here they are seen as she reads to him a particularly inept passage from a submitted screenplay. Frame enlargement. *Fine Line Features*

summaries of stories to be made into movies. Griffin processes hundreds of pitches a week, but the studio can produce only twelve movies a year.

Viewers quickly learn three aspects of Griffin's situation: an unidentified screenwriter is threatening Griffin; rumor has it that an outsider named Larry Levy will be brought in to take over Griffin's position; and Griffin is involved romantically with a subordinate, a story editor named Bonnie Sherow (Figure A.1).

After some hasty searching through office records, Griffin decides that the writer who has been threatening him is named David Kahane. That night, Griffin telephones Kahane from outside the writer's house. He sees Kahane's girlfriend, an artist named June Gudmundsdottir, answer the phone and is immediately attracted to her (Figure A.2). June tells Griffin that Kahane went to a movie. Later Griffin finds Kahane at the movie theater and afterward has drinks with him. The two men end up in a parking lot, tempers flare, and Griffin kills Kahane and then makes the murder look like an interrupted robbery (Figure A.3).

FIGURE A.2 Main character's new love interest
From outside the writer's house and looking in, Mill sees a luminous vision in the night, an artist who always dresses in white and works in a shimmering silvery white studio. Soon he pursues her as he tries to cope with the threat of the police arresting him for murder, changes in studio personnel, his relationship with Bonnie, and a persistent and increasingly threatening postcard writer. Frame enlargement. *Fine Line Features*

FIGURE A.3 Mill and the writer, tempers flaring
Mill finds Kahane, whom Mill assumes has been writing the threatening postcards. Kahane gets angry at Mill, but Mill fails to calm the writer's anger. One thing leads to another, and the two men face each other here, moments before Kahane pushes the car door against Mill knocking him backward and over a railing and Mill loses his temper, attacks back, and kills the man. Frame enlargement. *Fine Line Features*

a)   b)

FIGURE A.4 A pitch to Mill and Levy's pitch to the studio head
(a) An intense director—holding Mill's leather-encased scissors in one hand and a fake grenade from Mill's desktop in the other—pitches the story for *Habeas Corpus* to Mill. Mill thinks the story would be a disaster as a movie, so he OKs it but plans to let Levy propose it to the studio head. (b) Levy proposes the story of *Habeas Corpus* to the studio head as Mill waits behind clasped hands, probably enjoying that Levy is walking into the trap Mill set for him. Frame enlargements. *Fine Line Features*

The next day, Griffin returns to his job and finds that Larry Levy has come to work at the studio. Later, Griffin also learns that the writer who had been threatening him is still alive. Griffin attends Kahane's funeral and soon begins to pursue Kahane's girlfriend romantically.

Because Griffin is a suspect in the murder, the police come to Griffin's office and interview him. After a producer and director pitch Griffin their plans for *Habeas Corpus*—a grim story likely to be a huge flop if ever produced—Griffin "allows" Levy to take over championing the story in the hope that the movie will fail and Levy will be discredited (Figure A.4).

The police summon Griffin to the police station, where Detective Avery's questions and methods fluster him (Figure A.5). Later, Griffin and June slip off to a desert hideaway where at the conclusion of a romantic evening they become lovers. The next day, Griffin is called in for a police lineup, but the only eyewitness selects a police detective from among the possible suspects.

A year later, the director of *Habeas Corpus* has included stars and a preposterous happy

FIGURE A.5 Major threat to Mill's freedom and happiness
The main impediment to Mill's freedom and happiness is a clever police detective. She asks questions that catch Mill off-guard and interrogates him in an unorthodox manner (including twirling the tampon she holds in her hand here as she questions Mill). Frame enlargement. *Fine Line Features*

ending after all. After a screening at the studio, Bonnie Sherow points out the film has become a sellout, whereupon Levy fires her. Griffin now occupies the former studio head's office and is in charge of the studio. He and Levy are on good working terms. When Bonnie tries to make an emotional appeal to Griffin, he walks past her without looking at her and says she "will land on her feet."

In the final sequence, Griffin is cruising to his home in a Rolls-Royce convertible while listening to a pitch on his car phone. The caller obliquely identifies himself as the writer who had been threatening Griffin and proposes a story about a movie executive who gets away with murder—in fact, the story of the movie that viewers have just seen. Griffin's main concern is that the movie executive gets away with the murder and lives happily ever after married to the dead writer's girlfriend. The writer assures him that an OK to make the film will guarantee that outcome, and Griffin agrees. The writer proposes that the film be called *The Player*. Griffin arrives home and is greeted warmly by June, who is visibly pregnant.

MISE EN SCÈNE

In *The Player*, the mise en scène shows selected aspects of contemporary Hollywood and lets viewers mingle with the players, those exercising power, and the trappings of wealth.

Settings

The Player begins in an office interior; then the camera tracks up and back to give an overview of a movie lot in contemporary sunny southern California. The weather is clear yet nondescript; the parking lot is tidy and features an expensive car; the limited landscaping is well manicured. All players are nattily attired and perfectly coiffed. At once the setting suggests wealth (the clothes), power (the studio itself), and surface orderliness. The opening shot also introduces nearly all the main characters.

Griffin Mill's office is crammed with movie posters for *King Kong* (1933), *The Blue Angel* (1930), and six movies dealing with crime, especially murder: *Prison Shadows* (1936), *Hollywood Story* (1951), *Laura* (1944, Figure A.6a), *Murder in the Big House* (1942, Figure A.6b), *Prison Break* (1938, Figure A.6b), and *M* (the 1951 remake). The posters in Mill's office associate Mill with movies about murder. By contrast, the office of the studio head has a poster for *Casablanca* (1942), whose subject is not crime but romance, patriotism, and sacrifice (Figure A.4b).

Another component of the setting used especially expressively is the cars. For most of the film Mill drives a black Range Rover—a status symbol for moneyed Angelenos and a vehicle that can comfortably accommodate actor Tim Robbins's six-foot five-inch frame. The studio head, Joel Levison, drives a black Mercedes, and Mill's rumored rival, Larry Levy, drives a black Mercedes convertible. The cars suggest that Levy has the same tastes as the studio head and is a major player. In the film's last scenes, when Mill is now the studio head, he drives a Rolls-Royce convertible, an obvious symbol of his promotion.

The cars, car phones, car faxes, and clothing so expensive that the cost of a single suit would support a family in a barrio for a month—these are symbols of power within the industry.

Subjects

Except for the writer who is murdered, his girl-friend, and the police, all the main characters are involved in making studio movies. Of them, the central character is Griffin Mill. Because viewers see him in nearly every scene and in a variety of situations that are difficult for him, both professionally and personally, viewers get to know Mill fairly well, though we never get to know his thoughts directly. He is a complex character: calculating, guarded, professionally successful, vulnerable to rage and violence, adept at surviving—and lucky to survive his encounter with the law.

Even to a casual viewer, *The Player* includes an extraordinary number of cameos, mainly of famous actors but also of directors, a film critic, and others. As is typical of cameo performances, none affects the plot in any significant way. One could argue that the sixty-five cameos are part of the densely populated decor, part of the setting rather than subjects in their own right. The cameos also add an element of surprise—whom will viewers notice next?—though there is a danger that the cameos could distract viewers from the story. There are so many cameos, some of them inconspicuous, that attentive viewers may notice even more of them on later re-viewings.

a)

b)

FIGURE A.6 Symbolic setting
(a–b) Most of the many movie posters in Mill's office are for films involving crime and punishment, an appropriate backdrop for a man who has committed murder and hopes to evade punishment. *Fine Line Features*

Composition

The film's intended aspect ratio is 1.85:1. That makes it a wide-screen film but not as wide as it might have been—for example, an anamorphic version with a 2.4:1 aspect ratio. Rarely does *The Player* show subjects isolated from each other on opposite sides of the frame. Occasionally something significant is going on in both the foreground and the background simultaneously, as briefly in the opening shot where a man in a Porsche convertible (an investor's son) flirts with a woman as a group of Japanese are being given a studio tour behind them.

Much more typically the film uses a moving camera or zoom lens to follow a few characters for a while then pick up new characters and follow them. The mobile camera and many characters moving rapidly within the frame, and in and out of it, make for frequent changes in composition and a sense of exploration and perhaps restlessness.

Mise en Scène and the World outside the Film

The most obvious product placement is the Range Rover. It appears in many scenes and is photographed from a variety of distances and angles. Its logo (on both the front and the back of the vehicle) is legible at least four places in the film. Probably the Range Rover is so prominent because the film's producers and the vehicle maker struck a mutually advantageous deal. Among the people and businesses singled out for "Special Thanks" in the end credits is "Range Rover of North America" (see the appendix How to Read Film Credits for the closing credits for *The Player* on pp. 613-20).

CINEMATOGRAPHY

Aside from the opening shot, which is described on p. 121, the cinematography by Jean Lepine tends to be unobtrusive. It supports the story and helps make the movie easy to follow and pleasurable to watch. Viewers with training in film studies, however, are likely to notice some of the techniques that influence viewers' responses to the film.

Color

The film uses expressive color at various points. One occurs after dark when Griffin Mill drives to David Kahane's house. Mill drives up to a distinctly lit house whose windows glow with an unusual icy, crystalline blue. Unbeknownst to the woman inside, Mill watches her as she speaks to him on the phone while working at a canvas surrounded by a clutter of art paraphernalia—all in a variety of blues, whites, and silvers. She claims to have no particular interest in movies as she ranges languidly around in the liquid, shimmering bluish light, which is used to emphasize the icy environment. (Later Kahane will refer to her as the "ice queen.") Throughout the film Gudmundsdottir is associated with white. She even wears white shoes, dress, and hat and a light blue scarf to Kahane's funeral. Because she has been shown as a disengaged entity, we can understand this radical departure from tradition. Mill, in contrast, dresses in different colors. Initially he wears an off-white suit and generally wears darker and darker suits as the film progresses until he is wearing black in the last sequence.

Another particularly expressive use of color occurs the night Mill kills Kahane. Reddish tones are used to light the karaoke bar where they drink together. When Mill leaves the bar, a splash of red neon light colors his footsteps out the door. Just before Kahane mockingly asks to borrow Mill's cellular phone, another red flash originates from behind the camera and is directed onto the back wall. Seconds later, it again flashes against the wall as Kahane makes his imaginary phone call. Eventually, red dominates the scene and is reflected by the shallow pool of water where Mill kills Kahane. As is often the case in imaginative texts, the red underscores violence and the loss of blood and life.

Lighting

The Player is not a dark film. It begins in the outdoor morning light and concludes in sunny afternoon light. In between are some night scenes, though they are without deep atmospheric shadows; viewers can still see the subjects distinctly. As might be expected, the light is especially soft during the night scenes of romance between Mill and Gudmundsdottir at the desert resort. There are also numerous interior daytime scenes, many with light shadows from the open venetian blinds. All the daytime interiors are well and evenly illuminated. To accomplish a soft texture in the daytime interiors, cinematographer Jean Lepine used filters that create the feeling of naturally diffused light. Many filters are also used throughout the daytime shots to dampen the glare. The film's lighting supports its moods: mostly brightly lit day scenes that have minimal glare and some night scenes for murder, attempted assault with a serpentine weapon, romance, and sex.

The Camera

The camera is rarely positioned close to the subjects. When the subject is a talking individual, she or he is usually seen in a medium shot or a medium close-up. One exception is when viewers briefly see Mill's face in close-up as he holds Kahane's head under the puddle of water. Another notable exception is when Mill is with Detective Avery in the Pasadena police station. Avery is twirling a tampon and asking difficult questions; her assistant is stalking a fly and swatting it; and the three police personnel are laughing at Mill's desperate responses. Mill's bewildered, frightened reactions are seen in close-up and extreme close-up.

Lepine and Altman often use deep focus to capture group scenes that simultaneously portray the private interactions of famous people (without invading their conversations) and the "busyness" of the larger view. *The Player* also includes deep-focus shots during which the audience is made privy to activities and conversations in the foreground and background. Exemplary among them is a shot approximately 21¾ minutes into the film of Mill's breakfast meeting with Levison that begins with Burt Reynolds and film critic Charles Champlin at a table in the foreground, bicyclists in the middle ground, and Levison and Mill at a table in the background. On the other hand, when it suits the purposes of the scene, many shots of individuals and small groups are taken with a long lens so the background is out of focus and the viewer's attention can remain on the human subjects in the foreground.

The film also relies heavily on eye-level camera placements; viewers get to see players at an interactive level. Here, as in other films, the filmmakers play to the belief that viewers have a right both to explore the world of people who wield enormous power and to be on an equal footing with them.

As in other Altman films, many moving, exploratory camera shots are used throughout, as in the film's famous long opening shot (Table 3.1). The many shots of moving, fast-talking actors filmed by a moving camera or zoom lens (or both) contribute to the sense that people in the movie industry are an energetic group wrapped up in their work but not each other. Often scenes are filmed so that one character is walking away as another character walks alongside or behind, talking at rather than talking to each other—all the while without making eye contact.

EDITING

The Player is a suspenseful, satirical film in which the main character confronts several problems simultaneously. The editing by Geraldine Peroni[1] unifies the elements of Mill's story and moves the story along at a pace that entertains audiences and keeps them involved.

Continuity Editing

Continuity editing is used throughout *The Player*. An example of effective continuity editing is six consecutive scenes in which Mill tracks down a writer, meets him, and kills him:

1. *Tracking the writer*   Mill looks through the office datebooks and at data on a computer, identifies Kahane as the stalker, and gets Kahane's address and phone number.

---

[1]Geraldine Peroni is listed as the editor in the film's opening credits, in various printed sources, and on the laser disc jacket, the DVD cover, and the videotape box, but the concluding credits list Maysie Hoy as editor and many secondary sources list both people as coeditors.

2. *Calling Kahane's house*   Mill parks near a house and talks with the woman inside the house on his cell phone while he stands outside.

3. *The Rialto movie theater*   Mill sees the end of *The Bicycle Thief.*

4. *The theater lobby*   Mill talks with Kahane.

5. *The karaoke bar*   Mill and Kahane drink together and talk some more.

6. *The murder*   Mill and Kahane confront each other in a parking lot; Mill murders Kahane.

In this nearly sixteen-and-a-half-minute sequence, the film represents approximately two hours of story time. Each shot follows the preceding shot clearly; the characters' emotions and motives emerge; and the content and pace of the scenes are satisfying.

Another example of editing used to support continuity occurs a little more than seventy-one minutes into the film, when a match cut juxtaposes the dead snake Mill kills with the thick curvy line that June draws with blue chalk.

Image on Image and Image after Image

The film includes no lap dissolves or superimpositions. The only transitions between scenes other than cuts are two fade-out, fade-ins, between which appears the title card "One Year Later."

Among the most noteworthy cuts is one approximately $39\frac{2}{3}$ minutes into the film: the shift from the murder scene to the next day's executive conference. The image of the murder scene remains on the screen. Viewers subtly become aware that the sound has changed (although the picture hasn't) as background conversation (softly at first) begins to dominate the soundtrack. Within seconds the discussion assumes a normal volume, and viewers find themselves at a conference in which Larry Levy proposes making movies without using writers. In other words, the film cuts from a studio executive's murder of a writer to an executive's proposal to eliminate writers from the filmmaking process.

Also expressive is the cut from the lovemaking scene to the mud bath (nearly 106 minutes into the film). In the throes of passion Griffin Mill confesses his responsibility for David Kahane's death, but Gudmundsdottir does not want to hear such talk. There is a natural lack of clarity in this erotic exchange as the lovers are more concentrated on their physical arousal than on what is being said. Regardless of Gudmundsdottir's ardor, a murky element sullies their liaison. In fact, morally they are up to their necks. And that is what viewers can sense in the cut from the lovemaking scene to the mud bath scene where the lovers are immersed separately, do not touch, and make no eye contact.

At least two sets of reaction shots warrant discussion. The first, which occurs a little more than ten minutes into the film, concerns the scene in which Reggie Goldman, a banker's son, is trying to exercise his leverage in his pursuit of various attractive female actors. The scene includes multiple reaction shots of the amused and knowing Joel Levison, Walter Stuckel, and Griffin Mill.

The second set of reaction shots occurs approximately ninety-three minutes into the film, during the scene at the Pasadena police station where Mill has been summoned to review mug shots. Detective Avery nonchalantly unwraps a tampon and begins to twirl it while asking Mill whether he had gone out with Gudmundsdottir the night before. Avery wants to know how long Mill has known Gudmundsdottir and whether he has had sex with her. Mill becomes confused and incensed and says he won't answer that question without a lawyer present; then he contends in effect that his rights are being ignored. The camera cuts to Avery, who laughs in reaction to Mill's defensive behavior. Her laughter bubbles over as Detective DeLongpre joins in. Close-up and extreme close-up reaction shots of Mill accompanied by raucous background laughter complete the scene.

The film begins with the rare situation of one shot presenting multiple scenes (see Table 3.1 on p. 121). However, as in most scenes in movies, most of the scenes in *The Player* consist of multiple shots. Consider the scene in which Mill talks to Gudmundsdottir on his cellular phone. The scene runs 225 seconds and has twenty-six shots. This scene needs to be long enough to reveal something of Gudmundsdottir's character and allure and to make credible Mill's infatuation with her even though he is preoccupied with locating the threatening writer and dealing with him. The scene also needs to be visually varied and interesting. And it is. The moving subject (Mill) and the moving camera suggest Mill's restlessness and his curiosity about this luminous vision in the night; he wants to view her continually and from various distances and angles. Likewise Gudmundsdottir is usually in motion. It is not only the subjects' movements and the camera movement that inject vitality into the scene. The editing—as well as the varied camera distances and angles it makes possible—also contributes visual variety while excising uneventful time. Although the editing is not fast, its average shot length of 8.65 seconds is short enough to impart some energy to the scene.

Sometimes editing helps vary the pace within scenes. Consider the scene where Mill drives off from the St. James's Club,[2] receives a fax, uncovers a present on the floor of the Range Rover, and reacts to the snake. The first 45 seconds of the scene have an average shot length of 4.5 seconds. The last 54 seconds of the scene, after Mill discovers the rattler, have an even shorter average shot length of 2.7 seconds, with some shots lasting only a second or two. Given the danger to Mill (a crash, snake bites, or both), the fast cutting reinforces his panicky reaction after he uncovers the snake.

---

[2]The spelling is as given on the postcard Mill receives while sitting poolside at the club and talking with the producer and British director.

SOUND

Sound in *The Player* contributes to the varied moods. For example, in many scenes in which the characters display nervousness and tension, the music is jangling and edgy, not melodic. The few scenes featuring soothing music and relaxed conversation, such as when Mill and Gudmundsdottir dance at the desert hideaway, offer viewers (and Mill) a welcome break from the tension.

Spoken Words

Overlapping dialogue (a common experience in everyday life and in most Altman films) is used in group scenes to make some word and phrase recognition possible yet allow other snippets of language to function as ambient sound. In their rush, characters speak without being entirely heard, and the cacophonous mixture of voices suggests that the attempt to be heard may be in vain. In such an environment, communication can be stressful, fragmentary, and incomplete.

Each restaurant scene in *The Player* includes background din plus fragments of conversation that color the mood or drive the plot. The commentary on the laser disc version (but not the DVD) points out that for the scene of Larry Levy's first executive meeting, which occurs almost 39½ minutes into the film, each actor wore a separately wired microphone that allowed the sound editor to raise and lower the volume or shift the focus of dialogue interaction to replicate the flow of sound energy among participants in a high-level business meeting. Because the objective is so well achieved, viewers are more likely to feel like participants in that meeting. The breakfast meeting scene between Levison and Mill shifts viewers' awareness from foreground to background by combining a zoom-in with a soundtrack that simultaneously fades out the foreground sound as it fades in the background sounds. The result is a smooth, unobtrusive redirection of viewers' attention.

Spoken words are altered for effect when Griffin Mill cries out, "Keep it to yourself" during his rage that results in Kahane's murder, and the sound seems amplified by an echo chamber. It is loud enough to get the attention of anyone in the vicinity but does not; however, the distortion helps convey Mill's rage.

While film is not generally a medium in which spoken words dominate, *The Player* involves a protagonist who is a professional listener in a busy but never loud environment. Thus, it is appropriate that in many scenes conversations dominate and surround him.

Music

As in many movies, the soundtrack consists of previously recorded music and music composed specifically for the film, in this case by Thomas Newman. A major musical theme by Newman is introduced in the opening shot; it does not have a recognizable melody but is strongly rhythmical. What it does have is a certain feeling, busy and visceral yet at the same time light, shimmering, and chiming. As in most movies, including *The Player*, whenever dialogue is important, the music fades out to make room for it.

When Mill seats himself by the outdoor pool of the St. James's Club, the music includes a jazzy saxophone reminiscent of film noir. Background sirens and the sounds of a flying helicopter are blended in to enhance the feeling of a "big city at night." As Mill is driving home from the St. James's Club and discovers that a rattlesnake has been planted in his car, the music understandably becomes chaotic. It has an accelerated rhythm when Mill uncovers the snake; then it is dominated by loud, rapid bongo drums, horns, and a recurrent sibilant rattling sound.

Music is also a vital component of the lovemaking scene. Visually, there is simply the incontrovertible suggestion of sexual intercourse created by the screen filled with two glistening heads arranged horizontally and facing each other, kissing, moaning, breathing heavily, and speaking intimately. The music takes on complex rhythms while combining rapid chimes, a bongo drum, a snare drum, and various electronic sounds that together enhance the eroticism, simulate orgasm, then fade out. The music helps make the scene erotic.

In *The Player*, the music underpins, focuses, and helps blend the various film ingredients. Its power is achieved not through identifiable or memorable melodies but through its versatility and the appropriate feelings the music conjures up or supports.

Sound Effects and Silence

Sound effects are limited in *The Player* because spoken words and music play prominent roles, and the film does not showcase violence or action (traditional subjects requiring extensive sound effects). Where sound effects are used—as with the faint, distant offscreen barking dog after Kahane's murder—their presence melds so effectively with what is being shown that viewers are unlikely to notice them and are not meant to.

Silence is used briefly after David Kahane is murdered to emphasize that he is dead. Other than that, there are conventional split-second slivers of silence to differentiate scenes. Skillful sound editing allows these brief silences to be used as a subtle form of punctuation. Otherwise the silences might become awkward transitions inadvertently left unfilled.

In some scenes, two major types of sound help establish the setting. For example, a little more than ninety minutes into the film, as Mill arrives at the Pasadena police station, both spoken words and sound effects reveal the strident setting. Two suspects being hauled toward a hallway scream defiantly at the arresting officers, and immediately following a siren wails in the background.

Transitions

As in many movies, music is used to connect scenes, as between the end of the opening shot and the next scene, in Mill's secretary's office. Music is used again to connect the ending of that scene to the beginning of the following scene, where Mill and his secretary are outside walking and talking.

Spoken words, conversations particularly, are also used to ease the transitions between scenes. Twice an actor's name is mentioned, such as Anjelica Huston, and the next shot is of the actor named. An intriguing transition occurs immediately after Mill leaves Kahane for dead. The camera focuses on the murder scene, which is momentarily silent, but viewers' attention is soon diverted by a conversation that is fading in. Briefly, viewers' curiosity is in two places at once: the red pool of water where the body lies and the conversation that is slowly fading in.

SOURCES FOR THE FICTIONAL FILM

Michael Tolkin's novel *The Player* was first published in 1988. Tolkin also wrote the screen adaptation and acted the part of one of the two Schecter brothers, writers who are with Mill when Bonnie Sherow comes to his office to ask him if he is involved with someone new. For a discussion of the novel as a source for the film, see pp. 209-11.

Script and Film

The differences between the script and the film are similar to the differences between the novel and the film. In general, the film is more biting and satirical, and less emotional, than the script and certainly than the novel. For example, at Kahane's funeral the script calls for Kahane's brother to deliver the eulogy:

54 INT. CHAPEL—DAY

We hear Kahane's brother over a p.a. system. Mill takes a black yarmulke from a basket and puts it on.

BROTHER: Einstein said that God doesn't play dice. I'd like to say that we could console ourselves with the thought that in God's plan, David Kahane's death is necessary for the universe to unfold its majestic design . . .

He [Mill] opens the door to the chapel.

55 INT. CHAPEL—DAY

The coffin. About thirty mourners. The brother, 25, continues.

BROTHER: . . . but I can't say that, because David always laughed at mindless faith. Someone in the night killed him, and that person will have to bear his guilt, and he'll never know what he took from David's friends and family.

Griffin takes a seat in the back row. A few people in the front row turn to see who has come in. June looks at Griffin. She says something to the man sitting next to her, who turns around to see the last man who saw Kahane alive.

BROTHER: My brother died after seeing a movie, which I guess is sort of fitting. I hope you don't take this the wrong way, but he really loved movies, and I'm glad he didn't die on his way in, you know, before he saw it. That would have hurt me a lot more and this hurts a lot.

The pressure is too much for Griffin. He goes outside. We hear the Kaddish from inside.

56   EXT. HILLSIDE MEMORIAL—DAY

Mourners shovel earth onto the casket in the open grave. Finished. People walk away. (Tolkin script 44)

About 47½ minutes into the film, a fellow writer delivers Kahane's eulogy:

The Hollywood system did not murder David Kahane. Not the ninety-eight-million-dollar movie, not the twelve-million-dollar actor, not even the million-dollar deal that David Kahane never landed. No, the most that we can pin on Hollywood is assault with intent to kill because society is responsible for this particular murder. And it is to society that we must look if we are to have any justice for that crime. Because someone in the night killed David Kahane and that person will have to bear the guilt. And, if David were here right now, I know in my heart that he would have said, "Cut the shit, Phil. What did you learn from all of this? Did you learn anything from this?" I'd say, "Yeah, David, I've learned a lot. We here will, uh, take it from here and the next time we sell a script for a million dollars, the next time we nail some shit-bag producer to the wall we'll say 'That's another one for David Kahane.'" . . . David was working on something the day he died. I'd like to share it with you. "Blackness. A mangy dog barks. Garbage can lids are lifted as derelicts in the street hunt for food, buzzing as a cheap alarm clock goes off. INT—FLOP HOUSE ROOM—EARLY MORNING. A tracking shot moves through the grimy room. Light streams in through holes in the yellowing window shades. Moths dance in the beams of light. Track down along the floor. The frayed rug. Stop on an old shoe. It's empty." It's as far as he got. That's the last thing he wrote. So long Dave. Fade-out. Thank you.

In the script, the funeral is Jewish, and the eulogy is given by a grieving member of Kahane's family. In the film, the funeral is secular; the eulogy is given by an angry fellow writer; and there is no sign of Kahane's family. In the script, the eulogy and the mourners at the open grave show the devastating impact Kahane's death has had on his family. In the film, the eulogy is more about anger than grief.

The film's eulogy is longer than the one in the script and is supplemented by visual information. Thus, viewers can allow the droning speech to become background noise because they sense the visual information is more important. During the speech, viewers see Griffin Mill arrive silently in his black Range Rover; he approaches the gathering gingerly; he stands differentiated by his clothing (an expensive suit). June Gudmundsdottir, dressed in white, glances back to him. We also see Detective DeLongpre (who has not yet been identified) approach the mourners and stand at the other side of a broad monument next to a tree. Up to this point the audience has been teased with this character. He is curious-looking, suspicious perhaps, and viewers may be wondering whether he is the postcard writer.

The scene illustrates the point that typically films are more expressive visually than is indicated by the script. This combination of sounds and moving images is unique to the film and video media, and the differences between the script and the film allow us to see and hear how the filmmakers have capitalized on this distinctive capability.

Other Films

Films are called intertextual when they evoke or use other films and other forms of human expression. And *The Player* does this throughout. It is, after all, a movie whose main subjects are moviemakers and the early stages of making movies. Intertextuality in *The Player* runs from the lengthy opening shot and its inclusion of discussions of similar lengthy shots in other films, to the screening of *Habeas Corpus*, a parody of popular movies with serious subjects but distracting stars and last-minute rescues. In between, there are all those movie posters on the walls of Mill's and Levison's offices; the sixty-five cameos, most by famous movie actors but including the film's scriptwriter; the "one of us" allusion to the ending of *Freaks* (1932); the clips from the ending of *The Bicycle Thief*; and all the talk about other films and other filmmakers. *The Player* draws on a wealth of detail not merely from a novel and script but also from other films and a long tradition of moviemaking.

ASPECTS OF THE FICTIONAL FILM

As with all narrative films, *The Player* consists of selected and structured events presented over time.

Structure

The Player has two parts: five or six days of selected events; then, one year later, selected events from the day of the screening of the studio's latest offering, *Habeas Corpus*. The two parts are bridged by a title card informing viewers that the following action occurs one year later.

In the first and far lengthier part, viewers meet Griffin Mill and learn of his twin problems (the anonymous threatening writer and the rumor that

Levy is being groomed for Mill's job) and of his goals (retaining power at work and winning the love of a beautiful artist). To eliminate the first source of anxiety, Mill seeks out a man he believes is the stalker and ends up killing him. Thus, an action designed to help Mill eliminate one of his two major problems thrusts him into an arena where he lacks knowledge or leverage. A misstep or bad luck will unravel his career and plunge him into a legal abyss. He survives his brush with the law only by luck. At about this time, the Levy problem is also solved. Mill is not ousted from the studio; the studio head is. Interwoven with Mill's studio-related problems are scenes of his love life, first with Sherow, for whom he displays no ardor, then with Gudmundsdottir.

By a year later, Mill has assumed the helm of the studio; *Habeas Corpus* has been reworked beyond recognition; the former rival has become an ally; and Mill resumes his life with an even greater degree of power and prosperity than before. The story ends with Mill approving a story pitch that describes the movie we've just seen. The story promises to be circular.

Time

The story of *The Player* is conveyed chronologically. There are no flashbacks or flashforwards. The first part of the story—from the introduction of Mill and his problems and goals to his winning of Gudmundsdottir and getting away with murder—transpires over five or six days. As in most other films, *The Player* is usually vague about how much time elapses between scenes. If one notes when day scenes give way to night scenes, the first part of the story consumes at least five and a half days. The overall story time is approximately one week plus one year; the film's running time is 124 minutes. As usual in fictional films, the events of *The Player* are highly selective. There is nothing unconventional or even challenging about the film's handling of structure and time, except for the final twist that the anonymous writer's proposed story is the one viewers have just seen.

TYPES OF FICTIONAL FILMS

The Player is both classical Hollywood cinema and independent film. It has enough qualities of the former, such as some famous performers and a happy ending, to help ensure its commercial success and enough of the latter, such as satire, to win laudatory reviews and various awards and nominations including Cannes Film Festival awards, National Society of Film Critics' best film award, Independent Spirit award for best film, Golden Globe awards and nominations, British Academy Award nominations, and Academy Award nominations.

Classical Hollywood Cinema

The Player exemplifies all the major features of classical Hollywood cinema: the story is set entirely in a present, external world and is largely seen from outside the action, although point-of-view shots are sometimes included. *The Player* focuses on a character that has an initial goal: to survive in his position of wealth and power. In trying to attain his goal, Griffin Mill confronts two major problems: the anonymous threatening writer and an executive perhaps being groomed for Mill's job. Early in the film Mill develops a second goal: to win June Gudmundsdottir. The film has closure: the plot has no "loose ends" or unresolved issues, other than the identity of the threatening writer, which is unimportant. Mill reaches his goals: he gets free of the two threats to his success, gets away with murder, gets promoted, and settles down with the beautiful artist. Like so many popular Hollywood movies, *The Player* shows a male succeeding both professionally and personally. By the end of the film, what happens and why are unambiguous. Finally, the film uses continuity editing and, except for the opening shot, other unobtrusive filmmaking techniques.

Although *The Player* has a strong mystery component to it and the VHS videotape box categorizes it as a "thriller," it is not an example of the mystery genre: for one thing, much of the story is not devoted to the mystery of who is threatening Mill. The possible Levy threat and Mill's romances with Sherow and Gudmundsdottir also take up much of the plot.

American Independent Film

The Player also exhibits characteristics of the American independent film. Besides a lower budget than typical Hollywood products and freedom from studio creative control, *The Player* has other earmarks of an independent film. Its content has limited appeal, not because it is particularly controversial but because it requires a certain level of awareness of the film industry; more essentially, *The Player* is a complex and subtle satire that rewards attentive viewing. Finally, its plot is by no means formulaic—for example, unlike many movies, the main character gets away with murder, which would be inconceivable before the production code was abandoned in 1968. The story is surprising and unpredictable, and, like most independent films, *The Player* fits into no genre.

The movies made by the studio that Mill works for are classical Hollywood cinema of the most commercial stripe. As he explains to Gudmundsdottir approximately 103 minutes into the film, the films his studio makes need "suspense, laughter, violence, hope, heart, nudity, sex, happy endings . . . mainly happy endings." As initially proposed, *Habeas Corpus*, the movie within the movie, is to become an independent film: no stars, mostly true-to-life events, issues outside the mainstream, and a credible unhappy ending.

As made by Mill's studio, *Habeas Corpus* is an exaggerated example of crowd-pleasing classical Hollywood cinema, with stars, improbable action, and a happy ending.

UNDERSTANDING *THE PLAYER* THROUGH CONTEXTS

Any text is a product of its time and culture. Viewers who know some contexts of *The Player* can understand the film more completely than those who know only the film.

Society and Politics

Historically, Los Angeles fought for recognition amid aspersions that it was "sleepy," too much a part of the West to be considered a challenge to the East's position as the bastion of intellectual, financial, and social validity. The values that emerged and eventually grew to define Los Angeles are directly related to the emergence and eventual ascension to power of the movie industry. As a theatrical reviewer for the *Los Angeles Times* wrote in 1999, L.A. is "a city built on deception." The irony that Los Angeles has little to define itself other than its image is not lost on Angelenos. In fact, there is an air of pride rather than apology surrounding the statement. After all, it is a mesmerizing image.

The Player is L.A. on L.A. In this movie Los Angeles, unfiltered water is to be avoided even though Los Angeles water has long been rated among the best-tasting and safest of all large American cities. Business contacts are generated at AA meetings, and Range Rovers are equipped with faxes. Success requires that people recognize one another but remain unencumbered by relationships or obligations. These elements help re-create the Los Angeles of the late 1980s and early 1990s.

Censorship

The Player was made free of Hollywood studio control; thus the director, writer, and actors enjoyed a wide range of freedom to present the subjects as they saw fit, including gently satirizing Hollywood studio filmmaking. The film is rated R—presumably for its partial nudity; a sex scene of heavy breathing and two sweaty, bobbing heads; vulgar language; and one scene of murderous violence. The rating also allowed its makers to roam a broad field. The film does not attract audiences because of its sex and violence. In truth, there is little. Its concerns and appeal lie elsewhere—with Hollywood-style deal making and people who make movies and the pleasures of seeing them mocked genially.

Artistic Conventions

The Player follows certain filmmaking conventions, except for the film's virtuoso opening shot, which runs more than eight minutes and is described in Table 3.1. For instance, everyone, from principal characters to the studio mail carrier, is attractive. Some Angelenos would argue that that is true to life. It is, however, more an adherence to what viewers expect in movies (convention) than what is true of the gene pool in Los Angeles. All the "players" are white males. Women are portrayed as competent in a tough, competitive atmosphere, but they are not "players." The most sympathetic of them, Bonnie, gets fired and loses her footing. (That is not only adherence to film convention; it is part of the environment that must be shown if the story is to be credible.) The main female character, June, is represented as a beacon in the night dressed in white whose radiance allows her to stand out even among the Beautiful People.

Financial Constraints

By 1991, director Robert Altman had been relatively successful both at the box office and in the reviewers' columns, but in the years before he made *The Player* he had not had a recent popular or critical success. He also had (and maintains) the reputation of being a Hollywood outsider. With its satiric story of Hollywood studio moviemaking, lack of big stars in big roles, and a low quotient of sex and violence, *The Player* had virtually no chance of attracting big audiences. So how did the film get funding? Keeping the satire amusing and good-natured (what Altman himself calls "tame" in the DVD commentary) probably helped. Although the concluding credits list a stunt coordinator, special effects, and set medic, the film has no costly special effects or dangerous action scenes, such as a car crash described in the source novel. Instead of filming in Mexico, as the novel indicated, some scenes were filmed at a desert resort during the off-season. Certainly, the relatively modest budget of approximately $8 million and the willingness of many actors, some of them stars, to be involved in an Altman film at minimal rates also helped make possible the funding and the making of the film.

THINKING ABOUT *THE PLAYER*

The Player has multiple and unexpected story developments—especially the murder and the murderer's escape from conviction. It also has many possible meanings. In the following pages, only a few examples are developed, but others are sure to occur to anyone who has seen the film and thought about it.

Expectations and Interactions

Early in *The Player*, viewers read the title card "A Robert Altman Film." Those who have seen other Altman films—such as *M*A*S*H* (1970), *McCabe and Mrs. Miller* (1971), *The Long Goodbye* (1973), *Nashville* (1975), *A Wedding* (1978), *Short Cuts* (1993), *Cookie's Fortune* (1999), *Dr. T and the Women* (2000), and *Gosford Park* (2001)—will immediately have certain expectations: satire; surprises; some complexity in characterizations, plot, or meanings; and a potential for a viewing experience that will linger in the mind after leaving the theater.

A film entitled *The Player* may pique a viewer's curiosity to see which meaning(s) of the word will apply. By denotation, *player* has at least seven meanings about different types of people, including a person who engages in illegal activity. By connotation, the word can evoke shades of artifice, sleight of hand, and imposture. It may also suggest an elevated level of skill and competition.

In the opening shot, viewers discover immediately that they must process visual and verbal information at a demanding pace. We are going to get an insider's simultaneous, multichanneled view of Hollywood filmmakers at work. By reputation we know it to be a treacherous, illusory environment set in luxurious surroundings. By the film's conclusion, we understand that Griffin Mill is a player. Larry Levy is a player. Bonnie is not. Levison was a player—then suddenly and inexplicably was not. The director of *Habeas Corpus* has been converted into one.

Types of Meanings

There are only a few explicit meanings in *The Player*. Probably the most noteworthy one is heard while Griffin explains to June what makes for a successful Hollywood movie, especially a happy ending. Generally, fictional films invite viewers to construct their own character attributes and motivations and the film's meanings. Otherwise, it would be like playing cards with all hands dealt face up.

The Player is rich in implicit meanings. The film's portrayal of film industry personnel confirms the industry's reputation: Hollywood threatens constancy in human relationships. *The Player* shows only one lasting alliance, and that one (between Griffin and June) has the potential for survival only because she is outside the movie industry (she does not even go to movies).

In *The Player* actors and talk of them are plentiful, and, of course, writers are prominent, appearing in the initial scenes and often thereafter. The film exposes the low esteem in which writers are held. We see this most clearly when Larry Levy proposes doing away with them (expensive and unnecessary appendages) and suggests that the executives can create their own story lines from things as mundane as current newspaper headlines. Levy's next idea is to advocate production of *Habeas Corpus*, complete with unknown actors and unhappy ending. As pitched, beginning with the title, it is hard to imagine a less promising story for a commercial film. So after Levy's two false starts, what is his fate? Evidently when Griffin assumes control of the studio, Levy gets promoted to Griffin's old job. The continuity of the usual product is ensured.

When Bonnie cries at the end of *The Player*, she violates a cardinal principle of the filmmaking industry: at work, emotions must be kept under control. Near the film's end, Griffin breezes past her without so much as a backward glance and says that she "will land on her feet." In contrast to Bonnie's emotional reactions, recall Griffin's largely nonplussed demeanor when the studio's security chief questions him regarding Kahane's death. Remember Griffin's controlled response to each postcard. At one point he dismisses his secretary's suggestion that he involve studio security to help track down the threatening writer. Griffin knows he must not show fear if he is to remain a player, especially at this time when he believes that his job is in jeopardy.

Satire is the representation of an individual or a group that indirectly exposes and perhaps ridicules thinking or behavior for being foolish, evil, or stupid or for exhibiting some other shortcoming. *The Player* is wide-ranging in its satiric targets. Writers are satirized for being desperate and for wavering when they sense Mill's reluctance. Directors are satirized for selling out the integrity of a story for the sake of commercial success. Studio executives are shown as concerned more with profits than with creating quality products. Of course, the product of all these studio personnel—the studio movie— is parodied and satirized by the distracting presence of stars and the preposterous happy ending of *Habeas Corpus*.

Meaning is also suggested by symbols—for example, the main character's name. Hollywood is a griffin mill: a manufacturer of fabled creations. The product includes any number of chimerical masterpieces. But it likewise includes monstrosities. *Mill* has additional relevant meanings, including an institution or a business that makes a profit by turning out product without regard to quality, as in "diploma mill," a school that turns out graduates without regard to standards.

In its representation of the competition within and between companies, the use of consumer technology (such as cars, fax machines, and cell phones) in doing the work, and the immersion in work at the expense of personal connectiveness, *The Player* can be seen as symptomatic of much of life in late twentieth-century America.

As Chapter 10 illustrates, filmmakers decide how subtly to use techniques. Sometimes the expressive aspects of the settings—such as the movie posters—are seen only fleetingly. Another example of subtlety occurs nearly twenty-five minutes into the film as viewers glimpse a book in Mill's secretary's desk as Mill begins his search for leads about the threatening writer. For less than a second, viewers have a chance to read the title of the book, *They Made Me a Criminal*, which is also the title of a 1939 movie. In an interview with Geoff Andrew, Altman implies that the postcard writer is the eulogizer at Kahane's funeral (187), and in the Criterion laser disc version of *The Player* (but not on the DVD), Tolkin says that the actor who plays the eulogizer was used for the telephone voice of the blackmailing writer at the film's end. Both characters use the phrase "some shit-bag producer." That detail is too subtle for nearly all viewers to notice: the two speeches are brief, far apart, and the second is heard only as a telephone voice. Occasionally, though, significant details are not so much glimpsed as thrust into the viewers' faces, as when the camera zooms in on a movie poster or on a photograph of the cinematic master of mystery, murder, and suspense—director Alfred Hitchcock. Alert viewers have already understood the points about the poster and the photo.

Although *The Player* adheres to the basics of its source novel and screenplay, the film typifies Robert Altman's film work and could be a candidate for the auteurist approach. Like many Altman films, *The Player* relies heavily on satire without ever becoming venomous, and it is sometimes sprawling in terms of number of characters and intricacies of plot. And like other Altman films, there is also a heavy reliance on the moving camera, the zoom lens, and overlapping dialogue. Other viewers will see these and other meanings. Here is a sample:

Expectations and Interactions

"There's a chill at the center of *The Player*. Altman gets us rooting for Griffin by subtle degrees—first, because his job is threatened; later, because he's in love and in trouble. But the movie needles us by degrees, too, by gradually exposing Griffin's corruption. If we're cheering Griffin on even though he's a cad (and worse), that makes us somehow accomplices in his perfidy. And, in the end, when he prevails while the nice but decidedly less glamorous folk around him tumble, Altman slathers on the triumphant music and sunshine in a way that may make us squirm. He's not letting anyone off the hook—not even the audience. After all, we're part of the system, too. We're the ones clamoring for '*Ghost* meets *The Manchurian Candidate*'; we're the ones drooling over Bruce [Willis] and Arnold [Schwarzenegger] and Julia [Roberts] and Mel [Gibson]. No one leaves *The Player* with a clear conscience" (Schiff 143).

Explicit Meanings

A few commentators quoted the film's most prominent explicit meaning, Mill's explanation to June about the ingredients of a successful Hollywood movie: "suspense, laughter, violence, hope, heart, nudity, sex, happy endings . . . mainly happy endings."

IMPLICIT MEANINGS

Nearly always, *The Player* shows and suggests its meanings rather than states them, and as commentator Stephen Schiff observes, "Altman demonstrates all this [implicit meaning] without getting windy about it" (138).

"*The Player* is about how the industry crushes the originality out of anyone who participates in it—any Player, be he writer, director, or production chief. And that's because the Hollywood system makes it impossible to view the world afresh, to derive inspiration or even information from it" (Schiff 138).

"*The Player* . . . satirizes Hollywood mores and mannerisms, but, at the same time, never truly disturbs its audience and can easily be enjoyed, absorbed, and promoted by the industry itself" (Quart).

"The film should captivate anyone with a taste for bold cinematics, unpredictable storytelling, and pitch-black humor aimed at the worthiest of targets: a self-involved and self-congratulatory industry that often gives lip-service to art while worshipping the bottom line" (Sterritt 14).

SYMPTOMATIC MEANINGS

"*The Player* does capture L.A. and today's Hollywood with chilling exactness. It's more than the way the details are right, things like the cars, the houses, the restaurants, even the mineral water. . . . Tolkin and Altman are also hip to the mind set of a completely self-absorbed, not to say amoral, business awash in frenzied round-the-clock schmoozing" (Turan).

In a 1992 interview with Geoff Andrew, Altman said that *The Player* is "*of* Hollywood, but it's not really just *about* Hollywood. Hollywood is a metaphor for our society, which is based on greed—take, take, take, and don't give anything back to the system; lie and cheat. So though the film is about the stupidity of Hollywood, it's also about the moral problems of our society at large" ("The Player King," 185).

As with all films, the viewer's interactions with the film and the meanings the viewer formulates depend in part on the viewer and his or her contexts and ways of thinking.

WORKS CITED

Altman, Robert. Audio Commentary. *The Player* (DVD), N4032. New Line Home Video, 1997.

The Player. Screenplay by Michael Tolkin. Dir. Robert Altman. Fine Line Features, 1992. (The film's end credits are reprinted on pp. 613–20 of this book.)

The Player. Criterion Collection, 1993. CLV. 2 discs. Catalog: CC1318.

"The Player King." Robert Altman interviewed by Geoff Andrew. *Time Out* no. 1137 (3 June 1992): 18–20; rpt. *Robert Altman Interviews*. Ed. David Sterritt. Jackson: UP of Mississippi, 2000. 182–87.

Quart, Leonard, and Alissa Quart. Review. *Cineaste* 19.2–3 (1992): 60 ff.

Schiff, Stephen. "Auteur! Auteur!" *Vanity Fair* 55.4 (April 1992): 136–43.

Sterritt, David. "A Movie That Pokes Fun at Movies." *Christian Science Monitor*. 10 Apr. 1992: 14.

Tolkin, Michael. *The Player: A Novel*. New York: Atlantic Monthly, 1988.

———. *The Player*. Script, 20 Apr. 1989, first draft. Hollywood: Script City, [1993?]. Photocopy. 124 leaves.

Turan, Kenneth. Review. *Los Angeles Times* 10 Apr. 1992, Calendar: 1 ff.

Vicki Whitaker of Aztec, New Mexico, assisted me with much of this material during preparation for the first edition.

Studying Films: Reading, Researching, and Writing

WRITING ABOUT FILMS

No one ever has been able to give the exact measure of his needs, his concepts, or his sorrows. The human tongue is like a cracked cauldron on which we beat out tunes to set a bear dancing when we would make the stars weep with our melodies. (Flaubert 138)

To try to capture in speech the richness and nuances of human experience and thought can be frustrating. It is no easy task to capture them in writing, either, but writing can bring us closer to that goal than speech can. For understanding and communicating about something as complicated as our experiences of film, writing is indispensable.

Nearly everyone knows about the agony of committing words to paper. After all, the writer's job is to create clear and convincing prose that can be read without interruption, rereading, or puzzlement, often by a stranger, someone who knows nothing about the writer. It is no wonder effective writing requires much thinking and concentration and tends to be time-consuming.

Most writers find they work most efficiently if they don't work too long in a session and alternate periods of work with rest. They also know there's little time to do so in the last few days before an assignment is due. Nearly all successful writers divide their work into steps because they know that most writing is too complicated to do well in one sitting or even two.

Prewriting

For convenience, I have divided writing into three major parts: prewriting, writing (the first complete draft), and rewriting. I say *for convenience* because writing is rarely a 1-2-3 process. It defies formulas and predictions. For example, some writers may organize their main points (prewrite), write a first draft, then realize the structure is wrong, reorganize their outline, and redo the draft before moving on to rewriting. Other writers develop an effective structure for their writing by writing draft after draft with no prewriting (but this is usually a time-consuming way to discover a useful structure).

A few people can write well by composing and rewriting one page or paragraph or sentence at a laborious time (they are sometimes called "bleeders"). Probably fewer still compose and revise in their heads, then write and revise slightly. If one of those two approaches works for you, fine, but they probably won't, and you will find it useful to divide and conquer your work.

Dividing your work into manageable steps and using the strategies explained here will improve your chances of writing well but do not guarantee it. Extensive previous practice in writing (and reading) and much work and persistence are also required.

Here is one of my favorite ways of getting some of my responses to a film into writing. As I view the film, I write a few notes. After the viewing, I sometimes write a brief description and always write observations (analysis). Next I reread and revise what I have written so far. The next day I rewrite my notes, select the main points, and arrange them in a brief outline.

These are the stages I sometimes go through before I write a first draft. They take time, but they help me gather my thoughts and arrange them. I'm not saying the first draft is then easy for me. Often it is not. But because of the prewriting, the first draft is always less difficult.

Before you write the first draft, consider the following questions:

- Who are my readers?
- What needs to be explained?
- What does *not* need to be explained?
- How do I want my readers to react to what I write?

Then try one or more of these steps:

1. Write and rewrite a thesis statement: a sentence or a few concise sentences that summarize the main and unifying idea of the planned essay and, ideally, explain the major parts and their arrangement.
2. Make an outline.
3. Write a "discovery" draft.

1. **THESIS STATEMENT** A thesis statement early in an essay—often at the end of the first paragraph or the beginning of the second—helps both writer and readers. The following thesis statement, which appears at the end of the first paragraph of a student essay (p. 240), reveals the purpose and organization of the essay it helps introduce:

Despite its reputation for faithfulness, a careful analysis reveals that the film [*The Dead*] is unlike Joyce's novella in three major ways. First, the adaptation expands the scope of the original narrative by adding new scenes. Second, the adaptation deletes important contextual elements from its literary source. Finally, the adaptation modifies significant dramatic elements in the literary source.

Occasionally you can formulate a thesis statement before making an outline or writing a first draft. Sometimes the thesis statement is so well thought out and detailed that you can write a first draft without first making an outline. Often, however, the thesis emerges more clearly as you work on an outline or a first or second draft. It usually takes time and effort to figure out what you are trying to say, and often you may start out to make a point and end up saying something else. For the essay to be unified and forceful, though, the thesis statement must eventually step forward and introduce itself or be implied in the introduction and explained in the essay itself. Few students can create a focused, clear, and persuasive essay without stating the thesis; without it, the writer and the readers tend to get lost in a forest of words before emerging from page 2.

2. OUTLINE Outlines are useful for most writers most of the time, especially in writing long essays and books or in writing about a new subject, but some successful writers never use them. Instead they think out the major points and their arrangement, jot notes, or write draft after draft. Sometimes a short outline, however, leads to a more detailed one that is a partial first draft.

3. DISCOVERY DRAFT Some writers start to organize their material by rapidly writing a draft. Then they look at what they have written and perhaps underline the useful parts, perhaps rearrange its major points. Sometimes they toss out that draft and immediately write another one rapidly. For some writers it's a way to get something on paper and to start to discover what they have to say.

In outlines and early drafts, leave wide margins on all four sides of the lines and double-space. Leave room to improve.

Writing

While writing the first draft, most writers find it best to focus on organization (what are the major parts, and in what order should they be arranged?) and on examples (how can I illustrate my points to those who may misunderstand or disagree?). While writing the first draft, don't allow yourself to become sidetracked by spelling, punctuation, or even sentence structure. Like a sculptor, rough out the paragraphs; later, do the finishing work on the sentences and words. For most people, fussing over a spelling or a word, pausing to check a punctuation mark, or looking up a word or passage can halt their momentum and perhaps cause "writer's block," the inability to write anything.

In the first draft, try to see that your main points are arranged in a significant order and that they are explained and illustrated. Do not, as many ineffective writers do, try to rewrite while you write the first draft. Studies of writers show that few can write *and* rewrite well at the same time.

Rewriting and Rewriting: Some Strategies

What is written without effort is in general read without pleasure. (Samuel Johnson)

I never write five words but I correct seven. (attributed to Dorothy Parker)

There are days when the result is so bad that no fewer than five revisions are required. In contrast, when I'm greatly inspired, only four revisions are needed. (John Kenneth Galbraith)

As you rewrite and rewrite, remember three indispensable guidelines:

1. *Studies show that few readers will remember—let alone be impressed by—more than five major points in a speech or an essay.*
2. *Your goal should be to communicate—not to impress.* Writers who try to impress their readers often stumble and look silly, waste their readers' time, and puzzle them. Consider, for example, this sentence: "Another major meaning of Orson Welles's film *Citizen Kane* is that Charles Foster Kane has an abiding and persistent hunger to be loved by others" (twenty-five words). The writer misuses one word (*abiding*) and tries too hard to impress, with wordiness, passive voice, and formal words. In contrast, the writer of the following sentence, one of my former students, was more concerned with communicating: "The third trait to note about Kane is his need for love" (twelve words). That sentence is short, is easy to understand, yet says much the same as its longer counterpart. Indeed, this second sentence is more specific: it indicates that the *third* point is next.
3. *If you focus on only one major point in each paragraph and explain it fully, with detailed examples, you will be understood, probably even appreciated.* If you jump from generalization to unrelated generalization, especially within the same paragraph, you will not be understood by your unfortunate readers.

SOME REWRITING TECHNIQUES   Because it is difficult to spot errors in what we write (we are better at spotting errors in what *others* write), we writers need to reread our drafts often and in different ways. Unfortunately, many writers, especially inexperienced ones, reread their drafts once—maybe twice if they want to be thorough!—and they seldom spot what to improve, so they make only a few minor changes, such as in spelling and the use of commas. One or more of the following strategies may help writers see more clearly what they have indeed written so that they can rewrite and improve it:

1. After you finish the first or second draft, see if each paragraph explains one important point. Choose a paragraph at random, and read it at least twice (once aloud, once silently); underline the topic sentence or main point. (You may want to use a felt-tip pen so you can quickly spot each topic sentence later.) If a topic sentence is vague or misleading, rewrite it so it explains the main point of the paragraph. If the main point of the paragraph is not stated or clearly implied, write a topic sentence. If you have more than one important point in a paragraph, eliminate unimportant points and develop the main point, or explain each important point in its own paragraph.

   Next, select a different paragraph at random, and once again read it twice—once aloud and once silently. See that it has one major point that is fully and clearly explained. Proceed in this way until you have an underlined topic sentence for each paragraph. (Study your paragraphs out of order so that you can sneak up on what you wrote and see each paragraph for what it is.)

   Now that you have underlined the topic sentence of each paragraph, underline the main idea(s) of the essay (the thesis statement) with a double line; then read only the thesis statement and each topic sentence. If any topic sentences do not support the thesis or if the major points do not progress clearly, delete, add, or rearrange; then rewrite.

2. a. Reread your essay aloud at different speeds (rapidly one time, slowly the next). For many writers, reading a draft aloud—one time slowly, the next time rapidly—is the best way to spot weaknesses. They hear weaknesses they could not see.

   b. Read your essay aloud at different times (for instance, once after completing the first draft; once after a break; once more the next day).

   c. Reread your essay silently at different times looking for an aspect of writing that has given you trouble in the past—for instance, once for complicated, unclear sentences and at another time for wordiness. If you tend to write incomplete sentences, reread from the end of the essay to the beginning, a sentence at a time.

   d. Ask someone to read the draft aloud but without interruptions or commentary, perhaps as you close your eyes and listen (not recommended after lunch or late in the evening).

3. Another way to see what you have indeed written in each sentence is to read each sentence out of order. Pick up the latest draft; choose a sentence at random; read it twice (once aloud, once silently); then, if necessary, revise it. After you are finished with the sentence, place a check mark at the beginning of it; then repeat the process for every other sentence (out of order). You may be surprised how many weaknesses you can spot and eliminate using this method.

4. Are any sentences still not right? You've thought about them. You've put them aside. But you still frown as you read them. Imagine that you are

with a friend, and say aloud what you mean; then write what you just said. Chances are you'll be much closer to writing what you meant all along.

5. Reread your essay and underline or circle every general word; then consider replacing generalities with details from the film. Words like *good, great, wonderful, nice, interesting*, and *terrible* can be replaced by specific references to the film. "Vera Miles was great in *The Searchers*" neither communicates much nor convinces a reader who thought she was so-so. Instead, write a paragraph that includes examples from the film. Consider the following: "Vera Miles's Laurie is a complicated character. For example, she is not all patience and sweetness. In the scene where Martin is about to leave for the last time to rescue Debbie, Miles shows vehement and convincing frustration, wrinkling her brow and biting off her words." Although this second description is scarcely a full account of Vera Miles's performance, it is better than the original vague sentence.

While you are checking word choices, make sure that when you describe action in a film, you use present-tense verbs. For instance, "The soldiers blow up the house" (not "blew up").

Getting Feedback

Not long ago, most college instructors would tell their students to "not ask others for feedback about their draft(s)." During recent years, however, research on writing has confirmed that feedback from others can help writers, and increasingly college instructors are encouraging their students to work in groups and otherwise get feedback. However, if you do not follow certain procedures, getting feedback can be of little use and can even be counterproductive.

Find at least one good reader: someone who can read and explain accurately what the reading means. (Unfortunately, such readers may be scarce.) Show the assignment to your readers, and ask them to read your paper carefully (and at least twice) and tell you (1) what they understand from it and (2) where the paper is unclear or incomplete, or both. Do not tell your readers beforehand what you intended to convey; let your writing speak for itself.

If your readers rate your writing as excellent, good, or whatever, disregard their evaluations. Your classmates and outside readers are in a weak position to evaluate (or grade) your work: they do not know well the course work out of which the assignment emerged and lack training, experience, and perspective to grade college-level writing (so do you). If you ignore this advice and take the evaluation of your writing by others seriously, you may end up frustrated and perhaps in an unnecessary confrontation with your instructor.

Finally, take others' feedback, and rewrite your paper to make it fulfill the assignment more successfully. Do not let readers rewrite for you. And do not let them dictate wording either. *You* rewrite (and rewrite) the parts that need improving.

Of course, any rewriting you do will be *your* responsibility. For example, if none of your readers notices an important omission from your paper, do not blame them. *You* failed to include the material. You're responsible.

If misused, feedback can hurt your writing. However, if you follow these guidelines, feedback can help you improve your writing, often considerably.

Before you run off that last draft, be sure to consult reference sources, especially a college (not small paperback) dictionary. For example, you might want to look up words that you rarely use to make sure that you are indeed using them correctly. Remember that computer spelling checkers sometimes miss errors (for instance, when you wrote *it's* when you meant *its*). Remember, too, that computer "grammar checkers" often miss errors and, worse yet, are sometimes just plain wrong, as when they claim that a grammatical sentence is incomplete.

Most ineffective writers spend most of their time mired in the first draft, getting exhausted and demoralized by the ordeal. In contrast, effective writers tend to prewrite, divide the task into different work sessions, and spend much more time on rewriting than on writing the first draft.

Few writers do all the steps I suggest, nor do writers generally follow the same steps and same order of steps for every writing task. People are different, and writing is usually complicated. Let me repeat, too, that using the writing strategies I suggest will only improve your chances of writing well. Without extensive previous practice in reading critically and writing carefully, you will be limited in how well you can write, no matter what strategies you use. Similarly, even if you know the rules of a sport and follow them when you play it, you cannot play well unless you have worked hard and long at developing your skills. (Skillful coaches help, too.)

To write well about film requires much previous practice in reading and writing, practical strategies (such as some of those discussed in this essay), and patience and persistence. Writing well about anything you care about or enjoy, though, is well worth all the effort, for in writing and rewriting you think and learn, and you can communicate to others with more precision and permanence than you can any other way. When you write about a film or the film medium, you are unlikely to "make the stars weep" with your melodies, but by writing with care you can capture some of the magic.

The best writers have the satisfaction of knowing that people of distant times and places may learn from and enjoy their writing. What Carl Sagan said about ancient books applies as well to all writings that are preserved and read:

> One glance at . . . [a book] and you're inside the mind of another person, maybe somebody dead for thousands of years. Across the millennia an author is speaking clearly and silently inside your head, directly to you. Writing is perhaps the greatest of human inventions, binding together people who never knew each other, citizens of distant epochs. Books break the shackles of time. . . . If information were passed on merely by word of mouth, how little we should know of our own past. How slow would be our progress. Everything would depend on what we had been told, on how accurate the account. Ancient

learning might be revered, but in successive retellings it would become muddled and then lost. Books permit us to voyage through time, to tap the wisdom of our ancestors.

> For sample student essays, see the Close-Up sections near the end of Chapters 2, 5, and 7 and the Web site for this book: <bedfordstmartins.com /phillips-film>.

WRITING DEFINITIONS

Understanding the meanings of the terms used in political science, calculus, music, or any other subject helps one understand the subject more completely. An excellent way to gain a clearer and more precise understanding of what terms stand for is to write and rewrite definitions of them. To do so, indicate the category that the object or idea being defined belongs to and what differentiates it from other members of the same category. For example,

> **lap dissolve**: A transition between shots in which one shot begins to fade out as the next shot fades in, overlapping the first shot before replacing it.

Notice that a *lap dissolve* is not merely a transition between shots. It is, but so are *wipes*, *fade-outs*, *fade-ins*, and other transitions between shots. What distinguishes a lap dissolve from all the other transitions between shots is that one shot begins to fade out as the next shot fades in, overlapping the first shot before replacing it.

Do not phrase a definition in any of these four ways:

> _____ is when _____.
> _____ is where _____.
> This is when _____.
> This is where _____.

Do not attempt to define a word or phrase by giving only a synonym, especially when dealing with an abstract word. For example, to write that an *evaluation* is an appraisal will not be clear to readers who have only a fuzzy notion about what *appraisal* means. After you indicate the category and what distinguishes the term in question from other members of the same category, you may want to include a synonym—but only after you have *defined* the term in question.

A final pointer: in your definitions use the same part of speech as the word being defined. Do not define *composition* as "arranging settings, lighting, and subjects (usually people and objects) within the frame," but as "the arrangement of settings, . . .": "composition" (a noun) is a matter of "arrangement" (another noun). For more sample definitions, study some entries in the Glossary on pp. 621–648.

IMPROVING READING COMPREHENSION

Different types of readings make different demands on readers. For example, for most of us, reading a letter from a friend is a simple and straightforward task, but reading a contract that will affect our emotional and financial well-being for years to come requires more elaborate reading techniques.

Unfortunately, regardless of the reading assignment, some students use the same, limited reading strategies. Learn to adapt your reading techniques to the task at hand. You probably won't have time to use all of the following techniques, but for each important reading task preread, read, reread, and write. Don't just trust your memory and hope for the best.

Preread

These steps may take five to ten minutes, but they will help you get much more out of the reading the first time through:

- Consider the significance of the title.
- Consider the section of the book the reading selection is from. Examine the book's Table of Contents to see how the reading assignment fits into the book.
- Read the first paragraph (and perhaps the second) and the last paragraph to discover the main point and the conclusion.
- Examine the headings and subheadings (to find out the major parts).
- Read the summary or abstract (if one is included).
- Read the study questions (if any are included).

Read

To discover the structure and purpose of the writing, during the first reading it is crucial that you read without long interruptions and keep your marks, comments, and questions brief:

- Mark important passages.
- Write brief notes in the margins, especially your descriptions of important points and any questions that come to mind.
- Draw lines between related or contrasted points.
- Circle key words (often they are repeated).
- Mark words you don't understand.

Reread

Many readers use far too few rereading strategies. Using them, however, helps readers understand and remember the material in ways simply reading and quickly reviewing cannot:

- Reread passages you are still uncertain about, or reread the entire selection.
- Check a dictionary for words you still cannot figure out, and write the definitions in the margins.
- Study all marked passages; study your marginal notes, and rewrite and expand them as necessary.
- Study the summary (if one is included), *or* write a summary of the selection in your own words, *or* make an outline of the selection, *or* write a sentence explaining the main point.
- Read the study questions and try to answer them, preferably in writing.

ANNOTATED BIBLIOGRAPHY

BOOKS

Emmens, Carol A. *Short Stories on Film and Video.* 2nd ed. Littleton, CO: Libraries Unlimited, 1985. An alphabetical listing by authors of short stories adapted into films, usually short films. Supplied for each film are the title of short story, title of film, running time or number of reels, black-and-white or color designation, year, director, producer, cast, and a brief description of contents. Also includes indexes.

Enser's Filmed Books and Plays: A List of Books and Plays from Which Films Have Been Made, 1928–2001. 6th ed. Ed. Ellen Baskin. Burlington, VT: Ashgate, 2002. The main part of the book is an index arranged alphabetically by film titles, with brief information on each film and the name of the author of the source fiction or play. Also includes author and change of title indexes and information on made-for-TV movies and classic British television series.

Film Review Annual, 1981–2001. Ed. Jerome S. Ozer. Englewood, NJ: Film Review, 1982–. Reprints complete reviews of the feature films released in the United States during the previous year. Includes full credits, many different indexes, listings of major film awards.

Halliwell's Who's Who in the Movies. 15th ed. Ed. John Walker. New York: Harper, 2003. Formerly called *Halliwell's Filmgoer's Companion.* More than 12,000 entries on scriptwriters, actors, directors, and others; film terms; film movements; recurrent themes (or topics) in films; and some national cinemas. Also includes short quotations from actors, directors, and critics.

The International Dictionary of Films and Filmmakers. 4th ed. 4 vols. Ed. Tom and Sara Pendergast. Chicago: St. James, 2000. Critical essays, bibliographies, and filmographies. Vol. 1: Films; vol. 2: Directors; vol. 3: Actors and Actresses; vol. 4: Writers and Production Artists (including cinematographers, producers, editors, and designers).

Katz, Ephraim. *The Film Encyclopedia.* 4th ed. Rev. Fred Klein and Ronald Dean Nolen. New York: Harper, 2001. A comprehensive one-volume encyclopedia of world cinema. More than seven thousand entries on individual scriptwriters, producers, directors, and many others; studios and production companies; movements or styles of filmmaking; national cinemas; filmmaking personnel; and jargon and technical terms. For each person discussed, a selected list of films she or he worked on is also supplied.

Leff, Leonard J. *Film Plots: Scene-by-Scene Narrative Outlines for Feature Film Study.* 2 vols. Ann Arbor: Pierian. Vol. 1: scene-by-scene descriptions of sixty-seven films often studied or written about (1983); vol. 2: descriptions of fifty more feature films (1988).

Leonard Maltin's Movie and Video Guide. New York: Signet. Published annually. Brief description and evaluation of thousands of feature films, theatrical and made-for-TV. Indicates which titles have been released on videotape, which on laser disc, and which on DVD. For films made in a wide-screen process, an indication of which process was used. Also an indication of black-and-white titles available in a "computer-colored version."

Magill's Cinema Annual. Ed. Frank N. Magill and later Christine Tomassini. Englewood Cliffs, NJ: Salem Press. Published annually beginning in 1982. For major films of the previous year and occasional older films, includes credits, synopsis of the narrative, essay review, bibliography of reviews, and eight indexes.

Sadoul, Georges. *Dictionary of Films.* Trans., ed., and updated Peter Morris. Berkeley: U of California P, 1972. Brief essays on approximately 1,300 films.

Selected Film Criticism. 7 vols. Ed. Anthony Slide. Metuchen, NJ: Scarecrow, 1982–1985. Reprints original reviews of feature-length and short films; one volume includes foreign films.

Slide, Anthony. *The New Historical Dictionary of the American Film Industry.* Lanham, MD: Scarecrow, 1998. More than 750 entries on film studios, production companies, distributors, technical innovations, film series (such as *The Thin Man*), industry terms, organizations, and other subjects (such as nickelodeons).

The St. James Women Filmmakers Encyclopedia: Women on the Other Side of the Camera. Ed. Amy L. Unterburger. Detroit: Visible Ink Press, 1999. More than 200 entries—each of which includes a short biography, filmography, and analysis—on female filmmakers, mainstream and independent, from around the world.

Subject Guide to Books in Print. New York: Bowker. Under Moving-Picture and a noun (such as Direction) are listed appropriate books currently in print. Many cross-references. New edition every year.

Thomson, David. *The New Biographical Dictionary of Film.* New York: Knopf, 2002. More than 1,300 essays, ranging in length from one paragraph to several thousand words, arranged alphabetically, on filmmakers and key figures from film history. Many entries include a selective listing of films the person worked on.

The Video Source Book: A Guide to Programs Currently Available on Video. Detroit: Gale. Published annually. Comprehensive information on programs available on videotape, (laser) videodisc, and DVD and on sources for rental or purchase.

Welch, Jeffrey Egan. *Literature and Film: An Annotated Bibliography, 1900–1977.* New York: Garland, 1981.

———. *Literature and Film: An Annotated Bibliography, 1978–1988.* New York: Garland, 1993. Both volumes list and annotate books and articles published in North America and Great Britain having to do with the relation between literature and films.

The Women's Companion to International Film. Ed. Annette Kuhn and Susannah Radstone. London: Virago, 1990. Berkeley: U of California P, 1994. Approximately six hundred alphabetized entries, many including filmographies or bibliographies or both. Also includes an index of films directed, written, or produced by women.

Indexes for Periodicals

Film Literature Index. Albany: Film and Television Documentation Center. Published quarterly beginning in 1973. Indexes articles in more than three hundred international film and nonfilm periodicals. Entries are arranged alphabetically by author and subject (including film titles) and indicate the presence of filmography, credits, biography, and interviews.

Humanities Index. New York: Wilson. Published monthly beginning in 1974. At the end of each volume is a section on book reviews.

International Index to Film Periodicals: An Annotated Guide. New York: Bowker. Published annually beginning in 1972. Each volume lists articles and essays on film to appear during the past year in world film magazines. Some entries are annotated. Includes director and author indexes.

Readers' Guide to Periodical Literature. From 1910 to March 1977, film reviews are listed under Moving Picture Plays; after March 1977, film reviews are listed under Motion Picture Reviews. Since March 1976 (vol. 36), book review citations are listed at the end of each volume.

INDEXES FOR NEWSPAPERS

Los Angeles Times Index. Film reviews are listed under Motion Pictures.

New York Times Index. Film articles and reviews are listed under Motion Pictures.

The Times Index (London). Film reviews are listed under Films.

JOURNALS AND MAGAZINES

Because Web site addresses change so often, they are not included below, but they may easily be located by using one of the powerful Web search engines, such as Google (www.google.com) or Monster Crawler (www.monstercrawler.com).

Because film journals and magazines so often change their coverage, place of publication, frequency of publication, even their names or subtitles, some of the following information may no longer be accurate. For more current information on most of the following publications, use one of the powerful Web search engines, such as Google (www.google.com) or Monster Crawler (www.monstercrawler.com).

Afterimage: The Journal of Media Arts and Cultural Criticism. A journal of photography, independent film and video, alternative publishing and multimedia, and online communication. Published six times a year.

American Cinematographer. Includes many in-depth articles on the cinematography used in making particular movies, interviews with major cinematographers, and ads for such equipment as cranes, Steadicams, and cameras. Published monthly.

The American Historical Review. Beginning with vol. 96.4 (Oct. 1991), each October issue includes a section of films reviewed from a historian's perspective.

Camera Obscura. Published three times a year. Focus on feminist perspectives on film, TV, and visual media. Each issue may include debates, essays, interviews, and summary pieces.

CineAction. Film criticism in terms of race, gender, sexual orientation, and politics. Published three times a year in Toronto since 1984.

Cineaste. Provides coverage of the art and politics of world cinema. Includes film reviews, book reviews, and interviews. A quarterly published without assistance from the film industry or any academic institution.

Cinema Journal. Published four times a year in cooperation with the Society for Cinema and Media Studies, a professional association made up largely of college and university film teachers. Includes essays on a wide variety of subjects from diverse methodological perspectives.

Cinema Technology. Covers information of special interest to cinema managers, distributors, and projectionists. Published quarterly in London.

DOX. An international film magazine, which is published every two months and is dedicated to the documentary. *DOX* includes reviews of new films and important information about festivals, markets, funding bodies, and broadcasters.

Film & History: An Interdisciplinary Journal of Film and Television Studies. Articles, film reviews, and book reviews. Published quarterly since 1970.

Film Comment. Published by the Film Society of Lincoln Center (New York). Articles, interviews, and book and film reviews.

Film Criticism. Articles, interviews, festival reports, and book reviews. Published three times a year at Allegheny College.

Film Culture: America's Independent Motion Picture Magazine. Articles on experimental films and filmmakers. Published irregularly from 1955 to 1999, when it ceased publication.

Film History: An International Journal. Each issue includes articles on a special topic. Published quarterly.

Filmmaker: The Magazine of Independent Film. Published four times a year by the Independent Feature Project.

Film Quarterly. Interviews, discussions of film theory and film history, reviews of films and videos, and, especially in each summer issue, book reviews. Published since 1958 by the University of California Press.

Films in Review. Oldest film publication in the United States. Many short film reviews, longer articles on filmmakers, extensive obituaries. Published in print until 1997; since then, available only on the Web at <http://www.filmsinreview.com>.

The Independent Film & Video Monthly. Published ten times a year by the Foundation for Independent Video and Film (FIVF). Includes profiles of filmmakers, producers, and distributors; festival listings; information on new technology; coverage of political trends and legislation affecting independents; and reports from film festivals and markets.

International Documentary: The Magazine of the International Documentary Association is published ten times a year. Articles and departments, including information on premieres, funding, and festivals.

Journal of Film and Video. Quarterly published by the University Film and Video Association, which consists largely of filmmakers and university film teachers. Earlier known under the title *Journal of the University Film and Video Association*.

The Journal of Popular Film and Television (formerly *Journal of Popular Film*). Published quarterly. Articles on stars, directors, producers, studios, networks, genres, series, and other topics. Includes interviews, filmographies, bibliographies, and book reviews.

Journal of Religion and Film. Publishes articles, brief reviews of recently released films especially as they relate to religions and religious themes, and occasional book reviews.

Jump Cut: A Review of Contemporary Media. Published irregularly since 1974. Recent perspectives on film, television, video, and related media and cultural analysis. *Jump Cut* "is a nonsectarian left and feminist publication, open to a variety of left interpretations and to criticism which may not be explicitly left but which contributes to the development of a vigorous political media criticism."

Literature Film Quarterly. "Articles on individual movies, on different cinematic adaptations of a single literary work, on a director's style of adaptation, on theories of film adaptation, on the 'cinematic' qualities of authors or works, on the reciprocal influences between film and literature, on authors' attitudes toward film and film adaptations, on the role of the screenwriter, and on teaching of film." Also includes interviews, film reviews, and book reviews.

Monthly Film Bulletin. Detailed credits, summary of the story, and review of feature films and short films, contemporary and "retrospective." International coverage. Published from 1934 to April 1991. In May 1991, *Monthly Film Bulletin* was incorporated into *Sight and Sound* (see below).

MovieMaker. Published four times a year. Focuses on independent films and independent filmmakers.

New Review of Film and Television Studies. Twice a year, publishes articles about the results of "current research making a central contribution to film and television studies."

Quarterly Review of Film and Video. Articles on film production, history, theory, reception, and criticism, including the widest possible range of approaches and subjects plus book reviews and interviews.

Scenario: The Magazine of Screenwriting Art. Each quarterly issue includes three complete (mostly recent) feature-length screenplays, interviews with the writers, articles on screenwriting, and a short film script.

Sight and Sound. Published monthly by the British Film Institute. Articles, interviews, book reviews, and a review for each film released in the United Kingdom, each preceded by credits and a plot summary.

Sound & Vision. Published ten times a year with information on home theater, audio, video, multimedia, movies, and music. Test reports, evaluations, shopping tips, commentary, plus reviews of movies on DVDs and music on CDs.

Variety. A U.S. trade publication on the entertainment industry, including film reviews and many other types of information. Available in daily and weekly versions.

The Velvet Light Trap: A Critical Journal of Film and Television. Published twice a year. Critical essays, especially on American film and TV.

Wide Angle. Published quarterly. Usually each issue stresses a single topic. Also includes interviews with filmmakers and book reviews.

Widescreen Review. Devoted exclusively to "widescreen digital surround home theatre experience." Includes reviews of widescreen DVD and of equipment, such as DVD players.

WORKS CITED

Flaubert, Gustave. *Madame Bovary.* Trans. Paul de Man. New York: Norton, 1965.

Sagan, Carl. "The Persistence of Memory." Program 11. *Cosmos.* PBS. The wording is from the television program, not the book based on the series.

A Chronology: Film in Context (1895–2003)

SOME FILM HISTORY BOOKS, such as those by Gerald Mast and Bruce Kawin and by David Cook, are mainly aesthetic histories: they stress the artistic achievements of films that scholars regard as significant or representative. Then there are industrial histories: studies that help readers understand films as products of an industry. Other histories focus on film as one of the arts. Social histories emphasize how a society influences the films made, one of the topics discussed in Chapter 9. Sociological history focuses on how films influence viewers. There are many other types of histories of film, although increasingly historians blend different types of histories within the same written accounts because attempting to study films on their own (out of context) makes for incomplete and misleading history. Film scholar Dana Polan argues that films "are what they are because of the meanings given them by surrounding situations. A history of films is a history of films in history" (54).

Scholars now focus on how to study history ("historiography") and have concluded that there is no one history, only various histories. Professor Jack Ellis, for example, entitled his useful book *A History of Film* because he is well aware that his is only one selection and interpretation of cinema. Douglas Gomery's *Movie History: A Survey* interweaves four approaches: aesthetics, technology, economics, and sociology. Kristin Thompson and David Bordwell's second edition of their *Film History: An Introduction* is guided by three main concerns: the uses of the film medium over time; film production, distribution, and exhibition; and international trends in the film medium and the film market (7–8). Geoffrey Nowell-Smith coordinated the work of some international film scholars to create *The Oxford History of World Cinema*, which encompasses not just films but "the audience, the industry, and the people who work in it . . . and the mechanisms of regulation and control which determine which films audiences are encouraged to see and which they are not" (xix). The History of the American Cinema series, under the general editorship of Professor Charles Harpole, uses four approaches to cinema history: aesthetic, technological, sociological, and economic.

The following chronology supplies information from four major sources. In the first column, arranged chronologically, are world events that have affected the lives of many people. The other columns are given over to the arts, including many works that were sources for films or were derived from films (column 2), developments in the mass media (column 3), and varied critically acclaimed films and videos, innovative films, and films and videos about filmmakers or films (column 4). Although it is a long and complicated chronology, it is woefully incomplete. Unavoidably, everyone who has studied history will have quarrels with parts of it.

Nevertheless, the chronology can be useful in a number of ways. You can read an entire column to get a sense of the order and occasionally the connections between related events (for example, you might notice how conditions in Germany after World War I preceded the Nazis' rise to power). Or you can read all four columns one year at a time to get a sense of what happened in a particular year.

You can also use the chronology to place a film in other contexts. Imagine, for example, you are studying *Casablanca*, which was first shown in November 1942. From the chronology you can learn or be reminded about what else was happening before and during 1942. You might notice, for example, that Europe plunged into World War II in September 1939 and that the United States remained (officially) neutral for over two years (until the Japanese attacked Pearl Harbor in December 1941). On one level, *Casablanca* calls for Americans to put aside any inclination to isolationism and rally behind a traditional ally, the French, who at the time of the film's release were under German occupation. Once you consider when *Casablanca* was made, you can better understand its fervor in denouncing the Nazis, extolling the Free French, and criticizing the French government in Vichy that cooperated with the occupying Germans. The chronology can help you understand not only the times when a film was made but also the times a film is set in. For example, the information about events leading up to World War II can help you better understand *Saving Private Ryan* (1998).

The chronology also illustrates how widespread is the interaction of film and the other arts (for example, how plays have been made into films and vice versa) and how often film interfaces with other entertainments and the other media (especially TV). Then, too, the chronology repeatedly illustrates one of the major underlying messages of *Film: An Introduction*: film is pervasive in American and other societies, both drawing from and reflecting the infinite fascinating permutations of individual and group behavior.

The year given for a film is the year it was first shown publicly. Sometimes different sources disagree about a date. Whenever I have become aware of such discrepancies, I have tried to consult at least one additional authoritative source, but occasional inaccuracies may remain. When a film title in printed sources differs from the title in the film itself, I have used the title in the opening credits of a video or DVD version of the film. Some films do not fit neatly into one of the three distinct categories of films used in this book (fictional, documentary, and experimental), but to save space I have listed fictional films first then labeled most of the rest *documentary* or *experimental*.

Two notes about film titles: throughout the chronology, as throughout this book, film titles in quotation marks indicate films less than sixty minutes long. Titles in italics indicate films sixty or more minutes long. Parentheses included as part of a film's title indicate that the film is sometimes known by its longer title, sometimes by the shorter one (without the words in parentheses); thus, for example, the entry *(The Life and Times of) Rosie the Riveter* means that documentary film is sometimes known as *The Life and Times of Rosie the Riveter* and sometimes as *Rosie the Riveter*.

It is hoped that you will not use the chronology as your only historical source but will seek out more complete, coherent, and authoritative accounts, such as those cited following the chronology.

	World Events	Arts	Mass Media	Films and Videos
1895	Cuba fights for independence from Spain First U.S. automobile made for sale on a regular basis Roentgen discovers X-rays Invention of the diesel engine *Studies in Hysteria*, Sigmund Freud (book)	*The Red Badge of Courage*, Stephen Crane (fiction) *The Time Machine*, H. G. Wells (fiction) *The Importance of Being Earnest*, Oscar Wilde (play)	Lumière Brothers invent a portable motion-picture camera/projector to film short films and to show them publicly First U.S. demonstration of a motion picture shown on a screen, New York City Guglielmo Marconi sends and receives a radio signal	Lumière Brothers' first (and very brief) film, "Workers Leaving the Lumière Factory," is perhaps also the first documentary film Other Lumière films: "The Arrival of a Train at the Station" and "Feeding (the) Baby" "The Execution of Mary, Queen of Scots," Edison company
1896	Olympic games of ancient Greece reestablished Anti-imperialist violence in Africa: Ethiopian warriors defeat Italian soldiers and tribal rebellion erupts in Rhodesia Alaskan Gold Rush First "glider" flight	First major U.S. photography exhibition *Uncle Vanya*, Anton Chekhov (play) *Pont Boieldi in a Drizzle*, Camille Pissaro (painting)	Georges Méliès begins making short films Some U.S. vaudeville theaters include short films in their programs Some newspapers give synopses of film programs but little criticism of them Some films are hand-painted with colors	"The Kiss," Edison "The Vanishing Lady," Georges Méliès "The Fairy in the Cabbage Patch," first film by the world's first female film director, Alice Guy-Blaché
1897	Discovery of the electron United States annexes Hawaii	*Dracula*, Bram Stoker (fiction)	Fire kills 140 people at a charity film showing in Paris	Fitzsimmons-Corbett boxing match filmed and shown in theaters
1898	Spanish-American War; Spain cedes Cuba, Puerto Rico, Guam, and the Philippines to the U.S.	*The Turn of the Screw*, Henry James (fiction) *The War of the Worlds*, Wells (fiction) "J'accuse," Émile Zola (letter)	First photograph taken with artificial light William Randolph Hearst epitomizes the ethics of "yellow journalism" with his comment: "You furnish the pictures, I'll furnish the war."	"Tearing Down the Spanish Flag" (a staged documentary and perhaps the first propaganda film) "Express Train on a Railway Cutting," Cecil Hepworth (documentary)

	World Events	Arts	Mass Media	Films and Videos
1899	Aspirin first marketed, as a prescribed drug U.S. goes to war with insurgents in the Philippines	*McTeague*, Frank Norris (fiction) "Maple Leaf Rag," Scott Joplin (music)	First magnetic recording of sound Marconi sends a wireless signal across the English Channel	"The Dreyfus Affair," Méliès (a film that re-creates a political scandal) "Cinderella," Méliès
1900	Boxer Rebellion in China, mainly against foreigners *The Interpretation of Dreams*, Freud (book) Max Planck proposes quantum theory of energy King Humbert I of Italy assassinated by anarchist Russia annexes Manchuria	*The Wonderful Wizard of Oz*, L. Frank Baum (fiction) *Sister Carrie*, Theodore Dreiser (fiction)	At about this time, Edison uses artificial light in his roof-top film studio in New York City Lumière Brothers use a 70 x 53 foot translucent screen at Paris World's Fair so 25,000 people on both sides of the screen can see short films George Eastman introduces the cheap, popular portable Kodak camera	"One Man Band," Méliès, with the filmmaker himself playing the six band members and the conductor
1901	Queen Victoria of England is succeeded by Edward VII Nobel Prizes first awarded President McKinley assassinated by anarchist Australian Commonwealth established	*Three Sisters*, Chekhov (play)	Marconi sends a radio signal from Wales to Newfoundland by tapping out "S" in Morse code Electric typewriter invented	"Queen Victoria's Funeral" (documentary)
1902 (cont'd on next page)	Boer War ends in South Africa Riots rage throughout southern Russia Aswan Dam finished in Egypt	*The Virginian*, Owen Wister (fiction) *Heart of Darkness*, Joseph Conrad (fiction)	First English film studio is built in Ealing, near London Pathé builds film studio in France	"A Trip to the Moon," Méliès "Coronation of Edward VII," Méliès (documentary re-creation)

	World Events	Arts	Mass Media	Films and Videos
1902 (cont'd)		*The Wings of the Dove*, James (fiction)	First phonograph recording by the singer Enrico Caruso	
1903	Ford Motor Company founded and begins new assembly-line system for automobile construction Wright brothers fly airplane	*Call of the Wild*, Jack London (fiction) *Man and Superman*, Bernard Shaw (play) Isadora Duncan pioneers modern dance (1903–08)	Edwin S. Porter uses matte shots in "The Great Train Robbery" First radio message from U.S. to Britain	"The Great Train Robbery," "Life of an American Fireman," and "Uncle Tom's Cabin," all by Edwin S. Porter "La damnation de Faust," Méliès
1904	Theodore Roosevelt reelected president Russo-Japanese War Roosevelt Corollary added to Monroe Doctrine, asserts U.S. international policing rights	*Peter Pan*, J. M. Barrie (play) *The Cherry Orchard*, Chekhov (play)	A few nickelodeons—small storefront movie theaters showing programs of short films—open in U.S. Comic books, disk phonographs, and telephone answering machines are invented	"An Impossible Voyage," Méliès
1905	Police crush demonstration in St. Petersburg; general strike in Russia Russian sailors mutiny on battleship *Potemkin* Albert Einstein's theory of relativity	*The House of Mirth*, Edith Wharton (fiction) *Major Barbara*, Shaw (play) Fauvism and expressionism (art movements)	Pittsburgh theater is first to show films exclusively and regularly	"Rescued by Rover," Hepworth
1906	Britain launches the first large battleship, *Dreadnough* British Labour Party formed	*The Jungle*, Upton Sinclair (fiction) *Portrait of Gertrude Stein*, Pablo Picasso (painting)	Nearly 1,000 nickelodeons in the U.S. Movies are usually one reel (13–16 minutes) Victrola (record player) first marketed	"Dream of a Rarebit Fiend," Porter *The Story of the Kelly Gang*, Charles Tait (regarded as the first feature-length film)

	World Events	Arts	Mass Media	Films and Videos
1906 (cont'd)	In India, Mahatma Gandhi begins campaign of nonviolent protest			
1907	First completely synthetic plastic developed Ross Harrison grows human cells outside the body First blood test for syphilis	*The Playboy of the Western World*, John Millington Synge (play) Picasso's first cubist painting	Chicago creates its first film censorship board	"Ben Hur," Sidney Olcott
1908	Ford Motor Co. begins manufacturing the Model T Middle East oil boom begins in Persia	*A Room with a View*, E. M. Forster (fiction) Ashcan school of American realism (painting)	From 1908 to 1913, D. W. Griffith directs or supervises hundreds of short films at Biograph film production company	"The Adventures of Dollie," D. W. Griffith "The Last Days of Pompeii," Luigi Maggi
1909	Half of U.S. lives on farms or in small towns Congress passes the U.S. copyright law	The Italian book *Futurist Manifesto* exalts the beauty and dynamism of machines	At about this time, 35 mm becomes the standard film gauge throughout the world	"A Corner in Wheat" and "The Lonely Villa," Griffith
1910	Mexican civil war begins Portuguese monarchy ends after uprisings in Lisbon African American boxer Jack Johnson defeats white boxer Jim Jeffries, and race riots erupt throughout U.S.	*Howards End*, Forster (fiction) *The Dream*, Henri Rousseau (painting)	10,000 nickelodeons throughout the U.S. Film credits begin to identify U.S. actors First U.S. motion-picture newsreel exhibited Max Linder (France) writes, supervises, and performs in short comic movies	"A Child of the Ghetto," Griffith

	World Events	Arts	Mass Media	Films and Videos
1911	Mexican civil war ends First air flight across U.S. Indianapolis 500 mile auto race held for the first time	*Ethan Frome*, Wharton (fiction) *I and My Village*, Marc Chagall (painting)	The standard aspect ratio (4:3) is widely used in film showings	"The Battle" and "The Lonedale Operator," Griffith
1912	Revolution in China and abdication of the last Chinese emperor *Titanic* hits an iceberg and sinks on its maiden voyage; more than 1,500 die 2,000 Turks killed by soldiers of the Balkan alliance	*Death in Venice*, Thomas Mann (fiction) *Tarzan of the Apes*, Edgar Rice Burroughs (fiction)	About 5 million see American movies daily Most American films now made in Los Angeles, not the East coast Universal Studios founded Wireless communication is used when the sinking *Titanic* signals for help	"The Musketeers of Pig Alley," Griffith "Keystone Kops," Mack Sennett (series of short comic films) *Quo Vadis?*, Enrico Guazzoni (popular spectacle) *Queen Elizabeth*, Louis Mercanton and Henri Desfontaines
1913	Niels Bohr publishes his model of atomic structure Pancho Villa leads rebellion in northern Mexico; Mexican president deposed and killed in coup	First showing of avant-garde European art in the U.S. *Nude Descending a Staircase*, Marcel Duchamp (painting) *The Rite of Spring*, Igor Stravinsky (music)	Olga Wohlbruck becomes the first German female filmmaker	"Judith of Bethulia," Griffith "The Student of Prague," Stellan Rye and Paul Wagener
1914	World War I begins in Europe (1914–18) Panama Canal opens Term "birth control" coined	*Dubliners*, James Joyce (short stories, including "The Dead")	In the U.S., the feature film becomes the norm Strand Theater, perhaps the first movie palace, opens in New York	"Gertie the Dinosaur," Winsor McCay (series of short animated films) *Cabiria*, Giovanni Pastrone

	World Events	Arts	Mass Media	Films and Videos
1915	Germans use poison gas on western front German submarine sinks British liner *Lusitania*; approximately 1,200 die	*Of Human Bondage,* Somerset Maugham (fiction) *The Metamorphosis,* Franz Kafka (fiction) New Orleans jazz is popular in U.S.	First long-distance phone service established between New York and San Francisco	*The Birth of a Nation,* Griffith *The Cheat,* Cecil B. De Mille "The Tramp," Charles Chaplin *Les vampires,* Louis Feuillade (10-part series, 1915–16)
1916	Germans use gas against their enemies in the Battle of Verdun, which lasts from February to December Pancho Villa's forces attack the U.S. and kill 14 Irish insurrection on Easter Day ("Bloody Sunday")	*A Portrait of the Artist as a Young Man,* Joyce (fiction) Dada (art and literary movement founded in Zurich)	Camera crane used for filming parts of *Intolerance* *The Art of the Moving Picture* by Vachel Lindsay and *The Photoplay: A Psychological Study* by Hugo Münsterberg are early books on film theory	*Intolerance,* Griffith *Civilization,* Thomas Ince "The Pawn Shop," "The Vagabond," and "The Rink," Chaplin *Her Defiance,* Cleo Madison
1917	Puerto Ricans granted U.S. citizenship Revolution in Russia; provisional government is formed; tsar abdicates U.S. enters World War I In Russia, Bolsheviks seize power; later V. I. Lenin becomes chief commissar	Symphony 1 ("Classical"), Sergei Prokofiev	UFA (major German film studio) formed Technicolor Corporation is founded; experimentation with color film continues First jazz recordings	"The Immigrant" and "Easy Street," Chaplin
1918 (cont'd on next page)	World War I ends Romanov royal family executed in Russia	*The Magnificent Ambersons,* Booth Tarkington (fiction)	Warner Brothers Pictures incorporated by Harry, Albert, and Jack Warner	"Shoulder Arms," Chaplin *The Sinking of the Lusitania,* McCay (perhaps the first feature-length animated film)

	World Events	Arts	Mass Media	Films and Videos
1918 (cont'd)	World influenza epidemic kills 20 million people		During World War I, the U.S. film industry drastically increased its share of the world market	*Carmen*, Ernst Lubitsch
1919	U.S. states ratify prohibition amendment, which goes into effect in 1920, making the manufacture or consumption of alcohol illegal Civil war in Russia League of Nations founded Versailles peace treaty formally ends World War I	*Winesburg, Ohio: A Group of Tales of Ohio Small Town Life*, Sherwood Anderson (fiction) *Ten Days That Shook the World*, John Reed (nonfiction) Jazz arrives in Europe	United Artists (distribution company) formed by Chaplin, Griffith, Mary Pickford, and Douglas Fairbanks RCA founded	*Broken Blossoms*, Griffith *Blind Husbands*, Erich von Stroheim *The Homesteader*, Oscar Micheaux (first feature film about U.S. blacks written and directed by an African American) *The Cabinet of Dr. Caligari*, Robert Wiene *J'accuse*, Abel Gance (the "Griffith of Europe") *South: Ernest Shackleton and the Endurance Expedition*, Frank Hurley (documentary)
1920	Gandhi leads India's struggle for independence from Britain U.S. women get the vote Russian civil war ends	*Main Street*, Sinclair Lewis (fiction) *The Age of Innocence*, Wharton (fiction)	Lev Kuleshov founds workshop in Moscow and begins experimenting with editing U.S. films popular throughout much of the world KDKA in Pittsburgh offers regularly scheduled radio programs	*Way Down East*, Griffith *The Golem*, Paul Wegener and Henrik Galeen
1921	Adolf Hitler's storm troopers in Germany and Fascist blackshirts in Italy terrorize political opponents	*Six Characters in Search of an Author*, Luigi Pirandello (play)	British Broadcasting Corp. (BBC) begins U.S. President Warren G. Harding makes first presidential radio address	*The Kid*, Chaplin's first feature *Orphans of the Storm*, Griffith *Destiny*, Fritz Lang

	World Events	Arts	Mass Media	Films and Videos
1921 (cont'd)	Irish Free State (excluding Northern Ireland) established	*The Dream*, Max Beckmann (painting)		"Rhythmus 21," Hans Richter (experimental)
1922	Benito Mussolini forms Fascist government in Italy USSR formed by various Soviet states Fuad I begins rule of Egypt Insulin isolated and used to save diabetes patients King Tutankhamen's tomb discovered in Egypt	*Ulysses*, Joyce (fiction) "The Waste Land," T. S. Eliot (poem) Beginnings of surrealism (art and literary movement) *Twittering Machine*, Paul Klee (watercolor and pen and ink)	New York Philharmonic radio concert	*Foolish Wives*, von Stroheim *Nosferatu*, F. W. Murnau *La roue*, Gance *Nanook of the North*, Robert Flaherty (documentary) *Witchcraft through the Ages*, Benjamin Christensen (hybrid) *Kino-Pravda*, Dziga Vertov (creatively edited newsreels, 1922–25)
1923	In Germany, Hitler's attempted coup fails Former Mexican revolutionary Pancho Villa ambushed and killed by gunmen Massive earthquake kills 800,000 people in Japan	*St. Joan*, Shaw (play) "Stopping by Woods on a Snowy Evening," Robert Frost (poem)	Kodak produces first 16 mm movie film (black-and-white) Vladimir Zworykin develops television camera tube *Time* magazine begins	*Safety Last*, Sam Taylor and Fred Newmeyer (starring Harold Lloyd) *Our Hospitality*, Buster Keaton and Jack Blystone *The Ten Commandments*, De Mille "Retour à la raison," Man Ray (experimental)
1924	Lenin dies; struggle for succession begins in USSR American Indians given full U.S. citizenship by an act of Congress First winter Olympics held, in France Ottoman dynasty ends 600-year rule; modern country of Turkey formed	*A Passage to India*, Forster (fiction) *Juno and the Paycock*, Sean O'Casey (play) "Surrealist Manifesto," André Breton (essay) *Rhapsody in Blue*, George Gershwin (music)	MGM film studio formed 1.25 million radios in use in U.S. Introduction of the Moviola editing machine *Little Orphan Annie* comic strip begins Leica portable still camera invented in Germany	*Greed*, von Stroheim *The Last Laugh*, Murnau *Die Nibelungen*, Lang *(The Story of) Gösta Berling*, Mauritz Stiller *Strike*, Sergei Eisenstein "Entr'acte," René Clair (experimental) "Le ballet mécanique," Fernand Léger (experimental)

	World Events	Arts	Mass Media	Films and Videos
1925	Teacher John Scopes tried for teaching evolution in violation of a Tennessee statute Hitler publishes part of *Mein Kampf* (*My Struggle*) French build the Maginot Line for defense against an invasion	*The Great Gatsby*, F. Scott Fitzgerald (fiction) *The Trial*, Kafka (posthumous fiction) *Ralph 124C 41+*, Hugo Gernsback (science fiction) Art deco movement begins	Cinematographer Karl Struss uses colored makeup and color filters to depict the healing of lepers *Grand Ole Opry* radio show begins (eventually becomes longest continuously running radio show in the U.S.)	*The Gold Rush*, Chaplin *Ben-Hur*, Fred Niblo *Body and Soul*, Micheaux (film debut of singer and actor Paul Robeson) *The Joyless Street*, G. W. Pabst *Variety*, E. A. Dupont *(Battleship) Potemkin*, Eisenstein
1926	New York–London telephone service begins Rocket launched by R. H. Goddard (U.S.) Accession to the throne of Emperor Hirohito in Japan Chiang Kai-shek takes control of the Chinese government	*The Sun Also Rises*, Ernest Hemingway (fiction) *Orphée*, Jean Cocteau (play) Harlem Renaissance begins	*Don Juan* made with Vitaphone: film plus synchronized music from disks *The Black Pirate*: one of the first films to use the two-color Technicolor process	*The General*, Keaton *Metropolis*, Lang *Mother*, V. I. Pudovkin *Faust*, Murnau
1927	Charles Lindbergh flies alone nonstop from New York to Paris German economy collapses Physicist Walter Heisenberg introduces his uncertainty principle Mao Zedong's Autumn Harvest Uprising is crushed by the Chinese government	*To the Lighthouse*, Virginia Woolf (fiction) *Show Boat*, Jerome Kern and Oscar Hammerstein (musical) *Bird in Space*, Constantin Brancusi (sculpture) *Manhattan Bridge*, Edward Hopper (painting)	Warner Bros. releases *The Jazz Singer* using the Vitaphone sound system *Napoléon* (Abel Gance) includes triptych: wide-screen image made up of three standard images "To Build a Fire," experimental fiction by Claude Autant-Lara, first film to use anamorphic lenses developed by Henri Chrétien AM radio band created	*Underworld*, Josef Von Sternberg (early gangster film) *Sunrise*, Murnau *Napoléon*, Gance *The Italian Straw Hat*, Clair *Bed and Sofa*, Abram Room *Berlin, Symphony of a Great City*, Walther Ruttmann (experimental documentary)

	World Events	Arts	Mass Media	Films and Videos
1927 (cont'd)			Sales of radio sets increase dramatically in U.S.	
1928	German dirigible *Graf Zeppelin* makes first transatlantic crossing Penicillin, first antibiotic, discovered *The Oxford English Dictionary* published	*Lady Chatterley's Lover*, D. H. Lawrence (fiction) *Orlando*, Woolf (fiction) *The Front Page*, Ben Hecht and Charles MacArthur (play) *Greta Garbo*, Edward Steichen (photograph) *Three-Penny Opera*, Kurt Weill and Bertolt Brecht (musical)	First all-talking film, *The Lights of New York*, uses the Vitaphone sound system Feature films released on two rival sound-on-film systems, Movietone and Photophone Kodak introduces 16 mm color movie film First scheduled TV broadcast, in Schenectady, N.Y.	*The Circus*, Chaplin *The Crowd*, King Vidor *The Wind*, Victor Sjöström "Steamboat Willie," Walt Disney (first Mickey Mouse film released) *October*, a.k.a. *Ten Days That Shook the World*, Eisenstein *The Passion of Joan of Arc*, Carl Theodor Dreyer "Un chien andalou," Luis Buñuel (experimental) "The Seashell and the Clergyman," Germaine Dulac (experimental)
1929	U.S. stock prices plunge European economic crisis begins Josef Stalin becomes absolute ruler of USSR Mexico's dominant political party, the Partido Revolucionario Institucional (PRI), is founded	*A Farewell to Arms*, Hemingway (fiction) *All Quiet on the Western Front*, Erich Maria Remarque (fiction) "A Room of One's Own," Woolf (essay) Museum of Modern Art opens in New York	Sound film projector speed is standardized in U.S. at 24 frames per second Postdubbing (adding sound after filming) first used First Academy Awards ceremony held, for films for 1927–28 *Amos 'n' Andy* radio show debuts and quickly proves popular *Buck Rogers in the 25th Century* (sci-fi comic strip)	*Applause*, Rouben Mamoulian *Hallelujah!*, Vidor (first sound feature with all-black cast) "Big Business," James W. Horne and Leo McCarey (starring Stan Laurel and Oliver Hardy) *Blackmail*, Alfred Hitchcock (first British sound film) *Pandora's Box*, Pabst "Drifters," John Grierson (documentary) *Man with a Movie Camera*, Vertov (experimental documentary)
1930 (cont'd on next page)	Stalin orders collectivization of Soviet farms	*The Maltese Falcon*, Dashiell Hammett (fiction)	U.S. production code for certifying movies is instituted but only loosely enforced	*All Quiet on the Western Front*, Lewis Milestone

	World Events	Arts	Mass Media	Films and Videos
1930 (cont'd)	Major Indian cities in turmoil after Gandhi and his followers are arrested for civil disobedience against British rule	*Composition in Red, Yellow and Blue*, Piet Mondrian (painting)	Rear projection developed Worldwide, approximately 250 million people attend movies weekly 12 million U.S. homes have radios	*The Blue Angel*, Josef von Sternberg "The Blood of a Poet," Jean Cocteau (experimental)
1931	Cyclotron invented by Ernest Lawrence Big Bang theory is formulated U.S. unemployment reaches 16 percent, and over 800 banks close Japan occupies Manchuria	*The Persistence of Memory*, Salvador Dali (painting) "The Star Spangled Banner" becomes U.S. national anthem	*Dick Tracy* comic strip begins *Mädchen in Uniform*, by Leontine Sagan, early film with a lesbian character and all female cast	*City Lights* (includes sound effects and music but no spoken words), Chaplin *Frankenstein*, James Whale *Dracula*, Tod Browning *The Public Enemy*, William Wellman *M*, Lang
1932	First nuclear reaction U.S. unemployment: 24 percent Franklin D. Roosevelt elected U.S. president Neutron, a subatomic particle, is discovered	*Brave New World*, Aldous Huxley (fiction) *Mobiles*, Alexander Calder (mobile sculptures)	First international film festival: Venice Film Festival Technicolor three-color process first used, in a Disney cartoon: "Flowers and Trees" Radio City Music Hall, a huge and opulent movie palace, opens in New York	*Scarface*, Howard Hawks *I Am a Fugitive from a Chain Gang*, Mervyn LeRoy *Trouble in Paradise*, Lubitsch *Dr. Jekyll and Mr. Hyde*, Mamoulian *À nous la liberté* (*Freedom for Us*), Clair
1933	Hitler appointed German chancellor Revolution in Spain spreads to the south of Spain Nazis erect their first concentration camp and begin boycott of Jews in Germany	*Shape of Things to Come*, Wells (fiction) *Blood Wedding*, Federico García Lorca (play)	British Film Institute founded Nazis control German film industry World's first drive-in movie theater opens in Camden, New Jersey	*King Kong*, Ernest Schoedsack and Merian C. Cooper *Duck Soup*, McCarey (starring Marx Bros.) *Gold Diggers of 1933*, LeRoy (with choreography by Busby Berkeley)

	World Events	Arts	Mass Media	Films and Videos
1933 (cont'd)	First round-the-world airplane flight, by Wiley Post Prohibition ends in U.S.	*Man at the Crossroads*, Diego Rivera (temporary fresco for Rockefeller Center)	President Roosevelt uses radio for his Fireside Chats to the nation *The Lone Ranger* radio program debuts	"Lot in Sodom," James Watson and Melville Webber (experimental) "Zero for Conduct," Jean Vigo (experimental)
1934	Radar developed Stalin's purge of Soviet Communist Party begins Bank robbers Bonnie Parker and Clyde Barrow killed in police ambush	*The Postman Always Rings Twice*, James M. Cain (fiction) *The Children's Hour*, Lillian Hellman (play)	Production Code Administration seal of approval required for U.S. public film showings (1934–68)	*It Happened One Night*, Frank Capra *L'Atalante*, Vigo *Man of Aran*, Flaherty (documentary) "Composition in Blue," Oskar Fischinger (experimental)
1935	Germany begins massive military build-up Dust storms plague nearly half of the U.S. Italy invades Ethiopia Persia becomes the modern state of Iran Nuremberg Laws codify German anti-Semitism	*The Treasure of the Sierra Madre*, B. Traven (fiction) *Porgy and Bess*, Gershwin (opera) Popular songs: all five Irving Berlin songs from the film *Top Hat*, including "Cheek to Cheek"	Museum of Modern Art Film Library opens First three-color Technicolor feature film: *Becky Sharp*, directed by Mamoulian "The March of Time" newsreel series appears monthly in the nation's theaters, until 1951 Approximately 22 million U.S. homes have radios	*Mutiny on the Bounty*, Frank Lloyd *The Informer*, John Ford *Top Hat*, Mark Sandrich (starring Fred Astaire and Ginger Rogers) *The 39 Steps*, Hitchcock *Toni*, Jean Renoir *Triumph of the Will*, Leni Riefenstahl (Nazi-sponsored propaganda/documentary)
1936	Spanish civil war (1936–39) Mussolini and Hitler agree to be allies Jawaharlal Nehru becomes president of the Indian National Congress First Volkswagen ("people's car") built	Frank Lloyd Wright's Kaufmann House, Pennsylvania (architecture) "A Fine Romance" (popular song from the movie *Swing Time*)	La Cinémathèque Française (France's film archive) founded *Life* magazine begins publication	*Modern Times*, Chaplin *Swing Time*, George Stevens *Sabotage*, Hitchcock *Fury*, Lang "A Day in the Country," Renoir "The Plow That Broke the Plains," Pare Lorentz (documentary) *Olympia*, Riefenstahl (documentary)

	World Events	Arts	Mass Media	Films and Videos
1937	Stalin's purges result in millions of deaths and imprisonment in slave labor camps (1937–38) German warplanes bomb Guernica, Spain, killing hundreds of people, mostly civilians Japan invades China Italy withdraws from League of Nations	*Of Mice and Men*, John Steinbeck (fiction) *The Hobbit*, J. R. R. Tolkien (fiction) *The Cradle Will Rock*, Marc Blitzstein (opera) *Guernica*, Picasso (mural depicting results of German aerial bombardment in Spain)	Henri Chrétien links two cameras with an anamorphic lens to produce an image 200 feet wide by 33 feet high for a Paris exhibition Crash of dirigible *Hindenburg* broadcast live in the U.S. on transcontinental radio	*A Star Is Born*, Wellman *Snow White and the Seven Dwarfs* (first Disney animated feature) *Grand Illusion*, Renoir
1938	Germany annexes Austria House Committee on Un-American Activities (HUAC) formed United States and Germany sever diplomatic relations	*Our Town*, Thornton Wilder (play) *Les parents terribles*, Cocteau (play) *Recumbent Figure*, Henry Moore (stone sculpture)	Orson Welles's radio broadcast of *The War of the Worlds* causes panic nationwide on Halloween Superman first appears, in *Action Comics*	*Bringing Up Baby*, Hawks *The Lady Vanishes*, Hitchcock *Alexander Nevsky*, Eisenstein
1939	Spanish civil war ends with Francisco Franco's forces victorious Pan-American Airlines begins scheduled flights between U.S. and Europe World War II begins when Germany invades Poland Ho Chi Minh creates the Viet Minh Party, which opposes French colonialism in Indochina	*The Big Sleep*, Raymond Chandler (fiction) *The Grapes of Wrath*, Steinbeck (fiction) *Alexander Nevsky*, Prokofiev (cantata based on his film score) "Over the Rainbow" (popular song from the movie *The Wizard of Oz*)	Hollywood studios produce 400 movies National Film Board of Canada founded RCA demonstrates television at New York World's Fair First FM station begins operation, Alpine, N.J. Batman first appears, in *Detective Comics*	*The Wizard of Oz*, Victor Fleming *Stagecoach*, Ford *Gone with the Wind*, Fleming (last of several directors to work on the film) *Mr. Smith Goes to Washington*, Capra *The Rules of the Game*, Renoir

	World Events	Arts	Mass Media	Films and Videos
1940	Winston Churchill becomes prime minister of Britain German army enters Paris Germans begin all-night air raids on London France divided into the occupied northern zone and the collaborative Vichy southern zone	*Farewell, My Lovely*, Chandler (fiction) *The Ox-Bow Incident*, Walter van Tilburg Clark (fiction) "When You Wish upon a Star" (popular song from the Disney movie *Pinocchio*)	28½ million American homes have radios Edward R. Murrow's radio broadcasts from London during German air raids Republican and Democratic National Conventions broadcast on radio First American TV network broadcast	*The Grapes of Wrath*, Ford *The Great Dictator*, Chaplin *His Girl Friday*, Hawks *The Bank Dick*, Eddie Cline (starring W. C. Fields) *The Great McGinty*, first film directed by Preston Sturges *Dance, Girl, Dance*, Dorothy Arzner *Fantasia* and *Pinocchio* (Disney animated features) *Jud Süss*, Veidt Harlan (influential Nazi anti-Semitic film)
1941	First jet airplane flies German armies invade Greece and Yugoslavia Germany begins invasion of Russia Japan bombs Pearl Harbor United States and Britain declare war on Japan Germany and Italy declare war on U.S.	*What Makes Sammy Run?*, Budd Schulberg (fiction) *Moonrise, Hernandez, New Mexico*, Ansel Adams (photograph)	NBC and CBS granted commercial TV licenses	*Citizen Kane*, first film directed by Orson Welles *The Maltese Falcon*, first film directed by John Huston *Sullivan's Travels*, Sturges "Target for Tonight," Harry Watt (documentary)
1942	Germany begins killing Jews in gas chambers Japan invades the Philippines Heavy German air raids on London Fungus destroys Indian rice crops; 1.6 million die in famine	*The Stranger*, Albert Camus (fiction) *Nighthawks*, Hopper (painting)	In the U.S., radio is the main source of information about the war	*Casablanca*, Michael Curtiz *The Magnificent Ambersons*, Welles *To Be or Not to Be*, Lubitsch *Ossessione*, Luchino Visconti "The Battle of Midway," Ford (documentary) "Why We Fight," produced by Capra (series of seven wartime documentaries, 1942–45)

	World Events	Arts	Mass Media	Films and Videos
1943	Allied forces land in Sicily Mussolini dismissed as Italian premier Italy surrenders to Allies and declares war on Germany German forces fail to take Stalingrad after yearlong siege	*Oklahoma!*, Richard Rodgers and Oscar Hammerstein (musical)	*Perry Mason* radio series begins with Raymond Burr; later a TV series	*Shadow of a Doubt*, Hitchcock *The Ox-Bow Incident*, Wellman "Report from the Aleutians," Huston (documentary) *Fires Were Started*, Humphrey Jennings (documentary) "Meshes of the Afternoon," Maya Deren and Alexander Hammid (experimental)
1944	Allies land in northern France (D-Day) German V-2 rockets used against Britain Forces under the command of U.S. General Douglas MacArthur recapture the Philippines Roosevelt elected U.S. president for unprecedented fourth term	*The Glass Menagerie*, Tennessee Williams (play)	First general-purpose computer built, at Harvard University, funded in part by IBM	*Hail the Conquering Hero* and *The Miracle of Morgan's Creek*, Sturges *Double Indemnity*, Billy Wilder *Murder, My Sweet*, Edward Dmytryk *Laura*, Otto Preminger *Henry V*, Laurence Olivier "Memphis Belle," William Wyler (documentary)
1945	President Roosevelt dies unexpectedly United Nations charter signed in San Francisco War ends in Europe, 35 million killed, 6 million of whom were Jews United States drops two atomic bombs on Japan, and Japan surrenders Independent republic of Vietnam formed Nuremberg trials of Nazi war criminals begin	*Animal Farm*, George Orwell (fiction) *Carousel*, Rodgers and Hammerstein (musical) Beginnings of abstract expressionism (art movement)	*Meet the Press*, radio show 5,000 American homes have a TV set *Ebony*, first African American glossy magazine	*The Lost Weekend*, Wilder *Detour*, Edgar G. Ulmer *Open City* (a.k.a. *Rome, Open City*), Roberto Rossellini *Brief Encounter*, David Lean *Ivan the Terrible, Part I*, Eisenstein *Children of Paradise*, Marcel Carné (made in France during German occupation) "The Battle of San Pietro," Huston (documentary)

	World Events	Arts	Mass Media	Films and Videos
1946	Cold war begins between USSR and its allies and U.S. and its allies Juan Perón elected president of Argentina Philippine independence from the U.S., July 4 Nuremberg trials end French women get the vote France recognizes Vietnamese independence	*Zorba, the Greek*, Nikos Kazantzakis (fiction) *All the King's Men*, Robert Penn Warren (fiction) *Annie Get Your Gun*, Irving Berlin (musical)	Each week about 90 million Americans go to the movies, a record Cannes (France) Film Festival founded Sony Corporation founded in Japan	*My Darling Clementine*, Ford *The Killers*, Robert Siodmak *The Best Years of Our Lives*, Wyler *It's a Wonderful Life*, Capra *Beauty and the Beast*, Cocteau *Great Expectations*, Lean *Shoeshine*, Vittorio de Sica "Let There Be Light," Huston (documentary not released until many years later)
1947	India becomes independent of Britain Jackie Robinson first African American to play major league baseball India is divided into India and Pakistan U.S. jet plane flies faster than sound	*A Streetcar Named Desire*, Williams (play) The Actor's Studio, which teaches Method acting, is founded in the U.S.	House Committee on Un-American Activities (HUAC) investigates possible Communist influence in Hollywood British Film Academy formed Regular TV news broadcasts begin in the U.S. Zoom lens developed, at first for use in TV	*Out of the Past*, Jacques Tourner *Crossfire*, Dmytryk *Monsieur Verdoux*, Chaplin *Odd Man Out*, Carol Reed "Fireworks," Kenneth Anger (experimental) "Motion Painting No. 1," Fischinger (experimental)
1948 (cont'd on next page)	Gandhi assassinated in India U.S. Congress passes Marshall Plan: economic assistance for rebuilding Europe Israel proclaimed a country Apartheid becomes governmental policy of South Africa	*The Naked and the Dead*, Norman Mailer (fiction) *Cry, The Beloved Country*, Alan Paton (fiction) *The Loved One*, Evelyn Waugh ("black comedy" fiction) *Christina's World*, Andrew Wyeth (painting)	Drive-in theaters increase in popularity Hollywood Ten found guilty of contempt of Congress In "the Paramount case," U.S. Supreme Court rules that the major Hollywood studios' control of production, distribution, and exhibition violates antitrust laws	*The Treasure of the Sierra Madre*, Huston *The Naked City*, Jules Dassin *Force of Evil*, Abraham Polonsky *The Lady from Shanghai*, Welles *Fort Apache*, Ford *The Red Shoes*, Michael Powell *Oliver Twist*, Lean *The Fallen Idol*, Reed *The Bicycle Thief* (a.k.a. *Bicycle Thieves*), De Sica

	World Events	Arts	Mass Media	Films and Videos
1948 (cont'd)	USSR blocks all traffic between Berlin and the West; Western countries begin to airlift supplies into Berlin North Korea proclaims independence from Republic of Korea	*City Square*, Alberto Giacometti (bronze sculpture)	TV becoming a threat to the film industry Long-playing phonograph record introduced Transistor developed 135 million paperback books sold in U.S. during the year	*Les parents terribles*, Cocteau (film version of his own play of the same title)
1949	North Atlantic Treaty Organization (NATO) created, a collective defense alliance initially of twelve nations Berlin airlift ends USSR tests its first atomic bomb Chinese Communists come to power; Nationalists flee to the island of Formosa, later called Taiwan Republic of India begins	*1984*, Orwell (fiction) *Death of a Salesman*, Arthur Miller (play) *South Pacific*, Rodgers and Hammerstein (musical) Zither music from the film *The Third Man* is popular	1 million TV sets in U.S. *The Lone Ranger*, the first western TV series 45 rpm record introduced	*Gun Crazy*, Joseph H. Lewis *Pinky*, Elia Kazan *All the King's Men*, Robert Rossen *The Third Man*, Reed *Kind Hearts and Coronets*, Robert Hamer *Late Spring*, Yasujiro Ozu *The Quiet One*, Sidney Meyers (documentary) "Begone Dull Care," Norman McLaren (experimental)
1950	Senator Joseph McCarthy claims U.S. State Department is full of Communists North Korea invades South Korea, and Korean War begins Birth control pill developed	*The Third Man*, Graham Greene (fiction published after the film) *Guys and Dolls*, Abe Burrows and Frank Loesser (musical)	Live TV comedy show *Your Show of Shows* with Sid Caesar and Imogene Coca begins and runs until 1954 *The Jack Benny Show* (TV) begins *Peanuts* comic strip begins	*Sunset Boulevard*, Wilder *Night and the City*, Dassin *Asphalt Jungle*, Huston *All About Eve*, Joseph L. Mankiewicz *Rashomon*, Akira Kurosawa *Los olvidados* (literally *The Forgotten Ones*, but sometimes known as *The Young and the Damned*), Buñuel *Diary of a Country Priest*, Robert Bresson

	World Events	Arts	Mass Media	Films and Videos
1951	Japanese women get the vote Organization of American States (OAS) founded Chinese Communists occupy Tibet Libya becomes an independent state with the help of the United Nations	*The Caine Mutiny*, Herman Wouk (fiction) *From Here to Eternity*, James Jones (fiction) *Catcher in the Rye*, J. D. Salinger (fiction) *The King and I*, Rodgers and Hammerstein (musical)	Second congressional committee hearing on possible Communist influence in Hollywood (1951–52) Flammable nitrate base film, used for most 35 mm movies, replaced with cellulose acetate safety base *Cahiers du cinéma (Movie Notebooks)*, a French film magazine, first published Color TV introduced in the United States TV shows *I Love Lucy* and *Today* begin	*The African Queen*, Huston *A Streetcar Named Desire*, Kazan *Strangers on a Train*, Hitchcock *The Lavender Hill Mob*, Charles Crichton *Forbidden Games*, René Clément
1952	Juan Batista seizes power in Cuba Coup in Egypt deposes king and leads to establishment of Egyptian Republic Puerto Rico becomes a U.S. commonwealth U.S. explodes first hydrogen bomb (General) Dwight D. Eisenhower elected president	*Invisible Man*, Ralph Ellison (fiction) *The Old Man and the Sea*, Hemingway (fiction) *Waiting for Godot*, Samuel Beckett (play) "Do Not Forsake Me," from the film *High Noon* (popular song)	A three-projector version of Cinerama is introduced with the feature-length travelogue *This Is Cinerama* *Bwana Devil* starts a brief flurry of 3-D movies Eastman Color film, easier to process and cheaper than Technicolor, is introduced and results in increased use of color in Hollywood films Handheld transistor radios marketed in the U.S. *Mad* magazine debuts	*High Noon*, Fred Zinnemann *Singin' in the Rain*, Gene Kelly and Stanley Donen *Limelight*, Chaplin *Umberto D.*, De Sica *Ikiru (To Live)*, Kurosawa "Neighbours," McLaren (experimental fictional film)
1953 (cont'd on next page)	Stalin dies	*Fahrenheit 451*, Ray Bradbury (fiction)	U.S. theaters begin to show anamorphic wide-screen movies	*Shane*, Stevens *The Band Wagon*, Vincent Minnelli

	World Events	Arts	Mass Media	Films and Videos
1953 (cont'd)	Announcement that DNA's double-helix structure can be deciphered Elizabeth II of Great Britain crowned Korean War ends First humans scale Mt. Everest Women of Mexico earn the right to vote	*Picnic*, William Inge (play) *The Crucible*, Miller (play) *Apples*, Georges Braque (painting)	Academy Awards ceremony first telecast *The Moon Is Blue* released without a Motion Picture Association of America seal President Eisenhower's inauguration is broadcast live on TV *Playboy* magazine begins publication	*Peter Pan* (Disney animated feature) *Rififi*, Dassin *Mr. Hulot's Holiday*, Jacques Tati *I Vitelloni*, Federico Fellini *Ugetsu* (*Monogatari*), Kenji Mizoguchi *Tokyo Story*, Ozu *Gate of Hell*, Teinosuke Kinugasa
1954	Polio vaccine discovered U.S. Supreme Court rules school segregation unconstitutional French defeated in Vietnam; Vietnam divided into North and South Senator Joseph McCarthy discredited and censured by U.S. Senate	*Invasion of the Body Snatchers*, Jack Finney (fiction) *Lord of the Flies*, William Golding (fiction) First volume of *The Lord of the Rings*, J. R. R. Tolkien (fiction)	*White Christmas* filmed in VistaVision, a nonanamorphic wide-screen system Approximately half of American homes have TV Army-McCarthy hearings carried live on TV First U.S. TV color telecast, Rose Bowl parade *The Tonight Show* (with Steve Allen) debuts on TV	*On the Waterfront*, Kazan *Rear Window*, Hitchcock *A Star Is Born*, George Cukor *Salt of the Earth*, Herbert J. Biberman *La Strada*, Fellini *The Seven Samurai*, Kurosawa *Late Chrysanthemums*, Mikio Naruse *Godzilla*, Inoshiro Honda (science-fiction action)
1955	Civil war begins between North and South Vietnam Warsaw Pact signed by East European countries Blacks boycott segregated city buses in Montgomery, Ala. Coup overthrows the Perón regime in Argentina	*Lolita*, Vladimir Nabokov (fiction) *The Diary of Anne Frank*, Albert Hackett and Frances Goodrich (play) *The Family of Man*, Steichen (photographic exhibit)	Filming from helicopters becomes more practicable Todd-AO (a nonanamorphic wide-screen) process used in film version of *Oklahoma!* Disneyland opens in California Highest-rated TV show (1955–56): *The $64,000 Question* (quiz show)	*Rebel without a Cause*, Nicholas Ray *Night of the Hunter*, Charles Laughton *Smiles of a Summer Night*, Ingmar Bergman *Lola Montes*, Max Ophüls *Pather Panchali*, Satyajit Ray (first of three films featuring the character Apu)

	World Events	Arts	Mass Media	Films and Videos
1955 (cont'd)	McDonald's and Kentucky Fried Chicken start first fast-food franchises		*Alfred Hitchcock Presents*, TV show (1955–62)	
1956	Soviets crush Hungarian revolt Israel invades Sinai Peninsula Fidel Castro leads revolution in Cuba (1956–59) Britain, Israel, and France invade Egypt over Egypt's nationalization of the Suez Canal	*Long Day's Journey into Night*, Eugene O'Neill (posthumous play) *Look Back in Anger*, John Osborne (play) *My Fair Lady*, Alan Jay Lerner and Frederick Loewe (musical)	Elvis Presley appears on *The Ed Sullivan Show* (TV) TV westerns are popular Singer Nat King Cole becomes the first African American to host a network TV show *The Huntley-Brinkley Report*, a TV news program, debuts	*The Searchers*, Ford *The Killing*, Stanley Kubrick *The Seventh Seal*, Bergman *A Man Escaped*, Bresson "The Red Balloon," Albert Lamorisse "Night and Fog," Alain Resnais (documentary)
1957	Martin Luther King Jr. and others found the Southern Christian Leadership Conference President Eisenhower sends troops to help desegregate the University of Arkansas Soviets launch *Sputnik*, first satellite to circle Earth	*Doctor Zhivago*, Boris Pasternak (fiction) *On the Road*, Jack Kerouac (fiction) *The Cat in the Hat*, Dr. Seuss (fiction) *West Side Story*, Leonard Bernstein and Arthur Laurents (musical)	*Raintree County*, first film released in Ultra-Panavision 70 *Perry Mason* begins nine-season run on TV *American Bandstand* (with Dick Clark) is first shown on national TV Motown Records is founded and popularizes the music style that bears the company's name	*Paths of Glory*, Kubrick *A Face in the Crowd*, Kazan *The Sweet Smell of Success*, Alexander Mackendrick *Wild Strawberries*, Bergman *Throne of Blood*, Kurosawa "Two Men and a Wardrobe," Roman Polanski (experimental) "What's Opera, Doc?" Chuck Jones (animation) "A Chairy Tale," McLaren and Claude Jutra (experimental)
1958 (cont'd on next page)	European Common Market formed First successful launch of a U.S. satellite U.S. troops sent to intervene in Lebanese civil war	*Things Fall Apart*, Chinua Achebe (fiction) *The Birthday Party*, Harold Pinter (play)	More than 4,000 U.S. drive-in movie screens in operation Stereophonic LPs and phonographs come into use	*Touch of Evil*, Welles *Vertigo*, Hitchcock *Ashes and Diamonds*, Andrzej Wajda *Ivan the Terrible, Part II*, Eisenstein (completed in 1946)

	World Events	Arts	Mass Media	Films and Videos
1958 (cont'd)	General Charles de Gaulle becomes president of France's Fifth Republic	*A Raisin in the Sun*, Lorraine Hansberry (play) *Numbers in Color*, Jasper Johns (painting)	Most popular TV show (1958–59): the western *Gunsmoke*	*Room at the Top*, Jack Clayton *The World of Apu*, Satyajit Ray "A Movie," Bruce Conner (experimental)
1959	After leading a successful revolution against the Cuban president, Castro becomes premier of Cuba Yasir Arafat and others found Palestine Liberation Organization (PLO) Russia launches two monkeys into space Chinese suppress uprising in Tibet	*The Tin Drum*, Günter Grass (fiction) *Naked Lunch*, William Burroughs (fiction) "Happenings," multimedia events, first staged *Kind of Blue*, Miles Davis (jazz album)	TV quiz show scandal *The Twilight Zone* TV show begins *Adventures in Good Music*, classical music radio program by Karl Haas, begins on a Detroit station Microchip invented	*Ben-Hur*, Wyler *North by Northwest*, Hitchcock *Some Like It Hot*, Wilder *Imitation of Life*, Douglas Sirk *The 400 Blows*, François Truffaut's first feature *Breathless*, Jean-Luc Godard's first feature *Hiroshima, mon amour*, Resnais's first feature *Look Back in Anger*, Tony Richardson *Floating Weeds*, Ozu "Window Water Baby Moving," Stan Brakhage (experimental)
1960	FDA approves use of birth control pill Nigeria becomes an independent nation Laser invented South African government bans major anti-apartheid groups after protests turn violent Organization of the Petroleum Exporting Countries (OPEC) formed Wave of decolonization as France and Belgium give up African territories	*To Kill a Mockingbird*, Harper Lee (fiction) *Camelot*, Lerner and Loewe (musical) Minimalist style in painting, sculpture, and music *Coltrane Plays the Blues* and *My Favorite Things* (albums by John Coltrane)	*Echo 1*, the first communications satellite, launched First TV debate between presidential candidates (Kennedy and Nixon) *Harvest of Shame*, TV documentary film on migrant farm workers, Edward R. Murrow, commentator Approximately 100 million TVs in Europe and the U.S. The Twist dance craze influences songs, books, movies, and TV shows	*Psycho*, Hitchcock *Shadows*, John Cassavetes' first film as director *Saturday Night and Sunday Morning*, Karel Reisz *The Entertainer*, Richardson *L'Avventura*, Michelangelo Antonioni *La Dolce Vita*, Fellini *Shoot the Piano Player*, Truffaut *Cruel Story of Youth*, Nagisa Oshima *Primary*, (Robert) Drew Associates (documentary)

	World Events	Arts	Mass Media	Films and Videos
1960 (cont'd)	First Xerox photocopier U.S. Senator John F. Kennedy elected president	Fluxus movement begins in New York and Germany (multimedia arts)		
1961	U.S. establishes Peace Corps USSR begins manned space flights U.S.-sponsored Bay of Pigs invasion of Cuba fails Communists build Berlin Wall to deter East Germans from fleeing to the West Patrice Lumumba, first prime minister elected in Congo, is assassinated	*Catch-22*, Joseph Heller (fiction) *The Moviegoer*, Walker Percy (fiction) Comic-strip and comic-frame paintings, Roy Lichtenstein	First live TV coverage of a presidential news conference *The Dick Van Dyke Show* begins on TV and runs five years	*West Side Story*, Robert Wise *Jules and Jim*, Truffaut *Last Year at Marienbad*, Resnais (experimental fiction) *Viridiana*, Buñuel *Chronicle of a Summer*, Jean Rouch and Edgar Morin (documentary) "Prelude: Dog Star Man," Brakhage (experimental)
1962	John Glenn is first American to orbit earth in a spacecraft Algeria wins independence from France U.S. and USSR in tense confrontation over Soviet missiles in Cuba United Nations troops enter the Congo to control civil war *Mariner 2* spacecraft sends back first close-up photos of another planet, Venus	*A Clockwork Orange*, Anthony Burgess (fiction) *The Death of Artemio Cruz*, Carlos Fuentes (fiction) *One Flew over the Cuckoo's Nest*, Ken Kesey (fiction) *The Thin Red Line*, Jones (fiction) *Who's Afraid of Virginia Woolf?*, Edward Albee (play)	*The Alfred Hitchcock Hour*, TV show, airs from 1962 to 1965 Johnny Carson becomes host of NBC's late-night TV talk show, *The Tonight Show*, and remains host until 1992 Walter Cronkite becomes anchor (until 1981) of *CBS Evening News* *Telstar* satellite (for TV and telephone relays) launched Most popular TV show (1962–64): *The Beverly Hillbillies*	*The Man Who Shot Liberty Valance*, Ford *Dr. No*, Terence Young (first James Bond movie) *Lawrence of Arabia*, Lean *The Loneliness of the Long Distance Runner*, Richardson *Vivre sa vie* (*My Life to Live*), Godard *Knife in the Water*, Polanski "An Occurrence at Owl Creek Bridge," Robert Enrico (experimental fiction) "La jetée," Chris Marker (experimental fiction) "Cosmic Ray," Conner (experimental)

	World Events	Arts	Mass Media	Films and Videos
1963	Alabama civil rights march results in beatings of blacks, arrest of Dr. Martin Luther King Jr., and the sending of federal troops Four black girls killed in bombing of Birmingham, Ala. church President Kennedy assassinated and Vice President Lyndon Johnson becomes president By year's end, the U.S. has sent economic aid and 16,000 "advisers" to South Vietnam Kenya gains independence from British rule	*The Feminine Mystique*, Betty Friedan (nonfiction) *Cinema*, George Segal (life-size sculpture) *Mona Lisa*, Andy Warhol (painting)	New York Film Festival established "Movietone News" last presented in U.S. movie theaters First movie multiplex built, in Kansas City TV is now the major news source for most Americans TV networks expand evening news programs from 15 to 30 minutes Martin Luther King's "I have a dream" speech in Washington, D.C., is televised Unprecedented four-day TV coverage of President Kennedy's assassination and burial Abraham Zapruder's 26-second, 8 mm amateur film is the only moving picture record of Kennedy assassination Audio cassettes used to play back music	*The Birds*, Hitchcock *Tom Jones*, Richardson *Billy Liar*, John Schlesinger *Dr. Strangelove: Or, How I Learned to Stop Worrying and Love the Bomb*, Kubrick *Lord of the Flies*, Peter Brook *8½*, Fellini *Dead Birds*, Robert Gardner (documentary) *7 Up*, Michael Apted (first in documentary series tracing lives of same small group of British citizens in seven-year increments) *Sleep*, Andy Warhol (experimental documentary) "Scorpio Rising," Anger (experimental) "Mothlight," Brakhage (experimental) "Christmas on Earth," Barbara Rubin (experimental)
1964	Martin Luther King Jr. wins Nobel Peace Prize Zambia (formerly Rhodesia) becomes an independent nation	*The Woman in the Dunes*, Kobo Abé (fiction) *Little Big Man*, Thomas Berger (fiction) *Fiddler on the Roof*, Jerry Bock and Sheldon Harnick (musical)	Sports telecasts begin to use videotaped instant replay Beatles' first American TV appearance, on *The Ed Sullivan Show* *Understanding Media: The Extensions of Man*, Marshall McLuhan (book)	*Nothing But a Man*, Michael Roemer *A Hard Day's Night*, Richard Lester *The Gospel According to St. Matthew*, Pier Paolo Pasolini *Woman in the Dunes*, Hiroshi Teshigahara *A Married Woman*, Godard

	World Events	Arts	Mass Media	Films and Videos
1964 (cont'd)	Following an attack on U.S. warships, Congress passes Gulf of Tonkin Resolution, which justifies U.S. military build-up in Vietnam Nelson Mandela sentenced to life in prison in South Africa The Civil Rights Act is passed in the United States Nikita Khrushchev is ousted from power in the USSR	*Jackie*, Andy Warhol (painting of Jacqueline Kennedy) First Moog (electronic) synthesizer		*(The) Red Desert*, Antonioni *Point of Order*, Emile De Antonio (documentary) *A Stravinsky Portrait*, Richard Leacock (documentary) "Fuses," Carolee Schneemann (experimental 1964–67) *Dog Star Man*, Brakhage (experimental 1961–64)
1965	Malcolm X, a Black Muslim leader, murdered in New York City In U.S., growing demonstrations against U.S. involvement in Vietnam The U.S. deploys Marines to the Dominican Republic	*The Autobiography of Malcolm X*, Alex Haley (nonfiction) Luis Valdez founds Teatro Campesino in California *Campbell's Soup Can*, Andy Warhol (painting)	Super-8 film introduced TV expands coverage of Vietnam War Eight-track tape player is introduced	*The Pawnbroker*, Sidney Lumet *Pierrot le fou*, Godard *Juliet of the Spirits*, Fellini *The Shop on Main Street*, Jan Kadár and Elmar Klos "The Dot and the Line," Chuck Jones and Maurice Noble (animation) "The War Game," Peter Watkins (fake documentary) *To Die in Madrid*, Frédéric Rossif (documentary) "The Sins of the Flesh-poids," Mike Kuchar (experimental)

	World Events	Arts	Mass Media	Films and Videos
1966	Cultural Revolution— led by Mao Zedong— begins in China (ends in 1971), resulting in terrorism, purges, destroyed artworks, and restructuring of the education system Black Panther Party founded in Oakland, Calif. National Organization of Women (NOW) formed By year's end, 389,000 U.S. troops in Vietnam France withdraws its troops from NATO Indira Gandhi becomes prime minister of India	*The Last Picture Show*, Larry McMurtry (fiction) *Valley of the Dolls*, Jacqueline Susan (fiction) *In Cold Blood*, Truman Capote (nonfiction) *Cabaret*, John Kander and Fred Ebb (musical) *Sweet Charity*, Cy Coleman, Dorothy Fields, and Neil Simon (musical based on Fellini's film *The Nights of Cabiria*) *Witness to Our Time*, Alfred Eisenstaedt (photographs) *The State Hospital*, Edward Kienholz (mixed media)	Color TV becomes popular in U.S. *Star Trek* begins three-season run on TV *Mission Impossible*, TV adventure series, first airs and runs until 1973 William F. Buckley Jr.'s *Firing Line* TV interview show first airs; runs until 2000 *Amos 'n' Andy* reruns dropped from TV because of protests against the program's racial stereotypes *Sixteen in Webster Groves*, TV documentary "How the Grinch Stole Christmas," animation by Chuck Jones, first shown on TV	*Who's Afraid of Virginia Woolf?*, Mike Nichols *Seconds*, John Frankenheimer *Blowup*, Antonioni *Persona*, Bergman *Closely Watched Trains*, Jiri Menzel *The Battle of Algiers*, Gillo Pontecorvo *La guerre est finie*, Resnais *Black Girl*, Ousmane Sembène *The Chelsea Girls*, Warhol (experimental) *No. 4 (Bottoms)*, Yoko Ono (experimental documentary 1966–67) "Film in Which There Appear Sprocket Holes, Edge Lettering, Dirt Particles, Etc.," George Landow (a.k.a. Owen Land) (experimental) "The Flicker," Tony Conrad (experimental) "Lapis," James Whitney (experimental)
1967	Six-day war between Arab nations and Israel results in Israeli victory and acquisition of territory Thurgood Marshall first African American Supreme Court justice First human heart transplant, in South Africa By year's end, more than 500,000 U.S. troops in Vietnam	*One Hundred Years of Solitude*, Gabriel García Márquez (fiction) *Rosencrantz and Guildenstern Are Dead*, Tom Stoppard (play) *The Great White Hope*, Howard Sackler (play) *Hair*, Gerome Ragni and Jim Rado (rock musical)	American Film Institute founded *Rolling Stone* magazine founded *Ironsides* TV series, with Raymond Burr (1967–75) *The Carol Burnett Show*, TV show (1967–79)	*Bonnie and Clyde*, Arthur Penn *The Graduate*, Nichols *Weekend*, Godard *Playtime*, Tati *Belle de jour*, Buñuel *Accident*, Joseph Losey *Don't Look Back*, D. A. Pennebaker (documentary) *Portrait of Jason*, Shirley Clarke (documentary) *Titicut Follies*, first documentary by Frederick Wiseman

	World Events	Arts	Mass Media	Films and Videos
1967 (cont'd)	Five-year military dictatorship in Greece begins	First major rock festival, Monterey, California		"Quixote," Bruce Baillie (revised version; experimental documentary) "Wavelength," Michael Snow (experimental)
1968	Surprise Tet offensive demoralizes U.S. and South Vietnamese forces Martin Luther King Jr. assassinated Senator Robert Kennedy assassinated Soviets invade Czechoslovakia and end its liberal policies Riots and police brutality outside the Democratic Convention in Chicago Richard M. Nixon elected president	*2001: A Space Odyssey*, Arthur C. Clarke (fiction) *Black Rain*, Masuji Ibuse (fiction) *I Never Sang for My Father*, Robert Anderson (play)	Motion Picture Association of America institutes four-part audience rating system for films Recent Czech film movement ended by Soviet invasion of Czechoslovakia *60 Minutes*, TV magazine news show, begins *Rowan and Martin's Laugh-In* features very short satiric pieces on TV (1968–73)	*Faces*, Cassavetes *Night of the Living Dead*, first film by George Romero *2001: A Space Odyssey*, Kubrick *Once upon a Time in the West*, Sergio Leone *Shame*, Bergman *Memories of Underdevelopment*, Tomás Gutiérrez Alea *David Holzman's Diary*, Jim McBride (fake documentary) *High School*, Wiseman (documentary) "Pas de deux," McLaren (experimental)
1969 (cont'd on next page)	Yasir Arafat becomes head of Palestine Liberation Organization (PLO) U.S. astronauts land on moon for the first time and return Woodstock (N.Y.) music festival draws 500,000 Large U.S. demonstrations against Vietnam War continue Massacre of villagers in My Lai (Vietnam) by U.S. soldiers revealed	*Fat City*, Leonard Gardner (fiction) *The Godfather*, Mario Puzo (best-selling U.S. novel of the 1970s) *Portnoy's Complaint*, Philip Roth (fiction) *Slaughterhouse-Five*, Kurt Vonnegut Jr. (fiction)	Live TV broadcast from moon captures the world's attention PBS begins broadcasting TV programs, including *Sesame Street*, which uses techniques of TV commercials to teach children basic language skills Most popular TV show (1969–70): *Rowan and Martin's Laugh-In*	*Midnight Cowboy*, Schlesinger *Medium Cool*, Haskell Wexler *The Wild Bunch*, Sam Peckinpah *I Am Joaquin*, Luis Valdez (possibly the first film written, produced, and directed by Latinos in the United States) *My Night at Maud's*, Eric Rohmer *If . . .*, Lindsay Anderson *Boy*, Oshima *Monterey Pop*, Pennebaker (early rock documentary)

	World Events	Arts	Mass Media	Films and Videos
1969 (cont'd)	American Gay Liberation movement begins with the Stonewall Inn riot in New York City			*Salesman*, Albert and David Maysles (documentary) *In the Year of the Pig*, De Antonio (documentary) *Tom, Tom, The Piper's Son*, Ken Jacobs (experimental) "Back and Forth," Snow (experimental)
1970	U.S. Supreme Court allows school busing to achieve integration U.S. and South Vietnamese troops enter Cambodia At Kent State University, Ohio National Guard members shoot at demonstrating students and kill four Massive student demonstrations against the Vietnam War close hundreds of U.S. colleges and universities Muammar al-Qaddafi comes to power in Libya Coup in Cambodia leaves it under oppressive military dictatorship	*Deliverance*, James Dickey (fiction) *Spiral Jetty*, Robert Smithson (1,500-foot jetty, Great Salt Lake, Utah)	Rapid growth of film studies in U.S. colleges and universities IMAX ("image maximum"), extremely large-screen film format, introduced at world's fair National Public Radio (NPR) begins broadcasting *The Phil Donahue Show* is first seen nationally on TV and runs until 1996 About 231 million TV sets used throughout the world *The Mary Tyler Moore Show* (TV sitcom) begins *Doonesbury* (satirical) comic strip begins	*M*A*S*H*, Robert Altman *Patton*, Franklin Schaffner *The Great White Hope*, Martin Ritt *The Wild Child*, Truffaut *Even Dwarfs Started Small*, Werner Herzog *Woodstock*, Michael Wadleigh (documentary) *The Sorrow and the Pity*, Marcel Ophüls (documentary) *Gimme Shelter*, Maysles Brothers (documentary) *Zorns Lemma*, Hollis Frampton (experimental) "Remedial Reading Comprehension," George Landow (a.k.a. Owen Land) (experimental) "Runs Good," Pat O'Neill (experimental) "Serene Velocity," Ernie Gehr (experimental)
1971	Saddam Hussein seizes power in Iraq Pakistan attacks India but is defeated in two-week war Bangladesh established as independent nation	*Maurice*, Forster (posthumous fiction) *Being There*, Jerzy (N.) Kosinski (fiction)	Movie theater receipts are down sharply *Ms. Magazine* founded to promote the women's movement Ban on TV cigarette advertising goes into effect	*McCabe and Mrs. Miller*, Altman *The Last Picture Show*, Peter Bogdanovich *Sweet Sweetback's Baad Asssss Song*, Melvin Van Peebles *A Clockwork Orange*, Kubrick *Claire's Knee*, Rohmer

	World Events	Arts	Mass Media	Films and Videos
1971 (cont'd)	Failed coup attempt in China	*. . . And the Earth Did Not Devour Him*, Tomás Rivera (fiction)	*Masterpiece Theatre* begins on PBS, with Alistair Cooke as host Top U.S. TV show (1971–76): *All in the Family*, with Carroll O'Connor as Archie Bunker	*Walkabout*, Nicolas Roeg *The Conformist*, Bernardo Bertolucci "(nostalgia)," Frampton (experimental) "Kiri," Sakumi Hagiwara (experimental)
1972	White House announces the last U.S. ground combat units have left Vietnam Britain assumes direct control of Northern Ireland Men working for the Republican Party caught in the Watergate apartment building, Washington, D.C., breaking into the Democratic National Headquarters At Munich Olympics, terrorists invade Israeli compound and kill two; later developments lead to loss of more lives	*Bless Me, Ultima*, Rudolfo A. Anaya (fiction) *Story Show*, Laurie Anderson (multimedia performance) *Grease!*, Jim Jacobs and Warren Casey (musical) Christo wraps large section of Australian coastline in plastic sheeting	*M*A*S*H* TV series, based on movie of same title, begins and runs for 11 seasons Home Box Office (HBO) is first available through cable TV First International Festival of Women's Films held in New York City	*The Godfather*, Francis Ford Coppola *Cabaret*, Bob Fosse *Fat City*, Huston *Deep Throat*, Gerard Damiano (first sexually explicit feature to gain U.S. national audience) *Frenzy*, Hitchcock *The Discreet Charm of the Bourgeoisie*, Buñuel *Last Tango in Paris*, Bertolucci *Aguirre, The Wrath of God*, Herzog *Cries and Whispers*, Bergman "Near the Big Chakra," Anne Severson (experimental documentary)
1973 (cont'd on next page)	U.S. Supreme Court, in *Roe v. Wade*, rules abortion is constitutional Vietnam cease-fire agreement signed; U.S. combat deaths: around 58,000	*Fear of Flying*, Erica Jong (fiction) *The Gulag Archipelago*, Aleksandr Solzhenitsyn (first volume of three-volume fiction) *Equus*, Peter Shaffer (play)	Omnimax, huge dome screen for use with IMAX, developed Senate Watergate hearings broadcast on TV *An American Family*, 12-hour TV documentary series on PBS	*Mean Streets*, Martin Scorsese *American Graffiti*, George Lucas *The Long Goodbye*, Altman *Payday*, Daryl Duke *The Harder They Come*, Perry Henzell *Don't Look Now*, Roeg *Day for Night*, Truffaut

	World Events	Arts	Mass Media	Films and Videos
1973 (cont'd)	Salvador Allende, Marxist president of Chile, overthrown and reportedly commits suicide Amid scandal, Spiro T. Agnew resigns as U.S. vice president; U.S. Congressman Gerald Ford succeeds him During Yom Kippur, Egyptian and Syrian forces attack the Israeli-held Sinai Peninsula and Golan Heights	Scott Joplin's ragtime music popular after its use in movie *The Sting*		*Fantastic Planet*, René Laloux (animated) *Spirit of the Beehive*, Victor Erice *Distant Thunder*, Satyajit Ray *Touki Bouki* (*The Journey of the Hyena*), Djibril Diop Mambety "No Lies," Mitchell Block (fake documentary) "Three Transitions," Peter Campus (experimental videos)
1974	Nixon resigns presidency; Vice President Gerald Ford becomes president Ford pardons Nixon for possible criminal offenses committed while in office OPEC embargo causes oil shortages and serious economic problems in U.S. and elsewhere Turkish forces invade Cyprus; Greek forces mobilized to repel the invasion	*Jaws*, Peter Benchley (fiction) *Carrie*, Stephen King's first novel	*Little House on the Prairie*, TV show (1974–83) *The Rockford Files*, TV show (1974–80) *Happy Days*, TV show (1974–84) Ali-Foreman boxing match in Zaire, the "Rumble in the Jungle," is the best documented prizefight in history *Prairie Home Companion* radio program with Garrison Keillor as host begins Word processors hit the U.S. market	*The Godfather, Part II* and *The Conversation*, Coppola *Chinatown*, Polanski *A Woman under the Influence*, Cassavetes *Ali: Fear Eats the Soul*, Rainer Werner Fassbinder *Amarcord*, Fellini *Scenes from a Marriage*, Bergman *Xala* (*Impotence*), Sembène "Antonia: A Portrait of the Woman," Jill Godmilow (documentary) "8½ x 11," James Benning (experimental fiction) *Film about a woman who . . .*, Yvonne Rainer (experimental) "Print Generation," J. J. Murphy (experimental)

	World Events	**Arts**	**Mass Media**	**Films and Videos**
1975	U.S. ends all involvement in Vietnam Soviet space probes transmit first pictures of Venus's surface Franco of Spain dies; Juan Carlos sworn in as king Khmer Rouge kill at least one million Cambodians (1975–79)	*Ragtime*, E. L. Doctorow (fiction) *Heat and Dust*, Ruth Jhabvala Prawer (fiction) *American Buffalo*, David Mamet (play) *A Chorus Line*, James Kirkwood, Nicholas Dante, and Marvin Hamlisch (musical that opens in New York and runs 15 years)	Personal computers introduced Dolby film noise-reduction system introduced *Saturday Night Live*, TV show, debuts Sony introduces Beta home videotape format	*Nashville*, Altman *Shampoo*, Hal Ashby *One Flew over the Cuckoo's Nest*, Milos Forman *Barry Lyndon*, Kubrick *The Rocky Horror Picture Show*, Jim Sharman *Picnic at Hanging Rock*, Peter Weir *The Mystery of Kaspar Hauser*, Herzog *The Story of Adele H.*, Truffaut *Grey Gardens*, Maysles Brothers (documentary) *Jeanne Dielman*, Chantal Akerman (experimental documentary)
1976	Argentine military government begins "dirty war" against dissidents; tens of thousands disappear or are murdered or both Apple Computer company founded Two U.S. spacecraft land on Mars but find no signs of life Georgia Governor Jimmy Carter elected president	*The Woman Warrior*, Maxine Hong Kingston (fiction) *The Shining*, King (fiction) *The Kiss of the Spider Woman*, Manuel Puig (fiction) *Roots*, Haley (nonfiction)	Steadicam, a lightweight, portable mount for holding a motion-picture camera, first used in making a feature film (*Bound for Glory*) Louma (lightweight, modular, 25-foot) camera crane with remote-control camera head first used in filming a feature, *The Tenant* United States telecasts views from Mars worldwide *The McNeil-Lehrer Report* begins on PBS (TV)	*Taxi Driver*, Scorsese *Network*, Lumet *All the President's Men*, Alan J. Pakula *Face to Face*, Bergman *Seven Beauties*, Lina Wertmuller *In the Realm of the Senses*, Oshima *Harlan County U.S.A.*, Barbara Kopple (documentary) *Word Is Out*, Robert Epstein and Peter Adair (documentary) "Chulas Fronteras," Les Blank (documentary) "Projection Instructions," Morgan Fisher (experimental)

	World Events	**Arts**	**Mass Media**	**Films and Videos**
1977	American space probes *Voyager 1* and *Voyager 2* are launched and two years later send back data and photographs of Jupiter Indira Gandhi of India arrested on charges of corruption President Carter pardons all Vietnam War draft evaders	Pompidou Center, Richard Rogers and Renzo Pieno (Paris architecture) Cindy Sherman begins her photographic series of herself in various movie poses	Eight-part TV dramatization of Alex Haley's book *Roots* is popular and critical success *The Lou Grant Show*, TV show (1977–82)	*Annie Hall*, Woody Allen *Star Wars*, Lucas *Equus*, Lumet *Close Encounters of the Third Kind*, Steven Spielberg *Providence*, Resnais *1900*, Bertolucci *Ceddo*, Sembène "Video Weavings," Stephen Beck (experimental video) "Turn to Your ~~Gods~~ Dogs," Richard Beveridge (experimental)
1978	In Nicaragua, Sandinista guerrilla war develops into a civil war that lasts until 1988 Vietnamese occupy Cambodia and end Khmer Rouge slaughter of Cambodians First "test-tube" baby born, in England At Jonestown, Guyana, 909 American cultists commit suicide	*Zoot Suit*, Valdez (play) *Betrayal*, Pinter (play) *Ain't Misbehavin'*, jazz musical celebrating the music of Fats Waller Soundtrack albums for the movies *Saturday Night Fever* and *Grease* are popular	120 million people see the U.S. TV movie *Holocaust* *Dallas*, TV show (1978–91) Laser videodisc players and videodiscs first marketed in U.S. 98% of all U.S. households have at least one television set Gene Siskel and Roger Ebert first appear on a PBS film review show	*The Deer Hunter*, Michael Cimino *Grease*, Randal Kleiser *Girlfriends*, Claudia Weill *Get out Your Handkerchiefs*, Bertrand Blier *Autumn Sonata*, Bergman *The Marriage of Maria Braun*, Fassbinder *Gates of Heaven*, first film by Errol Morris (documentary) "Daughter Rite," Michelle Citron (hybrid)
1979	Shah of Iran forced into exile; new leader Ayatollah Khomeini Nuclear disaster averted at Three Mile Island, Penn. Margaret Thatcher becomes first female British prime minister Sandinistas overthrow Nicaragua's President Somoza and establish Marxist government	*Sophie's Choice*, William Styron (fiction) *The Right Stuff*, Tom Wolfe (nonfiction) Spalding Gray begins to write and perform mostly autobiographical monologues	Sony Walkman (portable audio cassette player) introduced in United States *The Far Side* comic strip by Gary Larson begins *I Know Why the Caged Bird Sings*, TV adaptation of Maya Angelou's autobiography	*Apocalypse Now*, Coppola *All That Jazz*, Bob Fosse *Breaking Away*, Peter Yates *Breaker Morant*, Bruce Beresford *My Brilliant Career*, Gillian Armstrong *Best Boy*, Ira Wohl (documentary) "Peliculas," Patrick Clancy (experimental) "Thriller," Sally Potter (experimental)

	World Events	Arts	Mass Media	Films and Videos
1979 (cont'd)	About 100 U.S. Embassy personnel taken hostage in Teheran, Iran Smallpox declared eradicated worldwide	*Evita*, Andrew Lloyd Webber and Tim Rice (musical)	C-SPAN (government) and ESPN (sports) cable networks founded	"Hearts," Barbara Buckner (experimental video) "A Portrait of Light and Heat," Bill Viola (experimental video)
1980	USSR continues its invasion of Afghanistan Rhodesia gains independence and becomes the new republic of Zimbabwe Lech Walesa becomes leader of Polish trade union, Solidarity Iraq invades Iran, starting a war that lasts until 1988 and kills more than a million Mariel boat lift brings tens of thousands of Cubans to Florida Ronald Reagan elected president	*The Name of the Rose*, Umberto Eco (fiction) *Amadeus*, Shaffer (play)	*Cosmos* TV series with scientist and educator Carl Sagan on PBS Home dish antennas to receive TV signals from satellites begin to gain in popularity Cable News Network (CNN) begins U.S. TV networks begin to offer some captioning for hearing-impaired viewers First interactive videodisc: *How to Watch Pro Football*	*Raging Bull*, Scorsese *Atlantic City*, Louis Malle *Melvin and Howard*, Jonathan Demme *The Empire Strikes Back*, Irvin Kershner *The Shining*, Kubrick *Berlin Alexanderplatz*, Fassbinder (TV miniseries later shown in theaters) *Moscow Does Not Believe in Tears*, Vladimir Menshev *Kagemusha*, Kurosawa *Model*, Wiseman (documentary) *(The Life and Times of) Rosie the Riveter*, Connie Field (documentary)
1981	Iran releases remaining U.S. hostages First U.S. space shuttle successfully flown Scientists first identify AIDS Sandra Day O'Connor becomes first female U.S. Supreme Court justice Some Egyptian soldiers assassinate Egyptian President Anwar Sadat	*Sixty Stories*, Donald Barthelme (fiction) *A Soldier's Play*, Charles Fuller (play)	Walter Cronkite retires from regular TV broadcasting *Hill Street Blues*, TV show, (1981–87) Highest rated TV show (1981–82): *Dallas* MTV, a 24-hour-a-day music video channel, begins	*Zoot Suit*, Valdez (first Chicano Hollywood film) *Gallipoli*, Weir *Pixote*, Hector Babenco *Das Boot (The Boat)*, Wolfgang Petersen *Céleste*, Percy Adlon *Mephisto*, Istvan Szabo "Ancient of Days," Viola (experimental videos, 1979–81)

	World Events	Arts	Mass Media	Films and Videos
1982	Argentina invades Falkland Islands, resulting in a war won by Britain Maya Lin's Vietnam Veterans' War Memorial, with 58,000 etched American names, dedicated in Washington, D.C. First permanent implant of a mechanical heart in a human	*The Color Purple*, Alice Walker (fiction) *Schindler's Ark*, Thomas Keneally (nonfiction) *Cats*, Andrew Lloyd Webber and Trevor Nunn (musical that opens on Broadway) Popular songs: "Eye of the Tiger," from the film *Rocky III* and the "Chariots of Fire" melody from the film of that title	28 million U.S. homes have cable TV *Cagney and Lacey*, TV show (1982–88) *Cheers*, TV show (1982–93) *USA Today*, newspaper available nationwide, begins publication Computer technology used to make images of settings and props for the film *Tron* Digital audio CDs first marketed	*Tootsie*, Sydney Pollack *E.T., The Extraterrestrial*, Spielberg *Blade Runner*, Ridley Scott *Fanny and Alexander*, Bergman *Night of the Shooting Stars*, Paola and Vittorio Taviani *Fitzcarraldo*, Herzog *Lola*, Fassbinder *Wend Kuuni (God's Gift)*, Gaston Kaboré *Burden of Dreams*, Blank (documentary) "Reassemblage," Trinh T. Minh-ha (experimental documentary) "Tides," Amy Greenfield (experimental)
1983	President Reagan backs Contra rebels in their war with Marxist Nicaraguan government U.S. troops are sent into Grenada International introduction of highly addictive and destructive drug "crack cocaine"	American Telephone and Telegraph Building in New York City designed by Philip Johnson and John Burgee and regarded as an important postmodernist structure	*The Day After*, a TV movie about nuclear war, is seen by half of U.S. adults Final episode of TV show *M*A*S*H* seen by an estimated 50 million HBO begins producing feature films First civilian cellular phones hit the market	*El Norte*, Gregory Nava *Betrayal*, David Jones *Local Hero*, Bill Forsyth *Entre nous*, Diane Kurys *Eréndira*, Ruy Guerra *Koyaanisqatsi*, Godfrey Reggio (experimental documentary)
1984	Apple Macintosh computer first sold Indian army troops invade Sikh temple and kill 1,000 Sikh fundamentalists using the temple as a haven and headquarters	*The Lover*, Marguerite Duras (fiction) *Love in the Time of Cholera*, García Márquez (fiction)	PG-13 film rating begins *The Cosby Show*, TV show (1984–92) *Murder, She Wrote*, TV show (1984–96)	*Stranger Than Paradise*, Jim Jarmusch *This Is Spinal Tap*, Rob Reiner *Blood Simple*, first film directed by Joel Coen *Frida*, Paul Leduc

	World Events	Arts	Mass Media	Films and Videos
1984 (cont'd)	Indian Prime Minister Indira Gandhi assassinated Ethiopia-Eritrea war, disease, and famine kill 1 million	*The Unbearable Lightness of Being*, Milan Kundera (fiction) *The House on Mango Street*, Sandra Cisneros (fiction) Soundtrack for *Purple Rain* is a huge success	U.S. Supreme Court rules that noncommercial private home videotaping of off-the-air programs is legal Criterion (company) releases *Citizen Kane* on laser videodisc	*Paris, Texas*, Wim Wenders *Yellow Earth*, Chen Kaige *The Times of Harvey Milk*, Robert Epstein (documentary) "In Heaven There Is No Beer?," Blank (documentary) *Marlene*, Maximilian Schell (documentary) "Thriller," Michael Jackson (video)
1985	Gorbachev becomes Soviet general secretary Rock Hudson, movie star, first known celebrity to die of AIDS Gorbachev and Reagan meet for a summit in Geneva Marxist Sandinistas gain control of Nicaragua; U.S. continues to support the Contra rebels The year is marked by terrorist hijackings, bombings, kidnappings, and murder, including at airports in Rome and Vienna	*The Handmaid's Tale*, Margaret Atwood (fiction) *Black Robe*, Brian Moore (fiction) *Old Gringo*, Fuentes (fiction) *The Accidental Tourist*, Anne Tyler (fiction) *Les Liaisons Dangereuses*, Christopher Hampton (play) *Les Misérables*, Alain Boublil and Claude-Michel Schönberg (musical)	Home movie video revenues exceed those of theatrical revenues Sundance Film Festival founded by Robert Redford to promote independent films First 3-D IMAX film shown, in Japan *Desert Hearts*, first lesbian love story on film to obtain mainstream distribution First laser videodisc players and videodiscs having digital sound	*Prizzi's Honor*, Huston *The Purple Rose of Cairo*, Allen *My Life as a Dog*, Lasse Hallström *Vagabond*, Agnès Varda *The Official Story*, Luis Puenzo *Ran*, Kurosawa *Shoah*, Claude Lanzmann (documentary) *George Stevens: A Film Maker's Journey*, George Stevens Jr. (documentary) *The Man Who Envied Women*, Rainer (experimental) *Naked Spaces: Living Is Round*, Minh-ha (experimental documentary) "Standard Gauge," Fisher (experimental)
1986 (cont'd on next page)	U.S. space shuttle *Challenger* explodes shortly after lift-off, killing entire crew	*Paco's Story*, Larry Heinemann (fiction) *A Summons to Memphis*, Peter Taylor (fiction)	Colorization of videos of older black-and-white films is controversial *L.A. Law*, TV show (1986–94) *The Oprah Winfrey Show*, TV talk show, begins	*Blue Velvet*, David Lynch *Platoon*, Oliver Stone *True Stories*, David Byrne *Mona Lisa*, Neil Jordan *Tampopo*, Juzo Itami *Sherman's March*, Ross McElwee (documentary)

	World Events	Arts	Mass Media	Films and Videos
1986 (cont'd)	Haitian dictator Jean-Claude Duvalier ousted by revolution and flees the country Corazon Aquino declared the winner of Philippine presidential election and President Ferdinand Marcos flees into exile Soviets orbit first long-term space station, *Mir* Nuclear accident at Chernobyl, Ukraine, pollutes Europe President Reagan admits that subordinates sold weapons illegally to Iran to raise money for Nicaraguan rebels 25,000 AIDS cases diagnosed in U.S.	*Phantom of the Opera*, Andrew Lloyd Webber and Charles Hart (musical)	Highest rated TV show (1986–89): *The Cosby Show* *Calvin and Hobbes* comic strip begins Nintendo video game system hits U.S. market	*Mother Teresa*, Ann and Jeanette Petrie (documentary) *Rate It X*, Lucy Winer and Paula De Koenigsberg (documentary) *Private Practices: The Story of a Sex Surrogate*, Kirby Dick (documentary) *Home of the Brave*, Laurie Anderson (documentary) "Street of Crocodiles," Timothy and Stephen Quay (experimental fiction)
1987	World population: 5 billion Iran-Contra congressional report faults President Reagan Gorbachev and Reagan sign a treaty banning all short- and medium-range nuclear weapons in Europe	*The Bonfire of the Vanities*, Wolfe (fiction) *Beloved*, Toni Morrison (fiction) *Fences*, August Wilson (play) *Driving Miss Daisy*, Alfred Uhry (play) Soundtrack for *Dirty Dancing* is a huge hit	Home videotape rentals in U.S. continue to grow Iran-Contra congressional hearings televised live *Eyes on the Prize*, TV series on the civil rights movement, shown on PBS	*The Dead*, Huston *Full Metal Jacket*, Kubrick *The Last Emperor*, Bertolucci *Red Sorghum*, Zhang Yimou *A Taxing Woman*, Itami *Yeelen (Brightness)*, Souleymane Cissé "Damned If You Don't," Su Friedrich (experimental fiction)
1988	Soviet troops begin retreat from Afghanistan	*The Satanic Verses*, Salman Rushdie (fiction)	Morphing first used in making parts of a feature film, *Willow*	*The Unbearable Lightness of Being*, Philip Kaufman

	World Events	Arts	Mass Media	Films and Videos
1988 (cont'd)	UN mediates ceasefire between Iran and Iraq; Iraq attacks rebelling Kurds Uprising by Palestinians in West Bank and Gaza Strip Crack cocaine increasingly used in U.S. cities Vice President George Bush elected president	(condemned by Muslim fundamentalists, who force Rushdie into hiding) *The Player*, Michael Tolkin (fiction) *The Heidi Chronicles*, Wendy Wasserstein (play) *Buster Keaton*, Jeff Koons (wood sculpture)	*P.O.V.* series of documentary films begins on PBS *Roseanne*, TV show (1988–94) TNT cable network founded *Oxford English Dictionary* becomes available on CD-ROM Apple Macintosh with CD-ROM player can play music CDs	*The Last Temptation of Christ*, Scorsese *Dangerous Liaisons*, Stephen Frears *Little Vera*, Vasily Pichul *Saaraba* (*Utopia*), Amadou Seck *The Thin Blue Line*, Morris (documentary) *Comic Book Confidential*, Ron Mann (documentary) *Hotel Terminus, The Life and Times of Klaus Barbie*, Ophüls (documentary)
1989	In Czechoslovakia, large peaceful opposition to Soviet dominance Prodemocracy students occupy Tiananmen Square in Beijing; two months later, government uses tanks to disperse them; thousands believed killed Berlin Wall torn down Playwright Vaclav Havel becomes president of Czechoslovakia	*The Mambo Kings Play Songs of Love*, Oscar Hijuelos (fiction) *The General in His Labyrinth*, García Márquez (fiction) *The Joy Luck Club*, Amy Tan (fiction) *Remains of the Day*, Kazuo Ishiguro *When Harry Met Sally*, popular film soundtrack	U.S. National Film Registry established to recognize significant American films; the first group announced includes *Citizen Kane* and *Casablanca* Time, Inc. buys Warner Communications, creating the world's largest entertainment group Sony Corporation purchases Columbia Pictures (thereby securing film production, distribution, and exhibition) and promotes its films in print and TV media under Sony's control Most popular TV shows (1989–90): *Roseanne* and *The Cosby Show*	*Drugstore Cowboy*, Gus Van Sant *Mystery Train*, Jarmusch *Do the Right Thing*, Spike Lee *sex, lies, and videotape*, Steven Soderbergh *The Little Mermaid* (Disney animation) *Lawrence of Arabia*, rereleased in revised and restored version *My Left Foot*, Jim Sheridan *The Killer*, John Woo *Yaaba*, Idrissa Ouedraogo *Roger & Me*, Michael Moore (satirical documentary) "You Take Care Now," Ann Marie Fleming (experimental documentary)

	World Events	Arts	Mass Media	Films and Videos
1990	Mandela freed from prison in South Africa Yugoslavia moving toward split-up Boris Yeltsin resigns from Soviet Communist Party Iraq invades Kuwait; various diplomatic solutions sought Germany reunited Walesa elected Poland's president Haiti holds first democratic elections	*The Snapper*, Roddy Doyle (fiction) *Possession: A Romance*, A. S. Byatt (fiction) *Orphée*, Philip Glass (music) and Jean Cocteau (libretto, screenplay for his film of the same title) *Mo' Better Blues*, Branford Marsalis (music from film of same title)	NC-17 rating instituted; *Henry and June* first film so rated *The Civil War*, 11-hour TV documentary on PBS, directed by Ken Burns *Twin Peaks*, TV show directed by David Lynch *Billboard* announces that home video movie revenue is now twice that of theatrical box offices	*GoodFellas*, Scorsese *Reversal of Fortune*, Barbet Schroeder *To Sleep with Anger*, Charles Burnett *The Grifters*, Frears *Life Is Sweet*, Mike Leigh *Ju Dou*, Zhang *Tilaï*, Ouedraogo *Finzan: A Dance for the Heroes*, Cheick Oumar Sissoko *Berkeley in the Sixties*, Mark Kitchell (documentary) *Paris Is Burning*, Jennie Livingston (documentary) *Privilege*, Rainer (experimental fiction)
1991	U.S. and its UN allies defeat Iraq in 100-hour battle and free Kuwait Rajiv Gandhi, prime minister of India, assassinated Boris Yeltsin elected president of Russia Bosnia and Herzegovina, parts of former Yugoslavia, wage civil war Coup against Gorbachev fails, Communist rule ends in the USSR, and cold war ends	*The Sweet Hereafter*, Russell Banks (fiction) *Maus II: A Survivor's Tale: And Here My Troubles Began*, Art Spiegelman (pictorial fiction) *Lost in Yonkers*, Simon (play)	Morphing used in parts of *Terminator 2* to show the transformation of a character into various other characters Highest-rated TV show (1990–91): *Cheers*	*Europa, Europa*, Agnieszka Holland *Raise the Red Lantern*, Zhang *Sango Malo* (*The Village Teacher*), Bassek ba Kobhio *Hearts of Darkness: A Filmmaker's Apocalypse*, Fax Bahr and George Hickenlooper (documentary) "First Comes Love," Friedrich (experimental documentary)

	World Events	Arts	Mass Media	Films and Videos
1992	Jury in Rodney King's state trial finds police defendants not guilty; parts of Los Angeles riot, leading to 58 dead and hundreds of millions of dollars in property damage USSR divides into fifteen nations, including Russia Leader of the Peruvian terrorist group The Shining Path is arrested Thousands die in Muslim-Hindu conflict in India Arkansas Governor Bill Clinton elected president	*All the Pretty Horses*, Cormac McCarthy (fiction) *The English Patient: A Novel*, Michael Ondaatje (fiction) *Angels in America*, Tony Kushner (two-part play) Soundtrack with Whitney Houston from *The Bodyguard* becomes best-selling soundtrack of all time	Johnny Carson retires as host of *The Tonight Show* (TV) and is replaced by Jay Leno Internet begins with the "Internet Society," a collection of 1 million linked host computers	*Unforgiven*, Clint Eastwood *The Player*, Altman *Reservoir Dogs*, Quentin Tarantino *Like Water for Chocolate*, Alfonso Arau *The Crying Game*, Jordan *Quartier Mozart*, Jean-Pierre Bekolo *Guelwaar*, Sembène *A Brief History of Time*, Morris (documentary) *Brother's Keeper*, Joe Berlinger and Bruce Sinofsky (documentary) "Women Who Made the Movies," Gwendolyn Foster and Wheeler Dixon (documentary) *Visions of Light: The Art of Cinematography*, Arnold Glassman, Todd McCarthy, and Stuart Samuels (documentary)
1993	Israel and PLO formally recognize each other Despite outside diplomatic pressures, parties in former Yugoslavia continue fighting Czechoslovakia divides into Czech Republic and Slovakia Agents of the Bureau of Alcohol, Tobacco, and Firearms attempt to enter the cult Branch Davidians compound in Waco, Texas; gunfights end in fatal fire	*The Shipping News*, E. Anne Proulx (fiction) *Before Night Falls*, Reinaldo Arenas (fiction) *Jesus' Son*, Denis Johnson (fiction) *Arcadia*, Stoppard (play) *Full Moon*, Bill Irwin and David Shiner (mime) *Marilyn*, Ezra Laderman (opera about Marilyn Monroe)	Last original *Cheers* episode draws record TV audience *The X-Files* first airs, on Fox Network	*Schindler's List*, Spielberg *Short Cuts*, Altman *The Ballad of Little Jo*, Maggie Greenwald *Orlando*, Potter *Naked*, Leigh *The Piano*, Jane Campion *Farewell My Concubine*, Chen *(Tim Burton's) The Nightmare before Christmas*, Henry Selick (animation) *Thirty-Two Short Films about Glenn Gould*, François Girard (documentary) *The Wonderful, Horrible Life of Leni Riefenstahl*, Ray Müller (documentary) *Blue*, Derek Jarman (experimental)

	World Events	Arts	Mass Media	Films and Videos
1994	Civil wars in Yemen, Georgia (part of former USSR), and Rwanda Mandela elected president in first multiracial South African election People from Chechnya, a southern Russian republic, seek independence from Russia and begin protracted guerrilla warfare U.S.-led occupation of Haiti leads to reinstatement of democratically elected president World Trade Center bombed in first foreign terrorist attack on U.S. soil Channel Tunnel (Chunnel) links Britain and France Mexican Indian guerrillas in southern state of Chiapas demand more land and self-rule; Mexican ruling party candidate assassinated and replaced by Ernesto Zedillo, later elected president	*Felicia's Journey*, William Trevor (fiction) *The Ice Storm*, Rick Moody (fiction) *Trainspotting*, Irvine Welsh (fiction) *The Hour We Knew Nothing of Each Other*, Peter Handke (100-minute wordless play with sound effects) *La belle et la bête*, Cocteau's film without soundtrack but with supertitles and live music composed by Philip Glass ("an opera for ensemble and film") *The Dangerous Liaisons*, Conrad Susa and Philip Littell (opera) Soundtrack for *The Lion King* is a huge hit Andy Warhol Museum opens in Pittsburgh	Steven Spielberg, Jeffrey Katzenberg, and David Geffen form DreamWorks SKG to produce theatrical films, animation, television programs, records, and interactive media Independent Film Channel offered on some cable systems (Short) IMAX 3-D films shown in U.S. (previously shown in Japan and Europe) More than 80% of all U.S. households have at least one VCR Marketing films first in video and perhaps later to theaters is a small trend DirectTV, Digital TV, offers multiple channels from a satellite Megaplexing of the U.S. begins when AMC Entertainment opens a megaplex in Dallas	*Pulp Fiction*, Tarantino *Vanya on 42nd Street*, Malle *Ed Wood*, Tim Burton *Natural Born Killers*, Stone *Exotica*, Atom Egoyan *Il Postino (The Postman)*, Michael Radford *Red*, Krzysztof Kieslowski *Burnt by the Sun*, Nikita Mikhalkov *To Live*, Zhang *Eat Drink Man Woman*, Ang Lee *The Lion King*, Disney animation *High School II*, Wiseman (documentary) *Crumb*, Terry Zwigoff (documentary) *The Troubles We've Seen*, Ophüls (documentary) *Hoop Dreams*, Steve James (documentary) *Carmen Miranda: Bananas Is My Business*, Helena Solberg (documentary) "A Great Day in Harlem," Jean Bach (documentary) "Cremaster 4," Matthew Barney (first of five experimental films)
1995	American astronauts dock with Russian space station *Mir* and work with cosmonauts	*Seven Guitars*, Wilson (play) *Rent*, Jonathan Larson (musical)	*Toy Story* is first feature film made entirely with computer animation	*Welcome to the Dollhouse*, Todd Solondz *A Little Princess*, Alfonso Cuarón *To Die For*, Van Sant

	World Events	Arts	Mass Media	Films and Videos
1995 (cont'd)	Separate terrorists use gas in Japan and a bomb in Oklahoma City to kill civilians U.S.-brokered peace plan for Bosnia-Herzegovina agreed to by presidents of Serbia, Bosnia, and Croatia Yitzhak Rabin, Israeli prime minister, assassinated by right-wing Israeli radical	Untitled 8½-by-11-inch film-related stills, Cindy Sherman *24 Frames per Second*, Bill T. Jones and Lyon Opera Ballet (dance homage to the Lumière Brothers, early French filmmakers)	Percentage of Americans reading a newspaper daily continues its decades-long decline Two studies show that the average American continues to spend more on books each year than on recorded music or home videos Disney and Capital Cities/ABC merge and form world's largest media company *Calvin and Hobbes* comic strip ends	*Richard III*, Richard Loncraine *Babe*, Chris Noonan *Hate*, Mathieu Kassovitz *Black is . . . Black ain't*, Marlon T. Riggs (documentary) *Orson Welles: The One-Man Band*, Vassili Silovic (documentary) *Theremin: An Electronic Odyssey*, Steven M. Martin (documentary) "A Cinema of Unease," Sam Neill and Judy Rymer (documentary on cinema of New Zealand) "Buried Secrets," Viola (experimental video and audio)
1996 (cont'd on next page)	Boris Yeltsin reelected president of Russia War and famine in Eastern Zaire kill massive numbers of people Suicide bombings by militant Muslims kill 61 in Israel, hamper peace talks, and contribute to election defeat of Israel's ruling party Unabomber captured and convicted after 17-year U.S. bombing spree Bomb explodes during Olympics in Atlanta, Ga.	*Angela's Ashes: A Memoir*, Frank McCourt (nonfiction) *The Tailor of Panama*, John Le Carré (fiction) *Last Orders*, Graham Swift (fiction) *In the Beauty of the Lilies*, Updike (fiction)	Sundance (independent) Channel offered on some cable and satellite systems *The Phil Donahue Show* (TV talk show) ends Federal Communications Commission standards for digital TVs include wider screens and sharper pictures than analog TVs 45 million people using the Internet, two-thirds of them in North America	*Fargo*, Coen *The English Patient*, Anthony Minghella *Trainspotting*, Danny Boyle *Secrets & Lies*, Leigh *Breaking the Waves*, Lars von Trier *Shall We Dance?*, Masayuki Suo *Hide and Seek*, Friedrich (fiction and documentary) *The Celluloid Closet*, Rob Epstein and Jeffrey Friedman (documentary) *A Personal Journey with Martin Scorsese through American Movies* (documentary) *The Devil Never Sleeps*, Lourdes Portillo (documentary)

	World Events	**Arts**	**Mass Media**	**Films and Videos**
1996 (cont'd)				*Lumière and Company*, Sarah Moon (documentary of 40 films, each by a different director, each less than a minute long and shot on the Lumière Brothers' original 1895 camera) *Sergei Eisenstein: Autobiography*, Oleg Kovalov (documentary) "Trouble in the Image," O'Neill (experimental)
1997	China's top leader, Deng Xiaoping, dies Scottish embryologist announces sheep cloning Labor Party's Tony Blair becomes U.K. prime minister and ends 18 years of Conservative rule Rebel forces capture the rest of Zaire; longtime dictator Mobutu Sese Seko flees into exile; country is renamed Democratic Republic of Congo and, later, Congo Britain returns control of Hong Kong to China, ending 156 years of British rule Unmanned *Pathfinder* lands on Mars; first mobile explorer of another planet sends data and photographs to earth	*Cold Mountain*, Charles Frazier (fiction) *American Pastoral*, Roth (fiction) *How I Learned to Drive*, Paula Vogel (play) *The Lion King*—a Disney musical based on the film and designed and directed by Julie Taymor—opens on Broadway Soundtrack for *Titanic* is a huge success *Film Noir*, Carly Simon (CD)	*Star Wars* revised slightly, rereleased to theaters, and passes *E.T.* as highest-grossing movie in history (until *Titanic* passes it in 1998) 413 movies released in the U.S., 125 more than in 1987 U.S. movie box office receipts set record Los Angeles Latino International Film Festival begins Broadcast and cable networks begin using a four-part age-based rating system for most of their programs Digital video disks (DVDs) and DVD players first marketed in the U.S., but not all studios agree to market their films on them; most of the DVD players also play music CDs	*L.A. Confidential*, Curtis Hanson *The Ice Storm*, Ang Lee *Eve's Bayou*, Kasi Lemmons *The Apostle*, Robert Duvall *The Sweet Hereafter*, Egoyan *The Full Monty*, Peter Cattaneo *The Wings of the Dove*, Iain Softley "T.R.A.N.S.I.T.," Piet Kroon (animation) *Will It Snow for Christmas?*, Sandrine Veysset *Life Is Beautiful*, Roberto Benigni *The Eel*, Shohei Imamura *Taste of Cherry*, Abbas Kiarostami *Welcome Back, Mr. McDonald*, Koki Mitani *Princess Mononoke*, Hayao Miyazaki (animation) *Fast, Cheap & Out of Control*, Morris (documentary) *Public Housing*, Wiseman (documentary) *Waco: The Rules of Engagement*, William Gazecki (documentary)

	World Events	Arts	Mass Media	Films and Videos
1997 (cont'd)	Algerian Islamic extremists continue to massacre civilians; more than 60,000 killed since 1992		Compaq introduces the PC theater: combination of computer and large-screen TV More than 31,000 movie screens in the U.S.	"2 or 3 Things But Nothing for Sure," Tina DiFeliciantonio and Jane C. Wagner (experimental documentary) "Bill Viola: Trilogy (Fire, Water, Breath)" (experimental installations)
1998 (cont'd on next page)	In Kosovo, the ethnic Albanian majority demands greater autonomy from Serb-dominated Yugoslavia Ireland, Britain, and the U.S. broker peace settlement for Northern Ireland, which Irish voters later accept President Suharto of Indonesia is forced to step down after 32 years in power Asian economic crisis continues to worsen and to hurt world economies Terrorist bombs near U.S. embassies in Kenya and Tanzania kill 258 India and Pakistan, declared enemies, conduct independent nuclear tests The U.S. and Britain bomb Iraqi targets in retaliation for Iraq's failure to cooperate with the U.N. weapons inspections	*Cloudsplitter: A Novel*, Banks *The Hours*, Michael Cunningham (fiction) *A Beautiful Mind*, Sylvia Nasar (biography of John Forbes Nash Jr.) *Wit*, Margaret Edson (play) *Art*, Yasmina Reza (play) *Elaborate Lives: The Legend of Aida*, Tim Rice and Elton John (first Disney musical not based on a film)	*Titanic* passes *Star Wars* as the highest-grossing movie in history, but *Gone with the Wind* has sold more tickets *Seinfeld* TV show airs its last episode Adrian Lyne's film version of *Lolita* is shown in the U.S.—first on Showtime Survey reveals that Internet use is up (an estimated 30 to 60 million users); TV- and VCR-watching and reading are all down Ticket sales for summer movies set U.S. record Four interactive movies released on DVD allow viewers to periodically choose plot developments Some high-definition television reception becomes available in more than 30 U.S. cities	*The Truman Show*, Weir *Happiness*, Solondz *Smoke Signals*, Chris Eyre *The Big Lebowski*, Coen *Touch of Evil* (1958) rereleased in a revised and restored version *Croupier*, Mike Hodges *Run Lola Run*, Tom Tykwer *Dreamlife of Angels*, Erick Zonca *Central Station*, Walter Salles *The Terrorist* (a.k.a. *Malli*), Santosh Sivan *Best Man*, Wohl (documentary sequel) *Wild Man Blues*, Kopple (documentary about Woody Allen) "Everest," David Breashears, Stephen Judson, and Greg MacGillivray (documentary initially shown in IMAX theaters) *Divorce Iranian Style*, Kim Longinotto and Ziba Mir-Hosseini (documentary) *The Farm: Angola U.S.A.*, Liz Garbus, Jonathan Stack, and Wilbert Rideau (documentary) "Human Remains," Jay Rosenblatt (documentary)

	World Events	Arts	Mass Media	Films and Videos
1998 (cont'd)				"Mother and Son," Alexander Sokurov (experimental)
1999	President Clinton impeached by U.S. House of Representatives but acquitted by Senate King Abdullah succeeds King Hussein of Jordan NATO sends ground forces into former Yugoslavia to protect the ethnic Albanian majority in Kosovo, and bombs Serbia Earthquakes kill 21,000 in Turkey United Nations declares East Timor independent of Indonesia; pro-Indonesian forces attack the new nation For the second time in a decade, Russia launches a major military offensive against separatist guerillas in Chechnya U.S. turns control of Panama Canal over to Panama Russian President Yeltsin resigns, succeeded by Vladimir Putin	*House of Sand and Fog*, Andre Dubus III (fiction) *Interpreter of Maladies*, Jhumpa Lahiri (fiction) *A Star Called Henry*, Doyle (fiction) *Close Range: Wyoming Stories*, Proulx (fiction) *Dinner with Friends*, Donald Margulies (play) *Betty's Summer Vacation*, Christopher Durang (play) *Songs and Stories from "Moby Dick,"* Laurie Anderson (stage multimedia production) Score for video reissue of the 1931 *Dracula*, Philip Glass *Jazz in Film*, Terence Blanchard (CD)	Highest summer movie revenues ever: $2.9 billion Nearly 91% of U.S. homes have a VCR; most have more than one *Big Brother* premieres in Europe, reality-based TV show features 9 people living under total surveillance for 100 days *The Sopranos*, TV show, is critical and popular success Video game software sales reach $6.2 billion, $1.1 billion dollars less than domestic movie box office revenues DVD audio and super CD recorded audio formats become available 150 million Internet users worldwide; over half are in the U.S. Digital projection (using computer equipment, prisms, and liquid crystal arrays) used to show *Star Wars: Episode 1* on selected standard theatrical screens	*Boys Don't Cry*, Kimberly Peirce *American Beauty*, Sam Mendes *The Matrix*, Andy and Larry Wachowski *Three Kings*, David O. Russell "George Lucas in Love," Joe Nussbaum (first shown on Internet) *Titus*, Julie Taymor *Topsy-Turvy*, Leigh *Il Mio Viaggio in Italia* (*My Journey to Italy*), Scorsese (documentary about postwar Italian films) *American Movie*, Chris Smith (documentary) *Buena Vista Social Club*, Wenders (documentary) *Keeper of the Frame*, Mark McLaughlin (documentary on film preservation and restoration) *Mr. Death: The Rise and Fall of Fred A. Leuchter Jr.*, Morris (documentary) *Belfast, Maine*, Wiseman (documentary) *Genghis Blues*, Roko Belic (documentary) *My Best Fiend: Klaus Kinski*, Herzog (documentary) *Cinéma vérité*, Peter Wintonick (a documentary about the documentary)

	World Events	Arts	Mass Media	Films and Videos
1999 (cont'd)			Silent American film classic *Greed* partially restored with inclusion of still photographs and premiered on *Turner Classic Movies* Disney's *Fantasia/2000* is first feature-length studio film produced for IMAX	"Encounter in the Third Dimension," Ben Strassen (documentary about 3-D films) "Negative Space," Christopher Petit (documentary) "Soliloquy," Shirin Neshat (film installation) "In Camera," Edward Stewart and Stephanie Smith (experimental) "Outer Space," Peter Tscherassky (experimental)
2000 (cont'd on next page)	Putin is elected president of Russia Former Chilean dictator Augusto Pinochet is ruled physically unfit to be extradited to Spain on charges of human rights abuses and is returned to Chile after four years of house arrest in Great Britain Long-time Syrian president Hafez al-Assad dies; succeeded by his son Human genome, the entire genetic code for a human being, mapped in a rough draft Yugoslav President Milosevic steps down from office after domestic protests, general strikes, and international appeals	*Blonde: A Novel*, Joyce Carol Oates (fiction based on Marilyn Monroe) *The Blind Assassin*, Atwood (fiction) *Cats*, Webber and Nunn, longest-running Broadway production, closes after a nearly 18-year run *Dead Man Walking*, Jake Heggie and Terrence McNally (opera) *Nighthawks*, Lynn Rosen (play based on Edward Hopper paintings)	Final original install-ment of *Peanuts* comic strip; thereafter past installments are reprinted First mass-market suc-cess in e-book format is Stephen King's *Riding the Bullet* *Life* magazine ceases publication (again) "Quantum Project," first major film production developed exclusively for Internet distribution "The New Arrival," first film allowing viewers to navigate around characters and props, shown at Cannes and later on the Internet "Dickson Experimental Sound Film" (approximately 1890) reunited with original, restored sound	*You Can Count on Me*, Kenneth Lonergan *Memento*, Christopher Nolan *Gladiator*, Scott *State and Main*, David Mamet *Shadow of the Vampire*, E. Elias Merhige *Cecil B. DeMented*, John Waters *Before Night Falls*, Julian Schnabel *Girlfight*, Karyn Kusama *George Washington*, David Gordon Green *Ratcatcher*, Lynn Ramsay *Amores perros*, Alejandro González Iñárritu *Faithless*, Liv Ullmann *Aimee and Jaguar*, Max Fäberböck *Beau Travail*, Claire Denis *Murderous Maids*, Jean-Pierre Denis *Blackboards*, Samira Makhmalbaf *The Circle*, Jafar Panahi

	World Events	Arts	Mass Media	Films and Videos
2000 (cont'd)	More than a month after a close election, Texas Governor George W. Bush declared U.S. president-elect The worst drought in 100 years strikes India, affecting about 130 million people In Mexican presidential election, Vicente Fox of the National Action Party defeats the candidate from the PRI, the political party in power since its founding in 1929		Museo Nazionale del Cinema in Turin, Italy opens, the world's biggest cinema museum *Time Code*, one of first major feature films recorded entirely with digital technology More than half of all U.S. households have a computer U.S. has 37,000 movie theater screens; number of foreign screens is about four times more Foreign cinema revenues now make up 55 percent of U.S. film industry income Modest, critically acclaimed films often earn much more in video than initial theatrical release; *Boys Don't Cry*, for example, takes in $3.7 million in the theaters but $17.5 million in 10 weeks of video rentals	*Yi-Yi* (a.k.a. *A One and a Two*), Edward Yang *In the Mood for Love*, Wong Kar-wai *Crouching Tiger, Hidden Dragon*, Ang Lee *Dark Days*, Marc Singer (documentary) *Divine Trash*, Steve Yeager (documentary) *Calle 54*, Fernando Trueba (documentary) "The God of Day Had Gone Down Upon Him," Brakhage (experimental) "Kyupi Kyupi I++," Kyupi Kyupi (a Japanese artists' collective) (experimental laserdisc)
2001	Democratic reformer, Zoran Djindjic, becomes prime minister of Serbia NATO forces collect arms from rebel forces in Macedonia, preventing civil war	*True History of the Kelly Gang*, Peter Carey (fiction) *Proof*, David Auburn (play)	The Academy Awards includes new category: Best Animated Feature Film	*Apocalypse Now Redux*, Coppola (expanded and rereleased film) *Mulholland Drive*, Lynch *Gosford Park*, Altman *The Lord of the Rings: The Fellowship of the Ring*, Peter Jackson

	World Events	Arts	Mass Media	Films and Videos
2001 (cont'd)	Mexico wins seat on UN Security Council The U.S. places severe restrictions on human cloning U.S. submarine accidentally strikes and sinks a Japanese fishing boat, killing nine Terrorists highjack four airliners, crashing two into the Twin Towers of the World Trade Center in New York, which collapse, and one into the Pentagon; the fourth plane crashes in Pennsylvania after passengers attempt to wrest control from the terrorists. These terrorist acts constitute the most destructive attack on U.S. soil in history U.S. postal system used by person or persons unknown to deliver anthrax spores to media companies and governmental centers The U.S. and Great Britain go to war in Afghanistan, and ruling Taliban government is toppled Energy trading giant Enron declares bankruptcy amid accusations of massive financial wrongdoing	The San Francisco Museum of Modern Art and the Whitney Museum hold first large-scale exhibitions of "digital art" *The Producers* (Mel Brooks), the Broadway musical based on the film of the same name, wins the Tony for best musical	DVD-RW (computer) drive allows a user who has transferred digital footage into the computer to then burn it on a DVD; with the DVD-RW drive, one can also play or record regular music and data CDs and play DVD movies Microsoft settles its antitrust case with the federal courts and avoids being broken up into smaller companies XM Radio launches the first digital satellite radio service nationwide, offering 100 channels of music, news, sports, and entertainment USA Patriot Act grants U.S. law-enforcement agencies sweeping powers to intercept computer communications	*Ghost World*, Zwigoff *Lantana*, Ray Lawrence *A ma soeur!*, Catherine Breillat *How I Killed My Father*, Anne Fontaine *No Man's Land*, Danis Tanovic *Kandahar*, Mohsen Makhmalbaf *Monsoon Wedding*, Mira Nair *Lan Yu*, Stanley Kwan *Shrek*, Andrew Adamson and Vicky Jenson (animation) *Waking Life*, Linklater (animation) *Spirited Away*, Miyazaki (animation) *Decasia*, Bill Morrison (documentary) *Startup.com*, Chris Hegedus and Jehane Noujaim (documentary) *The Endurance: Shackelton's Legendary Antarctic Expedition*, George Butler (documentary) "Shackelton's Antarctic Adventure," George Butler (IMAX documentary) *As I Was Moving ahead Occasionally I Saw Brief Glimpses of Beauty*, Jonas Mekas (documentary)

	World Events	Arts	Mass Media	Films and Videos
2002	Terrorist leader Osama Bin Laden continues to evade capture by the U.S. government The Taliban largely overthrown in Afghanistan; U.S. bombing raids continue to target al Qaeda terrorists; Hamid Karzai elected Afghan head of state as the country attempts to rebuild The war on terror gathers momentum and President Bush turns his attention to Iraqi leader Saddam Hussein UN food agency warns that more than 38 million Africans face the prospect of famine Child sex abuse claims against the Catholic Church make headlines Enron and WorldCom are at the center of a corporate governance scandal; world markets slump and investor confidence plummets World leaders turn a concerned look to North Korea after the communist state admits having a secret nuclear weapons program	*Atonement*, Ian McEwan (fiction) *Three Junes*, Julia Glass (fiction) *Hairspray* (musical), based on the 1988 John Waters's movie of the same name, opens on Broadway *Def Poetry Jam* with its hip-hop poets is a hit on Broadway	For the year, DVD sales were $8.7 billion and rental revenue was $2.9 billion More than $9 billion worth of movie tickets were sold in North America for the year; actual attendance reached levels not seen since Eisenhower was president More than 80% of U.S. households subscribe to cable or satellite service *The X-Files* TV series ends	*About Schmidt*, Alexander Payne *Adaptation*, Spike Jonze *All or Nothing*, Leigh *City of God*, Fernando Meirelles *Y tu mamá también*, Cuarón *Talk to Her*, Almodóvar *The Man without a Past*, Aki Kaurismaki *Hotel*, Mike Figgis (experimental fiction) "Baadassss Cinema," Isaac Julien (documentary about blaxploitation films) *The Kid Stays in the Picture*, Brett Morgen and Nanette Burstein (documentary about film producer Robert Evans) *Searching for Debra Winger*, Rosanna Arquette (documentary) *In the Mirror of Maya Deren*, Martina Kudlácek (documentary) *Domestic Violence*, Wiseman (documentary) *Bowling for Columbine* (satirical documentary), Moore *Lost in La Mancha*, Terry Gilliam (documentary) *To Be and to Have*, Nicolas Philibert (documentary) *Cremaster 3*, Barney (fifth and last of a cycle of experimental films) *Corpus Callosum*, Snow (experimental)

	World Events	Arts	Mass Media	Films and Videos
2002 (cont'd)	The search for life on Mars takes a step forward when the Mars *Odyssey* probe finds huge reservoirs of ice just beneath the surface			
2003 (cont'd on next page)	North Korea continues to taunt the U.S. with threats of nuclear proliferation SARS, a highly contagious and deadly respiratory syndrome, spreads throughout much of the world but is largely under control by year's end A "road map" outlining steps needed to bring peace between Israelis and Palestinians is advocated by the U.S., the European Union, the UN, and Russia U.S. space shuttle *Columbia* disintegrates over Texas while attempting re-entry, and all seven astronauts aboard are killed Without UN sanctions, U.S., Britain, Spain, and other countries—though not France, Germany, Canada, and many others—invade Iraq but find no "weapons of mass destruction," one of the main justifications	*Ten Little Indians: Stories*, Sherman Alexie (fiction) *Garbo Laughs*, Elizabeth Hay (fiction) *Anna in the Tropics*, Nilo Cruz (play) *Little Shop of Horrors*, one of off-Broadway's most enduring musicals and the source of film adaptations, opens yet again on a New York stage *The Movie Album*, Barbra Streisand (CD)	Although Hispanics make up 13.5% of the U.S. population, Hispanic characters received only 3% of screen time in fall 2002 programs on the six major networks, according to a UCLA study HBO's film adaptation of Tony Kushner's play *Angels in America* D-VHS videotape decks make it possible to record and play back high-definition material on tape Approximately 43 million U.S. households have a DVD player More and more theaters convert to digital projection, in some foreign countries more readily than in the U.S. *Devdas*, a remake of a popular Indian novel, wins seven awards, including best picture and best director, at the India International Film Awards	*Mystic River*, Eastwood *21 Grams*, González Iñárritu *House of Sand and Fog*, Vadim Perelman *American Splendor*, Shari Springer Berman and Robert Pulcini *Elephant*, Van Sant *The Company*, Altman *The Lord of the Rings: The Return of the King*, Jackson *Dracula: Pages from a Virgin's Diary*, Guy Maddin *28 Days Later*, Boyle *Whale Rider*, Niki Caro *Finding Nemo*, Disney animation *The Triplets of Belleville*, Sylvain Chômet (animation) *A Decade under the Influence*, Richard LaGravenese and Ted Demme (documentary about 1970s U.S. movies) *The Fog of War*, Morris (documentary) *Capturing the Friedmans*, Andrew Jarecki (documentary) *Amandla! A Revolution in Four-Part Harmony*, Lee Hirsch (documentary) *Spellbound*, Jeff Blitz (documentary)

	World Events	Arts	Mass Media	Films and Videos
2003 (cont'd)	for the invasion; the occupying forces have major problems ensuring safety and stabilizing the country, and nearly 500 U.S. soldiers have been killed by year's end; late in the year, U.S. forces capture Saddam Hussein Terrorist bombing in Saudi Arabian capital causes massive property damage and kills and maims many Charles Taylor, Liberia's warlord-turned-president, is forced out of office by rebel groups and regional peacekeeping forces Scientists prove the existence of *dark matter*, particles that do not emit or reflect light and are thought to take up most of the universe's space More than 40,000 die in Iranian earthquake		Increasingly, marketers of consumer products seek to capitalize on the movies that the studios unleash each summer by negotiating extensive and expensive movie tie-ins	*Love & Diane*, Jennifer Dworkin (documentary) *Tupac: Resurrection*, Lauren Lazin (documentary) *Decay of Fiction*, O'Neill (experimental)

SOURCES

Barnouw, Erik. *Tube of Plenty: The Evolution of American Television*. 2nd ed. New York: Oxford UP, 1990.

Beaver, Frank E. *Dictionary of Film Terms: The Aesthetic Companion to Film Analysis*. Rev. ed. New York: Twayne, 1994.

———. "An Outline of Film History." *Dictionary of Film Terms*. New York: McGraw-Hill, 1983.

Benét's Reader's Encyclopedia. 3rd ed. Ed. Katherine Baker Siepmann. New York: Harper, 1987.

Bohn, Thomas W., and Richard L. Stromgren. "A Film Chronology." *Light and Shadows: A History of Motion Pictures*. 3rd ed. Palo Alto: Mayfield, 1987. xiv–xlv.

Brooks, Tim, and Earle Marsh. *The Complete Directory to Prime Time Network and Cable TV Shows, 1946–Present*. 8th ed. New York: Ballantine, 2003.

Brownstone, David M., and Irene M. Franck. *Timelines of the Arts and Literature*. New York: Harper, 1994.

———. *Timelines of the Twentieth Century: A Chronology of 7,500 Key Events, Discoveries, and People That Shaped Our Century*. Boston: Little, Brown, 1996.

Chronicle of the 20th Century, North American Ed. Ed. Clifton Daniel. Liberty, MO: JL International, 1994.

Cinema: Year by Year, 1894–2003. Ed. Robyn Karney. London; New York: DK, 2003.

Cook, David A. *A History of Narrative Film*. 4th ed. New York: Norton, 2003.

Ellis, Jack C., *The Documentary Idea: A Critical History of English-Language Documentary Film and Video*. Englewood Cliffs, NJ: Prentice, 1989.

Ellis, Jack C., and Virginia Wright Wexman. *A History of Film*. 5th ed. Boston: Allyn, 2002.

Gomery, Douglas. *Movie History: A Survey*. Belmont, CA: Wadsworth, 1991.

Greenspan, Karen. *The Timetables of Women's History: A Chronology of the Most Important People and Events in Women's History*. New York: Simon, 1994.

Grun, Bernard. *The Timetables of History: A Horizontal Linkage of People and Events*. 3rd ed. New York: Simon, 1991.

Hilliard, Robert L., and Michael C. Keith. *The Broadcast Century and Beyond: A Biography of American Broadcasting*. 3rd ed. Boston: Focal, 2001.

Kane, Joseph Nathan. *Famous First Facts: A Record of First Happenings, Discoveries, and Inventions in American History*. 5th ed. New York: Wilson, 1997.

Katz, Ephraim. *The Film Encyclopedia*. 4th ed. Rev. Fred Klein and Ronald Dean Nolen. New York: Harper, 2001.

Mast, Gerald, and Bruce F. Kawin. *A Short History of the Movies*. 8th ed. New York: Longman, 2002.

McNeil, Alex. *Total Television: The Comprehensive Guide to Programming from 1948 to the Present*. New York: Penguin, 1996.

Monaco, James. *How to Read a Film: Movies, Media, Multimedia*. 3rd ed. New York: Oxford UP, 2000.

Nowell-Smith, Geoffrey, general ed. *The Oxford History of World Cinema*. Oxford: Oxford UP, 1996.

Ochoa, George, and Melinda Corey. *The Timeline Book of the Arts*. New York: Ballantine, 1995.

Polan, Dana. "History of the American Cinema." *Film Quarterly* 45.3 (Spring 1992): 54–57.

Rood, Karen L. *American Culture after World War II*. Detroit: Gale, 1994. Pages xix–xxx consist of two timelines: works and events.

Samuelson, D. "Equipment Inventions That Have Changed the Way Films Are Made." *American Cinematographer* 75.8 (1994): 74, 76.

Sklar, Robert. *Film: An International History of the Medium*. 2nd ed. Upper Saddle River, NJ: Prentice; New York: Abrams, 2002.

Strauss, William, and Neil Howe. *Generations: The History of America's Future, 1584–2069*. New York: Morrow, 1991.

Thompson, Kristin, and David Bordwell. *Film History: An Introduction*. 2nd ed. Boston: McGraw, 2003.

Thomson, David. *The New Biographical Dictionary of Film*. New York: Knopf, 2002.

Winston, Brian. "Z for Zoetrope." *Sight and Sound* July 1998: 28–30.

Other Sources

Various issues of *Billboard*, the *Los Angeles Times*, the *New York Times*, and the *World Almanac*.

On the Web: many newspapers, magazines, and journals accessed via Nexis; information on the Internet Movie Database (IMD); the History Channel (www.historychannel.com); and reviews accessed via Movie Review Query Engine (MRQE).

How to Read Film Credits

Most movies now run a list of credits at the end identifying the many people who worked on the film. Some movies, such as the theatrical version of *The Hurricane* (1999), use the closing credits to slip in the film's only disclaimer about the story's sources or about material that was not a source. In recent years, closing credits have generally become longer—and longer. Perhaps the closing credits for *The Lord of the Rings: The Return of the King* (2003) have set the record for length, running an eye-glazing 9½ minutes (Kennedy). So tedious have some closing credits become that some are broken up by outtakes of flubbed shots or whimsical messages. According to veteran film critic Andrew Sarris, the closing credits for one film included the reminder that if you had left the theater "at the beginning of these credits, you'd be home by now" (Fox). Other filmmakers have included whimsical fake credits, such as "Things to Do after the Movie" and, at the end of John Waters's *Serial Mom* (1994), "No Flies Were Harmed in the Making of This Film" (Fox). But did you ever wonder what all the other, more serious credits mean—what, for example, a gaffer does, or a best boy, or a grip? To help you appreciate the work involved in making a typical movie, the closing credits from *The Player* (1992) are reprinted here along with brief explanations of the terms that a typical viewer might not know.

Many of the chapters of this book explain the roles of the filmmakers with the high-profile jobs: writers, producers, directors, actors, designers, cinematographers, editors, and composers. As in many recent films, in *The Player* these people are identified in the opening credits. (In many older films, additional filmmakers are listed in the opening credits, but that is now rarely done.) The closing credits of *The Player*, listed here, identify all the actors and many other people who are associated with the production but are not listed at the film's beginning.

CLOSING CREDITS FOR *THE PLAYER*

CAST

These actors have major roles and appear in several scenes. Except for Sydney Pollack's name, their names also appear in the opening credits.

Griffin Mill	TIM ROBBINS
June Gudmundsdottir	GRETA SCACCHI
Walter Stuckel	FRED WARD
Detective Avery	WHOOPI GOLDBERG
Larry Levy	PETER GALLAGHER
Joel Levison	BRION JAMES
Bonnie Sherow	CYNTHIA STEVENSON
David Kahane	VINCENT D'ONOFRIO
Andy Civella	DEAN STOCKWELL
Tom Oakley	RICHARD E. GRANT
Dick Mellen	SYDNEY POLLACK
Detective DeLongpre	LYLE LOVETT
Celia	DINA MERRILL
Jan	ANGELA HALL

These actors have minor roles. Most of them appear in only one scene.

Sandy	LEAH AYRES
Jimmy Chase	PAUL HEWITT
Reg Goldman	RANDALL BATINKOFF
Steve Reeves	JEREMY PIVEN
Whitney Gersh	GINA GERSHON
Frank Murphy	FRANK BARHYDT
Marty Grossman	MIKE E. KAPLAN
Gar Girard	KEVIN SCANNELL
Witness	MARGERY BOND
Detective Broom	SUSAN EMSHWILLER
Phil	BRIAN BROPHY
Eric Schecter	MICHAEL TOLKIN
Carl Schecter	STEPHEN TOLKIN
Natalie	NATALIE STRONG
Waiter	PETE KOCH
Trixie	PAMELA BOWEN
Rocco	JEFF WESTON

AS THEMSELVES

These are all of the sixty-five cameos—brief roles played by well-known people.

STEVE ALLEN	MAXINE JOHN-JAMES
RICHARD ANDERSON	SALLY KELLERMAN
RENE AUBERJONOIS	SALLY KIRKLAND
HARRY BELAFONTE	JACK LEMMON
SHARI BELAFONTE	MARLEE MATLIN
KAREN BLACK	ANDIE MacDOWELL
MICHAEL BOWEN	MALCOLM McDOWELL
GARY BUSEY	JAYNE MEADOWS
ROBERT CARRADINE	MARTIN MULL

CHARLES CHAMPLIN
CHER
JAMES COBURN
CATHY LEE CROSBY
JOHN CUSACK
BRAD DAVIS
PAUL DOOLEY
THEREZA ELLIS
PETER FALK
FELICIA FARR
KASIA FIGURA
LOUISE FLETCHER
DENNIS FRANZ
TERI GARR
LEEZA GIBBONS
SCOTT GLENN
JEFF GOLDBLUM
ELLIOTT GOULD
JOEL GREY
DAVID ALAN GRIER
BUCK HENRY
ANJELICA HUSTON
KATHY IRELAND
STEVE JAMES

JENNIFER NASH
NICK NOLTE
ALEXANDRA POWERS
BERT REMSEN
GUY REMSEN
PATRICIA RESNICK
BURT REYNOLDS
JACK RILEY
JULIA ROBERTS
MIMI ROGERS
ANNIE ROSS
ALAN RUDOLPH
JILL ST. JOHN
SUSAN SARANDON
ADAM SIMON
ROD STEIGER
JOAN TEWKESBURY
BRIAN TOCHI
LILY TOMLIN
ROBERT WAGNER
RAY WALSTON
BRUCE WILLIS
MARVIN YOUNG

These are all of the sixty-five cameos—brief roles played by well-known people.

Manages the production crew and the business arrangements for each day's shooting, such as housing, meals, transportation, and payroll.

Often the film editor is listed only in the opening credits. For *The Player*, the opening credits list Geraldine Peroni as the editor; thus, this listing is a puzzle. Perhaps the credit here should have read "Assistant Film Editor." Or perhaps Maysie Hoy edited only the clip from *Habeas Corpus*, the film-within-the-film in *The Player*.

Creates the look of the film and runs the art department; ultimately responsible for all the visuals in the film, including architecture, locations, sets, decor, props, costumes, and makeup.

In *The Player*, one scene occurs in a karaoke bar, where videos are playing in the background. This person made those videos.

Associate Producer
Unit Production Manager
First Assistant Director
Second Assistant Director

Film Editor

Production Executives

Production Supervisor

Art Director
Set Decorator
Leadman
Location Manager

First Assistant Camera
Second Assistant Camera
Third Assistant Camera
Karaoke Videos

DAVID LEVY
TOM UDELL
ALLAN NICHOLS
CC BARNES

MAYSIE HOY

CLAUDIA LEWIS
PAMELA HEDLEY
JIM CHESNEY

JERRY FLEMING
SUSAN EMSHWILLER
PETER BORCK
JACK KNEY

ROBERT REED ALTMAN
CARY McKRYSTAL
CRAIG FINETTI
LARRY "DOC" KARMAN

Works closely with the producer(s) on artistic and financial matters. Unlike some "producers," the associate producer has day-to-day involvement with the making of the film.

The director's assistants; typically they keep track of scheduling, manage crowd scenes, supervise rehearsals, and prepare call sheets and production reports.

Responsible for the business and administrative aspects of making a film; assisted by the associate producer.

A.k.a. Production Manager. Supervises and coordinates all business and technical matters.

Decides how to decorate the indoor sets with furniture, props, art, and so on.

Finds locations for shooting and negotiates for their use.

The camera crew; they maintain the equipment, load the film, and use a clapboard or comparable electronic device to mark the beginning of each take.

The editor's assistants; they splice the film, maintain the editing equipment, and keep records.

Assistant Editor
Second Assistant Editor
Apprentice Editor

A. MICHELLE PAGE
ALISA HALE
DYLAN TICHENOR

Responsible for the final soundtrack; supervises the mixer, ADR (automated dialogue replacement) editor, dialogue editor, sound effects editor, music editor, and assistant sound editor.

Supervising Sound Editor
Dialogue Editors

MICHAEL REDBOURN
JOSEPH HOLSEN
ED LACHMANN
KEN BURTON
BILL WARD

Edits the music to make sure it complements the film's action and the other elements of the soundtrack.

Sound Effects Editor
Assistant Sound Editor

Music Editor
Music Scoring Mixer
Orchestration By

BILL BERNSTEIN
JOHN VIGRAN
THOMAS PASATIERI

Blends and balances the tracks of the various film scores.

Arranges the score for the parts of the orchestra.

Postproduction technicians who mix vocals, sound effects, music, and silence to produce the master soundtrack.

Re-Recording Mixers

Records sound during shooting; reports to the production sound mixer.

Recordist
Foley Artists

MATTHEW IADAROLA
STANLEY KASTNER
RICH GOOCH
JOHN POST
PAUL HOLTZBORN
BOB DESCHAINE
DAVID JOBE

Sound specialists who use various objects to simulate and record sound effects while synchronizing them with their corresponding movie images.

Foley Mixer
Foley Recordist

Mixes the sound produced during shooting to get the desired combination of vocals, sound effects, and ambient sound.

Production Sound Mixer
Boom Operator
Cable Puller

JOHN PRITCHETT, C.A.S.
JOEL SHRYACK
EMILY SMITH-BAKER

Sound technician who operates the boom, a pole with a microphone at one end.

Protects the cables and wires of the sound equipment from damage and the production crew from injuries from the cables and wires.

Gaffer
Best Boy Electric
Electricians

DON MUCHOW
ANDREW DAY
ROBERT BRUCE
VAL DE SALVO
TOM McGRATH
CHRIS REDDISH
ANTHONY T. MARRA II
MICHAEL J. FAHEY
WAYNE STROUD

The head electrician, assisted by the best boy electric. Supervises the electricians, who are responsible for supplying current and lights on the set.

Manages the grips, or stagehands, who set up and move equipment and props. Assisted by the best boy grip.

Key Grip
Best Boy Grip
Dolly Grip

Moves the dolly during shooting.

Stagehands or crew workers.

Grips

KEVIN FAHEY
SCOTT "EL GATO" HOLLANDER
TIM NASH

Obtains the costumes and takes care of them during filming. Assisted by the wardrobe assistants.

Wardrobe Supervisor
Wardrobe Assistants

LYDIA TANJI
ANGELA BILLOWS
VICKI BRINKKORD
DEBORAH LARSEN
SCOTT WILLIAMS
SYDNEY COOPER

Arranges the actors' hair.

In *The Player*, the character June is an artist, and her artworks are seen in her house. This person created that art.

Runs the makeup department; applies the makeup to the actors.

Make-Up Artist
Hairdresser
June's Artwork

Oversees acquisition and maintenance of all props. → Property Master — **JAMES MONROE**

Assistant Property Master — **JULIE HEUER**

Set Dressers — **MATTHEW ALTMAN / JOHN BUCKLIN / DAVID RONAN / JIM SAMSON / DANIEL ROTHENBERG / MARIO PEREZ**

Get the set ready for filming and disassemble it after filming.

Swing Gang — **PAUL BOYDSTON / JOHN BEAUVAIS**

The member of the construction crew who paints the sets. → Assistant Location Manager / Scenic Painter / Painter — **RICKY RIGGS / LOREN CORNEY / PAT MAURER**

Construction Coordinator / Construction Foreman — **CHRIS MARNEUS / DARRYL LEE** — Supervise the construction crew, who make the sets.

Build the sets, furniture, props, and camera tracks. → Carpenters — **KENNETH FUNK / THOMAS CALLOWAY / JOHN EVANS / JUSTIN KRITZER / MICHELE GUASTELLO**

Responsible for coordinating the visual elements of the film (other than the camera work). → Art Department Coordinator

Keeps track of all expenditures during production and supervises payment of salaries and bills. Assisted by the assistant accountant. → Production Coordinator / Assistant Coordinator / Production Secretary / Production Accountant / Assistant Accountant / Avenue Financial Representative / Additional Accounting Service / Post-Production Accountant — **CYNTHIA HILL** ← An administrator in charge of communication, correspondence, travel, accommodations, and bill paying. Assisted by the assistant coordinator and the production secretary.

BETSY CHASSE / STACY COHEN / KIMBERLY EDWARDS SHAPIRO / CHERYL KURK / SHERI HALFON ← Avenue Pictures was a small film production company. Its chairman at the time *The Player* was produced was Cary Brokaw, who served as executive producer of *The Player*.

JUDY GELETKO / CATHERINE WEBB / JIM McLINDON / ROBIN HAGE / DANIELLE KNIGHT / ALISON BALIAN / CELIA CONVERSE

Personal assistants, who help the director and producers. → Assistant to Robert Altman / Assistants to Cary Brokaw

Sandcastle 5 Productions, Inc., is a small film and TV production company closely associated with Robert Altman. → Assistant to Nick Wechsler / Sandcastle 5 Representative / Production Assistants — **ANGIE BONNER / JOHN BROWN III / SIGNE CORRIERE / STEVE DAY / KELLY HOUSEHOLDER** — Run errands for the director and assist him or her in various other small ways.

Plans, arranges, and supervises the stunts.

Keeps a log of the details in each shot to make sure continuity is maintained from shot to shot. → Script Supervisor / Stunt Coordinator / Special Effects — **CAROLE STARKES / GREG WALKER** ← The department responsible for the shots unobtainable by live-action cinematography.

JOHN HARTIGAN ←

Handles the animals on the set; in *The Player*, a rattlesnake appears twice. → Animal Trainer / Still Photographer / Set Medic — **JIM BROCKETT / LOREY SEBASTIAN** ← Takes photographs for publicity and advertising.

TOM MOORE

Responsible for maintaining and operating all vehicles.

Transportation Coordinator — DEREK RASER
Transport Captain — "J. T." THAYER
Drivers — CHRISTOPHER ARMSTRONG
RON CHESNEY
STEVE EARLE
DON FEENEY
D. J. GARDINER
GREG WILLIS

Drive the vehicles that transport equipment and personnel.

Perform odd jobs, such as getting coffee and snacks for the cast and crew.

Caterer — RICK BRAININ CATERING
Craft Service — STUART McCAULEY
ANDREA BERTY

Hires the actors who speak no lines and do not stand out as individuals.

Extras Casting — MAGIC CASTING
Location Security — ARTIS SECURITY ← Maintains security for scenes shot on location.

Lab person who adjusts the color of the negative as needed, often in coordination with the cinematographer.

Negative Cutter — BOB HART ← Cuts and splices the negative to make it match the final edited version of the film.
Color By — DELUXE ®
Color Timer — MICHAEL STANWICK
Titles & Opticals By — MERCER TITLE & OPTICAL ← Uses an optical printer or perhaps a computer to create the words that appear on the screen.

Designs the words that appear on the screen (such as the credits).

Title Design — DAN PERRI

Legal Services — SINCLAIR TENNENBAUM & Co.
WYMAN & ISAACS

This organization, here a Japanese-based bank, lent the producers money to produce the film.

Financing Provided By — THE DAIWA BANK LTD.
Completion Bond — FILM FINANCES, INC. ← The company responsible for drawing up the contract between the producers and the financiers that guarantees the film will be completed at a set time and within a set budget.

Publicizes the film through advertising and other publicity.

Promotions Arranged By — ANDREW VARELA
Publicity By — CLEIN + WHITE INC.

Arranges publicity events, such as interviews and appearances.

Title Painting By — CHARLES BRAGG

SPECIAL THANKS TO

PATRICK MURRAY   SUZANNE GOLDMAN   MIMI RABINOWITZ
RANDY HONAKER   TOYOKO NEZU   MORGAN ENTREKIN
LUIS ESTEVEZ   REEBOK   GEOWORKS
BASELINE   MARK EISEN   BALLY

These people or companies donated products or services or allowed the filmmakers to use certain locations. For *The Player*, companies such as Reebok, Bally, and Range Rover may have paid a fee for product placement.

GERALD GREENBACH & TWO BUNCH PALMS
BOB FLICK & ENTERTAINMENT TONIGHT
STEVE TROMBATORE & ALL PAYMENTS
RANGE ROVER OF NORTH AMERICA
MARCHON/MARCOLIN EYE WEAR
SPINNEYBECK/DESIGN AMERICA
HARRY WINSTON JEWELERS
L.A. MARATHON

These people or companies donated products or services or allowed the filmmakers to use certain locations. For *The Player*, companies such as Reebok, Bally, and Range Rover may have paid a fee for product placement.

THE LOS ANGELES COUNTY MUSEUM OF ART
JANIS DINWIDDIE
JULIE JOHNSTON
RON HAVER
THE LES HOOPER ORCHESTRA

THE BICYCLE THIEF
© RICHARD FEINER & CO., INC.

These are copyright acknowledgments, required whenever a film uses material that someone else claims copyright to.

"SNAKE" & "DRUMS OF KYOTO"
© Lia-Mann Music
Written & Performed By
KURT NEUMANN

"TEMA PARA JOBIM"
© Mulligan Publishing Co., Inc.
Music by GERRY MULLIGAN
Lyrics by JOYCE
Performed by JOYCE
MILTON NASCIMENTO
Courtesy of Estudio Pointer Ltda.
& RCA Electronica Ltda.

"PRECIOUS"
Written by LES HOOPER
© Chesford Music Publications

ENTERTAINMENT TONIGHT
Theme by
MICHAEL MARK
Published by ADDAX MUSIC CO. INC.

Re-Recording Facilities
SKYWALKER SOUND
A division of LucasArts Entertainment Company

This film recorded digitally in a THX Sound System Theatre.

RECORDED IN
ULTRA-STEREO

A caution: Film credits do not always indicate accurately who did what. Some job titles are largely ceremonial, favors to friends, supporters, or movie executives with clout. Two films may use a different term to indicate the same type of work. Then, too, some job titles are simply vague, and others (such as *construction coordinator* and *construction foreman* and *promotion* and *publicity*) are synonymous or overlapping. All these caveats aside, most titles and descriptions accurately describe who did what. Although you cannot always know what certain producers do, you can be certain what Foley artists and dolly grips do.

SOURCES

Fox, Margalit. "Where There's Life after 'The End.'" *New York Times* (Late ed.) 29 Nov. 1998: 2.17.

IMDb Film Glossary (Internet Movie Database Web site): <http://us.imdb.com /Glossary>. Accessed 20 Dec. 2003.

Katz, Ephraim. *The Film Encyclopedia*. 4th ed. Rev. Fred Klein and Ronald Dean Nolen. New York: Harper, 2001.

Kennedy, Randy. "Who Was That Food Stylist? Film Credits Roll On." *New York Times* (Final ed.) 11 Jan. 2004: 1.1.

Konigsberg, Ira. *The Complete Film Dictionary*. 2nd ed. New York: Penguin, 1997.

Law, Jonathan, and others, eds. *Cassell Companion to Cinema*. Rev. ed. London: Cassell, 1997.

Oakey, Virginia. *Dictionary of Film and Television Terms*. New York: Barnes, 1983.

Singleton, Ralph S. *Filmmaker's Dictionary*. Beverly Hills: Lone Eagle, 1990.

Illustrated Glossary

Filmmakers use many terms such as *frame-accurate effect* that most film critics and scholars have no occasion to use. Occasionally, filmmakers, film critics, and film scholars use the same term differently, such as *sequence*, or use different terms for the same subject, such as *deep focus* and *great depth of field*. In this glossary, I have tried to define and explain the main terms used in this book, normally with the same meaning(s) intended by film critics and scholars, and a few widely used but often misunderstood terms such as *irony* and *satire*. The number in parentheses at the end of an entry indicates the first page where that term is discussed most extensively in a chapter. Page numbers in *italic* type refer to illustrations, captions, or both. For additional terms or other explanations of the terms included in this glossary, see Robert Atkins's *ArtSpeak: A Guide to Contemporary Ideas, Movements, and Buzzwords, 1945 to the Present*, 2nd ed. (1997); Chris Baldick's *The Concise Oxford Dictionary of Literary Terms* (1990); Steve Blandford, Barry Keith Grant, and Jim Hillier's *The Film Studies Dictionary* (2001); Susan Hayward's *Cinema Studies: The Key Concepts*, 2nd ed. (2000); Kevin Jackson's *The Language of Cinema* (1998); Ira Konigsberg's *The Complete Film Dictionary*, 2nd ed. (1997); Ross Murfin and Supryia M. Ray's *The Bedford Glossary of Critical and Literary Terms*, 2nd ed. (2003); Roberta E. Pearson and Philip Simpson's *Critical Dictionary of Film and Television Theory* (2001); and Gerald Prince's *Dictionary of Narratology* (1987). Various glossaries of film terms, especially terms used by filmmakers, also appear on the Web.

abstract film: Experimental film whose subjects are shapes and perhaps sounds that do not represent the real world (left).

Academy leader: Numbered strip of motion picture film spliced to the beginning of a reel of film to be projected. Academy leader helps protect the beginning of a reel of film from scratches and tears and helps projectionists using older projectors to cue up each reel so that it can be started at the appropriate moment. On rare occasions, experimental filmmakers also incorporate pieces of Academy leader into the body of a film. See, for example, "A Movie" (Figure 8.18b & g).

allusion: A reference in a text to a person, an event, another text, or a part of a text. Unlike an homage or a parody, an allusion does not convey clear-cut admiration or amusing derision of the subject referred to but only briefly refers to it.

ambient sound: The sound atmosphere of a place that people tend not to notice. In a forest, for example, ambient sound may consist mainly of trees moving in the breeze and insects heard at a low volume.

ambiguity: An aspect of a text (such as a character's motivations for doing something) that is open to two or more plausible interpretations. Ambiguity can result because of the makeup of the text itself, perhaps because the writer deliberately withheld certain clarifying information or because viewers experience a confusing, truncated version of the original text. In fictional films and other imaginative texts, ambiguity is usually seen as a strength, whereas in texts that primarily convey information or ideas, such as a documentary film or a college student's essay, ambiguity is usually seen as a distracting flaw.

anamorphic lens: A lens that squeezes a wide image onto a film frame in the camera, making everything look tall and thin (bottom, left). On a projector, an anamorphic lens expands the image, returning it to its original wide shape (bottom, right). Many movies from the 1950s to the 1980s and some since then have been filmed and projected with anamorphic lenses. See also both **CinemaScope** and **spherical lens**. (*36*)

animation: The process of photographing or creating a series of individual images with visual variations from one frame to the next so that later a showing of the series of still images can give the appearance of movement. *Animate* means to give life to or to fill with life. Opposite of

live action. See also **stop-motion cinematography** and **time-lapse cinematography**.

animatronic: A puppet likeness of a human, a creature, or an animal whose movements are directed by electronic, mechanical, or radio-controlled devices.

aperture: (1) The adjustable opening in the camera lens that permits the operator to regulate how much light passes through the lens to the film. (2) The rectangular opening in a motion-picture projector that helps determine the size and shape of light sent from the projector to the screen.

aperture plate: (1) A small metal plate with a rectangular opening that is used in cameras to determine the shape and area of the light reaching the film. (2) A small metal plate with a rectangular opening used in front of a projector's aperture or opening to help determine the shape and area of the light reaching the screen.

art director: See **designer**.

aspect ratio: The proportion of the width to the height of the image on a TV or movie screen or on the individual frames of the film. A common aspect ratio for nontheatrical film showings is 1.33:1 (4:3); that is also the

---

1.85:1
The aspect ratio used for
most U.S. theatrical showings
since the 1960s

approximate aspect ratio of analog TV screens. Currently, most movies shown in American theaters have an aspect ratio of 1.85:1 (the image is nearly twice as wide as it is high) (on previous page). The aspect ratio has nothing to do with the size or area of the image; rather it indicates the shape (width in proportion to height) of film images. (35)

asynchronous sound: A sound that either precedes or follows its on-screen source, such as words that are not synchronized with lip movements. (184)

auteur ("oh TOUR") theory: The belief that some filmmakers—usually directors though sometimes producers, writers, or actors—function as the dominant creators of films and that the auteur's films embody recurrent subjects, techniques, and meanings. (505)

avant-garde film: See **experimental film**.

backlight or **backlighting:** Lighting from behind the subject. If used alone or if the backlighting is the strongest light used, the subject's identity may be obscured. Used in combination with other lighting, backlighting may help set the image of the subject off from the background. (72)

big studio era: See **studio era**.

big studio system: See **studio era**.

bird's-eye view: A camera angle achieved when the camera films the subject from directly overhead. (*91*)

black comedy: A narrative style that shows the humorous possibilities of subjects often considered off limits to comedy, such as warfare, murder, death, and illness. Black comedies are often also satiric. Examples of films using black comedy are the 1955 *The Ladykillers* (especially the five deaths and disposal of the five bodies that are treated comically toward the end of the film); *Kind Hearts and Coronets*; *Dr. Strangelove: Or, How I Learned to Stop Worrying and Love the Bomb*; *Life of Brian*; *Eating Raoul*; and *To Die For*. (276)

blaxploitation (film): A U.S. film movement from 1971 to 1975 or 1976 consisting of low-budget movies usually made by African American filmmakers, with black characters for black audiences. The first blaxploitation film is regarded as *Sweet Sweetback's Baad Asssss Song* (1971). (418)

Bollywood: Extremely popular Hindi-language movies made in India that usually feature complicated plots, large casts of mostly uncomplicated characters, fre-

quent extravagant musical interludes, and often happy endings. The word *Bollywood* was derived from a combination of Bombay (India) and Hollywood. Some use *Bollywood* affectionately, and others reject the term as derisive and condescending. (327)

boom: See **crane**.

bridge (music): Music used to link two or more scenes. Often used to enhance continuity.

cameo: A brief role in a narrative entertainment—such as a TV show or film (fictional or occasionally documentary)—performed by a well-known person, usually a famous actor, whose name is often not included in the credits or publicity. Cameos may also be played by famous people playing themselves or by insiders in the film community—a type of cinematic in-joke. (28)

canted framing: See **Dutch angle**.

catchlight: The light from one or more sources that is visible in the pupils of a subject's eyes. By examining the catchlight, one can discover the number and direction of some or all of the light sources (below).

cel: A thin sheet of clear plastic on which images are painted for use in making some animated films. To produce some animated films, a series of cels is superimposed on a painted background then each finished image is photographed.

celluloid: (1) Short for *cellulose nitrate*, film stock used until the early 1950s that could produce high-quality images that were subject to decomposition (see Figure 8.15 on p. 366) and combustion (illustrated by the projection room fire in *Cinema Paradiso*). (2) Any transparent material used as the base for motion-picture film (see Figure 2.1 on p. 62). (3) Synonym for *movie*, as in "celluloid heroes."

character actor: An actor who tends to specialize in well-defined secondary roles. Dennis Hopper, for example, is a character actor who has largely made a career of playing unstable secondary characters (right). (27)

cinéma noir: See **film noir**.

CinemaScope: A wide-screen process introduced in 1953 made possible by filming and projecting with anamorphic lenses.

cinematic: See **filmic**.

cinematographer: The person responsible for the motion-picture photography during the making of a film. Often called *director of photography* (DP).

cinematography: Motion-picture photography, including technical and artistic concern with such matters as choice of film stock, lighting, choice and use of lenses, camera distance and angle, and camera movement. (Chapter 2)

cinéma vérité: Literally, "film truth." A type and style of documentary filmmaking developed in France during the early 1960s whose aim was to capture events as they happened. To this end, cinéma vérité filmmakers used unobtrusive lightweight equipment to film and to record sound on location. Similar to direct cinema, which arose at about the same time in the United States, although the French filmmakers were likely to question their subjects during filming. Practitioners of cinéma vérité include Jean Rouch, Chris Marker, and Marcel Ophüls (as in his monumental *The Sorrow and the Pity*). See **direct cinema**. (362)

Cinerama: A wide-screen process involving the use of three synchronized projectors showing three contiguous images on a wide, curved screen (Figure 9.20a). Cinerama was first used commercially in the early 1950s and was available only in selected theaters in large cities. (441)

classical Hollywood cinema: Films that show one or more characters facing a succession of problems while trying to reach their goals and that tend to hide the manner of their making by using unobtrusive filmmaking techniques. (292)

close-up: An image in which the subject fills most of the frame and little of the surroundings is shown. When the subject is someone's upper body, the close-up normally reveals the entire head and perhaps some of the shoulders. Close-ups are used to direct viewers' attention to texture or a detail or, most often, the expressions on a person's face (left). (*86*)

closure: A sense of coherence and completion at the end of a narrative. A story that has closure leaves its audience with no major unanswered questions about the consequences of the narrative's most significant events. (260)

compilation film: A film made by editing together clips from other films. Sometimes used in creating a documentary film—as in *Point of Order*, *As I Was Moving ahead Occasionally I Saw Brief Glimpses of Beauty*, and *Decasia*—or in making an experimental film, as in Bruce Conner's "A Movie." (358, *370*)

composition: The arrangement of settings, lighting, and subjects (such as people and objects) within the frame. (35)

continuity (editing): Film editing that maintains a sense of uninterrupted time and action and continuous setting within each scene of a narrative film. (129)

contrast: In photography and cinematography, the difference between the lightest and darkest parts of an image. Low-contrast images show little difference between the intensity of the lightest part of the image and that of the darkest part. In high-contrast images, the dark parts are very dark and the light parts very light.

convention: In films and other texts, a subject or technique that makers of texts and audiences have grown to accept as natural or typical in certain contexts. For example, it is a convention that westerns include showdowns and shoot-outs, and it is a convention that audiences are allowed to hear both sides of a telephone conversation even if they see only one of the conversationalists. The authors of *The Film Studies Dictionary* point out, "conventions function as an implied agreement between makers and consumers to accept certain artificialities." Opposite of **revisionist**. (435)

crane: A mechanical device used to move a camera through space above the ground or to position it at a place in the air. A shot taken from a crane gives the camera operator many options: different distances and angles from the subject, different heights from the surface, fluid changes in distance and angle from the subject, and different speeds with which the camera moves through the air (below). (96)

critical approach: Related ideas on how to interpret texts. The ideas constituting a critical approach are sometimes only loosely connected and by no means agreed on by all those professing to use the same critical approach. Examples of critical approaches are Marxist criticism, cultural studies, auteur theory, feminist criti-

cism, viewer-response criticism, reception theory, and genre criticism.

crop: To trim or block out one or more parts of an image. For example, the photo from *Citizen Kane* on p. 54 is a publicity still that has been cropped so that the resultant image closely approximates one of the frames in the movie.

cross-cut: In editing, to alternate between events occurring at different settings and often presumably transpiring at the same time. See **parallel editing**.

cut: (1) The most common transition between shots, made by splicing or joining the end of one shot to the beginning of the following shot. When the two shots are projected, the transition from the first shot to the next appears to be instantaneous. (2) To change from one shot to the following shot seemingly instantaneously; this transition between shots is achieved whenever the end of the first shot has been spliced to the beginning of the following shot. (3) A version of an edited film, as in "director's cut," meaning the version the director intended. (4) To edit or edited, as in "They cut the movie in four months." (5) To sever film, splice film, or sever and splice film while editing. (*120*)

cutaway (shot): A shot that briefly interrupts the representation of a subject to show something else. Used in many ways, such as to reveal what a character is thinking, show reactions, maintain continuity, avoid showing sex or violence, or allow a passage of time. In *The Dead*, for example, viewers see the beginning of a dinner, a cutaway to the street outside, then the dinner table again where the guests have finished eating.

cutting continuity (script): A script that describes a finished film. Often contains detailed technical information, such as shot and scene divisions, descriptions of settings and events, dialogue, camera angles and distances, sometimes even the duration of shots and transitions between them. Extremely useful for studying a film, especially a foreign-language film, because any dialogue is usually translated more completely and more accurately than in the film's subtitles or dubbing. See **screenplay** and **shooting script**. (499)

dailies: The positive prints usually made from a day's filming (exposed negatives). The director, cinematographer, and perhaps editor usually check the dailies to see if the recently filmed shots are satisfactory and if additional takes or shots are needed.

deep focus: A term used widely by film critics to indicate photography in which subjects near the camera, those in the distant background, and those in between are all in sharp focus (below). Achieved in photography by use of wide-angle lenses or small lens aperture or both. In low illumination, fast lenses and fast film stock also help create deep focus. Filmmakers are likely to use the phrase *great depth of field* rather than *deep focus*. Opposite of **shallow focus**. (82)

depth of field: The distances in front of the camera in which all objects are in focus.

desaturated color: Drained, subdued color approaching a neutral gray. Often used to create or enhance an effect, as throughout Werner Herzog's *Nosferatu the Vampyre* and Tim Burton's *Sleepy Hollow*. Opposite of **saturated color**. (p. 67 and Plates 5 and 6)

designer: The person responsible for the appearance of much of what is photographed in a movie, including architecture, locations, sets, costumes, makeup, and hairstyles.

diffuser: (1) Material such as spun glass, granulated or grooved glass, or a silk or thin nylon stocking placed in front of the camera lens to soften the image's resolution. (2) Translucent material such as silk or spun glass placed in front of a light source to create soft light. (*84*)

digital effect: Image or a part of an image created or modified by use of computers and specially designed software. See also **optical effect**.

digital intermediate: A process available since the late 1990s in which filmmakers can transfer exposed film to

digital, manipulate the colors with a computer program, and then transfer the images back to film.

direct cinema: A type and style of documentary filmmaking developed in the United States during the 1960s in which actions are recorded as they happen, without rehearsal, using a portable 16 mm camera with a zoom lens and portable magnetic sound recording equipment. Editing is minimal, and usually narration and interviews are avoided. Similar to cinéma vérité, which developed in France at about the same time, though direct cinema attempted to be less directive and intrusive. Used by such American documentary filmmakers as Robert Drew and Richard Leacock, Albert and David Maysles, Donn Pennebaker, and Frederick Wiseman and an influence on some fictional filmmakers, such as John Cassavetes. See **cinéma vérité**. (361)

director of photography: See **cinematographer**.

dissolve: See **lap dissolve**.

docudrama: A film that re-creates and dramatizes occurrences from history, often recent history, by blending fact and fiction. The term is usually applied to TV movies that purport to be factual re-creations of newsworthy people or occurrences.

documentary (film): A film or video representation of actual (not imaginary) subjects. A documentary film may present a story (be a narrative film), or it may not. (345)

Dogme 95: Film movement begun by Danish filmmakers in 1995 when they drew up the "Vow of Chastity," a set of rules expressing their rejection of the expensive filmmaking techniques used by commercial film industries in Denmark, France, and the United States; "superficial actions," such as murders; and genre films. Instead, the focus was to be on realistic characters and settings. Although initially established in Denmark, the movement eventually spread to include directors from many countries. The most famous film from this movement is the first Dogme 95 film, Thomas Vinterberg's *The Celebration*. See also **Italian neorealism** and **French new wave (cinema)**. (332)

Dolby sound: Trade name for a system that reduces noise on optical and magnetic soundtracks. (*162c, d*)

dolly: (1) A wheeled platform most often used to move a motion-picture camera and its operator around while filming (below). (2) To film while the camera is mounted on a moving dolly or wheeled platform. See **track**, definition 1.

dominant cinema: See **classical Hollywood cinema**.

DP: director of photography. See **cinematographer**.

dub: (1) To add sound after the film has been shot. Sometimes used to supplement sounds that were recorded during filming. (2) To replace certain sounds in a film after the film has been shot—for example, to substitute native speaking voices for the original voices of a foreign-language film.

Dutch angle: A camera angle in which the vertical and horizontal lines of the film's image appear at an angle to the vertical and horizontal lines of the film's frame. For example, in a Dutch angle shot, the vertical lines of a door frame will appear slanted. Often used to suggest disorientation by the film's subjects or to disorient viewers or both (top, right). (92)

edit: To select and arrange the processed segments of photographed motion-picture film or videotape. Editors, often in collaboration with directors, determine the shots to include, the most effective take (version) of each shot, the arrangement and duration of shots, and transitions between them. To edit a film is sometimes called "to cut a film." (Chapter 3)

effect: See **sound effect** and **special effect**.

emulsion: A clear gelatin substance containing a thin layer of tiny light-sensitive particles (grains) that make up a photographic image. The emulsion and a clear, flexible base are the two main components of a piece of film. (Figure 2.1 on p. 62)

episodic plot: Story structure in which some scenes have no necessary or probable relation to each other; many scenes could be switched without strongly affecting the overall story or audience response. Episodic plots are used in *Nashville*, *Clerks*, and occasional other films. Such stories may be unified by means other than character and action, such as setting.

establishing shot: A shot, usually a long shot or an extreme long shot, used at the beginning of a scene to show where and sometimes when the events that are to follow take place.

event: In a narrative or story, either an *action* by a character or person or a *happening* (a change brought about by a force other than a person or character). Settings, subjects, and events are the basic components of a narrative. (249)

experimental film: A film that rejects the conventions of mainstream movies and explores the possibilities of the film medium. Probably the best-known experimental film is "Un chien andalou," a surrealist creation by director Luis Buñuel and the artist Salvador Dali (next page, top left). (367)

explicit meaning: A general observation included in a text about one or more of its subjects. In films, explicit meanings may be revealed by a narrator, a character's monologue or dialogue, a title card, a subtitle, a sign, a newspaper headline, or some other means. See **implicit meaning** and **meaning**. (472)

exposition: Information supplied within a narrative about characters (or people in a narrative documentary) and about events that supposedly transpired before the earliest event in the plot. Exposition is intended to help the audience better understand the characters or people and make sense of the plot. (258)

expressionism: A style of art, literature, drama, and film used to represent not external reality in a believable way but emotions in striking, stylized ways. As Ira Konigsberg says, in film this goal "was accomplished through distorted and exaggerated settings, heavy and dramatic shadows, unnatural space in composition, oblique angles, curved or nonparallel lines, a mobile and subjective camera, unnatural costumes and makeup,

and stylized acting" (126). The most famous example of film expressionism is *The Cabinet of Dr. Caligari.*

exterior: A scene filmed outdoors or on a set that looks like the outdoors.

extreme close-up: An image that shows one subject and largely or completely excludes the background. If the subject is someone's face, only part of it is visible (below). (86)

extreme long shot: A shot in which the subject appears to be far from the camera. If a person is the subject, the entire body will be visible (if not obstructed by some intervening object) but very small in the frame, and much of the surroundings will be visible. Usually used only outdoors, often to establish the setting of the following action. (*85*)

eye-level angle: A camera angle that creates the effect of the audience being on the same level as the subject. (*92*)

eyeline match: A transition between shots in which the first shot shows a person or animal looking at something offscreen, and the following shot shows what was being looked at from the approximate angle suggested by the previous shot. (129)

fabula: A term used by the Russian Formalist school of literary theory and some later film theorists to mean the chronological reconstruction of all the events of a nonchronological narrative. See also **plot**. (272)

fade-in: Optical effect in which the image changes by degrees from darkness (usually black) to illumination. Frequently used at the beginning of a film and sometimes at the beginning of a sequence.

fade-out: Optical effect in which the image changes by degrees from illumination to darkness (usually black). Sometimes used at the conclusion of a sequence and at the end of a film as a gradual exit from its world.

fade-out, fade-in: A transition between shots in which an image changes by degrees from illumination to darkness (usually to black); then, after a pause, the image changes from darkness to illumination (usually a new image). Sometimes used to suggest the passage of time. (124)

fake documentary: A film that purports to be a documentary film and seems to be one until viewers learn otherwise after the film has ended. Examples are *David Holzman's Diary* and *The Blair Witch Project*, which seem to be documentaries until viewers can figure out from the final credits that the films are fictional after all. See **mock documentary**. (387)

fast cutting: Editing characterized by frequent brief shots, sometimes shots less than a second long. Most recent American action movies, music videos, and trailers have extensive fast cutting. Opposite of **slow cutting**. (145)

fast film (stock): Film stock that requires relatively little light for capturing images. Fast film, especially before the last decade or so, has tended to produce grainy images. Opposite of **slow film (stock)**. (64)

fast lens: A camera lens that is efficient at transmitting light and thus transmits more light than a slow lens used in the same circumstances. Opposite of **slow lens**.

fast motion: Motion in which the action on the screen occurs more rapidly than its real-life counterpart, as when the cowboys in early 1920s films seem to ride horses faster than any yet seen by people outside movie theaters. Achieved whenever the projector runs significantly faster than the speed at which the camera filmed—for example, when the projector runs at 24 frames per second and the camera filmed at 14 frames per second. Opposite of **slow motion**.

feature (film): A fictional film that is at least sixty minutes long.

fill light: A soft light used to fill in unlit areas of the subject or to soften any shadows or lines made by other, brighter lights. (74)

film continuity: See **cutting continuity (script)**.

filmic: Characteristic of the film medium or appropriate to it, such as parallel editing or the combination of editing and a full range of spoken words, silence, and music. For example, a novel or play with many short scenes or frequent shifts between two locales (similar to parallel editing in a film) may be called filmic.

film(making) technique: Any aspect of filmmaking, such as the use of sets, lighting, sound effects, music, or editing. How well techniques are used is a strong determinant of a film's content, style, and impact.

film movement: A group of films sharing innovative styles or subjects (or both) that emerges from the same country or region over a period of a few years and that are in opposition to the dominant cinema(s) of the time. Examples are Italian neorealism, blaxploitation, and Dogme 95.

film noir ("film nwahr"): Literally, "black film." A type of film first made in the United States during and after World War II, characterized by frequent scenes with dark, shadowy (low-key) lighting; (usually) urban settings; characters motivated by selfishness, greed, cruelty, ambition, and lust; and characters willing to lie, frame, double-cross, and kill or have others killed. The moods of such films tend to be embittered, depressed, cynical, or fatalistic and their plots compressed and convoluted. Examples are *Murder, My Sweet*; *Out of the Past*; and *Touch of Evil* (below). (302)

film stock: Unexposed and unprocessed motion-picture film. Sometimes called *raw stock*. (61)

film theorist: A person who formulates a film theory or a general explanation of the film medium or a part of the medium. See also **film theory**.

film theory: "An evolving body of concepts designed to account for the cinema in [some or] all its dimensions (aesthetic, social, psychological) for an interpretive community of scholars, critics, and interested spectators" (Robert Stam, *Film Theory: An Introduction*, 6). As Dudley Andrew has pointed out in his *Major Film Theories*, a film theory often includes considerations of the properties of the film medium, its techniques, its forms, and its purposes and value. The concepts constituting a theory are sometimes only loosely related, evolve over time, and lack universal acceptance. Not all theorists calling themselves feminist, for example, will agree what "feminist theory" or "feminist criticism" entails.

filter: A sheet of transparent plastic or glass either in a color or a shade of gray attached before or behind the camera lens to change the quality of light reaching the film.

final cut: The last version of an edited film.

fine cut: A late version of an edited film, though perhaps not yet the final cut. See **rough cut**.

fisheye lens: An extreme wide-angle lens that captures nearly 180 degrees of the area before the camera and causes much curvature of the image, especially near the edges, as in some shots near the end of *Seconds* (below). (80)

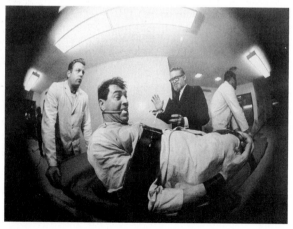

flashback: A shot or a few shots, a brief scene, or (rarely) a sequence that interrupts a narrative to show earlier events. (270)

flashforward: A shot, scene, or sequence—though usually only a shot or two—that interrupts a narrative to show events that happen in the future. For example,

GoodFellas begins with a few scenes that occur again late in an otherwise chronological narrative. Flashforwards are rarely used, though examples are found in *Don't Look Now* and *The Gift*. (270)

flat lens: See **spherical lens**.

Foley artist: Sound specialist who uses various objects such as different types of floor surfaces (usually in a Foley studio) to simulate sounds and synchronize them with corresponding movie images (below).

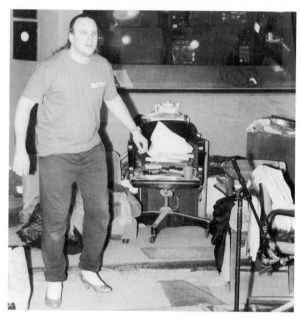

footage: A length of exposed motion-picture film (as in "They had enough footage to finish editing the film").

form: See **structure**.

form cut: See **match cut**.

found footage: Exposed motion-picture film or videotape, parts or all of which are incorporated into a later film or video.

frame: (1) A separate, individual photograph on a strip of motion-picture film. (2) The borders of the projected film, TV set, or monitor. (3) To position the camera in such a way that the subjects are kept within the borders of the image. (*120*)

frame enlargement: A photograph of an individual frame from a motion picture, blown up (enlarged) to reveal its details. Used in some publications, including this one, to illustrate certain features of a film or the film medium. See also **publicity still**. (*76* left)

freeze frame: An unmoving motion-picture or video image that looks like a still photograph, which is achieved by reprinting the same frame or two repeatedly. Sometimes used at the end of a film as in *Tom Jones* and *GoodFellas* and often used at the conclusion of TV sitcoms. Many videotape, videodisc, and DVD players also have a freeze frame option.

French new wave (cinema): A movement made up of a diverse group of French fictional films made in the late 1950s and early 1960s in reaction to the carefully scripted products of the French film industry and often as explorations of more current subjects sometimes rendered with untraditional techniques. Like cinéma vérité, some French new wave films were shot on location with portable, handheld equipment and fast film stock. Often new wave films include homages and surprising or whimsical moments. Examples of French new wave cinema are the early feature films of Truffaut (such as *The 400 Blows* and, more so, *Shoot the Piano Player*), Godard (*Breathless*), and Claude Chabrol (*Handsome Serge*). (320)

gauge: The width of a film, usually measured in millimeters, as in "The gauge of most theatrical movies is 35 mm." (63)

gender: A person's sexual identity as exhibited by various signals, including clothing, cosmetics, hairstyles, conversational styles, and body language. *Gender* is distinguished from *sex*, which means the biological or physical characteristics of men and women. (500)

genre ("ZHAHN ruh"): A group of fictional films—such as western, science fiction, horror, gangster, musical, and screwball comedy—that share enough similarities that both filmmakers and audiences recognize the films as members of the same group. As filmmakers bring forth more variations of a genre, the genre changes, and the genre changes as the times do. (294)

grain: One of the many tiny light-sensitive particles embedded in gelatin that is attached to a clear, flexible film base (celluloid). After the film is exposed to light and developed, a huge number of grains make up a film's finished images. (62)

graininess: Rough visual texture, as in "that film stock produces excessive graininess." In a film, graininess is caused when individual particles clump together in the film emulsion. Graininess also results if a film is magnified excessively during projection, as when a 16 mm print is used to fill up a large screen intended for 35 mm films.

grainy: Having graininess or rough visual texture. See also **graininess**.

habitat of meaning: See **interpretive community**.

happening: As defined by some narrative theorists, a change brought about by a force other than a person or character—for example, in the animated film "T.R.A.N.S.I.T.," a suitcase falling off the back of a sports car results in a man meeting and becoming infatuated with an attractive woman, which in turn leads to murders (see the description of the film's plot and fabula on p. 395). Happenings and actions by characters or persons constitute events in narratives.

hard light: Light that has not been diffused (scattered) or reflected before illuminating the subject. On subjects illuminated by hard light, any shadows are sharp-edged and surface details are more noticeable than with soft light (right). Examples: midday sunlight on a clear day or unreflected and focused light from a spotlight. Opposite of **soft light**.

high angle: A view of a subject from above, created by positioning the camera above the subject. (*91*)

high contrast: Photographic image with few gradations between the darkest and lightest parts of the image. Black-and-white high-contrast photos are made up mostly of blacks and whites with few shades of gray. Opposite of **low contrast**. See Figure 8.33 on p. 388.

high-key lighting: A high level of illumination on the subject. With high-key lighting, the bright frontal key lighting on the subject prevents dark shadows. Often used to create or enhance a cheerful mood, as in many stage and movie musicals. Opposite of **low-key lighting**. (75)

homage (in French and in film studies, pronounced "oh MAZH"): In film studies, a tribute in a text to a person, other text (such as a film), or part of a text. Examples of homages in a film are the inclusion of part of an earlier film, a re-creation of parts of it, or a respectful imitation of aspects of an earlier film. French new wave films often contain homages, especially to American movies. An homage may also be to a specific director's films. For example, entire films, such as some directed by Brian De Palma, are sometimes seen as homages to films directed by Alfred Hitchcock. (234)

hybrid film: A film that is not exclusively fictional, documentary, or experimental but instead shares characteristics of two or all three of the major film types. An example is *David Holzman's Diary*, which is not a fictional, documentary, or experimental film but contains aspects of all three. (384)

ideology: A frequently used term with different meanings in different contexts. In film studies, *ideology* means the influential underlying social and political beliefs of a society or social group. Often these beliefs are unexamined by the group's members and are assumed to be true and not the product of the group's way of thinking. For example, part of the ideology of the United States is the belief that individuals can influence major events in significant ways. This aspect of American ideology is often conveyed indirectly, or less often directly, by popular American movies. See also **symptomatic meaning**. (498)

IMAX (short for "image maximization"): A Canadian company's system for filming and showing very large screen motion pictures. The system consists of special cameras that can accommodate 70 mm film run horizontally through the camera (Figure 2.2d) and large theaters with special projectors, huge screens (some as high as an eight-story building), multiple speaker clusters behind the porous screens, and a multitrack sound system (now usually digital). With the steeply raked seating and large screen, typically the image extends beyond the viewers' peripheral vision and viewers feel a greater sense of presence and involvement than they do at any other type of film showing. See Figure 9.24c. Also available in some locales is IMAX 3-D, which creates a credible 3-D movie experience for viewers wearing IMAX 3-D glasses with polarizing filters or electronic liquid-crystal shutter glasses.

IMAX Dome: A theater in which film that was shot with a special lens onto 70 mm film running horizontally

through the camera (Figure 2.2d) is projected through a fisheye lens onto a huge curved screen. The projected images can be even more enveloping and involving than in the standard IMAX theater. See also **IMAX**.

implicit meaning: A generalization a viewer or reader makes about a text (such as a film) or subject in a text. An implicit meaning, for example, may be a viewer's generalization about the implications of a narrative's events (such as crime doesn't pay, or people are not always as they seem to be). An implicit meaning can also be a generalization about the significance of a symbol. See also **meaning** and **symbol**. (473)

independent film: (1) Film made without support or input from the dominant, established film industry. Usually an independent film is made without costly stars, director, and writer(s) and thus has a budget far below a big studio-backed movie. Sometimes called an *indie*. (2) In some publications, the phrase is used as an alternative to *experimental film*. (323, 326)

installation art: An art exhibit or ensemble, which is usually shown in a museum of modern or contemporary art, integrating various objects or arts, such as video images, furniture, and recorded voices (below). (382)

intercut: See **cross-cut**.

intercutting: See **parallel editing**.

interior: A scene filmed indoors, either in an existing building or one constructed for filming.

interpretive community: A group of people with common interests and a broadly shared outlook who tend to generate similar meanings from a text. Examples of two interpretive communities are film scholars and college students who see a lot of movies and like to talk about them. Meanings that one interpretive community formulate tend to be similar yet differ in general from the meanings formulated by a different interpretive community. (506)

intertextuality: The relation of one text (such as a film) to another text or texts (such as a journalistic article, play, or another film). Types of intertextuality in films include allusion, homage, parody, remake, prequel, sequel, and compilation film. Texts have always been dependent on earlier texts, but in recent decades intertextuality is more often employed than ever before. (195)

intertitle (card):   See **title card**.

iris-in: An optical effect usually functioning as a transition between shots in which the image is initially dark, then a widening opening—often a circle or an oval—reveals more and more of the next image, usually until it is fully revealed. (127)

iris-out: An optical effect usually functioning as a transition between shots in which the image is closed out as a constricting opening—usually a circle or an oval—closes down on it. Normally the iris-out ends with the image fully obliterated. See Figure 7.32c.

iris shot: Shot in which part of the frame is masked or obscured, often leaving the remaining image in a circular or an oval shape. The iris shot was widely used in films directed by D. W. Griffith, Sergei Eisenstein, and Abel Gance and in many other early films but is rarely used today (bottom, left).

irony: A statement, an event, or a situation involving an incongruity or a discrepancy between appearance and reality. As the authors of the second edition of *The Bedford Glossary of Critical and Literary Terms* illustrate, "A discrepancy may exist between what someone says and what he or she actually means, between what someone expects to happen and what really does happen, or between what appears to be true and what actually is true" (220). Irony is a frequent, useful tool of the satirist and other makers of texts.

Italian neorealism: As a film movement in Italy during and after World War II, neorealist films are a mixture of imaginary and actual events usually located in actual settings and showing ordinary and believable characters caught up in difficult social and economic conditions, such as poverty and unemployment. Other characteristics of this "new realism" are a heavy but not exclusive reliance on nonprofessional actors, use of available lighting, chronological narratives, few close-ups, straightforward camera angles and other unobtrusive filmmaking techniques, and natural dialogue that includes a range of dialects. Probably the best-known neorealist film is *The Bicycle Thief* (also known as *Bicycle Thieves*) (below). (317)

jump cut: A transition between shots that causes a jarring or even shocking shift in space, time, or action. A jump cut may be used to shorten the representation of an event or to disorient viewers, or both. It sometimes results unintentionally from careless editing or missing footage (below). Opposite of **continuity editing**. (123)

key light: (1) The main light in a shot. (2) The lighting instrument used to create the main and brightest light hitting the subject. (74)

kino: (1) In recent years, the term has come to stand for an informal group that meets periodically, often monthly, to show short films shot and edited digitally. Like those who follow the guidelines of Dogme 95, those making kino films are contributing to the democratization of filmmaking and film exhibition and the breakdown of the division between filmmakers and film viewers. (2) A short film shot and edited digitally, often in a short time, which is later shown at a gathering of other amateur digital filmmakers and other audience members. See also **microcinema**.

lap dissolve: A transition between shots in which one shot begins to fade out as the next shot fades in, overlapping the first shot before replacing it. Usually used between scenes or sequences to suggest a change of setting or a later time or both. Also frequently known as a *dissolve*, but *lap dissolve* better conveys what happens: (over)lapping (by the second shot) and dissolving (of the first). (124)

leader: Clear or opaque motion-picture film of any color that usually precedes and concludes a reel of film. It is used to decrease the chances of damage to the film print during shipment and projection, to carry verbal information about the reel of film, and to thread a projector. It has even been included in some experimental films, as in Bruce Conner's "A Movie." (Figure 8.18b & g)

letterbox format: A videotape, videodisc, and DVD format that retains the film's original theatrical widescreen aspect ratio (or a close approximation of it) by not using a portion of the top and bottom of the analog TV or monitor screen. (*38*)

limbo: An indistinct setting. In such a setting, the background may be all white (as in most shots in George Lucas's *THX 1138*), all black, or all the same color. Also called *limbo background* or *limbo set*. (13)

live action: Behavior by living (not animated) people or animals. Opposite of **animation**.

location: Any place other than a film studio that is used for filming. For example, the Monument Valley region in Utah and Arizona was a location for the 1939 John Ford film *Stagecoach* and other westerns, and *Schindler's List* was filmed on location in Poland, not on studio sets built to resemble parts of Poland. See **set**.

long lens: See **telephoto lens**.

long shot: A shot in which the subject may be seen in its entirety and much of its surroundings is visible. Not to be confused with **long take**. (*85*)

long take: A shot of long duration, as in the opening of *Touch of Evil*, *Halloween*, and *Boogie Nights*. The more than eight-minute opening shot of *The Player* is another example of a long take (Table 3.1). Not to be confused with **long shot**.

loose framing: An image in which the main subject has ample space and does not seem hemmed in by the edges of the frame and the background. Such framing can be used to give a sense of the subject's freedom of movement or of its being lost in or engulfed by its environment (next page). Opposite of **tight framing**. (16)

loose shot: See **loose framing**.

low angle: A view of the subject as seen from below eye level. (*92*)

low contrast: Photographic image with many gradations between darkest and lightest parts of the image. In black-and-white film, low-contrast images have many shades of gray. Opposite of **high contrast**. See examples on p. 136.

low-key lighting: Lighting with predominant dark tones, often deep dark tones. By using little frontal fill lighting, the filmmakers can immerse parts of the image in shadows. Often used to contribute to a dramatic or mysterious effect, as in many horror films and many detective and crime films (below). Opposite of **high-key lighting** .

magic realism: A style in which occasional wildly improbable or impossible events are included in an otherwise realistic story. For example, in *Like Water for Chocolate* the food one character prepares causes those who eat it to feel as she felt as she prepared it. (276)

masking: A technique used to block out part of an image (usually) temporarily. Normally used to block out extraneous details and focus viewer attention, to elongate or widen the image, or to exclude certain details for censorship reasons. Used more often in silent films than in sound films (below).

master-scene format: A screenplay that briefly describes scenes but does not break them down into shots. A film script in the master-scene format includes brief descriptions of setting and action and any dialogue but usually excludes instructions about the making of the film, such as indications about the camera setups. (198)

master shot: A shot usually made with an unmoving camera that records an entire scene, usually in a long shot. Parts of the master shot plus other shots of the same scene may be used as the final version of the scene, or the entire master shot may be used.

match cut: A transition between two shots in which an object or movement (or both) at the end of one shot closely resembles (or is identical to) an object or movement (or both) at the beginning of the next shot. (122)

matte: A partial covering placed in front of a camera lens so that another image (usually a matte painting) can be added to the unexposed area of the image. A matte shot is made by using one or more mattes in front of the camera lens and later by filling in the unexposed areas with images from other sources. Today, matte shots are usually made entirely in a film laboratory or in a computer.

meaning: An observation or a general statement about a subject, such as a film or an aspect of a film. Meaning in films may be explicit, a general observation in a text about one or more of its subjects; implicit, a generalization a viewer makes about a film or subject in the film; or symptomatic, an explicit or implicit meaning that is characteristic of the group that nurtured the film. (471)

medium close-up: Image in which the subject fills most of the frame, though not as much as in a close-up. When the subject is a person, the medium close-up usually reveals the head and shoulders. As with the close-up, the medium close-up is often used to direct viewer attention to a part of something or to show facial expressions in detail. (*86*)

medium shot: Shot in which the subject and surroundings are given about equal importance. When the subject is a person, he or she is usually seen from the knees or waist up. (*85*)

Method acting: Acting in which the performer studies the background of a character in depth, immerses himself or herself in the role, and creates emotion in part by thinking of emotional situations from his or her own life that resemble those of the character. (25)

microcinema: A program of untraditional short videos that may be shown on the Internet or in a casual atmosphere such as a coffeehouse or that may be purchased on videotape or DVD. See also **kino**.

mise en scène ("meez ahn sen," with a nasalized second syllable): French for "staging." An image's setting, subjects (usually people or characters), and composition (the arrangement of setting and subjects within the frame). (Chapter 1)

mix: (1) To select sounds from soundtracks of music, dialogue, and sound effects; adjust their volumes; and combine them into a composite soundtrack. (2) A final composite soundtrack consisting of a blend of other soundtracks.

mock documentary: A fictional film that parodies or amusingly imitates documentary films. Because mock documentaries have characteristics of documentaries—such as interviews, handheld cameras, and the absence of stars—viewers at first may think they are seeing a documentary but soon realize the film is an extended joke. Examples of mock documentaries are *This Is Spinal Tap*, purportedly a documentary about an aging heavy metal band, and *Fear of a Black Hat*, supposedly a

documentary film about the endless problems confronted by a hip-hop group. See also **fake documentary**. (230, 387)

montage ("mon TAZH"): From the French *monter*, to assemble. (1) A series of brief shots used to represent a condensation of subjects and time. *The Third Man*, for example, begins with a montage about the political and social conditions in Vienna after the end of World War II. (2) A type of editing used in some 1920s Soviet films (as in [*Battleship*] *Potemkin* and *October*) and advocated by some Soviet film theorists, such as the director Sergei Eisenstein. In films using this type of editing, the aim is not so much to promote the invisible continuity of a narrative favored in classical Hollywood cinema as to suggest meanings from the dynamic juxtaposition of many carefully selected details. (3) Editing, especially in European usage. (147)

morphing: *Morph* means shape, and *morphing* means changing shape. As used in filmmaking, *morphing* means altering or the alteration of a film image by degrees through the use of sophisticated computer software and multiple advanced computers. As Kevin Jackson has written, "Thanks to morphing, the director of live-action films can now achieve the kind of wild images previously reserved for the animator" (161). Used increasingly since 1988 in TV commercials and feature films, as in *Spawn*, *X-Men*, and many others (below).

movement: See **film movement**.

movie palace: An opulent type of movie theater built in the United States and Europe between the mid-1910s and the 1930s and seating at least 1,000 and as many as 6,200 patrons. Movie palaces were usually ornately decorated in both the lobbies and the auditoria, spacious, and extremely comfortable, in part because their lengthy programs included more than a feature film. With the steep decline in movie attendance beginning in the 1950s, most movie palaces were divided into smaller auditoria, torn down, or converted to other uses, such as churches. See Figure 9.24a–b.

narration: Commentary in a film about a subject in the film or some other topic, usually from someone off-screen. Occasionally the narration comes from a person on-screen, as in *Zoot Suit*, where the action sometimes freezes briefly as the character played by Edward James Olmos steps out of character and comments on some aspect of the story or the times of the story. Narration may be used off and on throughout a film or only occasionally. Sometimes it is used only at the film's beginning or ending, or both. Narration is sometimes used in documentary films, especially older ones, and in TV commercials, fictional films, and on rare occasions in experimental films.

narrative: A representation of a series of unified events (happenings and actions) situated in one or more settings. A narrative may be fictional or factual or a blend of the two. Its events may be arranged chronologically or nonchronologically. (248)

narrative closure: See **closure**.

narrative documentary: A film or video representation of an actual (not imaginary) narrative or story. Examples are *Hearts of Darkness*, *Hoop Dreams*, and *Genghis Blues*. See **docudrama**. (352)

narrator: A character, a person, or an unidentifiable voice in a film that provides continuous or intermittent commentary about subjects in the film or outside it, or both. As in written fiction, a narrator is not necessarily a reliable source for information.

negative: (1) Unexposed film stock used to record negative images. (2) Film (other than reversal film) that has been exposed but not yet developed. (3) Excluding reversal film, film that has been exposed and developed. It is normally then used to make (positive) prints for projection but is occasionally used in part of a finished film. In such films, negative footage is sometimes used to suggest death, as near the ending of *Gladiator*, where negative images suggest the main character is losing consciousness and approaching death. In color photography and cinematography, the colors of the negative image are complementary to those of the subject photographed. In black-and-white negatives, the light and dark areas are reversed (top, right).

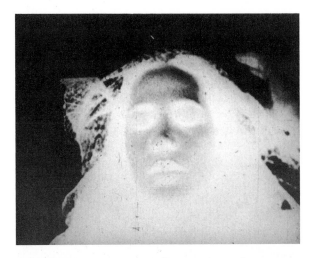

neorealism: See **Italian neorealism**.

new wave (cinema):   See **French new wave (cinema)**.

nickelodeon: Literally, "five-cents theater." A small, modest storefront converted into a theater for showing a brief program of short films (below). Nickelodeons were popular in the United States from 1905 to roughly 1915 and were the successors to one-person peephole machines and the forerunner of larger and more comfortable movie theaters, the largest and most elaborate of which were sometimes called *movie palaces*. See also **movie palace**. (450)

nitrate: See **celluloid**, definition 1.

nonfiction film: See **documentary film**.

nonlinear editing: Editing that involves using a computer and software to select and combine digitized shots.

nonnarrative documentary: A film or video that uses no narrative or story in its representation of mainly actual (not imaginary) subjects. Examples abound, such as Frederick Wiseman's *High School II* and *Public Housing*, many TV commercials, and many industrial and training films. See **documentary film**. (349)

normal lens: A camera lens that provides the least distortion of image and movement. The normal lens—50 mm on a 35 mm camera—comes closest to approximating the perceptions of the human eye (below). (*81*)

nouvelle vague: Literally, "new wave." See **French new wave (cinema)**.

objective camera: Camera placement that allows the viewer to see the subject approximately as an outsider would, not as someone in the film sees it. Opposite of **point-of-view shot**.

offscreen: (1) The area beyond the frame line, which has many possible uses. For example, someone may look offscreen at someone else; a shadow may be cast into the frame by something offscreen; or a sound may be heard from offscreen. (2) Life outside the movies. See **offscreen sound**.

offscreen sound: Sound that does not derive from an on-screen source, such as an unseen dog barking or music that is not made by anyone within the frame. (183)

OMNIMAX: See **IMAX Dome**.

180-degree system: Filming and editing so that all shots in a scene are from the same side of an imaginary straight line running between the scene's major subjects. The 180-degree system helps keep relationships between subjects and between subjects and setting consistent and clear (below). See also **continuity editing**. (129)

on-screen sound: Sound that derives from an on-screen source, such as someone viewers see and hear sneezing. (182)

optical effect: Special effect made with an optical printer or a computer. Examples are lap dissolves, wipes, and freeze frames. See also **digital effect**.

optical printer: A device consisting of a movie camera and one or more movie projectors used to reproduce images or parts of images from already processed film. An optical printer can be used to make lap dissolves, wipes, and many other optical effects, though increasingly such optical effects are made while doing nonlinear editing on a computer.

outtake: A take (version of a shot) not included in a film's final version, although occasionally outtakes are included during the ending credits, especially if they might be amusing, as in *The Nutty Professor* (1996) and in various Jackie Chan movies. During editing, often shots or even whole scenes or entire sequences are deleted because the film is running too long or the material is not functioning as the filmmakers had envisioned.

pace: A viewer's sense of a subject (such as narrative developments or factual information) being represented rapidly or slowly. A highly subjective experience that is influenced by many aspects in a film, such as the film's editing (fast cutting or slow cutting) and the frequency of the introduction of significant subjects. (144)

panning: Filming while a movie camera is pivoted horizontally on a stationary base (often a tripod). Used frequently to show the vastness of a setting, such as a sea, a plain, a mountain range, outer space, or the inside of an immense building. The term derives from the word *panoramic* because with this movement the camera shows an extensive area. When the camera pans too rapidly and the resultant images are blurred, the camera movement is called a *swish pan*. (94)

parallel editing: Editing that alternates between two or more events, often suggesting that the events are related to each other or are occurring simultaneously. Parallel editing may also be used to represent events from different times or eras (as in D. W. Griffith's *Intolerance*). See **cross-cut**. (140)

parody: (1) A representation that amusingly imitates human behavior or a (more serious) text, part of a text, or groups of texts, often to ridicule or criticize. For example, a parody may be of a famous narrative, part of a narrative, or a genre. Examples of film parodies are

Rocky Horror Picture Show, a musical parody of horror movies (bottom, left), and *Spaceballs*, a parody of sci-fi movies, especially of *Star Wars*. (2) To imitate and represent human behavior, a text, or part of a text in an amusing way. (229)

perspective: As used by painters, photographers, and cinematographers, the term means the relative size and apparent distances between objects in a created image. (88)

pixillation: A type of animation usually achieved by using stop-motion cinematography to show three-dimensional subjects (living or nonliving) moving continuously or discontinuously in ways impossible in the real world—for example, two men circling each other in a jumpy, impossibly rapid manner (below). See **stop-motion cinematography**. (393)

plot: The structure or arrangement of a narrative's events. (272)

plotline: A narrative or series of related events usually involving only a few characters or people and capable of functioning on its own as a story. Short films tend to have one plotline, but many feature films combine two or more. (261)

point-of-view shot: Camera placement at the approximate position of a character or person (or occasionally an animal) that gives a view similar to what that subject would see. Opposite of **objective camera**. (93)

pop art: An art movement begun in the United States and Britain in the 1950s and extending into the 1960s whose subjects were everyday objects—such as soup cans, clothespins, comic strips, graphic print ads, or celebrity images—that were represented archetypically, whimsically, or ironically or in a combination of these ways.

postproduction: All the work involved in making a film or video after the filming or taping is completed, usually including editing the shots, preparing a soundtrack, and making the credits.

p.o.v. shot: See **point-of-view shot**.

preproduction: All the work involved in making a film or video before the filming or taping begins, usually including such tasks as writing the script, casting, hiring the other necessary personnel, and selecting locations or designing and building sets.

prequel: A narrative film that shows some of the characters from a previous film at earlier stages of their lives. For example, *Butch Cassidy and the Sundance Kid* came out in 1969; ten years later the prequel *Butch and Sundance: The Early Days* was made. (234)

preview (of a coming attraction): See **trailer**.

producer: A person in charge of the business and administrative aspects of making a film. The (main) producer's job typically includes acquiring rights to the script and hiring the personnel to make the film. Sometimes producers influence the filmmaking process—for example, by changing directors before or during filming or insisting on changes in the script or editing. Producers may be known under a variety of titles, such as executive producer and assistant producer; the nature of their involvement (if any) remains obscure to those outside the production.

production: (1) All the work involved in making a film or video after the preproduction work is completed and before the postproduction work begins, including preparing the sets or locales for filming and filming the necessary shots. (2) The making of a film or video, which typically involves three stages: preproduction (which in a large production may include planning, budgeting, scripting, designing and building sets, and casting); production (filming or taping); and postproduction (which includes editing, preparing and mixing

sound, and making the credits). See also **preproduction** and **postproduction**.

production designer: See **designer**.

production still: See **publicity still**.

product placement: The practice of including commercial products or services, such as Coca-Cola cans or a particular airline, in films so that viewers can notice them. Makers of movies often make agreements with companies to display their products or services in exchange for money or, much more often, goods, services (such as airline tickets or hotel accommodations), or promotion of the movie (below). (52)

product plug: See **product placement**.

publicity still: A posed photograph taken with a still camera, usually during production, to later help publicize a film. (76 right)

pull focus: See **rack focus**.

rack focus: Changing the sharpness of focus *during* a shot from foreground to background or vice versa. (46)

reaction shot: A shot, usually of a face, that shows someone or occasionally an animal presumably reacting to an event. Used frequently in films to cue viewers how to react and to intensify the viewers' responses. (138)

reading: A term used in both filmmaking and film theory. (1) A tryout for a part in a film or play in which the applicant reads aloud from a script. (2) The amount of light or sound as measured by a light or sound meter. (3) Interpretation of a text or part of one, as in "Her reading of *Citizen Kane* stresses the contexts in which the film was made."

realism: Representation in a text that is widely believed to render its subjects accurately. A person's sense of what realism is largely depends on when and where the person lives and what that person's society deems as true-to-life representations; thus, what seems realistic in one place or time often seems unrealistic in another place or time.

rear projection: The process of projecting (usually moving) images on a screen behind actors seen in the foreground. Often used to create the illusion of characters in a moving vehicle.

rear-screen projection: See **rear projection**.

reel: (1) A metal or plastic spool to hold film, such as the two 16 mm reels in the background of Figure 8.33b. (2) One thousand feet of 35 mm motion-picture film stored on a reel. Since the speed of projection was not standardized before the late 1920s, early films were measured in terms of the number of reels. For example, the 1925 version of *Les Misérables* reputedly consisted of thirty-two reels (each reel could take from thirteen to sixteen minutes to project). Today, a 35 mm reel of sound film takes approximately eleven minutes to project if the film has leader attached to it or ten minutes if it has no leader.

reflexive: See **self-reflexive**.

representation: A likeness of a subject created in a text. A representation of an event (action or happening), for example, is not the event itself but someone's manufactured likeness or re-presentation of it in a text. As different people create texts, they unavoidably make different decisions, and different representations result. Even different representations of the same subject vary. For example, each group of filmmakers that creates another Tarzan movie makes many decisions about how to re-present the subject (for example, what to include) and ends up with a new representation of the story (see Figure 9.9).

resolution: (1) The degree of detail visible in an image; the greater the visible detail, the greater the resolution. One could say, for example, that with the appropriate film stock, lighting, and lens, high-resolution images are possible. (2) The culmination or concluding events of a plot. One could say, for example, "The resolution of the movie is implausible because it is not consistent with earlier events in the story."

revisionist: Referring to a new or revised interpretation or representation of a subject (such as history, a narrative, or genre). *Unforgiven* is a revisionist western, for example, in that most of the film is critical of violence and killing. Opposite of **conventional**. (297)

rough cut: An early version (usually the first complete or nearly complete version) of an edited film. See also **fine cut**.

running time: The time that elapses when a film is projected. The running time of most feature films is 80 to 120 minutes, though in recent years many features run longer than 120 minutes. (272)

rushes: See **dailies**.

satire: A representation that indirectly exposes and perhaps ridicules individual or group thinking or behavior for being foolish, evil, or stupid or for exhibiting some other shortcoming. Satire can be used to amuse but even more often to chide, perhaps inform, maybe even reform. In attempting to reach these goals, satirists often use such means as exaggeration, irony, and styles such as parody or black comedy. The tone of a satire may range from gentle and good-natured to scathing and bitter or somewhere in between. (482)

saturated color: Intense, vivid, or brilliant color. Opposite of **desaturated color**. See p. 67 and Plates 2–4.

scanned print: A version of a film made in the standard aspect ratio from an original anamorphic film. In making a scanned print, a technician—not the film's editor or director—decides which part of the width of the original anamorphic image to show at each moment of the film or video. (37)

scene: A section of a narrative that gives the impression of continuous action taking place in continuous time and space. Most feature films are made up of many scenes—often one hundred or more—as are narrative documentary films, such as *Hearts of Darkness*, *Hoop Dreams*, and *Genghis Blues*. (120)

scope lens: See **anamorphic lens**.

screenplay: The earliest version of a script, a script written before filming begins. Usually a finished film varies considerably from the original screenplay. See **shooting script** and **cutting continuity**.

self-reflexive: Characteristic of a text, such as a novel or film, to refer to or comment on itself as a text or as a medium. Self-reflexiveness draws reader or viewer attention to the text as something constructed and thus not inevitable in its techniques and subjects. For example, a movie may include a character interrupting the fictional story to speak directly to the audience. Examples of self-reflexiveness are found in Luigi Pirandello's play *Six Characters in Search of an Author*, John Fowles's novel *The French Lieutenant's Woman*, and the films *Man with a Movie Camera*, *Tom Jones*, and *High Fidelity*. Many experimental films are self-reflexive at times, as are occasional documentary films. (324)

sequence: A series of related consecutive scenes, perceived as a major unit of a narrative film, such as the Sicilian sequence in *The Godfather*. A sequence may be analogous to a chapter in a novel or an act in a play. (120)

serial: From the 1910s until the early 1950s, a low-budget action film divided into chapters or installments, one of which was shown each week in downtown and neighborhood movie theaters. Typically serials feature extensive fast-paced action, danger to the heroes, occasional touches of romance, and obvious cheap special effects. Villains often wear bizarre costumes, and the stories are often set in exotic locales (below). Usually, each chapter or installment ends with an unresolved problem. For example, one or more of the main characters is placed in mortal danger or seems to be killed. Serials have strongly influenced the *Star Wars* films, the series of *Raiders of the Lost Ark* films, *The Lord of the Rings* trilogy, and many other action movies.

set: A constructed setting where action is filmed; it can be indoors or outdoors (top, right). See **location**.

setting: The place where filmed action occurs, either a set, which has been built for use in a film, or a location, which is any place other than one built for use in a movie. Setting is often used to indicate a period and to reveal or enhance the film's style, characters, moods, and meanings. (11)

shallow focus: A term used widely by film teachers and scholars to indicate photography with sharp focus in only a short distance between the foreground and the background—for example, between ten and fifteen feet in front of the camera. Achieved in photography by using a telephoto lens or a large lens aperture, or both. The technique is often used to deemphasize the background and focus attention on the subject in the foreground (below). Filmmakers often use the terms *restricted depth of field* or *shallow depth of field* rather than *shallow focus*, the term favored by film teachers and scholars. Opposite of **deep focus**. (83)

shooting script: The version of the script used by the filmmakers during filming. Because usually many changes are made during filming and editing, the finished film typically varies considerably from the shooting script. See **screenplay** and **cutting continuity**.

short film: Variously defined, but often regarded as a film of less than sixty minutes. (256)

short lens: See **wide-angle lens**.

short subject: See **short film**.

shot: (1) An uninterrupted strip of exposed motion-picture film or videotape that represents a subject, perhaps even a blank screen, during an uninterrupted segment of time. (2) Filmed, as in "They shot the movie in seven weeks." (*120*)

shot/reverse shot: A filming and editing technique involving alternating a shot of one subject seen from one camera position with a shot of a second nearby subject seen from a different camera position. Most often used to show the face of the first person speaking or reacting as the camera looks from behind and to the side of the second person followed by a shot of the second person's face (perhaps speaking, perhaps listening) as the first person is now seen from behind and to the side. The shot/reverse shot technique is normally used in conjunction with the 180-degree system and helps contribute to continuity editing. See **continuity editing**. (130)

simulated documentary: See **fake documentary**.

slow cutting: Edited film characterized by frequent shots of long duration. Most of the early films directed by Michelangelo Antonioni and *2001: A Space Odyssey*, for example, have extensive slow cutting, as does the experimental film "(nostalgia)." Opposite of **fast cutting**. (145)

slow film (stock): Film stock that requires a large camera aperture or bright light for appropriate re-creation of images. Slow film produces images with fine grain and sharp detail. Opposite of **fast film (stock)**. (64)

slow lens: A camera lens that is inefficient at transmitting light and thus transmits less light than a fast lens used in the same circumstances. Opposite of **fast lens**.

slow motion: Motion in which the action on the screen is slower than its real-life counterpart, as when people are seen running more slowly than is possible.

Achieved whenever the projector runs at an appreciably slower speed than the speed at which the camera filmed. Opposite of **fast motion**.

socialist realism: A Soviet doctrine and style in force from the mid-1930s to the 1980s that decreed that Soviet texts, including films, must promote communism and the working class and must be "realistic" (actually, an idealized representation of the working class) so that they would be understandable to working people. After World War II, socialist realism was also enforced in the East European countries under Soviet rule. (425)

soft light or **soft lighting:** (1) Light that has been diffused or reflected before illuminating the subject. On subjects illuminated by soft light, any shadows are soft-edged and surface details are less noticeable than with hard light (right). One source is the so-called magic hour, the time after sunset but before dark or the time of increasing light before  sunrise. Another source of soft light is the light emitted through a frosted lightbulb then reflected off or through a cloth lampshade. Opposite of **hard light**. (2) A type of open-faced lamp that creates soft or diffused light. (72)

sound dissolve: A transition in which a sound begins to fade out as the next sound fades in and overlaps the first sound before replacing it. (165)

sound effect: A sound in film other than spoken words or music. Three examples of sound effects are a door slamming, a dog barking, and thunder. (165)

soundstage: A permanent enclosed area for shooting film and recording sound. A soundstage is especially useful because its controlled environment allows for filming and sound recording without unwanted sights and sounds.

Soviet montage: See **montage**, definition 2.

special effect: Shot unobtainable by live-action cinematography. Includes most superimpositions, freeze frames, and many others.

spherical lens: A lens used in cinematography that transmits the image to the film in the camera without squeezing or compressing the image. Movies shown in the widely used 1.85:1 aspect ratio are filmed with spherical lenses. See also **anamorphic lens**.

splice: (1) To attach the end of one piece of film to the beginning of another piece of film. (2) The connection between two pieces of film. See Figure 3.4.

spoof: See **parody**.

staged documentary: See **fake documentary**.

standard aspect ratio: For an image on a screen or on the film itself, the ratio of the width to the height is 4:3 or 1.33:1 (below). Until the 1950s, the usual shape of motion-picture screens throughout the world and the approximate shape of analog TV screens. (35)

1.33:1 or 4:3
Standard aspect ratio

Steadicam: A lightweight and portable mount for holding a movie camera that provides for relatively steady camera movements during handheld shots. Especially useful for filming in rugged terrain or tight quarters. (97)

stereotype: A commonplace, simplified, and in some ways inaccurate representation (likeness of a subject created in a text). As various scholars who have studied the representations of ethnic groups in films have shown, stereotypes of groups can help perpetuate the belief that certain groups are superior to other groups. Films and other texts may use stereotypes in many other ways—for example, as subjects to be represented in an exaggerated manner for the purpose of satire. See also **representation**.

still: See **publicity still**.

stock footage: Footage stored for possible duplication and use in other films. Often stock footage is of subjects and locations difficult, impossible, or costly to film anew, such as warfare or the Paris background in the flashback sequence of *Casablanca*.

stop-motion cinematography: The process of filming a two- or three-dimensional subject for only one or a few frames, stopping the camera and changing something in the image, filming again, and repeating this process many times (below). May be used to create the appearance of credible movement during the showing of the series of images, as in most animated films (Figure 8.37a) or pixillated movement (Figure 8.37b). See both **pixillation** and **time-lapse cinematography**. (390)

story: In this book, a narrative, which is a representation of a series of unified events situated in one or more settings. In some publications, *story* means the same as *fabula*. Still other writers use *story* to have a meaning other than narrative or fabula. See both **narrative** and **fabula**.

storyboard: A series of drawings (or occasionally photographs) of each shot of a planned film or video story, often accompanied by written dialogue, brief descriptions, or notes (below). (201)

story time: The amount of time represented in a film's narrative or story. For example, if a movie's earliest scene occurs on a Sunday and its latest scene takes place on the following Friday, then the story time is six days. The story time for a movie is nearly always much longer than its running time. (272)

straight cut: See **cut**, definition 1.

structure: The arrangement of the parts of a whole text. In a narrative film, structure can be thought of as the arrangement of scenes or sequences. In nonnarrative films, structure refers to the arrangement of discernible parts. In a nonnarrative documentary film, for example, the structure might consist of the arrangement of interviews and film clips. Sometimes called *form*. (250)

studio (era): The period of U.S. film history from the 1920s to the 1950s during which large studios such as MGM, Paramount, and Warner Bros. used a factory-style system with each worker employed in a specialized department such as editing and with creative control largely concentrated in the hands of senior studio executives. Using this system, studios mass-produced mostly genre movies that dominated film markets throughout the United States and much of the world.

studio system: See **studio era**.

style: The way that subjects are represented in a text, such as a film. Styles for films or parts of films include abstract, black comedy, expressionism, magic realism, parody, realism, and socialist realism. Style is sometimes contrasted with subject, though many theorists argue that the two are symbiotic. (275)

subjective camera: See **point-of-view shot**.

superimposition: Two or more images photographed or printed on top of each other. Can be achieved in the camera during filming or, more often, by using an optical printer or computer. At the beginning of many movies, the credits are superimposed on the opening events. During a lap dissolve, one image is momentarily superimposed on another. Sometimes, as in several scenes in *Drugstore Cowboy*, two or more shots are superimposed to suggest a character's emotional or physical instability. The technique is used often in experimental films, as in Carolee Schneemann's "Fuses," but rarely in documentary films. (132)

surrealism: A movement in 1920s and 1930s European art, drama, literature, and film in which an attempt was made to portray or interpret the workings of the subconscious mind as manifested in dreams. Surrealism is characterized by an irrational, noncontextual arrangement of subjects. The surrealist movement has been especially influential on some experimental filmmakers, such as Luis Buñuel ("Un chien andalou" and *L'age d'or*) and Jean Cocteau, especially his "The Blood of a Poet." Directly or through intermediate sources, surrealism has also influenced some music videos.

swish pan: (1) Pivoting a movie camera horizontally on a stationary base so rapidly that the resultant filmed images are blurred. (2) Blurred images that result from pivoting a movie camera horizontally too rapidly during filming. Used as a shot, within a shot, or as a transition between shots. (94)

symbol: Anything perceptible that has meaning beyond its usual meaning or function. Depending on the contexts, a sound, object, person, word (including a name), color, action, or something else perceived by the senses may all function as a symbol. In *Citizen Kane*, for example, many viewers believe that the glass paperweight that Kane drops at the beginning of the film and that is seen two other times is not simply an object serving its usual function (as a paperweight) but also a symbol. (479)

symptomatic meaning: A generalization about a text or part of one that is characteristic of a group that nurtured the film. For example, *Fatal Attraction*, which first appeared in 1987, suggests that casual sex can be dangerous, even deadly. This implied message is symptomatic of the growing concerns in late 1980s America about casual sex and the spread of AIDS and other sexually transmitted diseases. See **ideology** and **meaning**. (494)

take: A version of a shot. Directors often call for additional takes because of some mistake or imperfection in the original take. Different takes of each shot are usually made in shooting theatrical films. One of the major tasks of the editor is to select the most effective take of each shot to be used in the finished film.

technique: See **film(making) technique**.

telephoto lens: A lens that makes all subjects in an image appear closer to the camera and to each other than is the case with a normal lens (next page). With its long barrel, a telephoto lens resembles a telescope. Not to be confused with a zoom lens, which is capable of varying by degrees from telephoto range to normal, sometimes even to wide-angle range, while the camera is filming. (*81*)

text: Something that people produce or modify to communicate meaning. Examples are films, photographs, paintings, newspaper articles, operas, or T-shirts with a message.

theme: See **meaning**.

THX sound: A multispeaker sound system developed by Lucasfilm and used in selected movie theaters to increase frequency range, audience coverage, and dialogue intelligibility while decreasing low bass distortion.

tight framing: A shot in which there is little visible space around the main subjects. For example, the main subjects are near the edges of the frame and a wall behind them is nearby. Uses for such framing include giving a sense of the subject's confinement or lack of mobility (below). Opposite of **loose framing**. (16)

tilting: A movie camera pivoting vertically during filming, usually while the camera is attached to a stationary base, such as a tripod. Often used as a way of gradually revealing information, as when we first see someone's shoes, then the camera tilts up to reveal the wearer. This is done memorably near the beginning of Hitchcock's *Strangers on a Train*. See also **panning**.

time-lapse cinematography: The process of filming the same subject one frame at a time, usually at regularly spaced intervals—for example, one frame every thirty minutes or one frame every twenty-four hours. When the processed film or video is projected at normal speed, any change that was photographed is much accelerated, perhaps even blurred. Can be used to show quickly the changes of a long process, such as the building of a house or the budding of a flower. Time-lapse cinematography can also be used for many other purposes, as in parts of the experimental documentary *Koyaanisqatsi* to suggest the hectic pace of modern urban life (below). See **stop-motion cinematography**.

tinting: The process of dyeing a film with color. Sometimes used before the adoption of color film stock in the 1930s. In tinted movies, often each scene or sequence would be dyed the same color. For example, blue was often used for night scenes or scenes set in the cold, and red for scenes of violence, danger, passion, or heat. (66)

title card: A card or thin sheet of clear plastic on which is written or printed information included in a film. Before the late 1920s, title cards were used to supply credits, exposition, dialogue, thoughts, descriptions of actions not shown, the numbered parts of a movie, and other types of information. Since the late 1920s, they have been used less often, but they are seen, for example, in some documentary films, such as *The Thin Blue Line*, *Hearts of Darkness*, and *Hoop Dreams*; in occasional experimental films; and sometimes in fictional films, as in the 1995 *Richard III* and *The Blair Witch Project* (below).

In October of 1994, three student filmmakers disappeared in the woods near Burkittsville, Maryland while shooting a documentary.

A year later their footage was found.

track: (1) To film while the camera is being moved around. Sometimes the camera is mounted on a cart set on tracks. Other times, the camera is handheld, and the camera operator moves or is moved about in a wheelchair, on roller skates, or by some other means. In some publications, *to track* and *to dolly* are used interchangeably. (2) A film soundtrack, a narrow band on the film that contains recorded optical, magnetic, or digital sound. (*63, 162*)

trailer: A brief compilation film shown in movie theaters, before some videotaped movies, on DVDs, or on TV to advertise a movie or video release.

treatment: A condensed written description of the content of a proposed film, often written in paragraphs and without dialogue.

underground film: See **experimental film**.

virtual reality: "An illusion of reality derived from technological means [such as computer, headset, and display monitor before each eye] that gives the spectator the sense that he or she is immersed in and interacting with the created world" (Konigsberg 447). Images of virtual reality have been an occasional subject in movies, such as *Logan's Run*, *Lawnmower Man*, and the *Matrix* films. See Figure 9.21.

Vitaphone: Motion-picture sound system first used commercially in 1927 consisting of a movie camera synchronized to a phonograph recorder and a movie projector synchronized with the phonograph recording. See Figure 4.2.

voice-over: See **narration**.

wide-angle lens: A camera lens (significantly shorter than 50 mm on a 35 mm camera) that makes all subjects in an image appear farther from the camera and from each other than is the case with a normal lens. The wide-angle lens also renders subjects at all distances from the camera in sharp focus and captures more of the sides of the image than is possible with a normal lens, though at the cost of some distortion (below). (*81*)

wide-screen: A film format with an aspect ratio noticeably greater than 1.33:1 (a shape wider than that of an analog TV screen). Most current films shown in U.S. commercial theaters have a wide-screen aspect ratio of 1.85:1. Wide-screen film formats have been tried since nearly the beginning of cinema but have been used in most movie theaters only since the 1950s. (36)

wipe: A transition between shots, usually between scenes, in which it appears that one shot is pushed off

the screen by the next shot. Many kinds of wipes are possible; perhaps the most common is a vertical line (sharp or blurred) that moves across the frame from one side to the other, seemingly "wiping away" a shot and replacing it with the next one (previous page). (126)

zip pan: See **swish pan**.

zoom: To use a zoom lens on a movie or video camera to cause the image of the subject to either increase in size as the area being filmed seems to decrease (zoom in) or to decrease in size as the area being filmed seems to increase (zoom out).

zoom in: To use a zoom lens to cause the image of the subject to increase in size as the area being filmed seems to decrease.

zoom lens: A camera lens with variable focal lengths that can be adjusted by degrees during a shot so that the size of the subject and the size of the area being filmed both change. During filming, the lens may assume the properties of a telephoto lens, normal lens, or wide-angle lens. Since the 1960s, the zoom lens has often been used in documentary filmmaking and in making many other films. For example, throughout nearly all of the experimental film "Wavelength," the movie camera imperceptibly zooms in on a photograph on the background wall.

zoom out: To use a zoom lens to cause the image of the subject to decrease in size as the area being filmed seems to increase.

Acknowledgments

Front Cover Photos, from top to bottom:
Chicago
Breathless (1959)
Amores Perros
The Thin Blue Line
The Lord of the Rings: The Two Towers

Back Cover Photos, from top to bottom:
"Un chien andalou"
Spirited Away: © 2002 Nibariki: TGNDDTM
Intolerance
Bamboozled
Chinatown

All Photos: Photofest, except for "Un chien andalou"

Text Illustrations (in addition to individual captions):
Jon Jonik. Copyright © 1989 Jon Jonik/Cartoonists & Writers Syndicate. <www.cartoonweb
.com.> Reprinted by permission.
Gary Larson. THE FAR SIDE © 1991 FARWORKS, INC. Used by permission. All
rights reserved.
Wiley Miller. NON SEQUITUR © 1999 Wiley Miller. Distributed by Universal Press
Syndicate. Reprinted with permission. All rights reserved.

Index